T0190024

Lecture Notes in Computer Science   9298

Commenced Publication in 1973
Founding and Former Series Editors:
Gerhard Goos, Juris Hartmanis, and Jan van Leeuwen

More information about this series at http://www.springer.com/series/7409

Julio Abascal · Simone Barbosa
Mirko Fetter · Tom Gross
Philippe Palanque · Marco Winckler (Eds.)

Human-Computer Interaction – INTERACT 2015

15th IFIP TC 13 International Conference
Bamberg, Germany, September 14–18, 2015
Proceedings, Part III

 Springer

Editors

Julio Abascal
Universidad del País Vasco/Euskal Herriko
Unibertsitatea
Donostia-San Sebastián
Spain

Simone Barbosa
PUC-Rio
Rio de Janeiro
Brazil

Mirko Fetter
University of Bamberg
Bamberg
Germany

Tom Gross
University of Bamberg
Bamberg
Germany

Philippe Palanque
University Paul Sabatier
Toulouse
France

Marco Winckler
University Paul Sabatier
Toulouse
France

ISSN 0302-9743   ISSN 1611-3349   (electronic)
Lecture Notes in Computer Science
ISBN 978-3-319-22697-2   ISBN 978-3-319-22698-9   (eBook)
DOI 10.1007/978-3-319-22698-9

Library of Congress Control Number: 2015945606

LNCS Sublibrary: SL3 – Information Systems and Applications, incl. Internet/Web, and HCI

Springer Cham Heidelberg New York Dordrecht London

Springer International Publishing AG Switzerland is part of Springer Science+Business Media
(www.springer.com)

Foreword

The 15th IFIP TC.13 International Conference on Human–Computer Interaction, INTERACT 2015, was held during September 14–18, 2015, in Bamberg, Germany, organized by the University of Bamberg. The city of Bamberg is proud of its more than 1,000-year-old center. It has more than 2,400 historically listed buildings and became a UNESCO World Cultural Heritage Site in 1993. With 70,000 inhabitants, Bamberg is a small town in the heart of Europe.

The theme of the 2015 edition was "Connection, tradition, innovation." In its relatively short history, the human–computer interaction (HCI) area has experienced impressive development. Theories, methodologies, procedures, guidelines, and tools have been progressively proposed, discussed, tested, and frequently adopted by academia and industry. The protagonists of this development created in a short period of time a scientific and technological tradition able to produce high-quality interaction systems. However, the evolution of the computers and networks pose new challenges to all stakeholders. Innovation, based on tradition, is the only way to face these challenges, even if innovation often requires breaking the tradition. In order to make this process possible, INTERACT 2015 provides diverse and abundant connection opportunities. A multidisciplinary approach is characteristic of the HCI field. INTERACT 2015 aimed to connect all the matters able to contribute to the quality of the future interactions among people and computers.

The series of INTERACT international conferences (started in 1984) is supported by Technical Committee 13 on Human–Computer Interaction of the International Federation for Information Processing (IFIP). This committee aims at developing the science and technology of the interaction between humans and computing devices.

IFIP was created in 1960 under the auspices of UNESCO with the aim of balancing worldwide the development of computer technology and Science. Technical Committee 13 is fully conscious of the social importance of information and communication technologies for our world, today and in the future. Therefore, INTERACT 2015 made efforts to attract and host people from all over the world, and to pay attention to the constraints imposed on HCI by differences in culture, language, technological availability, physical, as well as sensory and cognitive differences, among other dimensions of interest.

INTERACT 2015 gathered a stimulating collection of research papers and reports of development and practice that acknowledge the diverse disciplines, abilities, cultures, and societies, and that address all the aspects of HCI, including technical, human, social, and esthetic.

Like its predecessors, INTERACT 2015 aimed to be an exciting forum for communication with people of similar interests, to foster collaboration and learning. Being by nature a multidisciplinary field, HCI requires interaction and discussion among diverse people with different interests and backgrounds. INTERACT 2015 was directed both to the academic and industrial world, always highlighting the latest developments in the discipline of HCI and its current applications. Experienced HCI researchers and professionals, as well as newcomers to the HCI field, interested in the design or evaluation of interactive software, development of new technologies for interaction, and research on general theories of HCI met in Bamberg.

We thank all the authors who chose INTERACT 2015 as the venue to publish their research. This was again an outstanding year for the conference in terms of submissions in all the technical categories.

We received 651 submissions. Of these, the following were accepted: 93 full research papers; 74 short research papers; eight demos; 30 interactive posters; four organizational overviews; three panels; six tutorials; 11 workshops; and 13 doctoral consortium papers.

The acceptance rate for the full papers was 29.6 % and 26.8 % for short papers.

In order to select the highest-quality contributions, an elaborate review system was organized including shepherding of 38 full research papers that went through a second and sometimes a third round of review. That process was primarily handled by the 32 meta-reviewers who willingly assisted and ensured the selection of high-quality full research papers to be presented at INTERACT 2015.

The final decision on acceptance or rejection of papers was taken in a plenary Program Committee meeting held in Tampere (Finland) in February 2015, aimed to discuss a consistent set of criteria to deal with inevitable differences among the large number of reviewers who were recruited and supported by the meta-reviewers. The technical program chairs and the track chairs, the general chairs, and the members of IFIP Technical Committee 13 participated in the meeting.

Special thanks must go to the track chairs and all the reviewers, who put in an enormous amount of work to ensure that quality criteria were maintained throughout the selection process. We also want to acknowledge the excellent work of the co-chairs of the different sections of the conference and the meta-reviewers of the full research paper track.

We also thank the members of the Organizing Committee, especially Mirko Fetter, local organization chair, who provided us with all the necessary resources to facilitate our work. Finally, we wish to express a special thank you to the proceedings publication chair, Marco Winckler, who did extraordinary work to put this volume together.

September 2015

Tom Gross
Julio Abascal
Simone Barbosa
Philippe Palanque

IFIP TC13

Established in 1989, the International Federation for Information Processing Technical Committee on Human–Computer Interaction (IFIP TC13) is an international committee of 37 national societies and nine working groups, representing specialists in human factors, ergonomics, cognitive science, computer science, design, and related disciplines. INTERACT is its flagship conference, staged biennially in different countries in the world. From 2017 the conference series will become an annual conference.

IFIP TC13 aims to develop the science and technology of human–computer interaction (HCI) by: encouraging empirical research, promoting the use of knowledge and methods from the human sciences in design and evaluation of computer systems; promoting better understanding of the relation between formal design methods and system usability and acceptability; developing guidelines, models, and methods by which designers may provide better human-oriented computer systems; and, cooperating with other groups, inside and outside IFIP, to promote user orientation and humanization in system design. Thus, TC13 seeks to improve interactions between people and computers, encourage the growth of HCI research and disseminate these benefits worldwide.

The main orientation is toward users, especially non-computer professional users, and how to improve human–computer relations. Areas of study include: the problems people have with computers; the impact on people in individual and organizational contexts; the determinants of utility, usability, and acceptability; the appropriate allocation of tasks between computers and users; modeling the user to aid better system design; and harmonizing the computer to user characteristics and needs.

While the scope is thus set wide, with a tendency toward general principles rather than particular systems, it is recognized that progress will only be achieved through both general studies to advance theoretical understanding and specific studies on practical issues (e.g., interface design standards, software system consistency, documentation, appropriateness of alternative communication media, human factors guidelines for dialogue design, the problems of integrating multimedia systems to match system needs and organizational practices, etc.).

In 1999, TC13 initiated a special IFIP Award, the Brian Shackel Award, for the most outstanding contribution in the form of a refereed paper submitted to and delivered at each INTERACT. The award draws attention to the need for a comprehensive human-centered approach in the design and use of information technology in which the human and social implications have been taken into account. 2007 IFIP TC 13 also launched an accessibility award to recognize an outstanding contribution with international impact in the field of accessibility for disabled users in HCI. In 2013, IFIP TC 13 launched the Interaction Design for International Development (IDID) Award, which recognizes the most outstanding contribution to the application of interactive systems for social and economic development of people in developing countries. Since the process to decide the award takes place after papers are submitted for publication, the awards are not identified in the proceedings.

IFIP TC 13 also recognizes pioneers in the area of HCI. An IFIP TC 13 pioneer is one who, through active participation in IFIP Technical Committees or related IFIP groups, has made outstanding contributions to the educational, theoretical, technical, commercial, or professional aspects of analysis, design, construction, evaluation, and use of interactive systems. IFIP TC 13 pioneers are appointed annually and awards are handed over at the INTERACT conference.

IFIP TC13 stimulates working events and activities through its working groups (WGs). WGs consist of HCI experts from many countries, who seek to expand knowledge and find solutions to HCI issues and concerns within their domains, as outlined here.

WG13.1 (Education in HCI and HCI Curricula) aims to improve HCI education at all levels of higher education, coordinate and unite efforts to develop HCI curricula and promote HCI teaching.

WG13.2 (Methodology for User-Centered System Design) aims to foster research, dissemination of information and good practice in the methodical application of HCI to software engineering.

WG13.3 (HCI and Disability) aims to make HCI designers aware of the needs of people with disabilities and encourage development of information systems and tools permitting adaptation of interfaces to specific users.

WG13.4 (also WG2.7; User Interface Engineering) investigates the nature, concepts, and construction of user interfaces for software systems, using a framework for reasoning about interactive systems and an engineering model for developing user interfaces.

WG 13.5 (Resilience, Reliability, Safety, and Human Error in System Development) seeks a framework for studying human factors relating to systems failure, develops leading-edge techniques in hazard analysis and safety engineering of computer-based systems, and guides international accreditation activities for safety-critical systems.

WG13.6 (Human–Work Interaction Design) aims at establishing relationships between extensive empirical work-domain studies and HCI design. It will promote the use of knowledge, concepts, methods, and techniques that enable user studies to procure a better apprehension of the complex interplay between individual, social, and organizational contexts and thereby a better understanding of how and why people work in the ways that they do.

WG13.7 (Human–Computer Interaction and Visualization) aims to establish a study and research program that will combine both scientific work and practical applications in the fields of HCI and visualization. It will integrate several additional aspects of further research areas, such as scientific visualization, data mining, information design, computer graphics, cognition sciences, perception theory, or psychology, into this approach.

WG13.8 (Interaction Design and International Development) are currently working to reformulate their aims and scope.

WG13.9 (Interaction Design and Children) aims to support practitioners, regulators, and researchers to develop the study of interaction design and children across international contexts.

New Working Groups are formed as areas of significance to HCI arise. Further information is available on the IFIP TC13 website: http://ifip-tc13.org/

IFIP TC13 Members

Officers

Chair
Jan Gulliksen, Sweden

Vice-chair
Philippe Palanque, France

Vice-Chair for WG and SIG
Simone D.J. Barbosa, Brazil

Treasurer
Anirudha Joshi, India

Secretary
Marco Winckler, France

Webmaster
Helen Petrie, UK

Country Representatives

Australia
Henry B.L. Duh
Australian Computer Society

Austria
Geraldine Fitzpatrick
Austrian Computer Society

Belgium
Monique Noirhomme-Fraiture
Fédération des Associations
   Informatiques de Belgique

Brazil
Raquel Oliveira Prates
Brazilian Computer Society (SBC)

Bulgaria
Kamelia Stefanova
Bulgarian Academy of Sciences

Canada
Heather O'Brien
Canadian Information Processing Society

Chile
Jaime Sánchez
Chilean Society of Computer Science

Croatia
Andrina Granic
Croatian Information Technology
   Association (CITA)

Cyprus
Panayiotis Zaphiris
Cyprus Computer Society

Czech Republic
Zdeněk Míkovec
Czech Society for Cybernetics &
   Informatics

Denmark
Torkil Clemmensen
Danish Federation for Information
   Processing

Finland
Kari-Jouko Räihä
Finnish Information Processing
   Association

France
Philippe Palanque
Société des Electriciens et des
   Electroniciens (SEE)

Germany
Tom Gross
Gesellschaft fur Informatik

Hungary
Cecilia Sik Lanyi
John V. Neumann Computer
   Society

Iceland
Marta Kristin Larusdottir
The Icelandic Society for Information
  Processing (ISIP)

India
Anirudha Joshi
Computer Society of India

Ireland
Liam J. Bannon
Irish Computer Society

Italy
Fabio Paternò
Italian Computer Society

Japan
Yoshifumi Kitamura
Information Processing Society of Japan

Korea
Gerry Kim
KIISE

Malaysia
Chui Yin Wong
Malaysian National Computer
  Confederation

The Netherlands
Vanessa Evers
Nederlands Genootschap voor
  Informatica

New Zealand
Mark Apperley
New Zealand Computer Society

Nigeria
Chris C. Nwannenna
Nigeria Computer Society

Norway
Dag Svanes
Norwegian Computer Society

Poland
Marcin Sikorski
Poland Academy of Sciences

Portugal
Pedro Campos
Associação Portuguesa para o Desen-
  volvimento da Sociedade da Infor-
  mação (APDSI)

Slovakia
Vanda Benešová
The Slovak Society for Computer
  Science

South Africa
Janet L. Wesson
The Computer Society of South Africa

Spain
Julio Abascal
Asociación de Técnicos de Informática
  (ATI)

Sweden
Jan Gulliksen
Swedish Computer Society

Switzerland
Solange Ghernaouti
Swiss Federation for Information
Processing

Tunisia
Mona Laroussi
Ecole Supérieure des Communications
  De Tunis (SUP'COM)

UK
Andy Dearden
British Computer Society (BCS)

USA
Gerrit van der Veer
Association for Computing Machinery
  (ACM)

Expert Members

Nikos Avouris (Greece)
Simone D.J. Barbosa (Brazil)
Peter Forbrig (Germany)
Joaquim Jorge (Portugal)
Paula Kotzé (South Africa)
Masaaki Kurosu (Japan)

Gitte Lindgaard (Australia)
Zhengjie Liu (China)
Fernando Loizides (Cyprus)
Dan Orwa (Kenya)
Frank Vetere (Australia)

Working Group Chairs

WG13.1 (Education in HCI and HCI Curricula)
Konrad Baumann, Austria

WG13.2 (Methodologies for User-Centered System Design)
Marco Winckler, France

WG13.3 (HCI and Disability)
Helen Petrie, UK

WG13.4 (also 2.7) (User Interface Engineering)
Jürgen Ziegler, Germany

WG13.5 (Resilience, Reliability, Safety and Human Error in System Development)
Chris Johnson, UK

WG13.6 (Human–Work Interaction Design)
Pedro Campos, Portugal

WG13.7 (HCI and Visualization)
Achim Ebert, Germany

WG 13.8 (Interaction Design and International Development)
José Adbelnour Nocera, UK

WG 13.9 (Interaction Design and Children)
Janet Read, UK

Conference Organizing Committee

General Conference Co-chairs
Tom Gross, Germany
Julio Abascal, Spain

Full Papers Chairs
Simone D.J. Barbosa, Brazil
Philippe Palanque, France

Short Papers Co-chairs
Fabio Paternò, Italy
Kari-Jouko Räihä, Finland

Posters and Demos Co-chairs
Stephen Brewster, UK
David McGookin, UK

Organization Overviews Co-chairs
Melanie Fitzgerald, USA
Kori Inkpen, USA

Panels Co-chairs
Anirudha N. Joshi, India
Gitte Lindgaard, Australia

Open Space Co-chairs
Christoph Beckmann, Germany
Achim Ebert, Germany

Tutorials Co-chairs
Christoph Beckmann, Germany
Regina Bernhaupt, France

Workshops Co-chairs
Christoph Beckmann, Germany
Víctor López-Jaquero, Spain

Doctoral Consortium Co-chairs
Geraldine Fitzpatrick, Austria
Panayiotis Zaphiris, Cyprus

Proceedings Chair
Marco Winckler, France

Madness Co-chairs
Artur Lugmayr, Finland
Björn Stockleben, Germany
Tim Merritt, Denmark

Local Organization Co-chairs
Mirko Fetter, Germany
Claudia Tischler, Germany

Student Volunteers Co-chairs
Robert Beaton, USA
Sascha Herr, Germany

Program Committee

Meta-reviewers

Birgit Bomsdorf, Germany
Gaëlle Calvary, France
José Campos, Portugal
Pedro Campos, Portugal
Luca Chittaro, Italy

Torkil Clemmensen, Denmark
Paul Curzon, UK
Achim Ebert, Germany
Peter Forbrig, Germany
Michael Harrison, UK

Anirudha Joshi, India
Denis Lalanne, Switzerland
Effie Law, UK
Célia Martinie, France
Laurence Nigay, France
Monique Noirhomme, Belgium
Fabio Paternò, Italy
Helen Petrie, UK
Antonio Piccinno, Italy
Aaron Quigley, UK
Kari-Jouko Räihä, Finland
Virpi Roto, Finland

Luciana Salgado Cardoso de Castro,
   Brazil
Paula Alexandra Silva, Ireland
Frank Steinicke, Germany
Simone Stumpf, UK
Allistair Sutcliffe, UK
Jean Vanderdonckt, Belgium
Gerhard Weber, Germany
Astrid Weiss, Austria
Marco Winckler, France
Panayiotis Zaphiris, Cyprus

Reviewers

José Abdelnour-Nocera, UK
Al Mahmud Abdullah, Australia
Silvia Abrahão, Spain
Funmi Adebesin, South Africa
Ana Paula Afonso, Portugal
David Ahlström, Austria
Pierre Akiki, Lebanon
Deepak Akkil, Finland
Hannu Alen, Finland
Jan Alexandersson, Germany
José Carlos Bacelar Almeida, Portugal
Florian Alt, Germany
Julian Alvarez, France
Junia Coutinho Anacleto, Brazil
Leonardo Angelini, Switzerland
Craig Anslow, New Zealand
Mark Apperley, New Zealand
Nathalie Aquino, Paraguay
Liliana Ardissono, Italy
Carmelo Ardito, Italy
Oscar Javier Ariza Núñez, Germany
Myriam Arrue, Spain
Ilhan Aslan, Austria
Simon Attfield, UK
Nikolaos Avouris, Greece
Chris Baber, UK
Myroslav Bachynskyi, Germany
Jonathan Back, UK
Gilles Bailly, France
Liam Bannon, Ireland

Emilia Barakova, The Netherlands
Javier Barcenila, France
Louise Barkhuus, USA
Barbara Rita Barricelli, Italy
Valentina Bartalesi, Italy
Mohammed Basheri, Saudi Arabia
Christoph Beckmann, Germany
Yacine Bellik, France
Vanda Benešová, Slovak Republic
Kawtar Benghazi, Spain
David Benyon, UK
François Bérard, France
Regina Bernhaupt, Austria
Karsten Berns, Germany
Nadia Berthouze, UK
Raymond Bertram, Finland
Mark Billinghurst, New Zealand
Dorrit Billman, USA
Silvia Amelia Bim, Brazil
Fernando Birra, Portugal
Renaud Blanch, France
Ann Blandford, UK
Mads Boedker, Denmark
Davide Bolchini, USA
Birgit Bomsdorf, Germany
Rodrigo Bonacin, Brazil
Paolo Gaspare Bottoni, Italy
Fatma Bouali, France
Chris Bowers, UK
Giorgio Brajnik, Italy

Anke Brock, France
Barry Brown, Sweden
Judith Brown, Canada
Gerd Bruder, Germany
Duncan Brumby, UK
Nick Bryan-Kinns, UK
Stéphanie Buisine, France
Sabin-Corneliu Buraga, Romania
Paris Buttfield-Addison, Australia
Maria Claudia Buzzi, Italy
Marina Buzzi, Italy
Cristina Cachero, Spain
Sybille Caffiau, France
Paul Cairns, UK
Roberto Caldara, Switzerland
Gaëlle Calvary, France
Licia Calvi, The Netherlands
José Campos, Portugal
Pedro Campos, Portugal
Katia Canepa Vega, Brazil
Maria-Dolores Cano, Spain
Maria Beatriz Carmo, Portugal
Francesco Carrino, Switzerland
Stefano Carrino, Switzerland
Luis Carriço, Portugal
Marcus Carter, Australia
Daniel Cernea, Germany
Teresa Chambel, Portugal
Stéphane Chatty, France
Monchu Chen, Portugal
Yu Chen, Switzerland
Kelvin Cheng, Singapore
Yoram Chisik, Portugal
Luca Chittaro, Italy
Elizabeth Churchill, USA
Torkil Clemmensen, Denmark
Gilbert Cockton, UK
Karin Coninx, Belgium
Tayana Conte, Brazil
Stéphane Conversy, France
Jeremy Cooperstock, Canada
Nuno Correia, Portugal
Joëlle Coutaz, France
Céline Coutrix, France
Nadine Couture, France
Chris Creed, UK

Martin Cronel, France
James Crowley, France
Jácome Cunha, Portugal
Paul Curzon, UK
Marie d'Udekem, Belgium
Florian Daiber, Germany
Girish Dalvi, India
José Danado, UK
Antonella De Angeli, Italy
Alexander De Luca, Switzerland
Maria De Marsico, Italy
Giorgio De Michelis, Italy
Leonardo Cunha de Miranda, Brazil
Boris De Ruyter, The Netherlands
Clarisse de Souza, Brazil
Alexandre Demeure, France
Giuseppe Desolda, Italy
Ines Di Loreto, France
Paulo Dias, Portugal
Shalaka Dighe, India
Christian Dindler, Denmark
Anke Dittmar, Germany
Pierre Dragicevic, France
Carlos Duarte, Portugal
Cathy Dudek, Canada
Henry Been-Lirn Duh, Australia
Bruno Dumas, Belgium
Sophie Dupuy-Chessa, France
Achim Ebert, Germany
Florian Echtler, Germany
Rob Edlin-White, UK
Jan Engelen, Belgium
Thomas Erickson, USA
Elina Eriksson, Sweden
Dominik Ertl, UK
Parisa Eslambolchilar, UK
Marc Fabri, UK
Carla Faria Leitão, Brazil
Ava Fatah gen Schieck, UK
Xavier Ferre, Spain
Eija Ferreira, Finland
Mirko Fetter, Germany
Sebastian Feuerstack, Germany
Vagner Figueredo de Santana, Brazil
Daniela Fogli, Italy
Joan Fons, Spain

Manuel Fonseca, Portugal
Peter Forbrig, Germany
Marcus Foth, Australia
Andre Freire, Brazil
Carla D.S. Freitas, Brazil
Jonas Fritsch, Denmark
Luca Frosini, Italy
Dominic Furniss, UK
Nestor Garay-Vitoria, Spain
Jérémie Garcia, France
Roberto García, Spain
Jose Luis Garrido, Spain
Franca Garzotto, Italy
Isabela Gasparini, Brazil
Miguel Gea, Spain
Patrick Gebhard, Germany
Cristina Gena, Italy
Giuseppe Ghiani, Italy
Patrick Girard, France
Kentaro Go, Japan
Daniel Gonçalves, Portugal
Rúben Gouveia, Portugal
Nicholas Graham, Canada
Andrina Granic, Croatia
Toni Granollers, Spain
Saul Greenberg, Canada
John Grundy, Australia
Nuno Guimaraes, Portugal
Jan Gulliksen, Sweden
Rebecca Gulotta, USA
Mieke Haesen, Belgium
Hans Hagen, Germany
Jonna Häkkilä, Finland
Jukka Häkkinen, Finland
Jaakko Hakulinen, Finland
Lynne Hall, UK
Arnaud Hamon, France
Chris Harrison, USA
Daniel Harrison, UK
Michael Harrison, UK
Ruediger Heimgaertner, Germany
Tomi Heimonen, Finland
Matthias Heintz, UK
Ingi Helgason, UK
Susan Catherine Herring, USA
Wilko Heuten, Germany

Martin Hitz, Austria
Thuong Hoang, Australia
Rüdiger Hoffmann, Germany
Jennifer Horkoff, UK
Heiko Hornung, Brazil
Ko-Hsun Huang, Taiwan,
   Republic of China
Alina Huldtgren, The Netherlands
Ebba Thora Hvannberg, Iceland
Aulikki Hyrskykari, Finland
Ioanna Iacovides, UK
Netta Iivari, Finland
Mirja Ilves, Finland
Yavuz İnal, Turkey
Poika Isokoski, Finland
Minna Isomursu, Finland
Howell Istance, Finland
Ido A. Iurgel, Germany
Mikkel R. Jakobsen, Denmark
Francis Jambon, France
Jacek Jankowski, Poland
Maddy Janse, The Netherlands
Nuno Jardim Nunes, Portugal
Caroline Jay, UK
Kasper Løvborg Jensen, Denmark
Mikael Johnson, Finland
Matt Jones, UK
Joaquim Jorge, Portugal
Rui Jose, Portugal
Anirudha Joshi, India
Christophe Jouffrais, France
Anne Joutsenvirta, Finland
Marko Jurmu, Finland
Eija Kaasinen, Finland
Jari Kangas, Finland
Anne Marie Kanstrup, Denmark
Victor Kaptelinin, Sweden
Evangelos Karapanos, Portugal
Kristiina Karvonen, Finland
Dinesh Katre, India
Manolya Kavakli, Australia
Patrick Gage Kelley, USA
Ryan Kelly, UK
Rabia Khan, UK
Hideki Koike, Japan
Christophe Kolski, France

Hannu Korhonen, Finland
Nataliya Kosmyna, France
Paula Kotze, South Africa
Christian Kray, Germany
Per Ola Kristensson, UK
Sari Kujala, Finland
Todd Kulesza, USA
Denis Lalanne, Switzerland
David Lamas, Estonia
Michael Lankes, Austria
Rosa Lanzilotti, Italy
Przemyslaw Lasota, USA
Yann Laurillau, France
Effie Law, UK
Shaimaa Lazem, UK
Xavier Le Pallec, France
Eric Lecolinet, France
Jong-Seok Lee, South Korea
Asko Lehmuskallio, Finland
Antti Leino, Finland
Juha Leino, Finland
Tuomas Leisti, Finland
Jair Leite, Brazil
Alexander Lenz, UK
Barbara Leporini, Italy
Sophie Lepreux, France
Karen Y. Li, UK
Edirlei Lima, Brazil
James Lin, USA
Mats Lind, Sweden
Agnes Lisowska Masson, Switzerland
Zhengjie Liu, China
Sara Ljungblad, Sweden
Corrado lo Storto, Italy
Steffen Lohmann, Germany
Fernando Loizides, Cyprus
Víctor López-Jaquero, Spain
Fabien Lotte, France
Maria Dolores Lozano, Spain
Yichen Lu, Finland
Paul Lubos, Germany
Stephanie Ludi, USA
Bernd Ludwig, Germany
Andreas Luedtke, Germany
Christopher Lueg, Australia
Jo Lumsden, UK
Christof Lutteroth, New Zealand

Kris Luyten, Belgium
Anderson Maciel, Brazil
I. Scott MacKenzie, Canada
Allan MacLean, UK
Christian Maertin, Germany
Charlotte Magnusson, Sweden
Ana Gabriela Maguitman, Argentina
Päivi Majaranta, Finland
Marco Manca, Italy
Nicolai Marquardt, UK
Célia Martinie, France
Paolo Masci, UK
Masood Masoodian, New Zealand
Maristella Matera, Italy
Denys J.C. Matthies, Germany
Peter W. McOwan, UK
Gerrit Meixner, Germany
Guy Melançon, France
Amaia Mendez Zorrilla, Spain
Maria Menendez Blanco, Italy
Zdenek Mikovec, Czech Republic
Jan-Torsten Milde, Germany
Nicole Mirnig, Austria
Giulio Mori, Italy
Roxana Morosanu, UK
Christiane Moser, Austria
Marcelle Mota, Brazil
Omar Mubin, Australia
Chrystie Myketiak, UK
Miguel Nacenta, UK
Lennart Nacke, Canada
Mathieu Nancel, Canada
Bonnie Nardi, USA
David Navarre, France
Ather Nawaz, Norway
Luciana Nedel, Brazil
Alexandra Nemery, France
Vania Neris, Brazil
Daniel Nesbitt, UK
Lene Nielsen, Denmark
Anton Nijholt, The Netherlands
Laurence Nigay, France
Manuel Noguera, Spain
Monique Noirhomme, Belgium
Julianne Nyhan, UK
Clemens Nylandsted Klokmose,
   Denmark

Michael O Grady, Ireland
Aisling Ann O'Kane, UK
Marianna Obrist, UK
Lars Oestreicher, Sweden
Jarno Ojala, Finland
Patrick Oladimeji, UK
Kathia Oliveira, France
Thomas Olsson, Finland
Dan Orwa, Kenya
Nuno Otero, Sweden
Benoit Otjacques, Luxembourg
Saila Ovaska, Finland
Janne Paavilainen, Finland
Xinru Page, USA
Ana Paiva, Portugal
Jose Ignacio Panach Navarrete, Spain
Eleftherios Papachristos, Greece
Konstantinos Papoutsakis, Greece
Avi Parush, Israel
Oscar Pastor, Spain
Fabio Paternò, Italy
Celeste Lyn Paul, USA
Andriy Pavlovych, Canada
Roberto Pereira, UK
Vinícius Carvalho Pereira, Brazil
Mark J. Perry, UK
Hele Petrie, UK
Antoinio Piccinno, Italy
Lara Piccolo, UK
Emmanuel Pietriga, France
Thomas Pietrzak, France
Frank Pollick, UK
Ravi Poovaiah, India
Roman Popp, Austria
Christopher Power, UK
Raquel Prates, USA
Costin Pribeanu, Romania
Angel Puerta, USA
Kai Puolamäki, Finland
Victor M.R. Penichet, Spain
Aaron Quigley, UK
Kari-Jouko Räihä, Finland
Roope Raisamo, Finland
Venkatesh Rajamanickam, India
Nitendra Rajput, India
Ismo Rakkolainen, Finland
Jussi Rantala, Finland

Alberto Raposo, Brazil
Dimitrios Raptis, Denmark
Umar Rashid, UK
Kirsten Rassmus-Gröhn, Sweden
Matthias Rauterberg, The Netherlands
Janet Read, UK
Mandryk Regan Lee, Canada
Patrick Reignier, France
Christian Remy, Switzerland
Karen Renaud, UK
Yann Riche, USA
Fabien Ringeval, Germany
Thomas Rist, Germany
Paola Rodriguez, Colombia
Markus Rohde, Germany
Teresa Romão, Portugal
Jose Rouillard, France
Virpi Roto, Finland
Thijs Roumen, Germany
Gustavo Alberto Rovelo Ruiz, Belgium
Elisa Rubegni, Switzerland
Simon Ruffieux, Switzerland
Jaime Ruiz, USA
Angel Ruiz-Zafra, Spain
Rimvydas Ruksenas, UK
Horacio Saggion, Spain
Pascal Salembier, France
Luciana Salgado Cardoso de Castro,
   Brazil
Antti Salovaara, Finland
Leonardo Sandoval, UK
Carmen Santoro, Italy
Corina Sas, UK
Andreas Savva, UK
Taufique Sayeed, Austria
Gianluca Schiavo, Italy
Antonio Giovanni Schiavone, Italy
Albrecht Schmidt, Germany
Stefan Schneegass, Germany
Kevin Schneider, Canada
Vinicius Segura, Brazil
Marcos Serrano, France
Ehud Sharlin, Canada
Sumita Sharma, Finland
Moushumi Sharmin, USA
Abhishek Shrivastava, India
Beat Signer, Belgium

Harri Siirtola, Finland
Paula A. Silva, Ireland
Bruno S. Silva, Brazil
Carlos CL Silva, Portugal
João Carlos Silva, Portugal
Jose Luis Silva, Portugal
Paula Alexandra Silva, Ireland
Milene Silveira, Brazil
Carla Simone, Italy
Shamus Smith, Australia
Andreas Sonderegger, Switzerland
Keyur Sorathia, India
Fabio Sorrentino, Italy
Hamit Soyel, UK
Oleg Spakov, Finland
Lucio Davide Spano, Italy
Mark Vincent Springett, UK
Jan Stage, Denmark
Christian Stary, Austria
Katarzyna Stawarz, UK
Frank Steinicke, Germany
Gerald Stollnberger, Austria
Markus Stolze, Switzerland
Simone Stumpf, UK
Noi Sukaviriya, USA
Allistar Sutcliffe, UK
David Mark Swallow, UK
Tapio Takala, Finland
Chee-wee Tan, Denmark
Franck Tarpin-Bernard, France
Carlos Teixeira, Portugal
Luis Teixeira, Portugal
Daniel Tetteroo, The Netherlands
Jakob Tholander, Sweden
Nigel Thomas, UK
Liisa Tiittula, Finland
Nava Tintarev, UK
Martin Tomitsch, Australia
Ilaria Torre, Italy
Marilyn Tremaine, USA
Daniela Trevisan, Brazil
Sanjay Tripathi, India
Janice Tsai, USA
Manfred Tscheligi, Austria
Huawei Tu, UK
Outi Tuisku, Finland
Phil Turner, UK

Susan Ellen Turner, UK
Markku Turunen, Finland
Blase Ur, USA
Heli Väätäjä, Finland
Stefano Valtolina, Italy
Judy van Biljon, South Africa
Jos P. van Leeuwen, The Netherlands
Paul van Schaik, UK
Jeroen Vanattenhoven, Belgium
Jean Vanderdonckt, Belgium
Jari Varsaluoma, Finland
Radu-Daniel Vatavu, Romania
Angel Velazquez-Iturbide, Spain
Hanna Venesvirta, Finland
Jayant Venkatanathan, India
Gilles Venturini, France
Arnold Vermeeren, The Netherlands
Karel Vermeulen, UK
Frédéric Vernier, France
Markel Vigo, UK
Nadine Vigouroux, France
Chris Vincent, UK
Giuliana Vitiello, Italy
Arnd Vitzthum, Germany
Dhaval Vyas, Australia
Mike Wald, UK
Jim Wallace, Canada
Tanja Carita Walsh, Finland
Robert Walter, Germany
Leon Watts, UK
Gerhard Weber, Germany
Rina Wehbe, Canada
Astrid Weiss, Austria
Janet Louise Wesson, South Africa
Graham Wilson, UK
Stephanie Wilson, UK
Marco Winckler, France
Theophilus Winschiers, Namibia
Chui Yin Wong, Malaysia
Wolfgang Wörndl, Germany
Volker Wulf, Germany
Yeliz Yesilada, Turkey
Salu Ylirisku, Finland
Nur Haryani Zakaria, Malaysia
Massimo Zancanaro, Italy
Panayiotis Zaphiris, Cyprus
Jürgen Ziegler, Germany

Sponsors and Supporters

Sponsors

 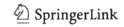

Supporters

Mensch-Computer-Interaktion
Human-Computer Interaction

Contents – Part III

Human-Robot Interaction

Interactive Tabletops

Mobile and Ubiquitous Interaction

Mullti-screen Visualization and Large Screens

Participatory Design

Pointing and Gesture Interaction

Social Interaction

An Interactive Approach for Inspecting Software System Measurements

Taimur Khan[1]([⊠]), Henning Barthel[2], Karsten Amrhein[1],
Achim Ebert[1], and Peter Liggesmeyer[1,2]

[1] University of Kaiserslautern, Gottlieb-Daimler-Str.,
67663 Kaiserslautern, Germany
{tkhan, ebert, liggesmeyer}@cs.uni-kl.de,
amrhein@rhrk.uni-kl.de
[2] Fraunhofer IESE, Fraunhofer-Platz 1, 67663 Kaiserslautern, Germany
{Henning.Barthel,
Peter.liggesmeyer}@iese.fraunhofer.de

Abstract. In recent times, visual analysis has become increasingly important, especially in the area of software measurement, as most of the data from software measurement is multivariate. In this regard, standard software analysis tools are limited by their lack of ability to process huge collections of multidimensional data sets; current tools are designed to either support only well-known metrics or are too complicated to use for generating custom software metrics. Furthermore, the analyst requires extensive knowledge of the underlying data schemas and the relevant querying language. To address these shortcomings, we propose an interactive visual approach that focuses on visual elements, their configurations, and interconnectivity rather than a data ontology and querying language. In order to test and validate our methodology, we developed a prototype tool called VIMETRIK (Visual Specification of Metrics). Our preliminary evaluation study illustrates the intuitiveness and ease-of-use of our approach to understand software measurement and analysis data.

Keywords: Software comprehension · Software measurement · Interactive visual analysis · Visual query specification · Software visualization

1 Introduction

Studies estimate that up to 80 % of the software costs occur in the maintenance phase, 40 % of which goes into understanding the software system [10]. In this context, various measurements or software metrics are often utilized to obtain objective, reproducible, and quantifiable measurements to assist software analysts in quality assurance testing, software debugging, and software performance optimization. Independent of the application area, such measurements are closely scrutinized to ensure that the system in question performs optimally, is safe and reliable, and is of high quality.

Analyses of such measurements of software systems tend to result in the scrutiny of a large amount of analysis data by means of software metrics. Most mainstream analysis tools, such as the Fraunhofer M-System [6], specify and examine these

J. Abascal et al. (Eds.): INTERACT 2015, Part III, LNCS 9298, pp. 1–8, 2015.
DOI: 10.1007/978-3-319-22698-9_1

software metrics using a database approach. In this case, an analyzable representation of the source code is generated, stored in a relation or graph database, and queried to create measurement data (e.g., quality or maintainability metrics) [3, 5].

However, these traditional approaches require the analyst to not only have in-depth knowledge of the underlying data schema but also expert knowledge of the relevant querying mechanisms. For using such an approach, the analyst needs an insight into the data ontology and must formulate queries using either the Structured Query Language (SQL) for relational databases [5] or a graph querying language such as GReQL [3] for graph databases. In contrast, we propose an interactive visual approach that focuses on visual elements, their configurations, and interconnectivity rather than a data ontology and querying language.

In this paper, the above-mentioned shortcomings are addressed through an innovative means for facilitating the specification and visualization of user-defined software system measurements. The key ingredients of our approach are a schema-less data access path to an underlying graph data model, a workflow-based approach for defining metrics, and the ability to visually depict the results of these queries not only in traditional forms (e.g., through tabular views, scatter plots, box plots, histograms, line charts, etc.) but also through modern interactive visualization paradigms (e.g., the city view [7]). The novelty of our approach lies in how we combine the specification and visualization of software measurements through data workflows. Ultimately, our goal is to empower end users with the ability to apply tailored metrics and visualization metaphors to visually explore the characteristics of a software system according to their individual needs and requirements.

In order to validate our ideas, we developed a live-data prototype tool called VIMETRIK (Visual Specification of Metrics). Our preliminary evaluation study indicates the prospects and the feasibility of our approach to analyze software measurement data.

2   Related Work

Our approach aims at providing easy and intuitive means for analyzing a software system at different levels of details in terms of software measurements or metrics, such as computing cyclomatic complexity, analyzing dependencies or call traces, or using statistical analysis to find issues. However, current software analysis tools (e.g., [4, 6, 11]) tend to be complicated as they require in-depth knowledge of the underlying data schemas and the relevant querying language.

Closely related tools are: Sextant [13], a tool for specifying and visualizing software metrics for Java source code and WiggleIndexer,[1] a tool that allows the indexing of Abstract Syntax Trees (AST) using a graph database. Although these tools have some similar features, they do not employ workflows in the visual analysis of software systems. WiggleIndexer has a similar graph database model and querying mechanism;

---

[1] WiggleIndexer – Indexing of AST using graph databases (https://github.com/raoulDoc/WiggleIndexer).

however, users need to have in-depth knowledge of both the model and the underlying Cypher querying language. On the other hand, although Sextant provides several visualization capabilities, it contains significantly fewer details about the system and the analysis needs to be performed in the Service Modeling Language (SML) instead of with workflows.

3 The Methodology

In this section, we present the details of our methodology, which consists of a graph database model capable of capturing full details of a software system's source code and a workflow-based approach for defining metrics.

3.1 The Graph Database Model

Generally, traditional measurement tools use a relational database to store information about the target software system, which leads to a trade-off between scalability and the number of source code details stored. Furthermore, relational databases are often faced with implementation-related issues, such as schema evolution over time, extensive joins of large tables, etc.

In contrast, we propose using a graph database approach aimed at storing full source code details, which scales to large programs and provides an easy means for restructuring. Our proposed graph model is designed to handle queries about software artifacts and is based on AST. The resulting Directed Acyclic Graph (DAG) contains additional links between the vertices of a syntax tree. Our aim in providing such a graph model is to address the many crosscutting queries that our domain experts may have.

For the sake of brevity, Fig. 1 shows only the top-level entities of our proposed graph model as well as the links between these entities. The key ingredients of this top-level model are: an *analysis* root, which may contain links to projects, primitives, arrays, and a literals root; *projects*, which may be connected to top-level packages or, for convenience, directly to compilation units; *packages*, which may have links to sub-packages; and *compilation units*, which contain a top-level type. By traversing the above-mentioned nodes, we touch upon nodes and edges that form the top-level hierarchy of a software system. Additional edges between these elements provide further insight into the various aspects of the underlying software system. For example: *IMPORTS* provides an understanding of the coupling between compilation units and *HAS_LITERAL* offers a means for tracking the usage of literals.

Similarly, our graph model contains representations of other source code elements such as fields, methods, statements, and expressions. It forms a tree-like structure that not only contains the hierarchy of each source file but, more importantly, links to elements found in other source files, too. These additional edges in our graph model connect related elements in a meaningful manner and are a key ingredient for cross-cutting queries, such as finding artifacts that connect method or variable usage to their declaration. Furthermore, nodes and edges in our graph model have properties that

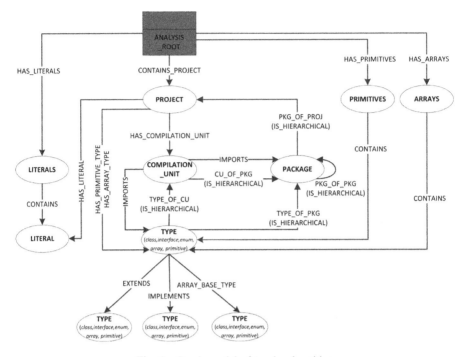

Fig. 1. Graph model of top-level entities

allow us to distinguish the graph elements according to their types, their access parameters, or through other artifacts.

Finally, it is important to mention that as graph databases rely on semi-structured data, they can be easily modified in order to cater to changing requirements. As a result, our model can be easily modified through the addition of new nodes, edges, or properties.

3.2 Querying Through a Workflow-Based Approach

The central focus of our methodology is on supporting users who have no prior knowledge of the underlying graph model, database, or query mechanisms. To do so, we break down larger software measurement concerns into smaller well-managed modules. The focal point of designing modules that process software entities, which we refer to as *Software Fact Extractors*, is to allow users to assemble and adapt an analysis flow comprised of standard building blocks. Thus, the main function of these modules is for users to combine them in a meaningful manner, through pipes that carry data, in order to produce useful software measurement results.

In order to highlight how the above-mentioned modules can be combined in a workflow to produce a software measurement, we present a simple workflow example in Fig. 2, which calculates the number of packages per project. In this figure, blue nodes represent our Software Fact Extractors, while the yellow node symbolizes a data manipulator. Since we are interested in projects that are part of the source analysis and not in external libraries, we configure the "AllProjects" module with the *INTERNAL* access option. From the user's perspective, this node produces a listing of all the internal projects in the database and connects to the "PackagesInProject" module. However, internally it needs to execute a Cypher query to produce the results. Similarly, the "PackagesInProject" node traverses the *PKG_OF_PROJ* and *PKG_OF_PKG* links of Fig. 1 to provide a project-to-package mapping. Finally, a data manipulation node labeled "Aggregation" groups the projects according to a count of project-to-package mappings.

4 The VIMETRIK Tool

In order to demonstrate our methodology, we have developed an interactive visual data exploration and data-mining tool called VIMETRIK. Our tool is built on top of the KNIME[2] Eclipse plug-in that enables users to model workflows. However, as a prerequisite to working with our workflows the user needs to extract source code facts, following the methodology described in Sect. 3, into a Neo4j graph database with the help of a pre-packaged library. From the user's perspective, this is a simple process as they just need to load Java projects into the Eclipse Java Package Explorer and click on "Extract Facts".

In KNIME, the most common processing unit is a "Node", which represents any of the visual workflow nodes. Our custom nodes gather the Cypher query results as "DataTables" and pass them to connected nodes for processing or visualization. Additionally, these nodes provide a token that contains the graph database connection details. This approach enables us to process elements of our graph database and at the same time have the full functionality of all the nodes available in KNIME. Interoperability between our Software Fact Extractors in KNIME and the Neo4j database is attained through the management of KNIME's DataTable data structure and the specification of our graph queries.

Using our VIMETRIK tool, we have developed several workflows that calculate metrics at different levels of the code structure, such as the Chidamber & Kemerer metrics suite [2], the QMOOD metrics suite [1], McCabe's cyclic complexity measure [8], etc. Figure 3a shows an example of such a workflow.

Once the relevant software metrics are modeled using our workflow-based approach, the measurement results can be analyzed using different coordinated views of the data. On the one hand, users can attach and configure standard KNIME "Data View" nodes that produce traditional views (i.e., parallel coordinates, scatter matrix, or tabular view). On the other hand, users can generate interactive software visualizations via a VIMTERIK "CustomNetworkViewer" node. This node allows the users to configure the type of visualization (i.e., city, sunburst, or hyperbolic), apply some generic settings, and map measurement results as entity properties. Figure 3b shows one of these possibilities, with the results being encoded in a city view [7].

---

[2] KNIME Analytics Platform (http://www.knime.org/knime/).

Fig. 2. A simple workflow for number of packages

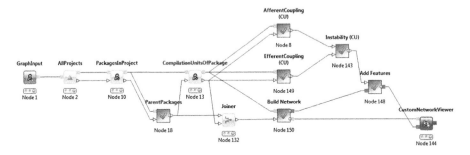

(a)   An example of the VIMETRIK workflow

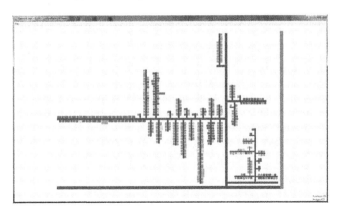

(b)   Custom view of the measurement results

Fig. 3. Integrated analysis and visualization approach

5   The Preliminary Evaluation Study

A preliminary evaluation study was conducted to determine if software analysts could use our proposed methodology to perform software measurement tasks effectively (in terms of completion and accuracy) and, importantly, without dealing with the complexity of a data ontology or querying mechanisms. To validate these claims, we chose experts (21 Master or PhD students, 4 females and 17 males) from the related fields of Software Engineering (SE), Computer Graphics (CG), and Database and Information Systems (DBIS). None of them had any prior experience with VIMETRIK or KNIME;

however, all had object-oriented programming experience and 19 had either SQL or basic query knowledge.

Our hypotheses were that by using our tool, users with no prior experience would be able to achieve a completion rate of at least 85 % (H_1) and an accuracy of at least 85 % (H_2) for basic software measurement tasks. Furthermore, we expected the participants to be highly satisfied (with regard to acceptability and usability) with our tool.

We selected the Apache Tomcat system as the target system for our investigation. The software measurement tasks (size, cyclic complexity, and coupling) were classified into three categories (lightweight, intermediate, and advanced) according to the number of Fact Extractor nodes required for each task. At the end of each test, a closed-ended Likert scale (ranging from 1 *"strongly disagree"* to 5 *"strongly agree"*) questionnaire and an open-ended questionnaire were used to collect user satisfaction feedback and suggestions.

Each subject was given a short tutorial and was asked to complete nine identical tasks. The subjects were awarded 0 % to 100 % for the completion or correctness of each task; however, the completion and correctness task results were weighted according to their difficulty: *lightweight = 1*, *intermediate = 3*, and *advanced = 5*. We applied descriptive statistical methods (i.e., sample mean, standard deviation, and median) to the gathered experiment data. We also tested our hypotheses statistically using the Wilcoxon T test, with a confidence level for rejecting the null hypotheses at 95 %. Due to space restrictions, we present only a summary of the results.

The overall completion percentage for all groups was 94.38 % (*SE = 94.03 %*, *CG = 95.43 %*, and *DBIS = 93.68 %*). The completion hypothesis H_1 was tested using the Wilcoxon T test (*Z = 4.04, p = 1.0E-04*), which justified our hypothesis (p<0.05; thus, the null hypothesis was rejected). Similarly, the overall correctness percentage for all groups was 94.22 % (*SE = 93.71 %, CG = 95.71 %*, and *DBIS = 93.24 %*). The correctness hypothesis H_2 was also tested using the Wilcoxon T test (*Z = 4.12, p = 3.78E-5*), which justified our hypothesis (p<0.05; thus, the null hypothesis was rejected).

In the closed-ended questionnaires (four questions from the performance and effort expectancy parameters of the TAM model [12] and eleven questions from the utility, intuitiveness, learnability, and personal effect parameters from the work of Nestler et al. [9]), the subjects (irrespective of the user group) gave an average score of 4 out of 5. This indicates that the subjects were highly satisfied with our tool. Furthermore, they provided a few useful suggestions in the open-ended questionnaires that we aim to tackle in the future.

6 Conclusion

This preliminary study shows both the prospects and the feasibility of our proposed solution. In particular, participants with no knowledge of the underlying database model, the querying mechanism, or software analysis in general were able to use our tool to understand software measurement and analysis data. The intuitive and easy-to-use nature of our approach is highlighted by the fact that independent of their expertise, they were able to complete basic software analysis tasks with a completion rate and accuracy of over 85 %. This would not be possible with current tools, which require users to have in-depth knowledge of data ontology and advanced querying skills. Furthermore, all participants were highly satisfied (with regard to usability and acceptance) with our approach.

This work has raised interesting issues for future work. One relevant extension is the addition of modules and mechanisms to include software measurements that handle source code analysis rules, such as those used by PMD, Checkstyle, and FindBugs. Another interesting future work is to monitor the evolution of these measurements in order to support various change requirements. Furthermore, as a consequence of the preliminary results a full-scale comparative study is planned with professional software analysts.

References

1. Bansiya, J., Davis, C.G.: A hierarchical model for object-oriented design quality assessment. IEEE Trans. Softw. Eng. **28**(1), 4–17 (2002)
2. Chidamber, S.R., Kemerer, C.F.: A metrics suite for object oriented design. IEEE Trans. Softw. Eng. **20**(6), 476–493 (1994)
3. Ebert, J., Bildhauer, D.: Reverse engineering using graph queries. In: Engels, G., Lewerentz, C., Schäfer, W., Schürr, A., Westfechtel, B. (eds.) Nagl Festschrift. LNCS, vol. 5765, pp. 335–362. Springer, Heidelberg (2010)
4. Hajiyev, E., Verbaere, M., de Moor, O.: *codeQuest:* scalable source code queries with datalog. In: Thomas, D. (ed.) ECOOP 2006. LNCS, vol. 4067, pp. 2–27. Springer, Heidelberg (2006)
5. Harrison, W.: A flexible method for maintaining software metrics data: a universal metrics repository. J. Syst. Softw. **72**(2), 225–234 (2004)
6. Münch, J., Wickenkamp, A.: M-System NT - Ein flexibles, datenbank-basiertes Mess- und Analyse-System. In: MetriKon, pp. 55–64. Shaker Verlag, Kaiserslautern, 14–16 November 2005
7. Khan, T., Barthel, H., Ebert, A., Liggesmeyer, P.: eCITY: a tool to track software structural changes using an evolving city. In: ICSM, pp. 492–495. IEEE (2013)
8. McCabe, T.J.: A complexity measure. In: ICSE, p. 407. IEEE Computer Society Press, Los Alamitos, (1976)
9. Nestler, S., Artinger, E., Coskun, T., Yildirim, Y., Schumann, S., Maehler, M., Wucholt, F., Strohschneider, S., Klinker, G.: Assessing qualitative usability in life-threatening, time-critical and unstable situations. GMS Med. Inf. Biomed. Epidemiol. 7(1) (2011)
10. Pollo, M., Piattini, M., Ruiz, F.: Advances in Software Maintenance Management: Technologies and Solutions. Idea Group Publishing, Hershey (2003)
11. Roover, C.D., Noguera, C., Kellens, A., Jonckers, V.: The SOUL tool suite for querying programs in symbiosis with Eclipse. In: Probst, C.W., Wimmer, C. (eds.) PPPJ, pp. 71–80. ACM (2011)
12. Venkatesh, V., Morris, M.G., Davis, G.B., Davis, F.D.: User acceptance of information technology: toward a unified view. MIS Q. **27**(3), 425–478 (2003)
13. Winter, V., Reinke, C., Guerrero, J.: Sextant: a tool to specify and visualize software metrics for Java source-code. In: WETSoM, pp. 49–55, May 2013

Non-response, Social Exclusion, and False Acceptance: Gatekeeping Tactics and Usability Work in Free-Libre Open Source Software Development

Mikko Rajanen[✉], Netta Iivari, and Arto Lanamäki

Department of Information Processing Science,
University of Oulu, Oulun yliopisto, PO Box 3000, 90014 Oulu, Finland
{mikko.rajanen,netta.iivari,arto.lanamaki}@oulu.fi

Abstract. Usability is an important aspect of Free-Libre Open Source Software (FLOSS), but barriers exist for usability specialists' participation in such projects. Organizational boundary literature is interested in the tensions of online communities, including FLOSS communities. While this literature recognizes the importance of managing boundaries in online communities, little empirical research has been conducted on actual gatekeeping tactics project members perform against outsiders' contributions. Based on several years of engaged research with FLOSS projects, we characterize three gatekeeping tactics in FLOSS projects: non-response, social exclusion, and false acceptance. They all have hindered usability work. We also offer examples of usability specialists and their contributions succeeding in avoiding these gatekeeping tactics in FLOSS projects. This paper provides an important contribution to the boundary management literature through detailed examination of gatekeeping tactics in action, as well as to the Human Computer Interaction literature interested in contributing to FLOSS projects through usability work.

Keywords: Usability specialist · FLOSS · Boundary management · Gatekeeping

1 Introduction

A young and enthusiastic usability expert wanted to volunteer in a Free-Libre Open Source Software (FLOSS) project developing a media-center software. He had seen how the project was strongly oriented in technical functionalities, while the usability aspects were lacking. Therefore, he saw how the project could benefit from his usability expertise. He went on the project's internet relay chat (IRC) channel and found active discussions going on. After a period of time, he introduced himself and proposed to volunteer as a usability expert in the project. No one answered him. After a while, he kindly restated his message. Soon, he received an answer: "don't be so *spammy*." He was confused and sad that the community disregarded his kind will to volunteer in the project, and to contribute to it using his expertise.

© IFIP International Federation for Information Processing 2015
J. Abascal et al. (Eds.): INTERACT 2015, Part III, LNCS 9298, pp. 9–26, 2015.
DOI: 10.1007/978-3-319-22698-9_2

This example is not how FLOSS projects are painted by the apologists. They, instead, emphasize the basic freedoms of software users: freedom to run software, freedom to study software, freedom to change software in any way that a user sees as necessary and freedom to distribute copies of software with or without changes to it [1] and characterize FLOSS projects as participatory and egalitarian settings in which individuals develop FLOSS due to their personal need, but also voluntarily reveal their solutions to be used and further developed by others [2]. In this kind of setting, user innovation flourishes as the reputation and status that can be gained as well as the community development model motivate people to reveal the solution also for others' use and further development [3]. The continuous improvement and refinement of the solution done by the community members is one driving force of FLOSS development [4]. All these indicate that FLOSS projects are to be seen as participatory and egalitarian places where people collaboratively develop FLOSS to serve their own needs as well as the needs of the others.

However, less attention has been paid to the aspects of inaccessibility and inequality in FLOSS projects. In a sense, Human Computer Interaction (HCI) research has already acknowledged FLOSS projects as not such participatory and egalitarian places; many HCI studies have revealed that usability experts are experiencing challenges when trying to enter FLOSS projects. HCI research has already established that usability specialists and their contributions are easily ignored, both in commercial software development (e.g. [5, 6]) and in FLOSS development (e.g. [7–12]. Hence, it is evident that power and politics play a role as regards usability work also in FLOSS projects; not all members get equal treatment in FLOSS projects, and usability specialists are often among the 'power-weak' in this respect [11, 12].

This paper tries to explain the challenges involved with usability specialists entering FLOSS projects with a focus on boundary management as the theoretical framework. Boundary management is generally interested in the "activities involved in defining, negotiating, and protecting organisational resources and domains of action, as well as managing relationships with external stakeholders, to achieve the organisational goals" [13]. This framework has already been utilized in the context of various kinds of online communities, including FLOSS communities (e.g. [14]). Online communities are considered as new forms for organizing, related to which boundaries are more permeable and dynamic [13, 15, 16]. Unlike traditional organizations that are hierarchical with quite clear boundaries, online communities are fluid objects "where boundaries, norms, participants, artifacts, interactions, and foci continually change over time" [15]. However, the framework has not yet been utilized to make sense of usability work in FLOSS projects. We consider the framework as a suitable lens to be utilized in this novel context: for examining the boundary management activities carried out by FLOSS project members when usability specialists are attempting to enter FLOSS projects. Here, we will especially rely on the concept of 'gatekeeping' to make sense of the challenges involved with usability specialists' work. This concept addresses the filtering and moderation of participation and content production in online communities [16]. Based on empirical analysis, we identify three gatekeeping tactics that have hindered usability work in our cases as well examples of situations in which usability specialists have succeeded to enter into and contribute to the FLOSS projects in questions, i.e., they and their contributions have succeeded in becoming 'filtered in'.

This study contributes both to the boundary management literature through examination of actual gatekeeping tactics in action and to the HCI literature interested in contributing to FLOSS projects through usability work.

The paper is structured as follows. The next section reviews research on boundary management and gatekeeping in the context of online communities and more specifically in FLOSS communities, indicating that these concepts have relevance also for FLOSS usability research. The third section describes the research method involved in this study, introduces the cases involved in this study as well as the procedures for data collection and analysis. The fourth section presents the empirical results of our analysis. The fifth section discusses the implications of the results while the last section summarizes the results and their implications for research and practice as well as outlines the limitations of the results and based on those, identifies a number of interesting paths for future work.

2 Background

This section introduces literature on boundary management and gatekeeping, and relates it to the FLOSS and HCI research on usability work in FLOSS projects.

2.1 Boundary Management and Gatekeeping in FLOSS Communities

FLOSS is computer software that is freely available as source code, and often also as a precompiled binary file. The license permits users to read, change, and modify the source code as derived works, recompile the modified source code to binary form, and distribute the modified source code as a derivative under the same license as the original source code [17].

While the letter 'O' in 'FLOSS' refers to openness *of the source code*, openness is often seen to apply to the whole ethos of development [18]. A fundamental idea of FLOSS is to enable software to evolve freely through community participation. In principle everyone can participate in FLOSS projects, and the more people participate, the better results will be achieved. This is reflected in Eric Raymond's [17] formulation of Linus' Law: "Given enough eyeballs, all bugs are shallow". This insouciant depiction of openness is visible in, for example, the article by Bach and Terry [19] who note that "members of the FLOSS community are highly accessible", and that "there are rarely 'gatekeepers' that control access."

On the other hand, studies have also shown that power and politics picture in FLOSS projects, too (e.g. [11]). The FLOSS community is often depicted with an onion model (e.g. [20]) with different layers representing the level of involvement within that particular FLOSS community. The layers also depict the level of decision power at each layer. In a typical FLOSS community, there is a lead developer or a small group of developers forming the core team that controls the overall architectural design and the course of the project [20–23]. Some FLOSS projects are relatively democratic, while in others the project leaders make decisions as "benevolent dictators". Indeed, one of the most common models in coordinating FLOSS development projects is that several contributors work under a single 'benevolent dictator' who is usually the founder of the project and who attracts committed and talented contributors [24]. An alternative to having one single benevolent dictator is rotating dictatorship or forming a voting committee from the developers [24]. Despite these differences, the core developers nevertheless have a significant position in FLOSS project as decision-makers: they make both low-level decisions regarding whether or not a particular contribution is accepted to the code, mid-level decisions regarding software features to be included in individual releases, and strategic decisions regarding the direction of the development in the future as well as the development roadmap.

For a developer to become an accepted contributor or even an acknowledged member of a FLOSS project certain procedures or 'joining scripts' need to be relied on [14, 25, 26]. A developer may have to provide *feature gifts*, i.e. whole modules or features as his contribution during that phase [26]. The core developers assess the value of the contribution and the contributor before accepting it. There is significant prestige motivation to get own contributions accepted and to become a member of the development team [20, 23]. However, many obstacles have been witnessed as regards entering FLOSS projects. In a recent systematic literature review, Steinmacher and colleagues [25] identified 20 published studies dealing with contribution barriers that newcomers face in FLOSS projects. These barriers represent 5 main types: social interaction, newcomers' previous knowledge, technical hurdles, finding a way to start, and documentation. Social interaction was the biggest category with 12 studies, and it divided into three subcategories: "lack of social interaction with project members", "receiving an improper answer", and "not receiving a (timely) answer" [25].

This leads us to consider how FLOSS projects balance between openness and control. Do FLOSS projects welcome newcomers and their contributions, stimulate creativity, and allow diversity? Or are they protecting the establishment, and relying solely on its tradition? These questions have already been addressed in the literature on boundary management, where it has been argued that in online communities "boundary management involves trade-offs between openness (attracting external participation, stimulating innovation, creativity and organisational growth) and control (over platform activities and content production and appropriation), or trade-offs between standardisation and formalisation of production processes and availability and accessibility of diverse resources" [13]. Here, we focus on a particular type of boundary management, namely gatekeeping. We adopted the concept of gatekeeping from Shaw [16], whose definition of gatekeeping reads as "the systematic reproduction of an unequal and regular flow of valued resources—especially influence—to an incumbent group or organization". Shaw borrowed the concept from Clayman and Reisner [27], who in turn credit its origin to Lewin [28]. Following Shaw [16], in this paper we formulate gatekeeping tactics to refer to the specific actions carried out by FLOSS project members relating to filtering and moderating outsiders' participation in and contribution to FLOSS projects to achieve the goals of the projects. We will offer an empirical analysis of it in relation to usability work in FLOSS projects.

2.2 Usability and FLOSS Development

HCI research has already addressed the FLOSS development context and HCI researchers have already argued that usability specialists should participate in FLOSS projects [7, 9, 10, 29–33]. Different kinds of usability methods have been suggested for FLOSS development. Several articles recommend conducting usability testing [7, 10, 32–34], while some argue also for usability inspections in FLOSS projects [33, 34]. For usability design, user interface design using blogs has been suggested [32], as has the establishment and use of usability infrastructure such as discussion forums, mailing lists, and design areas [8, 10, 30, 32].

Nevertheless, researchers have also revealed that problems might arise when combining the traditional usability methods and recommendations with the FLOSS development and philosophy [8–10, 31, 33, 35, 36]. Reluctance to heavyweight corporate usability processes might arise in FLOSS development; i.e., decentralized and engineering-driven FLOSS development might be in contrast with heavyweight corporate usability processes [8, 9, 31, 33, 35]. In addition, usability specialists might not be available in FLOSS projects, and, even if they were, they might be very few in number and they might be working in isolation [7–12]. Furthermore, the software development in FLOSS projects is almost always already ongoing when the projects gain enough visibility to be spotted by the usability specialists, making it difficult to apply usability methods from the beginning of the development when it is easiest [11, 37]. Usability specialists might have difficulties in showing their merits and gaining authority in FLOSS projects [7, 12, 30, 36]. They may be welcomed into the consultative role as feedback providers (cf. [6]), but they might find it difficult to gain any decision-making power regarding the design solution, which is recommended in the participative role endorsed in the HCI literature (cf. [6]). In FLOSS projects, as mentioned, the core developers make all of the decisions regarding what will be included in the code base. The usability specialists should try to utilize various kinds of lobbying, persuasion, and allying strategies in order to have an impact [12, 36, 38, 39].

Hence, several challenges for usability specialists' participation in FLOSS projects have already been identified. Our empirical data, along with these other studies, pinpoints these challenges. However, this paper contributes through making sense of these challenges. Three gatekeeping tactics hindering usability work are identified from FLOSS projects. Additionally, a few cases are identified in which usability specialists have succeeded in overcoming these challenges, and becoming 'filtered in'.

3 Research Method

Our arguments about boundary management and gatekeeping tactics in FLOSS projects are based upon intensive engagement in different FLOSS projects since 2007, with an overall aim of enabling usability specialists to enter into and contribute to FLOSS projects. Walsham [40, 41] has discussed different roles researchers can adopt in qualitative, interpretive research, i.e. the 'outside researcher' and the 'involved researcher' roles [40]. The former refers to the researcher having "no direct involvement in action in the field or in providing significant feedback to field participants", while the latter refers to researcher acting as a participant observer or action researcher who consciously and explicitly aims at changing things in the field. We have adopted the latter position, within a large research program that has included intensive work with a number of FLOSS projects during a 7 years timespan. The overall purpose has been the improvement of usability processes in FLOSS projects. The research program has resulted in the development and experimentation of various kinds of methods outlining for usability specialists how to enter into and contribute to FLOSS projects (reported in [11, 12, 35, 39, 42]). The methods have placed particular emphasis on participative approach of the usability specialists: they need to try to gain a thorough understanding the project in question and to actively collaborate with the developers [12, 35, 39]. Additionally, the results from the research program implies that usability work is more likely to have an impact if the results are provided by encultured insiders that have modified their usability work to fit the particular OSS project, because every OSS project is unique [42]. During our analyses, it has also become evident that power and politics sometimes truly complicate usability work in FLOSS projects [11]. The present paper aims to explain some of the challenges faced by usability specialists in the projects.

Our research program has included altogether 16 subprojects within which junior researchers, organized into usability teams, have introduced usability activities into FLOSS projects as part of their university studies. This has occurred under the guidance of more experienced HCI researchers. All junior researchers have had usability background from at least two previous usability courses about usability evaluation methods (e.g. heuristic evaluation and usability testing), user-centered design, and user interface design in both theory and practice. Each of the subprojects has consisted of three to five junior researchers working between 200 and 300 h each in planning the usability activities, carrying out these usability activities in the selected project, communicating with the project, following up the impact of these usability activities, collecting empirical data, and writing project reports. The senior HCI researchers have guided the usability teams during the entire process, including the selection of the project and the selection of suitable entrance strategies and usability methods to use. Altogether, our role has been that of involved researcher [40], i.e., we have consciously and explicitly tried to change things in the field and to make a valid contribution. During the 7 year research program and 16 different interventions organized, various strategies and methods have been experimented with, resulting in differing outcomes in involved projects with different domains, communities and cultures. After the interventions, the HCI researchers have been responsible of analyzing the collected data and developing and further refining the methods outlining ways for usability specialists to utilize their expertise and gain recognition in FLOSS projects.

In this paper, the empirical data included has been collected from six of these usability projects. This data includes online material of the involved FLOSS projects, such as websites, mailing list and discussion forum posts, IRC discussion logs, etc. In addition, the junior researchers, during their interventions, have produced numerous kinds of reports of their work and of the selected case projects that are included as research material. For the purposes of this paper, we inductively identified and analyzed the instances we encountered from this empirical data that somehow related to power and politics as regards usability specialists entering into and contributing to

FLOSS projects. We identified problems in that process as well as successes achieved. The data itself led to the categorization of the three different gatekeeping tactics, while only after the identification of those, the literature outlined in the previous section relating to boundary management and especially to gatekeeping was utilized as a sensitizing device to make sense of our findings.

Before describing our empirical findings on the gatekeeping tactics in FLOSS projects, we briefly introduce the six case projects involved in this analysis and our associated interventions into these case projects.

Case A was developing a media application, targeted at non-technical end users without programming skills or interest. The project was started in 2004 and had a total of about 30 developers. The usability team observed this FLOSS project for five months in 2007, while conducting heuristic evaluations, cognitive walkthroughs, and usability testing. The usability team reported the findings in the form of a report, which was sent to the core developers and mentioned in a post in the main discussion forum of the community.

Case B was developing a game targeted at non-technical end users. This project, started in 2003, had a total of 15 developers. The usability team observed this FLOSS project for five months in 2008, while performing heuristic evaluation and usability testing. The usability team was in close contact with the lead developer regarding their findings and possible redesign solutions, and also participated in discussions in the project's IRC channel. After the evaluations, the usability team wrote a usability report. This included suggestions for changes to fix the identified usability problems.

Case C was developing a 3D content creation software targeted at end users with 3D content creation skills but without skills or interest in programming. The project, started in 2002, had a total of 40 more or less active developers. The usability team observed this project for six months in 2009. During that time span, they carried out usability testing and heuristic evaluation and wrote several reports about usability problems and their suggestions for changes to fix those problems. These reports were made available on the usability team's blog and advertised in the project's IRC channels and discussion forums.

Case D was developing a media center software with target users of ordinary people. The project started in 2003 and had about 20 active developers. The usability team observed this FLOSS project for five months in 2009, while performing heuristic evaluations and usability testing. In this case the results report was sent to the FLOSS developers by email in a similar manner as in case A.

Case E was developing a game targeted at non-technical end users without programming skills. This project started originally in 1995, but the development team had changed many times since then. This project had 20 active developers with commit rights. The usability team observed this FLOSS project for four months in 2010, while conducting heuristic evaluations using game usability heuristics and usability testing. The usability team wrote preliminary and final usability reports about the usability issues and their suggestions for changes to the user interface to fix them. The final usability report was delivered to the wiki of the FLOSS project. In addition, the usability team submitted code patches and level design work, including new user interface menus and a new tutorial for the game.

Case F was developing a vector graphics software targeted at non-technical end users. The project, started in 2003, had a total of 6 core developers and 14 developers. The usability team observed this FLOSS project for six months in 2009 and 2010, while performing heuristic evaluation and prototyping. The usability team wrote a usability report based on the results from heuristic evaluation and redesigned an improved user interface as a mock up. These deliverables were sent to the core developers through email and discussion forum.

4   Gatekeeping Tactics in FLOSS Development

Our work with the FLOSS development projects has revealed that gatekeeping tactics to keep outsiders' unwanted contributions away truly take place. The gatekeeping tactics identified from each case are summarized in Table 1.

Next we offer empirical illustrations of the tactics, followed by examples that reveal that usability specialists occasionally have also been able to get 'filtered in'.

4.1   The Gatekeeping Tactic of 'Non-response'

In our first intervention, involving the case A, the junior researchers carried out two types of expert usability evaluations: heuristic evaluation and cognitive walkthrough. Next, they planned and executed usability tests based on the findings from these expert evaluations. A report of usability findings was written and sent to the developers by email. This was the first contact between the developers and the usability team, as it was planned. The purpose of this approach was to mimic the way the software patches are submitted in the FLOSS development projects: somebody writes the patch, which is then shared with the community. Eventually the core developers either accept this patch into the main branch or reject it.

As it turned out to be, the work of the usability team had no impact, but their message fell into deaf ears. At first, no answer was received from the emailed core developers. Thereafter, the same document containing the usability findings was posted to the discussion forum of the project. Then one of the core developers answered that

Table 1. Three gatekeeping tactics identified in the FLOSS cases

	A	B	C	D	E	F
Non-response	x			x		x
Social exclusion	x	x	x			
False acceptance					x	

they were discussing this document and its findings internally and could comment on it later. However, there has not been any answer or further communication from the developers and there are no signs of changes to the software that could be traced back to these usability findings. One can argue that the gatekeeping tactic of non-response was evidently utilized by the core-developers. This resulted in totally ignoring the attempts of the usability team.

A validation test was conducted in case D, in which a similar kind of FLOSS project was selected and the usability team followed a similar type of approach in their work. Hence, the result was also the same. The results report was sent to the FLOSS developers by email, they replied they had received it, but no further communication from their side emerged and the FLOSS in question has not been changed according to the results reported.

In another intervention, involving the case F, the usability team conducted heuristic evaluation and redesigned the user interface based on the results from the evaluation. The redesigned user interface was prototyped as a mock up so that it would be easy for the developers to understand the proposed changes. The results from heuristic evaluation and the prototype mock up were sent to the core developers by email and discussion forum posts. However, no answer was received from the core-developers despite multiple communication attempts. Not surprisingly, the work of the usability team had no impact and no signs of changes to the user interface could be noticed. Also in this case the gatekeeping tactic by the core-developers was simply to not respond to the communication attempts.

Finally, similar kind of behavior has been observable towards some users in FLOSS project discussion forums. In the case A, some users had expressed criticism towards the user-interface of the application and offered certain usability improvement suggestions. Also those had been disregarded by the developers who had only commented that the application "is not meant for girlfriends". This kind of response does not invite further discussion on the matter. Interestingly, this project had nevertheless stated on its website that it wanted to target 'non-technical end-users'. However, likely the suggestions provided by the users were not such that were preferred by the core developers, and thus they were hushed down.

4.2   The Gatekeeping Tactic of 'Social Exclusion'

The usability interventions arranged were not entirely ignored in all case projects. For example, in case B, after the failure encountered in case A, the HCI researchers decided that the junior researchers should familiarize themselves with the project before their usability intervention. Hence, the junior researchers followed the project's IRC channels and discussion forums for some time before making themselves and their intentions known to the project. Thereafter, they contacted the lead developer through email and offered their help. In this project, there was no prior knowledge about usability, but the usability team explained the concept of usability and its potential benefits to the project, and identified some possible areas for usability evaluation. They carried out expert usability evaluation and usability testing for the software. Additionally, they continuously communicated with the core developer and the community through the project's IRC channel. Also here, they delivered their results by email to the core developers. In this case, however, the core developers accepted and implemented the changes to the next version of the software. The usability team was even later on contacted and requested to carry out another usability evaluation.

However, although the work done by the usability team seemed to be a success, some problems were observed. The developers also gave some negative feedback on the work of the usability team. One of the main problems was the rapid development of the software. The pace of the usability evaluation was slower, and therefore some of the usability team's findings were obsolete by the time the report was ready. The usability team was in this case treated as an external resource and the core developers did not help the team to fit the usability activities into their overall development plan and bug fixing process. The usability activities were welcomed and encouraged, but the usability team did not become integrated into the community. In addition, the developers wanted concrete suggestions about how to fix the user interface problems and not just general comments about what the problems were. However, once the developers had a list of concrete improvement suggestions, they considered only those suggestions that they saw as fixing issues they saw as problems. If the core developers thought that some of the usability team's findings were not truly problems, these findings got a very low priority and were eventually discarded. All in all, one can say that in this case the usability team was allowed to work and was acknowledged by the FLOSS project, but they were excluded from the actual decision-making and planning processes, hindering the usability team's ability to offer meaningful and timely usability contributions.

Another observation can be connected with case C, within which another usability team consisting again of junior researchers carried out their intervention. Again, the junior researchers were expected to familiarize themselves with the project before their usability intervention. However, in this case there was a vast number of communication channels available both in the project's website and third party websites; e.g. mailing lists, IRC channels, wikis, and discussion forums. The usability team searched and followed multiple communication channels (e.g., various IRC channels, message boards, project news sites, and wiki pages) for a couple of weeks getting to know the project. Next, they contacted the core developers and offered their usability expertise in particular area of software that had already raised some discussion about complicated user interface and difficulties in use. The usability team conducted usability tests and expert usability evaluations, and documented them in open source fashion on a website, which was promoted in community forums and IRC channels, and also offered to several community news sites for publication. The reactions were mixed. One core developer was very supportive to the usability activities, while other core developers and community ignored the usability issues. The reports were downloaded about fifty times from the website, but no further discussion was generated. The news about the usability activities and their results were quickly buried beneath other discussions and news. Eventually, the usability intervention did not have an impact on the software in question. This FLOSS project had a multilayer hierarchical structure in which the leading core developer as the benevolent dictator was inaccessible to the usability team. The leading core developer communicated with other trusted core developers as his lieutenants. The usability intervention did not catch the attention of them, albeit the usability team was able to carry out their work and gain one supportive core developer on their side. However, their usability intervention results ultimately ended up as being socially excluded.

4.3   The Gatekeeping Tactic of 'False Acceptance'

An example that we label as "false acceptance" occurred in case E. The initial usability team working with the project clearly succeeded in having an impact on the software under development. The usability team, similarly to case B, followed the project IRC channels and discussion forums for some time before their intervention. Again, they conducted an expert usability evaluation and empirical usability testing. They sent their report to the mailing list of the project as well as to the community wiki. In this case, the results aroused a lot of interest. The developers actively commented the results. In addition, the usability team submitted code patches and game level design work that were accepted into the code repository of the project. Moreover, the usability report was referenced directly in commit messages of the core-developers four times. One of these commit messages asked for an input and contribution from the usability team. After this, changes were made based on their recommendations. One of the usability team members even got commit rights and gained a status as a developer. He was participating actively in discussions and was recognized within the community as being a skillful and committed user of the software.

However, the gatekeeping tactic of false acceptance can be connected with this case. Related to it, we emphasize that it is important to acknowledge that it may take place during a longer time span and in a discreet way, potentially leaving the usability contributors with an impression that they succeeded in improving the usability of the software. The usability team concentrated their efforts into the tutorial, which was found incomprehensible and frustrating to new users. The usability team streamlined the tutorial, cut the amount of data and descriptions presented to user and polished it with innovative new level design. The new tutorial performed well in usability tests. The core developers and the broader community were enthusiastic about it. However, later on it was revealed that the creator of the original tutorial had reverted the tutorial almost back to its previous version in the next major release. Hence, the usability improvements were obliterated. This did not involve any discussion on the matter or explicit criticism on the work of the usability team. The original creator of the tutorial had the right to modify the software the way he wished, and he exercised this right.

Subsequent usability teams working with the same project noticed later on that parts of the user interface and functionality changes requested by the first usability team working with the case project two years earlier that had already accepted and implemented by the core-developers, had been reverted almost completely to the original. This discarded the usability improvements. One core developer hinted to the later usability teams that another core developer had some very strong opinions on a certain part of the user interface and this core-developer had reverted back the changes to bring back this part of the user interface as it was originally and as he liked it, without a collective decision by all core-developers. None of the other core-developers had reacted to this in any way.

4.4   Usability Contributions Becoming Filtered In

Despite encountering these gatekeeping tactics when aiming to enter into and contribute to FLOSS projects, many successes have also been achieved by our usability teams. In particular, we view cases B and E as largely successful ones. In these two cases, the usability specialists and their contributions, at least partly, have succeeded in avoiding the gatekeeping tactics and become 'filtered in'. In case B, the usability team managed to avoid the gatekeeping tactics of non-response and false acceptance, albeit the gatekeeping tactic of social exclusion became visible through the usability team working on issues that already had become obsolete in the project due to the recent developments. We maintain that this success was due to the small size of development team and community as well as due to their willingness to have new people contributing to the development; the usability team was able to access the core developers and managed to contribute to the community in such a way that their contributions were accepted and appreciated. They were able to get in contact and interact with the core developers and the community before and during their intervention and they were able to address and convince the true decision-makers in this community. However, it may have been that the usability team accidentally succeeded in producing such a solution that the developers and the community were satisfied with, or at least beforehand the usability team did not specially consider the risk of false acceptance emerging nor tried eliminating it. In this case project there was no prior knowledge about usability, but instead the usability team educated the developers about the matter. Through this, however, it seems that the usability team succeeded in convincing the developers and the community of the value of their work and their redesigned solutions also happened to be compatible with the existing goals and visions of the decision-makers.

In case E, moreover, the usability specialists also managed to avoid most of the gatekeeping tactics, except for the false acceptance tactic. Also here we assume that this was due to the developers and community being very open to outsider contributions and the decision-makers being easy to contact and interact with. However, despite of this apparent openness for outsider contributors, the gatekeeping tactic of false acceptance was eventually utilized by at least some of the developers to block the contributions that they did not like. This happened even when these contributions were accepted by the other developers. In these instances, the usability team succeeded in arousing interest in the community and convincing the core developers initially, but this was not enough for their contribution to survive. This would likely have required another kind of design solution, but the usability team was unaware of their solution not meeting the needs or desires of some of the decision-makers.

5   Discussion

Several HCI studies have addressed the introduction of usability activities into FLOSS development context [7–12, 29–36, 38, 39, 42], but the challenges as regards this still seem to prevail. Moreover, there has not previously been reported this kind of long-term research intervention involving multiple FLOSS case projects, spanning multiple years and focusing on the boundary management and gatekeeping aspects of the interactions between the usability specialists and FLOSS developers. Based on the results of our analysis of usability work in FLOSS development, this study identified and characterized three tactics of gatekeeping: *non-response, social exclusion,* and *false acceptance*. Even though guidelines for introducing usability activities into FLOSS development have been proposed and experimented with earlier (see e.g. [12, 35, 39]), the gatekeeping tactics performed by FLOSS developers and communities against proposals to change have not been studied and categorized through this kind of longitudinal multiple case studies. Our studies imply that the usability specialists interested to conduct usability activities in FLOSS development context have to seriously take into account these forms of gatekeeping by the FLOSS developers and to be prepared for them. Next, the tactics are first summarized, after which some characteristics from successful cases are recapped.

As mentioned earlier, in cases A, D, and F the developers initiated a reply to usability specialists about the identified usability issues and proposed usability changes only after multiple attempts of contacting them. In these cases, the developers wanted not to open a public discussion about these proposed changes, but to silence the issue down. This kind of attitude was also indicated by certain discussion forum messages, where developers sometimes expressed open hostility towards any criticism or improvement suggestions about the user interface by the end-users. These occurrences indicate that the developers used the gatekeeping tactic labeled *non-response* to silence usability discussions even before they started. This tactic gains further support from the FLOSS literature in which "receiving an improper answer", and "not receiving a (timely) answer" have been reported as contribution barriers to newcomers [25]. These results have not been produced related to usability work, while our study shows that these are relevant also as regards usability work.

On the other hand, in cases B and C, the developers replied to and interacted with the usability specialists, but the usability specialists were, nevertheless, left out from the decision-making and planning processes. In case C, the usability specialists were free to conduct usability activities, but even though there were some words of encouragement and comments from core-developers regarding usability work, the usability specialists were left completely isolated from the decision-making arena, their voice was not heard within the community and the software was not changed as recommended. In case B, the planning process should have been visible also to the usability team to enable them to contribute in a meaningful way. Additionally, they were not allowed to take part in decision-making process in this project; hence the developers had the sole authority to decide which usability improvements ended up as being implemented and which ones were disregarded. These occurrences show that the developers used the gatekeeping tactic of *social exclusion*. Also this gatekeeping tactic can be connected with the existing FLOSS research that has indicated that "lack of social interaction with project members" acts as a contribution barrier for new members in FLOSS projects [25]. In our cases, the usability team should have been integrated into the planning and decision-making processes of the FLOSS projects or at least they should have been better informed of the outcomes of such processes. The lack of integration led to not keeping in pace with the development. As the rhythms of the development and usability were different, usability specialists ended up solving problems of yesterday. At the point of delivery, the development had already moved several steps ahead, and the usability efforts were obsolete. However, we acknowledge that it is a true challenge for any usability person to acquire a highly influential position in a FLOSS project and hence the gatekeeping tactic of social exclusion is very likely encountered by usability specialists working in FLOSS projects also in the future.

In cases B and E, on the other hand, the developers and the whole community were very enthusiastic about the work of the usability team and praised their reports of good quality. The developers implemented many of the suggested usability improvements and in the case E, the usability specialists and their work was referred to also in commit messages. However, in this case unfortunately some of the changes were rolled back in the next major release. These changes were not discussed in the community and even though other developers must have noticed the changes, they did not comment about them, at least not in public. All in all, in this case individual developers used the gatekeeping tactic of *false acceptance* directly to nullify the changes introduced by the usability team and it can be argued that also other developers utilized this tactic indirectly, because of their silence.

Despite all these challenges, many successes have also been achieved: the usability teams have succeeded in avoiding the gatekeeping tactics and become 'filtered in'. However, these gatekeeping tactics have been identified only after the fact and hence the usability teams could not prepare for them before or during their intervention. Still, these successful cases can be discussed here, as they may provide help for planning future interventions. It seems that the small size of development team as well as their willingness to have new people contributing to the development played a role in these successes. The usability team in these cases was able to access and directly interact with the core developers. In case B, it seems that the usability team also succeeded in convincing the developers of the value of their work and their redesign solutions also happened to be compatible with the project goals and visions.

However, we do not only wish to emphasize the negative aspect of boundary management and gatekeeping in online communities in general or in FLOSS projects in particular. Along with the existing literature, we highlight that boundaries and boundary management play a critical role in such communities: "Boundaries have an important dual nature. They *enable* the community to grow and thrive, but they also *protect and secure* the community from external threats." [13] Online communities need to protect their boundaries and ensure that only meaningful contributions get filtered in. For usability specialists, thus, it is of essential importance to understand what is considered meaningful in the particular community.

Regarding recommendations for practice, the boundary management literature can be utilized for offering advice for usability specialists on what kinds of things to consider when trying entering into a FLOSS project. The boundary management literature discusses different kinds of boundary logics that can be considered also in our context. The boundary logic of *identity* concerns the coherence of the community and its activities, the boundary logic of *power* relates to controlling key resources, defining the suitable domains of activity and influence in the community and managing external relationships, the boundary logic of *competence* addresses the critical competences for participation in these communities and the boundary logic of *transactional efficiency* relates to the resource view of the communities and economically efficient production models [13]. Applying these findings into our context leads to the following considerations. For enthusiastic usability specialists it might be essential to try to understand the identity of the community in question before entering into it and trying to introduce changes into it. This includes understanding the identity of the community as well as that of the software in question. In FLOSS projects there may be critical issues and ideological underpinnings underlying the design solution and usability specialists should understand those before messing with the solution. Otherwise the gatekeeping tactic of false acceptance may emerge when the decision makers notice that important aspects of their solution have become neglected. As regards power and politics in FLOSS projects, they have already been acknowledged as critical concerning usability work [11]. However, how to address them is still a question mark. Based on the boundary management literature we suggest that for usability specialists, figuring out the power related issues of interest may include finding out who controls the key resources in the project, defines the suitable domains of activity, has influence in the community and manages external relationships as well as how all these issues are accomplished in practice (cf. [13]). This should help usability specialists targeting right people at right time through right means. Finally, the issue of competence has already been brought up in the HCI literature on FLOSS projects: usability specialists tend not to have valued type of competence in FLOSS projects [11, 29, 30, 36, 38]. We do not have a solution for this problem, but our data points out (in case E) that usability specialists may benefit from having also technical skills. In our data one of the usability team members succeeded in getting commit rights and status as a developer. This usability team also contributed code to the FLOSS project in question. However, we do not wish to claim that technical skills are mandatory for usability specialists entering FLOSS projects. Many times usability specialists do not possess such skills and they should be allowed to contribute to FLOSS projects despite that. We suggest that usability specialists bring this issue to be openly discussed within the FLOSS project in question. Even this kind of a procedure may help the situation, albeit surely many challenges will still prevail for usability specialist attempting to enter into and to contribute to FLOSS projects.

One major takeaway from this study is the finding that FLOSS projects as fluid communities with blurred boundaries make also usability specialists' participation "blurry". In traditional closed source software development organizations, one knows who belongs to a project through an employment contract or other arrangement. In FLOSS development the boundary between inclusion and exclusion of potential participants is not that clear. The tactic of non-response signals that even when a newcomer has joined the project discussion forum, it may be difficult to actually enter the project and contribute to it in practice. The tactic of social exclusion shows that even after usability specialists have gained access within the boundary, they may remain on the peripheral edge of the FLOSS development onion unable to gain access to the deeper layers, and therefore be out of sync from the rhythm of how things develop in the inner layers of the FLOSS development onion. The tactic of false acceptance underscores that, even after usability has been accepted, integrated, and synchronized with the activities of the core developers, it may be disregarded retrospectively.

All in all, this paper contributes to the boundary management literature by providing a detailed examination of boundary gatekeeping tactics in action in FLOSS development context. By analyzing the FLOSS projects balancing between openness and control, we utilized the boundary management concept of gatekeeping and found that the concept of gatekeeping tactic applies in FLOSS development context in the sense of limiting outsider contributions, even though this goes against the philosophy of FLOSS movement, which highlights openness, participation, and lack of gatekeeping. Furthermore, this paper also contributes to Human Computer Interaction literature where there has been interest and several attempts to find ways to contribute to FLOSS projects through usability work. By identifying these gatekeeping tactics that were used by FLOSS projects to silence, block or revert usability work, we have made these kinds of actions visible in FLOSS projects. We recommend gatekeeping tactics as analytical lenses to study further the issue of contributing to FLOSS projects through usability work.

6   Conclusion

HCI research has identified numerous barriers for usability specialists' participation in FLOSS projects. Organizational boundary literature is interested in the tensions of online communities, including FLOSS communities. While this literature recognizes the importance of managing boundaries in online communities, little empirical research has been conducted on actual gatekeeping tactics project members perform against outsiders' contributions. Based on several years of engaged research with FLOSS projects, we characterize three gatekeeping tactics in FLOSS projects: *non-response*, *social exclusion*, and *false acceptance* that have hindered usability work.

By following the idea of Wittgenstein that "whereof one cannot speak, thereof one must be silent", we propose that the identification of the three tactics will have much practical relevance. As we have given names and visibility to these gatekeeping tactics, it is now possible to talk about them, to analyze them, and to be better prepared for them. When usability specialists face these barriers in action, they can try to identify the possible causes of them and communicate these issues on the broader forum.

Our choice of studying the FLOSS cases from the usability specialists' perspective has provided us with valuable insights, by allowing us to identify these three gatekeeping tactics. We can now analyze and understand better how online communities, including FLOSS projects, balance between openness and control. This choice of perspective is, however, also a limitation. The tactics may look different through the eyes of the insiders. Therefore, future research questions may involve: "How intentional are the gatekeeping tactics from within the boundary?", "Is it possible to create a greater transparency to alleviate the need of such tactics?", and "What are the strategies to help usability processes keep pace with the onwards moving core development?" Additionally, the usability specialists might use usability cost-benefit considerations to highlight the value of their usability work [37]. Although our research program has already proposed methods for usability specialists on how to enter into and contribute to FLOSS projects, the methods placing particular emphasis on understanding the project in question and active collaborate with the developers [12, 35, 39], many challenges still prevail. Further studies relying on a 'user-centered approach', the users here referring FLOSS developers, should be initiated to understand better the needs of the FLOSS developers, both as regards their work and as regards being more open to usability work.

References

1. Stallman, R.: The GNU manifesto. Dr. Dobb's J. Softw. Tools **10**(3), 30–35 (1985)
2. von Hippel, E., Krogh, G.: Open source software and the "private-collective" innovation model: issues for organization science. Organ. Sci. **14**(2), 209–223 (2003)
3. von Hippel, E.: Innovation by user communities: learning from open-source software. MIT Sloan Manag. Rev. **42**(4), 82–86 (2001)
4. Franke, N., Shah, S.: How communities support innovative activities: an exploration of assistance and sharing among end-users. Res. Policy **32**(1), 157–178 (2003)
5. Gulliksen, J., Boivie, I., Göransson, B.: Usability professionals – current practices and future development. Interact. Comput. **18**(4), 568–600 (2006)
6. Iivari, N.: Discourses on 'culture' and 'usability work' in software product development, Acta Universitatis Ouluensis, Series A, Scientiae rerum naturalium, vol. 457 (2006)
7. Andreasen, M., Nielsen, H., Schrøder, S., Stage, J.: Usability in open source software development: opinions and practice. Inf. Technol. Control **25**, 3A (2006)
8. Bødker, M., Nielsen, L., Orngreen, R.N.: Enabling user centered design processes in open source communities. In: Aykin, N. (ed.) HCII 2007. LNCS, vol. 4559, pp. 10–18. Springer, Heidelberg (2007)
9. Çetin, G., Verzulli, D., Frings, S.: An analysis of involvement of HCI experts in distributed software development: practical issues. In: Schuler, D. (ed.) HCII 2007 and OCSC 2007. LNCS, vol. 4564, pp. 32–40. Springer, Heidelberg (2007)
10. Nichols, D., Twidale, M.: The usability of open source software. First Monday **8**(1), 21 (2003)
11. Rajanen, M., Iivari, N.: Power, empowerment and open source usability. In: Proceedings of CHI 2015 (2015)
12. Rajanen, M., Iivari, N., Anttila, K.: Introducing usability activities into open source software development projects – searching for a suitable approach. J. Inf. Technol. Theory Appl. **12**(4), 5–26 (2011)
13. Jarvenpaa, S.L., Lang, K.R.: Boundary management in online communities: case studies of the nine inch nails and ccmixter music remix sites. Long Range Plan. **44**(5/6), 440–457 (2011)
14. O'Mahony, S., Ferraro, F.: Managing the boundary of an 'Open' project. In: Harvard NOM Working Paper No. 03–60 (2004)
15. Faraj, S., Jarvenpaa, S.L., Majchrzak, A.: Knowledge collaboration in online communities. Organ. Sci. **22**(5), 1224–1239 (2011)
16. Shaw, A.: Centralized and decentralized gatekeeping in an open online collective. Politics Soc. **40**(3), 349–388 (2012)
17. Raymond, E.: The cathedral and the bazaar. Knowl. Technol. Policy **12**, 3 (1999)
18. Coleman, G.: The political agnosticism of free and open source software and the inadvertent politics of contrast. Anthropol. Q. **77**(3), 507–519 (2004)
19. Bach, P.M., Terry, M.: The future of FLOSS in CHI research and practice. In: CHI 2010 Extended Abstracts, Atlanta, Georgia, USA. (2010)
20. Aberdour, M.: Achieving quality in open source software. IEEE Softw. **24**, 1 (2007)
21. Barcellini, F., Détienne, F., Burkhardt, J.M.: A situated approach of roles and participation in open source software communities. Hum.–Comput. Interact. **29**(3), 205–255 (2014)
22. Feller, J., Fitzgerald, B.: A framework analysis of the open source software development paradigm. In: Proceedings of the ICIS, pp. 58–69 (2000)
23. Mockus, A., Fielding, R.T., Herbsled, J.: A case study of open source software development: the apache server. In: Proceedings of ICSE, pp. 263–272 (2000)

24. Ljungberg, J.: Open source movements as a model for organizing. Eur. J. Inf. Syst. **9**(4), 208–216 (2000)
25. Steinmacher, I., Silva, M.A.G., Gerosa, M.A., Redmiles, D.F.: A systematic literature review on the barriers faced by newcomers to open source software projects. Inf. Softw. Technol. **59**, 67–85 (2015)
26. von Krogh, G., Spaeth, S., Lakhani, K.R.: Community, joining, and specialization in open source software innovation: a case study. Res. Policy **32**(7), 1217–1241 (2003)
27. Clayman, S.E., Reisner, A.: Gatekeeping in action: editorial conferences and assessments of newsworthiness. Am. Sociol. Rev. **63**(2), 178–199 (1998)
28. Lewin, K.: Frontiers in group dynamics: II. channels of group life; social planning and action research. Hum. Relat. **1**(2), 143–153 (1947)
29. Bach, P.M., Carroll, J.M.: FLOSS UX design: an analysis of user experience design in firefox and OpenOffice.org. In: Boldyreff, C., Crowston, K., Lundell, B., Wasserman, A.I. (eds.) OSS 2009. IFIP AICT, vol. 299, pp. 237–250. Springer, Heidelberg (2009)
30. Bach, P., DeLine, R., Carroll, J.: Designers wanted: participation and the user experience in open source software development. In: Proceedings of CHI 2009, pp. 985–994 (2009)
31. Benson, C., Müller-Prove, M., Mzourek, J.: Professional usability in open source projects: GNOME, OpenOffice.org, NetBeans. In: Extended Abstracts of the CHI 2004, (2004)
32. Nichols, D., Twidale, M.: Usability processes in open source projects. Softw. Process Improv. Pract. **11**, 149–162 (2006)
33. Zhao, L., Deek, F.: Improving open source software usability. In: Proceedings of the 11th Americas Conference on Information Systems (AMCIS2005), Omaha, USA (2005)
34. Zhao, L., Deek, F.: Exploratory inspection: a learning model for improving open source software usability. In: Extended Abstracts CHI 2006, pp. 1589–1594 (2006)
35. Rajanen, M., Iivari, N.: Open source and human computer interaction philosophies in open source projects – incompatible or co-existent? In: Proceedings of Academic MindTrek 2013, Tampere, Finland (2013)
36. Terry, M., Kay, M., Lafreniere, B.: Perceptions and practices of usability in the free/open source software (FOSS) community. In: Proceedings of CHI 2010, pp. 999–1008 (2010)
37. Rajanen, M., Iivari, N.: Traditional usability costs and benefits - fitting them into open source software development. In: Proceedings of ECIS 2010 (2010)
38. Bach, P., Twidale, M.: Social participation in open source: what it means for designers. Interactions **17**(3), 70–74 (2010)
39. Rajanen, M., Iivari, N., Keskitalo, E. Introducing usability activities into open source software development projects: a participative approach. In: Proceedings of NordiCHI, pp. 683–692 (2012)
40. Walsham, G.: Interpretive case studies in IS research: nature and method. Eur. J. Inf. Syst. **4**(2), 74–81 (1995)
41. Walsham, G.: Doing interpretive research. Eur. J. IS **15**(3), 320–330 (2006)
42. Iivari, N., Rajanen, M., Hedberg, H.: Encouraging for enculturation - an enquiry on the effort of usability specialists entering OSS projects. In: Proceedings of ACIS 2014 (2014)

Task Allocation Between UX Specialists and Developers in Agile Software Development Projects

Kati Kuusinen[(⌧)]

Tampere University of Technology, Tampere, Finland
kati.kuusinen@tut.fi

Abstract. Synchronizing efforts between developers and user experience (UX) specialists is one of the major challenges in agile UX work. In this paper, we report results of a study conducted over a release cycle of six agile software development projects in five companies, considering the task allocation and cooperation in the team. Team members (N = 31), including product owners, UX specialists, and developers, reported weekly on the UX-related tasks they had contributed to and whether the UX specialist had participated. We identified three forms of cooperation: minimal, product owner–UX specialist, and developer–UX specialist. Our study suggests that for projects operating in the minimal cooperation mode, the collaboration concentrates on the user interface (UI) design, while other aspects of UX work are downplayed. At the same time, many UX-related tasks were successfully handled by developers alone. Therefore, to support UX work integration, we suggest a task-oriented integration approach for projects with minimal UX resources.

Keywords: User experience (UX) · Agile development · Human-centered design (HCD) · UX design work · Agile UX · Human–computer interaction (HCI)

1 Introduction

In agile software development, small, cross-functional teams produce software in short, incremental iterations. The team should include all of the necessary expertise to enhance the team's efficiency and communication [14]. As agile methods [14] do not define the role of a UX specialist (UXS), it is often unclear how the UXS fits in the project team. Companies still struggle to integrate the UXS role into agile development practices [26]. Problems related to the amount and timing of UX work, as well as to the synchronization of tasks between developers and UXSs are common [26]. In addition, UX resources are often scarce in agile software projects [8, 31], which naturally reduces the amount of UX-related work that is possible. In many cases, development teams have to cope with only limited help from a UXS or, in extreme cases, with no UX support at all [25]. There have been attempts to improve team collaboration and to redistribute the workload of overburdened UXSs by creating the means to include developers in UX-related activities [5, 25, 29]. Regardless of the level of contribution by UXSs, certain activities that have a strong impact on UX, such as developing a UI, need to be conducted during development.

© IFIP International Federation for Information Processing 2015
J. Abascal et al. (Eds.): INTERACT 2015, Part III, LNCS 9298, pp. 27–44, 2015.
DOI: 10.1007/978-3-319-22698-9_3

Current recommendations for agile UX development suggest that work should be divided into activities that are conducted during agile development and those that are conducted prior to development iterations as upfront design work [7]. UX-related work is typically separated into its own stream directed by independent UXSs [6, 28]. However, it has been reported that organizations following these practices struggle with issues, such as balancing the amount of upfront design work and managing communication between developers and UXSs [7, 26]. Separating the UXS's activities seems to exclude the UXS from the core project team and affect the timing of feedback cycles between disciplines. Both of these issues blur the project vision, hindering within-project communication and endangering the realization of UX design [4, 15, 23].

In this paper, we concentrate on the cooperation and task allocation between developers and UXSs. Our goal is to clarify which UX-related tasks can or even should be handled by developers and which require the special competence of a UXS. We contribute to the understanding of how UX work is conducted in agile projects, explaining participating roles, and task and collaboration frequencies. Thus, we present a framework of collaboration between UXSs, developers, and product owners (PO), and offer process implications and suggestions to help improve collaboration in different collaboration setups. We report results from a longitudinal multiple-case study in which we studied the UX work-related task allocation and cooperation between the team members (N = 31), including developers, POs, and UXSs.

The rest of the paper is structured as follows: Sect. 2 presents related work. Section 3 discusses the research methodology we used to conduct the follow-up study and introduces the project contexts studied. Section 4 presents results from the weekly survey period. Section 5 presents results from a retrospective survey in which the participants shared their experiences of the ways of working in each project. Section 6 discusses the limitations of the research. Section 7 discusses the results and implications of the identified cooperation types. Section 8 concludes the paper.

2   Related Work

Agile software engineering refers to a collection of methodologies that share fundamental similarities in being lightweight and flexible [32]. Agile methodologies embrace change by reducing its cost throughout the project. Means to reduce the cost of change include prioritizing work based on business value, utilizing small incremental iterations and short feedback cycles, being cooperative and open in communication, and delivering software early and continuously [1, 14]. In addition, agile methodologies seek efficiency through a less hierarchical management structure, close cooperation with the customer, and the use of self-organizing, cross-functional teams [1, 14].

We consider UX in this paper to be *a person's perception of the value that results from the use or anticipated use of software in a certain context of use.* This definition is adapted from [13, 16]. By the term *agile UX work*, we refer to agile software development [14] that puts emphasis on developing software that the user values. There are differences between academic UX research and industrial UX development in terms of the conception of UX; whereas UX research concentrates mostly on hedonic aspects and emotions, companies concentrate more on functionality and usability issues [30].

Since our research considers UX work in the industry, the emphasis is on usability and functionality.

An agile team should include all of the expertise necessary to construct running software that satisfies user needs [14]. Including people from different disciplines makes communication generally more challenging [12], but separating UXSs into their own teams, instead of including them in agile development teams, may easily lead to degraded communication. UXSs become seen as outsiders, and developers tend not to take ownership of UX issues. When UXSs and developers are separated, teams encounter problems with timing and the implementability of the design [10, 20]. Hodgetts [15] considered it vitally important for UX practitioners to see themselves as part of a project team and to conduct their tasks according to that perception. Lee [24] stated that UXSs need to be active participants in order to be embedded in agile teams. Isomursu et al. [17] concluded that UXSs' responsibilities should be in line with the expectations of development teams.

UX resources are still often scarce in agile software projects [8, 31]. In many cases, development teams have to cope with only limited help from a UXS or, in extreme cases, with no UX support at all [20, 25]. Ferre [9] introduces usability techniques developers can utilize in their work. Ungar [29] has included developers in design work together with users and UXSs in the *Design Studio* method, and Leszek et al. [25] has supported developers through the *Office Hours* concept in which each development team can consult a UXS periodically for an hour or two at a time. Bornø et al. [5] described experiences from a one-day UI *Redesign Workshop* for developers and UXSs.

Little is known about the actual daily work and task allocation between developers and UXSs. The majority of agile UX research has concentrated on the development process or on endeavors to modify user-centered design (UCD) practices so that they will be better suited for agile development [6]. A systematic review listed the practices mentioned most often in agile UCD work [7]. These practices included conducting little upfront design work, ensuring close collaboration between UXSs and developers, designing iteration ahead of development, prototyping, and conducting user tests [7]. Joshi et al. [18] found the following activities most important for achieving usability goals: user studies, UI design, usability evaluation and development support. Boivie et al. [3] determined that usability designers allocate roughly 25–50 % of their time to analysis, 20–60 % to design, and 10–50 % to evaluation activities. The contribution of UXSs varies from single activities to full participation throughout the project [3]. In projects where there is no UXS involved, separate usability evaluation activities are more common [3]. Moreover, projects tend to favor informal feedback gathering methods, such as asking users' opinion, instead of conducting formal user tests [3, 22]. Most feedback gathering activities occur in the early stages before implementation [22]. Ferreira et al. [10] reported an observation study of a team with a separate UXS who fed the team with ready-made designs. The team coordinated its work by (i) inspecting the design and identifying mismatches with what had already been implemented, (ii) interpreting the design in terms of working software, and (iii) prioritizing the design and determining the parts that had already been implemented [10].

To conclude, the UXSs' role is often undefined in development projects [3, 17]. It is unknown what a UXS's daily work consists of in agile projects and how developers can contribute to UX. Moreover, UX resources are often scarce in companies [8, 20, 25, 31], and therefore it is important to utilize such resources wisely. This paper contributes to the understanding of the focal tasks of UXSs and how developers and POs can participate in UX work.

3   Methods and Participants

Our research goal was to increase the understanding of UX-related work in agile enterprise software development. We piloted the study in two projects, one of them reported in [19]. The results of the pilot study indicated that there seemed to be differences in both the emphasis of tasks and the degree of communication between projects in the same company, which could impact the satisfaction of team members. We expected to gain interpretive results from this study. Moreover, we aimed at comparing the ways of working to team members' experiences of the project and their conception of the success of the project and its outcome. Our research questions were as follows:

1. How do UXSs, POs, and developers contribute to UX?
2. Which tasks should be collaborative and which can be handled by a certain role?
3. Which practices do team members consider good or bad, and why?

Our research consisted of surveying agile projects about their ways of working in terms of UX-related work. We defined "UX-related work" in the survey as follows:

> Any work that contributes to understanding or defining user needs, designing and developing to meet the user needs, and evaluating or ensuring that the needs are being met. The work can be conducted by any project member; we do not limit the definition of UX work to a certain role (e.g. UX Specialist).

We surveyed members of each participating team using a weekly web questionnaire over a release cycle. We sent individual survey invitations before Friday morning in the earliest time zone of participants' locations and allowed response time until Monday evening in the latest time zone. We used three slightly different surveys, one intended for each of the following groups:

1. Developers and POs of teams that included a UXS.
2. UXSs.
3. Developers and POs of teams that did not have a UXS.

For the Group 1 survey, participants reported weekly which UX-related tasks they had participated in and whether the UXS had been involved in the task. UXSs (Group 2) reported tasks that they had contributed to and also the roles of persons who had participated in the activity, if applicable. Participants in Group 3 reported tasks that they had contributed to. In addition, they reported on an imaginary setting where a UXS would have been involved in the team. They reported the tasks that the UXS would have contributed to, if any. They also reported if they had needed a UXS during the week and the reason why or why not.

Respondents selected the tasks from a pre-defined list (Table 1), which included two open fields for tasks that were not listed. This list was based on our earlier research

Table 1. List of UX-related tasks in the weekly survey.

Task	Description
Created concepts	Designing and sketching early ideas
Clarified user requirements	Gathering and interpreting user requirements
Clarified user definitions or target user groups	Defining who the users and user groups are
Planning user data gathering	Planning the user participation, studies, and tests
Conducted user study	Studying users, their behavior, and contexts
Conducted user testing	Evaluating the system, prototype, concept, or idea by testing it on users
Created UI designs	Designing user interaction or flow, making graphic design etc. Design can be of any fidelity
Reviewed UI designs	Inspecting and evaluating UI design feasibility
Created architecture designs	Designing the software structure and deciding on the fundamentals of the system
Created or groomed product backlog	Deciding of the scope of the outcome and the order of implementation (Scrum practice)
Planned a feature	Planning new or modified features for the release
Shared understanding of the UI design	Discussing the UI design and decisions related to it, communicating the design idea to stakeholders
Shared understanding of the technology	Discussing technical feasibility, its limitations, and possibilities
Implemented UI	Implementing the user interaction and interface
Determined how to implement UI design details	Deciding on nuances and details related to the UI design, e.g. when implementing on different platforms
Made changes in the UI design	Modifying the UI design e.g. based on feedback or review
Reviewed implementation	Checking that the implementation corresponds to the design
Had a demo session	Demonstrating the software to customers, users or stakeholders (Scrum practice)

on important UX-related tasks conducted in two companies [20, 21]. In that study, 116 people in various roles related to software development responded to an open-ended question asking: *What are the most important tasks of UX Specialists?* We analyzed the responses utilizing the affinity wall method described in [2]. In addition, we evaluated and iterated the resulting task list with a group of UXSs and software architects in order to cover all of the focal tasks.

In addition to the weekly surveys, each participant filled in a retrospective survey about their experiences and their evaluation of the ways of working in terms of the UX-related work in the project. Through open-ended questions, the participants reflected on the good and bad practices and lessons learned from the ways of carrying out UX-related work in the project. At the beginning of the study period, we also interviewed one team member from each participating project who had a good understanding of the working methods of the project. We asked the interviewees about the ways of working in the project and about the company in general in order to understand the work context.

We analyzed the weekly data using descriptive statistics, including mean, standard deviation, count of occurrences, and ratios of different cases. We calculated counts of occurrences for each task role-wise. We compared task frequencies and ratios between collaborative and non-collaborative occurrences of reported tasks. We analyzed the retrospective survey responses using a qualitative content analysis method.

3.1 Participants

We selected projects using the following criteria:

- The project utilized agile methods. The basic criterion was that the PO considered the project agile; we did not want to interfere with the actual execution of the project.
- The project had a release cycle of six months or less.
- The outcome was enterprise software that would be used by a person.
- The outcome had a graphical UI that required design work. In particular, we excluded pure backend development projects and projects tailoring third-party systems.
- UX design work was ongoing or starting soon.
- Project members were willing to participate.

The participant population consisted of project team members. Table 2 presents characteristics of participating companies and projects, and Table 3 describes the participants. The PO and developer roles were defined similarly to Scrum [27], wherein the PO is responsible for maximizing the business value of the project, creating and maintaining the feature list (product backlog), and acting as a link between the developers and stakeholders; developers form a self-organizing team that is responsible for delivering working software in an iterative and incremental manner. At the beginning of each iteration, the development team selects those tasks from the product backlog that they will commit to delivering by the end of the iteration [27]. UXSs' responsibilities are inherited from human-centered design, as defined in [16]. Those include understanding and specifying the context of use, specifying the user and organizational requirements, producing design solutions to meet those requirements, and evaluating and redesigning until those requirements are met [16]. In all the projects, UXSs' roles were defined vaguely. Originally, the following tasks were assigned to UXSs. In P2 and P3 UXSs were to ensure the product viability and to create the UI design. In contrast, in P1 and P4, the UXS was to create the UI design while the PO was responsible for the product vision. In P5, the UXS was working as a consultant guiding the team while the PO was responsible for the vision.

Of all respondents, 45.2 % were from Finland, 25.8 % from Russia, 22.6 % from China, 3.2 % from Estonia, and 3.2 % from Latvia. In total, there were 38 team members working for the projects, of which 31 responded to our survey for a response rate of 81.6 %. Some of the non-respondents were backend developers who felt that the study did not concern them because of their minimal contribution to end-user UX. Altogether we collected 237 weekly sheets from the projects.

In P1, two developers had conducted some courses in HCI while the PO and the rest of the developers had had a short training in HCI. In P2, the PO and developers had

Table 2. Description of participating companies and project teams. P4 and P5 were conducted at the same company. Legend: PO = product owner, UXS = UX specialist, W = amount of studied weeks.

Project	Company description	Team size and location	W
P1	An engineering and technology company with around 20 000 employees worldwide. Utilized both waterfall and Scrum practices. Several small distributed UX teams and UXSs	11 of which 8 developers located in Russia, 1 PO and 1 part-time UXS co-located in Finland. 2 participating sites	24
P2	An IT service company with 100–500 employees in Finland. UXSs working in project teams	6 of which 4 developers, 1 PO, 1 UXS, all co-located in Finland. 1 participating site	17
P3	An IT service company with 100–500 employees in Europe. Utilized Scrum. A centralized UX team in one site and distributed specialists in others	5 of which 2 developers, 1 PO, 1 UXS, all co-located in Finland. 1 participating site	7
P4	An IT service company with around 20 000 employees worldwide. The company mainly utilized customer-defined processes	8 of which 5 developers and a scrum master in China, and 1 PO and 1 UXS in Finland. 2 participating sites	8
P5	It had a centralized UX team on one site and numerous distributed UXSs on several sites (Projects P4 and P5 were conducted at this company)	5 of which 3 developers in Finland at location A, 1 PO in Finland at location B, and 1 UXS in Latvia. 3 participating sites	7
P6	A mobile technology company with 100–500 employees worldwide. Utilized agile practices and customer processes. A centralized UX team	3 of which 1 developer and 1 PO in Finland co-located, the second developer in Estonia. Possibility to consult a UXS at another location in Finland. 3 participating sites	13

conducted some courses in HCI. In P3, one developer had majored in HCI and he also had ten years of experience in UX design work. The PO and UXS of P3 had conducted some studies in HCI. Developers of P4 had no training in HCI. A developer in P5 and P6 had conducted one course in HCI. The rest in those teams had no training in HCI. UXS of P2 had majored and UXS of P1 had minored in HCI. The rest of the UXSs had conducted some courses in HCI.

4   Results of the Weekly Survey

In this section, we present our results in terms of the description of ways of working in the projects, task allocation and the frequency of reported tasks, and the work roles that cooperated with UXSs in their work.

Table 3. Description of participants. Legend: PO = product owner, IT = information technology, M = mean, SD = standard deviation. Age and experience are expressed in years. *We did not get demographic data from one UXS and three developers.

Role	Developers (N = 19)*	POs (N = 6)	UX Specialists (N = 5)*
Mean age	M = 31.07 (SD 4.95)	M = 35.00 (SD 3.03)	M = 40.00 (SD 8.00)
Educational background	IT	IT	IT, society and culture, or industrial design
Education in HCI	None to major subject. The majority had some self-learning to some courses	Some self-learning to some courses	Some courses to major subject
Development experience	0–20, M = 8.46 (SD = 4.68)	2–9, M = 7.00 (SD = 2.53)	0–20, M = 8.75 (SD = 9.84)
UX design work experience	0–10, M = 2.46 (SD = 3.57)	0–1 M = 0.25 (SD = 0.27)	5–20, M = 11.25 (SD = 7.09)
Project management experience	0–5, M = 1.07 (SD = 1.43)	0–6, M = 4.50 (SD = 2.26)	0–5, M = 2.00 (SD = 2.45)
Agile work experience	0–8, M = 4.00 (SD = 2.04)	0–7, M = 4.92 (SD = 2.46)	5–9, M = 6.00 (SD = 2.00)

4.1 Task Allocation and Frequency as Reported by Developers and POs

In the Group 1 survey (developers and POs of teams that included a UXS, i.e. projects P1–P5; P6 is not included since it did not have a UXS), the most often reported tasks were related to clarifying user requirements, feature planning, and creating and reviewing UI designs (Table 4). Those tasks in which cooperation between UXSs and other team members was reported most often included conducting user study and discussions related to the UI design or technological issues, and carrying out other UX-related activity such as holding meetings (kickoff or status meetings), creating user documentation, and implementing test cases. UXSs participated least often in architecture design creation, the creation and grooming of product backlog, and implementation reviews.

Others collaborated most often with UXSs when conducting user studies (100 % of reported occurrences were conducted in cooperation with the UXS), sharing understanding of technical issues (88.9 %) or the UI design (86.4 %), creating concepts (50.0 %), reviewing (41.9 %) or creating the UI design (45.1 %), and clarifying user requirements (41.2 %).

4.2 Collaboration Types

We identified three collaboration types in the study. These collaboration types are not intended to be discrete; projects can have traits from several of them. Instead, the collaboration type indicates the emphasis of communication in the project. In P1 and

Table 4. Occurrences of UX-related tasks as developers and POs of P1–P5 reported. N = 23.

Task	Total reported times	Times without UXS	Times with UXS	Ratio with UXS /total
Clarified user requirements	68	40	28	0.412
Reviewed UI designs	57	29	28	0.491
Planned a feature	54	39	15	0.278
Created UI designs	51	28	23	0.451
Had a demo session	49	38	11	0.224
Made changes to the design	46	37	9	0.196
Reviewed the implementation	42	30	12	0.286
Created or groomed product backlog	40	24	16	0.400
Created architecture designs	39	36	3	*0.077*
Determined how to implement UI design details	31	22	9	0.290
Shared understanding of UI design	26	13	13	0.500
Created concepts	23	14	9	0.391
Clarified end user definitions or target user groups	22	3	19	*0.864*
Shared understanding of technical issues	18	2	16	*0.889*
Planned user studies or user tests	11	8	3	0.273
Other UX-related activity	6	1	5	0.833
Conducted a user study	2	0	2	*1.000*
Conducted user testing	2	2	0	0.000
TOTAL	**587**	**366**	**221**	

P3, collaboration in general was less than in P2 and P5 (Table 5). In P4, the majority of reported collaboration occurred between the PO and UXS. This was also the case for P6, which did not have a designated UXS in the team. In projects with the minimal collaboration type, others collaborated with the UXS most often when conducting a user study (100.0 % of the cases) and when sharing understanding about the UX design. By contrast, in the Developer–UXS type of collaboration, the rest of the team collaborated with the UXS most often during the following tasks: having discussions over the implementation of design details, sharing understanding of UI design, and creating concepts and UI design. Thus, we conclude that when there was less collaboration, it concentrated on the UI design and possible user studies. When the amount of collaboration increased, the team could also discuss the actual implementation and concepts behind UX design decisions. In effect, the quality of implementation in terms of the UI design was ensured beforehand through discussions over design details. Developers reported repeat occurrences of clarifying user requirements without the UXS in both the minimal and PO–UXS collaboration modes. This most likely indicates a form of rework; developers did not have direct contact with users, and the UXS clarified user requirements for themselves. Including developers in the clarification work might have saved developers time and increased their understanding of user requirements.

When there was no designated UXS involved, the team desired help primarily in conducting user studies, creating UX designs, clarifying target users, and reviewing the implementation. These might be the areas where problems become visible when working without a UXS. Of the 13 observed weeks, the P6 team reported 8 weeks that they would have needed the contribution of a UXS. The external UXS contributed for two weeks (weeks 2 and 10). The reasons mentioned most often for requiring the contribution of a UXS were the following: (i) to make better design decisions in terms of the user flow and UI (7 mentions in 6 weeks), and (ii) to get feedback on the current design of the user flow and UI (5 mentions in 5 weeks). The reasons why contribution from a UXS was not needed were the following: (i) we did not do or plan anything in the project this week that would affect the user experience, and (ii) we already had the needed competence within the project team (for both, 6 mentions in 5 weeks).

4.3   Roles that Cooperated with UX Specialists per Task

UXSs conducted the majority (62.8 %) of all reported tasks in collaboration with others. They collaborated most with POs; 51.5 % of all reported occurrences of collaboration included the PO role. Developers were involved in 34.9 % of all reported collaborative tasks. The proportion for customers or users was 26.6 %, and for other design-related roles it was 10.1 % (including other UXSs, usability experts, and graphic designers). POs most often collaborated when creating architecture design (100.0 % of reported collaborative occurrences related to this task), clarifying user requirements (84.0 %), holding demo sessions (81.8 %), and creating concepts (78.9 %). UXSs collaborated the most with developers during demo sessions, when discussing the UI design and when determining how to implement design details. Developers did not participate in conducting user studies or tests, clarifying end user definitions or target user groups, or creating architecture design together with UXSs.

UXSs reported the only collaborative occurrences of the following: conducting user testing, holding a demo session, and creating architecture designs. Other collaborative tasks included clarifying user requirements (85.3 % of reported task occurrences were collaborative) and planning user studies (84.7 %). UXSs worked alone most often when implementing UI (58.6 %), making changes to the design (50.7 %), and creating UI designs (46.9 %). Table 6 describes the proportional values per task of UXSs working alone and in cooperation with different roles. Cooperation with each role is represented as a proportion of the total number of reported cooperative occurrences of each task.

There were remarkable differences in cooperation between the projects. The UXS was in continuous collaboration with customers and users in P2, P3, and P4, whereas the customer or user was never mentioned in P1 and P5. The PO was responsible for collaboration with users and customers in both of those projects. In P5, the PO arranged two short sessions with users in order to understand their needs and to evaluate the

Table 5. Percentage of collaborative occurrences in minimal type projects (P1 and P3) and in Developer–UXS type projects (P2 and P5). Percentage of all reported tasks for which P6 members would have wanted the contribution of a UXS.

Task	P1 and P3 With UXS		P2 and P5 With UXS		P6 UXS
	M	SD	M	SD	Would
Created concepts	20.8 %	0.21	**90.00 %**	0.10	33.3 %
Clarified user requirements	29.7 %	0.05	61.9 %	0.05	40.0 %
Clarified user definitions or target user groups	16.7 %	0.17	50.0 %	0.00	**57.1 %**
Planned user studies or user tests	25.0 %	0.00	33.3 %	0.00	25.0 %
Conducted a user study	**100.0 %**	0.00			**100.0 %**
Conducted user testing	*0.00 %*	0.00			28.6 %
Created UI designs	26.7 %	0.07	**90.0 %**	0.10	**66.7 %**
Reviewed UI designs	37.5 %	0.13	**82.3 %**	0.01	47.6 %
Created architecture designs	*4.2 %*	0.04	9.1 %	0.00	0.00
Created or groomed product backlog	8.7 %	0.09	32.1 %	0.01	0.00
Planned a feature	20.0 %	0.00	22.5 %	0.23	14.3 %
Shared understanding of the UI design	**83.3 %**	0.17	**96.2 %**	0.04	
Determined how to implement UI design details	*9.4 %*	0.13	**100.0 %**	0.00	12.5 %
Made changes to the UI design	34.6 %	0.09	73.3 %	0.07	47.6 %
Reviewed the implementation	16.9 %	0.15	68.2 %	0.32	**57.1 %**
Had a demo session	20.8 %	0.08	35.0 %	0.00	28.6 %

product concept. In P1, collaboration with users was rare, and the project mainly concentrated on the technical problem it was trying to solve. By contrast, P2 was the most collaborative project in terms of both the frequency of collaboration and variety of roles with which the UXS continuously collaborated. In P4, the PO participated frequently in each task, except for conducting user studies and tests. The developers of P4 were involved primarily when the UXS explained the UI design to them, during demo sessions, and when making changes to the UI design. In P1, there was less reported cooperation, occurring almost solely between the PO and managers.

5 Results of the Retrospective Survey

This section presents results of the retrospective survey in which the participants evaluated the project and their ways of working. We present the results in terms of the identified collaboration types.

5.1 Minimal Cooperation Type Projects

After the weekly study period, we asked team members to share their opinions and experiences regarding the ways of working during the studied release cycle. POs evaluated the impact of UX-related issues on project success. The PO of P1 considered

Table 6. Average proportional occurrences of working alone and with others as reported by UX specialists (N = 5). PO = (with) product owner, DEV = (with) developer, CUS = (with) customer, OUX = (with) other UX specialists, including graphic designers.

Task	Alone	Together	PO	DEV	CUS	OUX
Conducted user testing	0.000	1.000	0.000	0.000	**1.000**	**1.000**
Created architecture designs	0.000	1.000	**1.000**	0.000	0.000	0.000
Had a demo session	0.000	1.000	**0.818**	1.000	0.818	0.000
Clarified user requirements	0.147	0.853	**0.840**	0.427	**0.588**	0.000
Planned user studies or tests	0.153	0.847	0.316	0.000	0.211	**0.789**
Shared UI design understanding	0.225	0.775	0.599	**0.588**	0.347	**0.080**
Reviewed UI designs	0.236	0.764	0.534	0.226	0.141	0.254
Created concepts	0.307	0.693	**0.789**	0.386	0.235	0.000
Clarified user definitions or target user groups	0.324	0.676	0.479	0.000	0.521	0.000
Created or groomed product backlog	0.329	0.671	0.571	0.265	0.204	0.000
Reviewed the implementation	0.333	0.667	0.300	0.340	0.180	0.000
Conducted a user study	0.420	0.580	0.000	0.000	0.538	0.000
Determined how to implement design details	0.428	0.572	0.000	0.182	0.000	0.000
Planned a feature	0.453	0.547	0.703	**0.618**	0.322	0.223
Created UI designs	0.469	0.531	0.435	0.383	0.094	0.081
Made changes to the UI design	0.493	0.507	0.307	0.396	0.247	0.074
Implemented UI	0.586	0.414	0.222	0.000	0.000	0.000

that having a UX engineer (instead of a design-oriented UXS) working in close collaboration with the developers and basically guiding the development work would have been a more suitable approach for the project. He also stated that the UX design was often late "*so most of the time developers just did it 'like before'.*" They also needed to do some UI-related rework, as no one, including the users, understood "*the functionality that end users actually wanted.*" They might have benefited from a rapid prototyping approach with repeat user evaluations, as it is often difficult for users to understand their own needs beforehand.

In P3, the PO explained that they had learned to be more aware of the UX budget; they had used too much too early, which had led to a situation whereby the UXS could not participate in the project as much as she should have in the later stages. The PO of P3 stated: "*We had a good intention to emphasize UX in the project and we did quite comprehensive designs early in the project. In some areas we did a bit of overdesign and at some point UX got ramped down due to tight budget.*" The PO summarized their lessons learned as follows:

- "*Create designs on as-needed basis as the project proceeds.*"
- "*Avoid overdesign because things tend to change during projects.*"
- "*UX is a continuous process, not one big push at the beginning of the project.*"
- "*Time spent on UX design pays off even if budget is tight.*"

To conclude, it seems that the POs of projects with the minimal collaboration type would have preferred the Developer–UXS collaboration type for their projects.

A developer of P3 stated: "*In the future I would do almost all the design together between developers and UX designers to avoid communication issues, as well as to avoid doing unnecessary work. Also, not burning the entire UX budget so early in the project to be able to review and improve UI-related implementations also later in the project.*" Also the UXS agreed: "*I would design more in co-operation with the developers (something I do today).*"

5.2 Developer–UXS Cooperation Type Projects

The P2 team was pleased with the UX work in general. They especially appreciated that the UXS was part of the team from the beginning: "*We got* [a UXS] *right from the start of the project. The person has been in the project all the time and not just conducting quick UX fixes*" (PO, P2). The PO also shared that they had been able to decrease project costs by negotiating with the customer about reasonable customer requirements, because the UXS had studied the actual user needs.

The P2 team reported frequent cooperation with users. The UXS had conducted user studies earlier and validated design decisions with users. Still, both the UXS and developers would have wanted even stronger user involvement. Developers in P2 wanted either to meet end users or to get better reasoning for design decisions: "*Reasoning behind design decisions could have been communicated better to developers, as the developers were in no direct contact to end users*" (developer, P2). Another developer mentioned that not being able to meet users decreased their motivation, as the developers did not really know for whom they were developing the software.

Developers in P5 were also pleased with the close collaboration with the UXS. One of them desired the "*shifting discussion from technical level to user level.*" Even though they had a user participating in the process, one developer wished for "*more iteration with end user.*" On the other hand, the PO of P5 complained that he did not have clear view of the UX work, since the UXS mostly collaborated with the developers. Also, the PO of P2 mentioned that "[UXS's] *tasks should be similarly visible on the* [*kanban* (a tool to visualize workflow)] *board as the other developers' tasks are.*" He added that breaking down tasks into chunks is important, because tasks described on too general a level can decrease developmental efficiency.

5.3 PO–UXS Cooperation Type Projects

The P6 team was only able to consult an external UXS occasionally. The PO of P6 reported that even the minor contribution of a UXS significantly improved the developed software. He expressed that he would never conduct a project again without the contribution of a UXS, adding: "*I would definitely emphasize regular short UX meetings, 1-1.5 h weekly. That would actually keep a small project more on track and to help the project be more successful. And it also prevents from rework. The whole team should participate in these UX meetings.*"

The UXS in P4 was pleased that UX issues were considered at the project level. The PO of P4 was able to learn how to conduct some UX work by himself. However, the developers were less pleased with the situation in which they had, in practice, no chance to impact design decisions, as ready-made designs were communicated to them to be implemented as-is. The PO felt that the developers were inexperienced, and, because of that, he thought that they would not have been able to challenge the UI design. Most of the developers also did not speak English very well.

6 Limitations

We studied only projects developing enterprise systems. All of the projects were Finland-based, although 54.8 % of the respondents were from other countries. We utilized theoretical sampling instead of random sampling for selecting the participant projects. The participants were aware of what was being measured, which could have made the study prone to performance bias. Moreover, prompting the participants to think about the UX work in their project weekly might have made participants more aware of UX work and its importance.

The results are based on self-reports from the team members, and, as such, the results are not as reliable as with observation studies. However, since observing geographically distributed projects over a release cycle is impossible in practice, we selected this research methodology despite its limitations. Participants reported their tasks using a pre-defined task list. Some tasks may not have been reported, since they were not included in the list; however, it was possible for participants to add other tasks. The list was based on earlier research on the most important UX tasks and was therefore not exhaustive. We did not define *collaboration* in the survey, which could have led to differences between participants in their perception of collaboration.

Not all of the project members responded the survey, which could have introduced possible attrition bias. However, the response rate was excellent at 81.6 %. Also, not every participant reported every week. Projects did not provide us with actual work-hour data. Thus, we asked the participants to report absences on the weekly survey in order to be able to distinguish between non-response and absence. However, there are non-responses in within-person data, which may also have introduced attrition bias. Because the UXSs and other team members reported independently on the same instances of collaboration, we were able to cross-check the data, and no significant outliers were found.

7 Discussion

To summarize our main findings, we observed the following three types of UX-related cooperation in the projects:

1. Minimal cooperation (P1, P3)

   • Either one single person responsible for UX work, mainly without project members' contributions, or several people conducting it separately

2. Close cooperation between the UXS and the PO (P4, P6)

   • PO and UXS conduct UX work together and ready-made designs are communicated to developers

3. Close cooperation between the UXS and developers (P2, P5)

   • Developers and UXS conduct the majority of UX work together; PO plays a smaller role in UX tasks

Of these, number 3 – the Developer–UXS collaboration type – was most favored among participants. However, implementing this mode of operation requires that both the UXS and the developers be experienced and willing to work together. The UXS should be able to allocate design tasks, which is challenging [26]. Moreover, it is important to have a PO who understands and appreciates UX work. By contrast, number 2 – the PO–UXS cooperation type – might be better for more inexperienced teams and for projects where the project scope is less clear. The rationale is that in this mode of operation, the PO always holds the reins, and there is a clear chain of command throughout the development. To our understanding, number 1, the minimal cooperation type, should usually be avoided because it introduces more problems than benefits. This was observed in our study and also previously in [11, 20]. Table 7 discusses the benefits and challenges related to each cooperation type in more detail.

We found that clarifying user requirements, feature planning, and reviewing and discussing UX designs were often collaborative activities. Developers conducted these activities irrespective of UXSs' contributions – either between developers or with the UXS. We interpret this as being because those are the core activities needed to be able to implement purposeful software. Thus, when there is insufficient communication between the UXS and developers, developers need to form their own understanding of the user need and UI design solutions. Moreover, their understanding might be significantly different from what the UXS designed. Thus, clarifying user needs, feature planning, and discussing UX design should be collaborative activities.

Developers and POs emphasized the importance of having a UXS as part of the team from early on and throughout the project. The PO of P5 mentioned that he would utilize a UXS even for small projects with tight budgets, since he saw how it had improved quality and efficiency due to the decreased amount of rework needed. The PO of P3 stated, *"Time spent on UX design pays off even if the budget is tight."* Also, developers from P1, P2, P3, and P5 mentioned that working with a UXS was an advantage in the project. Participants felt that the early work devoted to understanding user needs and thus the scope of the developed system had clarified the project vision and reduced uncertainty throughout the project. In addition, UXSs and developers should cooperate in order to create implementable UI designs: UXSs learn to take technical limitations into account, and developers learn basic UI design principles. Cooperation can also decrease the amount of rework when it is clearer for both the UXS and the developers which parts have already been implemented and how they impact on future designs. In addition, understanding the explicit user needs helps developers to design the implementation details in terms of the UI. Considering the PO role, the PO of P5 successfully gathered user feedback and organized workshop sessions in order to gain understanding of user needs. On the other hand, in P1 (in which

Table 7. Benefits and challenges in the identified types of cooperation

Type	Benefits	Challenges
Minimal	UXS can concentrate on UX tasks without disturbance [10]	Synchronizing work between UXS and developers. Maintaining the big picture of the project. Can lead to unfit design and double work. Spending the UX budget too early
PO–UX	UX issues at project level. Helps in maintaining the big picture of the project	High overhead cost especially in distributed projects. Developers have less impact on the design
Dev–UX	Developers have access to reasoning behind design decisions. Discussion about the design is easier. Enables making smarter compromises between design and technical limitations	Tendency to allocate no or too little time for planning and user studies, risk of piecemeal work and of compromising UX too much for technical reasons

the PO was also responsible for user communication), the user need remained unclear throughout the project. To conclude, it is beneficial to share the responsibilities of UX-related work among team members. However, it should be acknowledged that the PO and developers need to have a certain level of expertise to be able to successfully execute these tasks.

8 Summary and Conclusions

This paper reported on results of a longitudinal multiple-case study in which we studied six agile projects in five companies over a release cycle. Participants reported weekly the UX-related activities that they had participated in and whether the UXS had been involved. Developers and POs contributed the most to clarifying user requirements, reviewing UI designs, and feature planning. UXSs contributed most often in creating and reviewing UI design and changing the design. When there was no designated UXS involved, the team desired help primarily in conducting user studies, creating UX designs, clarifying target user groups, and reviewing the implementation.

We identified three descriptive types of cooperation, namely minimal, PO–UXS, and Developer–UXS cooperation. In projects with the minimal cooperation type, the UXS works mainly apart from the other team members, while with the PO–UXS and Developer–UXS cooperation types, the UXS works mostly with the PO and developers, respectively. The Developer–UXS cooperation was the most desirable cooperation type among the participant projects.

References

1. Beck, K., et al. Agile Alliance. Manifesto for Agile Software (2001). Accessed on http://agilemanifesto.org

2. Beyer, H., Holtzblatt, K.: Contextual Design: Defining Customer-Centered Systems. Morgan Kaufmann, San Francisco (1998)
3. Boivie, I., Gulliksen, J., Göransson, B.: The lonesome cowboy: a study of the usability designer role in systems development. IwC **18**(4), 601–634 (2006)
4. Budwig, M., Jeong, S., Kelkar, K.: When usability met agile: a case study. In: Proceedings of the 27th International Conference Extended Abstracts on Human Factors in Computing Systems (CHI EA 2009). pp. 3075–3084. ACM, New York (2009)
5. Bornø, N., Billestrup, J., Andersen, J.L., Stage, J.B.: A. redesign workshop: involving software developers actively in usability engineering. In: Proceedings of NordiCHI, pp. 1113–1118. ACM (2014)
6. Brhel, M., Meth, H., Maedche, A., Werder, C.: Exploring principles of user-centered agile software development: a literature review. Inf. Softw. Technol. **61**, 163–181 (2015)
7. da Silva, T., Martin, A., Maurer, F., Silveira, M.: User-centered design and agile methods: a systematic review. In: Proceedings of the Agile Methods in Software Development (Agile 2011)
8. da Silva, T., Silveira, M.S., Maurer, F.: Ten lessons learned from integrating interaction design and agile development. In: Proceedings of the. Agile Conference (AGILE 2013), pp. 42–49. IEEE (2013)
9. Ferre, X.: Integration of usability techniques into the software development process. In: proceedings of the Workshop on Bridging the Gaps Between Software Engineering and Human-Computer Interaction at International Conference on Software Engineering (ICSE 2003) (2003)
10. Ferreira, J., Sharp, H., Robinson, H.: User experience design and agile development: managing cooperation through articulation work. Softw. Prac. Exp. **41**(9), 963–974 (2011)
11. Ferreira, J., Sharp, H., Robinson, H.: Values and assumptions shaping agile development and user experience design in practice. In: Sillitti, A., Martin, A., Wang, X., Whitworth, E. (eds.) XP 2010. LNBIP, vol. 48, pp. 178–183. Springer, Heidelberg (2010)
12. Gulliksen, J.: Bringing the social perspective: user centred design. HCI **1**, 1327–1331 (1999)
13. Hassenzahl, M., Tractinsky, N.: User experience - a research agenda. BIT **25**(2), 91–97 (2006)
14. Highsmith, J., Cockburn, A.: Agile software development: the business of innovation. Computer **34**(9), 120–127 (2001)
15. Hodgetts, P.: Experiences integrating sophisticated UX design into agile process. In: Proceedings of the AGILE Conference (2005)
16. ISO 9241–210:2010. Ergonomics of human-system interaction. Part 210: Human-centered design for interactive systems (2010)
17. Isomursu, M., Sirotkin, A., Voltti, P., Halonen, M.: User experience design goes agile in lean transformation – a case study. In: Proceedings of Agile Conference (AGILE), pp. 1–10 (2012)
18. Joshi, A., Sarda, N.: Evaluating relative contributions of various HCL activities to usability. In: Proceedings of the HCSE 2010, pp. 166–181 (2010)
19. Kuusinen, K.: The impact of user experience work on cloud software development. Communications of Cloud Software, 2(1) (2013)
20. Kuusinen, K., Mikkonen, T., Pakarinen, S.: Agile user experience development in a large software organization: good expertise but limited impact. In: Winckler, M., Forbrig, P., Bernhaupt, R. (eds.) Human-Centered Software Engineering. LNCS, vol. 7623, pp. 94–111. Springer, Heidelberg (2012)

21. Kuusinen, K., Väänänen-Vainio-Mattila, K.: How to make agile UX work more efficient: management and sales perspectives. In: Proceedings of the 7th Nordic Conference on Human-Computer Interaction: Making Sense through Design (NordiCHI 2012), pp. 139–148. ACM (2012)

22. Lárusdóttir, M.K., Cajander, Å., Gulliksen, J.: Informal feedback rather than performance measurements–user-centred evaluation in Scrum projects. Behav. Inf. Technol. **2013**, 1–18 (2013)

23. Lárusdóttir, M.K., Cajander, Å., Gulliksen, J.: The big picture of UX is missing in scrum projects. In: Proceedings of the International Workshop on the Interplay between User Experience (UX) Evaluation and System Development (I-UxSED), pp. 49–54 (2012)

24. Lee, J.C.: Embracing agile development of usable software systems. In: Proceedings of the Conference on Human Factors in Computing Systems (CHI), pp. 1767–1770. ACM (2006)

25. Leszek, A., Courage, C.: The Doctor is In – using the office hours concept to make limited resources most effective. In: Proceedings of the AGILE Conference, pp. 196–201 (2008)

26. Salah, D., Paige, R., Cairns, P.: A systematic literature review on agile development processes and user centred design integration. In: Proceedings of the 18th International Conference on Evaluation and Assessment in Software Engineering (EASE 2014), 10 p., A. 5. ACM (2014)

27. Schwaber, K.: Agile project management with Scrum (Microsoft professional), 1st edn. Microsoft Press, Redmond (2004)

28. Sy, D.: Adapting usability investigations for agile user-centered design. J. Usability Stud. **2** (3), 112–132 (2007)

29. Ungar, J.: The design studio: interface design for agile teams. In: Proceedings of the AGILE Conference, pp. 519–524. IEEE Computer Society (2008)

30. Väänänen-Vainio-Mattila, K., Roto, V., Hassenzahl, M.: Towards practical user experience evaluation methods. EL-C. In: Meaningful Measures: Valid Useful User Experience Measurement (VUUM), pp. 19–22 (2008)

31. Wale-Kolade, A.Y.: Integrating usability work into a large inter-organisational agile development project: tactics developed by usability designers. J. Sys. Softw. **100**, 54–66 (2015)

32. Williams, L., Cockburn, A.: Agile software development: it's about feedback and change. Computer **36**(6), 39–43 (2003)

Breathe with Touch: A Tactile Interface for Breathing Assistance System

Bin Yu[✉], Loe Feijs, Mathias Funk, and Jun Hu

Industrial Design Department,
Technology University of Eindhoven, Eindhoven, The Netherlands
{B.Yu,L.M.G.Feijs,M.Funk,J.Hu}@TUE.NL

Abstract. Breathing techniques have been widely used as an aid in stress-reduction and relaxation exercises. Most breathing assistance systems present breathing guidance in visual or auditory forms. In this study, we explored a tactile interface of a breathing assistance system by using a shape-changing airbag. We hypothesized that it would help users perform the breathing exercise more effectively and enhance their relaxing experience. The feasibility of the tactile interface was evaluated from three aspects: stress reduction, breathing training and interface usability. The results showed that for most participants, the overall heart rate variability were improved after breathing training. Moreover, "Breathe with Touch" brought users better satisfaction during the exercise. We discuss these results and future design implications for designing tactile interfaces for breathing guidance.

Keywords: Tactile interface · Biofeedback · Breathing assistance · Relaxation

1 Introduction

In modern society, the pace of life is fast and the competition is fierce. An increasing number of people are suffering from chronic stress in their daily life. Breathing techniques have been widely used in mind-body practices for stress reduction and relaxation [1]. Breathing techniques offer a simple tool to improve the balance of autonomic nervous system, strengthen its capability to adapt to stress and further mitigate the negative effects of stress on the health [2]. With a variety of breathing assistance devices, individuals learn to regulate their breathing into an optimal pattern with the aim of stress reduction. But this is not an easy task for most people to achieve a real relaxed state physically and mentally; because besides an improved breathing skills, the users' psycho-physiologic relaxing experience also affects the stress mitigation. To put it simply, users should also "feel good" during a breathing exercise. Therefore, the interface of breathing assistance device should not only offer an effective breathing guidance, but also a "feeling good" relaxing experience.

In medical applications, breathing guidance is usually presented in graphic or numeric forms, which tend to be technical and performance-oriented. In recent years, several new audiovisual interfaces with more aesthetic qualities have been created for daily use. For instance, Yongqiang Qin et al. developed an immersive breathing training game "Balloon" to train the user to improve breathing pattern [3]. In [4],

© IFIP International Federation for Information Processing 2015
J. Abascal et al. (Eds.): INTERACT 2015, Part III, LNCS 9298, pp. 45–52, 2015.
DOI: 10.1007/978-3-319-22698-9_4

the authors presented "Sonic Respiration" to provide breathing feedback by modifying the quality of musical interface. However, very little work has explored the feasibility of tactile interface for breathing guidance.

The sense of touch enables us to interact with real objects around us, meanwhile, to perceive these interactions. In [5], the authors suggested that the characteristic bidirectional property of touch sense provides a basis to further enhance motor learning and somatic experience. Studies in [6] revealed that tactile feedback could also reduce the perceived workload in learning tasks and enhance the user's feeling of presence. Moreover, stimulating the tactile sense can give people strong relaxing experiences or even emotional experiences, which are beneficial for stress mitigation and health. Therefore, tactile stimuli are often used as a way to reduce stress and make people feel better, such as in massaging techniques and physiotherapy. Tactile feedback is often integrated into multimodal interfaces to enhance the user experience. For example in [7] the authors developed a breathing guidance system to provide the users with an immersive experience through a multimodal interface of auditory, vibratile and light stimuli.

In this study, we aim to investigate whether the tactile interface would help users perform breathing exercise more effectively and enhance user experience during the exercise. We present the concept of *"Breathe with Touch"*: a tactile interface of breathing assistance device that provides breathing guidance through a shape-changing airbag. The airbag inflates and deflates at a specific rhythm to simulate the targeted respiratory pattern. We assume that the changes in the shape of airbag can be mirrored by the user resulting in a better and more relaxing breathing pattern. The tactile interface was evaluated from three aspects: the effect on stress reduction, the efficacy of breathing guidance and the usability. We synthesized the results with valuable qualitative responses from users.

2 Design and Implementation

The concept *"Breathe with Touch"* entails a tactile interface for breathing exercises. By touching the interface, the user follows the shape change of the interface to receive the feedback information. To design the proper form of tactile feedback, we observe the nature of human's breathing movement. Breathing is accompanied by diaphragm fluctuation activities. As an individual inhale, the diaphragm contracts and flattens, causing the expansion of the lungs. Conversely, on exhale, the diaphragm relaxes and moves upward to reduce the space in the chest cavity (see Fig. 1). The lungs are like two air balloons inside of our body. The changes in its shape depend on the airflow.

"Breathe with Touch" simulates human's breathing movements through the shape changes of an inflatable airbag. The expansion and contraction of the lungs are mirrored by the inflation and deflation of the airbag. We assume that this kind of natural mapping between the targeted behavior and the interface could minimize cognitive workload thanks to the intuitive interpretation of the interface. Besides, we think the gradual shape-changing process of airbag could render the breathing guidance in a more soothing way, which helps users slow down their breathing and calm down as well. A hand-sized ellipsoid airbag was made of thermoplastic textile covered by a

Expansion and Contraction of Lungs   Inflation and Deflation of Airbag

Fig. 1. The shape change of the airbag might be naturally associated with breathing movements

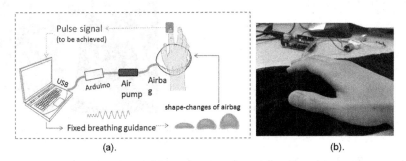

(a).   (b).

Fig. 2. (a). Touch Airbag schematic diagram. (b). The user's right hand on the airbag

layer of soft velvet. The user rests her hand on the airbag to "feel" the targeted breathing rhythm (see Fig. 2b).

The breathing guidance is mapped to the airbag in the following way: when the airbag inflates, an inhale activity is implied. When the airbag deflates, an exhale activity is implied. The maximum volume of airbag is around 120 ml that is the same size of a mouse approximately. This enables the user to identify subtle changes of the shape easily and accurately by hand. The sensitive tactile feelings from the hand and fingers ensure that users can receive the guidance precisely as well. An air pump and a solenoid vent valves implement the inflation and deflation of the airbag. During the inflation, the air-pump pumps air into the airbag and the valve is closed. During the deflation, the air-pump stops working and the valve turn opened. Then, with the hand own weight, the air will be pushed out of airbag gently.

In this study, we focus on the design and evaluation of the tactile interface. A feed forward system was built with a pre-set breathing rate of 6 breathing cycles per minute (c/min). According to literature [8], most people could achieve a high HRV level under a respiration of 6 c/min. The airbag starts from the deflated state to inflated state then return to deflated state again. The duration of this inflation/deflation process is 10 s and this process repeats for the whole training session. As shown in Fig. 2(a), the proposed tactile interface in this work can be embedded into a complete closed-loop biofeedback breathing assistance system in our future research.

3 Study One: Evaluation of the Effects on Stress Reduction

We administered the first user study to investigate whether the proposed tactile interface would enhance breathing training and reduce stress effectively. 12 subjects (six females and six males, age range: 25 to 35) participated in the study. Each participant performed two stress-induced tasks (mathematical test) before and after breathing training. For each task, the physiological data (pulse signals and respiration data) and subjective stress reports were collected (Fig. 3).

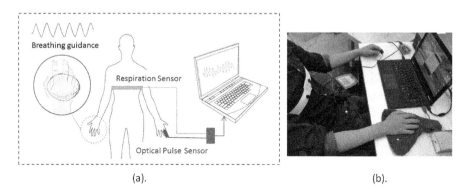

(a).   (b).

Fig. 3. (a). The experiment set up (b). Right hand on the airbag

For each participant, A PPG sensor was placed on the left index finger and a respiratory sensor was placed at the abdominal level. Pulse signals were measured by a data acquisition unit developed by our lab, and then beat-to-beat intervals (RR intervals) were calculated and transmitted to a Processing program for data storage. The standard deviation of the beat-to-beat intervals (*SDNN*) was calculated as the index of HRV. Respiration data was recorded by the ANT system[1] with a sampling rate of 256 Hz. The participant's stress level were measured by the state component of a Spielberger State-Trait Anxiety Inventory (STAIS) [9].

The experiment followed a procedure as shown in Fig. 4. On arrival at the laboratory, the participants were instructed how to use the breathing assistance system. The pulse sensor and respiration sensor were applied to the participants. Then participants were instructed to relax with their eyes closed for 5 min. After the resting period and without moving, participants were instructed to open their eyes and complete a pre-training mathematical task which lasted 10 min during which time measurements of HRV and respiratory rate were calculated. After the task, participants completed a pre-training STAIS questionnaire. After further 5-min rest with eyes closed, then participants completed a 10-min breathing training session with *"Breath with touch"*. The instructions given to participants were: *"Please follow the changes of the airbag to breathe, when the airbag inflates, you should breathe in. When airbag begins to deflate, you should breathe out. This session will last for 10 min."* After the training, participants completed a further 10-min mathematical task. Pulse signal and respiratory data were also recorded throughout this period. Then, a post-training STAIS questionnaire was completed.

The HRV, respiration rate and STAIS were calculated in Pre-training and Post-training periods separately. Differences were analyzed using an independent t-test.

---

[1] ANT, the Netherlands, http://www.ant-neuro.com/.

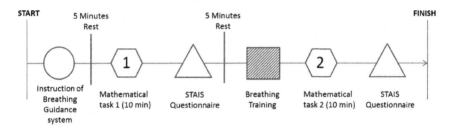

Fig. 4. The experiment procedure

All data are described as means ± standard deviation (SD). A p-value of < 0.05 was considered to be statistically significant.

Physiological data were missing from two participants because of technical problems. As the index of HRV, SDNN showed different degrees of increase among all participants after the breathing training, as shown in Fig. 5. The *SDNN* values of post-training period were significantly higher than pre-training period (49.5 ± 14.2 *vs.* 66.3 ± 20.4; Pre-training *vs.* Post-training, $p < 0.05$). Regarding the results of respiration data, seven participants showed a slower respiration rate during post-training task. However, there were no significant differences before or after training (18 ± 6 *vs.* 15 ± 2 circles; Pre-training *vs.* Post-training).

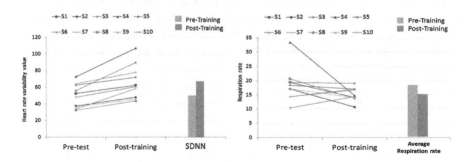

Fig. 5. HRV (*SDNN*) and respiration rate before and after the breathing training.

Psychometric data from the STAIS questionnaires are shown in Fig. 6. Nine participants reported a lower anxiety level during the post-training mathematics task; however, there were three participants showed a higher anxiety levels (subject #1, #4, and #5). The STAIS scores were not significantly different between Pre-training period and Post-training period (46 ± 11 *vs.* 39 ± 9 points; Pre-training *vs.* Post-training).

4 Study Two: Evaluation of Interface Usability

As tactile interfaces are seldom used in breathing assistance, we conducted another study to investigate the user's perception on the usability of tactile interface. To gain more insightful feedback and recommendations for further design, ten students with interaction design background (four females and six males, age range: 20 to 35) were

Fig. 6. Scores of STAIS questionnaires pre- and post- the breathing training (N = 12)

recruited for this study. All participants complete three 10-min breathing training sessions using the same breathing guidance, but with three different interfaces: visual, auditory and tactile interfaces. The experiment follows a within-subjects design with counter balancing to avoid carry-over effects.

We introduced visual and auditory interfaces for breathing assistance as shown in Fig. 7. In visual interface, an ellipse with varying radius represents the breathing guidance. When the ellipse grows, an inhale process is implied. In auditory feedback, we used the changes in sound volume to present breathing guidance. An increasing sound volume prompted user to breathe in, and the fading sound implied breathing out. The usability of the interface was measured using an adapted Lund's USE Questionnaire [10]. The questionnaire was designed for three dimensions: ease of use, ease of learning and satisfaction. All the questions used a seven-point Likert scale (1 = strongly disagree, 7 = strongly agree).

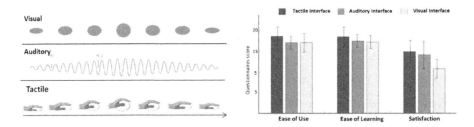

Fig. 7. The results of evaluation of interface usability

The results are shown in Fig. 7. In terms of "Ease of Use", all of three interfaces received high scores; there were no significant differences between tactile, auditory and visual interfaces (19 ± 2 $vs.$ 17 ± 2 $vs.$ 17 ± 2; Tactile $vs.$ Auditory $vs.$ Visual). In terms of "Ease of Learning", there were also no significant differences between three interfaces (19 ± 2 $vs.$ 18 ± 2 $vs.$ 17 ± 2; Tactile $vs.$ Auditory $vs.$ Visual). In terms of "Satisfaction", the score of visual interface was significant lower than tactile and auditory interfaces (15 ± 3, 14 ± 3 $vs.$ 11 ± 2; Haptic, Auditory $vs.$ Visual, respectively, $p < 0.05$). From the open-ended interview, we got more positive feedback about tactile interface. More than 70 % participants chose the tactile interface as their favorite interface. Specifically, they expressed a strong interest in working with the tactile interface and emphasized that it was more comfortable due to the touch experience.

5   General Discussion

During a breathing training, users need to recognize the breathing guidance and follow it to regulate their breathing. In other words, the breathing training is a learning process, in which the users should take an active role, rather than just being exposed to it. Therefore, in breathing training, although the learning tasks are very simple (i.e. to regulate breathing to a specific rate), some participants still regard it as a serious task, which keep them away from a pure relaxation. We think this might be an interesting "paradox" in the design of self-training system for relaxation. It appeals to us and drive us to think about the interaction design in these products or systems that aim to promote relaxation. The training session requires user's mental effort to achieve optimal training effect, such as improved breathing skills, positive imagination or more concentration. However, such mental effort of learning might leads to new stress.

In this design, we tried to lower the workload and enhance the relaxing experience by using a tactile interface. The touch airbag was used as a tangible communication media between the training system and the user. It is assumed that the user can adapt her breathing movements to an optimal pattern more effortlessly by mirroring the shape changes of the tangible interface. The results of user study confirm that the proposed "natural-mapping" interface could help the users perform breathing exercise more spontaneously. The users do not need to put much effort into understanding the instructions, and the transition between inflation and deflation of airbag might naturally trigger a slow and smooth transition between inhalation and exhalation.

The effectiveness of tactile breathing guidance in aiding relaxation and reducing stress was shown by the results of SAITS self-report. However, there is no significant reduction of stress level during the post-training mathematics task. There might be two possible explanations. For most participants, it was their first time to use breathing assistance system; the unfamiliarity with the system brings about new stresses. We also have reservations about the acute effect of 10-min breathing exercise on stress reduction. Although in some clinical use [11], the minimum time of each training session could be 5 min; a short-period exercise may be repeated several times throughout a day to achieve a greater effect on stress mitigation. From physiological measurements, the results suggested that there was a significant improvement in HRV during the post-training task, which suggests that tactile breathing training could enhance the users'physical ability to adapt to stress.

The users' ratings on the usability of visual, auditory and lighting interface were shown in Fig. 7. The tactile interface shows the potential in improving user experience during the relaxation exercise as seen from significantly higher user ratings on satisfaction. Improvements in user experience were also evidenced by the participants' feedback from the interviews at the end of the experiment. During a breathing training process, repeated breathing instructions become boring easily. This is a major problem of most breathing guidance systems for long-term use. To some extent, the touch airbag shifts the focus from the superficial interface to users' own regulating behavior, which helps to relieve users of tedium. Besides, the users thought tactile feedback offers a condition for them to perform breathing training with eyes closed, which also helped relax. They also gave us a lot of insightful recommendations for further design of the interface, for instance, changing the size or position of airbag, integrating the airbag into regular items, and combining tactile and auditory feedback.

References

1. Gilbert, C.: Clinical applications of breathing regulation. beyond anxiety management. J. Behav. Modif. **27**(5), 692–709 (2003)
2. Gevirtz, R.: Resonant frequency training to restore homeostasis for treatment of psychophysiological disorders. J. Biofeedback **27**, 7–9 (2000)
3. Qin, Y., Vincent, C.J., Bianchi-Berthouze, N., Shi, Y.: AirFlow: designing immersive breathing training games for COPD. In: CHI 2014 Extended Abstracts on Human Factors in Computing Systems, pp. 2419–2424. ACM (2014)
4. Harris, J., Vance, S., Fernandes, O., Parnandi, A., Gutierrez-Osuna, R.: Sonic respiration: controlling respiration rate through auditory biofeedback. In: CHI 2014 Extended Abstracts on Human Factors in Computing Systems, pp. 2383–2388. ACM (2014)
5. Hale, K.S., Stanney, K.M.: Deriving haptic design guidelines from human physiological, psychophysical, and neurological foundations. J. Comput. Graph. Appl. IEEE **24**(2), 33–39 (2004)
6. Gallace, A., Spence, C.: The science of interpersonal touch: an overview. J. Neurosci. Biobehav. Rev. **34**(2), 246–259 (2010)
7. Dijk, E.O., Weffers, A.: Breathe with the ocean: a system for relaxation using audio, haptic and visual stimuli. Spec. Symp. EuroHaptics **2010**, 50–60 (2011)
8. Vaschillo, E.G., Vaschillo, B., Lehrer, P.M.: Characteristics of resonance in heart rate variability stimulated by biofeedback. J. Appl. Psychophysiol. Biofeedback **31**(2), 129–142 (2006)
9. Marteau, T.M., Hilary, B.: The development of a six-item short-form of the state scale of the spielberger state—trait anxiety inventory (STAI). J. Brit. J. Clin. Psychol. **31**(3), 301–306 (1992)
10. Lund, A.M.: Measuring usability with the USE questionnaire. J. Usability Interface **8**(2), 3–6 (2001)
11. Muench, F.: The portable stresseraser heart rate variability biofeedback device: background and research. J. Biofeedback **36**(1), 35–39 (2008)

Low-Income Parents' Values Involving the Use of Technology for Accessing Health Information

David Muñoz[1]([⊠]) and Rosa I. Arriaga[2]

[1] IBM Watson, IBM, Pittsburgh, USA
dmunoz@us.ibm.com
[2] School of Interactive Computing, Georgia Institute of Technology,
Atlanta, USA
arriaga@cc.gatech.edu

Abstract. Technology is increasingly available to end users of low socioeconomic status (SES), yet little is known about how these users' values affect the interfaces they prefer when seeking information related to their child's health. We investigate low-SES parents' preferences when it comes to technology to track and learn about their child's developmental milestones using both qualitative and quantitative analyses. We follow the methods outlined by Value Sensitive Design (VSD) and found that the three most relevant values for information seeking are Convenience, Learning/Bonding and Trust. We also discuss how these values drive their technology preferences in tracking their child's developmental milestones. We also present a series of design principles for information communication technology for low-SES user groups that were derived directly from our qualitative research with 51 participants. We note that although working in this unique problem space necessitated following an abridged VSD paradigm our results align with the core set of values suggested by VSD.

Keywords: Value sensitive design · Public sector · Qualitative methods

1 Introduction

With the increasing prevalence of technology, researchers can use digital devices for addressing health-related research questions). Currently, there are over seventeen thousand general health-related mobile apps[1] [9]. However, there is little regulation of the accuracy of the mobile app's content. As long as a mobile app follows Apple or Google's design guidelines, it can be accepted into the App Store or Google Play Store, respectively [9]. Reliable health information is especially critical when it is related to young children because of their rapid growth. For example, developmental disorders affect 1 in 6 children in the US [4]. Early detection of these disorders is important for many reasons such as earlier intervention and treatment, as well as benefits like

---

[1] "Mobile apps" will be the term used in the rest of this paper to refer to applications developed for mobile phones (as opposed to desktop or web applications, or "apps").

© IFIP International Federation for Information Processing 2015
J. Abascal et al. (Eds.): INTERACT 2015, Part III, LNCS 9298, pp. 53–70, 2015.
DOI: 10.1007/978-3-319-22698-9_5

improved social skills and cognitive functioning [6, 24, 28]. There are now many mobile apps to help individuals with autism and their caregivers with various daily activities, including reference and messaging systems for social interactions [3, 16]. However, few programs provide parents with a comprehensive and holistic reference and log for their child's developmental progress [17, 19, 20]. Currently there are no mobile apps that focus on early tracking of developmental milestones. Children who are diagnosed with autism spectrum disorder (ASD) and other developmental disabilities may be late to show important developmental milestones. Thus, a parent's ability to know if his child is meeting these milestones may have important implications. However, keeping track of a child's developmental progress is made difficult by several factors. First, the quantity of developmental milestones a child should reach at certain ages can be overwhelming. Second, parents may need to reference milestones for older or younger age ranges to ensure the observed behavior is appropriate. Third, the fact that children develop in a unique fashion means that some milestones may be reached in a slightly different order than expected [37]. Due to these and other difficulties, less than half of children with developmental delays, including autism, are diagnosed before Kindergarten, leading to postponed treatment and intervention [35]. In this paper, we address the role technology can play in facilitating parents' ability to track their child's developmental milestones. We focus on families from low socioeconomic status (SES) because research indicates that their children are more likely to suffer the deleterious effects of late referrals and diagnoses of developmental disorders. For example, low-SES African American and Hispanic parents reported developmental concerns about 2 years later on average than Caucasian parents [29]. This in turn leads to the under-diagnosing of African American and Hispanic children with ASD [22]. A later diagnosis is associated with decreasing the impact that comes with receiving early treatment and intervention [10, 11, 33]. We used a Value Sensitive Design (VSD) methodology [12] to understand the underlying values that low-SES parents hold in terms of learning about their children's health in order to design the most appropriate solution (see Sect. 2 below for more discussion on VSD terminology). To reach low-SES parents of diverse racial backgrounds, we collaborated with the USA's Women, Infants, and Children (WIC) organization that provides nutritional and health services to mothers and children living 180 % below the poverty level [36]. As mentioned earlier it is important to test parents of diverse racial backgrounds because there are different developmental outcomes among these demographics [22, 29]. Additionally, WIC is an appropriate venue to carry out this study because their organizational mission includes the goal of educating parents about their child's development and developmental milestones, meaning that they are considering various approaches for effectively communicating this information. The study goal was to gather insights into technology use and attitudes towards technology that should be considered when developing tools for tracking developmental milestones for low-SES parents. Our work makes three contributions. First is the utilization of the VSD method with low SES parents in an ecologically valid setting, a community clinic. Here we show that the VSD was especially helpful given our collaboration with a client (the WIC) with limited HCI research experience. Second is an understanding of the values that low SES parents' have when tracking their child's milestones and how this relates to their interface preferences for tracking their child's developmental milestones. While there have been other research projects involving health-related information seeking [5, 7, 26, 27, 30], this work expands the utilization of VSD to health related information seeking on children's development, specifically. Finally, we present a series of design principles for information communication for low-SES user groups that were derived directly from our conceptual and empirical studies.

2 VSD Framework Overview

Values are "something that a person or group of people consider as important in life" [12]. Therefore, the goal of the VSD framework is to see which "enduring human values" are shared by users in a specific scenario [12]. Friedman et al. [12] provide 13 broad examples of values (e.g., "privacy", "informed consent"), though this list is not meant to be exhaustive and instead is meant to be adapted based on the context of specific research studies. By identifying these values, designers and researchers can consider the full range of user needs. This understanding of values is developed through a cycle of iterative studies as follows [12]:

- **Conceptual Study:** derives the values based on existent literature, observations and interviews with users, and other qualitative research methods.
- **Empirical Study:** measures users' responses to a system in terms of the values identified in the conceptual study.
- **Technological Study:** involves gathering value-related feedback from long-term usage of a system.

Given the lack of VSD-related work in our target user group, we focused our effort on conducting a conceptual and empirical study. This paper outlines the methods and findings from those studies that will help inform a future technological study. Our goal with these two initial studies was to explore low-SES parents' preferences for digital and non-digital systems for tracking children's development, including: mobile apps, websites, text messages, kiosks, and paper materials. We also took the opportunity to learn more about the existing WIC workflow, as well as the following research topics related to WIC clients: general use of technology at home, attitudes towards technology, and experiences tracking children's development.

3 Related Work

In the United States and other industrialized countries, mobile apps have great potential for promoting information to young mothers since this demographic is likely to own a smartphone. One study found that mothers with children from ages 0-5 in the U.S. used their phones more often than any other adult in the U.S. [6]. Both industry and researchers have bridged the connection between the ubiquitous nature of phones and parent's needs. Text4Baby is a text message[2] service phones that sends factoids about prenatal and infant health. The company's internal research found generally high usage (31 % of users responded to a text message). They also noted increased distribution of knowledge (75 % of users reported learning new medical information from the mobile app), and increased awareness of baby-related issues [32]. Other related approaches include a Twitter-based system [31] and a website [23]. Of these systems, @BabySteps is the only one that focuses on developmental milestones while the other two contain limited amounts of information relevant to these milestones.

Low-SES communities may have different preferences and access to technology than those in high-SES communities. Researchers have investigated these differences in needs and preferences through various health-related projects such as research on the communication between providers and low-SES patients with children [18, 27], low-SES adults at risk for cardiovascular disease [30], and low-SES African-American communities at risk for diabetes [15]. There has also been similar value-related work involving other topics concerning marginalized user groups such as the homeless [21] and low-literacy adults [26]. However, there is no previous work investigating values in these low-SES communities involving the use of technology for accessing health information on children's development. WIC has been the site of a number of studies but these have focused on technology preferences for learning about nutritional information. One study compared WIC client[3] satisfaction when using paper-based materials vs. a kiosk-based interactive program and found 87 % of clients preferred the kiosk over paper-based materials [34]. The second study found 93 % of WIC clients enjoyed using software for learning about nutritional information [5]. Neither study described the technology utilization of their cohorts nor addressed specific questions about values users had involving information seeking behavior.

4   Descriptive Study: Understanding the WIC Context

To address our study goals we needed to (1) systematically observe and understand the workflow of the WIC clinics and (2) develop an understanding of concerns parents may have about their child's development by interviewing WIC nutritionists.

4.1   Descriptive Study Logistics

Understanding the logistical aspect of the WIC visit would allow us to understand how to contextualize the VSD and allow us to infer how possible milestone tracking systems could fit into this environment. As stated earlier, WIC clients are homogenous with respect to financial income [15] but heterogeneous in other ways, including but not

---

[2] "Text message" will be used in the rest of this paper to refer to short text-based messages sent electronically between mobile phones. These "text messages" may also be referred to as "short message service" (SMS).

[3] "Client" is the WIC's preferred term for parents and children who receive WIC services.

limited to race[4] and access to technology (see Sect. 5.2, "Client Interviews", for more details). The research team's WIC contacts helped coordinate research activity in a single clinic with high racial diversity. To become more familiar with the WIC workflow and to select the most appropriate time to interview clients, the researcher shadowed a client throughout her visit to the clinic. Then, the researcher shadowed a mother and her child as they went through the WIC certification process.

4.2   Descriptive Study Materials

The researchers' university's institutional review board (IRB) approved study protocols to ensure the proposed research would uphold the university's requirements for ethical scientific research. Protocols were also approved by the review board of the district where the WIC clinic was located. All clients provided written consent to participate in the interviews. Given that the descriptive study's focus was to observe the current workflow at the clinic without directly speaking with WIC clients, the researchers did not need any materials for the observations. For the nutritionist interviews, 10 questions were asked about the kind of advice WIC clients seek from nutritionists and the resources that nutritionists recommend as references outside the clinic.

4.3   Descriptive Study Results

During check-in, a client was randomly chosen by WIC staff and asked about partic-ipating in a research study. The first client chosen in this manner agreed to participate. This process took one hour. Based on this shadowing, the research team developed a step-by-step diagram of the certification process and confirmed these steps with the clinic manager, avoiding the need to shadow additional clients. The manager suggested interviewing clients after the nutritionist consultation since the wait time for receiving WIC vouchers generally was the longest wait period for clients, lasting between 10-20 min. The manager also advised the team that clients usually try to get in and out of the clinic as soon as possible. Given this new constraint, the interview script was reduced from 25 min to 10 min.

The initial qualitative research conducted to familiarize the researchers with the WIC clinic and workflow provided insights into the values held by the WIC staff. One of WIC's goals is to find ways to provide educational content related to children's development to its various diverse clients regardless of access to technology. More generally, the overall goal of our collaboration with WIC emphasizes the values of universal usability and freedom from bias, as well as the value of human welfare given

---

[4] We consulted with the WIC's existing questionnaires to ensure that the terminology we used (e.g., "race") and the options available (e.g., "African American") were consistent with the terminology used in WIC's own questionnaires. After filling out the questionnaire, parents participated in a semi-structured interview focused on the research questions outlined below. We also include race in our study since it is a variable that has been associated with disparities in healthcare in general and child development in particular [22, 29].

that the information on children's development involves children's physical and psychological well-being [14]. Trust is also an important value present in the clinic given that clients consult with a health professional (the nutritionist) about their child or children's health. Lastly, given that the interviews were conducted in a cubicle nearby the other nutritionists' offices, away from the noisier public spaces and waiting room, privacy clearly is important to the clinic.

To understand more about the questions clients ask nutritionists, one of the researchers interviewed three of the six nutritionists in the clinic. The nutritionists mentioned that "[clients'] main concern is 'is my child physically growing?'" All three mentioned that in addition to questions related to height and weight, the next most common set of questions asked involved nutrition (e.g., picky eating). Questions about speaking and crawling were also fairly common. Overall, the questions typically asked involved milestones that are related to the child's physical development. This is a telling finding because many milestones that are critical for diagnosing autism are ones that involve social interactions (e.g., shared attention to an object between the child and caregiver) and cognitive development (ability to engage in pretend play).

5   Conceptual Study

The conceptual study consisted of having parents fill out (1) a survey related to their use of technology and (2) an interview about technology utilization, attitudes toward technology and experience tracking their child's development. The goal of this study was to gain qualitative insights about parents' use of technology and their attitudes towards technology in order to inform an analysis of the values parents hold.

5.1   Conceptual Study Logistics

Given that WIC clients are a disadvantaged population, the research team did not want to introduce possibilities for coercion or bias when asking clients to join the research study. The research team discussed this concern with the clinic manager, who suggested the WIC nutritionists should approach the client about the optional research study since they are familiar staff members who interact with parents each visit. Additionally, WIC nutritionists usually inform parents of programs or optional research studies they or their children may be eligible for. Careful attention was given to how nutritionists asked the clients if they wanted to participate. Particular emphasis was placed on making it clear that the research was optional and would not require the client to stay in the clinic longer then necessary. Clients were told that a student researcher was conducting the interview, that the interview topic was "technology usage at home" and that the interview could be done in English or Spanish. 30 % of clients agreed to participate. To minimize disruptions, the interviews took place in the same area where the nutritionist consultation took place. In one corner of this space was a large empty area that accommodated the researcher, the client, and a spouse/partner and/or children, if applicable. Participants were not provided with a stipend. The consent form and questionnaire were available in both English and Spanish. The consent form described that the interviews would be recorded, and the researcher made sure to emphasize this fact by showing the recording device before beginning the interview. Participants were reminded that the interview was optional and that they could stop at any time. First, clients each filled out a brief questionnaire on their own asking about demographic information (age, race, etc.). Given the lack of similar past research with low-SES parents, the researchers needed to record possible confounding variables, such as differences in race and age. For example, there could be cultural or other differences between parents of different ages, or between parents of different races (e.g., African American and Hispanic parents) that affect their technology usage, and therefore also affect the values they hold in regard to technology. Without recording this information, the researchers would have no way of accounting for this possible confound.

5.2   Conceptual Study Materials

The WIC team picked 5 systems to and probe evaluate WIC clients' values with respect to monitoring their child's developmental milestones. These were based on systems WIC currently had available (kiosk, website) as well as feasible future systems for which our research team had an existing prototype (mobile app, text message). A paper booklet was also included for two reasons. First, the WIC currently uses paper materials for distributing information, so feedback on parents' preferences related to paper sources would be valuable. Second, it is possible that low-SES parents may prefer paper materials depending on their values and access to technology. For the second set of questions, clients were presented with images of the five different systems that could be used to access information about their child's developmental milestones. The interviewer provided a one-sentence description of each system and asked to make sure clients understood the systems' functionality. The interviewer clarified that content would be identical in each system. Clients ranked these in terms of personal preference in order from least to most preferred system. Then, clients rated each option on a 5-point Likert scale with 1 corresponding to "not useful".

5.3   Survey Results

Demographic and technology utilization data was collected from 51 participants. The average age was 30 years and the average educational level was 12 years of schooling (high school degree). There were no significant differences in average age, educational level, or number of children (2 children) between races. We consulted with the clinic's records and confirmed that the racial diversity of the parents we spoke with was representative of the overall demographics of the clinics' clients (around 50 % African American, 40 % Hispanic, and 10 % Caucasian). 21 of the 51 participants spoke Spanish. Over half of Hispanic clients (12/21) did part of the protocol in Spanish. Participants were told that they should fill out the entire questionnaire if possible but given the sensitive nature of some questions, that they could withhold any answers they did not feel comfortable sharing. All 51 participants responded to 19 of 21 questions on the questionnaire. 15 parents did not answer the question on financial income, and 4 did not answer about their level of education. All 51 participants provided data that helped us understand their use of technology at home. Table 1 shows smartphone adoption is wide spread in this demographic (preference for the Android platform). Of the 10 participants that did not have Internet access on a smartphone, 6 of them had it at home. Four clients reported a lack of Internet access on their phone or at home. African Americans, when compared with Hispanics and Caucasians, were more likely to use other technologies such as laptops and tablets. Hispanics had the least overall technology adoption compared to African Americans and Caucasians.

Due to time limitations, 48/51 participants provided Likert data for their preferences on the 5 systems we presented. There was a statistically significant difference between parents' preferences for technology (Friedman's test value of $\chi^2(4) = 48.95$, $p < .001$). However, preference distribution was wide, showing that there is no "single" system to meet all parents' preferences (Fig. 1). A Wilcoxon signed-rank test was used

Table 1. Technology use by racial group

	Smartphone	Tablet	Laptop	Desktop
African American	21/24	16/24	18/24	7/24
Hispanic	15/21	3/21	8/21	4/21
Caucasian	5/6	2/6	2/6	3/6
All Clients	41/51	21/51	28/51	14/51

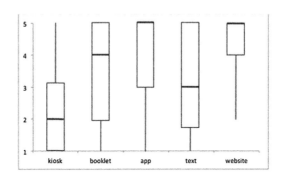

Fig. 1. The X-axis shows the 5 interfaces presented to parents. The Y-axis shows parents' preferences on a Likert scale for each system

Table 2. P-values from a Wilcoxon signed-rank test (highlighted cells for p < .05)

	Website	Booklet	Text	Kiosk
App	.222	.019	.004	<.001
Website		<.001	<.001	<.001
Booklet			.379	.001
Text				.003

to look at parents' preferences (Table 2). Parents significantly preferred the app and website over the other three systems. The booklet and text were the next most preferred systems, and the kiosk was significantly the least popular choice.

5.4   Interview Results

All 51 participants were interviewed about their values related to technology that could be used to help them track their child's development. The interview data was transcribed and two researchers used three research questions (technology utilization, attitudes toward technology and experience tracking their child's development) to guide the grounded theory (GT) analysis of clients' responses [14]. Values (i.e., categories, defined as conceptual elements that can stand on their own [14]) were identified, as well as related properties (i.e., the conceptual aspects of values [14]). Three core values emerged: (1) convenience, (2) learning/bonding, and (3) trust. These values were used to code individual parents' transcripts. All parents made comments alluding to each value, meaning that these 3 values are held consistently across the parents we spoke with. However, the value in which they placed the most importance (i.e., the value most frequently coded) affected their technology preferences [Table 3]. The following sections describe behaviors associated for each value, each of which was equally distributed across African American, Hispanic and Caucasian clients.

Convenience. This value involves finding a "convenient" answer to minimize time, energy, and money required. Given WIC clients' busy schedules, responsibilities to their children, and limited time and monetary resources, optimizing their time is crucial for conserving energy throughout the day. The value of convenience is multi-faceted and involves three properties described below.

Digital and Physical Access to Information. Clients who most valued convenience used their phones often and liked easily accessible systems for finding information, like websites and mobile apps. They liked forum sites like Yahoo! Answers that show feedback from other parents, indicating that these clients may seek validation for their questions. This group disliked the kiosk more than others since they "would have to come back to the WIC clinic and [clients] don't come here very often." These clients also did not like the paper booklet because "it's just something else that might be lost, something I'll have to remember to bring with me everywhere. If I lose it, where would I go for a new copy?"

Cost of Resources. Some clients said "a [mobile] app and website are free to access, but I have to buy the book." Others thought "the clinic would pay for the kiosk and

Table 3. Milestone tracking interface preference via value

	1st Choice	2nd Choice	3rd Choice
Convenience (N = 16)	Website	Mobile App	Booklet
Learning/Bonding (N = 16)	Mobile App	Website	Booklet/Text Message
Trust (N = 19)	Mobile App	Website	Text Message

could be very expensive." The interviewer did not mention the cost of the systems, so it is interesting to see which resources they inferred were more expensive.

Finding a Quick Answer. Some clients who valued convenience may do so because they are more or less familiar with certain websites and formats for finding answers to health-related questions (e.g.,. WebMD or a Google search). Many of these clients preferred Google, saying "that's the only place I know to go when I have a question." This suggests a potential lack of information literacy in terms of knowing which sources are most reliable since these parents expressed that they viewed the top results as the most reliable. Another client initially provided Google as their preferred resource but then paused for a moment before adding "maybe I should actually talk to a doctor instead of just trusting the Internet." When prompted as to why they might or might not talk to a doctor, however, the client again mentioned, "it can be too much of a hassle."

Learning/Bonding. These clients emphasized their interest and desire to grow and learn with their child. By learning more about their children, these clients grow a stronger bond between them and their child. These parents described themselves as "naturally inquisitive", regardless of the topic. One particular client mentioned that she was "hands-on. I like to read and learn more, so sites like Google and WebMD let me learn about stuff I didn't know about." While these clients also preferred websites and mobile apps for learning about children's health, their rationale was different than the group that valued Convenience. These clients also sought validation in the form of site reviews and online forum voting/ratings (such as Yahoo! Answers), like the clients who valued convenience. However, whereas the clients who valued convenience liked having a "Top Answer" to quickly scan, this second set of clients appreciated insights from other parents and also sought validation from these parents. This group was more receptive of the kiosk and booklet though they did not restrict themselves to using sources specifically backed up by research. This group particularly liked tips, activities, and other such add-ons. Due to their desire to learn, and be hands-on, these clients enjoyed learning about activities they could do with their child or any feature that suggested similar interactions. While it was heavily emphasized that all the systems would contain the same information, this group preferred the website, mobile app, and booklet. Perhaps these clients perceived those systems as having the clearest affordances and opportunities for providing interaction between client and child.

Trust. Given WIC clients' financial vulnerability and their children's physical vulnerability, trusting health professionals and related technological systems is crucial. WIC clients seek reassurance that their child is healthy, and this validation can only be obtained when they trust one or both of those sources of information. This value involves two properties: the information itself, and the feeling of reassurance that WIC clients seek through interactions with health professionals and technology.

Safety and Security of Information. Clients who most valued trustworthiness of information avoided reference material that was not backed by an expert. This group was the most likely to mention people (such as a doctor or mother) as a resource for learning about children's development. Many of these clients will not accept an answer from anyone other than a doctor or nurse. One client even mentioned that she would "wait until the next doctor's visit" to ask a question instead of finding an answer from another source. Several clients used their clinic hotline to talk with the next available doctor or nurse. One client was a nurse herself and said she "would never use a website, except maybe WebMD since real doctors review that. If I don't know it, I call the doctor right away." Some clients mentioned that the kiosk and text message could lead to losing private information. Several clients said they "would not feel secure using the kiosk because they would have to stand in front of everyone in the clinic. Someone walking by could see my information." For the text message, others mentioned they "would not feel comfortable responding to a system" and preferred recording information on their own.

Reassurance. Some clients expressed doubt in their ability to accurately record information about children's development, perhaps leading to their preference to rely on health professionals for reassurance. One client mentioned "each child is different, so I don't know what's 'normal' for a specific age. A doctor can help me since he has more experience than me." Similarly, one client said websites were "confusing to navigate." Possibly, these clients prefer speaking to doctors or health professionals because they do not have as much confidence in their use of technology as those clients who value convenience and regularly use their phones, tablets, or other type of computer. While clients in this group tended to review the booklet favorably, one client provided an interesting insight by mentioning "it's hard to update a booklet if there is new information." Perhaps these clients appreciate more trusted sources of content, such as their doctor or WebMD, since they are more aware of recent trends and findings. Indeed, one parent mentioned that "if a text [message] is coming to me from somewhere like webMD, maybe it will include advice, and I trust webMD and would try it." Another client mentioned they liked coming to the WIC since "the nutritionist can see my child in person and give me more specific advice for my child."

6 Empirical Study

The empirical study's goal was to get quantitative and qualitative feedback on prototypes to support the qualitative feedback from the conceptual study interviews.

6.1 Empirical Study Logistics

After completing the conceptual study (described above), parents proceeded to the Empirical study. The Kano method was used to gather feedback related to the features we implemented. Clients were asked to provide a 1-5 Likert scale rating on how they would feel if the feature (1) was included and (2) was not included [25]. This was done for each of the six features [Table 4]. Unlike the common use of Likert scales to express a continuum, the ratings 1-5 are slightly different. "1" is "unhappy" and "5" is "happy", but a "2" is "I could tolerate this", a "4" is "I would expect this feature to be present/not present", and "3" is "neutral". Clients were asked for qualitative explanations for the rating to provide a more complete picture. These comments were recorded to help refine the prototypes. Using established formulas [1] and visualization techniques [28], we identified the level of importance of features (Fig. 2).

Table 4. Technology features related to values

Value	Feature	Feature Description
Convenience	Reminders	Notifications of upcoming milestones a child should be reaching
Convenience	Search Function	A search engine that returns relevant milestones based on a term of interest
Learning/ Bonding	Milestone Tracker	A system for logging whether a child has or has not reached age-specific milestones
Learning/ Bonding	Suggested Activities	A list of activities that can help children's development (e.g., "use simple phrases")
Trust	Example Pictures	An example picture of what milestones look like (e.g., "plays simple pretend")
Trust	Photo Uploader	For each milestone, uploading a photo of one's child as a reference

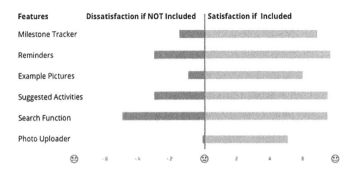

Fig. 2. Feature preference based on Value (N = 16)

6.2 Empirical Study Materials

Prototypes of the three most preferred technological systems (mobile app, website, text message) were developed to gather clients' feedback. All three systems had the same essential functionality: providing a static list of milestones (e.g., for an 18 month old child, "says and shakes head no"). Additionally, several features directly related to the values identified were added in each of the 3 systems (see Table 3). Given the nature of the different systems, the actual interaction differed slightly, though the ultimate functionality was the same (e.g., for "milestone tracker", the app allowed parents to track all milestones in real time, but in the text message prototype, parents would receive individual text messages for each milestone). This study's goal is to identify features that align with users' values and preferences that could help improve the use of the technology to track developmental milestones in a subsequent technological study. This is important given the difficulty involved in encouraging parents to adopt a new behavior (i.e., tracking developmental milestones). Based on the values identified in the conceptual study, a list of related features was created (described in detail in Table 4). While these features were created to appeal to a specific value, there is of course some overlap. For example, uploading photos could be useful for parents to bond with their children by creating a digital scrapbook to share with friends and family. "Example pictures" could be a convenient and visual way to check if your child has reached certain milestones.

6.3 Empirical Study Results

Time constraints limited the number of clients that completed the Empirical Study (N = 16). Thus, we limit our analyses to group statistics for the six features tested. The most compelling finding is that the two features related to convenience ("reminders" and "search function") would lead to the greatest satisfaction if included and also the greatest dissatisfaction if not included. Features related to trust ("uploading photos", "example pictures") would not necessarily be "missed" by parents if excluded but would lead to a moderate level of satisfaction if included. The responses for features related to learning and bonding ("milestone tracking", "suggested activities") were similar to those for convenience. "Suggested activities" is the only feature that leads to interaction with the child outside of the client/mobile app interaction, whereas the other features involve an interaction between the client and the mobile app. A technical study using these or other features should note to what extent these different kinds of interactions are seen as useful or not. Given that the empirical study involved a one-time interaction with a mobile app, it may be the case that suggested activities would be more cumbersome to follow in a more realistic long-term deployment.

7 Discussion

Parent's ability to know if his/her child is meeting milestones may have important medical implications since (1) children diagnosed with a variety of developmental disabilities may be late to show important developmental milestones and (2) children from low SES families are more likely to be diagnosed at a later age than their middle SES counterparts, leading to worse long-term outcomes [22, 29]. The goal of the present study was to gather insights into technology use and values that low-SES parents have for accessing information about their child's developmental milestones through a variety of interfaces. We did field research in a community clinic to gather ecologically valid information from low-SES Americans. We found that this demographic had high smart phone adoption and some differences among African Americans, Caucasians and Hispanics' utilization of other technology (laptops, desktops, and tablets). However, even with these differences, parents' values and technology preferences were consistent. According to our results, three values drove WIC client's technology adoption: (1) convenience, (2) learning/bonding, and (3) trust. We also found that values affected the client's interface preferences.

7.1 Designing Value-Sensitive Systems for Milestone Development for Low-SES Parents

None of the 51 clients knew what the term "developmental milestone" meant. Upon clarification, only one client mentioned tracking her child's developmental progress through a paper-based calendar system. Some clients mentioned asking their doctor at each visit if their child was developing normally. Based on these findings, it is clear that while clients used technology and other resources from time to time, logging developmental milestones is an unknown concept. Further, data from the nutritionists emphasized that most of these parents conceptualize development as being related to physical growth (e.g., eating certain foods, talking, crawling). However, indicators of developmental disabilities, such as autism, are associated with social milestones that may not be on the parent's radar. This further legitimizes the need for a tracking system that introduces parents to motor, cognitive and social milestones.

We found that WIC clients' attitudes greatly affect their technology utilization preferences. While clients who value trust strongly may avoid sources that aren't necessarily backed by expert sources such as Google and Internet forums, parents who most value convenience may prefer these quick ways to access answers. Additionally, search and forums allow for further exploration of content, an appealing feature for those clients who enjoy learning more about their children's development. In our specific use case, designing a single system that will satisfy the needs of these three client groups may not be possible. While the website and mobile app fared better on average, the features that drive each client group towards using these systems may differ. Additionally, these two systems may have been most popular with clients due to familiarity. Perhaps the website was more popular than the mobile app since there is no popular mobile app for developmental milestone information. Another interesting finding related to WIC clients is that previous research found that they preferred kiosk compared to paper based material to learn about nutritional information [5, 34] However, in this study the clients specifically mentioned that the kiosk was not the right interface to track their child's development. They did not feel comfortable recording personal information in a manner that could lead to a breach in privacy (e.g., someone could watch what they entered). This is an important reminder to designers that one interface does not fit all content.

In designing a system to meet our stated goal, we face two possible approaches. The first is to design one interface with multiple views within it to appeal to each of the three values our clients hold. The second consists of designing multiple systems, some of which may appeal to a single value and some of which may appeal to multiple values. In this second case, the system could potentially be more lightweight and easier to navigate due to the focus on one or two of the values rather than all three.

7.2 The Value of VSD in the Public Sector

VSD [12] provided guidance for assessing values among various stakeholders based on interviews and observations. As [2] states, there is a continuing need to "strengthen the voice of the participants in publications." Our GT analysis derived values directly from interviews with end users, preserving their voice and values. We also show that the 3 values we derived (Convenience, Learning/Bonding, Trust) align with 3 of the existing core set of 13 values suggested by VSD (Universal Usability, Autonomy, Privacy/Trust, respectively).

8 Conclusion

Tracking a child's developmental milestones is an important step to assuring that children with atypical development get the help they need. Technology, especially mobile devices, offers a powerful design space for assisting parents of various SES levels in logging their child's development. Equally important is that developmental information is available from credible sources (e.g., webMD). Using the VSD framework, we documented the values involving technology use for accessing health information by low-SES parents. Given the lack of VSD work in this user group and context, we focused this study on two of the three kinds of studies that are part of VSD: conceptual and empirical. The present findings will inform the third kind of VSD study, a technological study involving long-term deployment of preferred systems based on parents' values (i.e., mobile app, website). Our study has some limitations that cannot go unstated. As stated in the descriptive study, we only spent 10-15 min per participant during regular clinic visits, as suggested by WIC management. The time constraint led to only 16 participants in the empirical study, and perhaps those 16 are different than the other parents who did not complete the empirical study in the same time frame (N = 35). A second issue was that only 30 % of parents that were asked to participate in the study chose to do so, meaning our findings may not represent the WIC clients that chose not to participate. Also, the participants in this study were more educated (held a high school diploma) than would be expected given their income level. Unfortunately, there are no other studies with WIC clients that can help us clarify these points. Future research may investigate if providing remuneration would affect the sampling rate and in turn the values that parents embrace in regards to technology. As described in the methods section, we randomly asked parents to participate to avoid sampling bias. However, future research should obtain a larger sample in order to better control for possible differences such as these.

In the United States, race is an important factor to consider in studies that address health-related issues given disparities between whites, Hispanics and blacks. As stated in Sect. 5.3, our sample's demographics were consistent across race and comparable to the clinic's overall demographic distribution. We note that our study took place in one urban clinic, so our findings may not apply across all WIC clinics. For example parents we spoke with had a high usage of technology and African American parents owned more digital devices than either Caucasian or Hispanic parents (Table 1). Future research should study rural areas' technology adoption and values. However, one of our WIC advisors, who has traveled to over 95 % of the 200 clinics in the state, mentioned that our findings aligned with his observations of technology use by WIC clients. There is also evidence that the consumer purchasing trends we observed are generalizable (such as the shift towards mobile device ownership). Through our research, we show that developmental milestones and milestone logging are unfamiliar concepts to WIC clients, underscoring why this demographic is at risk for under or delayed diagnosis of developmental disorders. Our research suggests that technology usage in low-income families does not differ drastically from higher-SES parents. Given these two facts, we argue that the values identified as important to this low-SES cohort and their possible effects on technology usage preference will prove useful to HCI, clinical, and government researchers in their design goals. We expect that knowing low-SES parents' values will help maximize adoption of systems that facilitate tracking children's developmental milestones.

Acknowledgments. We thank Todd Stormant and Gregory Abowd for their advice on the project, Rushil Khurana and Naveena Karusala for help with interview transcription and analysis, and Barbara Stahnke and Marsha Canning for facilitating our research at WIC. This work was supported by NSF Award No. 1029679 and an NSF Graduate Research Fellowship under Grant No. DGE-1148903. This publication was also supported by the Disability Research and Dissemination Center (DRDC) through its Cooperative Agreement Number 5U01DD001007 from the Centers for Disease Control (CDC) and Prevention. Its contents are solely the responsibility of the authors and do not necessarily represent the official views of the DRDC or the CDC.

References

1. Berger, C., Blauth, R., Boger, D., Bolster, C., Burchill, G., DuMouchel, W., Walden, D.: Kano's methods for understanding customer-defined quality. Cent. Qual. Manage. J. **2**(4), 3–35 (1993)
2. Borning, A., Muller, M.: Next steps for value sensitive design. In: CHI 2012 Conference Proceedings, pp. 1125–113. ACM Press (2012)
3. Boujarwah, F.A., Hong, H., Arriaga, R.I., Abowd, G.D., Isbell, J.: Training social problem skills in adolescents with high-functioning autism. In: Proceedings of PervasiveHealth. ACM Press (2010)
4. Boyle, C.A., Boulet, S., Schieve, L.A., Cohen, R.A., Blumberg, S.J., Yeargin-Allsopp, M., Kogan, M.D.: Trends in the prevalence of developmental disabilities in US children, Pediatrics, pp. 1997–2008 (2011)
5. Carroll, J.M., Stein, C., Byron, M., Dutram, K.: Using interactive multimedia to deliver nutrition education to maine WIC clients. J. Nutr. Educ. **28**(1), 19–25 (1996)
6. Dawson, G., Jones, E.J., Merkle, K., Venema, K., Lowy, R., Faja, S., Webb, S.J.: Early behavioral intervention is associated with normalized brain activity in young children with autism. J. Am. Acad. Child Adolesc. Psychiatry **51**(11), 1150–1159 (2012)
7. Denning, T., Borning, A., Friedman, B., Gill, B.T., Kohno, T., Maisel, W.H.: Patients, pacemakers, and implantable defibrillators: Human values and security for wireless implantable medical devices. In: CHI 2010 Conference Proceedings, pp. 917–926. ACM Press (2010)
8. Draper, V.: Mobile moms, mobile first (2013). http://advertising.aol.com/blog/mobile-moms-mobile-first
9. Dufau, S., Duñabeitia, J.A., Moret-Tatay, C., McGonigal, A., Peeters, D., Alario, F.X., Grainger, J.: Smart phone, smart science: how the use of smartphones can revolutionize research in cognitive science. PLoS ONE **6**(9), e24974 (2011)

10. Durkin, M.S., Maenner, M.J., Meaney, F.J., Levy, S.E., DiGuiseppi, C., Nicholas, J.S., Schieve, L.A.: Socioeconomic inequality in the prevalence of autism spectrum disorder: evidence from a US cross-sectional study. PLoS ONE **5**(7), e11551 (2010)
11. Fountain, C., King, M.D., Bearman, P.S.: Age of diagnosis for autism: Individual and community factors across 10 birth cohorts. J. Epidemiol. Community Health **65**(6), 503–510 (2011)
12. Friedman, B., Kahn Jr., P.H., Borning, A., Huldtgren, A.: Value sensitive design and information systems. In: Doorn, N., Schuurbiers, D., van de Poel, I., Gorman, M.E. (eds.) Early Engagement and New Technologies: Opening up the Laboratory, vol. 16, pp. 55–95. Springer, Netherlands (2013)
13. Georgia Department of Health. Eligibility Income Guidelines (2012). http://dph.georgia.gov/eligibility-income-guidelines
14. Glaser, B.G., Strauss, A.L.: Awareness of Dying. Transaction Publishers, New York (1966)
15. Grimes, A., Grinter, R.E.: Designing Persuasion: Health Technology for Low-Income African American Communities. In: de Kort, Y.A.W., IJsselsteijn, W.A., Midden, C., Eggen, B., Fogg, B.J. (eds.) PERSUASIVE 2007. LNCS, vol. 4744, pp. 24–35. Springer, Heidelberg (2007)
16. Hong, H., Kim, J.G., Abowd, G.D., Arriaga, R.I.: Designing a social network to support the independence of young adults with autism. In: Proceedings CSCW 2012, pp. 627–636. ACM Press (2012)
17. Janssen, A.P., Tardif, R.R., Landry, S.R., Warner, J.E.: "Why tell me now?" the public and healthcare providers weigh in on pandemic influenza messages. J. Public Health Manage. Pract. **12**(4), 388–394 (2006)
18. Jeong, H.Y., Hayes, G.R., Yun, T.J., Sung, J.Y., Abowd, G.D., Arriaga, R.I.: Act collectively: opportunities for technologies to support low-income children with asthma. In: Proceedings of the 25th BCS Conference on Human-Computer Interaction, pp. 413–420. British Computer Society (2011)
19. Kientz, J.A., Arriaga, R.I., Chetty, M., Hayes, G.R., Richardson, J., Patel, S.N., Abowd, G.D.: Grow and know: understanding record-keeping needs for tracking the development of young children. In: CHI 2007 Conference Proceedings, pp. 1351–1360. ACM Press (2007)
20. Kientz, J.A., Arriaga, R.I., Abowd, G.D.: Baby steps: evaluation of a system to support record-keeping for parents of young children. In: CHI 2009 Conference Proceedings, pp. 1713–1722. ACM Press (2009)
21. Le Dantec, C.A., Edwards, W.K.: Designs on dignity: perceptions of technology among the homeless. In: CHI 2008 Conference Proceedings, pp. 627–636. ACM Press (2008)
22. Liptak, G.S., Benzoni, L.B., Mruzek, D.W., Nolan, K.W., Thingvoll, M.A., Wade, C.M., Fryer, G.: Disparities in diagnosis and access to health services for children with autism: data from the national survey of children's health. J. Dev. Behav. Pediatr. **29**(3), 152–160 (2008)
23. Liu, L.S., Hirano, S.H., Tentori, M., Cheng, K.G., George, S., Park, S.Y., Hayes, G.R.: Improving communication and social support for caregivers of high-risk infants through mobile technologies. In: CHI 2011 Conference Proceedings, pp. 475–484. ACM Press (2011)
24. Lovaas, O.I.: Behavioral treatment and normal educational and intellectual functioning in young autistic children. J. Consult. Clin. Psychol. **55**(1), 3–9 (1987)
25. Moorman, J.: Leveraging the Kano model for optimal results. UX Magazine (2012). http://uxmag.com/articles/leveraging-the-kano-model-for-optimal-results
26. Munteanu, C., Molyneaux, H., Maitland, J., McDonald, D., Leung, R., Fournier, H., Lumsden, J.: Hidden in plain sight: low-literacy adults in a developed country overcoming social and educational challenges through mobile learning support tools. J. Pers. Ubiquit. Comput. 1–15 (2013)

27. Ngo-Metzger, Q., Hayes, G.R., Chen, Y., Cygan, R., Garfield, C.E.: Improving Communication Between Patients and Providers Using Health Information Technology and Other Quality Improvement Strategies: Focus on Low-Income Children. In: Medical Care Research and Review, p. 67 (2010)
28. Perry, A., Cummings, A., Dunn Geir, J., Freeman, N.L., Hughs, S., LaRose, L., et al.: Effectiveness of intensive behavioral intervention in a large, community-based program. In: Research in Autism Spectrum Disorders, pp. 621–642 (2008)
29. Rosenberg, R.E., Landa, R., Law, J.K., Stuart, E.A., Law, P.A.: Factors affecting age at initial autism spectrum disorder diagnosis in a national survey. In: Autism Research and Treatment (2011)
30. Siek, K.A., LaMarche, J.S., Maitland, J.: Bridging the information gap: collaborative technology design with low-income at-risk families to engender healthy behaviors. In: Proceedings OZCHI 2009, pp. 89–96. ACM Press (2009)
31. Suh, H., Porter, J.R., Hiniker, A., Kientz, J.A.: @ BabySteps: design and evaluation of a system for using twitter for tracking children's developmental milestones. In: CHI 2014 Conference Proceedings, pp. 2279–2288 ACM Press (2014)
32. Text4baby.: Text4baby research and evaluation (2012). https://text4baby.org/index.php/about/data-and-evaluation
33. Thomas, P., Zahorodny, W., Peng, B., Kim, S., Jani, N., Halperin, W., Brimacombe, M.: The association of autism diagnosis with socioeconomic status. Autism 16(2), 201–213 (2012)
34. Trepka, M.J., Newman, F.L., Huffman, F.G., Dixon, Z.: Food safety education using an interactive multimedia kiosk in a WIC setting: correlates of client satisfaction and practical issues. J. Nutr. Educ. Behav. 42(3), 202–207 (2010)
35. U.S. Department of Education.: Part C Child Count (1997–2006). http://www.ideadata.org/PartCChildCount.asp
36. U.S. Department of Agriculture.: About WIC's Mission (2013). http://www.fns.usda.gov/wic/about-wic-wics-mission
37. Volkmar, F.R., Paul, R., Klin, A., Cohen, D.J.: Handbook of Autism and Pervasive Developmental Disorders, Diagnosis, Development, Neurobiology, and Behavior. Wiley, New York (2005)
38. Warren, Z., Stone, W.L.: Why Is Early Intervention Important in ASC? Autism Spectrum Conditions: FAQs on Autism, Asperger Syndrome, and Atypical Autism Answered by International Experts, p.167 (2011)

Probing the Potential of Multimedia Artefacts to Support Communication of People with Dementia

Alina Huldtgren[1,3(✉)], Fabian Mertl[1], Anja Vormann[2], and Chris Geiger[1]

[1] Department of Media, University of Applied Sciences Düsseldorf, Düsseldorf, Germany
{alina.huldtgren, fabian.mertl, geiger}
@fh-duesseldorf.de

[2] Department of Design, University of Applied Sciences Düsseldorf, Düsseldorf, Germany
anja.vormann@fh-duesseldorf.de

[3] Human-Technology Interaction Group, Eindhoven University of Technology, Eindhoven, Netherlands

Abstract. Communication between people with dementia and others becomes increasingly difficult as the disease progresses. Symptoms such as memory loss, speech impairments and limitations in higher cognitive functions affect people's abilities for communication and social interaction. At the same time, meaningful interactions with others are important for the quality of life of people with dementia. In this paper, we describe our work in designing technology probes and testing them with target users to understand how multimedia could be utilized to support the communication of people with dementia through memories.

Keywords: Dementia · Multimedia · Reminiscence · Communication

1 Introduction

Demographic changes and longer life expectancy lead to a growing number of people with dementia (about 36 million people worldwide[1]). Dementia is an umbrella term for decline in mental ability. Primary dementias (90 % of all dementias) are caused by irreversible brain damage, while secondary dementias are caused by other diseases and can be treated. Alzheimer's disease is the primary dementia most prevalent in the population (about 60-80 % of people suffering from dementia[2]). Over the course of the disease, dementia severely impacts memory, speech, thinking, orientation and social behavior. As a result people with dementia have difficulties in all areas of daily life, often become frustrated and experience lower life quality. Unfortunately, there are no medical treatments available at this point to cure primary dementias. Instead, psychosocial interventions play an important role in order to increase the wellbeing of

---

[1] www.alzheimers.net/resources/alzheimers-statistics/.
[2] www.alz.org/what-is-dementia.asp.

© IFIP International Federation for Information Processing 2015
J. Abascal et al. (Eds.): INTERACT 2015, Part III, LNCS 9298, pp. 71–79, 2015.
DOI: 10.1007/978-3-319-22698-9_6

people with dementia. Psychosocial interventions, e.g. reminiscence, have proven to positively and sustainably influence behaviors of people with dementia [1].

Technology has recently started to play an important role in the area of care, mostly in the form of assistive systems for the home care context (AAL). From experience we found that many system designs, however, emerge from a technology-push and not from real needs of seniors and caregivers. In addition, few developments focus on people with dementia. However, "living with dementia presents a range of challenges ripe for creative applications of technology" [2]. We believe, that especially in the area of designing for reminiscence, maintaining personhood and communication new media technologies can be utilized in supportive ways. At the same time, user-centered design is not easy, because the target group is hard to access, communicate with, and rarely aware of the potential of new technology, making it difficult to co-design solutions. This is why we decided to combine the strengths of ethnographic field research and design-led research through the use of technology probes. Probes – designed based on insights from a first field research phase – acted as triggers for discussions with experts and allowed observations of how people with dementia approach new interactive artifacts. In particular, our interdisciplinary team investigated ways in which multi-media technologies can be utilized to support and enhance the experience of reminiscence and communication for people with mild to moderate dementia. The paper outlines our approach and provides first insights from the use of probes in the field and in expert focus groups.

2 Background

2.1 Reminiscence as a Cue to Communication

Dementia limits communication abilities in diverse ways. In the early stages forgetfulness (e.g. of people's names) and associated embarrassment leads people with dementia to withdraw from their social network. As dementia progresses individuals experience extreme memory loss, disorientation in time and place and in later stages a loss of their sense of self. Many also experience problems finding words (similar to aphasia) at the medium and later stages. As such, it becomes increasingly difficult for them to engage in meaningful activities, which is of high importance for life quality [3]. "It is argued that reminiscence may be particularly important for demented individuals' psychological health given that the progressive deteriorating nature of the disease erodes the ability to achieve present successes and makes individuals increasingly dependent on past accomplishments for a sense of competency" [4]. Since remote memory is often spared for large parts of the dementia process, people are able to recall events from the past. While processing memories may be compromised due to brain damage, reminiscence can still provide structure in engaging with others [5].

2.2 Current Multimedia Applications for Dementia Patients

In the CIRCA project [6] researchers created a multimedia application using video, photo and music to support one-to-one reminiscence sessions. The authors reported positive results from user testing. More recent work of the same research team [7] focused on computer-generated 3D environments providing means for people with dementia to enjoy environments they once liked, but cannot visit anymore. Similar is the work of [8], who created 3D environments for reminiscence and meaningful activities. However, people in later dementia stages had problems with the interaction. Several works [9, 10] investigated the television as a medium to provide media from the past or personalized media to people with dementia and [11] found in an observation that generic video triggered more diverse comments and a broader spectrum of conversation topics in people with dementia. Thus, research showed that contents targeted to the individuals were catalysts for reminiscence and communication with others. Overall, there is some proof that multimedia provides support in reminiscence; however, existing work contains mainly single case studies. Our approach aimed to explore aspects of interaction and content with a range of stakeholders instead.

3   Research Approach

Designing for and with people with dementia is sensitive and requires an empathic design approach. In the first step (Fig. 1) we gathered information about dementia through literature research, expert presentations and documentary films. The first field visits were organized in close collaboration with the dementia service network. We established contacts to several welfare organizations and were transferred to the key staff in a care home and two support groups for people with dementia living independently in their homes. Several team members conducted (participant) observations and interviews with people with mild dementia and caregivers. The collected data in form of video, photos, field notes and interview transcripts were discussed with the team and used to develop six technology probes [12] specifically focusing on abilities of people with mild to moderate dementia, when memory, speech, orientation and learning is affected, but people are not entirely dependent yet.

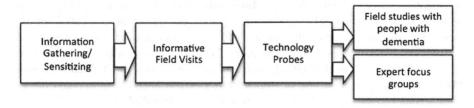

Fig. 1. Overall process of the research

4   Technology Probes

The collected material and first hand experiences served us to empathize with our target group, to understand their needs and challenges and, most importantly to inspire six designed probes (Fig. 2) that could be used in the diverse care contexts. The probes were designed as fully functional artifacts and underwent one review by a group of care professionals followed by a design iteration that focused on improving the content, aesthetics and interaction. (For detailed information about the design and implementation of a single artifact, see e.g. our previous publication on the Reminiscence Map [13]). The probes cover a range of interaction styles as well as media content ranging from public material to completely personal stories.

Fig. 2. Probes: Top row, left to right: Chrono TV with TV programs sorted by decade, Interactive Book with sound output based on opened page, Icho-Sphere reacting to user's touch. Bottom row, left to right: Music-Teddy playing songs from the 30 s when lifted, Reminiscence Map with users' stories linked to time and place, Memory Window with scenes of familiar places.

4.1   Media Contents

Three artifacts cue reminiscence through general content from the past: (1) **Chrono TV** plays video snippets of TV programs from past decades (50 s-70 s) including news, commercials, and entertainment, (2) the **Interactive Book** has a travelling theme (Italy in the 50 s), and combines photographs of, e.g., cars, or popular music artists from the time with audio tracks, and (3) the **Music Teddy** plays back music from the 30 s. More personalized content is used in the **Memory Window** that provides virtual window views to familiar places. Completely personal content is used in the **Reminiscence Map,** which stores a collection of stories from a person linked to a time and place. More abstract sounds and colored light are used in the **Icho-Sphere**.

4.2   Interactions

A range of interaction styles is used in the probes. All aim to be intuitive either by providing a well known interface or providing affordances for basic human interaction skills such as grabbing, lifting, or shaking an object. **Chrono TV** comes with a simple remote control for people with dementia with an on-off button and buttons for changing the channel and volume and an advanced remote control for caregivers offering functions to select a decade, a program or pausing a show, e.g. to be able to discuss the content with viewers. The **Interactive Book** can be used like a normal book by turning the pages. Additionally, it is augmented with different audio files per page (automatically recognized). The user can trigger the audio by pressing pictures in the book. The **Music Teddy** contains a gyroscope sensor, and plays back a random track when being sat up from a lying position. Users interact with the **Memory Window** by placing a postcard of choice on the windowsill. Thematic cards are provided with RFID chips that are recognized. The **Reminiscence Map** currently comes in two versions, a personal tangible object containing the story of one person. The user interacts with a time slider to select a year. LEDs light up in the places where the person was during that time. Respective stories can be listened to by clicking a speaker button. The digital version provides additional functionality to find out if people visited the same places. **Icho** is a sphere containing a range of sensors for measuring touch, movement and pressure. When touched it lights up, when shaken it plays ambient sounds, and when squeezed it vibrates. Icho was developed to provide sensory stimulation and engagement with an artifact (and possibly others).

5 Field Studies and Expert Feedback

5.1 Feedback from Testing the Probes in the Field

The design process of the probes was iterative with field tests involving people with mild to moderate dementia. These included, on the one hand, usability tests with small groups (e.g. three people tested the controls for Chrono TV). On the other hand, exploratory field studies were done, where we either deployed an artifact in the real context and reactions of people with dementia were observed (e.g. the Memory Window was placed in the common room of a care home, and groups of 3-5 users with mild to moderate dementia were observed throughout the day), or the artifact was actively integrated in a group activity (e.g. the Chrono TV in a dementia support group with six men with mild to moderate dementia). In addition, we organized a 2 h-workshop at a care home where all six probes were set up in the common room for residents to be tried out. About 20 people were present including residents (about 8 with dementia), relatives and caregivers. We collected written field notes.

5.2 Expert Workshop

Next, we conducted an expert workshop with 20 participants comprising caregivers, support group leaders, professionals from dementia research, social workers, and technology researchers. In the 1.5-h workshop participants first experienced all six probes in an interactive exhibition. They could discuss their experiences directly with developers and give voluntary feedback through a 5-item questionnaire about the user group, the attractiveness of the object, the expected potential to trigger communication, the expected effort to supervise the use, and the suitable care context. Afterwards, a 10-min presentation about the design of the probes was given. Then participants were divided into 4 discussion groups of five people with diverse backgrounds. Each discussed a different aspects of communication of people with dementia: (1) fostering communication, (2) non-verbal communication, (3) verbal communication, and (4) communication between young and old. The discussions were structured in three steps: (1) current practice and problems, (2) possible role of probes in different settings and (3) brainstorming of new ideas. We audio-recorded and transcribed the discussions for analysis.

6   Insights and Considerations

In the following we provide our first overall insights and design considerations that we derived from the field notes, short questionnaire, and focus groups.

Catering for Diversity and Personalization. One recurring aspect was the variability of symptoms and progression of dementia. Unlike other diseases it is difficult to foresee the progression and communication problems arising at different stages. In addition, how people experience their limitations and how they react in interactions with others is closely related to their personality and past life experiences. To cater for this diversity, experts suggested a strong focus on familiarity and personalized content. The latter could range from media targeted to the preferences and interests of the people (e.g. providing virtual views into a museum for the art-interested user) to completely personal media, such as own photographs.

Application Types. Three general types of applications suitable to support communication emerged: applications that (1) allow people to virtually visit places they cannot visit anymore (such as going to the opera, a museum, the old town), (2) use biographic content and storytelling as a basis for communication (as the book, or the Reminiscence Map), and (3) stimulate the senses to trigger reminiscence and reactions (as the teddy or Icho). The first type would be suited best for people with limited mobility to allow them to keep memories of familiar places and activities alive that could then be communicated to others. Storytelling about the past was identified as a major activity older people engage in, when new experiences are limited. Therefore, using content that triggers stories about the past by showing old videos or photos is useful for providing a basis in the communication, especially in the communication between young and old. As verbal communication plays a major role, these applications would be suited only for early stage dementia. For the later stages the role of emotional triggers was considered more important. The teddy was a good example of this. We observed that people, who did not communicate verbally, still sang along with the teddy's music. In addition, a care manager mentioned that also the soft fur, the familiar looks of the teddy (from the 30 s) and the shape probably reminded the person of familiar things from the past, like their own stuffed animals, or even holding a baby. In one discussion, an expert called it the "emotional memory" and said that sensory input often directly triggers memories without people undergoing a cognitive process to understand them. This was also a topic in the focus group on non-verbal communication where the possibility of adding olfactory input to the book (e.g. paper producing smell when being rubbed) came up to trigger emotional memories.

Communication While, Through and After Interaction. Generally, experts reported that all people have the need to communicate. However, while people with mild dementia often start communication with others, this diminishes throughout the disease. One aspect that should be explicitly considered in the design of such systems is the goal of the communication. While our initial intention was to design probes that foster communication during interaction, e.g. while two people look at the content together, we observed in the field tests that this was mainly true for objects like the book, the map and the window. In these cases people either explored the content together, or commented on it. In the field test with the TV we found that people with dementia were very concentrated on the program and little conversation took place. Although we had implemented a pause function for the group leader he did not use it, as he did not want to disturb the people's viewing experience. He decided to refer back to the content after it was consumed. We also observed that communication can take part through the artifact itself, meaning that the shared interaction could be considered communication or as one expert said "the artifact becomes the communication medium". This was the case with the teddy and the Icho-sphere, which are suited for non-verbal communication of people with extreme dementia.

Familiar Actions. Especially people with dementia have limited capacity to learn new interactions with digital user interfaces. Physical objects, however, provide at least three advantages: (1) interactions are based on familiar and basic actions (such as grabbing, moving or lifting objects), (2) they provide haptic stimulation, and (3) they often allow for shared interaction in a social setting. In the workshop at the care home we could observe that especially the objects that looked most familiar (the book and the teddy) attracted seniors and could be used by people with dementia without supervision. Although the users did not immediately see the buttons in the book, they were eager to touch the pages on different spots to trigger the sound. Many experts also liked the interaction with the window via RFID-enhanced postcards, but we observed in the field, that in the current implementation (card has to be placed on the windowsill) mobility was a limiting factor.

Practical Considerations. Practical considerations that were mentioned during the expert workshop were (1) hygiene, (2) data security and personal rights of people with dementia, and (3) effort of the communication partners (i.e. caregivers, social workers, relatives). Hygiene is important for artifacts to be used in the care home and where the haptic interaction is prevalent, such as the Icho sphere, and the teddy. Data security was discussed in consideration of the Reminiscence Map, which stores personal stories. It was highlighted that recurring informed consent to use the data is important, but difficult to obtain from people with extreme dementia. In addition, some people were concerned that the window would deceive people who do not realize that it is not real. Some experts were worried that the effort of relatives or caregivers to enter the data would be too high for the map. On the other hand, if integrated well into the existing practice (e.g. biographic therapy), it could be feasible. In addition, many thought that the artifacts needed to be used under supervision of a caregiver or relative. Our field experiences, however, showed that simple artifacts, e.g., the teddy or the book, were used by people with dementia alone or among each other.

7 Conclusions

The work presented here provides a snapshot of our larger research endeavor to design interactive multimedia artifacts for people with dementia to support reminiscence and communication with others. We presented six probes that were designed based on a first phase of exploratory field research. The probes were used in several field studies to observe reactions from people with dementia as well as an organized workshop with stakeholders from the care domain. We presented our preliminary design insights from these studies. In the future we intend to extend our investigations and provide general guidelines for the design of interactive multimedia artifacts that support people with dementia in reminiscence and communication in different care settings.

References

1. Gallagher-Thompson, D., Tzuang, Y.M., Au, A., Brodaty, H., Charlesworth, G., Gupta, R., Lee, S.E., Losada, A., Shyu, Y.-I.: International perspectives on nonpharmacological best practices for dementia family caregivers: a review. Clin. Gerontologist **35**, 316–355 (2012)
2. Astell, A.J., Alm, N., Gowans, G., Ellis, M., Dye, R., Vaughan, P.: Involving older people with dementia and their carers in designing computer-based support systems: some methodological considerations. Univ. Access Inf. Soc. **8**(1), 49–59 (2009)
3. Wood, W., Womack, J., Hooper, B.: Dying of boredom: An exploratory case study of time use, apparent affect, and routine activity situations on two Alzheimer's special care units. Am. J. Occup. Ther. **63**(3), 337–350 (2009)
4. Kasl-Godley, J., Gatz, M.: Pschosocial interventions for individuals with dementia: an integration of theory, therapy, and a clinical understanding of dementia. Clin. Psychol. Rev. **20**(6), 755–782 (2000)
5. Woods, B., Portnoy, S., Head, D., Jones, G.: Reminiscence and life review with persons with dementia: Which way forward? In: Jones, G.M.M., Miesen, B.M.L. (eds.) Care-Giving in Dementia: Research and Applications, December 6, 1st edn., pp. 137–161. Routledge (1993)
6. Gowans, G., Campbell, J., Alm, N., Dye, R., Astell, A., Ellis, M.: Designing a multimedia conversation aid for reminiscence therapy in dementia care environments. In: CHI 2004 Extended Abstracts, pp. 825–836. ACM (2004)
7. Alm, N., Astell, A., Gowans, G., Dye, R., Ellis, M., Vaughan, P., Riley, P.: Engaging multimedia leisure for people with dementia. Gerontechnology **8**(4), 236–246 (2009)
8. Siriaraya, P., Ang, C.S.: Recreating living experiences from past memories through virtual worlds for people with dementia. In: Proceedings of the 32nd Annual ACM Conference on Human Factors in Computing Systems, pp. 3977–3986 (2014)
9. Waller, P.A., Östlund, B., Jönsson, B.: The extended television: Using tangible computing to meet the needs of older persons at a nursing home. Gerontechnology **7**(1), 36–47 (2008)
10. Wallace, J., Thieme, A., Wood, G., Schofield, G., Olivier, P.: Enabling self, intimacy and a sense of home in dementia: an enquiry into design in a hospital setting. In: Proceedings of the SIGCHI Conference on Human Factors in Computing Systems, pp. 2629–2638 (2012)
11. Davis, B.H., Shenk, D.: Beyond reminiscence using generic video to elicit conversational language. Am. J. Of Alzheimer's Dis. Other Dementias **30**(1), 61–68 (2014)

12. Hutchinson, H., Mackay, W., Westerlund, B., Bederson, B.B., Druin, A., Plaisant, C., Eiderbäck, B.: Technology probes: inspiring design for and with families. In: Proceedings of CHI 2003, pp. 17–24 (2003)
13. Huldtgren, A., Vormann, A., Geiger, C.: Reminiscence Map: Insights to design for people with dementia from a tangible prototype. In: Proceedings of ICT4AgeingWell, Lisbon, Portugal (forthcoming) (2015)

Smartphone-Based Gait Measurement Application for Exercise and Its Effects on the Lifestyle of Senior Citizens

Takahiro Miura[1,2(✉)], Ken-ichiro Yabu[1], Atsushi Hiyama[2],
Noriko Inamura[3], Michitaka Hirose[2], and Tohru Ifukube[1]

[1] Institute of Gerontology, The University of Tokyo,
7-3-1 Hongo, Bunkyo-ku, Tokyo 113-8656, Japan
miu@iog.u-tokyo.ac.jp,
{yabu,ifukube}@human.iog.u-tokyo.ac.jp
[2] Graduate School of Information Science and Technology,
The University of Tokyo, 7-3-1 Hongo, Bunkyo-ku, Tokyo 113-8656, Japan
{miu,atsushi,hirose}@cyber.t.u-tokyo.ac.jp
[3] Urban Design Center Kashiwa-no-ha (UDCK),
178-4 Wakashiba, Kashiwa, Chiba 227-0871, Japan
inamura@udck.jp

Abstract. Population aging leads to more expensive social security and medical care in a society. In order to minimize national expenditure dedicated to providing support to the elderly, it is necessary to reduce the cost of treatment. Current prophylactic approaches mainly include training programs tailored towards seniors, who may be assisted by caregivers, for wellness maintenance and enhancement. However, these approaches are mainly administered by volunteers, who are often overburdened because of labor shortages. It is thus necessary to design and implement a system that enables seniors to maintain and improve their health by themselves. In this study, we propose and test a smartphone-based gait measurement application. Our results indicate that the mobile application can help motivate seniors to walk more regularly and improve their walking ability. Moreover, we found in our experiments that since our application helped improve our senior subjects' physical fitness, some of them became interested in participating in social activities and using new technologies as a consequence.

Keywords: Seniors · Smartphones · Walking · Changes in attitudes

1 Introduction

Population aging is among the most critical issues in the world today, particularly in developed countries. It causes reduced domestic productivity and increased expenditure on social security and medical care. In Japan, the population aging rate was 24.1 % in 2013 [14], and has been predicted to be as high as 40.5 % by 2055 [28]. Similarly, the ratio of the young to the elderly in Japan was 2.81 in 2009, and is predicted to be 1.26 by 2055 [28]. It is thus becoming increasingly difficult to continue with the conventional welfare and social security model in a situation where multiple young citizens support one senior [36, 49].

© IFIP International Federation for Information Processing 2015
J. Abascal et al. (Eds.): INTERACT 2015, Part III, LNCS 9298, pp. 80–98, 2015.
DOI: 10.1007/978-3-319-22698-9_7

The cost of national health care can be minimized by reducing medical expenses and increasing expenditure on preventive healthcare, especially with regard to long- term chronic diseases and sudden serious injuries [36]. Concrete prevention strategies include encouraging seniors to maintain and improve their health by themselves, often with support from caregivers. Numerous measures to quantify the state of the health of senior citizens have been proposed in order to support activities among them that are conducive to health maintenance and enhancement. To this end, medical organizations and research institutes regularly organize short-term group exercise courses and individual physical training for seniors. However, the regularity of the physical exercise depends on seniors themselves and on the support at their disposal. Effective and reasonable support methodologies for the daily activities of seniors have not yet been developed [12]. Several monitoring systems have been developed to address sudden contingencies among seniors, such as falls as well as acute heart attacks and brain aneurisms. Nevertheless, these activity measurement technologies primarily help monitor seniors' activities in their homes. Monitoring systems need a function to store and analyze seniors' outdoor activities in order to offer more effective assistance for their daily exercise. In particular with regard to walking, not only should such systems measure the user's walking distance, time taken, and the number of steps taken, but also walking velocity, which is closely related to muscle strength [11], as well as balance [37, 50].

In recent times, progress in mobile technologies, such as the development of smartphones, has provided highly functional applications that were hitherto available only on personal computers [44]. Mobile devices nowadays contain numerous sensors, including acceleration sensors and location sensors based on global positioning systems (GPS), and some mobile applications make interesting use of these sensors. In particular, these mobile applications can execute measurement functions with or without external sensors, e.g., measurement functions for the user's activity and physical condition, and support software designed for workouts, including aerobic exercises and progressive resistance training. These applications, if conveniently usable by seniors, would help seniors maintain and improve their health, and take advantage of several services geared toward improving their quality of life. Consequently, we assume that these mo- bile applications likely encourage seniors not only to maintain their health, but also to participate in social activities, such as community workshops and volunteer engagements, because of stable health. However, few studies have researched the measurement of gait parameters of seniors while walking through smartphones and analyzed factors that promote active lives among senior citizens. This is due to complications related to controlling the measurement conditions and long-term studies involving seniors.

In order to help senior citizens maintain their daily exercise schedule, improve their health, and to allow their caregivers to monitor their physical condition, we propose and test a smartphone-based gait measurement application to monitor daily walks taken by senior citizens. We do not test cases involving mobile applications with external devices, such as Fitbit or Jawbone, because our preliminary interviews with the senior subjects of our experiments indicated that they desired a mobile application that does not require external devices because they feared losing them. Moreover, they indicated that while they did not mind carrying their mobile devices, they were not used to carrying external devices with them, and hence found the idea uncomfortable.

Our research questions are as follows:

Q1.   Can the walk measurement application on smartphones help seniors maintain and promote their physical performance, including walking ability?

Q2.   What kinds of side effects does the continued use of the application have for seniors, if any? What is the mechanism, such as consciousness change interactions, of these side effects?

2   Related Work

Numerous studies have been conducted on helping seniors maintain and improve their physical fitness. These are classified broadly into two categories: analytic, diagnostic studies of seniors' gait as well as related exercise methods, and support systems for monitoring (and self-monitoring) their bodies and related neurological states. In this paper, we mainly focus on the latter.

2.1   Walking as an Exercise for Seniors

Since walking is one of the easiest regular exercises for seniors, much research has been conducted to analyze walking among seniors and related concepts. Several studies have proposed that seniors maintain muscle strength in order to prevent pelvic girdle weakness. Brisk walking has been recently recommended by many research groups [18, 40]. For a more active method to prevent adjustable exercise stress, Shimada et al. developed a treadmill-based walking exercise system [43]. Fiatarone et al. and Inaba et al. reported that heavy resistance training of muscles of the lower limbs has significant beneficial effects on muscle size in frail elderly people as well as healthy adults [19, 27]. Fiatarone et al. also indicated that seniors effectively improve muscle ability when they exercise based on progressive resistance training and receive appropriate nutritional supplements [20, 21]. A training method to improve standing balance among seniors proposed by Tanaka et al. used tactile feedback as well as moving auditory stimuli to guide their body sway [48]. Experimental results showed that the system influenced the body sway of elderly participants to a greater degree than that of young participants.

2.2   Monitoring Daily Activities and Health: Environmental and Portable Systems

This category mainly includes mounted or fixed systems attached to an environment, or constituting the entire environment, and portable or wearable systems that can be hand held, or whose sizes do not hinder daily activities of the users [9]. These systems can continually or continuously monitor users' activities or physical condition.

Examples of mounted systems include monitoring systems based on cameras [15, 33] or infrared rays [22, 35] installed at the user's home. With regard to studies on houses that can monitor residents' activity or health, the Georgia Tech Aware Home [31] and the Welfare Techno House [29, 47] are good examples. These houses can monitor the state of their dwellers' activities, their physiological parameters, and sudden risks of emergency that are detected and calculated by sensors in the house, e.g., in living rooms, bathrooms, etc. The need for a monitoring user interface for elderly people has also been investigated [39].

Portable monitoring systems can be used in special environments as well as in ordinary surroundings. With progress in wearable computing technology, various compact movable activity meters are commercially available these days [3, 6, 7]. These are based on research related to measurement systems using inertial sensor data [41], an algorithm to estimate a user's movement by analyzing the cell signal strength and visibility of the global system for mobile communications (GSM) [10]. Harris et al. reported that these kinds of devices were effective in encouraging user to exercise, based on the results of experiments that involved recording the step counts of a large group of elderly subjects [24].

2.3   Monitoring Applications Using Smartphones

The widespread use of smartphones [44, 53] enables users to monitor their health and physical condition much more easily than before because mobiles devices contain numerous applications that can determine user-related movements by using acceleration and gyro sensors, and GPS. Based on embedded sensors in smartphones, novel self- monitoring applications for physical and mental conditions have been proposed. For example, Brajdic et al. reported walk-detection methods [13], and Hammerl et al. pro- posed a semi-automatic personal digital diary [23].

Smartphone-based support applications for exercise and rehabilitation have also been proposed. Spina et al. developed a motion rehabilitation application that guides users in exercising by using auditory feedback [46]. Silva et al. applied embedded acceleration sensors to a dancing game to assess players' risk of fall [45]. Some systems used short messaging service (SMS) and social networking functions to enable users to manage their bodies and mental conditions themselves [30, 34]. Some case-specific support applications for monitoring the health of obese people [16], pediatric asthma patients [51], and persons requiring surgical pain therapy [42] have also been proposed. To assist medical staff, Mahmud et al. proposed a decision-making application for midwives [8]. Hurling et al. reported that an automated motivation and action support system implemented on mobiles can help increase and maintain the level of physical activity in healthy adults [26].

2.4   Issues Addressed in this Study

The aforementioned conventional studies analyzed physical conditions mainly in experimental or indoor environments, and helped users maintain their health by prompting them to exercise. However, a few studies have researched regular outdoor workouts, including walking and hiking, to maintain and improve health among senior citizens. It is true that traditional pedometers can help motivate walkers to continue exercising, but similar and advanced functions should be provided for smartphones with senior-friendly user interfaces to provide them opportunities to actively participate in social activities. We assume that our proposed application can enable seniors to not only maintain and improve their health, but also to find their motivation in life and improve their quality of life (QoL). However, these aspects were not evaluated in our clinical sites. We limit our research to answering the two questions posed by developing an application to monitor walking for smartphones, and then assessing the effects of this system on seniors.

3 Proposed System

3.1 System Overview

We implemented an application to measure walking characteristics based on sensors embedded in a representative smartphone: the Apple iPhone 4S. Smartphones with our application installed on them were distributed among seniors who were participants in our experiment. The user interface for this application was brushed up three times after a preliminary evaluation by a small group of participants who were senior citizens. They were then asked to use the application to log the details of their outdoor walking exercises. The walk-related parameters of each participant were calculated by a server once the logs were uploaded to it. These estimated gait parameters, including walking distance, time taken, and velocity, can be checked through our application.

In this procedure, the application recorded the logs of the embedded acceleration and gyro sensors and acquired location information from the GPS. The server calculated the walking distance, the time taken, and the velocity using the location information, and determined each participant's balance functions, body sways, and the number of steps taken using the acceleration and gyro sensors and referring to studies by Zheng et al., Arai et al., and Inaba et al. [11, 27, 52].

3.2 Interfaces

The views offered by our application named *AyuLog* (which means walk logger in Japanese) and shown in Fig. 1, include home, summary, and graph views that handle functions that log the sensor values, display walk summaries for the entire period of use of the application, and show detailed results. The design of these views, including button and font sizes, was developed by consulting the Apple iOS Human Interface Guidelines and a guideline for seniors proposed by Kobayashi et al. [1, 32]. To avoid confusion, the interface can be operated only by tapping a few buttons. We instituted this mechanism based on the results of three preliminary evaluation experiments involving a small group of senior participants. In this evaluation, which was based on a user-centered design (UCD) approach, the participants were asked to manipulate entire views of the application and then answer questions related to problems that they encountered as well as their suggestions for improvement, such as those regarding button size and allocations, and the method of checking the graphs. As a result, the number of buttons in the home and summary views was reduced following the preliminary evaluation, and the graph view was altered to use simple interactions to check users' monthly, weekly, and overall results.

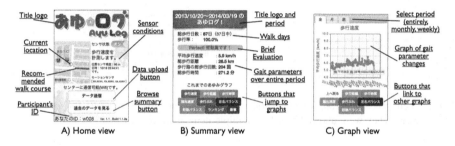

A) Home view   B) Summary view   C) Graph view

Fig. 1. The user interface of the proposed exercise measurement application for seniors. The characters in the views are Japanese.

When the home view shown in the left part of Fig. 1 was activated, the application stored sensor logs and displayed instantaneous sensor values. The sampling frequencies of the GPS and the acceleration/gyro sensors were set to 1 Hz and 10 Hz, respectively. When an experimenter sets recommended walking courses, this application can display these courses in deep blue color in the left-middle part of the view. When a user reaches and enters a course, the application records whether the relevant location is a recommended course. When a user enters the course, the audio guide announces, "You are in the recommended course." As a user exits a course, the audio guide informs him/her, "You have exited the recommended course." This view also has buttons to upload stored logs and browse user exercise results by accessing the server.

The summary and graph views shown in the middle and right parts of Fig. 1, respectively, inform users about the results of their exercise. These views are web views returned from the calculation server, and show the estimated gait parameters mentioned in Sect. 3.1 over the entire period of use of the application as well as periodic results. We used a server with Ubuntu Linux 12.04 operating system (OS) that can calculate and display the results, with the back end and front end coded in PHP, Javascript, Cascading Style Sheets (CSS), and especially jqPlot [4], jQuery mobile [5], and Twitter Bootstrap [2].

4 Evaluation

We carried out a three-month evaluation of the proposed system. Approval for our experiment was obtained from the Office for Life Science Research Ethics and Safety at our institute, and the consent of all participants was obtained. This evaluation was conducted from September to December, 2013 (87 days).

4.1 Participants

Fifty retired seniors citizens, whose age distribution is shown in the left part of Fig. 2, participated in this experiment. They comprised 30 males (mean age 69.7, ± 3.2 years) and 20 females (mean age 66.0 ± 4.1 years). All participants were recruited through an advertisement by a local volunteer group. Reasons cited in the right part of Fig. 2

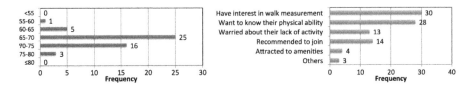

Fig. 2. Left: The age group of the participants. Right: Participants' reasons for joining this exper- iment. They were allowed to select multiple items as responses.

suggest that most participants joined the experiment because they were interested in learning more about their own physical condition. A total of 42.2 % and 48.9 % of them had a habit to walk outside almost every day and a few times a week, respectively.

As shown in the left part of Fig. 3, several participants had previously used information and communication technologies (ICTs) such as personal computers but had little to no experience of smartphones and tablets. However, as shown in the right part of Fig. 3, almost half of them wanted to use these touchscreen devices.

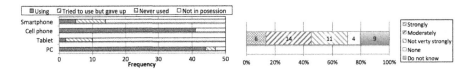

Fig. 3. Left: Participants' experience of use of ICTs. Right: Participants' willingness to use touch- screen devices.

4.2   Method

Experimental Procedure: We gave a smartphone, with our application installed on it, to each participant in the experiment. We explained to them the kinds of parameters that the application calculated and displayed in order to observe the effects of the exercise on them and to review the details of their past physical activity. We then instructed them on how to use the application, which required that each participant record his/her physical detail, including height, weight, and body fat percentage. Following this, they were asked to use the application for three months by attaching the device inside their jackets after having hung it around the neck, as shown in the left part of Fig. 4. This instruction was given because some seniors, who participated in the preliminary evaluation, reported feeling a sense of ease while walking with a smart-phone in a strapped case to prevent it from falling. They were then asked to regularly walk the recommended course during this period, as shown in the right part of Fig. 4. The course was approximately 100 meters long (111.5 m, strictly), was flat, and was located on a quiet street in a residential district of the participants to provide safe walking conditions for the seniors subjects of our experiments. The course also pro-vided suitable conditions for smartphone-embedded sensors to acquire walking-related motion changes. On this course, the horizontal accuracy of location estimation by the GPS was comparatively accurate, i.e., within 5–10 m (see Sect. 5.1). This course limitation was set in order not only to secure the participants' privacy and physical

Fig. 4. Left: User wearing the device. The device is slung around the user's neck and fitted inside the user's jacket. Right: A brief overview of the recommended walking course.

safety, but also to ad- just measurement conditions for the embedded sensors and develop a reference gait database for the seniors subjects at an outside location for medical usage in the future.

We also held monthly meetings with the participants to discuss problems they might have had in using the application and advised them accordingly. We conducted a few measurements during these meetings to calculate the above-mentioned physical parameters, mental conditions, and changes in attitudes regarding social activities and novel technologies by interviewing the participants' caregivers and having the participants fill out questionnaires.

Measured Items and Analysis: We employed height, weight, body fat percentage, skeletal muscle mass, grasping power, and boundary lengths of the thighs and upper arms as physical conditions. These parameters, excluding the boundary lengths, were measured by a Biospace InBody 430 whereas the boundary lengths were measured using a measuring tape.

The objective of the questionnaire was to collect the following data. These items were originally written in Japanese.

Preliminary Survey: Subjective health condition, subject's awareness of his/her health, fitness habits, and use of ICTs.

Midterm Survey: Subjective health condition, exercise awareness, walking environments, positive and negative effects of application use, and difficulty in using the application.

Post-experiment Survey: Subjective health condition, subjects' awareness of own health, fitness habits, positive and negative effects of application use, promotional and obstructive factors to continuing exercise, and difficulty in use of and shortcomings of the application.

A few items did not directly relate to maintenance and improvement of physical activity. However, because it is known that some healthy seniors are interested in participating in social activities, we would like to investigate the effects of improvement in physical performance on attitudes to social activities, and to novel things in general. Specific questionnaire items from our study are shown in the labels on the vertical axes in Figs. 6, 7, 8 and 9. Although these items include indirect elements related to physical ability, we wanted to check the range of positive effects of exercise facilitated by the proposed application.

Gait parameters were obtained by using data from the smartphone sensors and GPS logs, which were restricted to records of the recommended course for privacy reasons. These parameters included duration, distance, and velocity of walking based on GPS logs, as well as front-back/right-left body sways and balance based on acceleration logs. We also checked each participant's access counts to the summary views.

The results of the survey questionnaires were summarized by aggregating participant responses. In the following, we will compare the responses according to the frequency of the items, and will discuss the psychological effects of the application on the participants. In this analysis, the participants were categorized by performance changes in walking velocity based on the effect size of Cohen's d ($|d| < 0.2$: negligible, $|d| < 0.5$: small, $|d| < 0.8$: medium, $|d| \geq 0.8$: large).

5   Results and Discussion

In this section, we describe the results of our experiments involving GPS-related data and subjects' responses to our questionnaire.

5.1   Horizontal Accuracy of GPS in Experimental Location

Before distributing the smartphones, we evaluated the measurement accuracy of the application for the recommended walking course shown in the right part of Fig. 4. In this preliminary evaluation of the 50 smartphones, we measured GPS-related parameters, including horizontal accuracy, occurrence frequency of obtaining the location, and walking distance. The repeat count to go back and forth on the recommended road was six times one way.

The success rate of the GPS was 97.6 % in the 110-m recommended course. The mean values of horizontal accuracy and estimated walking distance for all devices were 5.8 m (Standard deviation (SD): 5.7 m, 95 % Confidence interval (CI): 0.65 m) and 109.9 m (SD: 9.2 m, 95 % CI: 1.06 m), respectively. However, when the statistical values were calculated by each device, the standard deviation was zero for 66 % of the devices whereas 8 % of the devices returned a value over 1.0 m. These results indicated that the horizontal accuracy of GPS location varied among the smartphones. However, disregarding cases where the horizontal accuracy was 60–80 m, the application correctly and consistently estimated the walking distance (e.g., the walking distance was estimated as 110.2 ± 1.4 m given 43.9 ± 26.2 m horizontal accuracy). This result suggested that even if the horizontal accuracy is not correct, the walking distance can occasionally be correctly estimated when the device obtains a broad location. Thus, because time lags among the clocks of the mobile devices clocks are remarkably small, the proposed application can measure the walking distance and the velocity with a probability of over 97 %.

5.2   Walking Days, Distance, and Velocity

During the experimental period, the mean distance walked by all participants and the number of days on which they went for walks were 11.5 km (SD: 4.5 km, 95 % CI:

1.2 km, Range: 5.0–27.3 km) and 61.1 days (SD: 13.8 days, 95 % CI: 3.8 days, Range: 23–87 days), respectively. Regarding their frequency of outside walks, 70.0 % of the participants said that they walked outside almost every day and 28.0 % reported doing so a few times a week. These results suggest that the proposed application helped seniors maintain their walking activity and encouraged it, or at least did not prevent them from continuing it.

The mean walking velocity of the participants was 5.42 km/h (SD: 0.44 km/h, 95 % CI: 0.12 km/h, Range: 4.41 ~ 6.33 km/h) for the experimental period. The left figure of Fig. 5 shows the trend of mean walking velocity change for all participants. The abscissa represents part of the experimental periods divided into 10 segments for each participant. We employed this normalized scale because the number of days on which a walk was taken and the distances walked varied among the participants. The figure shows that the walking velocity of the participants significantly improved after the three-tenth partial experimental period walk, and then remained constant until the end of the experimental period (Tukey's honest significant difference (HSD) test). Comments from most participants indicated that they found it helpful and exciting to check the results of their walks, and were motivated to continue their activity as a consequence. As shown in Table 1, the improvement in walking velocity improvement for each participant can be confirmed by the effect size (Cohen's d) between the one-tenth and ten-tenth experimental periods. These facts indicate that our application contributed to promoting walking among seniors and to increasing their pace.

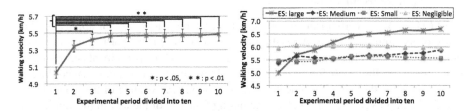

Fig. 5. Left: Change in mean walking velocity with change in the experimental period. The horizontal scale indicates the partial experimental period divided into 10 parts. The error bars represent standard error. Right: Examples of change in walking velocity during the experimental period. The lines in the graph represent participants the changes in whose walking velocities were large, medium, small, and negligible in effect size (ES) calculated by Cohen's d. The horizontal scale represents the experimental period divided into 10 parts.

Table 1. Mean velocity change, walking distance, and walk days by effect sizes between walking velocities at 1/10th and 10/10th experimental periods.

	Large	Medium	Small	Negligible
Number of participants	28	4	12	6
Ratio of mean velocity change	1.15	1.08	1.02	1.01
Mean walk distance [km]	11.6	9.1	12.6	10.3
Mean walk days	58.8	55.5	59.7	49.6

As shown in the right part of Fig. 5, trends of change in walking velocity varied among the participants. In this graph, we show examples of walking velocity transitions based on effect sizes (Cohen's d) shown in Table 1. The participants whose effect sizes were large or medium almost monotonically improved their walking velocity, whereas flat curves resulted in cases involving the participants whose effect sizes were small or negligible. In Table 1, the mean walking distance and the number of days a walk was taken of a small effect group were the largest because some active seniors belonged to this group: a ceiling effect was observed because some of them had exercised regularly and had comparatively better performances than when the experiment had begun.

In the analysis of the correlation coefficient, no significant or interesting relationships were revealed among changes of walking velocity and number of walking days, and distance. Furthermore, we cannot confirm regular tendencies in the correlation co-efficients representing changes in body fat percentage, body-mass index, the boundary length of the crus muscle, and access counts to the graph view page. It is true that the walking ability and health of most (88.0 %) participants improved, but the variation in these parameters was significant from one participant to another. The relationship be- tween body conditions and walking ability should be investigated for a larger participant group.

5.3 Difficulty in Using Our Application Interface, and Design Implications for Seniors

Most (94 %) of the participants reported that they could easily use our application because of its simple interface. According to the access log, these participants correctly uploaded their walk logs and checked their gait results. Three participants encountered difficulties with the small font size and the volume of the audio guide. According to their comments, they did not understand how to adjust the volume of the smartphone. Our future improvements will include increasing font size of the text in the application and writing an easier-to-read instruction manual. However, these three participants also successfully uploaded the sensor logs and browsed their gait results. Moreover, their walking days, distances, and velocity changes were almost identical to or greater than the average for the participants. This indicates that while the interface of our application presented a few complications, most seniors could easily use it.

Based on the lessons learned, the elements of application design should include appropriate font size and easily adjustable volume for the audio guide, support for applications, including easier-to-read instruction manuals for seniors, and a simple interface where most functions are accessible by explicit buttons.

5.4 Why Subjects Would Continue Exercising

According to Fig. 6, which shows participants' stated reasons for why they would continue walking regularly, over 80 % of the participants said that the fact that the proposed application could store their walking history was the most significant motivator for continuing to walk regularly. According to participants' comments, the walking velocity, distance, and days were satisfactory motivators for them because these parameters were intuitively understandable. Some participants also indicated that they appreciated being able to check their walking distances and days because these parameters were the results of their efforts, and gave them a sense of accomplishment. Half of them reported that they would carry on walking because they looked forward to measuring their physical condition at the monthly meetings, understood the importance of maintaining their health, received appropriate counseling from caregivers, and could easily use the proposed application. Comparing changes in participants' walking velocities with the questionnaire responses, we saw no significant difference between groups of participants that had witnessed an improvement in walking velocity (large Cohen's d) and those that had not (small and negligible d) (Fisher's test, $p > .10$). Based on this result and that shown in the right part of Fig. 5, we conclude that our application can effectively help most seniors continue exercising.

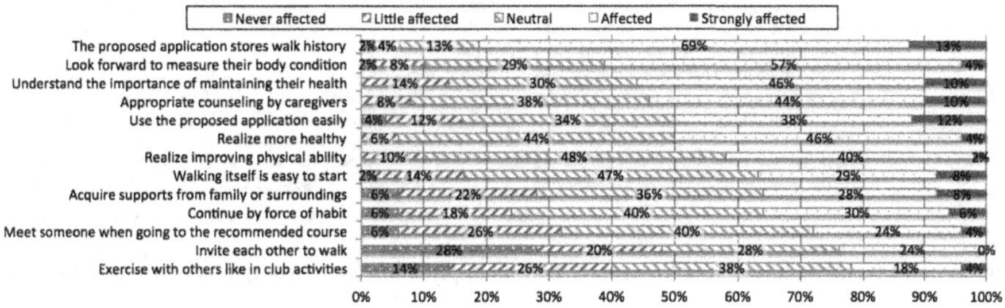

Fig. 6. Why participants would continue to walk regularly.

Most participants regarded exercising with others as a club activity and inviting each other to walk as unnecessary for continuing to exercise. However, comparing changes in walking velocities with the corresponding responses to these social factors, participants who had significantly improved their walking velocities according to Cohen's d reported positive effects in the questionnaire (Fisher's test, $p < .05$). The difference in the tendency to answer thus did not depend on the initial walking velocity of the participants.

These results suggested that the appropriate motivators for seniors to walk regularly were the functions to store and present the details of the results of their exercise, whereas social factors, such as the pleasure of exercising with someone, did not attract all participants. However, seniors who were conscious of the benefits of social activity were motivated more by our application, regardless of their initial physical ability, including walking speed.

5.5   Effects of the Application on Health Management Attitudes

Figure 7 shows the contribution of our application to the positive and negative effects in terms of changes in the participants' attitudes to health consciousness. Over 80 % of them indicated strong to moderately positive effects on health consciousness to continue regular exercise, maintain their health, and know their physical ability. Moreover, half of them reported having benefited by making a habit of walking, thus improving and maintaining their health. Comparing the improved and unimproved groups with regard to these items concerning health awareness, we found no significant differences (Fisher's test, $p > .10$) in any item. These results can suggest that the application contributed to raising participants' motivation to maintain and improve their physical fitness and health, and to exercise more regularly regardless of initial physical ability. However, participants who acquired a habit of walking as a result of the experiment mainly included those who did not regularly walk before. These results suggested that our application helps users improve the awareness of their health conditions and maintenances without depending on their exercise habit, and encourages seniors who do exercise regularly to continue to do so.

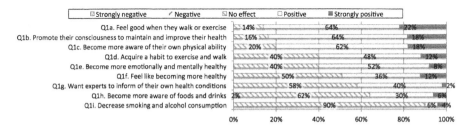

Fig. 7. The positive and negative effects of our application on participants' attitudes to their health.

However, the application had little positive effect in terms of participants' awareness of nutrition, and with regard to reducing tobacco and alcohol consumption. This may have been the case in part because most participants did not smoke or drink much to begin with. A few participants reported ill effects, such as increased consumption of food and drink. A few participants gained weight during the course of the experiment, but the body fat percentage of most participants decreased or remained more or less unchanged. Therefore, our mobile application contributed positively to the seniors' awareness regarding their own health.

5.6   Effects on Seniors' Awareness of Social Activity and Communication

Figure 8 shows the positive and negative effects of the application on participants' awareness of social activities and communication with others. Approximately half the participants reported beneficial effects on their participation in social activities, including volunteering, acquiring well-regulated lifestyles, increased communication frequency with others excluding their families, and improved communication with their families. These results are interesting because the participants' initially reported motivation to walk, as shown in the right part of Fig. 2, concerned reflective characteristics: most of the seniors were not driven by social factors to take up the activity.

According to the results of some statistical tests such as the χ^2 tests and the analysis of variance (ANOVA), there were no significant differences in the tendency of these changes in social activity between the group of participants whose walking velocity had improved and one whose walking velocity had not. According to research in gerontology, the lifestyles of seniors can be explained by and classified into activity, disengagement, and continuity theories [17, 25, 38]. These spectra of aspects can perhaps be explained by seniors' exercise situation.

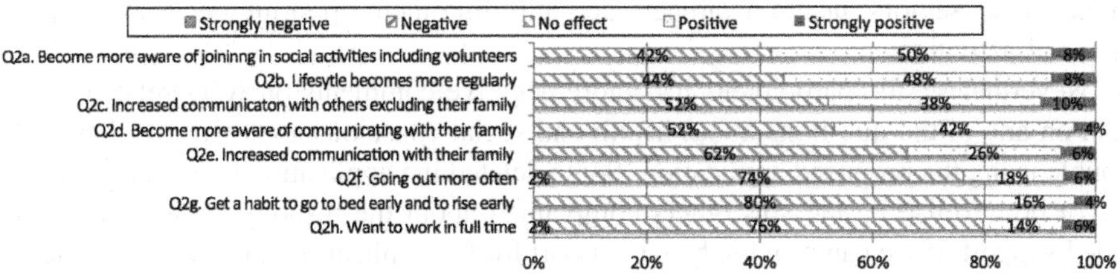

Fig. 8. The positive and negative effects of the application on participants' social activities.

On the other hand, there was little positive effect with regard to increased outdoor activity among the participants, who got into the habit of going to sleep early and waking up early. This may be because most participants were healthy and regularly went outdoors. The results indicate that our application can encourage people to walk out- doors but cannot always activate their awareness to go outdoors.

However, a small number of the participants became more aware of full-time work as a consequence of using our application. Participants who reported positive effects on this item stated that they had wanted to work but had not been confident to do so full-time. On the contrary, participants who reported no effect with regard to this item said that they had retired from full-time work and were reluctant to do so again, or that they had been full-time homemakers thus far. The results indicate that the proposed application can influence seniors to participate more in volunteer activities, but can affect only prompt a few to go to work full-time.

5.7   Effects on Seniors' Awareness of Novel ICTs

The positive and negative effects of our application on participants' awareness of ICTs are shown in Fig. 9. Almost half reported being less resistant to new ICTs, including smartphones. Further, 40 % said they wanted to learn more about smartphones. According to their comments, two participants had decided to switch from a traditional feature phone to a smartphone following this experiment. According to the results of Cohen's d, these two significantly improved their walking velocity during the course of the experiment. However, there was no significant difference in the preference for novel ICTs between the improved and unimproved groups in terms of walking velocity (Fisher's test, $p > .10$). On the whole, since they reported being more socially involved, including in volunteering activities, the proposed application can effectively contribute

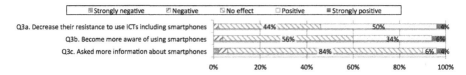

Fig. 9. The positive and negative effects of the application on participants' awareness of novel ICTs obtained through the application.

to increasing seniors' health awareness and affording them opportunities to participate in social activities.

Nevertheless, the participants had more negative comments on ICTs-related items than on any of the questions about health and social consciousness. Most of them had trouble using the proposed application. Some deleted the application by mistake, others forgot how to use it, and still others complained about the response time of the provided support. If we can provide better support for the application, these adverse effects can be mitigated. However, shortly after these issues, all participants became more skilled at negotiating our application with practice. To help seniors use support systems, it was important not only to develop senior-friendly interfaces, but also to organize an efficient service to solve their problems and teach them how to operate the application.

5.8   Relations Among Changes in Participants' Awareness

Figure 10 shows the relations among participants' responses to the questionnaire items mentioned above. This path diagram was generated through structural equation modeling (SEM) using a correlation matrix of the answers. The diagram suggests that health consciousness and awareness of social activities are closely related, as are awareness of social activities and novel ICTs. Hence, it is no coincidence that our application encouraged seniors to walk outdoors more regularly, and that this led to an increase in participants' health consciousness, social activities, and rendered them more accepting of ICTs. In order to disseminate comprehensive support for ICTs in order to encourage physical activity among seniors, it can be effective to appeal to the functions of health maintenance and social participation.

5.9   Limitations

In our experiments, we restricted the area of walking measurements in order to ensure participants' privacy and physical safety, and to appropriately adjust the measurement conditions of the embedded sensors. This setting led to the situation where some participants met and affected a little each other. However, according to some participants' comments, they were not too bothered about privacy, and were willing to be tested in areas other than the course that was used. Following further analysis of the embedded sensors used for our application, we would like to conduct a similar study without the course limitation.

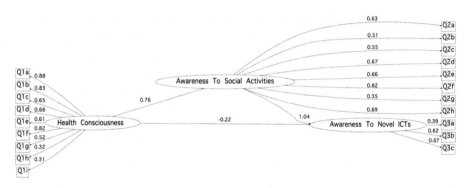

Fig. 10. Path diagram of awareness changes based on structural equation modeling. Sequential serial numbers "Qxx" correspond to the questionnaire items shown in Figs. 7, 8, and 9. The values are standardized solutions.

6 Conclusion

In order to help seniors maintain and improve their health and help their caregivers monitor their physical condition, we implemented a mobile measurement system to record the details of their regular walking exercise using sensors embedded in smartphones, and then tested its usability and effects on seniors. The contributions of this paper can be summarized as follows:

- A walking-monitoring application that can operate on a smartphone and present the results of the exercise was developed, and a group of seniors was asked to use and assess it.
- The implemented application, using GPS sensors, can measure a user's walking distance and velocity with an accuracy of over 97 % regardless of the time lags among the clocks of the devices and error in the horizontal accuracy.
- The application can motivate seniors to walk more because it presents them with their gait parameters, including walking velocity.
- The application has positive effects on health consciousness among seniors, who reported a resolve to continue exercising regularly in order to maintain their health and know their own physical ability.
- Half the participants reported being more socially aware and sociable, as well as being less resistant to novel ICTs as a result of using our application. This may be due to a successive "chain reaction" of awareness of health maintenance, social activities, and novel ICTs.

Our future work includes the following:

- Further analyses of the effects of, and correlations among, the gait parameters, based on the calculation of acceleration and gyro sensors, on improvements in the physical parameters and lifestyle of seniors.
- Further analyses of the effects of course limitations on participants' exercise habits based on further experiments and meta-analysis of related work.

- Improvements in the proposed application, including the implementations of edit and record modes of the walking course, functions of indoor measurement, and more senior-friendly user interfaces.

Acknowledgments. This material is based on work funded by S-innovation (Strategic Promotion of Innovative Research and Development) funding under Industry Academia Collaborative R&D Programs administered by the Japan Science and Technology Agency (JST). We are also grateful to the Healthcare Innovation Project (HIP) for their great help.

References

1. Apple iOS human interface guidelines. https://developer.apple.com/library/ios/#documentation/UserExperience/Conceptual/MobileHIG/Introduction/Introduction.html
2. Bootstrap. http://getbootstrap.com/2.3.2/
3. FitBit one. https://www.fitbit.com/one
4. jqPlot charts and graphs for jquery. http://www.jqplot.com/
5. jQuery mobile. http://jquerymobile.com/
6. Nike + fuelband se. http://www.nike.com/us/en_us/c/nikeplus-fuelband
7. UP by Jawbone. https://jawbone.com/up
8. Al Mahmud, A., Keyson, D.V.: Ubiquitous support for midwives to leverage daily activities. In: Proceedings of the UbiComp 2013 Adjunct, pp. 251–254. ACM, New York (2013)
9. Allet, L., Knols, R.H., Shirato, K., de Bruin, E.D.: Wearable systems for monitoring mobility-related activities in chronic disease: a systematic review. Sensors (Basel) **10**(10), 9026–9052 (2010)
10. Anderson, I., Maitland, J., Sherwood, S., Barkhuus, L., Chalmers, M., Hall, M., Brown, B., Muller, H.: Shakra: tracking and sharing daily activity levels with unaugmented mobile phones. Mob. Netw. Appl. **12**(2–3), 185–199 (2007)
11. Arai, T., Obuchi, S., Shiba, Y., Omuro, K., Nakano, C., Higashi, T.: The feasibility of measuring joint angular velocity with a gyro-sensor. Arch. Phys. Med. Rehabil. **89**(1), 95–99 (2008)
12. Arnrich, B., Osmani, V., Riva, G., Bardram, J.: Ubihealth 2010: the 5th international workshop on ubiquitous health and wellness. In: Proceedings of the Ubicomp 2010 Adjunct, pp. 497–500. ACM, New York (2010)
13. Brajdic, A., Harle, R.: Walk detection and step counting on unconstrained smartphones. In: Proceedings of the UbiComp 2013, pp. 225–234. ACM, New York (2013)
14. Cabinet Office: Annual report on the aging society (2013). http://www8.cao.go.jp/kourei/whitepaper/w-2013/gaiyou/s1_1.html. (in Japanese)
15. Caine, K.E., Zimmerman, C.Y., Schall-Zimmerman, Z., Hazlewood, W.R., Sulgrove, A.C., Camp, L.J., Connelly, K.H., Huber, L.L., Shankar, K.: Digiswitch: design and evaluation of a device for older adults to preserve privacy while monitoring health at home. In: Proceedings of the IHI 2010, pp. 153–162. ACM, New York (2010)
16. Chuah, M., Sample, S.: Fitness tour: a mobile application for combating obesity. In: Proceedings of the MobileHealth 2011, pp. 9:1–9:5. ACM, New York (2011)
17. Cumming, E., Henry, W.E.: Growing Old: The Process of Disengagement. Basic Books, New York (1961)
18. Earles, D.R., Judge, J.O., Gunnarsson, O.T.: Velocity training induces power-specific adaptations in highly functioning older adults. Arch. Phys. Med. Rehabil. **82**(7), 872–878 (2001)

19. Fiatarone, M.A., Marks, E.C., Ryan, N.D., Meredith, C.N., Lipsitz, L.A., Evans, W.J.: High-intensity strength training in nonagenarians. effects on skeletal muscle. JAMA **263**(22), 3029–3034 (1990)
20. Fiatarone, M.A., O'Neill, E.F., Doyle, N., Clements, K.M., Roberts, S.B., Kehayias, J.J., Lipsitz, L.A., Evans, W.J.: The boston ficsit study: the effects of resistance training and nutritional supplementation on physical frailty in the oldest old. J. Am. Geriatr. Soc. **41**(3), 333–337 (1993)
21. Fiatarone, M.A., O'Neill, E.F., Ryan, N.D., Clements, K.M., Solares, G.R., Nelson, M.E., Roberts, S.B., Kehayias, J.J., Lipsitz, L.A., Evans, W.J.: Exercise training and nutritional supplementation for physical frailty in very elderly people. N. Engl. J. Med. **330**(25), 1769–1775 (1994)
22. Hagler, S., Austin, D., Hayes, T.L., Kaye, J., Pavel, M.: Unobtrusive and ubiquitous in-home monitoring: A methodology for continuous assessment of gait velocity in elders. IEEE Trans. Biomed. Eng. **57**(4), 813–820 (2010)
23. Hammerl, S., Hermann, T., Ritter, H.: Towards a semi-automatic personal digital diary: detecting daily activities from smartphone sensors. In: Proceedings of the PETRA 2012, pp. 24:1–24:8. ACM, New York (2012)
24. Harris, T.J., Owen, C.G., Victor, C.R., Adams, R., Cook, D.G.: What factors are associated with physical activity in older people, assessed objectively by accelerometry? Br. J. Sports Med. **43**(6), 442–450 (2009)
25. Havighurst, R.J., Albrecht, R.E.: Older people. Arno Press (1980)
26. Hurling, R., Catt, M., Boni, M.D., Fairley, B.W., Hurst, T., Murray, P., Richardson, A., Sodhi, J.S.: Using internet and mobile phone technology to deliver an automated physical activity program: randomized controlled trial. J. Med. Internet Res. **9**(2), e7 (2007)
27. Inaba, Y., Obuchi, S., Arai, T., Satake, K., Takahira, N.: The long-term effects of progressive resistance training on health-related quality in older adults. J Physiol Anthropol **27**(2), 57–61 (2008)
28. Kaneko, R., Ishikawa, A., Ishii, F., Sasai, T., Iwasawa, M., Mita, F., Moriizumi, R.: Population projections for japan: 2006-2055 outline of results, methods, and assumptions. Jpn. J. Popul. **6**(1), 76–114 (2008)
29. Kawarada, A., Takagi, T., Tsukada, A., Sasaki, K., Ishijima, M., Tamura, T., Togawa, T., Yamakoshi, K.: Evaluation of automated health monitoring system at the "welfare techno house". In: Proceedings of the IEEE EMBC, 1998, vol. 4, pp. 1984–1987 (1998)
30. Kay, M., Morris, D., Schraefel, M., Kientz, J.A.: There's no such thing as gaining a pound: Reconsidering the bathroom scale user interface. In: Proceedings of the UbiComp 2013, pp. 401–410. ACM, New York (2013)
31. Kientz, J.A., Patel, S.N., Jones, B., Price, E., Mynatt, E.D., Abowd, G.D.: The georgia tech aware home. In: CHI EA 2008, pp. 3675–3680. ACM, New York (2008)
32. Kobayashi, M., Hiyama, A., Miura, T., Asakawa, C., Hirose, M., Ifukube, T.: Elderly User Evaluation of Mobile Touchscreen Interactions. In: Campos, P., Graham, N., Jorge, J., Nunes, N., Palanque, P., Winckler, M. (eds.) INTERACT 2011, Part I. LNCS, vol. 6946, pp. 83–99. Springer, Heidelberg (2011)
33. Lepri, B., Mana, N., Cappelletti, A., Pianesi, F., Zancanaro, M.: What is happening now? detection of activities of daily living from simple visual features. Pers. Ubiquit. Comput. **14**(8), 749–766 (2010)
34. Lin, R.J., Zhu, X.: Leverage user experience through social networking to improve health adherence. In: CHI 2013 Extended Abstracts on Human Factors in Computing Systems, CHI EA 2013, pp. 2341–2344. ACM, New York (2013)
35. Marie, C., Daniel, E., Eric, C.: Elderly daily activity habits or lifestyle in their natural environments. In: Proceedings of the PETRA 2011, pp. 26:1–26:4. ACM, New York (2011)

36. Muramatsu, N., Akiyama, H.: Japan: Super-aging society preparing for the future. Gerontologist **51**(4), 425–432 (2011)
37. Nakajima, K., Anzai, E., Iwakami, Y., Saito, M., Ino, S., Ifukube, T., Yamashita, K., Ohta, Y.: Development of the foot pressure measurement device and evaluation of ambulatory function for fall prevention on elderly. IEEJ MBE **60**, 67–70 (2012)
38. Neugarten, B.L., Havighurst, R.J., Tobin, S.S.: Personality and patterns of aging. In: Havighurst, R.J., et al. (eds.) The meanings of age. Chicago [ua]: Univ. of Chicago Pr, pp. 264–269 (1996)
39. Price, M.M., Pak, R., Müller, H., Stronge, A.: Older adults' perceptions of usefulness of personal health records. Univ. Access Inf. Soc. **12**(2), 191–204 (2013)
40. Sayers, S.P., Bean, J., Cuoco, A., LeBrasseur, N.K., Jette, A., Fielding, R.A.: Changes in function and disability after resistance training: does velocity matter?: a pilot study. Am. J. Phys. Med. Rehabil. **82**(8), 605–613 (2003)
41. Schuldhaus, D., Leutheuser, H., Eskofier, B.M.: Classification of daily life activities by decision level fusion of inertial sensor data. In: Proceedings of the BodyNets 2013, pp. 77–82. ICST, Brussels (2013)
42. Seiter, J., Feese, S., Arnrich, B., Tröster, G., Amft, O., Macrea, L., Maurer, K.: Evaluating daily life activity using smartphones as novel outcome measure for surgical pain therapy. In: Proceedings of the BodyNets 2013, pp. 153–156. ICST, Brussels (2013)
43. Shimada, H., Obuchi, S., Furuna, T., Suzuki, T.: New intervention program for preventing falls among frail elderly people: the effects of perturbed walking exercise using a bilateral separated treadmill. Am. J. Phys. Med. Rehabil. **83**(7), 493–499 (2004)
44. Siewiorek, D.: Generation smartphone. IEEE Spectr. **49**(9), 54–58 (2012)
45. Silva, P.A., Nunes, F., Vasconcelos, A., Kerwin, M., Moutinho, R., Teixeira, P.: Using the smartphone accelerometer to monitor fall risk while playing a game: the design and usability evaluation of dance! don't fall. In: Schmorrow, D.D., Fidopiastis, C.M. (eds.) AC 2013. LNCS, vol. 8027, pp. 754–763. Springer, Heidelberg (2013)
46. Spina, G., Huang, G., Vaes, A., Spruit, M., Amft, O.: Copdtrainer: a smartphone-based motion rehabilitation training system with real-time acoustic feedback. In: Proceedings of the UbiComp 2013, pp. 597–606. ACM, New York (2013)
47. Tamura, T., Kawarada, A., Nambu, M., Tsukada, A., Sasaki, K., Yamakoshi, K.I.: E-health-care at an experimental welfare techno house in Japan. Open Med. Inform. J. **1**, 1–7 (2007)
48. Tanaka, T., Kojima, S., Takeda, H., Ino, S., Ifukube, T.: The influence of moving auditory stimuli on standing balance in healthy young adults and the elderly. Ergonomics **44**(15), 1403–1412 (2001)
49. Tsutsui, T., Muramatsu, N.: Japan's universal long-term care system reform of 2005: containing costs and realizing a vision. J. Am. Geriatrics Soc. **55**(9), 1458–1463 (2007)
50. Yamashita, K., Iwasaki, Y., Imaizumi, K., Nakajima, S., Ino, S., Ifukube, T., Koyama, H., Kawasumi, M.: Evaluation of postural control of aging change by stabilogram diffusion analysis. J. Life Support Eng. **20**(1), 31–37 (2008). (in Japanese)
51. Yun, T.J., Arriaga, R.I.: A text message a day keeps the pulmonologist away. In: Proceedings of the CHI 2013, pp. 1769–1778. ACM, New York (2013)
52. Zheng, Y., Li, Q., Chen, Y., Xie, X., Ma, W.Y.: Understanding mobility based on GPS data. In: Proceedings of the UbiComp 2008, pp. 312–321. ACM, New York (2008)
53. Zickuhr, K., Madden, M.: Older adults and internet use. Pew Internet & American Life Project (2012)

Swimming the Channels: An Analysis of Online Archival Reference Enquiries

Joseph Pugh[✉] and Christopher Power

HCI Research Group, Department of Computer Science, University of York,
Heslington YO10 5GH, UK
{jjp513, christopher.power}@york.ac.uk

Abstract. Archives of historical and cultural data, such as the UK's National Archives, receive huge volumes of enquiries from users. These have been seldom systematically studied, despite the obvious benefits to the organisations concerned and interaction designers. The literature looking at the spectrum of remote communications carried out by a modern archive is sparse. Similarly, there is a lack of information about the problems users are having with archival information systems, and no information on the distribution of problems or where in users' information seeking journeys they occur. This paper reports on a mixed-method study using content analysis and grounded theory to address these gaps in the literature. The results of the study indicate that users primarily are encountering problems knowing where to start looking or where to look next in their information seeking journeys. Further, these problems seem to create a deep anxiety or uncertainty in archive users which drives them to seek reassurance and guidance from human archivists, who will provide the type of disambiguation and support that current information systems do not. The paper closes with implications of this work on the future prioritisation of design practice and research in online archives.

Keywords: Archives · Reference enquiries · Content analysis · Grounded theory social media · Email · Information seeking

1 Introduction

Archives of historical and cultural data, such as the National Archives in the UK (TNA), have millions of active users worldwide who approach them for a variety of different reasons. Whether it is students and professional researchers investigating the history of a nation, or members of the curious public mapping their family trees, each of them comes to archives with a need to find information. In the age of digitisation of documents and other resources, more often than not they are trying to find this information through online search engines and other interactive applications. These archival systems are difficult to navigate partly because archives are hard to navigate: they are a "crazy quilt" of inconsistent organisation and wildly varying metadata [6]. Some records may have extensive descriptions, approaching their full text, others may have lengthy lists of names to support genealogical researchers. However, many records have extremely terse, general descriptions which do not assist keyword

© IFIP International Federation for Information Processing 2015
J. Abascal et al. (Eds.): INTERACT 2015, Part III, LNCS 9298, pp. 99–115, 2015.
DOI: 10.1007/978-3-319-22698-9_8

searchers ("Correspondence", "Despatches" or the dreaded "Miscellaneous"). The challenge of users finding what they want is further complicated by the range of different systems available in any one archive, let alone across archives, that users have to learn, remember and apply in the right context.

As a result of this complexity, patrons of archives often have to contact archives directly for assistance. Just as interaction with the resources has changed in the digital era, the interactions with archives as organisations have changed. As opposed to coming into the archive, remote users try to access documents online, and will often put enquires to staff through a variety of different digital channels from telephone to email and onward into social networking. As an example, TNA fields over 100,000 research enquiries annually, with the majority of those enquiries now coming from remote users.

However, there is currently little research on what types of questions are being asked of archives through these different channels by their remote user base. Whereas libraries have extensively studied their interactions with users, there is no such tradition in archives and thus relatively scant information, despite a surge in interest by archives in user centred services in recent years.

Due to this lack of characterisation, it is difficult to judge how the different channels are serving either users or archives. Are all of the channels serving the same function or do particular types of enquiries come to specific channels? If the latter, then the characterisation of these queries could provide insight to archives as to how best to manage services across those channels.

More interestingly, these enquiries may offer an indication of the needs of users in regard to the key activity of *information seeking* in the archives and could provide indications of where users are getting "stuck" in their information seeking journey. Are they looking for help in interpretation? Or are they just trying to find where to locate a document? Characterisation of these types of enquiries will lead to a better understanding of what is working and not working in terms of online information seeking in archives.

In this paper we present a qualitative study involving a content analysis of the enquiries that come to a large national archive that offers multiple channels for user engagement. In addition to this, we include an analysis of a popular online genealogy forum, Rootschat, for comparison. This latter dataset is intended to improve the external validity of the analysis of the archive based enquiries, and help identify if the dataset is representative of more general problems in information seeking in archives. In the next sections we will motivate this problem from the relatively sparse literature available on the subject of archival interactions with their users, and then describe the overall design, conduct and results of the study.

2 Literature Review

There is no question that archivists have come late to the field of user studies. Since the early 1980s when Elsie Freeman pointed out that archivists had "never examined systematically who our users are" [7] there have been many calls for further research [11]. But a residual disinterest in user studies amongst archives professionals has ensured that the discipline knows far less about the behaviour and needs of its users than do librarians [8]. What progress has been made has appeared either in unpublished work commissioned directly by archives or published by a relatively small group of investigators. Foremost amongst them are Wendy Duff and her collaborator Catherine Johnson who together carried out seminal work in 2002 and 2003 when they examined the behaviour of two of the main user groups in archives, namely genealogists [5] and historians [4]. No collection of the views and strategies of these users in an archival setting had been available before, though researchers such as Samuel Wineburg had looked at how historians interpret documents in more artificial settings [17]. The same year, Elizabeth Yakel and Deborah Torres published their work on 'archival intelligence', for the first time seriously addressing the question of what skills an archival researcher needed to have [18]. Prior to this work archivists had little except their own experiences to guide them in trying to understand what their users needed.

The move from paper correspondence to enquiries received by email encouraged, almost simultaneously, Kristin Martin [13] and Duff and Johnson [3] to examine and categorise these enquiries. In Martin's case, her aim was assess the impact of email on the content of these enquiries within a single repository. In Duff and Johnson's case the aim was to inform the development of future digital archival information systems. The pair hoped that by categorising enquiries across a group of archives and examining the types of information supplied by users, they would uncover "clues as to how patrons seek information". Martin predicted that as more information about holdings became available online, users would form more specific enquiries relating to those holdings.

More recently, Kirschoff et al. have described the increasing profusion of archival information systems, digital libraries and other cultural databases as "digitisation islands" [9]. Archival users must undertake the difficult task of moving between these unconnected islands but little literature exists on how skilled they may be at achieving this. In fact, in spite of extensive library literature on offering digital services, the archival literature on topics such as answering enquiries via IM or "livechat" is virtually non-existent with Gary Brannan's paper discussing such sessions at West Yorkshire Archive Service a rare exception [1].

One might argue that libraries and archives are similar, and thus lessons from the library literature would carry forward to archives. However, there is insistence from authorities in the archival sphere, such as Mary Jo Pugh [14], that archival reference 'encounters' differ strongly from those in libraries, and thus are worthy of study in their own right:

> *"The most significant difference is that reference encounters in libraries are usually short and voluntary, each devoted to a single question. In contrast, reference transactions in archives are more likely to be substantive, obligatory and continuing."*

Is this view of archive interactions correct in the online space? When interacting with users online do archives maintain more substantive and continuing interactions? Today, archives are strongly focused on providing user centred services yet answers to these questions are not clear from current research.

A further theme that runs through the, admittedly small, user-based literature for archives is the study of information seeking behaviours and the problems encountered. For example, for family and other historians, it is impossible for their work to progress if they cannot find what they are looking for – indeed, to a great extent, the products of such searches *are* their work. Andrea Johnson examined the information seeking behaviour of over 500 archival users in the course of her doctoral work. Johnson summed up the three main problems encountered by these users as "where shall I look?", "what shall I say?" and "what is that?" [8].

Currently, it is very difficult to see if and how existing search and other information systems are meeting the needs of archive users, and subsequently, little information to drive future design. While Duff and Johnson's work provides a useful model for studying enquiries, their research was carried out on email exchanges between users and archivists. This valuable contribution is now over ten years old, and with the introduction of new means of remote online communication with archives being introduced in that time, there is no information about how this changes and shapes the interactions of users with the archive through these channels. Andrea Johnson ends her paper with a call for more empirical research in order to resolve the question of how to best support "the interaction between the user and digital archival material".

For these reasons, the study reported in this paper examines enquiries to the National Archives to address these gaps in the literature. The contributions of this study will allow us to know where and when users are encountering problems, through what channels they pose what kinds of questions to archivists, and what are the drivers of those requests. This will be of value to interaction designers as it will allow for prioritisation of putative design innovations and research that could help users address the most common problems at the appropriate point in their information seeking journeys.

3   Method

This mixed method qualitative study consisted of a combination of content analysis [10] and a grounded theory [15] of a variety of different sources of existing user-generated data stored at the National Archives in the UK and a selection of forum posts on the popular genealogy community forum Rootschat.

The content analysis used two existing coding schemes to answer the following two questions:

- What are the differences in the types of enquiries users make through different online channels?
- When users have information seeking enquiries, at what stage of information seeking behaviour are they in?

Further, the grounded theory analysis of the content was conducted using an open coding scheme, with the aim to understand what the drivers were behind information seeking enquiries.

3.1   Data Collection

The research team, in cooperation with TNA, identified four main channels through which remote enquiries are received and handled: email, telephone, livechat and

Twitter. In addition, a sample of enquiries to the Rootschat family history forums was also taken for comparison to the TNA channels. Each channel had data sampled from different time periods. This was to avoid the skewing of the data towards particular events or announcements from the National Archives - for example, the announcement of new records relating to the centenary of World War I would likely skew all channels towards requests for data from that era. Data was sampled in an incremental way with researchers coding data as it was retrieved. For each channel, when coding of the enquiries stabilised such that proportion of posts allocated to each code in the coding schemes did not change, sampling was ended for the channel.

At TNA, there is a Contact Centre which provides an email and telephone service. The purpose of this Contact Centre is to provide a positive advice service for callers, to enable them to pursue their research and to point users in the right direction with some suggestion but not to carry out their research for them, which is a service carrying a charge. The Contact Centre is staffed by a mix of administrative workers and records specialists.

TNA receives 1,000–2,000 emails per week to the enquiries inbox. These are responded to by staff working in shifts in the Contact Centre with a total of 37,613 responses logged in 2012/13. In order to manage this volume, the Contact Centre staff make heavy use of a collection of email templates maintained on the Archives' intranet. For example, in 2012 roughly 4,800 enquirers (nearly one in six) received a form response personalised by a link to a page on the National Archives website deemed relevant by the member of staff responding.

For this study, 150 emails received by the National Archives Contact Centre were examined. This comprised a sample from 31st May 2013 and another sample from January 15th and 16th 2014. In each case the Contact Centre were requested to send whatever had been received on a given date up to the number requested after filtering for spam messages. Requests for naturalisation records are handled via a separate web form containing structured fields and were therefore omitted from this study.

For the telephone channel, TNA collected a large amount of telephone enquiries in 2008 as part of their own internal auditing procedures. 51 telephone enquiries were analysed from four samples taken from between 27th February and 10th April 2008.

TNA staff run four hours of live chat sessions four days a week. Transcripts from fifty live chat sessions were analysed with twenty-two livechat sessions from 20th February 2014, three additional sessions from 21st February 2014, twenty three session from 3rd April 2014 and two session from 4th April 2014. The transcripts were anonymised to remove the names of the both the archives interlocutor and the user.

TNA has been using Twitter since July 2009 and has over 60,000 followers @uknatarchives. Fifty-five Twitter conversations were collected, covering the period from 3rd January to 24th May 2014. These conversation were collected by selecting every tweet where TNA participated in a discussion with the expectation that these would be have the highest likelihood of being in response to questions.

Rootschat is one of the world's largest freely accessible family history forums and the largest in the UK. It contains about 4.5 m posts, has around 200,000 registered members and records about a quarter of a million unique visitors a month. The site comprises a large number of different forums. The sample examined here was generated by collecting the top two posts from the most recently edited threads on 12th January 2014 and 2015 from a random selection of twenty-five (of forty) different English county boards to represent a snapshot of enquiry activity on this site.

For each data sample, each unit of communication (e.g. 1 email, 1 livechat session, 1 tweet conversation, 1 telephone session, 1 forum post) may contain more than 1 enquiry. Hereafter, for purposes of clarity and comparison, each channel is discussed in terms of the number of enquiries present within them as opposed to these units of communication. Further, not all enquiries are considered to be information seeking enquiries. For example, a copy request is not indicative of an information seeking activity. Accordingly, when talking about information seeking enquiries we see an expected dip in numbers. The total number of enquiries encountered for each channel is presented (Table 1).

Table 1. Final numbers of *enquiries* and *information seeking enquiries* identified in samples.

	Email	Telephone	Livechat	Twitter	Rootschat
Enquiries	153	51	63	57	71
Information Seeking Enquiries	115	36	56	21	64

3.2   Content Analysis

A content analysis was carried out on all of the above data with two researchers coding samples of the data and checking for reliable application of the codes. There were three different ways that the data was coded in order to answer the research questions.

The data was first coded using a version of the codes of the Duff and Johnson study. Duff and Johnson [3] This coding scheme allows us to characterize the types of enquiries that came in through each channel. The following are the codes used with a brief summary of what each means:

- **Administrative/Directional:** Enquiry asks about administrative information. Examples include costs of photocopying, opening hours or directions.
- **Fact-finding:** An enquiry requiring a specific factual answer.
- **Material-finding:** An enquiry about where to find sources about a particular person, place or event.
- **Specific form:** An enquiry about if a particular source type is available (e.g. census, military service records).
- **Known item:** An enquiry to know if a specific item known by the individual is held at the archive.
- **Service request:** An enquiry for a specific service provided by the organisation (e.g. copying).
- **Consultation:** An enquiry asking for advice that calls on the archivists' specific knowledge of resources. For example, does a specific series contain material relevant to the researcher.
- **User education:** An enquiry where the user has "vague sense" of the record they want or wants to know "how to get started". These may be statements that start with "how do I?"

In some instances, the enquiries did not fit into this classification scheme. These enquiries were subsequently labelled as *New*, with their contents analysed for possible common themes. In most cases these sets were quite small, but where there were patterns we discuss more information about these *New* types of enquiries in the results.

While the Duff and Johnson coding scheme provides a view of the type of enquiry in relation to the services offered by the archive, it does not provide insight into what users submitting the enquiries are really trying to achieve and in particular gives no view of progress in situations where users were in the process of information seeking.

A literature scan, a full reporting of which is beyond the scope of this paper, revealed many, many models of information seeking have been developed by a range of experts [16]. One model, proposed by Marchionini, seems a good fit for the archival domain [12] as it appears to include the key states for people working with information systems or collections. It also lacks the oversimplified 'one critical path' of a number of information seeking models which excessively privilege forward progress. It also seems to map well to the limited work with groups of archival users which has been carried out. Marchionini's "choose a search system" (sometimes "select source") is clearly analogous to Andrea Johnson's "where shall I look". Johnson [8] "Formulate query" is "what shall I say" and "what is that" is "extract information", which is the phase relating to the use of the information products (the documents) located in information seeking.

Using this model, a second coding was devised that characterises the stage of information seeking the user was at when the enquiry was made. The following were the codes used from the Marchionini model:

- **Define Problem**: An enquiry where the user cannot (or does not) define clearly what they are looking for.
- **Choose a search system /select source**: An enquiry where the user seeks direction as to where to begin a search. What types of information/source are available?
- **Formulate query**: An enquiry where the user has a clear sense of what they are looking for but is unable to generate the query terms required to meet their information need.
- **Execute query:** An enquiry where the user requests search be undertaken for them as they are unable to unwilling to do so.
- **Examine results:** An enquiry where the user is trying to understand the result set. Users may seek clarification or reassurance of their own understanding of the results, or the relevance of the results.
- **Extract information:** An enquiry about specific records where the user is trying to make sense of the record. This could include technical problems with document access (e.g. failed downloads).

3.3 Grounded Theory

A grounded theory method [15] was used to identify key categories, themes and patterns that were within the data. This method was undertaken without a pre-conceived hypothesis or theory regarding what the drivers were behind the enquiries. An open coding scheme, grounded in the data, identified key features of the enquiries and the attendant problems being experienced by users and solutions proposed by archivists.

4   Results

The following are the results from the content analysis and grounded theory analysis.

4.1   Content Analysis

The results of the application of the Duff and Johnson coding scheme are presented in Table 2. Further, in Fig. 1 the percentages of each enquiry type are presented by channel alongside the results from Duff and Johnson for purposes of comparison.

Table 2. Coding of enquiry types for each enquiry channel using the Duff and Johnson 3 coding scheme.

Category	Email	Telephone	Livechat	Twitter	Rootschat
Service Requests	15	6	10	10	0
Administrative	8	10	2	8	0
Fact-finding	19	2	12	6	24
Material-finding	28	14	14	4	13
Specific form	18	4	1	3	8
Known item	42	9	16	2	13
User education	8	6	6	3	8
Consultation	7	0	1	0	3
New	8	0	1	21	2
Total	153	51	63	57	71

Applying Duff and Johnson's coding to TNA emails produced some similarities between our data set and theirs. For example 10 % of Duff and Johnson's enquiries were considered to be fact finding and the proportion is 12 % in the TNA sample. 17 % were deemed to be material finding and the proportion is 18 % in the TNA sample. However some categories are very different. TNA received many fewer administrative and service enquiries and its largest block of enquiries were known item requests (27.5 %). In Duff & Johnson's sample only 4 % of requests were known item. It must be emphasised that it is not required that a user should be able to reel off a catalogue reference (COPY 1/400/254, say) in order to "know" an item. If they are accurately describing a discrete record that really exists (the will of Tobias Box, the log of HMS Brilliant) or should exist but perhaps has not survived, then it has been classed as a known item.

For the telephone-based enquiries, we see spikes of activity in the areas of administrative requests and material finding. In contrast to more modern channels, the telephone was the only channel in which material finding exceeded known item requests.

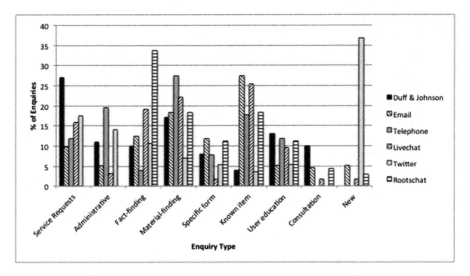

Fig. 1. Percentage of enquiry types for each enquiry channel. Results from Duff and Johnson [3] included for comparison.

While the main intention of the livechat sessions is to support research enquiries, we see that they in fact cover a much broader range of topics. Their profile actually looks very similar to the email sample. We can see, for example, similar proportions of known item requests (27 % to 25.4 %). We do see an increased proportion of service requests and fact-finding requests. This is not unexpected in a real-time medium: people are looking for quick answers to immediate queries that they have.

Twitter appears qualitatively different from any of the other media, and in particular highlights the *New* category introduced into the Duff and Johnson coding. Whereas in the other channels we largely were able to code within the Duff and Johnson coding scheme, Twitter deviated strongly from this trend. In other channels, there were very few outlying enquiries, but with Twitter nearly 37 % of enquiries to which TNA responded could not be categorised in this more traditional model. Many of these messages proved to be observations not questions, corrections to other users misconceptions (referring to the archive as an authority) or consisted of positive comments about TNA. These exchanges seem very distant from Mary Jo Pugh's characterisation of archival interactions [14] as "substantive, obligatory and continuing."

Turning to the coding using the Marchionini model of information seeking, the results are presented in Table 3.

Figure 2 shows the relative percentages of each code for each sample.

Using the Marchionini coding, in the majority of channels almost half of enquiries seemed to relate to the *choose a search system* phase; that is to say they were primarily concerned with asking "where do I look" type questions. Even in the livechat channel, where it is at its lowest percentage, we see that over a third of the sample are in this stage. Due to the dominance of that stage of information seeking, it is perhaps unsurprising that later stages have much lower percentages. There are relatively small numbers of issues in the "examine results" and "execute query" phase. If most enquiries indicate people do

Table 3. Coding of the information seeking stage for each enquiry channel using the Marchionini [12] model based coding scheme.

Information Seeking Stage	Email	Telephone	Livechat	Twitter	Rootschat
Define Problem	2	9	5	3	11
Choose a search system	55	18	20	10	32
Formulate query	19	1	9	1	13
Execute query	9	1	4	1	1
Examine results	11	4	13	4	7
Extract information	19	3	5	2	0
Total	115	36	56	21	64

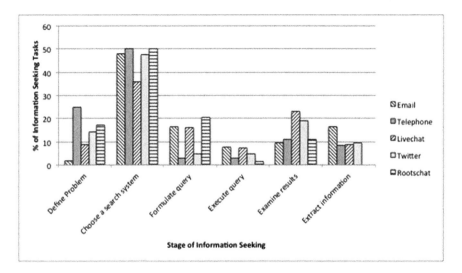

Fig. 2. Percentage of enquiries in each information seeking stage for each channel.

not know where to look, then the chances of them every reaching the point where they can execute and examine their queries is much lower.

4.2   Grounded Theory

A variety of different features in the enquiries were coded in the open coding scheme. On the enquirers' side, the codes encapsulated facts about why they conducted their queries, such as the users overall research question or reasons for their search. The actions users had taken in the system, such as previous searches tried, result sets checked, or sometimes reporting null results (e.g. "nothing comes up") or expectations of content not present (e.g. "there must be thousands of other files"). We also observed instances where users did not appear to understand how the archive was organised, such as advising the archivist, incorrectly, that documents belonged somewhere else. The codes also captured misunderstandings about the archives' services, such as requesting downloads of very large (sometimes non-digitised) volumes of material. We also captured any indicators of the overall user experience or emotional content as described by the enquirer. This often included feelings of frustration and expressions of anxiety.

On the side of the archivist interlocutors, the solutions proffered were coded by the mechanism by which they were resolved and associated information. These mechanisms included redirection of enquirers to prepared research guides on a web page, or a specific part of the archive, or a different archival catalogue or even an external organisation. In some cases, in particular when things could not be resolved, referrals to other colleagues were also observed and coded.

As the codes were developed, they were compared to each other for their content in an attempt to identify overall patterns of behaviour and subsequent impacts of that behaviour. These patterns of statements and enquiries were grouped together to form higher-level themes that were subsequently compared to the literature and each other to identify what the central core theme(s) were within the data.

After conducting the grounded theory analysis, a number of key themes emerged with one formal theory about what was driving the enquiries.

Archivist as Google. The first theme that emerges from the data is that the abundance of search engines and their related systems (e.g. websites), guides, manuals and other help mechanisms appear to not be sufficiently integrated to help users in their information seeking. While each of these different mechanisms for finding information are in themselves valuable, there is no mechanism to prompt users to go to particular pieces of help within the system. The absolute divide between searching the collections and searching guidance about those collections is immensely problematic.

This was evidenced by the large number of the enquiries across the channels which were handled by directing the enquirer to existing online record guidance. For example, two different livechat enquirers are both looking for unit war diaries relating to battalions of the Durham Light Infantry:

"I cannot find anything on your website....do you keep these please?" (Livechat Enquirer 14).

"...have been trying to locate it but without success" (Livechat Enquirer 3).

The war diaries are available at the archive, and through the primary Discovery search portal but more importantly, information on how to find unit war diaries is prominently displayed in a number of different places on the National Archives website. As a result, the archivist is easily able to direct the enquirers to the correct guidance. But the purpose of that guidance is to support users in finding the documents themselves and to free up archivists to focus on more difficult information seeking problems.

Situations where the archivist was 'acting as Google' in directing people to known resources was present in all channels. This type of interaction has an impact on archive resources in two ways. First, it impacts their ability to undertake more complex data seeking tasks, where individuals have hard to find or hard to access materials. Secondly, the resources that people are being directed to have been invested in to address specifically these types of requests.

Ability to Survey the Terrain.   When we look at the Marchionini model coding in combination with the grounded theory analysis, an interesting theme begins to emerge. The vast majority of enquiries that are coming from users fall squarely in the category of "where do I look?" This is a somewhat surprising result: given the availability of search technology we might assume that knowing where to look is a problem already solved.

One possible interpretation is this is all idiosyncratic to the National Archives. However, when we look at Rootschat, we see similar types of enquiries being made. Fact-finding, material finding or known item searches, users are predominantly getting stuck knowing where to look. This indicates to us that this is not unique to TNA.

A further possible explanation is a general laziness of the user base in trying to find out where to search. We all know that it is easier to ask someone else to undertake a task than to put in the effort ourselves. Within the dataset, such seeming lack of effort by users does occasionally appear:

> *"I am new to family research, please advise if it is possible to search the records online from Australia and what is required to help me do this."* (Email Enquirer 60).

> *"How do I get info on my grandad in Ww1 please? I have a name, DoB? Is there an email or tel number."* (Twitter Enquirer 33).

However, only a very small number of the enquiries across the channels appear to display this lack of effort. So, while this idea has face validity, we would expect a lot more of this type of interaction if it were the key reason for the enquiries. Further, when looking at the user base this explanation seems unlikely. People who are investigating their family histories, one of the largest groups now using archives, are doing so because they want to, not because they have to do so, and it seems unlikely they would hand over the task without making reasonably strenuous efforts. Trained professional historians also seem unlikely to 'outsource' their research in this way.

Other users seem to have all the information they need to conduct a search, yet still seem unclear even as to how to begin:

> *"Trying to trace my Grandfather ...who served in the Sherwood Foresters. Notts & Derby.Regt. in the Great War. How do I use the web site to get any information on him?? Got his Reg no [xxxxx]."* (Email Enquirer 42).

With the aid of a service number, many relevant records are easily available to this user. Similarly, an email enquiry about passage to Australia:

> *"My dad was in the Merchant Navy from 1948 - 1955. The only info. I have was that he was in Townsville, Australia in 1953 and he settled in South Africa in 1955.*

> *Is there any way of finding his record of service...His name was [xxxxx], DOB 30.11.1927."* (Email Enquirer 45).

We must ask ourselves, why, with an abundance of search systems to choose from, are these users contacting someone for instructions in place of trying to search for themselves?

The answer to this question perhaps lies in situations where users have tried to find information, but have ended up back near the start of the Marchionini model. There were several enquiries throughout the channels that indicate that users are seeking reassurance that what they have found is correct:

"Hi, was wondering if you could help find my Grandad's naval records and medals on here, I found him on your website ADM [yyyyy], the name [xxxxx]. I find it very confusing. Can you help me?" (Livechat Enquirer 30).

Furthermore, other users indicate that they do not trust their own findings:

"I am searching for records of my father's s service in WWI, he received his RAC pilots licence, aged 16, in 1916 and his wings from the Royal Flying Corps later that year. Despite flying for over 600 h there is no record of his war service with the RFC. I presume that this is because there are no RFC records for the period late 1916 - to early 1918, but would be grateful if you could confirm this?" (Email Enquirer 97).
"When I was young I was told that my Grandfather ([xxxxx]) fought in WWI with the Irish Guards. I found this person and army number [yyyyy] in the Irish Guards the information I paid for has not helped me in my quest to find if this is in fact my Grandfather, it tells me the same name but not where he lived or other useful information which indeed would confirm if this is the same person am looking for." (Email Enquirer 89).

Consider the case of Email Enquirer 97 above. This user is in fact correct to be suspicious of their lack of search progress (the documents are available); but they have no mechanism to know that a path has already been laid out for them in the research guides provided by TNA. To return to Kirchhoff's metaphor of digitised islands, the enquirer suspects he has passed his island by but there are no signposts to tell him if he is right or wrong - just as there were no signposts on any part of his journey.

Compare this to Email Enquirer 89 who is unable find information to confirm which individual is his grandfather. In this case, the information may be contained in a different part of the archive, but there is no way for the enquirer to know this is the case. If the enquirer understood the archive's structure, that might help their situation, but there are few mechanisms within existing search systems at TNA or at other archives that help teach users about the structure of archives as part of their ongoing search. This leads to frustration and anxiety on the part of the searcher. They are on one digitised island, and cannot even see the other islands in the distance they need to reach.

In the case of Email Enquirer 45, we have an even worse situation in that the individual finds the overabundance of choice so daunting that they are unable to even know where to begin their journey even though they appear to have all the information needed to successfully navigate to the end.

In all of these situations, the archival information systems have removed the archivist from the traditional assistive role they play in the physical reading room environment. This *disintermediation* [2] means that where systems fail to assist users in understanding the next step, the user must fall back on contacting the archivists through the channels available to them, even if it means trying to determine where to start.

Seeking Reassurance. There are a large number of enquiries where users indicate they have doubts and anxieties, often caused by a lack confidence either in what they have found or of what to do next. They then appear to seek reassurance from the archivist.

The disintermediation between user and archivist means that there is no opportunity for the user to seek reassurance that they have done the right thing and the archive's systems, primarily focused on finding materials, are not designed to fulfill this role. This, in turn, prompts users to try to engage with archivists through the various remote channels. At times, this is in regards to records, as seen in previous examples. In other cases, people seek to confirm facts they suspect but do not know:

> "I am aware that some libraries and archives require letters of recommendation to access certain resources, and was wondering if the National Archives follows any similar practices.... My time in London is limited, and (as I'm sure you'll understand) I am anxious to have everything necessary (including letters) before I arrive." (Email Enquirer 6).

Interestingly, this theme fits with prior research. Duff and Johnson's work with mid-career historians [4] exposed the stressful nature of negotiating an unfamiliar archival collection. Their participants described the experience as an "anxiety attack", "overwhelming" and referred to the "fear" they felt at having missed something in the course of their work. These same fears ring true in our own data.

Considering all of these themes, we drew out a formal theory of what drives enquiries to the archives: the disintermediation of the archivist creates anxieties in users regarding their search progress.

5   Implications for Design

From the results of content analysis using the Duff and Johnson coding, we see that there is definite variability in how different channels are used for enquiries. This indicates, at least in the case of TNA, there are distinct benefits to running these different channels. Users are opportunistically using the channels in different ways, and sometimes in ways that would not be predicted.

Looking at the content of the messages, the channels shape the enquiries in some way: either by drawing in users with certain forms of problem or by encouraging the framing of enquiries in certain ways. For example, livechat users can explore problems in a more naturalistic, conversational way than the Twitter users but these users lack the more casual, unplanned and spontaneous opportunities for interaction afforded by social networking.

Martin [13] predicted that there would be shifts in the types of questions that would be asked over time due to the availability of online archive tools, and this does seem to have happened, at least when comparing our data to the 11 archives studied by Duff and Johnson [3]. We do indeed see that the proportion of known item enquiries appears to have increased substantially, with users providing much more specific enquiries. This increase appears in email, livechat and telephone. Twitter users appear concerned with other topics than individual collections items.

This means that archives are in a better position to accommodate user needs than they have ever been. They are receiving, across a spectrum of channels, large numbers of detailed and specific enquiries, sufficient to identify the most significant issues faced by the main body of their users and attempt to resolve them. The use of models materially assists in this process. Overwhelmingly, plotting these enquiries against the

Marchionini model, tells us that users need more support within the archival interactive systems to improve their ability to choose a search system and navigate between digitised islands of archive data. Knowing 'where to look' remains a major problem for users, and they fall back on human support to solve this problem instead being able to rely on the system to aid them in being more effective or efficient in their information seeking tasks.

Kirchhoff et al. [9] advocate creating portals linking the islands together to solve this pervasive problem of users not knowing where to go. Interestingly, TNA now provides a form of portal, or federated search, through its Discovery search system that indexes archives across the UK and a number of other formally separate databases. But Discovery remains only one of a cluster of databases with which the historian or genealogist is likely to need to engage and in the data collected from TNA users it is clear that they still have difficulty knowing where to look. The lesson for online archives is that portals in and of themselves will not necessarily improve the users' ability to know where to start or where to go next in their search activities. In fact, creating such portals may exacerbate the problem further by offering so much choice in one place as well as adding another proverbial island.

As digitisation efforts continue (even accelerate) and further archival collections appear online, interaction designers must proactively seek solutions to solve this problem of knowing where to look. The results indicate that it is inadequate for support to exist somewhere separate from search systems; it must be proximal to and integrated within the system supporting the users' current task(s). This support might take the form of contextual help based on recognising broad types of queries ("looking for a person?"). It might make use of dynamic term suggestion, more thoroughly scoped search, result clustering (beyond the faceted browsing already available), wizards or relevance feedback.

However, what our results do not provide is the means by which to choose which of these design interventions, if any, are appropriate in specific contexts of use. The follow up work to this study will be focussing on what support human interlocutors provide to users. This information will provide insights into which particular design interventions are likely to help users at specific points along their information seeking journeys.

6   Conclusions

In this paper we have conducted a content analysis of several channels that users of the National Archives uses for interacting with their patrons. These channels comprised both traditional, such as phone and email, as well as modern media such as livechat, and Twitter. Further, we collected user-generated data from Rootschat for comparison and contrast with TNA's data.

From the analysis of the channels, disintermediation appeared to serve as a key driver for the enquiries seen in the different channels. This disintermediation, where the user is compelled to rely solely on the search systems and help documentation online without an archivist to assist them, leads to many users feeling unable to act. They find themselves with an abundance of choice, but very quickly do not know where to turn.

Users are, essentially, lost in a sea of islands of digitised data not knowing where their journey began, where they are now, or whether they have reached their destination. This lack of awareness leads to anxiety in the users, which manifests in them reaching out to real world archivists for direction and reassurance when they have found something, that they have proceeded correctly.

This has implications on how we design new search and interactive systems for archives. These systems must integrate support for navigating the archive structure so that users can grasp how to start their information seeking journeys, and direct or signal them onward to their next location. This, when combined with user education facilities to help the user learn where to find particular types of information that are relevant to them, could lead to a powerful step change in the types of interactions that would come in through the channels of enquiry. Instead of the archivist having to act like a search engine, they could instead collaborate with users in developing more sophisticated information seeking strategies.

Acknowledgments. This work has been supported by the Engineering and Physical Sciences Research Council (EPSRC).

Research Data Access. Researchers wishing access to the data used in this study should visit the following URL for more information:

http://www.cs.york.ac.uk/hci/jjp513

References

1. Brannan, G.: Talking in the night: exploring webchats at the west yorkshire archive service. In: Theimer, K. (ed.) Reference and Access: Innovative Practices for Archives and Special Collections. Rowman & Littlefield, Blue Ridge (2014)
2. Butterworth, R.: The Accessing our Archival and Manuscript Heritage project and the development of the Helpers website. Middlesex University, Interaction Design Centre, The Burroughs (2006)
3. Duff, W., Johnson, C.: A virtual expression of need: an analysis of e-mail reference questions. Am. Archivist. **64**, 43–60 (2001)
4. Duff, W., Johnson, C.: Accidentally found on purpose: information-seeking behavior of historians in archives. Libr. Q. **72**, 472–496 (2002)
5. Duff, W., Johnson, C.: Where is the list with all the names? Inf. Seeking Behav. Genealogists. Am. Archivist. **66**, 79–95 (2003)
6. Duff, W.M., Stoyanova, P.: Transforming the crazy quilt: archival displays from a user's point of view. Archivaria. **1**(45), 66 (1998)
7. Freeman, E.: In the eye of the beholder: archives administration from the user's point of view. Am. Archivist. **47**, 111–123 (1984)
8. Johnson, A.: Users, use and context: supporting interaction between users and digital archives. In: Craven, D.L. (ed.) What are Archives?: Cultural and Theoretical Perspectives: A Reader. Ashgate Publishing Ltd, Aldershot (2012)
9. Kirchhoff, T., Schweibenz, W., Sieglerschmidt, J.: Archives, libraries, museums and the spell of ubiquitous knowledge. Arch. Sci. **8**, 251–266 (2008)
10. Krippendorff, K., Bock, M.A. (eds.): The Content Analysis Reader. Sage, Thousand Oaks (2008)

11. Malbin, S.L.: The reference interview in archival literature. Coll. Res. Libr. **58**, 69–80 (1997)
12. Marchionini, G.: Information Seeking in Electronic Environments. Cambridge University Press, Cambridge (1997)
13. Martin, K.: Analysis of remote reference correspondence at a large academic manuscripts collection. Am. Archivist. **64**, 17–42 (2001)
14. Pugh, M.J.: Providing Reference Services for Archives and Manuscripts. Society of American Archivists, Chicago, Ill (1992)
15. Strauss, A., Corbin, J.: Basics of Qualitative Research: Grounded Theory Procedures and Techniques. Sage Publications, Inc., Thousand Oaks (1990)
16. Wilson, T.D.: Models in information behaviour research. J. Documentation. **55**, 249–270 (1999)
17. Wineburg, S.S.: Historical problem solving: a study of the cognitive processes used in the evaluation of documentary and pictorial evidence. J. Educ. Psychol. **83**, 73–87 (1991)
18. Yakel, E., Torres, D.: AI: archival intelligence and user expertise. Am. Archivist. **66**, 51–78 (2003)

"Not Some Trumped Up Beef": Assessing Credibility of Online Restaurant Reviews

Marina Kobayashi, Victoria Schwanda Sosik[(✉)], and David Huffaker

Google, Inc., Mountain View, CA, USA
{kobayashim, victoriasosik, huffaker}@google.com

Abstract. Online reviews, or electronic word of mouth (eWOM), are an essential source of information for people making decisions about products and services, however they are also susceptible to abuses such as spamming and defamation. Therefore when making decisions, readers must determine if reviews are credible. Yet relatively little research has investigated how people make credibility judgments of online reviews. This paper presents quantitative and qualitative results from a survey of 1,979 respondents, showing that attributes of the reviewer and review content influence credibility ratings. Especially important for judging credibility is the level of detail in the review, whether or not it is balanced in sentiment, and whether the reviewer demonstrates expertise. Our findings contribute to the understanding of how people judge eWOM credibility, and we suggest how eWOM platforms can be designed to coach reviewers to write better reviews and present reviews in a manner that facilitates credibility judgments.

Keywords: eWOM · Online review credibility · Online review platforms

1 Introduction

Imagine you're in the market for a new computer or that you want to choose the perfect vacation destination. How do you decide the model that is best for your needs or pick from all the Caribbean islands? In these situations we have traditionally relied on word of mouth (WOM), or oral, person-to-person, non-commercial communication regarding a brand, product, or service [1]. Word of mouth has a huge impact on consumer behavior, holding more influence over people's choices, expectations, and attitudes than other types of information such as advertisements and neutral print sources [17, 32].

Much of this power comes from the perception that WOM is from other like-minded consumers who are not motivated to sell a product or service. However while it sometimes comes from this altruistic place, people also express opinions for reasons of self-enhancement, vengeance [11], or even satire (see Fig. 1). Given these different motives, we must assess the credibility of others' opinions to decide how they will impact our own consumer decisions.

Beyond traditional ways to share opinions, use of the internet for WOM (eWOM) has become increasingly popular via online discussion forums, eCommerce sites (e.g., Amazon.com), and targeted opinion platforms (e.g., tripadvisor.com) [18]. These eWOM sources have extended the reach and altered the nature of WOM, allowing

© IFIP International Federation for Information Processing 2015
J. Abascal et al. (Eds.): INTERACT 2015, Part III, LNCS 9298, pp. 116–131, 2015.
DOI: 10.1007/978-3-319-22698-9_9

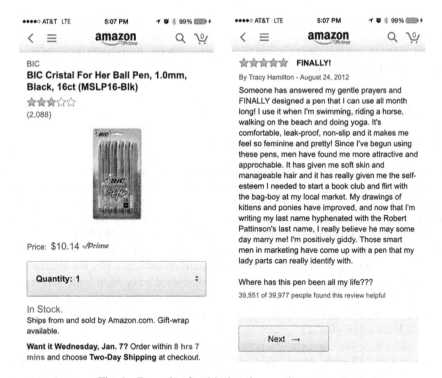

Fig. 1. Example of satirical review on Amazon.com

people to share opinions with a much larger audience of people whom they do not know personally. While such sites are great consumer resources, they've also been criticized as less credible than other information sources [15, 24]. Furthermore, they tend to lack standard means for assessing credibility, such as the identity of the information source [7].

In order to help people sort through the large volume of conflicting reviews that is common on eWOM platforms, and to do so in the absence of standard credibility signals, it is important to determine what other types of information may help people judge eWOM credibility. Yet there is very little work in this area of how people develop perceptions of credibility, especially in online environments [23]. Much of the prior work on credibility of online information has focused on traditional, institutionally created news media sites instead of user-generated content (e.g., [13]), which is often created by people lacking institutional authority. Some more recent work has investigated the credibility of user-generated content like blogs (e.g., [2]), wikis (e.g., [22]), and tweets (e.g., [8]), however with respect to verifiable, factual news events, not subjective opinions about products and services. Another line of work has developed algorithms to detect fake online reviews (e.g. [29]), however this work does little to explain the process that people go through when making similar credibility judgments.

With the current research we strive to fill this gap and contribute an understanding of what types of information can help people judge the credibility of subjective eWOM reviews. These findings have implications for the design of eWOM platforms, suggesting ways such platforms can help reviewers write more helpful reviews and suggesting types of information that can be displayed alongside reviews to help readers make credibility judgments.

2   Related Work

2.1   Characteristics of Effective WOM

While the potential power of WOM is largely accepted (e.g., [1, 10]), it is not enough for WOM to simply be generated, it also needs to be judged as credible and recipients must be influenced by its content [36]. Despite the importance of understanding how WOM is received and the processes leading to its outcomes, the majority of research around WOM has focused on its generation [36]. However a smaller body of work has investigated factors impacting outcomes, finding that characteristics of the WOM's source are among the most important in explaining its influence [9]. For example the source's expertise and whether or not they are considered an opinion leader can impact a recipient's assessment [3, 14]. The tie strength between the source and recipient is also one of the strongest predictors of WOM influence, as closer friends have more personal knowledge of and a greater interest in the recipient [3, 5].

In addition to the source's characteristics, the content of the WOM message can also impact its influence. More vivid and strongly delivered messages–which can be conveyed by both message wording and body language—are more influential [36]. The valence of a message–whether it is positive or negative—also affects individuals' responses to WOM [20]. However findings around valence and influence have been inconsistent, with some work showing that positive messages have stronger impact [21] and other work showing the opposite [28].

2.2   Credibility Signals in eWOM

However as noted above, many of these factors impacting the assessment of WOM are absent in the case of eWOM [7]. Sources may be unknown to the recipient, may hide their identity behind pseudonyms, or may even post completely anonymously. eWOM is also written instead of oral, which may impact the interpretation of message content while removing accompanying body language and introducing the possibility for grammatical and spelling errors. As such, credibility judgments must be based on different factors in online eWOM environments than in traditional WOM.

Among the few studies that have begun to investigate this topic, source identity has been a focus. Studies have found that reviewers who disclose their identity information are viewed as more credible than those who don't [23, 37]. However the identity manipulation in these studies provided extensive profile information such as name, location, age group, length of membership, picture, and a brief bio. While this type of information can help people judge similarity between themselves and the eWOM source, which can impact influence [4], people are not likely to include such detailed information in their profiles due to privacy concerns [27]. Prior work also shows that identity disclosures as simple as whether or not people use their real names can impact others' evaluation of online information such as news articles [12]. We therefore consider a simpler and more practical identity manipulation, focusing just on username:

RQ1: Is eWOM by reviewers who use their real names judged more credible than by those who use pseudonyms or post anonymously?

In the absence of detailed source information, people often rely on other cognitive heuristics to assess the credibility of online information, such as reputation and endorsement from others [26, 34]. Online eWOM platforms have the opportunity to provide their audiences with cues to facilitate the use of these heuristics, yet what exactly these cues look like and whether they are effective has not be explored in prior work. Studies modeling the credibility of factual information in tweets show that information like the number of tweets people have made or the number of followers they have predicts credibility [8, 16], and these cues may likewise be useful for eWOM. In order to evaluate the efficacy of such signals, our second research question asks:

RQ2: How do reviewer status signals such as review or follower counts impact credibility judgments in eWOM?

In addition to attributes related to source identity and reputation, valence has also been shown to impact assessments of credibility in eWOM. In one study, negative reviews were rated as more credible than positive ones, an effect that was strengthened when the reviewer disclosed their identity [23]. However given the mixed results of valence in traditional WOM (e.g., [21, 28]), we also investigate the influence of valence on eWOM credibility judgments in the current study. Furthermore, we extend prior work by considering more than just the extremes of positively and negatively valenced reviews. It is often the case that people express both positive and negative aspects of a product or service in a single, more balanced review and it is well established that balanced sentiment increases credibility in advertising [19]. Therefore we ask:

RQ3: How does eWOM valence (positive, negative, or balanced) influence credibility judgments?

Fig. 2. Example of stimuli that respondents were asked to rate

3   Methods

To answer our research questions, we recruited 1,979 U.S. respondents via Amazon Mechanical Turk (MTurk) to complete a survey, compensating them each with $1. MTurk has been used as a recruiting platform in several studies (e.g., [21, 31]) and allows researchers to collect high-quality data from a more diverse population than the typical university student sample [6].

Each respondent was shown three restaurant review stimuli (see Fig. 2) and asked to rate how credible they found each reviewer on a 7-point Likert scale. In order to understand how different signal variations impacted perceived credibility, we varied three elements of the review stimuli: reviewer identity, review valence and a UI signal related to the reviewer's status or reviewing history (see Table 1 for stimuli variations). Each respondent was presented with each of the three review sentiments in random order and reviewer identity and status variations were randomly combined with the review texts. When selecting real names to use in review stimuli, we generated a total of 118 names representing people from various nationalities and both genders (e.g., "Ellen Romano", "Hoang Kim"). We similarly included 6 different pseudonyms (e.g., "Natalie247", "DreamTeam4ever") in order to avoid effects due to a specific type of reviewer identity (e.g. American female who likes to cook).

Table 1. Review stimuli variations.

Reviewer Identity	Reviewer Status	Review Valence
Real Name ex: *Ellen Romano, Hoang Kim*	**Stats: social, activity** *3 Followers* *357 Followers* *3 Reviews* *357 Reviews*	**Positive** *I've loved everything I've had here. It's the best-kept secret in this neighborhood. The gnocchi is to die for, but really all the small plates are top notch! Cool, hip ambience.*
In Lieu of Real Name *Anonymous* *A Google User*	**Labels: status, authentication** *City Expert* *Local Guide* *Verified Visit*	**Negative** *Overrated. We waited in line for what seemed like an eternity, only to get slow, impossible service and greasy, over-salted food. Will not be going back. Not worth the hype.*
Pseudonym ex: *Natalie247, DreamTeam4ever*		**Balanced** *Easy place to go for a quick bite. It gets pretty busy around dinner time, so you might want to consider getting takeout. All the dishes are reasonably priced and the portions are decent.*

We used linear mixed models to analyze how different review attributes affect credibility ratings, nesting credibility ratings within respondents. This method accounts for potential non-independence of observations since each respondent rated three different review stimuli. Note that the denominator degrees of freedom in linear mixed models are estimated using a Satterthwaite's approximation, which can yield non-integer degrees of freedom [35].

For the first review, we also asked respondents to describe in text why they rated the reviewer as they did. This allowed us both to verify that respondents were basing their rating on the stimuli presented and to understand what attributes of the review led to their credibility assessment. To understand factors that contributed to credibility judgments, we analyzed open-ended responses using open coding procedures [33].

Two researchers started by independently reviewing a random sample of 100 responses and iteratively generating a coding scheme. Note that in this scheme multiple codes can be assigned to a single response, if applicable. After arriving on a final scheme, we then individually reapplied it to the original set of 100 responses. We then resolved disagreements and calculated interrater reliability metrics, determining that another round of coding was necessary to reach acceptable reliability. We repeated this process with another set of 100 responses, this time reaching an average percent agreement of 97 % (Krippendorff's alpha = 0.68). After resolving disagreements, we each coded an additional 150 responses, leading to a total of 500 coded responses (just over 25 % of our data set).

4 Results

Together, our 1,979 respondents rated the credibility of 5,937 review stimuli. The average credibility rating across all stimuli was 5.0 on a 7-point Likert scale (SD = 1.39). Figure 3 presents the average credibility rating for different types of review attributes. We will discuss these differences in the following sections. While we model our three different types of attributes individually for ease of interpretation in the sections below, when including all of the attributes together, we find that our model explains 25 % of variance in credibility ratings, as calculated using Ω_0^2 statistic for measuring explained variance in linear mixed models [38].

4.1 Effects of Review Attributes on Credibility Judgments

Reviewer Identity. To answer RQ1, we analyzed how credibility ratings differed based on reviewer identity. We found that perceived credibility was significantly different between identity variations, $F[3, 4710.5] = 16.64$, $p < 0.001$ (see Table 2). Reviews from those who disclose their real name were judged as the most credible while reviews from those who posted anonymously were the least credible. We did not find significant differences between more traditional pseudonyms (e.g. Natalie247) and the "A Google User" identity.

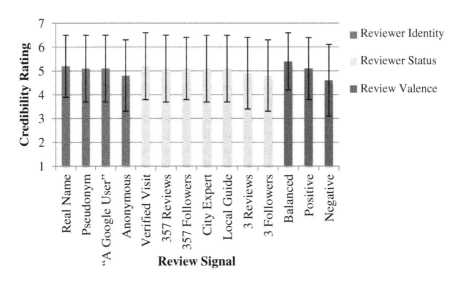

Fig. 3. Average review credibility by review signal

Reviewer Status. Our second research question investigates the impact of different types of signals about reviewer status on the judged credibility of reviews. We evaluated the effects of three different types of status signals. One signal acts to show the recipient how many reviews the reviewer has posted in the past, which can demonstrate expertise as a reviewer. The second type communicates the reviewer's reputation in the community by showing how many followers a reviewer has. The final type uses status labels like "Local Guide" to convey topic expertise.

We found that different types of status signals significantly impacted perceived credibility, $F[6, 5434.4] = 9.25$, $p < 0.001$ (see Table 2). Reviewers that were labeled with "Verified Visit" were judged the most credible, followed by those who demonstrated review expertise and reputation through their reviewing activities. Other types of status labels like "City Expert" and "Local Guide" were the next most credible. The least credible of all reviewers were those who were labeled as having less expertise or a small number of followers.

Review Valence. To answer our third research question, we analyzed how different review valences influence perceived credibility ratings. We found review valence did significantly impact credibility, $F[2, 3956] = 223.56$, $p < 0.001$ (see Table 2) and balanced reviews were the most credible, followed by positive reviews then negative reviews. Based on prior work showing interactions between identity and valence in credibility judgments [23], we also modeled interactions between valence and status and valence and identity, however neither of these interactions were significant.

Table 2. Coefficients from three separate mixed models predicting credibility ratings based on different reviewer identities, reviewer status signals, and review valence.

Reviewer Identity[a]	Estimate (Std. Error)
Real Name	0.10 (0.05)*
Pseudonym	0.03 (0.05)
"A Google User"	--
Anonymous	-0.23 (0.05)***
Reviewer Status[b]	*Estimate (Std. Error)*
Verified Visit	0.42 (0.07)***
357 Reviews	0.34 (0.07)***
357 Followers	0.32 (0.07)***
City Expert	0.28 (0.07)***
Local Guide	0.27 (0.07)***
3 Reviews	0.13 (0.07)*
3 Followers	--
Review Valence[c]	*Estimate (Std. Error)*
Balanced	0.86 (0.04)***
Positive	0.49 (0.04)***
Negative	--

*$p < 0.05$, **$p < 0.01$, ***$p < 0.001$; a. Identities were dummy coded with "A Google User" as the reference identity; b. Status levels were dummy coded with "3 Followers" as the reference status; c. Valences were dummy coded with Negative as the reference valence*

4.2   Qualitative Factors Influencing Credibility Judgments

To gain a deeper understanding of what review attributes impact people's perceptions of review credibility, we also analyzed respondents' descriptions of their credibility judgments. Table 3 presents the data-driven codes that we arrived at along with example responses and the observed frequencies of each code. In line with prior work on assessing credibility of WOM, our codebook includes two different types of codes, those relating to the reviewer themselves and those relating to the content of the message.

We also find that people described attributes of reviews that would both increase and decrease their credibility ratings. Exactly half of our response codes led to reported increases in credibility ratings (e.g. Displays Expertise, Relatable Reviewer, Many Followers), while the other half lead to reported decreases (e.g. Anonymous, Few Followers, Not Detailed). This finding is supported by looking at the average credibility rating for each code, which shows that all codes leading to reported decreases in credibility ratings had average ratings below the mean of 5.0, while all codes that were reported to increase credibility had average ratings above the mean.

Table 3. Frequencies of different factors reported to influence credibility judgments with respective average credibility ratings and regression coefficients for a model predicting credibility ratings.

Review Content	Example	Freq. (%)	Mean (SD)	Estimate (Std. Error)
Displays Expertise	*It sounds like she has been to a few restaurants in the area so she has some experience in how food should be. Not only that... but who orders gnocchi.. someone that knows food that is who*	63 (12.6 %)	5.7 (1.0)	0.59*** (0.15)
Actually Visited	*He mentioned a specific dish which tells me he was actually at the restaurant*	59 (11.8 %)	5.5 (1.0)	0.38* (0.16)
Relatable Reviewer	*This person seems like a friend who I would ask about restaurants*	50 (10.0 %)	5.7 (0.8)	0.65*** (0.17)
Many Followers	*The person had hundreds of followers and gave a review that seemed very plausible*	18 (3.6 %)	5.1 (1.1)	−0.06 (0.26)
Anonymous	*The anonymous listing makes them less credible...I have no idea who they are*	13 (2.6 %)	4.3 (1.1)	−0.70* (0.31)
Not Relatable Reviewer	*Writing is mismatched forced. Like it's fake, no one says "hip" and why would you rave about a restaurant having small portions?*	12 (2.4 %)	4.5 (1.3)	0.24 (0.32)
Many Reviews	*I gave him higher than I initially thought because of the 357 reviews he has given*	10 (2.0 %)	5.7 (0.9)	0.83* (0.35)
Few Followers	*They're semi credible. They only have 3 followers. I'd prefer to see more*	8 (1.6 %)	3.4 (1.1)	−1.44*** (0.39)
Few Reviews	*The person only has 3 reviews, so you can't really gauge whether or not she is credible*	6 (1.2 %)	4.0 (1.5)	−0.53 (0.45)
Pseudonym	*Scrubs999 does not sound like a credible reviewer, so I would be unlikely to believe what they are telling me. If the signed their name or even first name and last initial I would think this would be more credible*	4 (0.8 %)	2.8 (1.2)	−1.81** (0.55)

(Continued)

Table 3. (*Continued*)

Review Content	Example	Freq. (%)	Mean (SD)	Estimate (Std. Error)
Detailed	*It seems quite thorough. Succinctly stated his experience from beginning to end*	115 (23.0 %)	5.7 (1.0)	0.77*** (0.13)
Not Detailed	*They gave no specifics about the restaurant such as recommended dishes. It was too general*	107 (21.4 %)	3.9 (1.4)	−0.98*** (0.13)
Reasonable Review	*They listed several reasons for the rating they give. The reasons sounded realistic and not some trumped up beef*	78 (15.6 %)	5.7 (1.0)	0.79*** (0.14)
Biased Experience	*It sounds like emotion got in the way of a fact-based or purely observational review*	48 (9.6 %)	3.7 (1.4)	-0.74*** (0.18)
Well written	*The reviewer wrote in full sentences using good language/grammar*	44 (8.8 %)	5.5 (1.2)	0.29 (0.18)
Not Exaggerated	*There's nothing dramatic about the person's statement. I don't see exclamation marks saying it's sooo fantastic!!!*	37 (7.4 %)	5.5 (1.0)	0.36 (0.19)
Exaggeration	*Instead of giving a thorough review of the food, the reviewer attacked the establishment with over-exaggerations.*	21 (4.2 %)	3.6 (1.3)	−0.80** (0.03)
Balanced Sentiment	*The review doesn't seem over the top, one way or the other. Just a balanced view of things*	19 (3.8 %)	5.8 (0.9)	0.60* (0.26)
Too Positive	*The review is overly positive, which can raise some red flags*	12 (2.4 %)	4.2 (1.3)	−0.04 (0.33)
Poorly Written	*It is written in very basic language, something I expect to see a teenager write or someone with no experience*	6 (1.2 %)	4.0 (2.4)	−0.46 (0.45)

We also find that some reasons to judge a review more or less credible are more frequently cited than others. The top three factors influencing credibility (by frequency) are how detailed, not detailed, or reasonable a review is. All of these codes were related to the review content instead of the reviewer, suggesting that respondents were more often focusing on review content than reviewers when making credibility judgments.

Table 3 also presents regression coefficients for a linear regression model predicting credibility rating based on the presence or absence of coded response factors. Note that we use linear regression here instead of linear mixed models since we are only modeling one rating per respondent. We find that our model explains 42 % of the variance in credibility ratings, and the factors that most positively impact credibility ratings are the reviewer having many reviews, writing a reasonable review, and including much detail with balanced sentiment, respectively. The factors that most negatively impact credibility ratings are the use of pseudonyms, followed by having few followers displayed, the review not being detailed, and exaggerated or biased experiences.

5 Discussion

In summary, by showing people different types of review stimuli, we find that reviewer identity, reviewer status, and review valence all impact credibility judgments of online restaurant reviews. People find reviewers who use their real names more credible than those who post anonymously, which extends prior work by showing that differences in credibility can be seen even when just varying the reviewers' name as opposed to requiring a more drastic identity manipulation like hiding or revealing detailed profiles [23]. We also find that people judge reviewers with a labeled status signaling their expertise or reputation in a community as more credible than those lacking this signal. This finding provides empirical support for work suggesting different cues and heuristics that people use to judge the credibility of online information [26, 34]. We find support for these heuristics in the case of eWOM specifically, and inspired by work on judging factual information in tweets [8] we also suggest concrete signals to facilitate heuristic credibility judgment in eWOM. Signaling domain expertise by showing that a reviewer had actually visited a restaurant led to the highest credibility ratings, followed by signals that show a reviewer has posted many reviews and has many followers. Finally, we find that balanced reviews were judged the most credible, followed by positive and then negative reviews. Our finding contributes to the conflicting body of work evaluating how review valence impacts credibility, because unlike prior work [23], we find that positive eWOM is judged more credible than negative eWOM. This suggests that in an online environment, the impact of review valence is just as unclear as in traditional WOM [21, 28] and further work is needed to better understand when and how review valence impacts credibility judgments. Although consistent with longstanding research in advertising [19], we find that a balanced review was judged to be even more credible than either a positive or negative review, and suggest that future work consider this case in addition to the typically studied positive/negative valence dichotomy.

Our qualitative analysis of people's descriptions detailing why they judged credibility in the way that they did also provides a deeper understanding of how review attributes impact eWOM credibility ratings. People reported attending to each of the three different types of signals that we manipulated: reviewer identity (codes: *Anonymous, Pseudonym*), reviewer status (codes: *Displays Expertise, Actually Visited, Many Followers, Many Reviews, Few Reviews, Few Followers*), and review valence (codes: *Biased Experience, Too Positive, Balanced Sentiment*). They also used other criteria to judge credibility of reviews, considering how relatable (or not) a reviewer seemed, how detailed (or not) a review was, how reasonable the review content felt, whether or not it was exaggerated, and whether or not it was well written. We find that these codes are consistent with other data-driven heuristics that people base credibility judgments on, but are more detailed and apply specifically to the case of eWOM instead of online information more generally [26, 34]. For example, in eWOM *authority* and *reputation* can be gained by displaying expertise about a particular topic (e.g. demonstrating via status signal or detailed review content that one has actually visited a restaurant) and by showing that one has an extensive review history. Having a large number of followers also suggests that one has been *endorsed* by others, leading to increased credibility. People's consideration of whether the review seemed reasonable to them is also in line with the *expectancy violation* heuristic, stating that people find information more credible when it is consistent with their expectations [26]. Additionally, people talked about how relatable the reviewer was, which follows from [26]'s *persuasive intent* heuristic, or the fact that people find commercial information less credible than information from someone like themselves. Finally, we find further evidence that in the case of eWOM, presentation attributes like the quality of writing in a review can impact its credibility rating [25] just as presentation attributes like body language can impact judgments of traditional WOM [36].

5.1   Relative Importance of Reviewer and Review Attributes

Our work also contributes an understanding of the relative importance of different types of signals in eWOM. Studies of WOM have prioritized attributes of the reviewer in making credibility judgments [3, 5, 14], however we find that attributes of the review tended to be the most influential. Examining model coefficients shows that differences in review valence most strongly predicted credibility ratings, beyond reviewer identity or status. The most commonly cited explanations for credibility ratings in our open-ended responses were also attributes of the review, not the reviewer, suggesting that people were consciously paying more attention to the review content. Furthermore, five of the top eight explanations that actually impacted credibility ratings were related to the review content. It is therefore likely that while signals as to reviewer identity, expertise, and reputation are still useful, in the absence of first-hand knowledge of these attributes (such as is the case in eWOM), people focus more on the content itself when judging credibility.

5.2   Implications for Designing EWOM Platforms

Our work has implications for the design of platforms that solicit and present eWOM content, like Amazon.com and tripadvisor.com. Based on our findings showing how important the content of a review is in judging credibility, such sites should provide people with more guidance during the review creation process. For example, review valence can be automatically determined [30] as people write a review, and if a review appears overly positive or negative, the site could make suggestions that the reviewer try to include a more balanced account of their experience with the product or service. Likewise they could be given tips on writing a more detailed review if the review appears to be too short or lacking in descriptive words. This type of reviewer coaching could facilitate the creation of more helpful and eventually more influential eWOM.

It also suggests types of signals that should be presented alongside reviews in order to support people in judging credibility. Selecting and verifying types of information that can signal a reviewers' domain expertise is important, as we saw that the "Verified Visit" signal most positively impacted credibility judgments of restaurant reviews. These platforms do not always have access to such information, but often they do by way of purchase records or records of online restaurant reservations. When this information is lacking, it can still be useful to show a record of how many reviews a reviewer has written or how respected they are in the community, via the number of people that have read and/or subscribe to their reviews and/or find them helpful.

5.3   Limitations

While we make several contributions to the understanding of how credibility is signaled and assessed in eWOM, our work is not without limitations. We used MTurk as a recruiting platform, and while this allowed us to quickly collect high-quality data, studies have found that those on MTurk are more likely female than male, averaging 36 years of age and more highly educated than the general US population [29]. Our methods also asked respondents to evaluate the credibility of individual reviews, while reviews more often appear amongst others in eWOM platforms. This allowed us to isolate specific variations of different types of review signals, but does not consider the effect that groups of reviews have on each other, as has been studied in other work [10]. Finally, some of our model coefficients were small, representing significant but not substantial changes in credibility ratings; this is particularly true for the model predicting reviewer identity. Therefore even though we find reviewers who use their real names to be most credible, we're hesitant to suggest that eWOM platforms require all users to use their real names due to potential privacy concerns [27] and related drops in contribution rates for not all that great of an increase in review credibility.

6   Conclusion

Our work contributes to the understudied topic of how review attributes impact judgments of eWOM credibility, focusing on attributes of the review and of the reviewer. We also present a deeper qualitative analysis of factors that respondents describe focusing on when making their credibility judgments. We find that many of the same factors important in traditional WOM assessments are also important in eWOM judgments, however they are signaled differently. We also see that people may place more emphasis on the review content itself as opposed to the reviewer when judging eWOM. This work has implications for designing eWOM platforms that both coach reviewers to write better reviews and present reviews to recipients in a manner that facilitates credibility judgments. Future work should continue to investigate the impact of review valence on eWOM credibility as well as evaluate a more exhaustive list of concrete signals that can help people to make use of cognitive heuristics in assessing online review credibility.

Acknowledgements. We would like to thank Judy Zhao and Samantha Sachs for their work designing and writing the review stimuli used in this study. We would also like to thank Jeff Tamer for his help with data collection.

References

1. Arndt, J.: Role of product-related conversations in the diffusion of a new product. J. Mark. Res. **4**, 291–295 (1967)
2. Banning, S.A., Sweetser, K.D.: How much do they think it affects them and whom do they believe? Comparing the third-person effect and credibility of blogs and traditional media. Commun. Q. **55**, 451–466 (2007)
3. Bansal, H.S., Voyer, P.A.: Word-of-mouth processes within a service purchase decision context. J. Serv. Res. **3**(2), 166–177 (2000)
4. Bart, Y., Shankar, V., Sultan, F., Urban, G.L.: Are the drivers and role of online trust the same for all web sites and consumers? a large-scale exploratory empirical study. J. Mark. **69**, 133–152 (2005)
5. Brown, J.J., Reingen, P.H.: Social ties and word-of-mouth referral behavior. J. Consum. Res. **14**(3), 350–362 (1987)
6. Buhrmester, M., Kwang, T., Gosling, S.D.: Amazon's mechanical turk a new source of inexpensive, yet high-quality, data?. Perspect. Psychol. Sci. **6**(1), 3–5 (2011)
7. Callister Jr., T.A.: Media literacy: on-ramp to the literacy of the 21st century or cul-de-sac on the information superhighway. Adv. Reading/Lang. Res. **7**, 403–420 (2000)
8. Castillo, C., Mendoza, M., Poblete, B.: Information credibility on twitter. In: Proceedings of WWW 2011, pp. 675–684 (2011)
9. Dichter, E.: How word of mouth advertising works. Harvard Bus. Rev. **44**(6), 147–160 (1966)
10. Doh, S.-J., Hwang, J.-S.: How Consumers Evaluate eWOM (Electronic Word-of-Mouth) Messages. CyberPsychol. Behav. **12**(2), 193–197 (2009)
11. Engel, J.F., Blackwell, R.D., Miniard, P.W.: Consumer Behavior, 8th edn. Dryden Press, Fort Worth (1993)
12. Fitch, J.W., Cromwell, R.L.: Evaluating internet resources: identity, affiliation, and cognitive authority in a networked world. J. Am. Soc. Inform. Sci. Technol. **52**(6), 499–507 (2001)
13. Flanagin, A.J., Metzger, M.J.: Perceptions of internet information credibility. Journalism Mass Commun. Q. **77**, 515–540 (2000)
14. Gilly, M.C., Graham, J.L., Wolfinbarger, M.F., Yale, L.J.: A dyadic study of interpersonal information search. J. Acad. Mark. Sci. **26**(2), 83–100 (1998)
15. Gretzel, U., Fesenmaier, D.R., O'Leary, J.T.: The transformation of consumer behaviour. In: Buhalis, D., Costa, C. (eds.) Tourism Business Frontiers, pp. 9–18. Elsevier/Butterworth-Heinemann, Burlington (2006)
16. Gupta, A., Kumaraguru, P.: Credibility ranking of tweets during high impact events. In: Proceedings of the 1st Workshop on Privacy and Security in Online Social Media (PSOSM 2012) (2012)

17. Herr, P.M., Kardes, F.R., Kim, J.: Effects of word-of-mouth and product attribute information on persuasion: an accessibility-diagnosticity perspective. J. Consum. Res. **17**, 454–462 (1991)

18. Horrigan, J.: The Internet and consumer choice, 7 January 2015 (2008). http://www.pewinternet.org/Reports/2008/The-Internet-and-Consumer-Choice.aspx

19. Hunt, J.M., Smith, M.F.: The persuasive impact of two-sided selling appeals for an unknown brand name. J. Acad. Mark. Sci. **15**(1), 11–18 (1987)

20. Ilgen, D.R., Fisher, C.D., Taylor, M.S.: Consequences of individual feedback on behavior in organizations. J. Appl. Psychol. **64**(4), 349–371 (1979)

21. Kittur, A., Chi, E.H., Suh, B.: Crowdsourcing user studies with mechanical turk. In: Proceedings of the ACM Conference on Human-factors in Computing Systems (CHI 2008), pp. 453–456 (2008)

22. Kittur, A., Suh, B., Chi, E.H.: Can you ever trust a wiki? impacting perceived trustworthiness in wikipedia. In: Proceedings of Computer-Supported Cooperative Work (CSCW 2008), pp. 477–480 (2008)

23. Kusumasondjaja, S., Shanka, T., Marchegiani, C.: Credibility of online reviews and initial trust: The roles of reviewer's identity and review valence. J. Vacation Mark. **18**(3), 185–195 (2012)

24. Litvin, S.W., Goldsmith, R.E., Pan, B.: Electronic word-of-mouth in hospitality and tourism management. Tourism Manag. **29**(3), 458–468 (2008)

25. Mackiewicz, J.: Reviewer motivations, bias, and credibility in online reviews. In: Kelsey, S., Amant, K.S. (eds.) Handbook of Research on Computer Mediated Communication, pp. 252–266. IGI Global, Hershey (2008)

26. Metzger, M.J., Flanagin, A.J., Medders, R.B.: Social and heuristic approaches to credibility evaluation online. J. Commun. **60**(3), 413–439 (2010)

27. Milne, G.R., Rohm, A.J., Bahl, S.: Consumers' protection of online privacy and identity. J. Consum. Aff. **38**(2), 217–232 (2004)

28. Mizerski, R.W.: An attribution explanation of the disproportionate influence of unfavorable information. J. Consum. Res. **9**, 301–310 (1982)

29. Ott, M., Cardie, C., Hancock, J.: Estimating the prevalence of deception in online review communities. In: Proceedings of WWW 2012 (2012)

30. Pennebaker, J.W., Francis, M.E., Booth, R.J.: Linguistic inquiry and word count (LIWC) [computer software]. Erlbaum, Mahwah (2001)

31. Shay, R., Ion, I., Reeder, R.W., Consolvo, S.: My religious aunt asked why I was trying to sell her viagra: experiences with account hijacking. In: Proceedings of CHI 2014, pp. 2657–2666 (2011)

32. Sheth, J.N.: Word of mouth in low risk innovations. J. Adv. Res. **11**, 15–18 (1971)

33. Strauss, A., Corbin, J.: Basics of Qualitative Research: Grounded Theory Procedures And Techniques. Sage, Newbury Park (1990)

34. Sundar, S.S.: The MAIN model: a heuristic approach to understanding technology effects on credibility. In: Metzger, M.J., Flanagin, A.J. (eds.) Digital Media Youth Credibility, pp. 73–100. The MIT Press, Cambridge (2008)

35. SPSS Technical report-linear effects mixed modeling. http://www.spss.ch/upload/1107355943_LinearMixedEffectsModelling.pdf

36. Sweeney, J.C., Soutar, G.N., Mazzarol, T.: Factors influencing word of mouth effectiveness: receiver perspectives. Eur. J. Mark. **42**(3/4), 344–364 (2007)

37. Xie, H., Miao, L., Kuo, P.-J., Lee, B.-Y.: Consumers' responses to ambivalent online hotel reviews: The role of perceived source credibility and pre-decisional disposition. Int. J. Hospitality Manag. **30**, 178–183 (2011)
38. Xu, R.: Measuring explained variation in linear mixed effects models. Stat. Med. **22**(22), 3527–3541 (2003)

An Empirical Investigation of the Practices and Challenges Specific to International User Studies

Sabine Madsen[1], Lene Nielsen[1(✉)], Heidi Hautopp[2], and Iben Jensen[2]

[1] IT University of Copenhagen, Rued Langgaardsvej 7, 2300 Copenhagen S,
Denmark
sabinemadsen@live.dk, lene@itu.dk
[2] Aalborg University, A C. Meyers Vænge 15, 2450 Copenhagen SV, Denmark
heidi.hautopp@gmail.com, ij@learning.aau.dk

Abstract. In today's globalized world, it is increasingly important for companies to gain knowledge about international markets and to understand the differences and similarities between international users. As a result, international user studies have become more common. However, they still pose a challenge for most companies. In this paper, we present the results of an empirical investigation of how companies conduct international user studies. We describe the empirical findings in detail, with an emphasis on the practices and challenges that are specific to the process of doing international user studies. Key findings concern where, geographically, companies choose to collect data; the scope and scale of the studies; as well as the preferred data collection methods and employed control mechanisms. Our research shows that strategic/pragmatic considerations, perceived differences in national culture, and concerns about data quality shape and delimit the approach that companies take to international user studies.

Keywords: Design · International user studies · Application · Practice-study

1 Introduction

The HCI field has traditionally focused on two key research areas, namely (1) methods, tools and guidelines for designing and testing interfaces to enhance the usability hereof and (2) approaches for understanding the users and the context and situational aspects that influence their use of a given (IT) product or service. Within both of these research areas, the implications of globalization and the internationalization of products and services have over the years become important topics of study [2, 3, 14, 16].

Our research is positioned within the second stream of research concerned with approaches for understanding users and contextual product use. In particular, we aim to contribute to the HCI literature with insights about how companies conduct international user studies to get a foundation for meeting the needs of and designing products and services for users on international markets.

An earlier research project discovered that companies found it difficult to decide which markets to approach and how to incorporate cultural differences when

© IFIP International Federation for Information Processing 2015
J. Abascal et al. (Eds.): INTERACT 2015, Part III, LNCS 9298, pp. 132–148, 2015.
DOI: 10.1007/978-3-319-22698-9_10

communicating the findings from the user studies as personas [10]. Looking at the literature within HCI very little address these aspects in a scientific way and most address data collection and communication from an experience-based perspective, see e.g. [13, 14]. An exception is [1], who draws on empirical data to propose a conceptual framework that, among other things, assists designers in global companies in planning user studies that take local and cultural aspects into account.

The purpose of this research is to investigate how companies conduct international user studies; and more specifically to identify the practices and challenges that are particular to the process of collecting data and presenting insights about users on international markets.

The research is based on a qualitative interview study with 15 practitioners from 11 different companies. All interviews were held in Denmark, either in Danish companies that have users and subdivisions around the world or in Danish subdivisions of large international corporations. This means that what is considered "international" is seen from a Danish perspective.

2   On Culture and Intercultural Communication

All user studies are concerned with understanding the important differences and similarities among users. However, one of the aspects that make international user studies different from national user studies is that they are explicitly concerned with culture and intercultural communication. Thus, international user studies require attention to cultural differences and similarities during the planning and data collection phases of the study. Moreover, an important outcome of these studies is an increased understanding of which cultural differences and similarities that exist among users on different markets and which of these that are - and are not – important to take into account when designing a given product.

Recent theories point out that in today's globalized world it is useful to think about culture as a concept and phenomenon that refers to much more than just national culture [7]. This allows for other understandings of the significant differences and similarities between groups of people and of the complexity of peoples' everyday lives. A complex understanding of culture facilitates ways of grouping people based on their everyday practices and the communities (i.e. cultures) they participate in; e.g., by focusing on their practices with regard to work, leisure, sport, parenting, language, gender, and religion [8].

A complex understanding of culture does not exclude a focus on national culture; rather the emphasis is on, for example, understanding what it means to be Danish and at the same time that there are many ways in which to be Danish. However, as the theories stress, even for people with a high level of intercultural competence it remains a challenge to avoid interpretations, linguistic expressions, and actions that are informed by more simplistic national and geographical stereotypes. This is due to, among other things, the strong influence of the very notion of national culture as well as to the often more one-sided representations and discourses presented in the media.

This complex understanding of culture is very different from the understanding of culture as represented by methods, tools and guidelines for designing interfaces as suggested by e.g. [9] or the application of methods on new frontiers as described by e.g. [12, 15].

In this paper, we use the distinction between the concept of national culture and the complex understanding of culture as our theoretical foundation for understanding the role that perceptions of cultural differences and similarities play when companies collect and present data about international users.

3   Research Method

The research presented in this paper is based on a qualitative interview study with 15 user researchers from 11 different companies. The aim of the interviews was to investigate how companies collect and present data about users on international markets.

The companies/interviewees were selected from the involved researchers' professional network based on the following criteria. (1) The most important criterion was that they were operating on international markets. (2) The second criterion was that they had experience with international user studies and/or that they were using methods (such as, e.g. the persona method or segmentation into target groups) to delineate and incorporate user insights into their work and design processes.

The interviews were carried out from February - April 2014. All interviews took place in Denmark, either in Danish companies that have users and subdivisions around the world or in Danish subdivisions of large international companies.

The interviews were semi-structured and held in accordance with an interview guide. Each interview lasted 1−1,5h, was audio-recorded and subsequently transcribed. All interviews were held in the Danish language. The included interview quotes have therefore been translated from Danish to English by the paper authors.

As all interviews took place in Denmark what constitutes "international" is viewed from a Danish perspective. This can be useful to keep in mind when reading interview quotes that compare Denmark to other countries or when differences and similarities are mentioned. For example, when the interviewees make comparisons and statements about differences and similarities they seem to do so based on a number of taken-for-granted notions, such as the assumption that the Danish work culture is less hierarchical and more characterized by employee autonomy than work culture in other countries and that Danes in general are task oriented and prioritize efficiency.

Moreover, as all interviews were held in Danish it means that the two interviewers and the interviewee shared the same language and that much could be taken for granted with regard to contextual understandings, body language, humor, etc. It has been suggested that in such data collection situations (characterized by shared language and background) interviewer(s) and interviewee(s) create an 'ad hoc' national community as 'fellow travellers' [4, 5] that jointly aim to understand the world around them. However, it also means that taken for granted notions, national stereotypes, etc. might go unnoticed and that statements about national differences and similarities might be more expressed, because they are intended − and understood - as jokes in the interview situation. This is also useful to keep in mind when reading the interview quotes in this paper.

Table 1. Overview of the participants

Interviewee	Job title	Type of company	Method for presenting user insights
A	Design researcher	Danish subdivision of a large international software development company	More than 10 years of experience with the persona method (international personas)
B	Senior interaction designer		
C	Design researcher	Large financial company with headquarter in Denmark and subdivisions in Northern Europe	Around 5 years of experience with the persona method (international personas)
D	Head of digital experience and global marketing	Large financial company with headquarter in Denmark and subdivisions around the world	Preferred method: Segmentation; considers using personas
E	Technical writer	Software development company (financial systems), headquarter in Denmark and subdivisions around the world	Development of a set of international personas is under consideration
F	Senior UX researcher	Software development company (content management systems), headquarter in Denmark and subdivisions around the world	Development of a set of international personas has been initiated
G	Innovation consultant	Organization that specializes in development of digital health-care solutions; many projects are funded by EU and involve development of solutions for several EU countries at a time	The method for presenting user insights is chosen from project to project; experience with national personas
H	Innovation consultant		
I	Senior innovation consultant		
J	Consultant	Design agency that specializes in tourism, events and city development (project work for clients)	(National and international) Personas often constitute an important result of the projects/for the clients
K	User researcher		
L	Design researcher	Design agency that specializes in product, service, graphical and digital design (project work for clients), headquarter in Denmark and subdivisions around the world	One-page profiles of actual users, with pictures and quotes

(Continued)

Table 1. (*Continued*)

Interviewee	Job title	Type of company	Method for presenting user insights
M	Company owner	Design agency that specializes in national and international user studies, UX design and test of solutions (project work for clients)	Profiles of actual users, with pictures, quotes and video sequences
N	Innovation specialist	Hearing aid company, headquarter in Denmark and subdivisions around the world	Several years of experience with the persona method (international personas)
O	Audio engineer	Hearing aid company, headquarter in Denmark and subdivisions around the world	Several years of experience with the persona method (international personas)

All interviewees work in companies, where digital solutions and/or software development is the main area of expertise or an important part of the products and product portfolio. They have many years of professional experience and are currently holding positions as design researchers, user experience (UX) researchers, innovation consultants and so on. A part of their job is to plan and carry out user studies. We will hereafter refer to them as user researchers. Table 1 provides an overview of the characteristics of the involved companies and participants.

The analysis of the interview data was structured into several rounds of analysis, where we used a thematic approach to organize the interview data into relevant units of text and themes, which were then interpreted and meaning condensed into our research findings [6].

An important part of the analysis was to distinguish between on the one hand, themes that the interviewees described as specific to *international* user studies and on the other hand, themes related to national studies or inherent to all types of user research. In this paper, we focus on the practices and challenges that are *specific* to (or magnified by) the process of doing international user research.

4   Empirical Findings: A Process Perspective on International User Studies

In this section, we describe the strategies and practices that the companies and interviewees use when conducting international user studies.

We present our research findings in accordance with a process perspective, because this was how the interviewees structured their practice descriptions. Thus, we look at the practices and challenges related to: (1) Initial planning, (2) International data collection, (3) Perceptions of end users, and (4) Presentation of user insights.

We do not address data analysis and implementation of user insights into design processes. This delimitation has been chosen, because the interviewees reported that the practices and challenges for these two process steps (i.e. analysis and implementation) were similar for national and international user studies. See [10] for research findings about the practices and challenges that relate to analysis and implementation of user insights in a national context.

4.1   Initial Planning

There are a number of initial decisions and planning activities that have to be made before an international user study can commence.

Strategic Markets are Prioritized. For companies operating on international markets a key decision is where, geographically, to collect data about the users. In most cases it is the management/client who makes the decision about which countries/regions to include in the study. The decision is typically based on what they consider to be the company's most important strategic markets.

> *"It has to do with which strategic markets we want to be strong in. It is not so much that now we need to find four [countries] that are very different...of course India is included because they are very different from the US, but India is also included because they have a very large population who could use [our products]..." (Innovation specialist, N)*

Thus, our analysis shows that the management's/client's decision about where to collect data is driven more by strategic business considerations and a market-orientation than by a focus on specific countries and national culture. Moreover, while it is not possible to say that it is a distinct pattern in the interview data, there does seem to be a slight difference in the way the interviewees use the words "markets" and "countries". When the word "market" is used, it seems to have more of a business connotation and to be used in connection with economic and pragmatic considerations. When the word "country" is used, it more intuitively invites the interviewee to talk about differences and similarities between countries/regions, and whether they matter or not for decision-making, data collection, and the product in question.

Pragmatic Issues Sometimes Overrule Strategy. The interviewees report that normally it is quite clear which markets the management/client want to collect data about or what kind of knowledge they want to obtain about a particular geographical area. However, economic and pragmatic considerations related to, e.g., easier and cheaper travelling and language barriers mean that data sometimes is collected in other countries than originally decided. And also in other countries/regions than what might yield optimal knowledge. For example, it might be decided to do user interviews in England instead of an Eastern European country, because it reduces the language barrier for all involved.

Strategies for Planning the User Study. While it typically is the management/client that makes the decision about where to collect data, it is the task of the user researchers to plan the study. There are two different strategies for planning an international user study:

- A research design oriented strategy. Some user researchers plan the study to cover as many users and user groups in the chosen countries/regions as thoroughly as the budget allows. This planning strategy is driven by the notion of validity and tends to lead to large-scale studies that involve many end users.
- A use oriented strategy. Other user researchers plan the study with the aim of being able to provide the employees (i.e., product designers, system developers, and marketing personnel) with insights about the important differences and similarities – between countries/regions, between the employees and their users, and between the many different types of users. When this planning strategy is used, the notion of validity still plays a role, but designing a study that addresses knowledge gaps is considered just as or more important than scientific method and rigor.

4.2   International Data Collection

The planning and the logistics that surround data collection for international user studies are much more demanding and time consuming than for national studies. This is because they typically involve: planning of international field studies, travel planning, use of external resources (e.g., agencies and translators from the countries where the study takes place), and many end users.

All this adds to the scale and complexity of carrying out this type of user studies. In this section we look at the interviewees' reported practices and concerns about data collection.

The Importance of Going to the Field.   User researchers consider it very important to go to the field and participate in the data collection, for two reasons:

- To gain rich insights, i.e. to gain contextual knowledge and to interact directly with each of the users. It is also considered important for other employees, such as designers and developers to go to the field and meet the users.
- To ensure the quality of the data, i.e. to ensure the consistency of the data collection across countries and in general to ensure that the data collection is carried out in the way the user researchers has planned it. This is considered especially important if the data collection takes place in "new" or less familiar countries.

We have identified three different field study strategies. Thus, when user researchers go to the field they use one or more of the strategies mentioned below.

Strategy 1: The user researchers prefer to perform the data collection themselves, if possible from a language perspective. This approach provides much contextual knowledge about the particular country. Moreover, the experience of interacting with each of the users in person allows for a nuanced understanding of who the users are, how they live and work, and what their needs and motivations are.

Strategy 2: The user researchers perform the data collection with the help of a translator. This provides all the advantages of the abovementioned approach. However, different experiences are reported. Some state that it works well with a translator and especially if the translator is skilled and unobtrusive; others feel that they miss out on many nuances in what the user is saying and that they are unable to build a relationship with the user in the same way.

"It is always a challenge to use a translator because you never really have that direct contact. You always depend on the translator. But when it is a good translator it works surprisingly well." (Design researcher, L)

Strategy 3: The user researchers participate as observers despite language barriers. Five of the 15 interviewees mention that they have used this strategy, and while they consider it the least desirable option, it has advantages. Thus, even in cases where language barriers mean that they cannot understand the actual interaction between a local resource and a user, observation provides them with contextual knowledge and is a great aid to memory during the subsequent data analysis.

"We made sure that at least one of us was present at all interviews in all countries…" (Design researcher, C)

External Resources: A Matter of Trust and Control. International user studies often involve the use of external resources, such as:

- Recruiters/recruitment agencies
- User research agencies
- Local resource persons (e.g. freelance user researchers and translators)
- Danes with a relevant ethnic or educational background (e.g. a person with Danish-Kenyan ethnicity or a Danish anthropologist)

Choosing which external resources to use is an important decision. The user researchers state that it is essential for them to be able to trust that the external resources can perform and deliver the results of the study with the expected quality.

"…Just to find an agency that understands what we are talking about and…is able to do it with the quality we expect. We don't understand Russian for example…how can I know that what they are talking about is a good persona interview? A good observation? And they will probably report back with phrases and language that has many implicit understandings, which I might not get, so, yes, there are many challenges." (Senior interaction designer, B)

The user researchers prefer to use resources that they have used before. If this is not possible, e.g., because the study is performed in a country where they have not pre-viously collected data, they prefer to participate in all or selected data collection activities to control the process.

As the data collection often involves the use of different agencies and resources in different countries, the external resources are typically briefed very thoroughly. Thus, to ensure that the data is collected in the same way and with the desired quality, the user researchers provide the external resources with:

- Detailed criteria for recruiting relevant users
- An interview guide with detailed explanations of why and how to ask each question
- Detailed guidelines for how to transcribe the interviews

"We used agencies in all four countries...it has the advantage that they speak the language and that they do it for us...but it of course also has the disadvantage that we used quite a lot of time on explaining very thoroughly what it was we wanted...When we delivered something to them there was a column with a question and then there was a long explanation of why we were asking about this and what we wanted to do with it...so we were very thorough and it also worked." (Design researcher, C)

The common way of working with external resources is to be very thorough when choosing and briefing the resources. In general, the user researchers view international data collection as a collaborative effort and they work closely with the external resources throughout the data collection process to ensure that they get good quality data.

Large-Scale Studies Involving Many End Users. International user studies typically involve many end users. The prevailing approach is that data collection should cover the same number of users in each country/region that is included in the study. In other words, a research design oriented approach informed by the notion of validity is preferred. As one of the interviewees explain:

"...of course, identical in the four countries" (Design researcher, C).

This means that if a company normally performs 15 user interviews for a national study, they will plan an international user study in four countries to cover 60 interviews.

Another example is from a user study that involved two countries, Denmark and an Eastern European country. It was prioritized that the same number of interviews should be held in both countries and that several user groups should be covered in each country. As a result, the number of interviews became quite extensive.

"...we did 72 qualitative interviews in total, half in Denmark and half in Hungary." (Design researcher, L)

Strategies for Recruitment of End Users. As international user studies typically involve many end users, recruitment is a big task that takes up much time in the initial phases of a project. The user researchers choose between or mix two different strategies, depending on whether money or time is the more important aspect for the particular project.

The prevailing strategy is that the user researchers do all, most or some of the recruitment themselves. This is primarily because it is expensive to use external recruiters, but also because it often is possible (if time-consuming) for them to find the end users, based on customer lists or by drawing on their own social network.

Another strategy is to use external recruiters to minimize the time spend, and also because it sometimes is not possible (or too time-consuming) to find relevant users in other countries.

The user researchers state that they give much thought to determining the recruitment criteria and that they typically use the same criteria to recruit the end users in all the involved countries/regions.

Concerns About National Culture Create Barriers for Data Collection. In addition to travel expenses, language issues, and data quality, concerns about national culture create barriers for data collection.

The user researchers express many concerns about lack of education in culture and about insufficient understandings of particular countries and national cultures.

"...if you are going to do user studies, e.g., with Chinese people, it has to be in collaboration with somebody who knows something about China, about the Chinese market. Someone with an education. We wouldn't know enough." (Consultant, J)

They are especially worried about their lack of knowledge about Asia and Africa, but also areas that are geographically closer to Denmark such as Eastern European countries.

Some interviewees explain that they are much more comfortable doing user studies in countries and regions they are familiar with and where they do not perceive the culture to differ significantly from Danish culture. In some cases, the consequence of this respect for differences in national culture is that they do not conduct user studies in countries/regions they feel too unfamiliar with, even when these countries/regions are or could be relevant for their business.

"...India, China, Brazil, which are big markets, and yes, well, we know that we have a huge knowledge gap and we haven't really done anything..." (Senior interaction designer, B)

Dealing with Cultural Differences in the Data Collection Situation. Our analysis shows that (too much) focus on differences in national cultural can give rise to concerns that significantly delimits a company's approach to international data collection. However, our analysis also shows examples of user researchers that acknowledge cultural differences as inherent to the data collection situation, also in a national context. They therefore see it as an important part of their job and skill set to be able to build a trusting and empathic relationship with the user, despite such differences (in nationality, educational background, work culture etc.).

"I try to achieve this closeness and that is difficult to achieve...[when] you meet a complete stranger and also from a different country...even in that cultural distance, which always is there, I have to establish empathy, trust, so she also can tell me about those aspects of her job where she is not so successful or where she does workarounds, how they tinker [with the system]..." (Design researcher, A)

4.3 Perceptions of International End Users

In this section, we focus on perceptions of international end users, as an important outcome of the process as well as something that shapes the way the user study is planned and carried out.

End Users Share Many Similarities Across Nationalities. The user researchers stress that one of the most important outcomes of international user studies is the insight that there are many similarities among end users across nationalities - as humans, consumers (of particular products), parents, workers, etc. This insight reflects a complex understanding of culture, i.e. an understanding that foregrounds the similarities of the users' everyday practices and the communities they participate in rather than national differences.

However, the user researchers also explain that employees have many preconceptions about different nationalities and the (large) role that national culture plays. It is therefore important to explicitly communicate insights about the similarities that the company's end users share across nationalities to the employees. Otherwise stereotypical understandings of national differences might go unquestioned and influence the designers' work and ultimately the company's products.

"The user studies we have done have shown that at the personal level our end users have very similar motivations and approaches across borders...and this is very, very important and we make a big deal out of communicating this to employees." (Design researcher, C)

"...[this disability] effects end users in the same way no matter where they live in the world." (Innovation specialist, N)

There Are Important Differences in Market Conditions. There are also important differences among end users. Interestingly, it is pointed out that the most important differences often do not stem from national culture as such, but instead from differences in the economy, legislation, education, and societal structures and structural developments in different countries and regions.

"...it has to do with how the economy is...[and the] legislation. Legislation promotes a particular behavior in a particular country. And this is actually the two things [i.e. economy and legislation] that we have seen consequences of." (Design researcher, C)

"...the differences that we see when we talk about [our end users] are that there can be a difference in how much money they have and this has something to do with whether the country they live in gives refunds, or health insurance, or whether the state is paying the full amount, and things like that. There are many different [health care] models in the different countries. And that effects this very much." (Innovation specialist, N)

Knowledge about differences in national/regional market conditions cannot be obtained through user studies alone. Other types of internal data from databases, reports, social network, etc. as well as secondary sources about the socio-economic situation, societal structures and legal systems are also important in order to be able to distinguish between and understand the different types of users.

Perceived Differences in National Culture Are Used to Explain Behavior. In addition to the complex understanding of culture demonstrated above, the interview data contains many examples of how perceived differences in national culture are used to explain expected and experienced behavior when collecting data in other countries.

The interviewees explain that challenges might arise because the communication partners have different expectations and may place different emphasis on efficiency and/versus politeness.

*"I have just received an email from one of my colleagues who is trying to get [a user study] in Japan in place for me. He says that you just have to be aware that they are...**traditionally speaking**, they are not so willing to say what they really think...you have to be aware of that, especially if their opinion is negative, so I have to take that into account." (Senior UX researcher, F)*

*"We have experienced **the classical thing**, in Brazil [they] were expressive about it and in Asia much shorter replies. We have used the same type of test in both places, and in Brazil they were very expressive, the Japanese gave very short statements, the Chinese were very polite and the Germans made jokes that were kind of dirty, which was a little strange, but it was also in Berlin [laughs] so maybe it was that." (Company owner, M)*

In the examples, perceived differences in communication styles are associated with and explained by national culture. The consequence of this is that more general understandings based on one factor, namely national culture, are foregrounded, while the more complex aspects of culture and the uniqueness of the actual situations and the individual communication partners are played down. As can be seen from our high-lights in the quotes, the interviewees use words such as "traditionally speaking" and "the classical thing" to signal that they are aware of using general and somewhat stereotypical descriptions to explain the behavior of people from the countries in question.

National stereotypes develop over time as stories, examples, and jokes about the characteristics of people with a particular nationality are told and retold in the media, in literature, at social gatherings, etc. Moreover, they tend to cohere well with the experiences we have of interacting with people from these countries [11]. In this way, stereotypes come to influence the way we make sense of and talk about other nationalities. This can be problematic if stereotypical understandings gain too much explanatory power. Moreover, it can be problematic if stereotypes shape interpretations and decision-making in unreflective or unrecognized ways, e.g., when interacting with a person from a particular nationality or when making decisions about where and how to conduct international user studies.

Linguistic Simplifications Create Distance Between People. In addition to stereo-types, language can in subtle, and often unconscious, ways serve to create distinctions between "us" and "them". For example, when the interviewees say that *"those from Norway"* prefer this or that *"some lady from Mongolia"* has that type of education, a distance is created. This is because the choice of the seemingly insignificant words "those" and "some" refer to a generalized group or person different from oneself – and therefore by implication more difficult to understand and relate to.

Likewise, communication theory shows that we always position ourselves as either: superior, equal, or subordinate in relation to other people when we communicate [7, 8]. This can be seen in the above examples, where the generalization to "those" and "some" positioned the interviewee as superior and the others as subordinate. Other examples include the interviewees' use of linguistic images to explain that even though their company has a very diverse user group much data collection is conducted with *"the white middle class"* and *"pale Europeans"*. Or to explain that the software their company produces is used by different groups, and therefore has to be designed so that it can be used by both *"engineering types"* and *"a Russian cosmetologist"*. Such expressions are very powerful in communicating a point, because (positive and neg-ative) stereotypes are used to create a vivid image. However, they also gloss over complex understandings and create distance (rather than empathy and identification) because of the use of general, value-laden categories.

Such linguistic images and simplifications cannot be avoided no matter how culturally competent one becomes. However, it is possible to become more aware of the language that one self and others use and to gain a better understanding of how linguistic structures create distance and cause people to take value-laden positions in relation to others.

This awareness of language is especially important when presenting the obtained user insights to the employees who have to use them for product design.

4.4   Presentation of the User Insights

The companies that have participated in this research project use three different types of methods for presenting the user insights that they obtain through international user studies, namely personas, segmentation, or profiles of actual users. It is clear from our interview data that different types of companies use the three methods for different reasons.

- Personas is used by companies that wish to capture and apply the user insights for a period of time and for several purposes, i.e. in design activities, development projects, marketing campaigns, etc.
- Segmentation is used in companies where the company culture enforces a focus on logical arguments and decisions based on quantitative data.
- Profiles of actual users (rather than personas) are used by design agencies. For the design agencies we have talked to, the priority is to identify design insights for a particular client project. The profiles and user insights are not meant to live on after the project is over and therefore in-depth analysis leading to personas is not economically feasible unless they constitute an outcome, which the client is interested in and willing to pay for.

In this section, we look first at how the companies work with international personas and subsequently we describe the use of the two other methods.

Strategies for Creating International Personas. The user researchers stress that the strength of the persona method is its ability to create recognition and empathic identification, but they disagree about how to achieve this in international personas. There are two different overall strategies for presenting international user insights as a set of personas:

(1) To create personas according to nationality. When this strategy is used there is typically one persona per country/region covered by the user study (e.g., if the user study was conducted in Denmark, India and USA, there will be one Danish, one Indian, and one US persona). In other words, this strategy results in country specific persona descriptions.
(2) To create personas according to other criteria, such as, e.g., differences in user preferences, profession, education level, level of involvement, learning styles, digital maturity, autonomy at the work place, etc. This is similar to the criteria that are used to create national personas. This results in general persona descriptions.

"We have tried two different models. One is to have a persona that is very focused on how people in this job think and what kind of goals they have. It [the persona description] can be quite general...the other model we have tried is to map different personas to different regions." (Senior interaction designer, B).

However, some compensate for what the choice of main strategy leaves out by adding text fields that delineate:

- What would be different about the persona compared to the country specific description if s/he was living in different countries/regions
- What would be unique to the persona compared to the general persona description if s/he was living in a particular country/region

This indicates that neither strategy is entirely successful. In line with this, one of the interviewed user researchers states that he would prefer if people did not have to read about the differences between, e.g., Japan and Europe, in added text fields and that he is planning to experiment with other ways of presenting the information about cultural differences.

When it comes to the content of the persona descriptions, some user researchers prefer to use pictures or drawings that contain very little background that could place the persona in a specific context. Moreover, they avoid geographical references in the text and they give the personas as general names as possible. The argument for this is that employees around the world should be able to recognize and use the personas and therefore the focus should be on the persona as a person rather than a person in a specific place.

Other user researchers prefer to use pictures, names, titles, etc. which draw attention to and challenge the employees' stereotypical understandings of who the users are. The argument for this is to communicate the diversity of the users to the employees and therefore the focus is on the persona as a person who has both expected and unexpected features. One of the interviewees explain that she puts much effort into finding the right pictures for the personas and that she deliberately chooses pictures that challenge stereotypical understandings: *"Generally for personas in firms: the top manager is a woman, the creative leader is a dark man. That is how you try to challenge stereotypes." (Design researcher, A).*

The Choice of Strategy is Not Only Based on Data. In general, the user researchers have strong opinions about which strategy they prefer. One of the interviewees for example states that:

"I would rather not divide [personas] according to nationality." (Innovation specialist, N).

There are also several examples of how the choice of strategy for creating personas is made based on other considerations than the differences that emerge during data analysis. In one example, political considerations led to the use of strategy one, i.e. one persona for each of the company's main markets (even though nationality was not reflected as a significant difference in the data).

In another example the client had requested personas specifically to be able to develop 'the Swedish market', 'the Norwegian market', etc. and it was therefore natural to use strategy one. In other words, the decision to create personas based on nationality was made early on in the project, due to the client's way of conceptualizing their users in terms of markets that could be developed.

Profiles and Segments. Not all the companies we have talked to use personas. In the design agencies, for example, they do not use personas. Instead they create a profile of each user who has participated in the user study. The profile contains one or more pictures of the user and the home- or work context where the data collection took place as well as quotes and key insights. Thus, if the study covers 72 interviews, 72 user profiles are subsequently created – and in this particular example hung in a project room in order for the project team to be continuously reminded of the users and whom they were designing for.

Another company currently uses segmentation as the method for gathering and presenting user insights. Some companies conduct and use quantitative segmentation surveys, among other things, for planning a qualitative user study that results in personas. Yet again, in other companies they use and need both personas and segmentation as: *"Personas are a strong tool to communicate user behavior and intentions, but many "number people" want to be able to use them to prioritize, so they want to know exactly how many "of those" there are in each country." (Innovation specialist, N).*

5   Conclusion

In this paper, we have presented the results of an empirical investigation of how companies conduct international user studies. Key findings are as follows.

Companies do not collect data about end users in all the countries/regions they operate in. Instead, they focus on a few strategic markets. These can be new markets the company wants to develop, but more often it is relatively well-known markets where the company is already conducting much of its business.

Our research also shows that for some geographical areas and countries the companies/user researchers have almost too much respect for the national culture. This in turn means that, even though it would be highly relevant for the business, there are parts of the world where they do not conduct user studies.

International user studies tend to be large-scale studies that involve many human resources, including company employees as well as external agencies, translators, etc. from the countries where the studies take place. The studies typically cover 2–4 countries/regions and many end users in each country/region. It is not uncommon that more than 50 qualitative interviews are conducted (in total), among other things, to ensure validity.

The preferred data collection method is field studies. If possible, user researchers choose to go to the field themselves to gain rich insights and to control the data collection process.

The main insights that companies gain from international user studies are (1) that there are many similarities among end users across nationalities and (2) that it often is more important to focus on and take differences in market conditions (i.e. legislation, socio-economic situation, healthcare system, education, etc.) into account rather than national culture per se. This indicates that one of the important outcomes of international user studies is a complex understanding of the role of culture. However, we also saw examples of stereotyping the users and of an "us versus them" attitude, even though the goal of the user studies is to gain a nuanced understanding of the users and to provide other employees with user insights that allow for recognition and empathic identification.

Companies are in the process of finding out how best to present the insights about international end users to the employees (i.e., product designers, project participants and marketing personnel). Currently, two strategies are used, namely to distinguish among end users (1) according to nationality or (2) according to other criteria (e.g., user preferences, education level, and IT maturity). However, neither strategy is entirely successful, as it either foregrounds the differences between nationalities or downplays the unique aspects of the different countries/regions.

Thus, so far, no best practice for incorporating both national differences and cross-cultural similarities into persona descriptions, segmentations, etc. has been established.

This study contributes to the HCI literature with empirical findings about how companies conduct international user studies and the specific practices and challenges hereof. In particular, we show that strategic considerations, perceived differences in national culture, and concerns about data quality play an important role in shaping and delimiting the approach that companies take to international user studies.

Our findings points to the need for more research that addresses how to plan and carry out user studies in countries that are perceived as culturally very different, how to ensure data quality and understand the notion of validity when conducting multi-country studies, and how to incorporate both national differences and cross-cultural similarities into persona descriptions, segmentations, etc.

Acknowledgement. This research is supported by InfinIT- Danish Network for Innovative Utilization of IT.

References

1. Boztepe, S.: Toward a framework of product development for global markets: a user-value-based approach. Des. Stud. **28**, 513–533 (2007)
2. Camara, S.B., Oyugi, C., Abdelnour-Nocera, J., Smith, A.: Augmenting usability: cultural elicitation in HCI. In: Katre, D., Orngreen, R., Yammiyavar, P., Clemmensen, T. (eds.) HWID 2009. IFIP AICT, vol. 316, pp. 46–56. Springer, Heidelberg (2010)
3. Clemmensen, T., Roese, K.: An overview of a decade of journal publications about culture and human-computer interaction (HCI). In: Katre, D., Orngreen, R., Yammiyavar, P., Clemmensen, T. (eds.) HWID 2009. IFIP AICT, vol. 316, pp. 98–112. Springer, Heidelberg (2010)
4. Gabriel, Y.: Storytelling in Organizations: Facts, Fictions And Fantasies. Oxford University Press, Oxford (2000)
5. Gertsen, M.C., Søderberg, A.M.: Intercultural collaboration stories: on narrative inquiry and analysis as tools for research in international business. J. Int. Bus. Stud. **42**, 787–804 (2011)
6. Kvale, S.: InterView. Hans Reitzel (1997)

7. Jensen, I.: Introduction to Cultural Understanding. Roskilde University Press, Frederiksberg (2006)

8. Jensen, I.: If culture is practice …? a practice theoretical perspective on intercultural communication and mediation. In: Finch, J., Nynäs, P. (eds.) Transforming Otherness, pp. 9–34. Transaction publishers, New Jersey (2011)

9. Marcus, A., Gould, E.: Cultural dimensions and global user-interface design: What? So What? Now What? In: 6th Conference on Human Factors and the Web (2000)

10. Nielsen, L., Hansen, K.S: Personas is applicable: a study on the use of personas in denmark. In: Proceedings of CHI2014, pp. 1665–1674. ACM, Toronto (2014)

11. Risberg, A., Søderberg, A.M., Tienari, J., Vaara, E.: National talk: the construction of national stereotypes in a merging multinational. In: Søderberg, A.M., Vaara, E. (eds.) Merging Across Borders: People, cultures and politics, pp. 61–86. Copenhagen Business School Press, Copenhagen (2003)

12. Putnam, C., Rose, E., Johnson, E.J., Kolko, B.: Adapting user-centered design methods to design for diverse populations. Inf. Technol. Int. Dev. **5**(4), 51–73 (2009)

13. Schumacher, R.: The Handbook of Global User Research. Morgan Kaufmann, Boston (2009)

14. Siegel, D.A., Dray, S.M.: International contextual field research. In: Douglas, I., Liu, Z. (eds.) Global Usability, pp. 57–88. Springer, London (2011)

15. Walsh, T., Vainio, T., Varsaluoma, J.: Cross-cultural design of mobile mathematics learning service for South African schools. In: Proceedings of Mobile Learning, 2014 (2014)

16. Young, P.A.: Integrating culture in the design of ICTs. Br. J. Educ. Technol. **39**(1), 6–17 (2008)

Entity-Centric Visualization of Open Data

Sajan Raj Ojha[(✉)], Mladjan Jovanovic, and Fausto Giunchiglia

Department of Information Engineering and Computer Science,
University of Trento, Via Sommarive 9, 38123 Trento, Italy
{sajanraj.ojha,Mladjan.Jovanovic,Fausto.Giunchiglia}
@unitn.it

Abstract. The diversity, which is intrinsic to open data, affects intuitiveness and acceptance from the end users perspective. While the existing visualization techniques provide various ways to exploit open data in different domains, they still lack mechanisms to capture generality and flexibility across highly heterogeneous data representations that are crucial in the open data domain. We propose a novel visualization approach that exploits an entity-centric representation of open data. The key idea is that people intuitively perceive things as entities and categorize them according to their similarities and differences. The approach is supported by a UI architecture that allows aligning underlying open data described by the entities with a meaningful user experience. A preliminary user study shows the feasibility of our approach and its potential in turning the exploitation of open data catalogues into a positive user experience.

Keywords: HCI · Open data · Linked open data (LOD) · Usability · User experience (UX) · Visualization

1 Introduction

Open data[1] are data that can be freely used, reused and redistributed by anyone - subject only, at most, to the requirement to attribute and share alike. A huge volume of information is made available through data portals[2] that supports citizen to access data. In its original form, open data are not known in advance and varied in format and content. Moreover, different datasets have different provenances and use different modeling approaches which make it even harder for consumers to consume the content of data catalogue.

The Semantic web community is facing similar challenge in linked data consumption [35]. Linked open data has already made a big step by adding both diversity and machine-readable semantics of data on the Web. However, the scale of the Web provides unlimited amounts of cross-domain data whose contexts impose various perspectives and interpretations from a human side. This requires a general method to handle open data, which is domain-independent and user-centered at the same time. Research done in [41] shows that people want more interactivity than simply downloading and manipulating files. The major research challenge currently faced by the

---

[1] https://okfn.org/.
[2] http://datahub.io/dataset: As of November 2014 there are 8733 datasets registered.

© IFIP International Federation for Information Processing 2015
J. Abascal et al. (Eds.): INTERACT 2015, Part III, LNCS 9298, pp. 149–166, 2015.
DOI: 10.1007/978-3-319-22698-9_11

linked open data community is to figure out how to present the structured data in an intuitive and generic way for common users [8].

Various visualization applications are being developed in Open Linked Data community. Most of these applications are domain-specific and serve specific purposes [11]. They work with specific scenarios and require fixed, predefined data. Moreover, these applications use different visualization and navigation techniques. They usually require certain level of technical knowledge and thus add an extra effort for the common users [12, 21, 37].

We propose a novel approach to align open data with user experience. In this approach people intuitively perceive things as entities and categorize them according to their similarities and differences. We describe open data as a network of interrelated entities. On top of this entity-centric description of open data, we build visualization layer.

An entity represents any unique object that can be described by a set of attributes and relations to other objects. Each entity has a reference class that actually determines its type. Entity type is defined in terms of attributes (such as name, age), relations (such as located-in, friend-of), services (such as computeAge or computeInverseRelation) and categories of Meta attributes (such as timespan, validity and provenance). Entity types are organized into hierarchy of domains, with an ordering on attributes, relations and services. There are relatively few commonsense entity types (such as person, event, location) and many domain dependent entity types.

The paper is organized as follows: Section 2 gives a brief overview of visualization tools found in Open Data and Linked Open Data communities. Then it describes UX in general. In Sect. 3, we show a motivating problem. Section 4 gives a solution methodology and proof-of-concept prototype. Section 5 describes the user study we have conducted on the prototype. Section 6 concludes the paper.

2   State of the Art

Open Data are being used for different purposes and in different domains, including business, military intelligence, research and innovation, tourism and others. Since our focus is in effective visualization, navigation and exploration of open data, we describe existing solutions relevant to our problem domain. Then we describe general UX dimensions that we aim to exploit in our solution.

2.1   Open and Linked Data Visualization Tools

In this section, we give comparative analysis of the open data visualization systems found in literature. Comparison is done against a set of criteria adapted from [11]. The criteria are:

1. *Interactive Visualization (IV)*: Refers to the use of interactive representation through different kind of widgets (such as images, buttons and maps). Here, human perception is considered in understanding the complexity of the data structure and discovery and analysis of the data [3, 8, 10, 25].

2. *Relations (R)*: Denotes different kinds of relationships within one or multiple datasets to understand the data and discover new data [4, 7, 16, 21].
3. *Details on demand (DOD)*: Deals with exposing different level of details for the data as needed [10, 25].
4. *Scalability (S)*: Denotes the ability to manage and link large amount of heterogeneous data, which are loosely coupled [4, 10, 22].
5. *Filtering (F)*: Refers to an ability to suppress irrelevant information and focus only on information relevant for particular context or user session [4, 10].
6. *History (H)*: Describes the ability to record history of interaction allowing the user to review or retrace paths, undo/redo their actions [8, 27].
7. *Faceted exploration and Navigation (FEAN)*: Refers to flexible mechanism that enables setting particular context for search and exploration, and switching to another context based on relations the user explores during the session [9, 15, 39].
8. *Domain Independency (DI)*: Means that applications are not coupled with the specific domain and can exploit wide range of underlying datasets [6, 8, 20, 25].
9. *Target User Group (TUG)*: Means we differentiate three target user groups [11, 35].
   (a) Common User (CU): End user who does not have any background in ontologies.
   (b) Tech User (TU): End user who has understanding of the underlying technology and ontologies.
   (c) Domain Expert (DU): End user with expertise in data of a particular domain. DU might or might not have knowledge of an underlying technology.

Table 1 provides a brief comparison of existing Open Data applications. When visualizing open linked data to make them accessible for common end users who are not familiar with Semantic Web languages, it is important not to present data as URIs or triples but in a more user-friendly way. Although some systems provide high-level interactivity and emphasize different kinds of relations in visualized datasets, they mostly use RDF to describe the data. From the usability viewpoint, it adds an extra effort to the end user to interpret and understand what is being visualized. Applications like Dipper[3], Disco[4], Marbels[5], Piggy Bank[6], Sig.ma, URI Burner[7], Zitgist[8] and Isa-Viz[9] employ complex notations for visualization. They mainly use knowledge graphs that quickly become cumbersome as users drill down the data. Tools like OpenLink[10], RDF Gravity[11], RelFinder[12], SIMILE/Exhibit[13] and LESS[14] provide good visualization

---

[3] http://api.talis.com/stores/iand-dev1/items/dipper.html.

[4] http://www4.wiwiss.fu-berlin.de/bizer/ng4j/disco.

[5] http://www5.wiwiss.fu-berlin.de/marbles.

[6] http://simile.mit.edu.

[7] http://linkeddata.uriburner.com.

[8] http://dataviewer.zitgist.com.

[9] http://www.w3.org/2001/11/IsaViz.

[10] http://lod.openlinksw.com/ode.

[11] http://semweb.salzburgresearch.at/apps/rdf-gravity.

[12] http://relfinder.dbpedia.org.

[13] http://www.simile-widgets.org/exhibit/.

[14] http://less.aksw.org.

Table 1. Comparing functionality of different tools

Application	IV	R	DOD	S	F	H	FEAN	DI	TUG
Dipper	L	L	L	L	L	L	L	L	TU
Disco	L	L	M	L	L	L	L	H	TU
Marbels	L	M	M	L	L	L	L	H	TU
Piggy Bank	L	M	H	L	L	H	H	H	CU
Sig.ma [43]	L	L	M	H	H	M	L	H	TU
URI Burner	L	L	M	L	L	L	L	H	TU
Zitgist	L	L	H	M	H	M	H	H	TU
DBPediaMobile [4]	H	L	H	M	H	H	L	M	CU
Fenfire [25]	H	H	H	H	M	L	L	H	CU-M; TU
IsaViz	H	H	H	H	H	H	H	H	CU; TU
LESS	H	L	M	L	L	L	L	H	CU-M; TU
OpenLink	H	H	H	M	H	H	L	H	CU-M; TU
RDF Gravity	H	H	H	M	H	L	L	H	CU-M, TU
RELFinder	H	H	H	H	H	L	L	L	CU-M; TU
Tabulator [7]	H	M	H	L	L	M	L	H	TU
SIMILE/Exhibit	M	L	L	L	H	L	L	L	CU
Rhizomer [17]	L	M	H	L	M	L	H	L	TU
Sgvizler [40]	H	M	L	L	L	L	L	L	TU
LODWheel [42]	L	H	M	M	M	M	L	L	TU
Calluna [36]	H	H	H	L	H	H	L	M	CU

Low (L) - The system has no or low support for the category.
Medium (M) - The system supports the feature to some extent.
High (H) - The system has full support for the category.

support, but are highly contextualized and does not support better filtering and tracking history of interaction. In terms of cross-domain support, most of the systems allow to visualize in a predefined context, without the ability to switch to another context based on the relations user perceives during the session. This limitation also comes from the automated production of Linked Data which raises the problem of the accuracy and completeness of the datasets. In particular, incorrect or missing values, or incorrect links makes it hard to correlate data [11]. All the factors above require a certain level of expertise, either in ontologies or domain of the visualized data or even knowledge of specific UI notation. This is the reason why majority of systems is well suited for more experienced users. Thus, LOD community is still struggling to come up with common visualization tool that captures open data diversity and unexpectedness in a user-friendly way.

2.2   Common UX Dimensions

An overall positive UX is the key to the wide acceptance and increased usage of the open data. In scoping UX for open data, we use existing body of knowledge that expresses UX through a set of the measurable attributes [43]. Here, we enumerate these properties as follows:

1. **Visual and Aesthetic Experience**: Shows how aesthetics affects user perception of the system. It deals with the pleasure that users gain from immediate perception of the system [2, 23, 29, 32].
2. **Emotion**: Describes affective side of UX in terms of feelings and emotions elicited as an outcome of the interaction with the system [2, 14, 29, 33].
3. **Identification**: Addresses the human need to express one self through the interaction with the system [30, 34].
4. **Stimulation**: Relates to the quality of the system to encourage user to use it [24, 31, 38].
5. **Meaning and Value**: Denotes the quality of the system to reflect or represent values that are important to the user [29, 30].
6. **Social relatedness/coexperience**: Describes the pleasure that comes from the social interactions [18, 30].

3   A Motivating Example

Open data is widely used in various kinds of services aimed at different categories of users (citizens, domain experts, technical users) [11]. Figure 1 illustrates the inherent property of open data - variety in format and content. This feature of open data is critical from the usability viewpoint. With respect to the example, we enumerate major elements of this variability:

1. **Variability in data formats**: Datasets referred by data catalogue are stored in various formats such as XML, XLS, CSV JSON and so on. It is assumed that end user knows how to deal with multiple formats and use them [13]. This extra effort creates a barrier in utilizing the datasets by most of the users. In Fig. 1, record B[15] is stored in XLs format, whereas record C[16] is written as JSON CSV.
2. **Tabular presentation**: On one hand, it provides a concise overview of information to the user as data are aggregated and list view flattens the depth of the data itself [1, 35]. On the other hand, different types of data require proper visualizations to be perceived and to extract needed information. For example, numbers can be expressed as chart and/or graphs, whereas map-like presentations are more convenient for spatial data [28]. Coming up with a uniform generic visualization is rather difficult, as data from different domains require different ways to visualize information. In the example above, it would be more convenient to display location-based data on a map.
3. **Inefficient search and exploration of datasets**: In general, open data lacks a proper interface that allows for an efficient interaction and exploration [1]. Finding a specific tuple in the dataset requires an extra effort for a user. The data may overlap,

---

[15] http://goo.gl/iH0xfD.

[16] http://goo.gl/77UbzF.

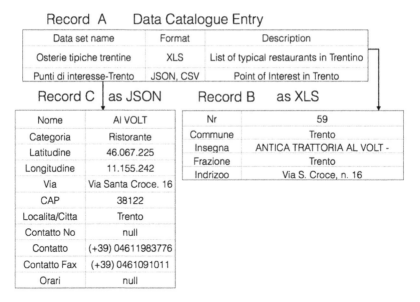

Fig. 1. An excerpt from open data catalogue that illustrate the feature of open data critical for end-users acceptance - variety in format and content. It shows data catalogue entry that points to different data structures representing the same data. Record A shows the data catalogue entry for restaurants. Record B points to the tabular representation. Record C refers the JSON representation. Both records B and C contain information about the same restaurant Al Volt.

be incorrect or incomplete (as shown in Fig. 1). An interface that allows for multi-faceted interaction and supports exploratory search is still missing [26].

4. **Complex data correlation process**: The process of discovering related data tuples within the datasets is rather difficult. Looking at the record B from Fig. 1, we can notice that extracting different points of interest located nearby or within the address via Santa Croce is almost impossible from the dataset.

5. **Multiple languages**: Datasets are usually localized. For example, all datasets in Fig. 1 are in Italian. This requires a potential user to have knowledge of the language.

6. **Scope of specific domain**: Existing open data visualizations are tailored to specific domains and aimed to be used in different contexts. They often use different ways to interact with the data. This requires users to use different tools in different manner and increases cognitive effort when users switch among the tools.

4   Entity-Centric Open Data Visualization

In this chapter, we propose a generic user interface framework that aims to bridge the gap between what is called data-driven and user-centered approach to describe open data. In general, we describe a method that captures diversity and unexpectedness of open data in a generic way.

We see two basics steps to this process. First we describe and encode open data in a domain-independent manner. We do that by identifying fine-grained elements that can be modeled individually and used to compose and encode open data for different domains. On top of this model, we build UI layer that brings the open data to the level of a user experience. In this section, we describe basic principles and concrete elements that make our solution.

4.1 Entity-Centric Open Data

In an entity-centric view on open data, instances (objects) are described as entities [19]. Accordingly, tabular view on open data (Fig. 1) is transformed into the knowledge graph showing relevant entities and their attributes and relations (Fig. 2).

Entity: Denotes representation of real-world object that can be found in different contexts in our everyday life. Each entity is described with a set of attributes and relations with other entities.

Attribute: Represents a property of an entity. Each attribute has a name and one or more values. Except the value of the property it represents, each attribute has associated meta attributes such as provenance (describes the origin), permanence, dependency (whether it is computed) or validity time periods (case of an attribute whose value has changed over time). In addition, we distinguish different kinds of attributes like qualitative (numeric), quantitative (expressed as an adjective) or descriptive (given in natural language).

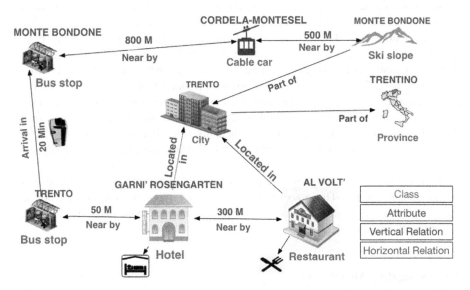

Fig. 2. Simplified entity-centric knowledge graph that describes open data as linked entities. Each entity is described with the class and with the name attribute. It also gives different types of relations. Vertical relations are defined on the level of classes, whereas horizontal are generated at runtime.

Relation: Defines links between entities. In general, we differentiate between two types of relations - vertical (ontological) and horizontal (epistemic). Vertical relations are used to compose hierarchies and mainly for the purpose of classification. These relations are created at design time, on the level of classes. The examples are *is-a* and *part-of*. Horizontal (epistemic) relations link entities according to their specific properties. In this case, the entities can be instances of different, unrelated eTypes. They are defined at the level of instances and are computed at runtime from attribute values. The examples include *located-in* and *near-by*.

eType: Presents a reference class of an entity. It is a template that defines the constraints for creating attributes and relations of an entity. Some common examples of eTypes include Location (geospatial entities), Facility (physical entities providing services to the people) or MindProduct (the result of a human intellectual effort).

Clear separation of concepts of attributes, relations and entity classes leads to flexible mechanism that combines these elements to represent domain knowledge.

Lightweight ontology: Refers to a method to dynamically compose entity classes, attributes and relations to create the background knowledge about the domain of interest (e.g., tourism, transportation). Thus, we have hierarchies of entity classes (eTypes), attributes and relations. These hierarchies are also known as facet ontologies. Facet is a term widely used in knowledge representation community and denotes aspect of meaning. Each facet contains group of homogeneous terms, where each term in the hierarchy denotes a primitive atomic concept (whether it is a class, a relation or an attribute). Then the lightweight ontology is dynamically created by linking the elements belonging to respective facets into unique hierarchy. The mechanism basically enables construction of multi-perspective representation schemes combining the terms from the facets. This concretely means we can view an entity from different perspectives. While vertical relations provide precompiled classification and description of entity types, horizontal relations are created at runtime. For example, a restaurant can be described as a refreshment facility, as part of the city, as near-by hotel, as on the lake, as where the event is being held, depending on the context provided. Context can be defined by a user request. In this sense, they provide flexible and scalable mechanism to represent domain-specific knowledge that combines different views on the same concept. From the technical side, it brings performance benefits since it may be generated at the beginning of a user session and thereby provide flexible, but also efficient navigation and search.

Figure 3 provides a simplified example of using lightweight ontology to generate UI navigation control. The ontology classifies entity types from a tourism domain according to their purpose. The level of a menu item matches to the depth of a node that represents the entity type.

4.2   Navigation Modalities

Based on the type of relations among entities, we define two basic kinds of navigation modalities. Combined together, they allow flexible navigation among open data entities. The are as follows:

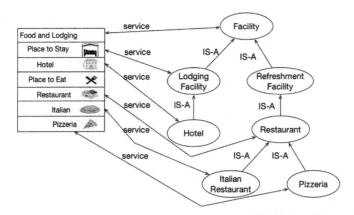

Fig. 3. An example that illustrates the usage of a lightweight ontology to generate a menu for navigating domain entities.

10. **Vertical (Ontological) Navigation:** Follows vertical relations that exist in hierarchical structures of entity classes. If we look at the Fig. 2, we can see *part-of* relations between location-based entities (province, mountain, city). On the other hand, Fig. 3 shows lightweight ontology with *is-a* relations between eTypes, starting from Facility as the highest level propagating to more specific types of Italian Restaurant and Pizzeria.

11. **Horizontal (Epistemic) Navigation:** Follows the relations that exist between entities. In the Fig. 2, it might not be easy to find Restaurants near Hotel using vertical relation. Horizontal relations connect entities that can belong to different eTypes. They are generated at runtime (for example on a user request). If we look at Fig. 2, Hotel and Restaurant are connected with *near-by* relation. In addition, the network of horizontal relations gives the possibility to reach different means of transportation.

4.3   Reference Architecture

We describe our solution with the general, high-level architecture (Fig. 4). The architecture consists of the three main components:

1. **Domain Component**: Describes source open data from the domain of interest. These data are taken from the open data catalogue.
2. **Semantic Component**: Handles entity-centric representation of open data. This component contains mechanisms that transform source open data into entities. The process and the platform behind are described elsewhere [5]. Converted open data are stored in an entity base.
3. **Interaction Component**: Provides UI layer on top of the entity base.

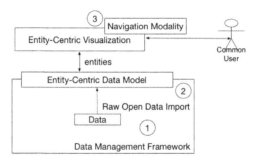

Fig. 4. System architecture

4.4   Experimental Prototype

We have developed experimental prototype[17] that uses the entity base containing open data from the province of Trento[18]. The Entity Base is called Entitypedia. It is a large-scale knowledge base. Currently, it provides 98 percent of correctness with the goal and tendency to improve it. Aside from serving as an entity repository, it provides entity-based services ranging from simpler (such as standard CRUD operations) to more advanced (such as context-dependent operations of search, matching or navigation) The contents of the Entity Base is described in Table 2.

Figure 5 shows main components of the UI. The UI calls the Web API endpoint which is responsible for querying the data from the Entity Base. The UI components are responsible for visualizing the entities returned as the query result.

Developed prototype is shown in Fig 6. It contains four main parts: ontological menu, map, information container, and relational menu. Ontological menu is placed on the left side and contains different eTypes. It is created from a lightweight ontology. Currently, it supports Italian and English. Based on the selected menu item (eType), the entities are retrieved and visualized on the map.

Table 2. Entities classified according to eType inside an entity base

eType	Total
Location	20704
Facility	141
Lodging Facility	442
Shopping Facility	219
Refreshment Facility	229
Transportation Facility	3379

---

[17] http://www.opendata.entitypedia.org/spacetime.

[18] http://dati.trentino.it: It is one of the major data catalogue with 875 datasets from different sectors.

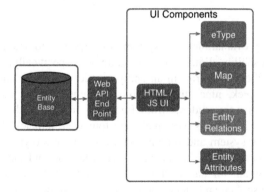

Fig. 5. Main architecture

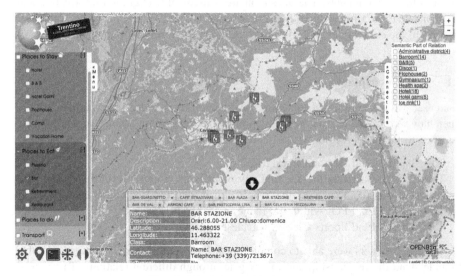

Fig. 6. UI of the working prototype

Users can also select multiple menu items. Once an entity is selected on the map, the information about that entity is shown on the screen and relational menu is created on the right side of the screen. The relational menu lists the entities that are either near or located in the same place. There are also standard settings, such as the default language, the radius to search within, and geo-locational search for the entities relative to the user's position. More detailed demonstration of the prototype can be seen in accompanied video.

5   Experiment

The goal of the initial evaluation of the system prototype was to obtain insights on how different UX and usability dimensions are addressed, specifically, how people perceived entities and their categories in an entity centric world was understood. During the period of one week, nine students from different faculties participated in the evaluation. The users were students from Bachelors to PhD with age ranging from 21 years to 29 years. Five users were male and four were female. They were given a brief overview of the system and shown how to use the prototype application called Trentino Entitypedia (TE). The users were then asked to find entities in TE. Each session lasted maximum for half an hour. All the interaction of the users and their comments were transcribed and video was recorded for future analysis. The users were instructed to think aloud and they were asked to perform the task in normal way without feeling any discomfort or stress. After completing the task, respondents were asked to fill questionnaires. The questionnaire consists of background information and questions that use 5-point Likert Scale to assess different usability and user experience criteria. In the subsections that follow we describe the results of the evaluation.

5.1   Task Description

Each user was asked to spend some time on the interface in order to get familiar with it. Then they were asked to read the instructions about the system. Four related tasks were assigned to the users as follows:

- Task 1 (T1): Find Bed and Breakfast.
- Task 2 (T2): Based on the T1, find any other Point of Interest (POI) that is in the same location (commune) as that of previously selected Bed and Breakfast.
- Task 3 (T3): Find POI within the range of 500 m in Cavalese.
- Task 4 (T4): Find Sports Club in Cavalese.

Most of the users were able to complete task 1 within minutes. They were also able to understand the relationship and to navigate through different relations. Task 2 also took less time to complete. The possibility to set the radius made the task 3 simple to be achieved and users were also excited to see the results. Task 4 was also easily performed by most of the users.

5.2   Usability Evaluation

On average, users' assessments were quite high for all measured variables. The overall assessment of the system was positive. Five usability dimensions were selected as follows: Usefulness, Learnability, Memorability, Satisfaction and Visibility of system status. Evaluation study is summarized in Table 3. Detailed evaluation dimensions and statistics can be found elsewhere[19].

---

[19] http://goo.gl/6KtFLe.

Table 3. Usability evaluation based on five-point likert scale.

User	Usefulness		Learnability		Memorability	Satisfaction	Visibility of System Status	
	Q1	Q2	Q3	Q4	Q5	Q6	Q7	Q8
1	4	3	5	2	2	3	3	3
2	5	5	4	2	2	4	4	5
3	4	3	4	3	3	3	4	4
4	5	4	4	2	2	4	4	4
5	4	4	4	2	2	4	4	4
6	4	4	5	2	2	3	3	5
7	4	4	5	1	1	4	5	5
8	4	5	5	2	1	4	5	5
9	4	3	4	3	2	3	4	5
Mean	4.22	3.88	4.44	2.11	1.89	3.55	4.0	4.4
S.D	0.44	0.78	0.52	0.60	0.60	0.52	0.70	0.72

Q1 - I find the application simple to use.
Q2 - The system meets my needs.
Q3 - It is easy to learn how to use the system.
Q4 - I had to put extra effort to use the system.
Q5 - It takes some time to remember application controls.
Q6 - I didn't notice any inconsistencies while using it.
Q7 - I receive timely feedback on my actions.
Q8 - The information provided by the system is easy to understand.

Overall, the TE system was assessed as quite useful. Standard deviation from the mean value for each of the questions for the usability dimensions is also minimum. This proves that system was useful for almost all of the users.

Ontological menu on the left and the semantic menu were both considered as user-friendly. Left menu proved to be well organized as it allows user to find specific service in less time. Users also liked the possibility of setting entity search range on the system. Overall, the interactivity and the integrated environment was interesting for users. Some minor bugs were also discovered during the process. The check-box on the left menu behaved with certain issues. When an item was checked on semantic menu (right menu), the users expected that the previously selected entity will also be shown on the map. Some suggestions about font size and type were also provided. The system was little slower and users expected results in less time.

For the future version, users also suggested some features. Directional features like in Google Maps, direct search functionality, facet level service on attribute level. More interactive help was also pointed out as needed. Users also requested putting icon on both the menus. Some users also suggested accommodating the relational menu (right menu) directly inside the information container.

5.3   UX Evaluation

The system was evaluated considering five UX dimensions i.e. Aesthetics and Visual appearance, Emotion, Identification, Stimulation and Meaning and value. Table 4 shows responses related to specific UX dimensions.

On average, the users' assessments were positive for all of the UX variables. User 7 and 8 gave negative remarks for Q3 and Q7, respectively. This resulted in higher deviation for those questions from the mean. We explain this with the comments they have provided. User 7 noted that the system has easy traversal mechanism, but the discovery of information may not be intuitive. Similarly, User 8 mentioned that though it is easy to find entities and relations, the meaning of the words in Italian was not intuitive in some cases. For example, Cateratta was used to describe waterfall, whereas the Cascata may be an appropriate word. This issue comes from the quality of underlying entity-centric open data.

Table 4. UX evaluation based on five-point likert scale

	Aesthetics and visual appearance		Emotion		Identification	Meaning and Value	
User	Q1	Q2	Q3	Q4	Q5	Q6	Q7
1	4	4	4	3	4	3	5
2	4	5	5	4	4	4	4
3	3	4	4	3	4	4	4
4	4	4	4	4	4	4	4
5	4	4	4	4	4	4	4
6	5	5	5	4	4	4	4
7	4	5	1	3	5	5	5
8	3	5	5	5	5	5	1
9	2	4	4	4	4	4	4
Mean	3.66	4.4	4.0	3.77	4.2	4.11	3.88
S.D	0.86	0.52	1.22	0.66	0.44	0.60	1.16

Q1 - Seeing different types of entities on the same page is visually pleasant

Q2 - Icons clearly reflect the purpose of the specific entity on the map

Q3 - I like the idea that, using the system, I can discover new information connected to what I was looking for in the first place

Q4 - The fact that I can propagate through the network of connected entities makes this application somehow playful

Q5 - I see myself in using the application.

Q6 - The application gives me reliable evidence of entities in a sense that I get the information I expect

Q7 - The meaning of entities and their relations enables me to quickly navigate and extract the information I find useful

Table 5. Application features rating with respect to UX dimensions

Application Feature	Identification	Stimulation
Relations/links between entities on the map	63%	63%
Entities details on demand	38%	38%
Entities view scalability	25%	25%
Entities view filtering	38%	50%
History of browsed entities	25%	13%
Flexible exploration and navigation through entities		50%
Flexibility /Contextual switch in showing entities from different domains		38%

The idea of seeing entities of different types on the same page really excited the users. Users felt it is less time-consuming and can get a clear picture of what they were looking for. User 1 mentioned that the interface was intuitive and exciting. Users liked the idea of consistency between menu color with the color of an icon color which showed clarity and symmetry. For some users, the green icon was not helpful as it also matched with the color of the map. Icon for street also did not make any sense to the users. For most of the users finding new information was an innovative thing. User 6 expressed that she enjoyed the way in which connected entities can be traversed. User 4 was surprised to see the opening and closing time for POI. All users asked if they could start using the application immediately. They also suggested that it will be extremely helpful for them if the application can be made mobile. User 3 liked the menu. The arrangement of menu items seemed logical for him. User 2 was doubtful whether the menu item 'Things to do' was expressive. He also thought that menu ski and club should be placed together under same menu.

Table 5 gives percentage of users that indicated application features with respect to specific UX dimensions. With respect to the identification, the users were asked to choose the features that reflect their habits in using similar systems. Regarding stimulation, the users were asked to choose the specific features that encourage them to use the application.

The table shows that the most interesting application features are relations between entities, view filtering and flexible exploration and navigation through entities. It also shows that some of the features were not noticed by the users. These features require further improvement.

6   Conclusion and Future Work

The paradigm shift to make the data free raises an issue of the effective usage by common users. This requirement comes from the fundamental properties of open data - diversity in format and content and unexpectedness (meaning they are not known in advance). Thus far, they are handled with predefined, hard-wired solutions.

We handle open data explicitly through entities as a domain-independent and a user-centeric methodology. From the data perspective, entities address fundamental issues of open data. By design, they capture context very well by encapsulating all the relevant properties (attributes) in a component. Once designed, they serve as good data aggregators (such as People, Locations, Events, Facilities). Moreover, different kinds of relations among entities make them usable across domains. From the usability perspective, we perceive that people intuitively think in terms of entities as objects (such as friends, events and places) and we aim to exploit this notion in human mental model.

In this paper, we have proposed an entity-centric solution to visualize open data. The solution is supported by the high-level, reference architecture. Upon the architecture, we have developed proof-of-concept prototype. Insights that are gained from the user study demonstrate the feasibility of our solution.

Our next step is to design entity-centric UI framework that will use generic UI components - entigets to improve development of open data applications for different domains and contexts of use.

References

1. Agrawala, M., Li, W., Berthouzoz, F.: Design principles for visual communication. Commun. ACM **54**(4), 60–69 (2011)
2. Alben, L.: Defining the criteria for effective interaction design. Interactions **3**(3), 11–15 (1996)
3. Amar, R.A., Stasko, J.T.: Knowledge precepts for design and evaluation of information visualizations. IEEE Trans. Vis. Comput. Graph. **11**(4), 432–442 (2005)
4. Becker, C., Bizer, C.: Exploring the geospatial semantic web with dbpedia mobile. Web Seman. Sci. Serv. Agents World Wide Web **7**(4), 278–286 (2009)
5. Bedini, I., et al.: Open government data: Fostering Innovation. JeDEM-e J. eDemocracy Open Gov. **6**(1), 69–79 (2014)
6. Berners-Lee, T., Hollenbach, J., Lu, K., Presbrey, J., Schraefel, M.C.: Tabulator Redux: Browsing and Writing Linked Data. Citeseer (2008)
7. Berners-Lee, T.: Linked data-design issues (2006). http://www.w3.org/DesignIssues/LinkedData.html. 2011
8. Bizer, C., Heath, T., Berners-Lee, T.: Linked data - the story so far. Int. J. Seman. Web Inf. Syst. **5**(3), 1–22 (2009)
9. Cao, N., Sun, J., Lin, Y.-R., Gotz, D., Liu, S., Qu, H.: Facetatlas: multifaceted visualization for rich text corpora. IEEE Trans. Vis. Comput. Graph. **16**(6), 1172–1181 (2010)
10. Card, S.K., Mackinlay, J.D., Shneiderman, B. (eds.): Readings in Information Visualization: Using Vision to Think. Morgan Kaufmann Publishers Inc., San Francisco (1999)
11. Dadzie, A.-S., Rowe, M.: Approaches to visualising linked data: a survey. Semant. Web **2**(2), 89–124 (2011)
12. Davies, S., Hatfield, J., Donaher, C., Zeitz, J.: User interface design considerations for linked data authoring environments. In: LDOW, p. 628 (2010)
13. Davies, T.: Supporting open data use through active engagement. In: Position Paper: W3C Using Open Data Workshop. W3C (2012)
14. Desmet, P.M., Hekkert, P.: Framework of product experience. Int. J. Des. **1**(1), 57–66 (2007)
15. Farazi, M.S.F.: Faceted lightweight ontologies: a formalization and some experiments. Ph.D. thesis, University of Trento (2010)

16. Fekete, J.-D., van Wijk, J.J., Stasko, J.T., North, C.: The Value of information visualization. In: Kerren, A., Stasko, J.T., Fekete, J.-D., North, C. (eds.) Information Visualization. LNCS, vol. 4950, pp. 1–18. Springer, Heidelberg (2008)

17. García, R., Gimeno, J.M., Perdrix, F., Gil, R., Oliva, M.: The rhizomer semantic content management system. In: Lytras, M.D., Damiani, E., Tennyson, R.D. (eds.) WSKS 2008. LNCS (LNAI), vol. 5288, pp. 385–394. Springer, Heidelberg (2008)

18. Gaver, B., Martin, H.: Alternatives: exploring information appliances through conceptual design proposals. In: Proceedings of the SIGCHI Conference on Human Factors in Computing Systems, pp. 209–216. ACM (2000)

19. Giunchiglia, F., Dutta, B.: Dera: A Faceted Knowledge Organization Framework. University of Trento (2011)

20. Giunchiglia, F., Maltese, V., Dutta, B.: Domains and context: first steps towards managing diversity in knowledge. Web Seman. Sci. Serv. Agents World Wide Web 12, 53–63 (2012)

21. Halb, W., Raimond, Y., Hausenblas, M.: Building linked data for both humans and machines. In: LDOW (2008)

22. Hassenzahl, M., Tractinsky, N.: User experience-a research agenda. Behav. Inf. Technol. 25 (2), 91–97 (2006)

23. Hassenzahl, M.: The thing and i: understanding the relationship between user and product. In: Blythe, M.A., Overbeeke, K., Monk, A.F., Wright, P.C. (eds.) Funology, pp. 31–42. Springer, Netherlands (2005)

24. Hastrup, T., Cyganiak, R., Bojars, U.: Browsing Linked Data With Fenfire (2008)

25. Hearst, M.: Design recommendations for hierarchical faceted search interfaces. In: ACM SIGIR Workshop on Faceted Search, pp. 1–5. Seattle, WA (2006)

26. Heath, T.: How will we interact with the web of data? Internet Comput. IEEE 12(5), 88–91 (2008)

27. Heer, J., Bostock, M., Ogievetsky, V.: A tour through the visualization zoo. Commun. ACM 53(6), 59–67 (2010)

28. Hekkert, P.: Design aesthetics: principles of pleasure in design. Psychol. Sci. 48(2), 157 (2006)

29. Jääskö, V., Mattelmäki, T.: Observing and probing. In: Proceedings of the 2003 International Conference on Designing Pleasurable Products and Interfaces, pp. 126–131. ACM (2003)

30. Karapanos, E., Zimmerman, J., Forlizzi, J., Martens, J.-B.: Measuring the dynamics of remembered experience over time. Interact. Comput. 22(5), 328–335 (2010)

31. Lavie, T., Tractinsky, N.: Assessing dimensions of perceived visual aesthetics of web sites. Int. J. Hum. Comput. Stud. 60(3), 269–298 (2004)

32. Mahlke, S., Thüring, M.: Studying antecedents of emotional experiences in interactive contexts. In: Proceedings of the Sigchi Conference on Human Factors in Computing Systems, pp. 915–918. ACM (2007)

33. Marc, H.: Aesthetics in interactive products: Correlates and consequences of beauty.

34. Mazumdar, S., Petrelli, D., Ciravegna, F.: Exploring user and system requirements of linked data visualization through a visual dashboard approach. Seman. Web 5(3), 203–220 (2014)

35. Otjacques, B., Stefas, M., Cornil, M., Feltz, F.: Open data visualization keeping traces of the exploration process. In: Proceedings of the First International Workshop on Open Data, pp. 53–60. ACM (2012)

36. Rutledge, L., van Ossenbruggen, J., Hardman, L.: Making rdf presentable: integrated global and local semantic web browsing. In: Proceedings of the 14th International Conference on World Wide Web, WWW 2005, pp. 199–206. ACM, New York, NY, USA (2005)

37. Sheldon, K.M., Elliot, A.J., Kim, Y., Kasser, T.: What is satisfying about satisfying events? testing 10 candidate psychological needs. J. Pers. Soc. Psychol. 80(2), 325 (2001)

38. Shneiderman, B.: Designing the User Interface: Strategies for Effective Human-Computer Interaction, vol. 2. Addison-Wesley, Reading (1992)
39. Skjæveland, M.G.: Sgvizler: a javascript wrapper for easy visualization of sparql result sets. In: Extended Semantic Web Conference (2012)
40. Socrata: Open Government Data Benchmark Study Report. Technical report (2010)
41. Stuhr, M., Roman, D., Norheim, D.: Lodwheel–javascript-based visualization of rdf data. Citeseer (2011)
42. Tummarello, G., Cyganiak, R., Catasta, M., Danielczyk, S., Delbru, R., Decker, S.: Sig. ma: live views on the web of data. Web Seman. Sci. Serv. Agents World Wide Web 8(4), 355–364 (2010)
43. Winckler, M., Bach, C., Bernhaupt, R.: Identifying user experience dimensions for mobile incident reporting in urban contexts. IEEE Trans. Prof. Commun. 56(2), 97–119 (2013)

Mindful Gaming: How Digital Games Can Improve Mindfulness

Jacek Sliwinski[✉], Mary Katsikitis, and Christian Martyn Jones

University of the Sunshine Coast, Queensland, Australia
jacek.sliwinski@research.usc.edu.au,
{mkatsiki,cmjones}@usc.edu.au

Abstract. In recent years, attention has increased around the delivery of mindfulness interventions by means of new technology such as via the smartphone [1]. However, less research has been devoted to investigating how digital games can enable and facilitate mindfulness training. This study demonstrates how mindfulness can be improved by using technology, in particular digital games. Based on the work of Bergomi et al. [2], mindfulness is defined as an inherent capacity in human beings that can be trained, which is explored within the structure of an eight-factor model. For each mindfulness factor identified by the research of Bergomi et al., appropriate games are presented together with research evidence showing their efficacy for mindfulness training. Effective games are disaggregated according to their mechanics, dynamics, and aesthetics [3] to provide design recommendations for game developers.

Keywords: Mindfulness · Meditation · Games · Mobile applications

1 Introduction

Mindfulness is growing in popularity as attention and emotion regulation training, and as a subject for scientific research. Numerous studies have demonstrated the positive impact of mindfulness on psychological wellbeing, with mindfulness meditation the traditional and predominant mindfulness practice. Meditation refers to techniques that self-regulate body and mind [4], which is predominantly achieved by conscious sitting, during which the core skills of systematic deployment of attention and non-reactive observing of experiences are trained. As simple as this may sound, meditation is difficult to learn and practise for beginners [5]. Challenges include physical discomfort (e.g. back pain), inability to concentrate and unpleasant side-effects like tiredness and boredom. These challenges make meditation difficult for most beginners, disrupting regular practice and even being the cause to cease meditation completely [5].

Mindfulness meditation has been developed in the absence of modern technology and there is so far little scientific exploration of innovative solutions to develop a technology-based mindfulness training that overcomes beginner challenges [1]. This study focuses on exploring how technology, and in particular digital games, can be used to develop an engaging mindfulness practice. Applying the concept of mindfulness into a modern technological context and to translate it into a beginner-friendly

© IFIP International Federation for Information Processing 2015
J. Abascal et al. (Eds.): INTERACT 2015, Part III, LNCS 9298, pp. 167–184, 2015.
DOI: 10.1007/978-3-319-22698-9_12

form of mindfulness practice, fills a significant research gap between mindfulness research and human computer interaction.

Digital games provide a promising technology for the research of mindfulness because the interactive nature of games allows the development of experiential knowledge, at which mindfulness is cultivated. Games can be so engaging that they make their players forget about time and create an absorbing interaction [6], which is why gaming has been described as a meditative practice by itself [7]. These qualities are parallel to those of mindfulness meditation (facilitating deep concentration); however, games are generally seen as a fun medium that do not require much persuasion to be used [8], while meditation is sometimes perceived as a daunting task [5]. Games are designed to be motivating, engaging and entertaining and furthermore have the potential to elevate players into a 'Flow' state of higher consciousness [6]. Both mindfulness practice and gaming are often described as a non-striving effortless effort or doing nothing [9, 10].

A recent study comparing self-reported mindfulness with gaming experience found gamers to be generally more mindful, which supports the potential of digital games as mindfulness practice [11]. Although this study was only correlational (without experimental conditions), it does reflect the potential of this medium. In recent years more atypical games have been released, which are purely explorative and with no definite goal (e.g. Proteus, Dear Esther, Bientôt l'été) and audio-visual experiences that can be described as "meditative" (e.g. SoundScape, Mountain, Journey). This trend can be interpreted as a mirror of the general demand for deeper game experiences and predicts a positive acceptance of a mindfulness game. In the context of training mindfulness, an interactive application provides the ability to externalise some aspects of the mindfulness practice and thus decrease a practitioner's cognitive load, which facilitates training by making it less demanding. Furthermore, digital games can provide clear instructions and multisensory feedback, which can be essential in guiding the user to practise mindfulness independently and with opportunity to check and correct practice.

This research aims to investigate the relationship between mindfulness and digital games. The research investigates which aspects of mindfulness can be trained by interactive technology, in particular games, and which game elements influence aspects of mindfulness and how must they be designed to have a positive impact. The feasibility of such an approach is supported by the acceptance of games as a medium of daily use [8], and the general view that 'games are fun' (especially among children and young adults). On average, people are using their mobile device for 3.6 h per day, spending most time engaged with applications (apps) of which the majority are games [12].

2   Research Study

2.1   Defining Mindfulness

Contemporary psychology describes mindfulness inconsistently [13], suggesting a lack of operational consensus. It has been defined as self-regulatory capacity [14], an acceptance skill [15], and a meta-cognitive skill [16]. There is a multitude of questionnaires available to measure mindfulness [17], with great conceptual differences [18]. This study uses a recent questionnaire, the Comprehensive Inventory of Mindfulness Experiences (CHIME) by Bergomi et al. [2], developed to unify other available questionnaires and provide a comprehensive measure of mindfulness. Nine aspects of mindfulness were identified that are covered by previous operationalisations of mindfulness. Those aspects were assimilated, and using factor analysis reduced to eight factors. The final definition of mindfulness and resulting measurement instrument consists of eight individual mindfulness factors.

2.2   Scan of Literature and Software

This study explores digital games and interactive applications with regards to their fit to individual mindfulness aspects, based on the CHIME eight-factor mindfulness model [2]. After briefly describing each factor, relevant games and interactive applications are reviewed.

A thorough search was conducted on popular websites, search engines, and app stores with the inclusion criteria of at least one mindfulness aspect. The initial search was conducted in October 2014, while subsequent searches were performed to keep the results up to date. To identify relevant research studies, the search engines Scopus, Web of Knowledge, and Google Scholar have been searched for the terms ["mindfulness" OR "meditation"] AND ["game" OR "application" OR "interactive"]. Additionally, applying the same search algorithm, the first 50 results pages of Google were used to identify any other relating studies and programs. Game databases Steam (incl. Greenlight), moddb, and GamesForChange were searched using the terms ' "mindfulness" OR "meditation" '. The same terms were used to search through the popular app-stores Google Play and Apple App Store (both iPhone and iPad), though the search was limited to the first 100 hits. For all searches, the range of keywords was extended to match individual mindfulness factors. The final search included the following additional terms: present moment, mindful, attention, focus, concentration, ADHD, mind wandering, affect, mood, self-compassion, compassion, irrational, inspire, inspiration, openness, insight (ful), explore, exploration, acceptance, accept, act, body scan, emotion, Zen, Vipassana, balance, equilibrium, uplift, ego, inner, Buddhist, Buddhism, sati, rumination, kindness, depression, self-esteem.

Several exclusion criteria were applied. Non-interactive presentations of mindfulness training (e.g. web pages with audio and video instructions or guided meditation mobile apps) were deliberately excluded from this study. Although these kinds of applications can teach mindfulness techniques, they do not tap into the potential of building experiential knowledge through interactivity. Likewise, research studies that presented art installations and case studies that do not relate to at least one of the eight CHIME mindfulness factors were excluded. For example, the 'Sonic Cradle', an installation, where participants lie in the dark on a hammock while respiratory biofeedback sensors control the soundscape to create an interactive 'meditative' experience, did not reveal any significant effects on measures of mindfulness [19]. Likewise, 'The Meditation Chamber', a mindfulness and relaxation training environment that uses virtual reality and biofeedback, was excluded because of a lack of evidence for its efficacy [20]. For the same reason, the 'Mind Pool' was not included, a brainwave feedback installation to foster self-reflection [21]. For the purpose of brevity, only those interactive programs and games most relevant to this study are discussed.

2.3   Analysis

The mechanics, dynamics and aesthetics (MDA) framework [3] is used to analyse those games aligned with the eight mindfulness factors. Mechanics refer to the lowest level of the game such as game objects and rules. Dynamics describe the run-time behaviour of mechanics, for example the translation of user input into the program and the expression of mechanics (e.g. time pressure or freedom to explore). The resulting user experience of dynamics is aesthetics and can be described by qualitative properties of game play (e.g. challenge, expression or discovery). Taking Tetris [22] as an example, this game's goal is to clear lines so that they do not stack to the top (which is game over when reaching a certain altitude). The game mechanics involve moving and rotating falling blocks so that they fill gaps to eliminate lines. The dynamics of Tetris include time pressure and increasing game speed. Its aesthetics are challenge and sensory pleasure.

Each section reports on empirical evidence that games can increase particular mindfulness factors. Furthermore, the specific mechanics, dynamics and aesthetics responsible for the effectiveness of the program are detailed to provide specific HCI recommendations.

3   Results

3.1   Mindfulness Factor 1: Awareness Towards Inner Experiences

This factor encompasses the ability to be aware of one's own experiences such as thoughts, feelings and sensations [2, 18]. It can be characterized further as interoceptive or body-awareness, which is a form of self-awareness, drawing on the ability to direct one's own attention to specific parts of the body (like the shortness of breath and tightness in the chest after seeing a big snake in the garden). The main challenge for the training of this skill within digital games is that most games create external experiences (on the screen) and do not stimulate the exploration of the player's own mind and body. Although the game creates the virtual world and is therefore aware of all aspects within it, it is difficult for the game to understand the player's inner thoughts and feelings. Therefore, the question arises whether a game that stimulates present awareness in the virtual world can transfer this ability to the player's inner world. Generally, gamers have been found to outperform non-gamers in tasks relating to executive and sustained attention [23, 24], however, those were measured by external stimuli and it remains unclear whether training external attention also trains internal attention and interoceptive awareness.

Training interoceptive awareness could be achieved by using parts or processes of one's own body as the object of concentration, for example, the breath. The practice of observing the breath (or by observing the sensations caused by the breath, for example, around the nostrils) is also an integral part of teachings in traditional Buddhist meditation (known as ānāpānasati), with the goal to 'sharpen' the mind (i.e., train concentration) before confronting own sensations deliberately [25]. One smartphone application that is based on this approach is 'Mindfulness TS' [26], which requires the user to tap the screen when breathing in and out. The mobile application 'Breathe Daily' [27] works in a similar way by instructing the user to hold the finger on the screen when inhaling and releasing when exhaling. Additionally, visual feedback is provided by a gradual change of the background colour when a finger is touching/releasing the screen. Starting from blue, the background turns into yellow and after that into blue again. Users are recommended to wait until the screen turns to its original blue again until inhaling again, providing guidance for regular breathing. Furthermore, users count their breath and slide their finger after each tenth inhalation. The background colour then turns into green or red to indicate whether the count is correct and focus was maintained successfully. A report screen at the end of 5 or 15 min meditations shows the total amount of inhales and the amount of focused key breaths.

The method of breath counting was recently evaluated in four independent studies [28] with positive results, using a digital breath counting task similar to the apps discussed above. In study one, counting accuracy was found to be associated with better mood, decreased mind-wandering and increased meta-awareness and correlated with trait mindfulness [28]. Study two revealed that the significance of mind-wandering and mood did not change after controlling with individual scores obtained from the Sustained Attention to Response Task [SART; 29], suggesting that it is not just a result of sustained attention [28]. Also, breath counting accuracy was found to be uncorrelated to working memory capacity (as measured by the automated operation span test [OSPAN; 30]), supporting the method's independence. The third study [28] found counting accuracy to be associated with less attention capture, as measured by a monetarily rewarded task in which participants had to identify/ignore targets with specific colours. The authors interpreted this result as a reduced influence of wanting, representing nonattachment (i.e., reduced craving as a state reflecting higher mindfulness [31]). The fourth study [28] confirmed the prior result that participants with an improved counting accuracy had also increased mindfulness scores, while two comparable control groups did not.

In contrast to breathing apps that help visualise the process of breathing, the discussed study evaluated the effectiveness of breath counting for mindfulness. The hypothesis that the engagement with the associated internal process of breath counting is necessary for its efficacy was recently rejected [32]. In an experimental study, three different designs for breathing apps have been tested. An audio-only design was found to be inferior to two breathing training programs that visualise the process of breathing, on both, physiological parameters (deeper breathing) and participants' self-assessment. [32]. Although mindfulness was not included as a measure, awareness of the breath was included in the questionnaire, and which revealed significant better scores for the designs with breathing visualisation [32]. A wave visualisation showing the current state (inhale/exhale) with temporal detail was found to be superior to a circle-based visualisation with two states (green/red) and a textual counter (using seconds) to indicate change [32].

Breath counting can be used to increase certain aspects of mindfulness, although the specific relationship with Awareness towards inner experiences was not explicitly investigated [28]. Though training the awareness of one's own breath as an inner experience corresponds to training inner awareness in a specific task and results showing decreased mind-wandering and increased meta-awareness suggest an increased awareness toward inner experiences in general. This application's simplicity in instruction as well as the property of minimising distractions with no visual or audio stimuli during the exercise are believed to be vital elements for its feasibility and the development of the ability of inner awareness.

Design recommendations for improving Awareness towards inner experiences include the integration of a control mechanic for the process of breathing, such as holding alternate buttons when inhaling/exhaling, and a detailed breath visualisation. If the aim is to manipulate the user's breath, then the design should also include a preview of the next change from inhale to exhale or exhale to inhale. Assessment measures could include key breaths requiring a unique user action.

3.2   Mindfulness Factor 2: Awareness Towards Outer Experiences

Awareness towards outer experiences relates to the clear perception and experience of external stimuli [2, 18], e.g. being aware of birds chirping or the different shades of green of a forest. Studies on visual attention comparing non-gamers with gamers of first-person shooters found that gamers are aware of more visual details and can distinguish subtle visual stimuli more accurately [24, 33, 34]. The games in these studies where predominantly using war scenarios (like those from the Call of Duty and Battlefield series) and the tests to measure the players' attentional skills included several versions of the Useful Field of View Task [35] in which gamers identified more visual details in a clutter, and visual discrimination tests where gamers were able to distinguish more accurately different shades of grey. Additionally, studies show that those gamers are able to track more independent moving visual objects simultaneously compared to non-gamers [23, 36, 37].

Evidence about the benefits from playing shooter games has been furthermore extended to auditory attention [38]. The administered tests were visual and auditory discrimination tasks, in which gamers outperformed non-gamers. On a simultaneity judgement task, participants had to distinguish whether stimuli were presented simultaneously or slightly offset. Additionally, on temporal order judgement tasks, participants had to determine the temporal sequence of multisensory stimuli. In all tasks gamers showed a higher performance compared to non-gamers. Therefore, it can be argued that playing shooter games increases the awareness towards outer experiences by inducing a state of alertness and training attentional skills and multisensory perception. It is believed that crucial for this process is the use of stimuli rich virtual environments that provide a very detailed representation of the real world. The player's challenge to move and focus (aim) constantly requires fast information-processing and reactions, which is believed to train awareness.

Most traditional and popular practices of mindfulness, including sitting meditation (e.g. Zazen, Vipassana), do not target the awareness of outer stimuli and instead aim to train Awareness towards inner experiences, i.e., self-awareness [31]. Conceptual considerations and statistical evidence [2] are suggesting that training inner awareness is associated with an increase in outer awareness as well, which implies that targeting outer awareness for the purpose of cultivating mindfulness through an interactive program might not be required if inner awareness is practised.

Practical recommendations for the design of programs aimed to improve Awareness towards outer experiences include the modelling of a realistic virtual world with moving objects that challenge the perception, decision-making, and dexterity of users. Limited health and consequences for under-performance may be used to increase the user's sense of alertness and presence.

3.3   Mindfulness Factor 3: Openness to Experience

This factor expresses a non-avoidant (confrontational) attitude towards experiences that is characterised by openness and curiosity [2, 18]. People scoring high on this dimension try to perceive all the richness of stimuli in their environment and don't suppress their emotions or distract themselves but deliberately direct their attention to all of them (including pain and other negative experiences). It might sound paradoxical to look for games that increase Openness to experience since one motivation for its usage is escapism, thus distraction from real world experiences. This is however only one of many motivations for playing digital games [39]. On the other hand, it could be argued that people who are open to play (various) games and engage in various virtual worlds and experiences have a high openness to experience. Prior research indicates that people with high openness to experience tend to prefer games with a high level of exploration such as role-playing games [RPGs; 40].

In the context of mindfulness, openness to experience refers to inner experiences like sensations and emotions. Interactive media that increase this trait should therefore aim to stimulate the user to try out new things and cultivate an open mind towards all kinds of experiences, even seemingly unpleasant ones. An openness to experience program might be a gamified app that poses its users daily challenges to do unusual things that they haven't done before (like for example eating an olive together with a gummy bear or walking backwards for 10 min). At the same time, instructions should be given to keep an open and non-avoidant mind while doing the task consciously. By completing challenges, in-app awards could be offered e.g. stars could be earned, and the player's status increased and more challenges unlocked. The drawback of such a game is the issue of preventing users from cheating by falsely stating that challenges were completed.

An already available mobile application that uses an approach similar to described above is the 'Positive Activity Jackpot' [41]. Designed as a slot machine, users choose a category and press the lever, which spins a 'wheel of fortune' of activities. The resulting activity can be chosen or another spin can be made. After selecting an activity the program asks the user where the activity should be done and if the user wants to invite friends to the activity. Finally, the app recommends the user to schedule the activity in his/her personal calendar.

The Positive Activity Jackpot uses the Pleasant Events Schedule [PES; 42] technique that helps people with mental illness (such as depression) by reinforcing positive behaviour. Users, however, are also allowed to deactivate individual activities from the list and add own activities. Additionally, the application provides an augmented reality (AR) mode that lets the user hold the device like a camera and shows possible positive activities and places in the near environment (e.g. parks and museums). The Positive Activity Jackpot is believed to be a promising candidate to increase this mindfulness factor, however activities should be selected that improve the openness to inner experiences instead of outer experiences that are likely to be used as a distraction from internal discomfort. The beneficial key mechanic of this app is encouraging users to perform novel tasks for interoceptive awareness in a playful way.

Openness to experience might be well suited to be combined with Awareness towards inner experiences. By using a proven program that increases the skill of interoceptive awareness (for example a breath counting game), it could be extended to improve the attitude of openness as well. Game elements to achieve this goal might include priming instructions and rewards for spotting and enduring experiential states. In addition to that, opportunities to collect in-game rewards by doing daily challenges will encourage some users to engage for longer with the game. Design implications for improving Openness to experience comprise of gamified activities that stimulate inner exploration. The use of gambling elements, such as a wheel of fortune or a slot machine mechanic, intriguing sound effects, and tactile stimuli, enhance the motivation and engagement in use.

3.4   Mindfulness Factor 4: Decentering

Decentering refers to the ability to experience non-reactively [2, 18], e.g. not trying to control an emotion or not trying to engage in cognition. Thoughts, emotions or sensations are perceived as detached (i.e., non-identifying with them).

Chittaro and Vianello [43] have developed an app called AEON to train decentering or thought distancing (that is observing thoughts in a non-judgemental way and without identification). Users are asked to formulate and type in a (worrisome) thought into the program, which is then displayed on a neutral background. By touching and swiping the screen, ripples on the water (above the thought) are animated accompanied by water sounds. The longer a user swipes the screen, the more the visualised thought fades away. By watching the thought disappear, the authors suggest that thought distancing and mindfulness is practiced.

AEON was tested on 22 undergraduate students, where the interactive application has been compared to two other non-digital practices of thought distancing. The first control group task was a mental cloud imagery task [44] in which participants were asked to imagine their thoughts on flying clouds and (mentally) observe how they fly away. In the second control condition participants were asked to perform a card-tossing exercise [45], which instructs participants to write down their thought on index cards and then look at them one at a time and toss them into a basket. Measured by the 7-item Decentering sub-scale from the Toronto Mindfulness Scale [46], AEON achieved significantly higher scores compared to the card-tossing task but not to the cloud-imagery exercise. The authors explain this result by suggesting that AEON is better than the card-tossing task to sustain attention on the thoughts and work on their perception instead on the process of throwing them away. Attention, however, was not measured in this study. The non-significant difference between AEON and the cloud-imagery exercise might be due to the similar nature of both applications. The difficulty was perceived lowest for the interactive smartphone app, which the authors attribute to the computational off-loading by the app, thus decreasing cognitive load by externalising the mental process of keeping in mind a particular thought. Thought distancing apps similar to AEON use different metaphors. While AEON [43] visualises thoughts and lets them slowly disappear in the water, other apps shred negative experiences or shoot them with a rocket into the universe.

Mobile applications like AEON may be a feasible approach to increase Decentering. Recommendations for HCI and mindfulness are deduced from its functional design. The mechanic of the AEON app to enter a troubling thought and watching how it disappears has been found to be effective in the initial evaluation study [43]. However, its dynamics and aesthetics might play an important role as well, since the time watching a troubling thought slowly disappear is controlled by the user's swiping speed. The control, and with it the association of the content to the self ("my thought"), and the representation of slowly fading text (in a calm and visually enjoyable way), are believed to enhance the process of decentering.

3.5 Mindfulness Factor 5: Acceptance

This dimension of mindfulness portrays the encounter of experiences with an accepting attitude and without judgement, e.g., good or bad [2, 18]. Moreover, it involves a self-compassionate orientation towards one self (e.g. being kind with one self in difficult situations) such that personal mistakes are accepted without blame and resentment. The name of this factor is therefore somewhat confusing, since it refers to self-acceptance in particular rather than general acceptance.

McEwan et al. [47] studied the effect of facial cues on self-criticism, which is an outcome behaviour of low self-compassion and acceptance. The measure for self-criticism that was used is the Forms of Self-criticism/reassurance Scale [FSCRS; 48], which measures self-criticism vs self-reassuring of which the latter is identical to the Acceptance factor. The stimulus set that was developed for this study is currently being tested in a self-compassion game, which is believed to be an effective candidate to increase Acceptance in the context of mindfulness. Results show improved measures of self-reported well-being including self-criticism [49]. In this game's evaluation study [49], 125 participants played the game for over two weeks for 5 min daily. Results revealed a significant increase in self-criticism and self-reassurance (the equivalent to Acceptance) after playing the compassion game. The effect was maintained after a follow-up period of one month.

The game by McEwan et al. [49] to increase self-compassion has been found to be effective, and may be feasible to increase Acceptance in the context of mindfulness. Its game mechanic presents the user with a 4 × 4 matrix of faces of which one has a compassionate expression while all others are critical, and instructs the user to click on a compassionate face as quickly as possible. Design implications comprise an element of repeated training to shift the user's attention towards accepting positive emotional stimulus, while ignoring other negative stimuli. Time pressure, point systems and leader boards are believed to increase motivation and performance.

3.6   Mindfulness Factor 6: Relativity of Thoughts and Beliefs

This construct draws upon the recognition that thoughts and beliefs do not possess universal truth but are completely subjective and might not always correspond to reality [2, 18]. Thus, people scoring high on this dimension would recognise that their evaluations about situations and other people can easily change. It also means that one is not taking one's thoughts too seriously for they are "only" thoughts.

A game-based approach to increase Relativity of thoughts and beliefs might be to put the player in the shoes of somebody who perceives the world differently. Interpreting reality as a virtual character might promote realisation that there are different realities and that beliefs are subjective as well. In the text-based adventure game 'Depression Quest' [50] players control a depressed avatar and experience events through his/her eyes. Furthermore, the game shows the limitations of actions that result from the avatars interpretations of reality. While Depression Quest is a good example for confronting players with different thoughts and beliefs, the content of the game is generally negative and thus might also have negative effects to the players' psychological wellbeing.

Illustrating human susceptibility to false beliefs can be achieved by the experience of illusions. Visual illusions in particular are often used in classes of cognitive psychology to show students how the manipulation of attention and beliefs alter perceptions. In 'The Bridge' [51] players have to walk through different levels that look like visual mazes to reach the exit door. Perspective and presentation of forms is often ambiguous and stimulates the player's interpretation of the game world. Controls of The Bridge comprise the avatar's movement and rotation of the world. Letting players experience the relativity of perception and misinterpretation of situations is believed to increase the mindfulness factor Relativity of thoughts and beliefs.

Training Relativity of thoughts with digital games has not been undertaken and any research in this field will be pioneering. Taking a virtual avatar's perspective and experiencing illusions is believed to influence this factor positively through the development of experiential knowledge about the volatility of thoughts and beliefs.

HCI recommendations comprise the use of ambiguous visual stimuli to stimulate interpretation and self-reflection. As in The Bridge, a stylized cartoonish visual style may be appropriate, which allows easy manipulation of forms and shapes to create a visual illusion.

3.7   Mindfulness Factor 7: Insightful Understanding

Insight derives from understanding that the quality of an experience is influenced by its subjective evaluation [2, 18]. Seeing through the link between evaluation and perception makes it easier to spot negative cognitions that might cause catastrophic interpretation of situations (e.g. getting very sad or angry because of a small challenge), hence making it possible to counter-act (for example by just smiling, taking a deep breath and re-assessing the situation). It is probably this very insight which causes the defusion of (highly intensive) thoughts and emotions, which is supported by the fact that this factor was found to have the highest correlation with emotion regulation in the preliminary version of the CHIME questionnaire [18].

In the game 'Dinner Date' [52] the player is in the role of the subconsciousness of his avatar Julian who is waiting for his date to arrive. The player is forced to observe all the thoughts and worries of Julian as time passes by and nobody arrives. In Dinner Date, all thoughts of the protagonist are verbalised and the player cannot avoid them. This game is believed to influence the mindfulness factor Insightful understanding because the player is actively confronted to hear worries from a third-person perspective and by doing that, seeing through its exaggerated absurdity. Although insightful, this game might be problematic when intended to be used for cultivating mindfulness because of the negative nature of the content.

A positive version of this general idea, spiced with a substantial amount of humour, is the game 'Octodad: Dadliest Catch' [53]. The player impersonates Octodad, the protagonist of the game, who is an octopus, masquerading as a human. This means that everyday human tasks have to be performed with tentacles instead of hands and legs, which is both difficult and funny, with controls made intentionally clumsy. It is believed that the humour derived from mistakes in the game can be transferred to the player's personal perspective on life, thus playing Octodad might increase Insightful understanding. This claim, however, needs yet to be verified.

No scientific exploration has been conducted to research the intersection between games and Insightful understanding. To influence this factor, the game Octodad is believed to be a promising approach by making the player see life with ease. Implications for design focus around the unique characteristic of Octodad. The key effective element of this game is believed to be its dynamics, which is the challenge of control that cause unintended results (damage in the game world), while the system is very forgiving. This takes out the seriousness of the interaction and facilitates a humorous experience.

3.8 Mindfulness Factor 8: Acting with Awareness

Central to this factor is that the mental focus stays in the moment and does not wander away to reflections about the past or predictions about the future, thus being fully conscious of the here and now [2, 18]. It implies a high level of concentration with everything that is performed and indirectly refers to a high performance by not being distracted with thinking.

For the purpose of sustaining focus, 'ReWire' [54] was developed as a support tool for mindfulness meditation practice. It addresses the significant challenge for meditators, especially novice meditators, which is keeping the mind from wandering off (i.e., keeping sustained attention on the current experiences). ReWire is used during meditation and the meditator places the smartphone on his/her lap and wears earphones. The app plays music and at random short intervals the music slowly fades out and when it completely disappears, the user must tap the screen (causing the music to slowly fade in again). If the user does not notice the fade out of the music the smartphone vibrates. In this way the program sustains and controls for a level of presence and alertness. It can happen that the meditator's mind wanders off and is not being noticed for a relatively long time (i.e., dreaming away). ReWire makes the practice of meditation more effective by shortening these times of unawareness so that the process of observing experiences non-judgementally can be given more time. This second process has been shown to be the key beneficial mechanism in mindfulness practice [55].

Attention has been studied extensively in cognitive psychology and a wide range of measures and tasks have been developed. The general mechanics have been redesigned Gamification, however, usually does not go beyond adding points (and a player score) and leader boards. Furthermore, it is unclear whether training attentional control in an abstract virtual context transfers into real-world applications.

The method of not altering the breath with a defined pattern, but observing it naturally while counting breaths, was already tested [28], as described in Mindfulness factor 1: Awareness towards inner experiences. The ongoing cognitive demand for counting breaths requires the participant to sustain a focused attention and its practice was found to significantly decrease mind-wandering [28], which is a symptom of inattention. Therefore, breath counting, as a method for counter-conditioning the mind from being susceptible to distraction and thereby training focus, is believed to be a valuable method to train Acting with awareness in the context of mindfulness.

With already proven beneficial effects on attention, shooter games in general might be suitable to increase the factor Acting with awareness. Comparing gamers of action video games (predominantly first person shooter games) with non-gamers, gamers were found to be better at resisting attentional capture [56]. The conducted experiment used a target search task in which gamers responded quicker than non-gamers in all conditions, suggesting that these gamers were more successful in ignoring distractions and thus showed a better executive control. Findings of this study furthermore show that the beneficial effects are extended to exogenous (bottom-up) attentional control as opposed to only an endogenous mechanism (top-down), implying the successful transfer of the skill to other domains. These findings are supported by another study, which used the steady-state visual evoked potentials technique to investigate the neural functioning of attention in action gamers and non-gamers [57]. Participants viewed multiple streams of rapid sequences of alphanumeric stimuli presented at different distinct temporal frequencies, which evokes independent brain signals and allows tracking brain activation of both attended and unattended streams. The gamers were more efficient at suppressing the distracting streams than non-gamers in this attention-demanding task, supporting prior findings of action shooter games increasing focus. In another study, using the Test of Variables of Attention (T.O.V.A.™) confirmed the positive effect of action video games on sustained attention [58]. In this experiment, gamers responded quicker to targets, while being no less accurate, and showing at the same time no difference in impulsivity (withholding a response to a non-target).

Approaches exist that can train attention to achieve general concentration that is associated with the mindfulness factor of Acting with awareness. Research on action video games (especially shooters) yields very promising results to train the desired

Table 1. Effective training aspects of interactive media to increase mindfulness. Disaggregated accordingly to the MDA framework [3].

Mindfulness factor	Evaluated programs	Training aspect	Game design recommendations		
			Mechanics	Dynamics	Aesthetics
1 Awareness towards inner experiences, 8 Acting with awareness	Awareness online [28], breathing training visualisations [32]	Keeping interoceptive attention through ongoing cognitive demand by counting breaths	Single button input (/tap) by user for each inhale/exhale, every 10th time different button has to be pushed	Warm-up block (tutorial) provided, key breaths (10th) used to calculate accuracy score	Awareness Online: Visual feedback on tap (in warm-up). Breathe daily app only: Visual feedback (fading colours) indicate inhale/exhale Breathing training: Animated wave form design
2 Awareness towards outer experiences	Action/shooter games [23, 24, 33, 34, 36–38]	Training multisensory perception through stimuli rich virtual environments	Players have a weapon with which they have to shoot enemies. Limited health and ammo	Aiming is challenging, constant movement is required to not get shot. Sensory challenge through vast amount of stimuli, requiring fast information-processing and reactions	Very detailed (realistic) representation of the world
3 Openness to experience	Modified version of the Positive Activity Jackpot (untested)	Encouraging users to perform novel tasks for interoceptive awareness	User pulls the lever, slot machine starts spinning, activity (task to increase interoceptive awareness) gets drawn. Users confirm activity (and schedule it in calendar)	Spinning slot machine creates sense of excitement and luck	Spinning animation is accompanied by authentic sound and vibration pattern of the phone. Users can choose to swipe instead of tap the lever (natural behaviour)
4 Decentering	AEON [43]	Watching a visualised thought or emotion fading out	User enters text, text is displayed, text disappears by swiping	Disappearing of text is gradual to total length of swipe, sound (water ripple on touch)	Calm backgrounds (e.g. sand), animated water surface, disappearing of

(Continued)

Table 1. (*Continued*)

Mindfulness factor	Evaluated programs	Training aspect	Game design recommendations		
			Mechanics	Dynamics	Aesthetics
					text by gradual black to transparent fade.
5 Acceptance	Compassion game [49]	Training Acceptance through cognitive bias modification	User is presented with a 4 × 4 matrix of faces of which one has a compassionate expression while all others are critical. User is instructed to click on the compassionate face as quickly as possible	After user input, next matrix of faces is presented. Challenge is created by a sense of time pressure	All faces are monochrome
6 Relativity of thoughts and beliefs	The Bridge (untested)	Demonstrating volatility of thoughts and beliefs through visual-illusionary experiences	Player navigates through an ambiguous 2D world. Player is allowed to rotate the world	Sensory challenge through ambiguous interpretation of architecture	Monochrome cartoonish world
7 Insightful understanding	Octodad: Dadliest Catch (untested)	Making the player see life with ease and humour	Player impersonates an octopus with tentacles with which everyday tasks (e.g. walking) have to be executed	Very challenging controls cause unintended results (/damage), system is forgiving	Presentation of narrative and gameplay is humorous
8 Acting with awareness	Action/shooter games [11, 56–58]	Training sustained and focused attention through the presentation of context-relevant stimuli in virtual worlds	The system provides many clear objects of interest whose focus upon is vital for the player	Game objects are not static but moving (and shooting)	Very detailed (realistic) representation of the world

attentional skills that are associated with Acting with awareness. In further support of this assumption are the results of a study showing that gamers of this genre show increased mindfulness scores for present-centred awareness compared to other genres [11].

To address implications for HCI, the common property of those games is the presentation of context-relevant stimuli (mechanic) in very detailed virtual worlds (aesthetics). The system provides many clear objects of interest, where focus is vital for the player, and game objects are not static but moving (and shooting), which is believed to be the key dynamic that enhances focused and sustained attention.

4 Summary

This study reviewed digital games and interactive applications for the context of mindfulness interventions, as well as smartphone apps and games to increase mindfulness or skills and states related to this concept. Relevant programs were investigated for each individual mindfulness factor. A summary, including the specific mechanics, dynamics and aesthetics that influence each individual mindfulness factor, is presented in Table 1.

In general, the field of 'mindful gaming' lacks scientific evaluation, however provides huge potential due to its high accessibility and motivation through design. No single game could be identified to train more than two mindfulness factors and be easy to use and engaging at the same time. Thus, developing a game to train all factors of mindfulness will be an original and innovative contribution to the fields of mindfulness research and human computer interaction. The results of this study are believed to contribute to this endeavour, to which the authors invite fellow game developers to join.

References

1. Plaza, I., Demarzo, M.M.P., Herrera-Mercadal, P., García-Campayo, J.: Mindfulness-based mobile applications: literature review and analysis of current features. JMIR Mhealth Uhealth **1**(2), e24 (2013)
2. Bergomi, C., Tschacher, W., Kupper, Z.: Konstruktion und erste validierung eines fragebogens zur umfassenden erfassung von achtsamkeit. Diagnostica **60**(3), 111–125 (2014)
3. Hunicke, R., LeBlanc, M., Zubek, R.: MDA: A formal approach to game design and game research. In: Proceedings of the AAAI Workshop on Challenges in Game AI (2004)
4. Cahn, B.R., Polich, J.: Meditation states and traits: EEG, ERP, and neuroimaging studies. Psychol. Bull. **132**(2), 180 (2006)
5. Lomas, T., Cartwright, T., Edginton, T., Ridge, D.: A qualitative analysis of experiential challenges associated with meditation practice. Mindfulness **6**, 1–13 (2014)
6. Sherry, J.L.: Flow and media enjoyment. Commun. Theor. **14**(4), 328–347 (2004)
7. Gackenbach, J.: Video game play and consciousness development: a transpersonal perspective. J. Transpersonal Psychol. **40**(1), 60–87 (2008)

8. Brand, J.E., Lorentz, P., Mathew, T.: Digital Australia 2014. Bond University, Queensland (2014)
9. Kabat-Zinn, J.: Wherever You Go, There You Are: Mindfulness Meditation in Everyday Life. Hyperion, New York (1994)
10. Sweetser, P., Wyeth, P.: GameFlow: a model for evaluating player enjoyment in games. Comput. Entertainment (CIE) **3**(3), 3 (2005)
11. Gackenbach, J., Bown, J.: Mindfulness and video game play: a preliminary inquiry. Mindfulness **2**(2), 114–122 (2011)
12. Pearson, C., Hussain, Z.: Smartphone use, addiction, narcissism, and personality: a mixed methods investigation. Int. J. Cyber Behav. Psychol. Learn. (IJCBPL) **5**(1), 17–32 (2015)
13. Brown, K.W., Ryan, R.M., Creswell, J.D.: Mindfulness: theoretical foundations and evidence for its salutary effects. Psychol. Inquiry **18**(4), 211–237 (2007)
14. Brown, K.W., Ryan, R.M.: The benefits of being present: mindfulness and its role in psychological well-being. J. Pers. Soc. Psychol. **84**(4), 822 (2003)
15. Linehan, M.M.: Cognitive-Behavioral Treatment of Borderline Personality Disorder. Guilford Press, New York (1993)
16. Bishop, S.R., Lau, M., Shapiro, S., Carlson, L., Anderson, N.D., Carmody, J., Segal, Z.V., Abbey, S., Speca, M., Velting, D.: Mindfulness: a proposed operational definition. Clin. psychol.: Sci. Pract. **11**(3), 230–241 (2004)
17. Park, T., Reilly-spong, M., Gross, C.R.: Mindfulness: a systematic review of instruments to measure an emergent patient-reported outcome (PRO). Qual. Life Res. **22**(10), 2639–2659 (2013)
18. Bergomi, C., Tschacher, W., Kupper, Z.: Measuring mindfulness: first steps towards the development of a comprehensive mindfulness scale. Mindfulness **4**(1), 18–32 (2013)
19. Kitson, A., Riecke, B.E., Vidyarthi, J.: Sonic cradle: investigating meditative aspects of an interactive technology (2014)
20. Shaw, C.D., Gromala, D., Seay, A.F.: The meditation chamber: enacting autonomic senses. In: Proceedings of ENACTIVE/07 (2007)
21. Long, K., Vines, J.: Mind pool: encouraging self-reflection through ambiguous bio-feedback. In: CHI 2013 Extended Abstracts on Human Factors in Computing Systems, ACM (2013)
22. Pajitnov, A.: Tetris (1984)
23. Boot, W.R., Kramer, A.F., Simons, D.J., Fabiani, M., Gratton, G.: The effects of video game playing on attention, memory, and executive control. Acta Psychol. **129**(3), 387–398 (2008)
24. Green, C.S., Bavelier, D.: Action video game modifies visual selective attention. Nature **423**(6939), 534–537 (2003)
25. Gilpin, R.: The use of Theravāda Buddhist practices and perspectives in mindfulness-based cognitive therapy. Contemp. Buddhism **9**(2), 227–251 (2008)
26. Mindfulapps. Mindfulness TS (2013). https://play.google.com/store/apps/details?id=com.rep.MindFul
27. Mu Studios. Breathe Daily (2013). https://itunes.apple.com/us/app/id659230503
28. Levinson, D.B., Stoll, E.L., Kindy, S.D., Merry, H.L., Davidson, R.J.: A mind you can count on: validating breath counting as a behavioral measure of mindfulness. Front. Psychol. **5**, 1202 (2014)
29. Robertson, I.H., Manly, T., Andrade, J., Baddeley, B.T., Yiend, J.: 'Oops!': performance correlates of everyday attentional failures in traumatic brain injured and normal subjects. Neuropsychologia **35**(6), 747–758 (1997)
30. Unsworth, N., Heitz, R.P., Schrock, J.C., Engle, R.W.: An automated version of the operation span task. Behav. Res. Methods **37**(3), 498–505 (2005)

31. Hart, W.: The art of living: Vipassana meditation as taught by SN Goenka. Pariyatti, Onalaska (2011)
32. Chittaro, L., Sioni, R.: Evaluating mobile apps for breathing training: The effectiveness of visualization. Comput. Hum. Behav. **40**, 56–63 (2014)
33. Green, C.S., Bavelier, D.: Learning, attentional control, and action video games. Curr. Biol. **22**(6), R197–R206 (2012)
34. Bavelier, D., Davidson, R.J.: Brain training: games to do you good. Nature **494**(7438), 425–426 (2013)
35. Ball, K.K., Beard, B.L., Roenker, D.L., Miller, R.L., Griggs, D.S.: Age and visual search: expanding the useful field of view. JOSA A **5**(12), 2210–2219 (1988)
36. Green, C.S., Bavelier, D.: Enumeration versus multiple object tracking: the case of action video game players. Cognition **101**(1), 217–245 (2006)
37. Trick, L.M., Jaspers-Fayer, F., Sethi, N.: Multiple-object tracking in children: The "Catch the Spies" task. Cogn. Dev. **20**(3), 373–387 (2005)
38. Donohue, S.E., Woldorff, M.G., Mitroff, S.R.: Video game players show more precise multisensory temporal processing abilities. Atten. Percept. Psychophys. **72**(4), 1120–1129 (2010)
39. Yee, N.: Motivations for play in online games. CyberPsychology Behav. **9**(6), 772–775 (2006)
40. Johnson, D., Gardner, J.: Personality, motivation and video games. In: Proceedings of the 22nd Conference of the Computer-Human Interaction Special Interest Group of Australia on Computer-Human Interaction, ACM (2010)
41. T2. Positive Activity Jackpot (2014). https://play.google.com/store/apps/details?id=t2.paj
42. MacPhillamy, D.J., Lewinsohn, P.M.: The pleasant events schedule: studies on reliability, validity, and scale intercorrelation. J. Consult. Clin. Psychol. **50**(3), 363 (1982)
43. Chittaro, L., Vianello, A.: Computer-supported mindfulness: evaluation of a mobile thought distancing application on naive meditators. Int. J. Hum. Comput. Stud. **72**(3), 337–348 (2014)
44. Wells, A.: Detached mindfulness in cognitive therapy: a metacognitive analysis and ten techniques. J. Rational-Emot. Cognitive-Behav. Ther. **23**(4), 337–355 (2005)
45. Leahy, R.L.: The worry cure: stop worrying and start living. Hachette, UK (2012)
46. Lau, M.A., Bishop, S.R., Segal, Z.V., Buis, T., Anderson, N.D., Carlson, L., Shapiro, S., Carmody, J., Abbey, S., Devins, G.: The toronto mindfulness scale: development and validation. J. Clin. Psychol. **62**(12), 1445–1467 (2006)
47. McEwan, K., Gilbert, P., Dandeneau, S., Lipka, S., Maratos, F., Paterson, K.B., Baldwin, M.: Facial expressions depicting compassionate and critical emotions: the development and validation of a new emotional face stimulus set. PLoS ONE **9**(2), e88783 (2014)
48. Gilbert, P., Clarke, M., Hempel, S., Miles, J., Irons, C.: Criticizing and reassuring oneself: an exploration of forms, styles and reasons in female students. Br. J. Clin. Psychol. **43**(1), 31–50 (2004)
49. McEwan, K., Gilbert, P., Dandeneau, S., Maratos, F., Gibbons, L., Chotai, S., Elander, J.: Evaluations of a 'Compassion Game' to promote wellbeing. In: Preparation
50. Quinn, Z.: Depression Quest (2013)
51. The Quantum Astrophysicists Guild. The Bridge (2013)
52. Stout Games. Dinner Date (2011)
53. Young Horses. Octodad: Dadliest Catch (2014)
54. Redmer, M.: ReWire (2013). https://itunes.apple.com/us/app/rewire/id529696522?mt=8
55. Kang, Y., Gruber, J., Gray, J.R.: Mindfulness and de-automatization. Emot. Rev. **5**(2), 192–201 (2013)

56. Chisholm, J.D., Hickey, C., Theeuwes, J., Kingstone, A.: Reduced attentional capture in action video game players. Atten. Percept. Psychophys. **72**(3), 667–671 (2010)
57. Mishra, J., Zinni, M., Bavelier, D., Hillyard, S.A.: Neural basis of superior performance of action videogame players in an attention-demanding task. J. Neurosci. **31**(3), 992–998 (2011)
58. Dye, M.W., Green, C.S., Bavelier, D.: Increasing speed of processing with action video games. Curr. Dir. Psychol. Sci. **18**(6), 321–326 (2009)

The Affordances of Broken Affordances

Martin Gielsgaard Grünbaum and Jakob Grue Simonsen[(✉)]

Department of Computer Science, University of Copenhagen (DIKU),
Njalsgade 128-132, 2300 Copenhagen S, Denmark
{grunbaum, simonsen}@diku.dk

Abstract. We consider the use of physical and virtual objects having one or more affordances associated to simple interactions with them. Based on Kaptelinin and Nardi's notion of instrumental affordance, we investigate what it means to break an affordance, and the two ensuing questions we deem most important: how users may (i) achieve their goals in the presence of such broken affordances, and may (ii) repurpose or otherwise interact with artefacts with broken affordances. We argue that (A) thorough analyses of breakdowns of affordances and their associated signifiers and feedbacks have implication for design, particularly so for virtual artefacts, and that (B) there is a largely unexplored design space for designing, and redesigning objects with broken affordances, rather than broken or decayed objects.

Keywords: Affordances · Technology affordances · Mediated action · Breakdown · Design

1 Introduction

Affordance is a ubiquitous term in interaction design whose– very rough and high-level–meaning designers seem to have an understanding of, but whose precise semantics has been the subject of intense refinement, discussion, and disagreement [7, 8, 12, 14, 18, 20–22, 26, 30–32, 34]. Regardless of the specific semantics, awareness of, and manipulation of, affordances is used in practice by designers. In addition, specific interpretations of "affordance" may be used for analysis of the properties of an artefact, for example–as suggested in [18] for uncovering usability problems in finished products or prototypes, and hence employed in re-design. In a different vein of research, the interaction and design opportunities for objects that are working, broken down or otherwise damaged, have recently been the subject of intense scrutiny with researchers starting to explore the design space around objects that are already broken, or even deliberately designing both physical and virtual objects with broken or decayed parts [15–17, 19, 24, 27]. The aim of this paper is to explore and analyze the implications of a designer–deliberately or inadvertently–breaking one or more affordances of an object—as opposed to breaking the object itself. We posit that among the many extant definitions of affordance, only some are operational in the sense that they allow for non-trivial analysis, and experimental exploration, of breakage, and we take our departure in the notion of *instrumental technology affordance* [18] and its constituent elements of handling affordance and effecter affordance. Through analysis of the

© IFIP International Federation for Information Processing 2015
J. Abascal et al. (Eds.): INTERACT 2015, Part III, LNCS 9298, pp. 185–202, 2015.
DOI: 10.1007/978-3-319-22698-9_13

difference between breaking affordances of physical and virtual, and through two explorative experiments, we reach two conclusions: (A) that systematically breaking the different facets of instrumental affordances, either by thought experiment or by prototyping, can be a useful tool for analyzing and refining interface design, and (B) that there is an untapped design space to be explored in breaking affordances as part of deliberate design of objects that are not intended to be ephemeral; and that this design space is distinct from one where brokenness is a quality of the object. Space constraints prevent us from treating all the reasonable variations of the difficult concepts of affordance and brokenness, from treating the notions of physical and virtual as anything but mutually exclusive. We are convinced that our analysis, and our assessment of the possibilities of the design space of brokenness, may be extended to encompass many of these variations.

1.1   Related Work

Previous studies have investigated user interaction and coping with broken (hardware) interfaces [27], investigating continued use and re-purposing of damaged artefacts, and have explored design possibilities [13]. Ikemiya and Rosner [15] investigate design strategies using deliberate wear and degradation of objects to explore how to use breakage and wear to inform and cultivate design practices. Jackson and Kang [16], and Kang et al. [17] investigate interactions with broken and discarded technologies by letting artists explore disassembly, reassembly and design, and having people playfully interact with the resulting artworks. However, none of these studies analyze the strategies of users when interacting with specific broken affordances, or the differences between broken affordances in physical and virtual objects. A related vein of research considers digital heirlooms and virtual objects with which users have emotional attachment, e.g. Kirk and Sellen [19] and Odom et al. [24], but consider mostly data (e.g., electronic diaries or photographs) rather than technological mediators such as programs, making for a very different set of affordances; in this vein of research, Gulotta et al. mention the mostly untapped design space of using wear or decay on virtual objects [11], but from an aesthetic perspective rather than treating breakdown or obsolescence of affordances. De Souza, Prates and Carey [6] consider the actions of users missing affordances (essentially equivalent to users not perceiving affordances intended by designers, and equivalent to the defective signifiers treated later in this paper) and declining affordances (deliberately not acting on affordances intended by designers). Finally, Oshlyansky et al. [25] investigate the effect of culture on perception of and interaction with affordances, but do not consider deliberate breakage.

2   Affordances in HCI and Other Disciplines

The psychologist J.J. Gibson first coined the term "affordance" [9, 10] as part of an ecological alternative to cognitive perception. Cognitive perception posits that an individual only has direct access to sensations, and that those sensations are integrated with memories, which in turn build up symbolic representations of the environment and its potential for goal-oriented action [7]. Ecological perception, on the other hand, suggests that the environment is not merely a physical environment. In ecological perception, an individual collects information from a meaning-laden environment, which provides, amongst other things, affordances. Gibson wrote that "The affordances of the environment are what it offers the animal, what it provides or furnishes, either for good or ill" [10, p. 127]. Several post-Gibsonian definitions were proposed in eco-logical perception (see, e.g., [5, 29, 32]).

2.1 Affordances in Human-Computer Interaction

Norman applied the term "affordances" to everyday artefacts in his book "The Psy-chology of Everyday Things" [21] as part of an attempt to understand how humans manage in a world with thousands of objects, many of which we encounter only once. In later clarification, Norman calls his original affordances "perceived affordances" [22]. In this view, roughly, "affordances are the fundamental", actual properties of an object that define how it can be physically interacted with. These properties are rela-tional properties of the environment, that exist independently of whether a particular user perceives them or not. In contrast, "Perceived affordances" are actions that a user perceives to be possible and meaningful. These perceived affordances inhere solely in the user, but can be "encouraged" or suggested through good design. Under this–strict–view of a perceived affordance, it is not possible for an external agent to create or add a perceived affordance, as these depend solely on the user's perception of the situation and not what is actually possible. Gaver explores the notion of affordances and the role of perception and context [7], separating affordances from their perception, and accounts for 'complex' affordances through exploration and sequential/nested affor-dances. To Gaver, the perception of affordances is determined in part by the observer's culture, social setting, experience and intentions [7]. After Norman and Gaver, many authors have attempted to clarify or re-conceptualize the notion of affordance in technology and interaction (a sample: [7, 14, 20–22, 26, 29–32]). We briefly treat some of the most influential of these. McGrenere and Ho detail the differences between Gibson's and Norman's notions of affordance and argue for a grading of the presence of affordances rather than a binary view where the affordance is either there or not, and advocate separating affordances from the perception of them. Bærentsen and Trettvik suggest using activity theory for conceptualizing affordances and advocate using a much more general and encompassing notion of activity than earlier work. Turner [31] suggests expanding the notion of affordance to cover both the classic Gibsonian notion of affordance and the context of use. Conceived from a socio-cultural approach inspired by Vygotsky [35] and theoretically grounded in mediated action, Kaptelinin and Nardi argue that Gibson's concept of affordances is purposefully limited in scope; they hold that the limited focus of Gibson's affordances fits into his conceptual framework of ecological psychology, a framework which is difficult to work within for HCI [18].

2.2   The Instrumental Affordances of Kaptelinin and Nardi

Kaptelinin and Nardi identify tool usage as a particularly problematic area of the Gibsonian view in which tools are presented as part of the animal-environment system. Kaptelinin and Nardi [18] find this insufficient for three reasons (i) Gibson does not recognize that the facets of a tool may be independent of one another, particularly in technology, (ii) Gibson's affordances do not deal with the social aspects that may occur through use and production of tools, and (iii) in Gibson's view, tool usage is unrelated to the capabilities of the actor.

In the mediated action perspective, technology (tools) can be a mediational means between an actor and the environment, in the pursuit of a goal. If we think of technology as an instrument, Kaptelinin and Nardi suggest that such an instrument offers two related facets: (a) possibilities for interacting with the technology, handling affordances; and (b) possibilities for using the technology to cause an effect on an object, effecter affordances. These two facets define Kaptelinin and Nardi's instrumental technology affordances: possibilities for acting through technology on an object. For example: a pair of scissors offers an instrumental affordance of cutting, consisting of a handling affordance (scissor handle) and an effecter affordance (the blade of the scissor). This concept extends to virtual technologies as well. For example: a scroll-bar offers dragging either horizontally or vertically (handling affordance), and this typically scrolls an object of interest, e.g. by moving what part of something is visible appropriately (effecter affordance). More generally, software widgets are comprised of these two facets: a handling affordance for interacting with the widget, and an effecter affordance which is the consequence of interacting with the widget.

Kaptelinin and Nardi distinguish between instrumental affordances as defined above, auxiliary affordances "determined by the embeddedness of a technology in 'webs of mediators' typical of real-life uses of technology [4], and learning affordances. Examples of auxiliary affordances are maintenance and aggregation affordances concerned respectively with the maintenance of objects and the possibility of actions afforded by several objects acting in concert (e.g., a mobile phone connected to a headset). Learning affordances are the affordances of objects by which users understand how to act on instrumental and auxiliary affordances, for example tooltips, standardized icons, or embedded manuals in software.

We stress that the notion of instrumental affordance is *operational* in the following sense: the separation of instrumental and auxiliary affordances, and further subdivision of instrumental affordance into handling and effecter affordance allows for separate design considerations to be made to each of the constituent parts. We believe that this clear subdivision (a) more readily affords analysis and possibilities of re-design than the psychology-focused approaches of both the earlier Gibsonian notions and the later refined work by several authors (see [20, 30] for related discussions), (b) is better specified and well-grounded than the ground-breaking, but early, approaches of Norman [21–23] and Gaver [7], and (c) complements earlier operationally-oriented approaches to interface design that did not specifically focus on affordances, for instance [3].

3   Making Perception Explicit

Whereas perception does not play an explicit role in the model of Kaptelinin and Nardi, the user's perception of instrumental affordances becomes a tricky issue when devising an operational definition of breaking (see Sect. 4); we now briefly discuss and make the issue of perception explicit. It is fruitful to consider the typical timeline involved in the activation of an affordance: the user needs to perceive the presence of the affordance (and, consciously or not identify it correctly), whereupon the user activates the handling affordance, which subsequently activates the associated effecter affordance, and finally the user receives feedback. Thus, temporally:

Perceive and understand signifier(s) → *Activate handling affordance* → *(effecter affordance)* → *Receive feedback*

The parentheses around effecter affordance above are a reminder that the effecter affordance need not be directly perceivable to the user. We stress that the above simplified sequence can be replaced by more refined models of interaction, for example by Norman's classic Stages of Action model [21]. The word "signifier" here means the cues to the user about the entire instrumental affordance; more fine-grained notions exist, for example Vermeulen et al., though not working within Kaptelinin and Nardi's framework, consider signifier to–roughly–mean cues about the handling affordance and feed-forward to mean cues about the effecter affordance [33]. For some affordances, there may be no perceivable difference between some of the steps above: for example, in a soda vending machine there is the instrumental affordance of seeing a button with the desired soda and recognizing it as such (signifier), pushing the button (handling affordance) and receiving a soda bottle in the dispenser tray (effecter and feedback). As an aid for better user-centered design, and as a guide for exploring the design space, we argue that all steps should be considered separately, echoing McGrenere and Ho [20].

Following Norman, we stress that signifiers are distinct from affordances; indeed, Norman argues strongly that the notion of affordance should be replaced by signifier, leading to better design. In the mediated action perspective of Kaptelinin and Nardi, signifiers do not seem to play a role insofar as they are not part of the reconceptualization of the notion of affordance [18], and the issue of the "Role of perception" is relegated to something that "can be an outcome of learning" [18, Table 2].

From a design perspective, there is an obvious incentive to explicitly consider signifiers: signifiers tell the user that a specific affordance is present, based on learning and context; and as we make clear in the discussion on breaking affordances in Sect. 4, there is ample reason to consider signifiers as distinct phenomena from instrumental affordances when exploring the design space unfolding when breaking affordances.

While signifiers serve as cues that an affordance is present, and is perceived by the user prior to acting on the affordance, affordances may also have one or more *feedbacks* serving as cues that the intended action was performed (i.e., that the affordance indeed was present when the action was taken). For some technology artefacts, in particular physical ones, feedbacks associated to affordances may be obvious: when pressing a selector button on a soda vending machine (the handling affordance), the desired soda bottle drops to the dispenser tray (the effecter affordance, and the feedback). For some affordances, feedback may occur long after the affordance has been acted upon (e.g., submitting a physical reimbursement form to a university bursar, not receiving any receipt, and only observing the reimbursement appear on a back account some time later). For affordances of virtual objects, feedbacks for simple interface affordances such as scrollbars or widgets for closing windows, may also be tightly bound to the effecter affordances: the window scrolls, or closes. However, interaction with modern devices are replete with instrumental affordances whose handling affordance is simple (e.g., a button), but whose effecter requires separate feedback: consider the instrumental affordance of submitting an online form by pressing a button labeled "submit"; the form may be submitted and end in the right place on a system elsewhere in the world, but the user has no way of knowing unless some explicit feedback is given (e.g. a confirmation page appears, a confirmation email is sent to the user's account, etc.).

4 Breaking Affordances

We now propose an operational notion of brokenness and describe how it can be used to understand the actions and propensities of users interacting with technological affordances.

4.1 What Is Brokenness?

We define a technology affordance to be *broken* if (i) the designer intended the affordance, and the user either (iia) perceives the presence of the affordance but the affordance is not present, or (iib) perceives that the affordance was supposed to be present, but is not present (the user may or may not discover the brokenness after attempting to activate the affordance).

As affordances in the mediated action perspective may depend on cultural or other contexts, different users may perceive distinct affordances. We thus view the property of being broken as relative to the context, and relative to the particular user. An example: a user perceiving an obviously smashed "on" button on a TV, sees a broken (handling) affordance. A user perceiving an unbroken "on" button that fails to turn on the TV when pressed sees a broken (effecter) affordance. The above definition of broken is *absolute* and *binary*: the affordance is completely absent if broken (and completely present if unbroken). For many affordances, in particular aggregate affordances, it may be fruitful to consider grades of brokenness: For instance, Schaub et al. [27] show that many users still use smartphones with cracks in the display for viewing and interaction, and that more severe cracks negatively affect the kind, and the quality, of interactions more than less severe ones. However, a full discussion and exploration of these issues is beyond the scope of this paper.

Note that we consider brokenness to be a quality of a technology affordance intended by a designer (hence, not of natural objects as in the Gibsonian view, and not of unintended or emergent affordances). These restrictions in scope are due to our focus on the operational aspect of affordance to designers and to reduce the number of special cases to be considered. For example, if we removed "the designer intended the affordance" from the definition, the perceived presence of an affordance where there is none can be due to a defective signifier (e.g., a graphical widget with the visual appearance of a button, but with no underlying functionality at all); this is an interesting phenomenon, but beyond the scope of the paper.

4.2   Breaking Handling and Effecter Affordances Separately

In an instrumental affordance, the handling affordance can–informally–be "shared" between several instrumental affordances with different effecter affordances: (opening) the lid of a physical mail box may afford dropping of envelopes to adults and dropping of firecrackers to wayward children. More subtly, there is a definitional choice of whether to allow the theoretical possibility of distinct instrumental affordances having different handling affordances, but sharing an effecter affordance.

Fig. 1. Two instrumental affordances with equivalent effecter affordances but distinct handling affordances: opening the print dialog of a word processor, using a keyboard shortcut (left) and by pressing the left mouse button (right). In both cases, the effecter affordance is a print window.

For example, highlighting a specific entry field in a virtual text entry form can typically be done by tabbing through fields (if the window is already highlighted), or by selecting the field with a pointing device–two distinct instrumental affordances with distinct handling affordances, but accomplishing the same action. While breaking a handling affordance breaks the instrumental affordance that it is part of, several instrumental affordances may have effecter affordances accomplishing the exact same goal, and a user may often still complete the desired action by switching to a different instrumental affordance of the same object (e.g., use a keyboard shortcut or a drop-down menu instead of pressing a button). If a user acts using two distinct instrumental affordances of the same object with a result indistinguishable to the user, we say that the two effecter affordances are *equivalent*, see Fig. 1. To avoid confusion due to inconsistent language, we also say that two handling affordances are equivalent if they are indistinguishable to the user (but their associated effecter affordances may be different), see Fig. 2.

The reader may deem the notion of "equivalent handling affordances" unnecessary: in most mediating technology objects, two (visually or otherwise) similar handling affordances are cognitively associated with distinct instrumental affordances unless the user is given explicit cues that it is not the case. For example, two distinct, but identical-looking, buttons are for accomplishing two different things, but a single button (or a mailbox lid) with two distinct effects is cognitively a single entity, and it may seem to be useless semantics to talk about handing affordance of opening a mailbox lid to "be" two distinct, but equivalent affordances.

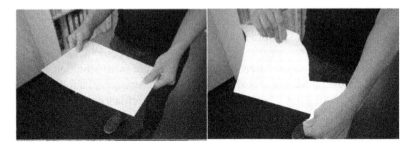

Fig. 2. Two instrumental affordances with equivalent handling affordances but distinct effecter affordances. Left: handing a piece of paper to someone. The handling affordance is grasping the paper, and the effecter affordance the giving of paper. Right: tearing a piece of paper. The handling affordance is grasping the paper, and the effecter affordance is the paper being torn.

The notion of "equivalence" becomes clearer when considering what happens if handling or effecter affordances are broken: For many simple mediating tools, breaking the handling affordance also breaks the effecter affordance: consider a hammer where the handle is burned off–the hammer no longer affords hammering. However, for more complex tools, the handling affordance may appear broken upon activation, but the effecter affordance could still be present: when pushing a button on a touch-sensitive keyboard, it may not depress, but the touch sensor could still send the appropriate signal and activate the effecter affordance; if in doubt, the user may often use another input device (say, a pointing device) to accomplish the same effect as pushing the button (i.e., act on an affordance with effecter equivalent to the one activated by the button push). For complex instrumental affordances, the effecter affordance of an instrumental affordance in general is easy to break without breaking the handling affordance: for a software object, a button may work, but the intended effect, e.g. submission of a form, may not occur.

4.3   "Breaking" Perception: Defective Signifiers and Feedbacks

In investigating the actions of users, and in particular the design space associated to, breaking affordances, we argue that signifiers and feedbacks have an important role to play independently of affordances: Namely that signifiers and feedback can be changed to signal that an affordance is broken (in the above sense), or can them-selves be defective in several ways without the associated affordance being broken. Consider the instrumental affordance of submitting a data form by clicking on the 'Submit' button. The handling affordance is pressing the button (by a mouse click), and the effecter affordance is the (supposed, but invisible to the user) submission of the data. There is at least one signifier present: The widget suggesting a button with the word "submit" is a signifier of the handling affordance. There are–at least–the following scenarios where the signifier or feedback is somehow defective, but the associated instrumental affordance is affected in different ways: (a) the button no longer visually depresses, and so does not alert the user to having been pressed /activated correctly. But the button action still activates correctly (handling and effecter affordances work, feedback is defective); (b) the computer responds, on pressing the submit button, with an 'Error' beep, as if the user is trying to press or activate something they cannot. But the button action still activates correctly (handling and effecter affordances work, feedback is defective). (c) The button is greyed out from the beginning, i.e. the signifier introducing the button as clickable is defective from the get-go. But the button action still activates correctly (handling and effector affordances work, signifier is defective). (d) The button is visually marred (e.g., by "cracked" graphics or an unintended visual artifact such as a red "X" across the button), but the button still activates correctly (handling and effector affordances work, signifier is defective). (e) There is no follow-up result from clicking the 'Submit' button, alerting the user of the success or failure of their submission (handling and effecter affordances work, feedback is defective). As the above example shows, signifiers and feedback can be defective independently from brokenness of handling and effecter affordances. The philosophical question of whether an affordance exists if the user does not perceive its existence is beyond the scope of this paper, and we have consequently deftly defined brokenness in such a way that if a user does not perceive an affordance to be there, then it cannot be broken. The technology may fail to work in an absolute sense, but this does not matter to the particular user if she was never conscious of the possibility of using the technology for a particular purpose. Hence, a sufficiently defective signifier prevents an affordance from being broken.

We posit that there is a very useful distinction between considering the user's perception of an affordance (the signifier(s) and feedback) and the user's possibility to carry out an action (the affordance). Whereas the notion of "broken" can be applied in an absolute sense to affordances (they "work", or "do not work"), the question of the user's perception is more subtle, hence our use of the word "defective" for signifiers and feedback instead of "broken". For example, a signifier can be missed by the user, or refer to another affordance entirely, or misdirect leading to accomplishing the wrong goal. "Breaking" a signifier in an absolute sense–i.e., either the user perceives the affordance or not–is less interesting as an analysis tool than breaking an affordance; rather it is an important question of good design, which we do not treat here.

5   The Affordances of Objects with Broken Affordances

For some simple tools, their instrumental affordances are tightly coupled with their identity: a hammer that cannot be used for hammering is not a hammer (and for most hammers, the affordance of being used for hammering, is the only intended affordance). For complex tools, say a car, or a word processor, the designers intended a multitude of instrumental affordances for accomplishing subtasks and interacting with the tool. Some high-level aggregate affordances may still be closely tied with the identity of the object (a word processor that cannot be used for writing is not a word processor), but low-level instrumental affordances may potentially be broken without the object itself losing its identity. Thus, an object may have broken affordances without a user deeming the object itself broken. Objects with broken affordances afford–at least– repair, maintenance, or replacement, though this may be highly dependent on the object and user: decay of objects may be viewed as positive and engender affection and memory, also for virtual objects such as photos [19, 24]. Furthermore, they may afford repurposing where the object is changed or combined with other objects to form a new object with distinct affordances, and exploration where the inside of complex technological objects are investigated by the user [16].

In addition, objects with broken affordances may afford *repurposing*, to be used for something else or having some of its affordances that were already there take the foreground, even though they were not what the object was originally produced for, as already remarked by Bærentsen and Trettvik [2]. For example, an old CRT TV with a broken screen may be used as a table, or a polystyrene packing box cracked in two may be used as two bathtub toys.

5.1 Physical Versus Virtual Objects

Physical objects may have emotional significance that is harder to find for virtual objects: a blanket that has been worn thing and no longer affords warmth or insulation may have belonged to a beloved family member. This is also true for virtual objects such as photos or video [24]. A difference between physical and virtual objects, in particular of tools, is the permanence and common irreplaceability of physical objects: a well-crafted saw, or a vintage car, may have belonged to a loved one, and retained for sentimental value even if they have lost key affordances, as may a leaky teapot made by a pre-schooler; and the objects are very hard to replace.

Similarly, physical objects are often repurposable, but software tools that have broken affordances are much harder to repurpose: even an expert user or programmer will be hard pressed to repurpose a program (though parts of the program code may be re-used). We hold that there are two primary reasons for this. The first is simply the intangibility of virtual objects: if users cannot experience an object with a full sensory apparatus, the objects will in general fail to be repurposable: if a user cannot feel, or hear, or smell an object, fewer possibilities for creative reuse present themselves. The second reason is cultural and holds equally for many quickly replaceable technological physical artefacts: objects have a very limited lifespan before obsolescence–when today's high-schooler passes away in 70 years, her grandchildren may keep her old yearbook as a family heirloom, but probably not her currently favorite smartphone. A key difference between virtual tools such as programs, and physical tools, is that they are often maintained actively through patching or releases of new versions, and lend themselves well to rapid prototyping: adding an instrumental affordance with an effecter equivalent to an existing one (e.g., adding a quick-access button to an action otherwise hidden deep in layers of menu) can often be done, and tested, quickly, as opposed to (high-fidelity) physical prototyping. However, for highly complex and non-modular software, testing of a quickly-produced prototype can be highly cumbersome.

6 Experimental Exploration

To challenge our analysis above, and to explore the actions of users and designers when faced with broken affordances, we facilitated an explorative workshop with usability experts and artists, and devised a user study where users were faced with combinations of broken handling and effecter affordances, and with defective signifiers and feedback. The scenarios used in the workshop and the software and questions used for the user study can be obtained by contacting the authors.

6.1 Explorative Workshop

Two usability consultants from industry, and a visual designer and a visual artist were recruited for a workshop. All were professionals making their primary income from their profession. Participants were remunerated by standard rates for consultancy work (the usability consultants), respectively by standard rates for expert participants (visual designer and artist). Participants were not informed about the purpose of, or tasks to be covered in, the workshop prior to its beginning, and were only informed about the purpose in the debriefing following the workshop. Scenarios were prepared for the workshop, consisting of a description and an associated physical artefact, software mockup or image of a physical artefact (Fig. 3). The scenarios were divided into: (i) 8 goal-oriented scenarios, describing an artefact and what was broken about it, along with a particular goal to attempt to achieve, and (ii) 4 open scenarios, describing an artefact and encouraging users to both find out what was wrong with it, and what they would like to use the artefact for. The first half of the workshop involved goal-oriented scenarios, the second half open scenarios. The first scenario was to be treated and reflected upon individually. For the remaining scenarios, participants were divided into pairs consisting of a usability consultant and visual designer or visual artist. At the conclusion of each of the two halves of the workshop, a facilitated plenary discussion

Fig. 3. Foreground: two physical artefacts from the workshop: a conference room chair with defective backrest (breakage behind the leather flap visible in the picture center), and a plastic bottle with a hole near the bottom (indicated by red marker outline on the bottle in the center-left). Background: the workshop lab.

was held. At the conclusion of the workshop, a facilitated discussion was held concerning desired behaviors of more complex software system with broken affordances. The workshop was recorded on video and audio devices and later coded by the authors.

Results. We identified a number of recurring themes in the response to, and discussion of, the scenarios, all of which supported our original analysis: Firstly, simple physical objects with broken affordances afford repair by the user: A hole in a bottle can be plugged, a chair with a faulty backrest can be mended if the user has the skill, or can simply be placed against a wall. Secondly, some physical objects with broken affordances afford repurposing: A chair with a faulty backrest can be made into a footstool, a bottle with a hole can be made into a bird feeder.

For the goal-oriented scenarios, the amount of workarounds and tinkering with physical objects was context-dependent (this observation was explicitly articulated several times by the participants): for example, a cardboard ballot box with tape across the slit could be easily used by either removing the tape, cutting a hole in the side, or removing the entire lid, but all participants agreed that they would not tinker with a wooden ballot box with a padlock. Likewise, virtual objects with broken affordances were treated in a manner entirely different from the physical objects: all participants first attempted to verify that it was not themselves who had made an error (this was most evident in the text entry box with a greyed-out "submit" button). Virtual objects were clearly treated as tools that were replaceable (participants faced with a program with broken affordances all suggested using a different program to accomplish scenarios), reinforcing the view of affordances as facets of mediated human action. In contrast, physical objects were treated as having a variety of roles: tools (to be repaired or replaced by similar tools), objects of affection (a broken coat hanger could have been made a cherished family member), or repurposable objects (often completely replacing the original affordances of the object with new ones).

Asked to provide scenarios – explicitly unconstrained by their knowledge of current technology constraints – where virtual objects with broken affordances could be retained (as opposed to worked around, replaced, or reinstalled) participants volunteered that this would only happen if the object had emotional significance, for instance if it was a program that they had themselves contributed to in some way.

6.2   Goal-Oriented User Study

To investigate user interaction with instrumental affordances where signifiers, handling affordances, effecter affordances, and feedback could be broken separately, we conducted a small user study concerned with accomplishing a simple task using interface metaphors that would be immediately recognizable to users, but deliberately decontextualized: the user was placed in front of a screen and asked to interact with a program clearly not embedded in any standard software they used (i.e., not browser-based, with color scheme and icon placement clearly distinct from the usual suite of software they were used to). This setup allowed us to put the users in a position where they would recognize the standard WIMP metaphors (e.g., dragging-and-dropping, or WASD keyboard mappings), but such that the ambient software of

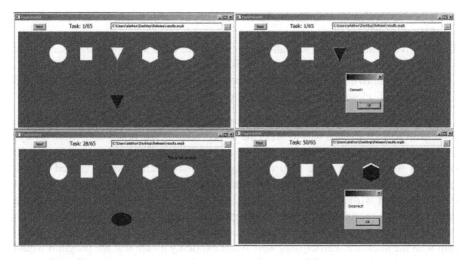

Fig. 4. The shape-sorter task. Top left: the green oval affords dragging to one of the white holes. Top right: feedback for correctly solving a task. Bottom left: Broken signifier: the green oval still affords dragging and dropping to the oval hole, but the text above the hole reads "this is not an oval". Bottom right: Broken feedback: the hexagon is dropped correctly on top of the white hexagon, but the software responds with 'Incorrect!'. The task has actually been completed correctly, so the software moves on to the next task (not depicted) (Color figure online).

the OS did not afford obvious alternatives to complete the task. A classic shape-sorter toy was used for the study. In a shape-sorting toy, the user is presented with a number of differently-shaped holes and a number of shapes to be put into the "right" holes; the holes are shaped such that only a single shape can fit into a given hole, but occasionally smaller objects may fit into holes intended for larger objects. The layout of the shape-sorting task is shown in Fig. 4. The user is presented with one task at a time, with an option to skip to the next task by clicking a 'Next' button. At the beginning of each task, a green-colored shape is provided to the user at the bottom of the screen. One or more white shapes appear at the top of the screen, and the user can drag the green-colored shape into a white shape, and if it is the correct shape then the task is completed, a popup box appears stating, 'Correct!', and the program advances to the next task. Moving the green shape into a shape where it does not fit, or anywhere else, will prompt a popup box stating, 'Incorrect!'. All shapes can be put in a hole whose geometry and area would allow it (e.g., all shapes except the oval can be dropped in the circular hole). We defined five variations of the 'default task':

1. Broken handling affordance, broken effecter: The green shape is impossible to move by any means.
2. Broken effecter, defective feedback, intact handling affordance: Despite moving the green shape onto the correct target shape, the task does not complete.
3. Broken handling affordance, intact effecter: The green shape shows no visual indication of being moved, but still moves.

4. Defective feedback, no broken affordance: The task will display 'Correct!' instead of 'Incorrect!' and vice versa.
5. Defective signifier, no broken affordance: Text intended to mislead the user will be displayed on the screen, such as 'This is not an oval.' above the white oval, 'Triangle.' above an empty space where the triangle would normally be, and 'Pentagon??' close to where the hexagon would usually be.

Variations 1 and 2 present an unsolvable task. In such a case, the only option the participant had to advance was to press the 'Next' button. The first 5 tasks were always chosen to be the 'default task' with nothing broken, and a randomized list of 60 variations were chosen for a total of 65 tasks. 6 participants were recruited from a graduate programme in game design (all male, age 23-27, median 24). Each participant received a short written instruction prior to the study, was provided a laptop with the shape-sorter toy program open. Each participant received a short oral instruction, and a facilitator was present to answer general questions about the study, but to provide no help with the interface. Participants were made explicitly aware that the program would only proceed to the next task by itself (i.e. without the user pressing the 'Next' button), if they had correctly solved the task. Participants were asked to think aloud, and complete a short questionnaire after the study asking for (free, user-defined) categorization of the various problems encountered and a free-text description of what they would normally do if a program exhibited these kinds of problems, and were asked to rank their self-defined types of errors from most to least annoying. An audio device recorded the utterances of each participant. The study took between 45 and 60 min per participant.

Results. By coding participants' think-aloud utterances and examining the error counts for the task variations, we observed the following: P1-5 all attempted to use arrow keys several times in Variations 1 and 3 (broken handling affordances); P6 did not try using the keyboard at any point in time during the study. Erroneous feedback (Variation 4) when the user correctly/incorrectly solved a task caused frustration and confusion amongst all participants. All participants initially indicated that they blamed themselves for solving the task wrong, not understanding that in fact the feedback was incorrect and they had correctly solved the task. P1,P3,P5 and P6 realized that the program would occasionally lie to them or give them wrong feedback, while P2 and P4 considered all feedback to be correct, and faults to lie with them self and not the program. P1-4 and P6 considered the tasks with a broken handling affordance to be most annoying, all of them likening it to a program freezing. P2 and P4 proclaimed that they would rather receive incorrect feedback, or have the program simply not work (read: broken effecter), rather than not be able to manipulate the elements of the software at all. The *part(s)* of an affordance broken in the different task variations had effects as follows: (i) broken handlers (variations 1 and 3) caused immediate frustration for several participants, (ii) defective feedback (variations 2 and 4) prompted participants to try a wide range of different actions to solve the task. When only defective feedback was present, but the task still worked (variation 4), there was little frustration amongst the participants. When defective feedback was coupled with a broken task (variation 2), several participants became frustrated very quickly, more than in variations 1 and 3. Participants displayed widely varying levels of effort with regards to the number of different actions attempted upon a non-obvious or unsolvable task: some participants attempted dozens of different combinations of keyboard and mouse input, while others almost immediately stopped trying.

7 Discussion: Implications and Opportunities for Design

The user studies, in conjunction with the theoretical treatment of Sects. 2, 4 and 5, give rise to several intriguing observations:

- From a design perspective, there are several design guidelines that may be gleaned. Specifically: (A) *Create several instrumental affordances with equivalent effecter affordances* (but with different handling affordances and signifiers). This entails ensuring several ways to accomplish the same goal. A classic instance of this is to provide keyboard shortcuts to supplement point-and-click interfaces. For OS designers, an example is to allow access to a bricolage of clients rather than chaining the user to a specific application (e.g., allowing several browsers on a smartphone). As mentioned by all participants in our workshop, this was a preferred strategy when using web interfaces. (B) *Couple handling and effecter affordances tightly* (also advocated by Kaptelinin and Nardi [18]): the outcome of a user action should be clear. In the user study, all participants were confused when they received no visual feedback upon trying to drag a shape (i.e., a broken handling affordance). This confusion, in some cases, led to completely incorrect assumptions about how the program worked and how input affected it. (C) *Do not remove expected interaction possibilities, even if no effecter affordance is intended by the designer.* If a user expects to be able to drag-and-drop a file to move it and, for some reason, it cannot be moved (i.e., a broken effecter from the user's perspective), let the user drag-and-drop instead of "freezing" the file or returning an error message when clicking the file. If possible, give feedback after the drop that the action could not be completed. (D) *Make the background logic of virtual objects with affordances accessible to the user, if possible.* This is a difficult task, and may not lend itself well to the current generation of users. Workshop participants stated clearly that if they could program, they would like to examine the source of the page to ascertain whether they had made an error, or more closely inspect what the problem could be (supposedly, instead of looking for alternative instrumental affordances sharing the same effecter). Note that (A)-(D) vindicate, and provide additional support for, existing design heuristics. There is one novelty evident in (A) and (C), namely that the explicit focus on handling and effecter affordances may provide the designer with a specific terminology and mental model to work with.
- While we have focused on user *experience*, e.g., by considering user's utterances in the experimental explorations, it is hard to draw firm conclusions for the implications for *usability*: in the goal-directed user study, several users rank the brokenness of different parts of an instrumental affordance on a self-devised scale of annoyance; but this says little about the *effectiveness* or *efficiency* with which they solve tasks. We expect that effectiveness will be hampered by, say, a broken effecter if the designer's intent matches that of the user; but the impact on effectiveness of, say,

breaking a handling affordance compared to breaking an effecter may be small even though users may report it as more annoying.

- We have studied artefacts where the notion of brokenness was absolute and, for most users, not subject to discussion. Our definition of brokenness concerns the *designer*'s intent, but a broken object may add to the user experience *by virtue* of its brokenness, especially in cases where there is discrepancy between the intent of the designer and the needs of the user. Consider the typical SMS app found on smartphones; this app often comes with an auto-correcting language dictionary that cannot be easily disabled. If this functionality were to break, users who find the dictionary to be annoying might see this as a benefit, not a problem.
- We have argued that the reconceptualization of the notion of affordance by Kaptelinin and Nardi is "operational" in a sense that the earlier notions of Norman and Gaver (and the original ecological perspective of Gibson) are not. We hold that both user studies completely vindicate this view: Participants clearly reacted differently, and with different coping strategies when signifiers and feedback, respectively handling and effecter affordances, were independently defective or broken. We believe that this fact alone makes the case for a rich notion of affordance (in the style of Kaptelinin and Nardi) to be used for design purposes (see also [20]).

8   Conclusions and Perspectives

We have argued that the notion of instrumental technology affordances of [18] is "operational" in the sense that the notion of deficiency or breakdown of various components of an affordance, and the consequences, is much more clearly elucidated than in much of the early literature; however, work in activity theory, notably [1, 2], while taking its inspiration in work closely aligned with [18], could conceivably be used to perform a structured study of the concept and implications of brokenness of affordances. Similarly, recent attempts to give detailed accounts of cognition in interaction with technology could be used for a similar purpose [28], as may more fine-grained analyses of the roles of signifiers and feedback [33]. We have used this operational view to analyze the interplay between notions of brokenness for affordances in both physical and virtual objects, and outlined the differences between these. Through analysis and explorative experimental work we have identified opportunities for concrete identification, and circumvention or improvement, of usability problems, using systematic breaking of instrumental affordances. A novelty of this approach is that breaking handling or effecter affordances separately forces the designer to consider the constituent parts of each affordance (and how malfunction of each part may lead to different coping strategies by the user), and may lead to new design choices or opportunities by re-appropriation or alternative use of objects or interfaces. We welcome longitudinal field studies "in the wild" of designers, artists, and developers using brokenness as a means of expression, and analysis. As noted in Sect. 7, the naïve notion that "broken = bad" may be challenged due to the discrepancy between the intent of the designer and the needs of the user; we expect that this challenge may be used creatively. Finally, we have posited that exploration of the design space of wear and brokenness of objects, as put forth in recent work [13, 15–17], would be informed by both systematic and playful breaking of facets of the affordances (e.g., breaking of handling affordances, not effecter affordances, and vice versa) of objects. The payoff, we believe, is a further sensitization of designers of the consequences when affordances break down and objects are repurposed, repaired, or complemented by affordances of other objects.

References

1. Albrechtsen, H., Andersen, H.H.K., Bødker, S., Pejtersen, A.M.: Affordances in activity theory and cognitive systems engineering. Technical report Risø-R-1287(EN), Risø National Laboratory (2001)
2. Bærentsen, K.B., Trettvik, J.: An activity theory approach to affordance. In: Proceedings of NordiCHI 2002, pp. 51–60 (2002)
3. Beaudouin-Lafon, M.: Instrumental interaction: an interaction model for designing post-wimp user interfaces. In: Proceedings of CHI 2000, pp. 446–453 (2000)
4. Bødker, S., Andersen, P.B.: Complex mediation. Hum.-Comput. Interact. 20(4), 353–402 (2005)
5. Chemero, A.: An outline of a theory of affordances. Ecol. Psychol. 15(2), 181–195 (2003)
6. de Souza, C.S., Prates, R.O., Carey, T.: Missing and declining affordances: are these appropriate concepts? J. Braz. Comput. Soc. 7(1), 26–34 (2000)
7. Gaver, W.W.: Technology affordances. In: Proceedings of CHI 1991, pp. 79–84 (1991)
8. Gaver, W.W.: The affordances of media spaces for collaboration. In: Proceedings of CSCW 1992, pp. 17–24 (1992)
9. Gibson, J.: The concept of affordances. In: Shaw, R., Bransford, J. (eds.) Perceiving, Acting, and Knowing, pp. 67–82. Wiley, Hoboken (1977)
10. Gibson, J.J.: The Ecological Approach To Visual Perception. Psychology Press, New York (1986)
11. Gulotta, R., Odom, W., Forlizzi, J., Faste, H.: Digital artifacts as legacy: exploring the lifespan and value of digital data. In: Proceedings of CHI 2013, pp. 1813–1822 (2013)
12. Hartson, H.R.: Cognitive, physical, sensory, and functional affordances in interaction design. Behav. IT 22(5), 315–338 (2003)
13. Huang, E.M., Truong, K.N.: Breaking the disposable technology paradigm: opportunities for sustainable interaction design for mobile phones. In: Proceedings of CHI 2008, pp. 323–332 (2008)
14. Ihara, M., Kobayashi, M., Sakai, Y.: Human affordance. Int. J. Web Based Communities 5(2), 255–272 (2009)
15. Ikemiya, M., Rosner, D.K.: Broken probes: toward the design of worn media. Pers. Ubiquit. Comput. 18(3), 671–683 (2014)
16. Jackson, S.J., Kang, L.: Breakdown, obsolescence and reuse: HCI and the art of repair. In: Proceedings of CHI 2014, pp. 449–458 (2014)
17. Kang, L., Park, T., Jackson, S.J.: Scale: human interactions with broken and discarded technologies. In: Proceedings of CHI 2014, pp. 399–402 (2014)
18. Kaptelinin, V., Nardi, B.: Affordances in HCI: toward a mediated action perspective. In: Proceedings of CHI 2012, pp. 967–976 (2012)
19. Kirk, D.S., Sellen, A.: On human remains: values and practice in the home archiving of cherished objects. ACM Trans. Comput.-Hum. Interact. 17(3), 10:1–10:43 (2010)

20. McGrenere, J., Ho, W.: Affordances: clarifying and evolving a concept. In: Graphics Interface 2000, pp. 179–186 (2000)
21. Norman, D.A.: The Psychology of Everyday Things. Basic Books, New York (1988)
22. Norman, D.A.: Affordance, conventions, and design. Interactions **6**(3), 38–43 (1999)
23. Norman, D.A.: The way I see it: signifiers, not affordances. Interactions **15**(6), 18–19 (2008)
24. Odom, W., Pierce, J., Stolterman, E., Blevis, E.: Understanding why we preserve some things and discard others in the context of interaction design. In: Proceedings of CHI 2009, pp. 1053–1062 (2009)
25. Oshlyansky, L., Thimbleby, H., Cairns, P.: Breaking affordance: culture as context. In: Proceedings of NordiCHI 2004, pp. 81–84 (2004)
26. Şahin, E., et al.: To afford or not to afford: a new formalization of affordances toward affordance-based robot control. Adapt. Behav. **15**(4), 447–472 (2007)
27. Schaub, F., Seifert, J., Honold, F., Müller, M., Rukzio, E., Weber, M.: Broken display = broken interface: the impact of display damage on smartphone interaction. In: Proceedings of CHI 2014, pp. 2337–2346 (2014)
28. Still, J.D., Dark, V.J.: Cognitively describing and designing affordances. Des. Stud. **34**(3), 285–301 (2013)
29. Stoffregen, T.A.: Affordances as properties of the animal-environment system. Ecol. Psychol. **15**(2), 115–134 (2003)
30. Torenvliet, G.: We can't afford it!: the devaluation of a usability term. Interactions **10**(4), 12–17 (2003)
31. Turner, P.: Affordance as context. Interact. Comput. **17**(6), 787–800 (2005)
32. Turvey, M.T.: Affordances and prospective control: An outline of the ontology. Ecol. Psychol. **4**(3), 173–187 (1992)
33. Vermeulen, J., Luyten, K., van den Hoven, E., Coninx, K.: Crossing the bridge over norman's gulf of execution: revealing feedforward's true identity. In: Proceedings of CHI 2013, pp. 1931–1940 (2013)
34. Vicente, K.J., Rasmussen, J.: Ecological interface design: theoretical foundations. IEEE Trans. Syst. Man Cybern. **22**(4), 589–606 (1992)
35. Vygotsky, L.S.: Mind and Society. Harvard University Press, Cambridge (1978)

Deploying Robots in a Production Environment: A Study on Temporal Transitions of Workers' Experiences

Daniela Wurhofer[(✉)], Thomas Meneweger, Verena Fuchsberger,
and Manfred Tscheligi

Christian Doppler Laboratory "Contextual Interfaces", Center
for Human-Computer Interaction, University of Salzburg, Salzburg, Austria
{daniela.wurhofer, thomas.meneweger,
verena.fuchsberger, manfred.tscheligi}@sbg.ac.at

Abstract. Understanding a worker's perspective when introducing robots at humans' workplaces is crucial to improve human-robot interaction in production environments. Taking a temporal perspective on workers' experiences with robots, we explored expectations and general attitudes as well as actual feelings and reflections regarding the deployment of robots in a semiconductor factory. To evoke reports on workers' experiences, we applied a narrative interview technique with 10 workers. To characterize the temporal transition of workers' experiences, we distinguished between three phases in the deployment process: expectations before the deployment of the robots, familiarization with the robots, and experienced consequences of working with the robots. We present characteristic experiences of each phase and describe how these experiences change over time regarding the perceived functional value of the robots, work organization, feelings, social environment, and attitudes. Overall, our research contributes leverage points towards a more positive experience of workers when deploying robots in a factory.

Keywords: Temporality · Experience · Factory · Human-robot interaction

1 Introduction

Introducing robots at humans' workplaces is a critical endeavor. Specific expectations, attitudes, familiarization processes and experiences may be relevant as they presumably influence actual, future human-robot interactions. In particular, workers' experiences with interactive artifacts, i.e., user experience (UX), are crucial as they influence the course of actions in a factory [22]. Robots represent such interactive artifacts and thus can be a focus of UX research in a factory.

To facilitate a better collaboration between humans and robots, it is important to understand the temporal process of deploying a new robot from a worker's point of view, ranging from workers expectations before the introduction of robots to their actual experience of working together with such a robot. Previous work already showed that time can be a crucial factor regarding workers' experiences in human-robot interactions [5]. Initial experiences positively changed with prolonged interaction and

© IFIP International Federation for Information Processing 2015
J. Abascal et al. (Eds.): INTERACT 2015, Part III, LNCS 9298, pp. 203–220, 2015.
DOI: 10.1007/978-3-319-22698-9_14

remained stable after one year. To extend the contribution of Buchner and colleagues, details about temporal influences at different stages in the deployment process of a robot regarding the workers' experience would be beneficial, as this could provide important hints on how to improve human-robot collaboration in general.

By explicitly taking a process-oriented perspective (beginning from expectations to familiarization issues up to long-term consequences) on workers experiences regarding robots, we extend the current state of the art. In particular, we were interested in the characterization of workers' experiences within the deployment process of robots in a semiconductor factory. Further, we aimed to find out how the workers' experiences changed across different stages in the deployment process of the robot.

In the following, we motivate our research aims that led to the research questions, then we present related work on human-robot interaction (HRI), user experience (UX) and temporal aspects of UX. Next, we point out the objective of our study, the study set-up, participants and procedure, as well as our approach. We then explain the data analysis process and present our findings on workers' experiences at different stages of the deployment process of a robot. Finally, we discuss transitions of workers' experiences over time as well as leverage points for potential interventions during the deployment process.

2 Background

2.1 HRI and UX

UX comprises all aspects of how people interact with a product: the way it feels in their hands, how well they understand how it works, how they feel about it while they are using it, how well it serves their purposes, and how well it fits into the entire context in which they are using it [1]. Interactions – with systems or individuals – are key elements in many working environments, e.g., in factories. Obrist et al. [22] emphasized that research on workers' experiences in a factory is important, as UX aspects like collaboration and reliability, usability or even emotions influence working routines in the factory. The experiences that result from these interactions in turn may influence motivation, compliance and performance and are, thus, relevant to investigate in order to improve them. This work was extended by Wurhofer et al. [30], who explored workers' everyday experiences and contextual influences on it in a semiconductor factory.

In general, industrial contexts pose a variety of challenges and restrictions, for instance, fieldwork must not impact work practices [3, 27]. The challenges of these contexts led to a limited number of studies. In particular, introducing robots in a factory is a critical endeavor. A recently conducted quantitative study in the cleanroom of a semiconductor factory focused on how UX of industrial robots with and without safety fences changes over time [5]. By deploying a self-developed UX questionnaire consisting of five scales – cooperation, perceived usability, perceived safety, stress, and general UX - different facets of UX were measured at different points in time. Results showed that time can be a crucial factor in human-robot interaction, as initial experiences positively changed with prolonged interaction. In order to understand the reasons for this change, however, more details about what accounts for these changes, i.e., what influences how a robot is perceived in the course of time, are needed.

There are studies on how to raise the workers' acceptance of industrial robots, for instance, by transferring anthropomorphic features to the industrial robot [8, 12]. Next to the appearance of the robot, other factors probably play a role regarding the acceptance of robots as co-workers. For example, in previous studies it was found that the fear of being replaced by a robot is crucial regarding how the robot is experienced and accepted [22, 28].

In contrast to industrial robots, investigations of service robots over a longer period became more frequent, e.g., in schools [6], or health care settings [7, 18]. In such studies, it was reported that the users' attitude towards the robot changed over time, e.g., became more accepted over time [7]. Further studies highlight that it is important to keep up the users' interest [9], to match the functionalities of the robot to its appearance [15], and to give feedback at the right time [20]. As Karapanos et al. [14] pointed out, usability becomes more important over time; studies in HRI have also shown that it is crucial to consider usability aspects for long-term human-robot interaction [18].

2.2   UX Over Time

In recent years, research on UX over time has been intensified and became an important area of research within the HCI community (e.g., [14, 16]). However, the temporality of UX, i.e., how the quality of the users' experience develops over time [14], is still an area of research to be further explored [2]. As soon a new technology is deployed, acceptance becomes an issue (e.g., [10, 25]), and technology adoption is crucial. Technology adoption represents a process that ends with a user embracing a technology, i.e., accepting it [24].

Regarding UX over time with robots in an industrial context, we already pointed out the limited number of studies due to the challenges and restrictions of this context. The study of Buchner et al. [5] represents an exception, however, still leaves open some issues (see Sect. 2.1).

In contrast to the industrial context, consumer contexts are better researched. For example, Karapanos et al. [14] contributed a five-week study with six participants purchasing an Apple iPhone. They found that prolonged use was motivated by different qualities than the ones that provided positive initial experiences. According to their results, early experiences seemed to relate mostly to hedonic aspects of product use, whereas prolonged experiences became increasingly more tied to aspects reflecting how the product becomes meaningful in one's life. Their findings showed that many different kinds of experiences may take place during the same day, but their distribution changes over time, starting from an orienting learning phase to a final emotional attachment phase. They identified three phases of how the experience with a product develops over time: (1) orientation, (2) incorporation, and (3) identification.

Recent research in the consumer context further demonstrated that the factor usability is becoming more important with increasing time [16]. In the study of Kujala and Miron-Shatz [16], emotions and experience episodes during real-life mobile phone use were examined over a five-month period. Their results indicated that both emotions and how people remember them had strong unique roles in the overall evaluation of the product. Positive emotions were mostly related to good user experience, whereas negative emotions were mostly related to low usability. Further, users seemed to focus on user experience in the early stages of use, whereas the importance of usability increased over time. The importance of usability as crucial factor for long-term interactions was also pointed out by Coradeschi et al. [7], who studied long-term human-robot interaction.

The decreasing importance of hedonic aspects with increasing time was also reported by Von Wilamowitz-Moellendorff et al. [26], who found that the perceived stimulation and other hedonic aspects of user experience of mobile phones seem to fade away during the first 20 months of use. Studies further showed that sustaining perceived attractiveness can be a differentiating factor in the user acceptance of personal interactive products such as mobile phones [17].

3 Method

3.1 Objective of the Study

In our study, we aimed to explore how people working in the production line of a semiconductor factory experience the deployment of industrial robots. Following Alben [1], Wright and McCarthy [29] and Karapanos et al. [14], we conceive experience broadly, including users' expectations and general attitudes as well as actual feelings and reflections. In particular, we addressed the following research questions:

- RQ1: How can the workers' experience be characterized within the deployment process of robots in a semiconductor factory (by taking a temporal point of view)?
- RQ2: How does the workers' experiences change at different stages in the deployment process of the robot?

The outcome from our research contributes leverage points for improving the introduction of robots in a factory environment (regarding workers' UX) as well as deepens the general knowledge on temporal transitions of UX regarding human-robot collaboration.

3.2 Study Set-Up

In order to understand how workers have experienced the introduction of the robots, one researcher conducted 10 narrative interviews on two consecutive days in a semiconductor factory. We aimed to assess how workers experience the interaction with robots and the transition to working together with robots (i.e., we sought to interview workers that witnessed the deployment of robots in the factory). The interviews were conducted in a quiet and comfortable atmosphere (i.e., a meeting room). Each lasted about one hour and all were audio recorded.

3.3 Narrative Interviews

By applying a narrative interview approach, we aimed to reveal workers' experiences, attributions and reflections regarding the robots. To get insights about the deployment process of robots, we adopted a retrospective method. Such an approach implies that people reconstruct personally meaningful experiences from memory [13, 29], representing one possibility to access experiences over time.

The set-up of our narrative interviews was based on Meneweger and colleagues' [19] classification of textual data specifically developed for accessing user experience. Using an open structured interview guideline, the interviewer encouraged the interviewees to report their personal experiences in form of stories and situation narratives. The focus of the interviews was based on the three main stages of the deployment process: Stage 1 – before the actual deployment of the robots; stage 2 – briefing, training and first interactions with the robot; stage 3 – daily work with the robots.

An exemplary question triggering personal experiences associated with stage 1 is the following: "Can you tell me about the situation when you got to know that you will work together with a robot? Please tell me about that." Regarding stage 2, an exemplary question is the following: "Can you remember the first day working with the robot? Please tell me about that." An exemplary question for stage 3 is represented by this one: "Can you tell me about specific events regarding your daily work with the robots? Please tell me about that." Thus, we collected episodes (situation narratives) of certain human-robot experiences, ranging from pre-expectations regarding the robots, first time experiences, to current experiences of workers.a>

Narrative interviews are open-structured qualitative interviews that aim to evoke reports of personal experiences by the participants [11]. The main task of the interviewer is to stimulate these reports by asking narrative trigger questions. Meanwhile the participants are reporting their experiences, the interviewer should be mainly a listener and her/his influence on the participant's story is limited [11]. By making use of people's reports about their experience of a certain process or an event, we considered a narrative interview technique to be appropriate for accessing the experiences of workers, who are directly interacting with industrial robots. In addition to narrative questions, Flick [11] proposes to additionally ask semantic questions, which are questions that do not trigger reports of personal experiences, but argumentations regarding the interviewee's assessments and ascriptions of meaning. These semantic questions aim at accessing additional information, which cannot be narrated, but which is nevertheless relevant (like subjective meanings). An exemplary semantic question was the following: "What does 'robot' mean to you?".

3.4 Participants and Procedure

The narrative interviews were conducted with people that are actually working together with the robots as they are directly affected by the transition from working without robots to working with them. Working with robots basically means that the product (i.e., silicon wafer) to be processed by the equipment is handed to the robot (by the workers). The robot then puts the wafers into the equipment and passes it back to the workers after the processing is finished.

The manager of the automation department recruited the participants. In the selection process, diversity was sought in terms of age, working experience, and role. In particular, we aimed for a sample of participants that ranged from novice participants (their first interaction/encounter with robots not being longer ago than one month) and advanced/expert workers (being familiar with the robot in their environment). Overall, seven operators, two shift leads, and one dispatcher were interviewed,[1] all working in the same department. We interviewed eight male and two female workers, with a mean age of 40 years (SD = 12), ranging from 22 to 57 years. Their average working experience at the specific factory was 16 years (SD = 11), ranging from 0.5 to 30 years.

The procedure of the study was as follows. At the beginning the researcher introduced the participant to the study purpose and its goal. Each participant filled in the informed consent form as well as short demographic questionnaires. After the interview, participants were thanked for their participation.

3.5 Analysis Approach

The audio recordings were transcribed verbatim and analyzed in a team of two researchers following a thematic analysis approach [4]. This analysis approach is used to organize qualitative data sets by identifying different themes within the collected data. For our purpose we aimed to structure and describe the participants' reports about their personal experiences with the newly introduced robots by revealing the prevalent thematic issues regarding the different phases of the deploying process.

In a first step we selected relevant data with regard to our research questions. Then, taking a temporal focus, we structured the collected experience reports and assigned them to different (temporal) phases in the deployment process: *(1) anticipated experiences before the deployment of the robots, (2) initial experiences immediately after the deployment of the robots, and (3) long-term experiences in the daily work with the robots.* As a next step, to further structure the data, we assigned initial codes to the data and searched for themes within the phases based on the codes. The identified themes aimed to describe commonalities and differences regarding the worker's experiences and assessments during the introduction process of the robots. Finally, based on the revealed themes, we aimed to identify changes and transitions regarding the participants' experiences of working together with the robots within the deployment process.

4 Findings

4.1 Workers' Experiences Within the Deployment Process of Robots

With our first research question we aimed to describe workers' experiences within the temporal process of deploying robots in a semiconductor factory. Based on the stages of the deployment process addressed in the interviews (see Sect. 3.3), we distinguished

---

[1] In this paper, we refer to all of them as *workers*, as they are interacting with the robots during daily working routines.

between the following three phases from the workers' (experimental) point of view (see Fig. 1 for an overview): Phase 1 deals with workers' expectations before the deployment of the robots. Phase 2 describes the workers' familiarization with the robots as a process, which is influenced by learning and training. Finally, phase 3 points out the experienced consequences of working with the robot. In the following sections, we characterize these phases with regard to workers' experiences in detail.

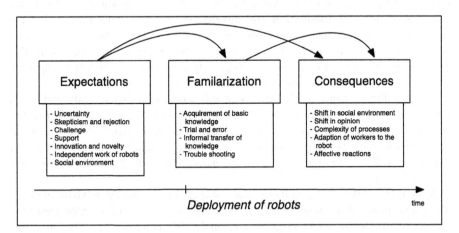

Fig. 1. Phases in the deployment of the robots and associated experiences of workers.

Phase 1: Expectations Before the Deployment of the Robots. When being asked about expectations they had before the robot was actually deployed at their workplace in the semiconductor factory, the workers experienced the following aspects to be crucial:

- Uncertainty
- Skepticism and rejection
- Challenge
- Support
- Innovation and novelty
- Independent work of robots
- Social environment

As the workers did not know how the future with robots will look like, **uncertainty** was a key issue. In particular, workers faced the fear of being replaced by the robot. For example, P1 wondered *"Are you going to be replaced, will you be supported, or will you be completely replaced?"* Workers were unsure how working with the robot will look like or did not recognize the benefit of the robot. P9 stated, *"How will this work out at all? How shall this work out at all?"*

Next to uncertainty, **skepticism and rejection** characterized this phase. Workers' negative attitudes or emotions towards robots led to negative expectations. *"In the beginning, no one actually wanted it* [the robot]," stated P2. P4 said, *"Somehow, I wasn't happy about it... I did feel anger,"* while P8 claims that *"In the beginning, everyone was shocked, for sure, because everyone fears losing their job."*

Further, working with robots was considered as demanding or challenging by the workers. Thus, **challenge** was also a crucial expectation regarding the collaboration with robots. For example, P3 stated, *"It was challenging to work hand-in-hand with the robot. Let's see how it* [the robot] *will behave."*

Support in the sense that robots could relieve stress from factory workers by taking over work from them was another expectation. For example, P10 indicated, *"Maybe* [they introduced the robots] *to disburden the operators."* Introducing a robot was further associated with **innovation and novelty**. In this case, workers were looking forward to new developments due to the introduction of robots. This is illustrated by the following statement of P1; *"Well, at that time* [when the robots were installed], *I was in a positive mindset and also a bit happy. Just because it is something different, because it is innovative, because it is just new."*

Workers further expected that the robot was **working independently** and on its own, arguing that the human was not involved in the work. *P7 claimed, "The first few days I didn't have any contact with it* [the robot] *... I thought it would do everything on its own and we wouldn't have to do anything with it... gradually in the course of time, it* [working with the robot] *became more and more... fixing all the errors, moving* [the robot], *unloading."*

Moreover, workers' expectations were shaped by the **social environment**, as information from others, who already worked together with a robot, influenced their anticipations of future interactions. For example, P4 indicated, *"... thus they* [the colleagues, who already worked with the robot] *cursed. Because from time to time the robot did not work correctly and did not do exactly what they* [the operators] *wanted them* [the robot] *to do...you then get a negative image already in advance, which makes you think that if you also get such a robot, it will go crazy as well and not do what I want it to do."*

Overall, some of the expressed expectations indicate the workers' ambiguity towards robots: they are torn between positive and negative expectations regarding the collaboration with robots.

Phase 2: Familiarization as Process Which is Influenced by Learning and Training. The time after actually deploying a robot in the semiconductor factory may be considered as a phase of reorganization for workers in terms of a change of the workflow and spatial rearrangements. When learning how to handle the robot after deploying the robot in the factory, we found the following aspects to be characteristic for workers' experiences in this phase:

- Acquirement of basic knowledge
- Trial and error
- Informal transfer of knowledge
- Trouble shooting

First, workers got a mini training in which they **acquired basic knowledge** to solve minor problems of the robot. This training took place on-site. The worker was explained the most important functions of the robot in the production line directly at the robot. If there were more severe problems, workers were instructed to call the technicians to get support. As P2 explained, *"We got a brief training over just the most* *important things, so if something happens, like small issues, they told us what to do. However, if there were more in-depth issues, then we had to inform these people* [technicians], *who had been previously here all the time* [during the installation of the robots]. *Therefore, we learned a little bit."* P8 also stated that, *"Training also happens within the cleanroom, on site and at the machine. Otherwise, it does not make any sense."*

Knowledge acquisition for handling the robot was often characterized by individually trying and exploring. Thus, when interacting with the robot, **trial and error** was prevalent in the early phase of human-robot interaction. This learning process took place on-site, next to the robot. The following statements point out this kind of knowledge acquisition. P1 had to *"learn 80% of it on my own; I had to deal with it by myself. Then you just tried it yourself." "I mean, I have to say, we found out a lot by ourselves, because at night no one is here and we are doing overnight shifts. This means we have to be able to find solutions by ourselves and, thus, we were able to fix some errors with the manual, the electronic one, thankfully. Also without the technicians,"* stated P10. Also P1 said, *"Exactly, that happened exclusively on-site. You can do it with learning by doing, that's clear anyway. Some error has to occur and then someone, who knows about it, can show it to you. If there is no one around, you just have to decide by yourself."*

Another important aspect of knowledge acquisition was the **informal transfer of knowledge**. This means that information about the robot and how to handle it was generated by asking or observing others. Informal information channels were important, e.g., information was passed on by other people (rumors). On one hand, knowledge was transferred from worker to worker, on the other hand, from technician to worker. This is illustrated by P1, *"It seemed there have been trainings, but most information had been shared from worker to worker."* P3 agreed that *"In case of an error, someone fixed it and you observed it. This person told you how it worked or that you only have to confirm* [at the robot's interface]. *Then suddenly you took that over."* P1 further stated that *"when you talked to them* [technicians], *when you stood next to them, when they installed it, they certainly showed you where to push, where it moves to the right, where it moves to the left..." "Not everyone got trained from the robots team... in each finger* [sub-department] *or in a department, only one gets trained from the robots team, maybe two, and they pass it on,"* stated P8, while P10 claimed that *"when someone from the technicians was around, than you pepper them with questions. How is this? And how can I do that?"*

The main interaction the workers had with the robot was problem solving: Skills and knowledge regarding the robot were mainly needed for **trouble shooting**, i.e., in case of problems. The situatedness of the problem was also characteristic. This means that workers had the feeling that the robot will never be fully understood, as problematic situations are changing. For example, P1 stated that *"There are always new situations. Well, this will go on forever. You cannot say, I know everything about that."* P3 said, *"Confirming* [on the robot's interface], *moving* [the robot] *to its home position, or bringing back the wafers because there had been a problem... You handle all these things on the screen. We are not allowed to do anything else and we don't do it. Certainly, when you talked to them* [technicians], *when you stood next to them when they installed the robots, they certainly showed you where to push, where it moves to* *the right, where it moves to the left, but when something happened to please give them a call." "We never had a special training. It was just like this, that, … when there is an error you have to push this button and if it does not help give us a call,"* recalled P10.

Phase 3: Experienced Consequences of Working with the Robot. After getting familiar with the robots and restructuring work routines, workers' predominately experienced the following aspects as a consequence of deploying the robots:

- Shift in social environment
- Shift in opinion
- Complexity of processes
- Adaption of workers to the robots
- Affective reactions (non-involvement, resignation)

The operators were faced with a **shift in their social environment**, as they got new working colleagues due to the introduction of the robot. These new working colleagues were, for example, technicians, who were responsible for the technical functioning of the robot. This change was considered as a positive one, as reported by P1, *"Yes, this had actually been a very positive aspect, that new faces occurred, young people, motivated people, who take care."* Introducing a new robot further attracted attention of other workers, who did not know the robot. Thus, workers from other working areas came and had a look at the robot or wanted to get information about the robot. An example for this was given by P3, *"In the beginning, it was interesting, people asked you whether you are in a finger with a robot because it had been the first finger with robots. People asked how is it with the robots and observed how it worked. Especially when they got to know that their finger would get a robot as well."*

Another issue we identified in this phase was a **shift in the workers' opinion**, as initial skepticism and rejection turned out to be arbitrary. For example, there was no reduction of staff due to the introduction of the robots as initially expected by the workers. This change of opinion was expressed by P2 in the following way, *"Yes, well, in the beginning, we were all a bit skeptical towards it, but over the time, we grew with this* [development] *and now it is as it is."*

A consequence related to the introduction of a robot was an increased **complexity of processes**. Due to the robot, some procedures were more complex than before, resulting in the perception that the robot was not as supportive as expected. Further, the deployment of the robot required an **adaption of the workers' behavior** in a way that the workers had to adjust their behavior to the robot's behavior. This means that workers' tried to anticipate or react to the robot's behavior in order to execute their work properly. For example, workers had to take care where to position things as the robots took physical space, which was not demanded before. P3 stated, *"To some extent, you have to be careful where to put the cart* [where the wafers are stored and carried].*"*

Affective reactions linked to the deployment of robots were, for instance, the feeling of **non-involvement, resignation,** or **malicious joy**. The feeling of non-involvement was characterized by the fact that workers saw no possibility to contribute or influence the introduction process, or that they felt excluded from the decision process. P6 expressed this, saying *"We have been confronted with an* *accomplished fact, it is as it is."* P8 indicated that *"At some point we were con-fronted... At some point, they installed tracks, and then it was there, and at some point we got angry. Yes, that's ho it is."* P10 confirmed the questionable reasonability of the robots, as they had not been asked about that: *"But no one really asked us, whether they would make sense where they installed them. That has been decided from the higher authorities and that's it."* Resignation means that workers got used to the robot as there was no other option. To conduct one's work properly, interacting with the robot was required. The following statement from P2 expressed the non-involvement as well as the resignation linked to the introduction of the robot, *"... it* [the robot] *was just there and we worked with it and tried to get the best out of it."*

Another reaction to the robot was related to a feeling of malicious joy. Workers felt joy or satisfaction when the robot did not work as expected. In such cases, workers often stated that they would have told the management about such problems before-hand, if they would have been asked. P10 illustrated such feelings in saying, *"How-ever, yes, again we came up with a grin. We knew it anyway, but they have to recognize it themselves."* *"We certainly made a little fun of the company, because that did not work from the beginning,"* agreed P1.

4.2   Transitions of Workers' Experiences

Our second research question targeted changes regarding the workers' experiences across the deployment process of the robots. Therefore, we compared initial expecta-tions and dominant themes before the deployment of the robots with actual experiences and prevalent topics of production workers who actually work together with the robot. We identified several substantial changes over time. In particular, we found changes regarding the attitude towards the robots, the functional value of the robot, work organization, feelings, as well as the social environment.

Change in the Perception of the Robots' Functional Value. Before the actual deployment of the robot, workers expected that the robot would take over work and thus relieve them from stress. However, after actually working with the robot, the workers recognized that the robot led to an increased complexity of some working procedures. Thus, the robot turned out not to be as supportive as supposed, but to increase complexity in some working issues. For example, the robot's tasks are not fully automated so that the workers' assistance is needed, representing an additional task for the workers. Thus, initially expected support of the robots turned into the perception of increased complexity of processes.

Change in Work Organization. Regarding work routines, workers expected that robots would work autonomously and independently from the workers, with no contact between human and robot. However, it turned out that this initial expectation was not true in their daily work. In fact, the workers had to interact with the robot and adjust their behavior to the robot's behavior, e.g., by providing (physical) space to the robot or adapting their work routines to the robot's routines, e.g., waiting until the robot finishes its task. Consequently, initially expected independent work of robots changed to the necessity to adapt to the robot.

Change in Feelings. The prospect of a robot being deployed in the production line was often linked to feelings of uncertainty, but also to feelings of challenge and novelty. This was closely related to the aspect that workers did not feel informed about the deployment process and the robots to be deployed. Whereas uncertainty is often manifested in fears (losing one's job due to the robot), novelty is connected to aspects of innovation (new developments due to the introduction of the robot). After actually deploying the robot, feelings of non-involvement, resignation, or malicious joy were in the foreground. Workers accepted the robot, but felt excluded from decision processes, thus resigned with their (new) working situation, or felt a kind of satisfaction in case the robot made a mistake. This change of feelings ranged from initial feelings of uncertainty and novelty to feelings of non-involvement and resignation. Although the feelings towards the robots were still ambiguous when actually working with the robot (i.e., both positive and negative), the workers' had a more differentiated picture of the robot.

Change in Social Environment. Before the deployment of the robot, providing information about the robot was considered as the main social activity in relation to robots. This means that information regarding the robot and its introduction was passed on from other workers (i.e., in particular from those already working with a robot in the production line) and shaped the workers' expectations of future interactions with the robot. After deploying the robot in the production line, the social environment changed (e.g., new working colleagues due to the introduction). Further, the robot attracted attention from other workers, who came to look at the robot or requested information about it. Consequently, the information provision function of the social environment was replaced by a change of the social context.

Change in General Attitude Towards the Robots. Before the deployment of the robots, rather negative attitudes and expectations were expressed. This was reflected in workers' statements showing skepticism and rejection before actually working with the robot. However, the experience of actually working with the robot changed the workers' attitude towards the robot in a positive way. Expected negative consequences due to the deployment of the robot did not occur (e.g., reduction of staff) and thus led to a more positive attitude towards the robot. As a consequence, initial skepticism and rejection turned out to be arbitrary, and robots were not perceived as negative as initially expected. These changes do not mean that the robot was considered as completely negative before its deployment and entirely positive after the deployment. Rather, the daily worklife with the robots was different than expected, leading to a refined perception of the robots.

5   Reflection and Discussion

The aim of this work was to investigate workers' experience when deploying robots in a production environment. In this chapter, we reflect on our results regarding potential interventions ("leverage points") during the deployment process. Further, we discuss benefits and limitations of our research.

5.1   Leverage Points

Through creating awareness of which aspects or themes are foregrounded in which phase of the deployment process, we point out potential interventions (i.e., leverage points) towards more positive experiences of workers regarding future human-robot interactions. Based on the insights from our study, we suggest the following leverage points. In general, these leverage points are feasible at all stages of the deployment process, although we suggest to apply them as early as possible.

Increased Transparency and Information. Overall, workers reported uncertainties regarding the future deployment of robots that would not have been necessary, as they turned out to be arbitrary afterwards. Many of these uncertainties evolved because workers hardly had any information about the robots. In such situations, rumors from the social environment can reinforce negative expectations so that workers have negative associations regarding the robots. Informing the workers as much as possible about facts regarding the deployment of the robots represents a way to reduce some of these uncertainties and rumors. We therefore suggest giving workers a relatively realistic estimation of how the situation will change and inform about benefits as well as potential negative consequences. For example, informing the workers beforehand how the robot will look like combats rumors and speculations about the robots' appearance (e.g., space requirements). Further, information about planned tasks of the robot and interactions with the workers would be beneficial. As negative aspects of robots seem to overshadow positive aspects especially at times when few facts are known, positive aspects of the robots' introduction should be foregrounded, but potential consequences should nevertheless not be neglected.

A Platform for Workers' Thoughts and Reflections. Our study showed that both – positive as well as negative expectations and attributions regarding the forthcoming deployment of the robot – were mentioned by the workers. Fears and uncertainties as well as challenges and innovations were associated with the robots. Based on the workers' statements and the interviewer's reflections, we believe that the workers felt not being heard and taken seriously. On the one hand, the workers felt not involved in the decisions of the management regarding the introduction of the robot, although they knew the working context very well and felt that they could give advice. On the other hand, the workers showed a desire to talk and reflect about the robot in the interviews. Therefore, we think that providing a way to express thoughts and reflections continuously (and as soon as possible when the introduction of robots is discussed for the first time) can combat feelings like non-involvement or inferiority. We think that openly discussing positive and negative aspects of the deployment of robots (e.g., in workshops, via an online platform) reduces uncertainties and a-priori rejection regarding the robot

Improved Training and Enhanced Competences. In the interviews, workers expressed that they felt inferior, incompetent or helpless regarding the interaction with the robots. Workers reported that they wanted to understand the robot and strived for more training and skills regarding their handling of the robot. Some of them were even actively asking for information about the robots' handling, which, mainly consists of error handling. Not knowing how to handle the robot conveyed negative feelings regarding one's competences. In turn, providing workers with sufficient competences regarding the handling of the robot will support the avoidance or reduction of negative associations. Thus, adequate training and courses are crucial, especially at the beginning to allow positive first interactions. Successful initial interactions convey a feeling of competence in the workers and may impress future attributions and associations regarding the robot.

5.2   Benefits and Limitations

Overall, our interviews were appreciated by the workers as a platform for expressing thoughts and reflecting about the deployment process of the robots. Although the interviewees initially expressed a kind of astonishment that they were interviewed about the robots, they soon showed that they valued to be taken seriously as experts regarding the robots. Thus, we think that our interviews represent a positive intervention for workers towards a critical reflection on human-robot interaction in their daily work.

Our research is beneficial in several aspects. First, we want to highlight the peculiarity of our data. Our sample is exceptional in terms of experiencing the change from working without robots to working with robots. Interviewing workers about their personal experiences regarding this change provided us with valuable insights, which have not been reported in related literature so far.

Moreover, investigating workers' experiences from a process-oriented, temporal perspective in a factory extends the current state of the art, as long-term studies and in-situ investigations in production environments have rarely been conducted. This may be due to lacking accessibility, since such studies may interrupt the workflow, which, in turn, restricts access and possibilities. Our work thus extends knowledge on how workers' experience the changes in their daily work and experiences due to the deployment of robots from a long-term perspective. Taking such a temporal perspective allows to focus on experiental changes and how these changes evolved and developed. This knowledge provides leverage points for interventions (before and after the introduction), as discussed earlier in the paper.

Further, we showed that the workers' experience regarding the interaction with the robots already started before the deployment of the robot. Indeed, human-robot interaction at the workplace is more than just working with robots. Emotions and expectations are crucial. Attributions and interpretations of the robots' behavior play an important role, as workers aim to "understand" the robot. Thus, we also found the recently emphasized importance of expectations and anticipated experiences [23, 31] in a factory / robots context. Further, studying the transitions of the workers' experiences over time (i.e., relating the different phases of the deployment process as done in Sect. 4.2) revealed valuable insights regarding workers' experiences, e.g., how initial uncertainties and fears turned into a still ambiguous but more differentiated picture of the robot.

In this study, we applied a narrative interview approach to access workers' thoughts and reflections regarding the (self-experienced) deployment process of robots – which is only possible retrospectively. Further, we had to consider not to interfere with the production itself, which was feasible by applying a retrospective approach. At the beginning of the interviews, it seemed that the workers were rather unaffected by the deployment of robots. However, in the course of the interview, the actions and experiences reported by the workers during the conversation revealed that the workers were indeed affected regarding the deployment of the robots. These insights were enabled by adopting a narrative approach, giving the interviewee the opportunity to extensively express his personal reflections and thoughts.

In our study, we specifically addressed the memories of the workers (after deploying the robots), as they represent the salient aspects kept in mind and which are associated with robots. Furthermore, the challenges that are inherent to the specific context of production environments require approaches that do not influence the production itself. Thus, the narrative interview approach was the most feasible and promising way to assess workers' temporal experiences in such a setting. Certainly, memory effects need to be taken into account in a retrospective approach on UX, relating to the question whether "memory" or "actuality" of an experience is more important [21].

With this work we addressed the change of workers' experiences over time. Work that focuses on the temporal transitions of experience so far exists in the area of consumer products [14]. According to Karapanos et al. [14], the act of anticipating an experience results in the formation of expectations, happening prior to any experience of use. This corresponds to our phase 1, i.e., expectations before the deployment of the robots regarding anticipated human-robot collaboration. In line with Karapanos et al., this phase is characterized by both positive and negative anticipations. Their phase of orientation corresponds to our phase 2 (familiarization), dealing with users' initial experiences with an interactive product. In both the consumer and the factory context, learning and familiarization characterize this phase. The last two phases – incorporation and identification – deal with the integration and meaning of the product in our daily life. This corresponds to our third phase considered as consequences of the robots' deployment. Long-term usability and social aspects are crucial here. To this extent, our findings confirm the work of Karapanos and colleagues [14]. However, when going in-depth, differences reflecting the specific application context become significant. In particular, we found affective reactions, a shift in opinion, as well as a change in working routines to be further characteristic regarding long-term experiences in the factory context.

6 Conclusion

In which ways – if at all – does the deployment of robots affect workers' daily experiences and routines? Our study showed that the workers were indeed affected. Information was sought actively from others, rumors were dispersed, routines were adapted, and affective reactions towards the robots were set. By taking an experience-centered perspective and focusing on the transitions of workers' experiences in the course of the deployment of robots, such inherent actions and experiences became obvious.

We found different aspects of workers' experiences to be foregrounded in different phases of the deployment process. Before the actual deployment of the robot, uncertainty as well as skepticism and rejection were predominant issues. Further, challenges as well as innovation and novelty were associated with the robots. Support as well as independent work of the robots was expected. Overall, the workers' expectations were strongly influenced by their social environment. Immediately after deploying the robots, getting familiar with the robots and learning how to handle them was in the foreground. This included the acquirement of basic knowledge, learning to correct errors of the robots' through trial and error, actively looking for knowledge regarding the handling of the robot, as well as trouble shooting as the prevalent kind of interaction with the robots. After getting familiar with the robots, workers experienced increased complexity, the need to adapt to the robots' behavior, and affective reactions like non-involvement, resignation, or malicious joy in their daily work. This was accompanied by a shift in the workers' opinion as some of their initial fears turned out to be arbitrary, as well as a shift in their social environment in terms of new colleagues. Regarding changes of the workers' experiences, we identified changes regarding the perception of the robots' functional value, work organization, feelings associated with the robots, the social environment, as well as the general attitude towards the robots.

In this paper we argued that it is crucial to understand workers' experience in the temporal process of deploying a new robot (ranging from workers expectations before the introduction of robots to their actual experience of working together with such a robot) to facilitate a better collaboration between humans and robots. By adopting such a temporal perspective, we were able to identify salient aspects of the workers' experiences and their changes during the deployment process of robots. Thus, this work contributes insights towards interventions for a better experience of workers in the interaction with robots.

Acknowledgments. The financial support by the Austrian Federal Ministry of Science, Research and Economy and the National Foundation for Research, Technology and Development is gratefully acknowledged (Christian Doppler Laboratory for "Contextual Interfaces").

References

1. Alben, L.: Quality of experience: defining the criteria for effective interaction design. Interactions **3**(3), 11–15 (1996)
2. Bargas-Avila, J.A., Hornbaek, K.: Old wine in new bottles or novel challenges: a critical analysis of empirical studies of user experience. In: Proceedings of CHI 2011, pp. 2689–2698. ACM, New York (2011)
3. Björndal, P.S., Ralph, M.B.: On the handling of impedance factors for establishing apprenticeship relations during field studies in industry domains. In: Proceedings of the NordiCHI 2014, pp. 1107–1112. ACM (2014)
4. Braun, V., Clarke, V.: Using thematic analysis in psychology. Qual. Res. Psychol. **3**(2), 77–101 (2006)

5. Buchner, R., Wurhofer, D., Weiss, A., Tscheligi, M.: Robots in time: how user experience in human-robot interaction changes over time. In: Herrmann, G., Pearson, M.J., Lenz, A., Bremner, P., Spiers, A., Leonards, U. (eds.) ICSR 2013. LNCS, vol. 8239, pp. 138–147. Springer, Heidelberg (2013)
6. Castellano, G., Aylett, R., Dautenhahn, K., Paiva, A., McOwan, P.W., Ho, S.: Long-term affect sensitive and socially interactive companions. In: Proceedings of the 4th International Workshop on Human-Computer Conversation (2008)
7. Coradeschi, S., Kristoersson, A., Lout, A., Von Rump, S., Cesta, A., Cortellessa, G., Gonzalez, J.: Towards a methodology for longitudinal evaluation of social robotic telepresence for elderly. In: 1st Workshop on Social Robotic Telepresence at HRI 2011 (2011)
8. Duffy, B.R.: Anthropomorphism and the social robot. Robot. Auton. Syst. **42**, 177–190 (2003)
9. Fernaeus, Y., Hakansson, M., Jacobsson, M., Ljungblad, S.: How do you play with a robotic toy animal? A long-term study of pleo. In: Proceedings of the 9th International Conference on Interaction Design and Children, pp. 39–48 (2010)
10. Fink, J., Bauwens, V., Kaplan, F., Dillenbourg, P.: Living with a vacuum cleaning robot. Int. J. Soc. Robot. **5**(3), 389–408 (2013)
11. Flick, U.: Episodic interviewing. In: Bauer, M.W., Gaskell, G. (eds.) Qualitative Researching with Text, Image and Sound, pp. 75–92. Sage, London (2000)
12. Hinds, P.J., Roberts, T.L., Jones, H.: Whose job is it anyway? A study of human-robot interaction in a collaborative task. Human-Comput. Interact. **19**(1), 151–181 (2004)
13. Karapanos, E., Martens, J., Hassenzahl, M.: Reconstructing experiences with iScale. Int. J. Hum. Comput. Stud. **70**(11), 849–865 (2012)
14. Karapanos, E., Zimmerman, J., Forlizzi, J., Martens, J.: User experience over time: an initial framework. In: Proceedings of the CHI 2009, pp. 729–738 (2009)
15. Kidd, C.D.: Designing for long-term human-robot interaction and application to weight loss. Ph.D. Thesis, Massachusetts Institute of Technology (MIT) (2008)
16. Kujala, S., Miron-Shatz, T.: Emotions, experiences and usability in real-life mobile phone use. In: Proceedings of CHI 2013, pp. 1061–1070. ACM, New York (2013)
17. Kujala, S., Roto, V., Väänänen-Vainio-Mattila, K., Karapanos, E., Sinnelä, A.: UX Curve: a method for evaluating long-term user experience. Interact. Comput. **23**(5), 473–483 (2011)
18. Lee, M.K., Forlizzi, J.: Designing adaptive robotic services. In: Proceedings of IASDR 2009 (2009)
19. Meneweger, T., Wurhofer, D., Obrist, M., Beck, E., Tscheligi, M.: Characteristics of narrative textual data linked to user experiences. In: CHI EA 2014, pp. 2605–2610. ACM, New York (2014)
20. Mutlu, B., Forlizzi, J.: Robots in organizations: the role of workflow, social, and environmental factors in human-robot interaction. In: Proceedings of HRI 2008, pp. 287–294 (2008)
21. Norman, D.A.: The way I see it: memory is more important than actuality. Interactions **16**(2), 24–26 (2009)
22. Obrist, M., Reitberger, W., Wurhofer, D., Förster, F., Tscheligi, M.: User experience research in the semiconductor factory: a contradiction? In: Campos, P., Graham, N., Jorge, J., Nunes, N., Palanque, P., Winckler, M. (eds.) INTERACT 2011, Part IV. LNCS, vol. 6949, pp. 144–151. Springer, Heidelberg (2011)
23. Olsson, T.: Layers of user expectations of future technologies: an early framework. In: CHI EA 2014, pp. 1957–1962. ACM, New York (2014)
24. Renaud, K., Van Biljon, J.: Predicting technology acceptance and adoption by the elderly: a qualitative study. In: Proceedings of the SAICSIT 2008, pp. 210–219. ACM (2008)

25. Venkatesh, V., Bala, H.: Technology acceptance model 3 and a research agenda on interventions. J. Decis. Sci. **39**(2), 273–315 (2008)
26. von Wilamowitz Moellendorff, M., Hassenzahl, M., Platz, A.: Dynamics of user experience: How the perceived quality of mobile phones changes over time. In: User Experience - Towards a unied view, Workshop at NordiCHI 2006, pp. 74–78 (2006)
27. Weiss, A., Buchner, R., Fischer, H., Tscheligi, M.: Exploring human-robot cooperation possibilities for semiconductor manufacturing. In: International Workshop on Collaborative Robots and Human Robot Interaction (2011)
28. Weiss, A., Igelsböck, J., Wurhofer, D., Tscheligi, M.: Looking forward to a "Robotic Society"? - imaginations of future human-robot relationships. Special issue on the Human Robot Personal Relationship Conference in the Int. Journal of Social Robotics (2010)
29. Wright, P., McCarthy, J.: Experience-centered design: designers, users, and communities in dialogue. Synth. Lect. Hum. Centered Inform. **3**, 1–123 (2010)
30. Wurhofer, D., Buchner, R., Tscheligi, M.: Research in the semiconductor factory: insights into experiences and contextual influences. In: Proceedings of HIS 2014, pp. 123–128 (2014)
31. Yogasara, T.: Anticipated user experience in the early stages of product development. Ph. D. Thesis, Queensland University of Technology (2014)

Finding Objects Faster in Dense Environments Using a Projection Augmented Robotic Arm

Hind Gacem[1,2]([⊠]), Gilles Bailly[1,2], James Eagan[1,2],
and Eric Lecolinet[1,2]

[1] Télécom ParisTech, Paris, France
{hind.gacem, gilles.bailly, james.eagan, eric.lecolinet}
@telecom-paristech.fr
[2] CNRS LTCI UMR 5141, Paris, France

Abstract. Locating an object in an unfamiliar and dense physical environment, such as a control room, supermarket, or warehouse, can be challenging. In this paper, we present the *Projection-Augmented Arm (PAA)*, a motorized robotic arm augmented with a pico-projector to help users to localize targets in such environments. The arm moves and displays a projected spotlight on the target. We present the results of a study that shows that the PAA helps users to more quickly locate target objects in a dense environment. We further study the influence of the visibility of the projected spotlight while moving versus that of the physical movement of the projection arm on user performance and search strategy, finding that (1) information about the orientation of the arm has a stronger impact on performance than moving spotlight projected on the search space; (2) the orientation of the arm is useful (24 % improvement) and especially when the target is behind the user (26 % improvement); and (3) users' strategies relied mainly on the arm when it is visible.

Keywords: Guidance techniques · Augmented arm · Steerable pico-projector

1 Introduction

Finding and locating physical objects can be challenging, especially in dense environments such as control rooms, supermarkets, warehouses, etc. These environments may contain several hundreds or even thousands of objects, which may look similar and be spread about the space, including behind the user. Even when the user knows what the target looks like (e.g. color, shape, size, etc.) and has a general idea of the organization of the space, finding an object in such an environment is already difficult. Even in such situations, one might look several times over several areas before finding the target, such as when looking for, say, a yoghurt pot in the refrigerator. For unfamiliar targets or unfamiliar environments, locating an object can be even more challenging. Generally, one must first orient oneself to find the general vicinity of the target and then perform a visual search on this area to pick out the target.

Although this localization task occurs frequently in many application areas (maintenance, training in control rooms, libraries, warehouses, etc.), proposed guidance techniques for such environments [2, 10, 19–21] focus separately on how to help the

J. Abascal et al. (Eds.): INTERACT 2015, Part III, LNCS 9298, pp. 221–238, 2015.
DOI: 10.1007/978-3-319-22698-9_15

user to orient himself or how to show him precisely the location of the target, but not both.

Existing work mainly focuses on outdoor way-finding and guidance techniques for people with visual impairments [4, 5], for small environments [14, 18, 22, 23] and/or guidance techniques requiring instrumenting users (e.g. with a head-mounted display (HMD)) [12, 29], which may be cumbersome, expensive, and sometimes incompatible with other constraints. Our goal is to provide guidance support to help users to orient themselves and to precisely locate targets in dense environments, such as controls in a control room, by augmenting only the environment and not the user.

In this paper, we introduce the Projection Augmented Arm (PAA), illustrated in Fig. 1b. It consists of a motorized arm with a pico-projector mounted on the end to project a spotlight on a given target. It can be mounted to a cart (e.g. a shopping cart in a supermarket or to a delivery cart in a warehouse) in front of the user (Fig. 1b) or handled by the user to allow multiple usages. The design of the PAA draws inspiration from the way that humans gesture toward targets by pointing. An observer can easily recognize the general direction of the target without looking directly at the arm of the person pointing it out. However, because pointing at an object is insufficiently precise, we extend the arm with a projected spotlight, as if the person were carrying a flashlight in her hand (Fig. 1a).

The design of the motorized arm (1) offers a large projection surface: the projector can target anywhere in area from 0 to 300-degrees horizontally and vertically. Moreover, by placing the arm within the user's field of view, (2) the general direction of the arm remains visible in the user's peripheral vision, thus (3) reducing the search area by orienting the user toward the desired object while (4) the spotlight precisely indicates the location of the target. Moreover, the projector could display additional information

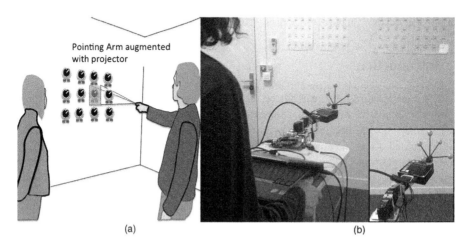

(a)   (b)

Fig. 1. (a) The metaphor of the PAA: a user points to a specific component on the wall, which contains several similar targets. The observer follows the direction of the user's pointing arm, which is augmented with a projector to precisely highlight the target. (b) The PAA prototype. A user fills out a form on a rolling table, on which an automated arm is fixed and projects toward the desired target on top right of the wall.

around the target, using the same device. It is straightforward to attach the system to a cart, making it (5) mobile. Further, it (6) alleviates occlusion problems and (7) can be less intrusive than guidance techniques requiring users to wear additional devices such as glasses or HMDs. Finally, (8) PAA may be visible by several users simultaneously when performing a collaborative task.

We conducted a user study to better tease out the impact of having a physical pointer perceivable in the periphery on the performance on object localization tasks. More precisely, we investigated the influence of the projected spotlight versus the physical movement of the projection arm on user performance and search strategy. Results show (1) information about the orientation of the arm has a stronger impact on performance than moving spotlight projected on the search space; (2) the orientation of the arm is useful (24 % improvement) and especially when the target is behind the user (26 % improvement); and (3) users mainly relied on the arm for guidance in conditions where it was visible.

Our primary contributions are:

An application of the metaphor of the way humans use pointing to orient each other for improving guidance techniques.

The design and implementation of PAA, a mechanical, motorized pico-projector for localizing physical targets in dense environments.

Findings of a user study investigating the influence of the projected light while moving versus the physical movement of the projection arm on user performance.

2 Informative Study

Our primary context of interaction is control rooms of nuclear plants. To better understand the specificities of this environment, we conducted both observations as well as interviews with five domain experts.

We learned that these control rooms are quite large and contain numerous panels densely filled with buttons, gauges, and alarm indicators that are difficult to quickly distinguish, especially for novice users (typically, people performing maintenance or when training novice or experienced operators on a new type of control room). The environment can be noisy and is manned by several personnel who move about the room. Moreover, operators generally bring with them a wheeled high-top table to transport documents.

Regarding the task, we learned that operators typically follow a paper procedure document, which references the appropriate controls. Paper is used rather than an electronic device for safety and verifiability reasons. This document is generally placed on a high-top table cart, which also serves to store auxiliary documents. For each step of the procedure, operators first move with the cart to the position of a specific element in the room and then take notes according to the state of this element on the paper procedure (e.g. to mark that a button has been pressed, report the value of a sensor, etc.).

We thus derive several requirements for our guidance system:

1. Users should be able to move about freely. Not only must they roam around the control room, but their hands must also be free to manipulate pens and various

documents (they may have to find supporting information in other documents, including large books with complex diagrams).

2. Users' senses should not be obstructed. In particular, audio does not seem an appropriate modality in such a noisy environment and in which operators frequently communicate.

3. Glasses and HMDs are problematic for the same reason. The operator must maintain an environmental awareness and be able to rapidly detect any visual alarm, regardless of the panel it is displayed on. Moreover, operators often work in pairs, and, occasionally, in larger groups. It is thus convenient and advantageous to use equipment that several people can see simultaneously. This is also less constraining for the people working permanently in the control room (they do not have to wear a device all day long) and for those working in several rooms (they do not have to put on and take off a device multiple times). Augmenting a cart or wheeled table offers a straightforward solution to these problems.

4. The guidance system should accommodate multiple operators. In particular, some operators may temporarily occlude some elements with their body. Moreover, the guidance system should minimize the disruption of other operators. Hence, on the one hand, people working together should all be able to see the system, but, on the other hand, other people should not be bothered by the system.

5. Due to the size of the room and the density of the elements, the guidance system should be precise enough to unambiguously identify a single 4 cm × 3.5 cm control in a control panel.

Because of this specific context of use, we focused the design of the PAA for command and control rooms. Nonetheless, we believe our guidance approach can be readily generalizable to other contexts such as a supermarket, a warehouse or a library. As in our case, these are dense environments where it is difficult to augment objects and where users often use carts (either a shopping cart, a library shelving cart, or a warehouse delivery cart).

3   Related Work

3.1   Guidance Techniques

Guidance techniques have been proposed for a variety of purposes. Generally, they can be categorized in terms of the granularity of the guidance they provide: from helping the user to navigate within a space (e.g. by moving one's feet) to helping her to orient herself (e.g. turning in place) [12] to precisely locating a target in front of the user (e.g. visual search) [2, 27]. The PAA focuses on these last two categories.

Body/Head Orientation. Several techniques have been proposed for orienting the user toward a given direction using different modalities. For example, Yamano et al. [32] rely on sound (frequency or amplitude panned sound), while Erp et al. [8] rely on haptics by using a vibrating waist. As our technique should work in noisy areas and allow for precise localization, we focus on visual guidance techniques (e.g. [12, 20]).

Precise Guidance. Techniques generally help the user to find a target that is already in his/her field of view. Again, the use of audio [27] and haptics [18] has been considered, but vision is more appropriate in our case as in [2] where a steerable projected spotlight highlights a target. The projector is, however, ceiling-mounted, outside the view of the user. As such, it provides precise guidance, but does not provide orientation guidance to help a user who might be facing in the wrong direction.

Few techniques support both of these guidance granularities. Henderson and Feiner [12] use left/right arrows displayed on augmented reality goggles to help orient the user. Once the target is in the field of view of the user, a 3D virtual arrow directly points to the target in the glasses, providing for precise guidance. This technique is promising, but requires the user to wear additional equipment, notably augmented reality glasses. Gröhn et al. [9] combine 3D sound to help orient the user with a spotlight to precisely locate a target, but the use of sound precludes this approach from noisy environments in which the user cannot wear headphones. For the reasons explained in Sect. 2, our goal is to provide guidance without requiring the user to wear special equipment. Control rooms may have strict safety requirements that prevent the use of such equipment, as in our direct case. In supermarkets or libraries, providing clients with a cart is feasible whereas requiring them to share wearable devices may not be.

3.2   Projector-Based Augmented Reality

Based on these considerations, we now focus on projector-based techniques that do not require the user to wear any special equipment such as augmented reality glasses or Google glasses. From the literature review, we have identified two main dimensions: whether the projection system is motorized or not, and whether it is fixed (the environment is augmented) or not fixed (the user or environment are augmented) (Table 1).

Fixed Projectors Without a Motorization System. Single-projector solutions can only project on a limited surface area. They may also be susceptible to occlusion if a person or object passes between the projector and the projection surface. To overcome these limitations, Jones et al. [15] enlarge the projection area and minimize occlusion problem by deploying several fixed projectors in a room with shared projection areas. Ehnes and Hirose [6] proposed to minimize the degradation of projection quality by selecting the projector that is closest to the projection surface and that has the best orientation. However this approach may be costly and hard to implement for complex and dense environments composed of many projection surfaces such as in supermarkets or control rooms.

Fixed Projectors with a Motorization System. Pinhanez [25] proposed using a steerable mirror mounted on a fixed projector to enlarge the projectable surface of a single projector. Some other systems [2, 26, 31] can also augment moving objects, possibly in

Table 1. Motorized vs. Fixed projection systems.

		Motorized projection system	
		Yes	No
Fixed projection system	Yes	[2, 7, 25, 26, 31]	[6, 15]
	No	PAA, [3, 16]	[11, 24, 30]

real-time [7]. However, these solutions suffer from possible occlusion problems because they rely on a single projector at a predefined position. They may also introduce degradation in the projection quality [6] because of the distance and the orientation (for non-perpendicular angles) between the projector and the projection surface. Moreover, because of their fixed location, these platforms will not be always directly visible to the user if he moves freely. The user must then follow a projected spotlight to be aware of its location. Keeping track of the moving spotlight may be problematic (1) if another task occupies the attention of the user (he may be doing something else while the spotlight moves), (2) the projection passes over a light-absorbing surface (such as a computer screen) and becomes barely visible, or (3) the projection moves too rapidly, especially if the target is outside the user's field of view.

Mobile Projectors Without a Motorization System. When fixed on the user's body [11], such techniques have the advantages to support user mobility using a single and inexpensive projector. However, because their orientations and height are fixed, they have a limited available projection area. Ota et al. propose using several projectors to solve this problem [24], but this solution tends to be cumbersome and expensive and still does not allow projecting in all directions. Hand held mobile projectors are another solution [30], but using them may be tiring, they suffer from unsteady projection (especially when the users move), and they may disturb the user's attention (who must worry about how to keep the projection steady). However, such solutions may improve projection quality because the projector can be moved close to projection surface.

Mobile Projectors with a Motorization System. In contrast with the previous category, motorized projectors allow projecting anywhere around the user. Either the user adjusts the projector direction [3], or it is automatically controlled in real time by a computer to improve steadiness [16], such as by mounting the motorized camera-projector on the backpack of the user and above the shoulder height. Hence, contrary to our own system, the projector is not visible by the user because it is located behind her head. As will be seen in the following sections, this is a major difference in the approach. Our key insight is to exploit the physical movement of a motorized projection arm to help guide the user to the target. We thus study the impact of using a projected spotlight from an out-of-view movable projector versus the physical movement of a projection arm on user performance and search strategy. Obviously, the user cannot benefit from this alternate modality (the projection arm) without seeing the device.

4 PAA: Projection Augmented Arm

We present PAA, a Projection Augmented Arm consisting of a pico-projector fixed to a motorized arm that is attached to a wheeled high-top table (Fig. 1). The user selects the name of an object on a piece of paper (such as by pointing with an Anoto pen) to indicate to the system which object he is looking for. The system extracts the physical location of this object in the room from a database and (1) moves the motorized arm to make it point towards this object and (2) highlights this object by a spotlight emitted from the pico-projector. In the current implementation, arm movement time is under 1 s, with a standard deviation of pointing error of approximately 4 mm at a 2.5 m distance. As explained later, the spotlight can either be shown while the arm is moving or only once it is oriented to the proper direction. The orientation of the arm (hence the projector) is automatically updated when the table is moving.

4.1 Properties

PAA has several advantages:

Projection Area. PAA offers a large surface of projection thanks to its capability to orient itself. In practice, the projector can target anywhere in an area of 0 to 300-degrees horizontally and vertically.

Precision. Standard motorized projectors attached at a fixed position (typically, the ceiling) cannot provide a high resolution when the targets are far from the projector. Moreover, a small error in the orientation of the projector can shift the spotlight from a couple of centimeters from the target and highlights another target. In contrast, PAA is movable: when the operator is in the vicinity of the target, the projector is also in the vicinity of the target: this increases the resolution of the projected surface and reduces the risk of shift. Finally, PAA reduces occlusion problems that can occur with fixed projectors.

Pointing Metaphor. We further use the metaphor of a human arm pointing towards a target. Although imprecise, people have a lifetime of experience following such gestures. With PAA, users can look at the system to get an idea of the location of the target. This is especially useful when users do not know where the target or the spotlight are located (e.g. when the spotlight is behind users). As the augmented arm is in the close vicinity of the users (see Fig. 1b), users can get an idea of the location of the target by looking at the direction of the arm. In fact, they can even use their peripheral vision without explicitly looking at the arm. This differs from fixed projectors, which are not easily visible, especially if fixed to the ceiling. Users can thus maintain their attention on their primary task. Moreover, a physical 3D pointer should be easier to follow than a 2D one, such as an arrow displayed on the top of the cart. The PAA thus provides general and precise guidance with the same device and therefore it is less expensive compared to a system using several display devices.

Spotlight. The spotlight is a useful visual cue to help users to localize the targets not only when focused on the target but also when the arm is moving. A large, dynamic and colorful spotlight can help users to follow it when the arm is moving. However, a moving spotlight can also disturb the other people located in the room. As said in the Informative Study section, the guidance system should be both easy to follow and minimally intrusive so as to minimize the disruption of other operators. Augmenting the arm with projection addresses this problem by providing an alternate modality. We considered a simpler approach of using a laser pointer, but laser pointers are restricted to a limited size. With a projector, we can vary the size of the spotlight, to make the spotlight visible when it is projected on distant targets, or show additional information around the target. It can even be switched off while the arm is being moved.

Our user study aims at better understanding the respective impact of the arm and the spotlight on visual search performance. One potential advantage of the arm compared to a moving spotlight is that the user does not necessarily need to follow it while it is moving: The user can be doing another task while the arm is moving and only look at its final position when she is ready. Thanks to the pointing metaphor, she will still know where to search the object.

Attachment. We primarily designed PAA to be attached on a table/cart. Using a table to carry the device frees the user from having to wear any special equipment that may cover the eyes or ears. Such a system could also provide sound feedback or haptic feedback. However, we have also imagined other scenarios involving a handheld version of the system that could provide haptic force feedback resulting from the acceleration of the PAA, subtly suggesting the direction of movement of the arm. In the future, when the servomotors and projectors become small enough to fit in the hand, the users could sense the orientation of the arm just by touching the arm.

4.2 Implementation

Hardware and Software. The PAA prototype hardware consists of five primary components: two Dynamixel AX-12A robotic actuators, mounted in series, a Philips PicoPix 3610 projector, an Arduino-based controller, a laptop computer and an ARTTrack 3D motion tracking [1]. The ARTTrack is composed of 8 IR cameras connected to a controller, which estimate the coordinates of tracked objects at 60 fps with a precision of about 0.05 mm on the position and 0.0015 rad on the orientation.

Additionally, the prototype is target-aware, meaning that the system maintains a list of all of the possible targets and their coordinates and a calibrated model of the room. This model is composed of six equations of the walls of the room. To compute these equations we measured manually the dimensions of the walls and their distance from the origin of an absolute referential (R_0) (Fig. 2a). In more complex environments, it is

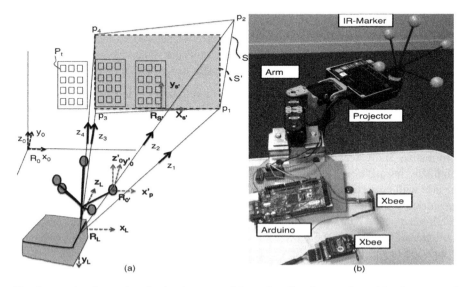

Fig. 2. (a) The distorted projection is corrected from S to S' and target Pt position is computed relative to the referential related to S'. (b) The actual PAA prototype and its components.

possible to use approaches based on depth cameras to build the 3D model of the projection surfaces that compose the environment [13]. The problem with such approaches is the limited precision of the obtained models.

For a given target, a controller running on the laptop looks up the target's position in this model and queries the ARTTrack [1] tracker for the position and orientation of the projector. From these positions, it calculates the necessary movements and relays the appropriate heading and tilt angles to the Arduino control board, which drives the robotic actuators.

The ARTTrack follows the position of the projector during movement, creating a feedback loop to ensure that the projector is properly aimed at the desired target in real time. Finally, the laptop calculates the appropriate affine transform to compensate for any keystone effects introduced by projecting at a non-perpendicular angle. Using the current prototype, the projector can target an object within 300-degrees horizontally and vertically, in under a second.

Operating of PAA. By using a pre-calibrated model of the room and its targets ($P_{t/R0}$), the PAA can dynamically adapt its keystone correction to project an undistorted spotlight on a given target, even while the PAA is moving. This pre-calibration allows us to use a simpler tracking model that does not require dynamic recalibration [17] or a separate camera to correct the distortion [28, 31]. The coordinates of the projector, the target, and the equation of projection plane it is on suffice.

When selecting a new target, the PAA performs up to two simultaneous angular movements (heading and tilt) to bring the target within the projection range. Closed-loop tracking enables the system to dynamically compensate if the PAA over- or undershoots the target (e.g. due to inertia).

Control of the Arm Angular Movement. In order to determine the necessary angular movements to update the arm's position, we first use the measurements of the coordinates of the projector expressed in terms of an absolute room referential, R_0. A transformation, ${}^{0}T_L$, maps between R_0 and the projector lens referential, R_L. Then we compute the position of the target in lens-coordinates, $P_{t/RL}$. Then, we compute the spherical coordinates of the target and thus correspond to the angular deviations between the PAA and the targets, $\rho, \Delta\phi, \Delta\theta$. In our setup, the roll angle in R_0 is fixed to zero for the projector and for the targets. Finally, we compute the input controls to the servomotors, C_h, C_t. Two constants, k_h and k_t represent gain for both tilt and heading control loops.

$$P_{t/R_L} = \left({}^{0}T_L\right)^{-1}.P_{t/R_0}$$

$$C_h = k_h.\Delta\theta$$

$$C_t = k_t.\Delta\phi$$

Computation of Target Location in the Projection Area. We dynamically compute the position of the target, $P_{t/S'}$, in the referential of the undistorted projection area, S', where ${}^{l}T_{S'}$ is the transformation between the projector lens referential and S'. Each time, the target comes within S', we compute its position $P_{l'}$ in the undistorted OpenGL frame.

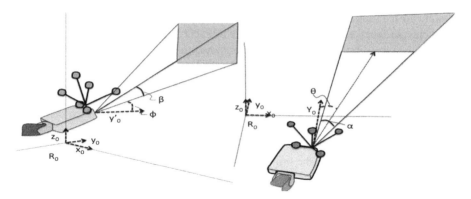

Fig. 3. Left: side view of the projector with tilt angle ϕ and vertical focal length β. Right: top view with heading angle θ and horizontal focal length α.

$$P_{t/S'} = ({}^{0}T_L.{}^{L}T_{S'})^{-1}.P_{t/R_0}$$

Distortion Correction. To provide precise guidance, the PAA projects a spotlight, which has the same shape as the target (rectangular) and with fixed size regardless of the orientation and distance between the target and the projector.

To correct any keystone distortion, we first estimate S, to do that we compute the intersection points $P = (p_1, p_2, p_3, p_4)$ between projection plan equation and unit vectors $(\overrightarrow{z_1}, \overrightarrow{z_2}, \overrightarrow{z_3}, \overrightarrow{z_4})$ pointing in the direction of the light beam emitted from the projector (Fig. 2a), the components of these vectors are function of the orientation of the projector (Φ, θ) and the projector characteristics (α, β) (Fig. 3). Then we compute S', the maximal rectangular area included in S. We then compute homographic transformation H between S and the original image I, using A and B: the matrix based on P that delimits S, and the coordinates of the corners of I:

$$H = A^{-1}.B$$

Finally to compute the new location of a given point $P_{I'}$ in the undistorted image, we apply the following formula, using the (x, y) coordinates in the referential of the undistorted projection area:

$$P_{I'} = \begin{bmatrix} H_{1,1} - H_{3,1}.x & H_{1,2} - H_{3,2}.x \\ H_{2,1} - H_{3,1}.y & H_{2,2} - H_{3,2}.y \end{bmatrix}^{-1} \begin{bmatrix} x - H_{3,1} \\ y - H_{2,3} \end{bmatrix}$$

$H_{i,j}$ is the element of H 3×3 matrix at the i line and j column.

5   User Study

Our intuition is that, by making the motorized projection arm visible, we can help the user to more quickly narrow down the search space for the target. In this user study, we try to identify the relative contributions of being able to see the arm versus a moving spotlight that also guides the user to the target. As mentioned earlier, the PAA provides several cues to guide the user's search, including the movement of the spot or the direction of the arm. In this laboratory study, we wanted to investigate two of these properties by controlling (1) the visibility of the arm and (2) the visibility of the spot while moving the arm. The four resulting techniques are illustrated on Table 2.

Arm & Spot is the PAA technique: Users can look at the direction of the arm and follow the spotlight to help locate the target. The Arm and Spot techniques derive from PAA by removing one property: Arm does not let users follow the spotlight (which only appears once the final direction of the arm has been reached) while Spot does not let users look at the direction of the arm. The Baseline condition completes our design space so that we can precisely understand the relative contributions of the arm and the spotlight.

5.1   Participants and Apparatus

12 participants (6 female) aged from 20 to 38 (M = 27.83, SD = 4.8) were recruited from our institution. They were compensated for their participation with candy.

Room. The study was conducted in a room (5 × 5m2) under standard overhead lighting condition. The room was equipped with an ARTTrack tracking system [0] to track the position and orientation of the pico-projector and the user. Figure 1b shows the room.

Targets. Each wall contained 8 paper panels of 20 targets (total = 480) to mimic the real-world control dials in a control room. We used the three walls to compare three conditions: Targets located in front, behind, or on the side of the participant (Fig. 4). Each target was a rectangle (4 × 3.5 cm2) containing an id of two characters (letter + digit). The font size was 64 to ensure that each participant could easily read them. The distance between targets of 4 cm was superior to the precision of the system.

Techniques. Each of the four tested techniques relies on the same hardware presented above to avoid possible confounded variables (e.g. inertia of the arm): PAA was installed in the center of the room as shown on Fig. 4, with the participant located on its left side. The spotlight has the same shape as a target. We fixed its size to be big

Table 2. The four guidance techniques we explore in this study. They are organized according to two dimensions: the visibility of the arm and the visibility of the spotlight while moving the arm.

		Visibility of the spot while moving	
		No	Yes
Visibility of the arm	No	Baseline	Spot
	Yes	Arm	Arm & spot

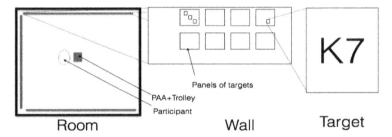

Fig. 4. Left: map of the room; Right: example of a target part on a panel

enough to be visible from across the room yet not overlap the objects in the vicinity of the target. We also wanted to maintain a small enough size to avoid being overly intrusive while moving. We used the same size and shape of spotlight in all conditions to ensure the same level of difficulty and to avoid to biasing the results. This included correcting for distortion and resizing the spotlight during movement to compensate for the effects of non-perpendicular projection angles on the wall ($\Phi \neq 0$ or $\theta \neq 0$) (see Fig. 3). In the Arm condition (spot not visible), the spotlight was switched off during arm movement. In the Spot condition (arm not visible), participants wore basketball dribble glasses that prevented them from looking down at the arm. Finally, participants wore a hat to track head position as well as earphones with a gentle white noise to ensure that they could not hear the sound of the servomotors, which could serve as a hint about relative distance to the target. This was done to prevent confounding factors and to be in accordance with our primary context (control rooms) which is noisy and where users cannot rely on auditory feedback.

5.2   Task and Procedure

The task consisted of finding a target as quickly and accurately as possible. Participants started a trial by pressing button. The arm then moved from its current position (that of the last target) to highlight the next target. Participants then searched for the target on the three walls by using the arm or the moving spot depending on the conditions. As soon as the participants identified the target, they pressed the same button to stop the trial, at which point the spot disappeared and participants orally indicated the ID of the target to the experimenter. Participants could take a short break between each trial and between each block. Participants were videotaped during the experiment. After the experiment, they answered a questionnaire and were debriefed via a semi-structured interview.

5.3   Design

We used a within-participants design: each participant tested the four techniques. The order of techniques was counter-balanced using a Latin square design. Participants performed two blocks per technique. Each block contained 25 different target selections (from 460 targets). The location of the targets was randomized in order to appear either on the wall in front of the user, on a lateral wall on his side or on the wall behind him. In summary, the design of this study was: 12 participants × 4 techniques (baseline; arm; spot; arm&spot) × 2 blocks × 25 targets = 2400 selections.

6 Results and Observations

6.1 Completion Time Analysis

We assumed the normal distribution of our data (Shapiro-Wilk test) and we used a three way ANOVA which showed a significant effect on completion time of the location of the target relative to the initial orientation of the participant ($F2,22 = 225.17$, $P < 0.001$). Post hoc Tukey tests revealed that this effect is significant for each pair of relative locations between the user and the target. Indeed, the search time was faster if the target was: on the wall in front of the participant (1.6 s) rather than on the wall behind him (2.6 s, 38 % improvement); on the front wall rather than on the lateral wall (2.4 s, 33 % improvement); and on the lateral wall (2.4 s) rather than on wall behind (2.6 s, 8 % improvement).

ANOVA also showed a significant effect of the visibility of the arm on completion time ($F1,11 = 91.79$, $P < 0.001$) (see Fig. 5). Indeed, participants were faster when they could see the arm (1.9 s) than when it was not visible (2.5 s).

ANOVA also revealed a significant interaction effect between the visibility of the arm and the relative location of the target from to the initial orientation of the user ($F2,22 = 5.20$, $P < 0.05$) with a highest improvement (26 %) when the target is behind the user (see Fig. 6). Post hoc Tukey tests confirmed a significant effect for all possible interactions between visibility and relative location, except in two cases: (a) when the arm is visible, for lateral (2.0 s) vs. behind (2.2 s), locations; (b) for lateral locations when the arm is visible (2.0 s) vs. for front locations when the arm is not visible (1.9 s). For the remaining cases, we found significant decreasing completion time with increasing location distance whether the arm is visible or not.

Finally, there was no significant effect of the visibility of the spotlight while moving (See Fig. 5).

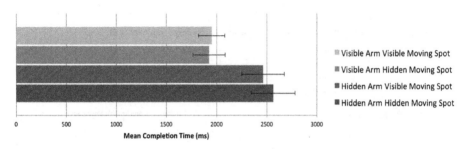

Fig. 5. Mean completion time (ms) according to the visibility of the arm and the visibility of the spot while moving.

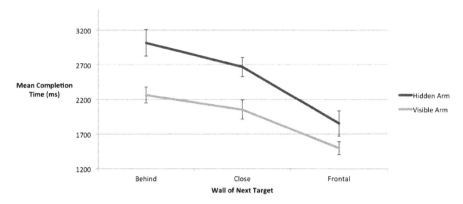

Fig. 6. Completion time according to the visibility of the arm and the relative location of the target from the orientation of the user (behind, close to (on the lateral wall), and in front of the user).

6.2   Observations and Questionnaire

The participants rated the ease of the search task for each technique. They preferred the two conditions where the Arm was visible. Then, for each case (Arm visible and Arm not visible), they preferred having a spotlight (Fig. 7).

We also made the following observations:

When the arm is visible, users seem to orient themselves faster from the beginning to the end of the search task and stop on the correct direction without exceeding the target. When the arm is hidden and the spot visible, users start moving rapidly but become slower at the end.

Unsurprisingly, when the arm and the spotlight are not visible, users seem to be slower than in any other condition at all stages of the searching task. They also occasionally go on the wrong direction, which never happened when both the arm and the spot were visible.

All participants stated that they were aware about the movement of the arm in their peripheral field of view. Some also said they just followed the arm automatically, without thinking.

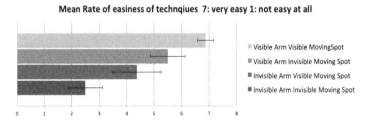

Fig. 7. Subjective feeling of easiness for the four conditions (7 corresponds to very easy /1 to uneasy).

The interviews show that users rely on different strategies depending on whether the arm and the moving spot are visible or not. Surprisingly, more than half of the participants (55 %) reported that, when the arm was visible, they did not care about the spotlight while it was moving. However, they all tried to follow the spotlight when the arm was not available.

7 Discussion

Moving Arm. Results confirm our hypothesis that the visibility of the arm reduces completion time. However, the results are surprisingly good with a decrease of 24 % in average, regardless of the visibility of the moving spotlight and relative location of the target. The visibility of the arm is especially useful when the task is complex (i.e. the target is not in front of the user). Participants provided several possible explanations: The arm provides an efficient visual cue for localizing the general direction of the targets, presumably because the movement could easily be perceived in the peripheral field of view. This explains why users relied on the arm even when the spotlight was visible. When the arm was visible, participants always oriented their body in the correct direction without overshooting the target. As a result, they did not perform unnecessary movements, which could be time consuming and tiring. This effect could explain the completion time gain. Moreover, several participants mentioned that they were aware of the direction of the arm even without looking at it thanks to the use of their peripheral vision. This is especially useful in scenarios where users have to share their attention (for instance between a paper procedure and verifying and activating controls).

Moving Spotlight. We expected that the introduction of the moving spotlight would reduce the completion time. However, our results did not reveal a significant effect regardless the conditions (visibility of the arm and location of the targets). Participants explained that the speed of the spotlight was too fast and that they had some difficulties to track it. It results that some participants sometimes tried to anticipate the movement of the spotlight and overshoot the target. As a consequence, the spotlight was not as useful as expected. It would have been possible to use a larger spotlight or reduce its speed. However, both have some drawbacks. Increasing the size of the spotlight can disturb other users (operators in nuclear plants; consumer in a supermarket) working in the same environment. Reducing the speed of the spotlight would also reduce the speed of the arm, which was not judged too fast. When the moving spotlight was combined with the moving arm, participants explained that they primarily used the arm because they found it more useful.

Finally, in light of the obtained results, it would be interesting to explore several potential optimizations: depending on the density of the projection area and whether it is shared by other users or not, the speed of the arm and the size of the spot may be controlled dynamically during the movement of the arm. For example, if it is possible to model shared and non-shared spaces, the moving spotlight could be made bigger when moving the arm so as to allow the user to more easily following it, and to reduce its size in shared areas. Also, the motors could adjust their speed based on the difficulty of following the spotlight on the particular projection surface. In the future when the servomotors and projectors become smaller and the PAA could fit in the hand, we could explore the impact of haptic feedback on localization performance.

8   Conclusion and Future Work

We have designed, implemented and evaluated a novel guidance technique, PAA, which is inspired from the way humans perform in air pointing gestures with their arms to orient each other. Moreover, this technique also relies on a projection system to allow precise indication of the target. Our user study provides two main findings: (1) the moving arm helps users to localize the target especially when the task is complex (i.e. the target is not in front of the users) because users can quickly get a raw idea of the direction of the target: the arm is always localized at the same location, in the peripheral vision of the user. In contrast, (2) the moving spot does not provide real benefits because it requires a lot of attention to track it. A challenge would be to design a spotlight easier to track without disturbing other operators and impairing the performance of the arm.

In the present study, we focused on a fully automated PAA: the system controls the direction of the arm. As a future work, we plan to investigate scenarios where users (partially) control the arm and how shared control will impact visual search performance. Moreover, we plan to evaluate PAA with multiple operators (and possibly multiple PAAs) to better understand the impact of our system on cognitive load, global awareness and concentration. We also plan to investigate the impact of 3D pointing using the arm vs. 2D pointing using a display to indicate a direction in 3D space.

Acknowledgement. This work is supported by the French ANR/Investissement d'Avenir "Cluster Connexion" and by the ÉQUIPEX DigiScope ANR-10-EQPX-0026.

References

1. http://www.ar-tracking.com
2. Butz, A., Schneider, M., Spassova, M.: SearchLight – a lightweight search function for pervasive environments. In: Ferscha, A., Mattern, F. (eds.) PERVASIVE 2004. LNCS, vol. 3001, pp. 351–356. Springer, Heidelberg (2004)
3. Cauchard, J.R., Fraser, M., Han, T., Subramanian, S.: Steerable projection: exploring alignment in interactive mobile displays. Pers. Ubiquitous Comput. **16**, 27–37 (2012)
4. Cosgun, A., Sisbot, E.A., Christensen, H.I.: Evaluation of rotational and directional vibration patterns on a tactile belt for guiding visually impaired people. In: 2014 IEEE Haptics Symposium (HAPTICS), pp. 367–370 (2014)
5. Dramas, F., Oriola, B., Katz, B.G., Thorpe, S.J., Jouffrais, C.: Designing an assistive device for the blind based on object localization and augmented auditory reality. In: Proceedings of the 10th International ACM SIGACCESS Conference on Computers and accessibility, pp. 263–264. ACM (2008)

6. Ehnes, J., Hirose, M.: Projected Reality - Enhancing Projected Augmentations by Dynamically Choosing the Best Among Several Projection Systems. In: IEEE Conference on Virtual Reality, pp. 283–284 (2006)

7. Ehnes, J., Hirota, K., Hirose, M.: Projected augmentation - augmented reality using rotatable video projectors. In: IEEE & ACM ISMAR 2004, pp. 26–35 (2004)

8. Van Erp, J.B.F., Van Veen, H.A.H.C., Jansen, C., Dobbins, T.: Waypoint navigation with a vibrotactile waist belt. ACM Trans. Appl. Percept. 2(2), ACM (2005)

9. Gröhn, M., Lokki, T., Takala, T.: Comparison of auditory, visual, and audiovisual navigation in a 3D space. ACM Trans. Appl. Percept. 2(4), 564–570 (2005)

10. Harada, S., Takagi, H., Asakawa, C.: On the audio representation of radial direction. In: Proceedings of the SIGCHI Conference on Human Factors in Computing Systems, pp. 2779–2788. ACM (2011)

11. Harrison, C., Benko, H., Wilson, A.D.: OmniTouch: wearable multitouch interaction everywhere. In: UIST 2011, pp. 441–450. ACM (2011)

12. Henderson, S.J., Feiner, S.: Evaluating the benefits of augmented reality for task localization in maintenance of an armored personnel carrier turret. In: IEEE ISMAR 2009, pp. 135–144 (2009)

13. Henry, P., Krainin, M., Herbst, E., Ren, X., Fox, D.: RGB-D maping:using kinect-style depth cameras for dense 3D modeling of indoorenvironments. IEEE Int. J. Rob. Res. (IJRR) 31(5), 647–663 (2012)

14. Ishii, K., Yamamoto, Y., Imai, M., Nakadai, K.: A navigation system using ultrasonic directional speaker with rotating base. In: Smith, M.J., Salvendy, G. (eds.) HCII 2007. LNCS, vol. 4558, pp. 526–535. Springer, Heidelberg (2007)

15. Jones, B., Sodhi, R., Murdock, M., Mehra, R., Benko, H., Wilson, A., Shapira, L.: RoomAlive: magical experiences enabled by scalable, adaptive projector-camera units. In: UIST 2014, pp. 637–644. ACM (2014)

16. Kratz, S., Rohs, M., Reitberger, F., Moldenhauer, J.: Attjector: an attention-following wearable projector. In: Kinect Workshop at Pervasive (2012)

17. Lee, J.C., Dietz, P.H., Maynes-Aminzade, D., Raskar, R., Hudson, S.E.: Automatic projector calibration with embedded light sensors. In: UIST 2004, pp. 123–126. ACM (2004)

18. Lehtinen, V., Oulasvirta, A., Salovaara, A., Nurmi, P.: Dynamic tactile guidance for visual search tasks. In: UIST 2012, pp. 445–452. ACM (2012)

19. Li, M., et al.: ProFi: design and evaluation of a product finder in a supermarket scenario. In: UbiComp 2013, pp. 977–984. Adjunct (2013)

20. Li, M., Arning, K., Sack, O., Park, J., Kim, M.-H., Ziefle, M., Kobbelt, L.: Evaluation of a mobile projector-based indoor navigation interface. Interact. Comput. 26(6), 595–613 (2013)

21. Lindeman, R.W., Sibert, J.L., Mendez-Mendez, E., Patil, S. Phifer, D.: Effectiveness of directional vibrotactile cuing on a building-clearing task. In: CHI 2005, pp. 271–280. ACM (2005)

22. Ngo, M., Spence, C.: Auditory, tactile, and multisensory cues facilitate search for dynamic visual stimuli. Attention Percept. Psychophys. 72, 1654–1665 (2010)

23. Ogata, K., Seya, Y., Watanabe, K., Ifukube, T.: Effects of visual cues on the complicated search task. pp. 478–485. ACM (2012)

24. Ota, S., Takegawa, Y., Terada, T., Tsukamoto, M.: A method for wearable projector selection that considers the viewability of projected images. Comput. Entertain. 8, 17:1–17:16 (2010)

25. Pinhanez, C.: The everywhere displays projector: a device to create. In: UbiComp 2001, pp. 315–331. ACM (2001)

26. Pinhanez, C., Kjeldsen, R., Levas, A., Pingali, G., Podlaseck, M., Sukaviriya, N.: Applications of steerable projector-camera systems. In: ICCV Workshop on Projector-Camera Systems, IEEE (2003)

27. Pulkki, V.: Virtual sound source positioning using vector base amplitude panning. J. Audio Eng. Soc. **45**(6), 456–466 (1997)

28. Sukthankar, R., Stockton, R.G., Mullin, M.D.: Smarter presentations: exploiting homography in camera-projector systems. In: ICCV 2001, (1) pp. 247–253 (2001)

29. Umlauf, E.J., Piringer, H., Reitmayr, G., Schmalstieg, D.: ARLib: the augmented library. In: The First IEEE International Workshop on Augmented Reality Toolkit, p. 2 (2002)

30. Willis, K.D.D., Poupyrev, I., Hudson, S.E., Mahler, M.: SideBySide: Ad hoc multi-user interaction with handheld projectors. In: UIST 2011, pp. 431–440 (2011)

31. Wilson, A., Benko, H., Izadi, S., Hilliges, O.: Steerable augmented reality with the beamatron. In: UIST 2012, pp. 413–422. ACM (2012)

32. Yamano, S., Hamajo, T., Takahashi, S., Higuchi, K.: EyeSound: single-modal mobile navigation using directionally annotated music. In: Augmented Human, p. 1. ACM (2012)

It's Not the Way You Look, It's How You Move: Validating a General Scheme for Robot Affective Behaviour

Jekaterina Novikova, Gang Ren$^{(\boxtimes)}$, and Leon Watts

Department of Computer Science, University of Bath, Bath, UK
{j.novikova,g.ren,l.watts}@bath.ac.uk

Abstract. In the emerging world of human-robot interaction, people and robots will work together to achieve joint objectives. This paper discusses the design and validation of a general scheme for creating emotionally expressive behaviours for robots, in order that people might better interpret how a robot collaborator is succeeding or failing in its work. It exemplifies a unified approach to creating robot behaviours for two very different robot forms, based on combinations of four groups of design parameters (approach/avoidance, energy, intensity and frequency). 59 people rated video clips of robots performing expressive behaviours both for emotional expressivity on Valence-Arousal-Dominance dimensions, and their judgement of the successfulness of the robots' work. Results are discussed in terms of the utility of expressive behaviour for facilitating human understanding of robot intentions and the design of cues for basic emotional states.

Keywords: Human-robot interaction · Social robotics · Nonverbal communication · Artificial emotions · Body language

1 Introduction

People tend to treat interactive systems as if they are social agents [20]. McCarthy famously argued that people routinely attribute mental states even to simple systems, such as a thermostat, to make sense of their operational dynamics when their state is otherwise uninspectable [15]. When treated as social agents, interactive systems are additionally attributed with social qualities, such as helpfulness or obstinacy, which can influence a person's readiness or ability to make use of them. These qualities could serve to facilitate social coordination in Human-Robot Interaction (HRI) by reflecting aspects of an agent's ability to take action. From a design perspective, this depends upon the creation of cues that can effectively encode relevant social qualities. Researchers in Computer-Supported Cooperative Work have a long-standing interest in the design of systems that provide cues about the status of ongoing collaborator activity. These fall under the general theme of support for awareness [24] and range from the mechanistic articulation of work by coordinating action [18], through to general

© IFIP International Federation for Information Processing 2015
J. Abascal et al. (Eds.): INTERACT 2015, Part III, LNCS 9298, pp. 239–258, 2015.
DOI: 10.1007/978-3-319-22698-9_16

activity-based indications of social action with a powerful influence on the attitudes and feelings of collaborators [1].

Although awareness is a multifaceted problem, Schmidt argues that its support always depends on combining a selective aspect of the world of work with abstractions that span the material and computational world [24]. In this paper, we consider the problem of designing a set of emotional cues for robots that could help a person to maintain awareness of relevant states of a robot collaborator. We describe an approach to the systematic design of such cues that depends on qualities of emotional expression. By drawing on affect research in the animal world, we translate a set of design rules for generating expressive behaviours for robots into the design of five basic emotions for two robots of very different construction and behavioural capability. We argue that this general approach could be mapped to any physical robot form, thus advancing the design potential for the use of affect in HRI.

Bodily expression of emotion is an important part of human socio-emotional communication in both humans and animals [2]. Prior studies have shown that affective cues can be interpreted successfully by people when expressed by robots [12,22]. Research on artificial expressions of emotion has made use of a variety of approaches, typically tailored towards particular conceptions of the form of robot on which they will be displayed. In some studies, animators are employed to design emotional movements for a robot [21]. In other studies, body movements of humanoid robots are copied from a human actors' body language [4]. However, humanoid robots represent a highly restricted physical form. Some researchers define more general high-level design patterns for creating an emotionally expressive behavior in robots [12,22,26] but have struggled to establish their general utility [17].

There is a considerable gap between high-level design guidelines for bodily expression of emotion and the implementation of a specific robot with expressive movements. We extrapolate from the design scheme of Novikova and Watts to treat non-humanoid robots in terms of their expressivity [17]. In addition to our goal of establishing the validity of a general framework for designing intelligible emotional cues for social robots, we shall describe in detail how a particular scheme [17] can be implemented into different types of non-humanoid robots. We validate the design scheme with a user study, based on Valence-Arousal-Dominance (VAD) ratings of behavioural expressions as judged by human observers. We thus present data on the consistency of interpretation of expressive behaviours enacted by two non-humanoid robots with very different degrees of expressivity. The contributions of the paper reflect both design and validation considerations:

1. Refinement and generalisation of a design scheme proposed by [17] by presenting a new way of classifying robots based on expressivity, illustrated with five basic emotions as a sequence of VAD parameters.
2. Validation by exposing similarities and differences in the perception of VAD after applying the design scheme to non-humanoid robots of different expressivity.

2   Related Work

2.1   Emotional Body Language (EBL) in Robots

Nonverbal communication through body movements plays an important role in human communication. Expressing emotions is one of the main functions of bodily communication [2]. But people and animals don't only *express* emotional feelings, they also *communicate* certain information through their emotional postures and gestures. Thus expressive behaviors can serve as a rich source of information in inter human communication. Heider and Simmel [11] demonstrated in 1944 already that people are biased to interpret moving figures and motion patterns in social or emotional terms. Their experiment showed that it's possible to communicate emotional meaning to people through very basic forms and thus created the base for future work on emotionally expressive robots.

For designing expressive and communicative robot movements it is important to know which features cause the interpretation of intentions and emotions [8]. Up to date, the researchers mostly focused on identification of features related to animacy [25]. However, there exist a small number of studies investigating the relation between robot movements and perceived emotion. The biggest part of these studies use humanoid robots as examples and almost directly transfer human emotive gestures to humanoid robot bodies [4,28].

Karg et al. [12] in their study analyzed if a hexapod robot can express emotion in the way it walks and if these expressions are recognizable. The authors mapped human emotive gait parameters to a hexapod by changing a step length, height and time for one step depending on the emotion. The results of the study revealed that different levels of pleasure, arousal and dominance were recognizable in the way the hexapod walked. Furthermore, higher velocity of a gait resulted in a higher level of preceived arousal, while lower velocity resulted in lower pleasure and lower dominance. Saerbeck and Bartneck [22] also analyzed the relationship between motion characteristics of a robot and perceived affect. They systematically varied two motion characteristics, acceleration and curvature, and found a strong relation between these motion parameters and attribution of affect. Specifically, they found that the level of acceleration is correlated with perceived arousal. They didn't find a direct relationship between acceleration or curvature and perceived valence. Two different robotic embodiments - the iCat robot shaped as a cat with an animated mechanical face and the Roomba robot of a circular shape - were used in this experiment. The authors didn't find significant differences between the embodiments, thus suggested that motion design tools can be used across embodiments.

In a recent study, Singh and Young [26] investigated how a dog-inspired tail interface can be applied to utility robots and communicate high-level robotic states through affect. The study indicated that people were able to interpret a range of affective states from various tail configurations and gestures. As a result, the authors presented a set of guidelines for mapping tail parameters to intended perceived robotic state, e.g. a higher speed projects a higher valence and arousal while a lower speed projects a lower valence and lower arousal, a large horizontal wag results in a higher valence.

There also exist several recent studies on the use of Laban Movement analysis (LMA) for design of emotionally expressive robots with non-humanoid shape. For example, [3] discusses design parameters for designing the movement of a robot with a circular shape using Laban movement analysis which helped to improve the recognition of emotions in the context of a game. Another study [23] develops a computational model for recognizing and generating affective hand movements for display on anthropomorphic and non-anthropomorphic structures. These studies provide an evidence that even very low actuated robots or non-anthropomorphic structures can make expressive movements based on LMA.

Based on this research, in our recent study recent study [17] we presented an integrated account of the effect of a range of characteristics of robot movement on human perception of affect. We used anatomical body planes as a reference for combining research on animal social behaviour with Shape and Effort dimensions derived from the Laban theory of movements so present a scheme for designing emotionally expressive robotic behaviours. The scheme includes two concepts to define emotionally expressive behaviours for robots: Expressive Shape and Expressive Quality. Expressive Shape defines how the overall posture of a robot should change in terms of its physical form, and relates this change to the emotional significance of approach and avoidance in the animal world. It is associated with ten distinct parameters of body motion (see Table 1). Expressive Quality defines the performative characteristics of robot movement, i.e. strength or frequency, again grounding the meaning of these characteristics in prior work on signals of affective state in animals. It is associated with a further thirteen parameters of motion. The general grounding of the scheme is intended to reflect its generality in application for different types of non-humanoid robots. However, it has not been validated in a design context and does not explain how this design scheme might be implemented with different forms of non-humanoid robots. Thus in this current work we introduce a new concept of a robot *expressivity* that allows us to further generalize earlier proposed scheme for designing expressive behaviour and validate it with two very different types of robots.

It is common for non-humanoid robots to vary greatly in terms of the number of embodied degrees of freedom, and the maximum amplitude, velocity and frequency of motions they are able to perform. However, there are some similarities in the influence of the parameter on perceived dimensions of emotional meaning, e.g. higher speed of expressive movement often increases perceived level of arousal, or that reduction of size (shrinking) can reduce the perceived level of dominance. Thus, it may be that all robots are capable of expressing basic emotional states, regardless of their form factor, as long as their behavioural capabilities are mobilised appropriately. So, from a design perspective, we propose that all robots can be described in terms of their general *expressivity* whilst still being able to convey emotional meaning through their movement. As a property, we argue that expressivity refers to aspects of the construction of a robot that constrain the robot's ability to vary in terms of Expressive Shape and Expressive Quality. This leads us to our first hypothesis:

Fig. 1. The more expressive Lego robot E4 (left) and less expressive Sphero robot (right).

H1. Perceptions of emotionally expressive movements do not vary as a function of the degree of a non-humanoid robot's expressivity.

We provide a detailed description of expressivity as it applies to this study in the method section, so that its treatment as an independent variable is clear.

2.2 Value of Emotions

Organizational behavior researchers have investigated the social influence of human emotions in a workplace [10]. The way individuals conduct their individual work is often conditioned by inferences about the emotional state of other people. Appraisal theories state that emotions can tell a story about the agent that expresses them. Thus, people may draw inferences about the beliefs and intentions of other expressive agents, given perceptions of their emotional state [9]. Prior research in HRI suggests that the same can be true in human-robot teams. Even the non-emotional non-verbal signals of a robot can improve the performance of tasks and decrease perceived human's workload [14]. Beck et al. [4] suggest that emotionally expressive tutoring robots would help people to learn better and faster. The findings of [13] indicate that a social robot with emotional behavior can serve as a better assistant in a gaming situation than functionally equivalent robots that do not have emotional behaviours.

From a collaboration perspective, the value of such inferences is to facilitate social coordination. They define expectations for the action that other agents may take, given a basic common sense frame of reasoning [15], but also with an understanding of the ongoing status of their activity. With social agency, it is highly likely that an observer's perceptions of robot affective state will also be conditioned by their general understanding of the task context. More specifically, emotional expressions reflect beliefs about the progress of the work an agent is carrying out. Task progress is a joint function of changes that result from an individual's actions and changes to the environment in which they operate. Consequently, alongside the contribution of emotional expression, it is important to consider how positive and negative task-related events might influence an observer's situational awareness. We shall also treat task context as an important control variable for an observer's expectations about a robot's next actions, in particular whether or not the robot will continue with its current course of action.

All these findings lead us to the third hypothesis:

H2. An observer's beliefs about the successfulness of a robot's actions varies consistently with the nature of the robot's expressive behaviour.

In this paper, we treat beliefs about successfulness through the two complementary observer ratings: judgement of whether the robot successfully completed its task, and judgement of the robot's intention to continue or abandon its current activity.

3   Method

We designed a mixed-model experiment, in which participants observed and rated video clips of a robot in action. We used a between-subject design for presenting clips of two different robots - a more expressive non-humanoid robot E4 with several limbs for the first group of participants and a less expressive abstract robotic ball Sphero for the second group. Within each group, we used a within-subject design for presenting subjects with a sequence of expressive behaviours performed by their respective robot.

3.1   Classifying Robot Expressivity

We used the scheme proposed by [17] for designing emotional body language in our robots. The scheme presents a hierarchical system of design characteristics combined into two large movement groups: *Shape* and *Quality*. The lowest level of the scheme consists of 23 parameters. We linked each parameter of the *Shape* group to the capability of a robot to move its body in a specific way, depending on its construction. We also linked each parameter of the *Quality* group to an ability to program robot actions in a specific way. The list of *Shape* and *Quality* design parameters (DPs) with an associated ability to program robot movements are listed in the right-hand part of Table 1.

The list of expressive parameters, allowed us to define the level of expressivity for any type of robot simply by summing the parameters that can be activated in a specific robot. Thus, the maximum expressivity level for any type of robot is determined by its ability to make use of all 23 parameters. This is a simplistic method for contrasting the base expressivity of any form of robot since it does not privilege any particular parameter. It may be that specific parameters of Expressive Quality or Expressive Shape, or combinations thereof, invoke higher emotional significance. We shall return to this point in our general discussion.

Each design parameter is associated with one or several emotions, as we'll discuss later in the section on *Emotional Expressions*. Thus, the higher a robot's expressivity, the greater its potential ability to express emotion through body language.

Table 1. Parameters of a *Shape* (left) and *Quality* (right) group with associated robot's programming abilities.

SHAPE				QUALITY			
Group	ID	Parameter Name	Body Part or Ability	Group	ID	Parameter Name	Ability to Program
Approach	1	Transfer weight forward	ability to bend or bow forward	Energy	11	High strength	motor's speed at high level
Approach	2	Move limbs forward	movable limbs	Energy	12	Low strength	motor's speed at low level
Approach	3	Move its body forward	wheels, tracks, legs. Roll, fly, swim, drive, go, move the body forward	Intensity	13	Sudden	sudden start/finish
				Intensity	14	Not sudden	smooth start/finish
Approach	4	Move visible appendage(-s) away from the body	movable limbs, visible movable appendage(-s) not used for moving forward/backward, movable head	Flow	15	Short duration	movement able to finish in a short time
				Flow	16	Medium duration	movement able to finish in a medium time
Approach	5	Extend or expand its body	ability to extend or expand itself	Flow	17	Long duration	movement able to finish in a long time
Avoidance	6	Transfer weight backward	ability to bend or bow backward	Flow	18	High change in tempo	motor's speed change
Avoidance	7	Move limbs backward	movable limbs	Flow	19	High frequency	high level of vibration, spinning or frequent movements of the limbs
Avoidance	8	Move its body backward	wheels, tracks, legs. Roll backward, fly backward, swim backward, drive backward, go backward, move the body backward	Flow	20	Medium frequency	medium level of vibration, spinning or frequent movements of the limbs
Avoidance	9	Attract limbs close to the body	movable limbs, visible movable appendage(-s) not used for moving forward/backward, movable head	Flow	21	Low frequency	low level of vibration, spinning or frequent movements of the limbs
				Flow	22	Direct trajectory	straight, linear, direct movement of the whole body
Avoidance	10	Reduce its body	ability to reduce itself	Flow	23	Indirect trajectory	curved movement of the whole body

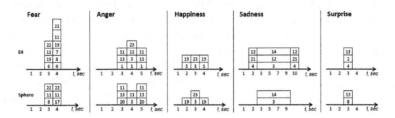

Fig. 2. The combination of design parameters for the emotional expressions of fear, anger, happiness, sadness and surprise, as implemented in a more expressive E4 robot (top) and a less expressive Sphero robot (bottom).

3.2   Emotional Expressions

We created five emotional expressions for the robots, namely: (1) afraid, (2) angry, (3) happy, (4) sad and (5) surprised. The emotions were selected as a subset of commonly known *discrete* or *basic* emotions, as defined by [7]. We used design parameters shown in Table 1 to create emotional expressions in robots, based on the mapping from animal behaviours to general parameters of body movement in [17]. We were able to make use of more design parameters for creating expressions in the high expressivity robot E4 than in the less expressive Sphero because of differences in their construction. One of the contributions of this paper is to demonstrate how a general scheme for designing robot emotional expressions can be mapped to non-humanoid robots with very different expressive possibilities. The precise mappings require the designer to exercise judgement, as it true of all design, but the general scheme does not privilege any particular parameter. Thus, design freedom is preserved for at least basic emotions. Figure 2 presents the combinations of design parameters used for creating each emotional expression in both robots, where block numbers correspond to the ID numbers allocated to design parameters and the horizontal axis represents time of onset and offset in seconds. For example, to create an expression of happiness in the Sphero robot, we used a parameter No. 19 (vibration at a high level) at two seconds, parameters No. 3 and 23 at three seconds (moving forward in a curved trajectory), and parameter No. 19 (fast vibration) at four seconds, creating an expressive behaviour that lasted for three seconds in total. As seen from the Fig. 2, both robots use the same initial DPs for expressing each of five basic emotions e.g. parameters No. 8, 11 and 22 for expressing Fear; 3, 11 and 13 for expressing Anger etc. Such a similarity in designing emotional expressions makes the comparison of the movements valid although the capabilities of the actuators are very different in two presented robots.

Some previous studies [4, 19] showing an importance of a context in interpreting robot's affective cues encouraged us to include a context in the design of our study. We linked a situational context in which robots were acting to the three emotional dimensions of valence, arousal and dominance in accordance with a VAD space proposed by [16]. For each dimension, we designed a positive and negative context thus getting six contextual environments. For creating the context of a positive valence (V+) something positive happened in the robot's environment, e.g. robot managed to finish its task successfully. For the context of a negative valence (V-), something negative happened in the environment due to robot's fault. Similarly, the context was linked to both positive and negative arousal and dominance, as shown in the Table 2. The neutral context was the same for all the dimensions and ment that nothing happened in the robot's environment.

Table 2. The combination of a context and a consistent/inconsistent/neutral emotional expression. Here, A+,V+,D+ means a context of a positive arousal, valence, dominance, A-,V-,D- means a context of a negative arousal, valence, dominance. Number in brackets is a number of a test condition.

Type of context (more detailed explanation)	Consistent emotional expression	Inconsistent emotional expression	Neutral emotional expression
A+ (a block suddenly falls down from above in front of a robot)	sad (1)	surprised (2)	none (3)
A- (the task is already finished, robot's help is not needed)	surprised (4)	sad (5)	none (6)
V+ (robot finishes its task successfully)	happy (7)	sad (8)	none (9)
V- (all the blocks fall and scatter due to robot's fault)	sad (10)	happy (11)	none (12)
D+ (a dangerous big obstacle prevents a robot from completing a task)	afraid (13)	angry (14)	none (15)
D- (a harmless small obstacle prevents a robot from completing a task)	angry (16)	afraid (17)	none (18)

3.3   Independent Variables

The two main independent variables in our experiment were *expressivity* of robot (high expressivity vs. low expressivity), *Design Parameter group* (approach/avoidance; high/low energy; high/low intensity; high/medium/low frequency). We also varied the influence the occurrence of positive and negative events in the robot's environment to examine the *consistency of emotional ratings* as an indication of the robustness of expressive behaviours (consistent; inconsistent; not emotional).

Robots. We used two robots in our experiment: E4 and Sphero (see Fig. 1).

Robot with Higher Level of Expressivity. The more expressive robot, E4, was implemented with Lego Mindstorms NXT, was based on a Phobot robot design [6]. The robot had two motors which allowed it (1) to move forwards and backwards on a surface, (2) to move the upper part of its body. The upper body part was constructed such that the robot's hands moved together with its neck and eyebrows. Its neck could move forwards and backwards, and its hands and eyebrows could move up and down. The overall expressivity level of the E4 robot was 19. The RWTH Mindstorms NXT Toolbox for MATLAB[1] was used to program E4's behaviours. This software is a free open source product and is subject to the GPL.

Robot with Lower Level of Expressivity. The less expressive robot, Sphero, is a robotic ball[2] with a ARM Cortex M4 processor, two RGB LEDs and two internal motors that allowed it (1) to roll on a surface at different speeds and directions, (2) to spin or vibrate at different frequencies. Although it is also possible to change Sphero's colour, we did not use this function in our study. The outer shell is made of white polycarbonate. The overall expressivity of the Sphero robot was 12.5. We used the Android SDK provided by Sphero[3] to program Sphero's rolling direction, speed and directional pattern. We used a Samsung TabPRO 8.4 tablet to control Sphero via Bluetooth for creating the video clips.

Design Parameters (DPs). Four groups of design parameters (DPs) were used as independent variables in our study. For the high-level group of *Shape*, we used *Approach* and *Avoidance* DPs. For the high-level group of *Quality*, we used low and high *Energy*, low and high *Intensity* and low, medium and high *Frequency*, which is a sub-level of the *Flow* group.

Consistency of Emotional Ratings. We recorded a set of videos where an event in the robot's task environment was combined with a specific emotional expression of the same and the opposite level of the appropriate dimension, e.g. an event of a positive valence was recorded with the robot expressing an emotion of a positive valence, of negative valence and a neutral one. If the sign of context's emotional dimension matched the sign of a robot's expressed emotion on the same dimension, we treated the emotion as *consistent*. If a sign of the context was opposite to the sign of a presented robot's emotional expression, we treated it as *inconsistent*. If robot only performed the actions related to its task and didn't perform any emotional expression in addition, we called such an emotion *neutral*.

3.4 Test Conditions

We recorded five emotional expressions performed by each robot in a neutral environmental context. In addition, we recorded eighteen combinations of each context and a consistent, inconsistent and neutral emotion. The combination of a

---

[1] http://www.mindstorms.rwth-aachen.de/.

[2] http://www.gosphero.com.

[3] https://github.com/orbotix/Sphero-Android-SDK.

context and a consistent/inconsistent/neutral emotional expression is presented in the Table 2.

Five emotional expressions without context plus eighteen test conditions described in the Table 2 resulted in a list of twenty three emotional expressions of each robot in different contexts, each of the duration of 3-13 s.

We used video recordings in our study instead of real robot's observations in order to overcome the limitations of live trials. The method of using a real robot has several important limitations for our study: (1) the beginning and end times of an interaction trial are not clearly defined, (2) the context is not clearly defined, and finally, (3) while using a real robot its movements are not exactly the same from trial to trial due to the noise in motors' accuracy. Thus, live HRI trials would make it very difficult to control the conditions and to ensure that statistically valid results are obtained. Videotaped HRI trials, on the other hand, overcome these limitations: the movements of the robot are observed as exactly the same by each participant, there is no ambiguity about the duration of interaction, its beginning and end. There is also no ambiguity about the presented situational context in which the robot operates. Woods et al. verified in their study [27] whether videotaped HRI trials for various scenarios could be used in certain situations instead of live HRI trials and concluded that for certain HRI scenarios including the issues of speed, space and distance videotaped trials are representative and realistic, and do have potential as a technique for prototyping, testing and developing HRI scenarios and methodologies. These are the issues that play a crucial role in the context of robot affective expressions thus the conclusions of the Woods et al. study [27] are applicable to our study and justify the choice of videos over the real robot.

3.5   Dependent Variables

Our dependent variables included emotional ratings of robot expressive behaviours; ratings of robot task intention, and ratings of robot task success. We also collected demographic information on age and gender.

Perceived Emotional Dimensions. Participants rated valence, arousal and dominance of robot expressive behaviours with a validated questionnaire called the 'Self assessment manikin' (SAM) [5]. SAM has been used to rate the affective dimensions of valence, arousal and dominance in a wide variety of settings [5].

Judgement of Robot Intentions. Judgements of robot intentions were scored on a 5-point Likert scale, where score 1 means *'Definitely not going to continue'* and score 5 means *'Definitely going to continue'*.

Judgement of Robot Task Success. Judgement of task success was again scored on a five-point Likert scale, in response to the question *Do you think the robot's task was completed successfully?*. The scale ranged from *Definitely No* to *Definitely Yes*.

3.6   Experimental Procedure and Participants

A between-subject design for the robot expressivity variable. 34 participants (9 females and 25 males; age from 18 to 46, M=23.21, SD=7.42) rated video clips of the high-expressivity E4 robot. 20 participants (7 females and 13 males; age from 23 to 38, M=29.25, SD=3.60) were assigned to the low-expressivity Sphero robot.

A within-subject design was used to assign participants to a specific task condition, i.e. each participant was exposed to all the twenty-three experimental conditions with one of the robots. In order to overcome limitations of a within-subject design and decrease the impact of a learning effect, the videos presented to each participant in pseudorandom order but also ensuring that two expressions of the same type were never presented one after another.

Participants watched the video clips whilst seated in a quiet room, completing ratings after each separate clip. They were recorded the whole way through the experiment and at the end of the experiment participants were invited for a 5-10 mins recorded interview, after which they were debriefed. The duration of the experiment did not exceed thirty-five minutes and though participants were informed that they could leave at any time, none decided to do so.

3.7   Data Analysis

Cronbach's α was used as a measure of internal agreement between subjects. For the videos showing only the context the α value for the ratings was 0.835, and for the videos showing only the emotional expressions the α value was 0.607. The ratings for the videos showing the combinations of the context and emotional expressions, the α value for the ratings was 0.708. All these α values are acceptable, indicating a good level of internal agreement between all subjects across all the scenarios and respective video conditions.

Mixed measures ANOVA was used to examine the relation between each design parameter and the SAM ratings for the two robots. The same test with different factors was used to evaluate the potential influence of context consistency.

4   Results

We conducted several tests of two factor mixed measures ANOVA to analyze an influence of different design parameters on the perception of robot's valence, arousal and dominance. We also analyzed the influence of both between- and within-subject factors on the perceived level of a robot's intention to continue its job.

4.1   Perceived Emotional Dimensions

We only report significant results in this section. The overview of all the ANOVA tests results showing the effect of different DPs on a perceived valence, arousal and dominance are shown in the Table 3.

Table 3. ANOVA results, showing the effect of different design parameters (DPs) on perceived Valence, Arousal and Dominance, using the more expressive E4 and less expressive Sphero robots.

	SHAPE			QUALITY								
	2 (Robots: Sphero, E4) x 3 (DPs: Approach, Avoidance, Neutral) ANOVA			2 (Robots: Sphero, E4) x 2 (DPs: High Energy, Low Energy) ANOVA			2 (Robots: Sphero, E4) x 2 (DPs: High Intensity, Low Intensity) ANOVA			2 (Robots: Sphero, E4) x 3 (DPs: High, Medium, Low Frequency) ANOVA		
	DPs	DPs xRobots	Robots	DPs	DPs xRobots	Robots	DPs	DPs xRobots	Robots	DPs	DPs xRobots	Robots
Perceived Valence	$F_{1.8,57}$ =15.14, p<0.001	$F_{1.8,57}$ =0.54, p=0.566	$F_{1,315}$ =1.69, p=0.195	$F_{1,157}$ =51.02, p<0.001	$F_{1,157}$ =2.84, p=0.094	$F_{1,157}$ =0.99, p=0.320	$F_{1,477}$ =1.48, p=0.224	$F_{1,477}$ =2.79, p=0.096	$F_{1,477}$ =1.36, p=0.244	$F_{1.83,2}$ =15.84, p<0.001	$F_{1.83,2}$ =8.71, p<0.001	$F_{1,158}$ =0.14, p=0.705
Perceived Arousal	$F_{1.9,60}$ =191.33, p<0.001	$F_{1.9,60}$ =38.54, p<0.001	$F_{1,314}$ =0.04, p=0.835	$F_{1,157}$ =93.57, p<0.001	$F_{1,157}$ =0.01, p=0.949	$F_{1,157}$ =3.79, p=0.053	$F_{1,475}$ =261.15, p<0.001	$F_{1,475}$ =35.01, p<0.001	$F_{1,475}$ =0.44, p=0.507	$F_{2,310}$ =56.73, p<0.001	$F_{2,310}$ =4.94, p=0.008	$F_{1,157}$ =3.93, p=0.049
Perceived Dominance	$F_{2,614}$ =20.14, p<0.001	$F_{2,614}$ =5.63, p<0.005	$F_{1,307}$ =006, p=0.810	$F_{1,156}$ =31.60, p<0.001	$F_{1,156}$ =5.69, p<0.05	$F_{1,156}$ =0.05, p=0.831	$F_{1,467}$ =0.02, p=0.877	$F_{1,467}$ =12.97, p<0.001	$F_{1,467}$ =0.13, p=0.716	$F_{2,310}$ =1.66, p=0.193	$F_{2,310}$ =6.01, p<0.005	$F_{1,155}$ =1.89, p=0.171
Perceived Intention	$F_{2,636}$ =5.11, p=0.006	$F_{2,636}$ =2.50, p=0.083	$F_{1,318}$ =0.57, p=0.452	$F_{1,157}$ =9.15, p<0.005	$F_{1,157}$ =6.71, p<0.05	$F_{1,157}$ =0.08, p=0.781	$F_{1,477}$ =6.35, p<0.05	$F_{1,477}$ =0.16, p=0.693	$F_{1,477}$ =4.94, p<0.05	$F_{2,314}$ =2.19, p=0.114	$F_{2,314}$ =0.69, p=0.505	$F_{1,157}$ =5.12, p=0.025

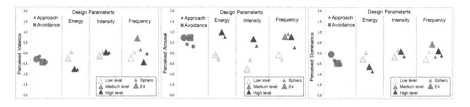

Fig. 3. Plot of the mean values of perceived Valence (left), Arousal (center) and Dominance (right) for the expressions with implemented parameters of approach-avoidance, energy, intensity and frequency, using the more expressive E4 and less expressive Sphero robots.

We found a significant difference in the effect of *Approach* and *Avoidance* design parameters SAM ratings. The first column of the left part of the Fig. 3 shows that the mean valence rating for the avoidance behaviours for both robots (mean=-0.43, 95 % CI=[-0.54, -0.31]) was lower than approach behaviours (mean=-0.22, CI%=[-0.36, 0.08]). The mean dominance rating for avoidance behaviours (mean=-0.49, 95 % CI=[-0.61, -0.37]) was lower than for approach (mean=-0.20, 95 % CI=[-0.33, -0.07]), as shown in the first column of the right part of the Fig. 3. The effect of interaction between a robot and DP was significant for the perception of arousal and dominance, although the interaction only influenced the observers' ratings when the design factor changed from neutral to not neutral. While changing from approach to avoidance, the interaction effect did not differ significantly.

We found a significant difference in the effect of high and low *Energy* DP on valence, arousal and dominance ratings. The mean valence rating for high-energy behaviours (mean=-0.77, 95 % CI=[-0.93, -0.60]) was lower than that of a low energy expression (mean=-0.09, 95 % CI=[-0.24, 0.05]). The mean score of arousal for the expression of a low energy (mean=-0.19, 95 % CI=[-0.37, -0.02]) was significantly lower than that of a high energy expression (mean=0.88,

95 % CI=[0.74, 1.02]). The mean score of dominance for the expression of a low energy (mean=-0.13, 95 % CI=[-0.31, 0.05]) was significantly higher than that of a high energy expression (mean=-0.75, 95 % CI=[-0.92, -0.58]). The mean scores are presented in the second columns of each plot in the Fig. 3. The effect of interaction between a robot and DPs was significant for the perception of dominance: for the more expressive E4 robot the effect of a high-energy DP was stronger than for the less expressive Sphero.

We found a significant difference in the effect of high and low *Intensity* DP on ratings of arousal. The mean arousal rating for the behaviours of low intensity (averaged for both robots; mean=-0.54, 95 % CI=[-0.64, -0.43]) was significantly lower (p<0.001) than for those with high intensity (mean=0.51, 95 % CI=[0.42, 0.61]). The interaction between Robot and DP was significant for dominance: for E4 robot, the mean rating of valence for low-intensity expressions (mean=-0.13) was lower than that of high-intensity expressions (mean=0.05) although the difference between these two values was not significant. For Sphero, mean valence rating for low-intensity (mean=0.06) was higher than that of high-intensity behaviours (mean=0.03) although this difference was either not significant (see third columns of each plot in Fig. 3.

Finally, we found a main effect for the *Frequency* DP on ratings of valence and arousal. Expressive behaviours of medium frequency received the highest valence ratings (mean=0.44, 95 % CI=[0.23,0.65]) comparing to those of low (mean=-0.09, 95 % CI=[-0.23,0.05]) and high frequency (mean=-0.22, 95 % CI=[-0.40, -0.04]). Medium frequency behaviours also received the highest arousal ratings (mean=0.85, 95 % CI=[0.69, 1.01]) comparing to those of low- (mean=-0.20, 95 % CI=[-0.38, -0.03]) and high-frequency (mean=0.53, 95 % CI=[0.39, 0.66]) (see last columns of each plot in Fig. 3.

With respect to a *Consistency*, our data suggest that valence, arousal and dominance of a robot's expression are not strongly influenced by positive and negative events in the robot's operational context. However, we found positive context to significantly (p<0.001) increase the mean ratings of both valence (mean=0.58, 95 % CI=[0.41, 0.75]) and dominance (mean=0.93, 95 % CI=[0.75, 1.10]) when compared to negative contexts. Additionally, the context of a negative arousal significantly (p<0.005) decreased the mean arousal rating (mean=-0.42, 95 % CI=[-0.60, -0.25]).

4.2   Value of Emotional Expressions

We treated the value of emotional expressions primarily in terms of their ability to support inferences about a robot's intentions to continue cleaning the room, and the successfulness of its cleaning actions.

Observer Judgement of Robot Intentions. Row four of Table 3 presents ANOVA results for the four types of DP on perceived Intention. We only discuss contrasts that reached statistical significance.

We found a significant difference main effect of *Approach* and *Avoidance* on judgement of robot intention. The mean score of intention for the approach expression (mean = 2.81, 95 % CI=[2.67, 2.95]) was significantly higher than either neutral (mean=2.54, 95 % CI=[2.40, 2.68]) or avoidance expression (mean=2.59, 95 % CI=[2.46, 2.72]). We also found that ratings of intention for differed by *Energy* levels. The mean score of intention for the expression of a low energy (mean=2.81, 95 % CI=[2.60, 3.01]) was higher than that of a high energy expression (mean=2.46, 95 % CI=[2.28, 2.63]). Although the size of effect is small in both cases, our participants were highly consistent in their ratings on these two measures so confidence in these results is high. The main effect of type of robot did not reach significance for Energy or Approach/Avoidance, but robot type did interact with the Energy DP.

There was a main effect of *Intensity* for judgements of robot intention, with a mean score for low-intensity expressions (mean=2.63, 95 % CI=[2.52, 2.75]) significantly lower than that for high-intensity expressions (mean=2.82, 95 % CI=[2.71, 2.92]). In this case, scores also varied by type of robot, with both high- and low-intensity behaviours of Sphero rated higher overall than their equivalents for E4.

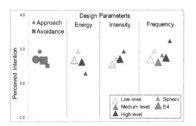 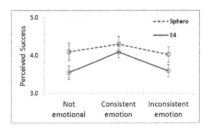

Fig. 4. Left: Plot of the mean values of perceived robot's Intention and standard errors for the expressions of Low, Medium and High Frequency, using the more expressive E4 and less expressive Sphero robots. Right: Plot of the mean values of Success and standard errors for robot expressing emotion consistently, inconsistently and not expressing them, using the E4 and Sphero robots. Based on videos where task was completed successfully.

Observer Judgement of Robot Task Success. Judgement of task success differs from robot intention, as it depends on the interplay between changes in the task environment (its operational context) and the expressive behaviour of the robot. We assume that a person would jointly assess the robot's behaviour and its operational context to decide whether or not its task was completed successfully. If behavioural and operational context both suggest a positive outcome, they are consistent and thus should present a clear signal of success. Similarly, if both are negative, they should clearly signal failure. This is why we use a *consistency of emotion* factor for analyzing the data using ANOVA test.

A two- (E4 vs. Sphero) x three- (Not emotional, Consistent emotion, Inconsistent emotion) mixed measures ANOVA was used to analyze the influence of expressive behaviour on judgements of task success. In this paper, we limit our analysis to video clips that objectively show that the block-moving task was in fact completed successfully (see Fig. 4 Right). The mean rating of success was significantly different for each robot ($F(1.76, 182.98)=3.67$, $p=0.03$, observed power=0.63). Post-hoc tests revealed that observers judge successfulness significantly higher ($p<0.05$) for robots with context-consistent emotional expressions (mean=4.20, 95% CI=$[3.95, 4.44]$) than for neutral (mean=3.82, 95% CI=$[3.54, 4.11]$) or context-inconsistent expressions (mean=3.81, 95% CI=$[3.54, 4.07]$). The difference between two types of robots ($F(1, 104)=4.29$, $p=0.04$) does not interact with this result.

5   Discussion

This paper has reported the implementation of the five basic emotions as robot expressive behaviours in two forms of robot, based on a design scheme for expressing and interpreting emotional body language. The use of two very different robots was intended illustrate the general utility of the design scheme, accompanied by empirical data on human interpretation of the emotional content of these expressive behaviours. Our findings partially support the first hypothesis:

H1. Perceptions of emotionally expressive movements do not vary as a function of the degree of a non-humanoid robot's expressivity.

We found that some design parameters, such as high energy level or avoidance, have a similar influence on observer perceptions of valence, arousal and dominance for both forms of robot i.e. regardless of robot expressivity. These results are consistent with the findings of [26], who showed that (a) high speed of tail movements increased perceived arousal of a robot, and (b) low tail height decreased perceived valence. The latter could be mapped to the *Reduce Yourself* parameter of the *Avoidance* DP group.

Our findings also suggest that some parameters, e.g. approach, high and low intensity or medium and high frequency of movements when implemented into robots of different expressivity level, exert a similar influence on perceptions of a subset of emotional dimensions. For example, high frequency consistently increased ratings of arousal for both types of robots, although its influence on valence differed by robot type. Table 4 presents all the similarities between a more expressive and a less expressive robot revealed by our study. These findings partially supported our first hypothesis.

However, our study also suggests that there are some significant differences in how some parameters influence perceptions of emotion in robot as a function of expressivity, contrary to our expectations:

– Both types of robots showed that avoidance behaviours were rated as low dominance. However, for the low-expressivity robot, the ratings was significantly lower than for the highly expressive robot.

Table 4. Similarities in parameters' influence on valence, arousal and dominance between a more expressive robot E4 and a less expressive robot Sphero. Arrows ↑ and ↓ show whether the parameter increased or decreased a perceived value of valence, arousal and dominance. Signs "-" and "+" show whether the value is negative or positive.

Group of design parameters	Perceived Valence	Perceived Arousal	Perceived Dominance
Approach	↓ " − "	↑ " + "	
Avoidance	↓ " − "	↑ " + "	↓ " − "
Low intensity		↓ " − "	
High intensity		↑ " + "	
High energy	↓ " − "	↑ " + "	↓ " − "
Medium frequency		↑ " + "	
High frequency		↑ " + "	

- Only the high-expressivity robot was rated with a lower level of dominance for low-frequency expressive behaviours than for high-frequency expressions. In addition, the value of dominance ratings in this case was positive for the low-expressivity robot but negative for the high-expressivity robot.
- The high intensity DP increased the level of perceived valence for the highly expressive robot and made it positive, while for the low-expressivity robot the level of perceived valence was decreased and negative.

Table 5 presents all the differences between a more expressive and a less expressive robot revealed by our study. These findings didn't support our first hypothesis. They also add to the current knowledge of the design of emotional expressions in robots, as no previous studies suggested that there could be different consequences of applying expressive movements to different types of robots.

Table 5. Differences in parameters' influence on perceived valence, arousal and dominance between a more expressive robot E4 and a less expressive robot Sphero. Arrows ↑ and ↓ show whether the parameter increased or decreased a perceived value of valence, arousal and dominance. Wider arrows ⇓ and ⇑ show a stronger decrease/increase effect. Signs "-" and "+" show whether the value is negative or positive.

Group of design parameters	Perceived Valence		Perceived Arousal		Perceived Dominance	
	E4	Sphero	E4	Sphero	E4	Sphero
Approach					NA	↓
Avoidance					↓	⇓
Low intensity	↓ "-"	↑ "+"			↓ "-"	↑ "+"
High intensity	↑ "+"	↓ "-"			↑ "+"	↓ "-"
Low frequency	↓ "-"	NA "+"	NA	↓	↓ "-"	NA "+"
Medium frequency	↑	NA			↑ "+"	NA "-"
High frequency	↓	NA	⇑	↑		

In addition to the current knowledge, the Consistency findings of our study revealed that the context of positive valence specifically has a significant effect on perceived valence and dominance of an expressive robot. With respect to perceived arousal, our findings revealed that the context of a negative arousal decreases it significantly. Other contexts, i.e. of a positive or negative dominance, positive arousal or negative valence do not have a significant effect on interpretation of an expressive robot.

In contrast to [19], the results of our study did not provide any evidence that the consistency of context can override the interpretation of emotional expression of a robot. Our findings showed that inappropriate emotional context was not different to the neutral context cases in interpretation of valence, arousal, dominance and robot's intention. However, our findings correspond to the results of [19] in the part stating that alignment of robot's action and affective context enhanced the affective interpretation.

H2. An observer's beliefs about the successfulness of a robot's actions varies consistently with the nature of the robot's expressive behaviour.

The findings of the study revealed that consistent emotional expressiveness increased the rating of a task success and it was significantly different from the cases when a robot completing the task was inconsistently expressive, e.g. expressed sadness after successfully completing the task, or not expressive, e.g. just completed the task and didn't follow it with any emotional expression. Such a result shows that participants' awareness of a situation they observed improved when robot behaved in a consistently emotional way thus supporting our third hypothesis. Our findings conform to those of [13] and [14] by showing an additional value of expressive robot on a neutral one. However, our study also resulted in additional finding that extends the state-of-the-art of HRI and shows that inconsistently expressive robot doesn't create an additional situational understanding in human observers although it doesn't reduce a situational awareness either.

The ratings of robot's Intention varied significantly depending on its expressive movements. This means that emotional expressions of a robot can not only communicate emotional signal but also let people draw additional inferences of that robot. These findings support the second hypothesis and they are consistent with [9] who stated people may presume other things about affective agents based on their expressiveness in addition to how he or she is feeling. However, the study of [9] only made this statement about human agents. Our findings make a first step to generalize this idea to a broader set of agents, including robots.

6   Conclusions

We attempted to address a gap in the literature between high-level design guidelines for robotic emotional expression using a body language and the implementation of expressive movements into specific non-humanoid robots. We have presented a refinement of the general design scheme proposed in [17]. We made this design scheme usable for HRI researchers working with different types of non-humanoid robots in two ways. We presented a new technique for classifying non-humanoid robots based on their expressivity. We also demonstrated representations of five basic emotions of fear, anger, happiness, sadness and surprise as sequence of parameters in accordance with the general design scheme. The results of our validation study show both the similarities and differences in the perception of valence, arousal and dominance after applying the design scheme to non-humanoid robots of different expressivity. The Energy and Approach/Avoidance group of DPs were robust across the two robot forms. However, our data suggest a need for a more considered mechanism for describing combinations of parameters, especially in terms of the frequency and intensity of expressive behaviours. There is also a need to create a more sophisticated statistical model instead of performing a series of ANOVA calculations, thus reducing the risk of Type I errors.

Although we adopted a very simple model for estimating the general expressivity of any robot, it proved adequate for the questions we posed in this paper. Simple summative models are attractive from a design viewpoint, since they create opportunities for creating equally expressive robots with rather different form factors. They reflect a crude assumption that interpretations depend only on the total number of available cues - a basic bandwidth argument - rather than their choreography. Further work is required to probe the limits of our main finding: interpretations of robot expressive behaviours are consistent, regardless of salient differences in their expressive possibilities. It is hard to imagine non-humanoid form factors of robots that would differ much more than Sphero and E4 but, as we have consistently argued in this paper, it's not the way they look, it's the way they move that counts from the viewpoint of the observer. We have deliberately limited our enquiry to basic emotional states. Were a designer to explore sophisticated robot emotional expressions, such as guilt, regret or schadenfreude, a different picture may emerge. However, there are also ethical considerations which have directed our work away from matters such as these.

References

1. Ackermann, M., Starr, B.: Social activity indicators: interface components for cscw systems. In: Proceedings of the UIST 1995, the 8th ACM Symposium on User Interface Software and Technology, Pittsburgh, USA (1995)
2. Argyle, M.: Bodily Communication. Routledge, New York (2013)
3. Barakova, E.I., Lourens, T.: Expressing and interpreting emotional movements in social games with robots. Pers. Ubiquit. Comput. **14**(5), 457–467 (2010)
4. Beck, A., Hiolle, A., Mazel, A., Cañamero, L.: Interpretation of emotional body language displayed by robots. In: Proceedings of the 3rd International Workshop on Affective Interaction in Natural Environments, pp. 37–42. ACM (2010)
5. Bradley, M.M., Lang, P.J.: Measuring emotion: the self-assessment manikin and the semantic differential. J. Behav. Ther. Exp. Psychiatry **25**(1), 49–59 (1994)
6. Cramer, H., Kemper, N., Zwijnenburg, A., de Rooij, O.: Phobot: Hri 2008 student design competition winner
7. Ekman, P.: An argument for basic emotions. Cogn. Emot. **6**(3–4), 169–200 (1992)
8. Gaur, V., Scassellati, B.: Which motion features induce the perception of animacy? In: Proceedings of the 2006 IEEE International Conference for Development and Learning, Bloomington, Indiana (2006)

9. Gopinath, R.: Employees emotions in workplace. Res. J. Bus. Manage. **5**(1), 1–15 (2011)
10. Hareli, S., Rafaeli, A.: Emotion cycles: on the social influence of emotion in organizations. Res. Organ. Behav. **28**, 35–59 (2008)
11. Heider, F., Simmel, M.: An experimental study of apparent behavior. Am. J. Psychol. 243–259 (1944)
12. Karg, M., Schwimmbeck, M., Kuhnlenz, K., Buss, M.: Towards mapping emotive gait patterns from human to robot. In: 2010 IEEE RO-MAN, pp. 258–263, IEEE (2010)
13. Leite, I., Pereira, A., Martinho, C., Paiva, A.: Are emotional robots more fun to play with? In: The 17th IEEE International Symposium on Robot and Human Interactive Communication, RO-MAN 2008, pp. 77–82. IEEE (2008)
14. Lohse, M., Rothuis, R., Gallego-Pérez, J., Karreman, D.E., Evers, V.: Robot gestures make difficult tasks easier: the impact of gestures on perceived workload and task performance. In: Proceedings of the 32nd Annual ACM Conference on Human Factors in Computing Systems, pp. 1459–1466. ACM (2014)
15. McCarthy, J.: Ascribing mental qualities to machines. In: Formalizing Common Sense: Papers, pp. 93–118. Ablex (1990)
16. Mehrabian, A.: Basic Dimensions for a General Psychological Theory: Implications for Personality, Social, Environmental, and Developmental Studies. Oelgeschlager Gunn & Hain, Cambridge (1980)
17. Novikova, J., Watts, L.: A design model of emotional body expressions in non-humanoid robots. In: Proceedings of the Second International Conference on Human-Agent Interaction (HAI 2014) (2014)
18. Pinelle, D., Gutwin, C., Greenberg, S.: Task analysis for groupware usability evaluation: modeling shared-workspace tasks with the mechanics of collaboration. ACM Trans. Comput. Hum. Interact. 281–311 (2003)
19. Read, R., Belpaeme, T.: Situational context directs how people affectively interpret robotic non-linguistic utterances. In: Proceedings of the 2014 ACM/IEEE International Conference on Human-Robot Interaction, 41–48. ACM (2014)
20. Reeves, B., Nass, C.: How People Treat Computers, Television, and New Media like Real People and Places. CSLI Publications/Cambridge University Press, Stanford/Cambridge (1996)
21. Ribeiro, T., Paiva, A.: The illusion of robotic life: principles and practices of animation for robots. In: Proceedings of the Seventh Annual ACM/IEEE International Conference on Human-Robot Interaction, pp. 383–390. ACM (2012)
22. Saerbeck, M., Bartneck, C.: Perception of affect elicited by robot motion. In: Proceedings of the 5th ACM/IEEE International Conference on Human-Robot Interaction, pp. 53–60. IEEE Press (2010)
23. Samadani, A.-A., Kubica, E., Gorbet, R., Kulić, D.: Perception and generation of affective hand movements. Int. J. Soc. Rob. **5**(1), 35–51 (2013)
24. Schmidt, K.: The problem with 'awareness'. Computer Supported Cooperative Work. J. Collaborative Comput. **11**, 3–4 (2002)
25. Scholl, B.J., Tremoulet, P.D.: Perceptual causality and animacy. Trends Cogn. Sci. **4**(8), 299–309 (2000)
26. Singh, A., Young, J.E.: A dog tail for utility robots: exploring affective properties of tail movement. In: Kotzé, P., Marsden, G., Lindgaard, G., Wesson, J., Winckler, M. (eds.) INTERACT 2013, Part II. LNCS, vol. 8118, pp. 403–419. Springer, Heidelberg (2013)

27. Woods, S., Walters, M., Koay, K.L., Dautenhahn, K.: Comparing, human robot interaction scenarios using live and video based methods: towards a novel methodological approach. In: 9th IEEE International Workshop on Advanced Motion Control, pp. 750–755. IEEE (2006)
28. Xu, J., Broekens, J., Hindriks, K., Neerincx, M.A.: Robot mood is contagious: effects of robot body language in the imitation game. In: Proceedings of the 2014 International Conference on Autonomous Agents and Multi-Agent Systems, International Foundation for Autonomous Agents and Multiagent Systems, pp. 973–980 (2014)

HoverSpace

Analyses of the Perceived Spatial Affordances of Hover Interaction Above Tabletop Surfaces

Paul Lubos[1]([⊠]), Oscar Ariza[1], Gerd Bruder[1], Florian Daiber[2],
Frank Steinicke[1], and Antonio Krüger[2]

[1] Human-Computer Interaction, Department of Informatics,
Universität Hamburg, Hamburg, Germany
{lubos,ariza,bruder,steinicke}
@informatik.uni-hamburg.de
[2] German Research Center for Artificial Intelligence, Saarbrücken, Germany
{florian.daiber,Krueger}@dfki.de

Abstract. Recent developments in the area of stereoscopic displays and tracking technologies have paved the way to combine touch interaction on interactive surfaces with spatial interaction above the surface of a stereoscopic display. This holistic design space supports novel affordances and user experiences during touch interaction, but also induce challenges to the interaction design. In this paper we introduce the concept of hover interaction for such setups. Therefore, we analyze the non-visual volume above a virtual object, which is perceived as the corresponding hover space for that object. The results show that the users' perceptions of hover spaces can be categorized into two groups. Either users assume that the shape of the hover space is extruded and scaled towards their head, or along the normal vector of the interactive surface. We provide a corresponding model to determine the shapes of these hover spaces, and confirm the findings in a practical application. Finally, we discuss important implications for the development of future touch-sensitive interfaces.

Keywords: Hover space · Touch interaction · Stereoscopic displays · 3D interaction

1 Introduction

Recently, the combination of two different technologies has attracted enormous attention. Several setups have been released, which combine touch-sensitive surfaces with 3D mid-air finger tracking [5]. These technologies provide direct interaction with two-dimensional (2D) or three-dimensional (3D) data sets, respectively, which is primarily leveraged in the fields of natural interaction for spatial application domains such as geo-spatial applications, architectural design, games or entertainment [6]. While multi-touch technology is available for several years, recently multiple hardware solutions from the professional as well as consumer domains have been released, which provide the means to sense hand and finger poses as well as gestures on 2D surfaces or in 3D space without the requirement to wear gloves or use other encumbering instrumentation (e.g.,

© IFIP International Federation for Information Processing 2015
J. Abascal et al. (Eds.): INTERACT 2015, Part III, LNCS 9298, pp. 259–277, 2015.
DOI: 10.1007/978-3-319-22698-9_17

Leap Motion [13], Microsoft Kinect [17]). The combination of these technologies and the resulting expanded interaction space consisting of 2D touch input and 3D mid-air sensing provides enormous potential for novel interaction techniques.

Until recently, research on interaction techniques in the scope of tabletops and interactive surfaces have mainly been focused on (multi-)touch 2D input with mono-scopically displayed data. The direct nature of multi-touch gestures and interaction including haptic feedback has great potential for natural and intuitive interaction for novice and expert users. The matching perceptual and motor space during direct touch interaction proved beneficial over less direct interaction techniques [23].

Spatial interaction above tabletop surfaces has received much attention over the last years, in particular since Hilliges et al. [12] discussed the limitation of 2D input on surfaces for natural 3D interaction and proposed interactions above the tabletop. With the advent of stereoscopic display on interactive tabletops, the interaction space has to be extended to the third dimension in order to facilitate a coherent space for input and output of such interactive systems. With stereoscopic display, objects can appear detached from the display surface, i.e., in front of or behind the display surface. Such situations induce challenges for natural touch interaction due to missing haptic feedback when interacting with stereoscopically displayed floating objects (cf. "touching the void" [6]). Schöning et al. [19] considered general challenges of multi-touch interaction with stereoscopically rendered projections and conclude that most of the existing interaction techniques have in common that the interaction and visualization is limited to a region close to zero parallax (i.e., the interactive surface) [5, 21].

While the described setups provide interesting challenges to the interaction with stereoscopically displayed 3D objects on a touch surface, it is often not clear for users with which objects they can interact, i.e., 3D stereoscopically objects often miss the affordance of touch [5, 6]. In mouse-based interaction setups, such affordances are often presented by hover effects. Hence, it sounds reasonable to transfer this concept to tabletop setups. However, with touch-based interaction such hover effects are difficult to implement since a hover movement on the surface already induces a touch event. Such hover interaction has been successfully applied for monoscopic displays to support multi-touch tabletops with contextual information [12]. However, we are not aware of existing solutions considering hover interaction for stereoscopic multi-touch environments.

In this paper we focus on hover interaction, which does not require users to touch an object in 2D or 3D spaces, e.g., by moving a finger inside the object or on the surface, but is rather based on hovering "over" the object with a finger or hand relative to the considered object. However, so far it is not clear how users perceive affordances of hover spaces above the interactive surfaces, especially, if objects are displayed stereoscopically. In particular, it is not clear which shapes and sizes of volumes match the perceived affordances of hover interaction. For these reasons, we determine a perceptually-inspired model for volumes used for hover interaction, which we call the *HoverSpace*. We evaluate the model and compare it with a naive approach in a confirmatory study. The results of these experiments provide guidelines for interactive applications using hover gestures in tabletop setups.

In summary, our contributions are:

- An analysis of above-surface volumes for hover interaction in tabletop setups,
- a usability comparison of perceptually-inspired and naive hover volumes, and
- guidelines for designing hover interaction in touch-sensitive tabletop setups.

The remainder of this paper is structured as follows. Section 2 presents an overview of related work on hover and above-surface interaction in tabletop setups. Section 3 describes the experiment in which we analyze perceived spatial affordances of hover interaction. In Sect. 4 we derive the perceptually-inspired HoverSpace. Section 5 validates the results in a confirmatory experiment. Section 6 provides a general discussion of the results and guidelines for hover interaction in tabletop setups. Section 7 concludes the paper.

2   Related Work

In this section we provide an overview of related work on hover interaction in 2D and 3D user interfaces as well as mid-air interaction on 3D stereoscopic touch surfaces.

2.1   2D Hover

As Buxton describes in his three state model of graphical input, for traditional input devices, like a mouse, there is a so-called tracking state, as in the state where the cursor can be moved without pressing a button. The position and movement of the cursor can be directly transferred to input in user interfaces [7]. One of the most common uses of such a tracking state is for so-called hover effects in classic 2D user interfaces [7]. The tracking state is often used for highlighting or tooltips and can declutter interfaces by providing context sensitive information. In most touch interfaces, for example using capacitive sensing technology, this tracking state is missing [9, 18]. While dragging is possible, when pressing down on the screen, the hovering usually cannot be detected. Especially during the design of touch-enabled tabletop and mobile user interfaces, such as mobile versions of websites, the missing tracking state becomes obvious and many design principles, such as flat design, become complicated [9].

To compensate for the missing hover capability in 2D multi-touch setups Benko et al. [2] simulated a hover state with techniques that make use of a secondary finger which adjusts the control-display ratio while the primary finger controls the movement of the cursor, thus resulting in more precise selection.

Beyond hover interaction in multi-touch setups other input modalities have been investigated as well. Grossman et al. [9] presented Hover Widgets, which extend the expressiveness of pen-operated touch surfaces by using the tracking state of the pen as hover input. In particular, they proposed a special hover technique that activates a widget by a short discrete gesture that is followed by a pen-down action. The Hover Widget technique shows that the space between the hover state and the touch state can be effectively used.

2.2   3D Hover

With recent advances in 3D sensing technologies it becomes possible to track a user's fingers above touch surfaces which allows for a tracking state to be leveraged for user interfaces [3, 12]. Different interaction techniques have been proposed for monoscopic and stereoscopic display environments which make use of this capability.

Han and Park [10] explored hover-based zoom interactions in monoscopic display environments. They proposed a technique that relies on a magnifying lens metaphor. This approach allows users to quickly zoom in and out in a restricted range of multiple zoom levels that are defined by layers above a multi-touch display. Initial evaluation results revealed that their technique outperforms the common pinch-to-zoom technique in both speed and user preference. However, in their implementation zoom layers were discrete and no continuous zooming in a 3D hover volume above the multi-touch display was possible.

Echtler et al. [8] presented a multi-touch tabletop that was extended with a ceiling-mounted light source to create shadows of hands and arms. By tracking these shadows with the rear-mounted camera of their frustrated total internal reflection (FTIR) setup they augmented the multi-touch tabletop with mouse-like hover behavior. With this setup users can control multiple cursors by hovering above the tabletop and trigger a "click" event when touching the surface. They evaluated their system with respect to tracking accuracy, which indicated that users were aware of their hand position above the display and tried to avoid occlusion by orienting their hand in an unnatural pose parallel to the edge of the tabletop so that the cursor pointed perpendicular to the user's viewing direction.

Annett et al. [1] presented Medusa, a proximity-aware multi-touch tabletop that is capable of tracking multiple users and differentiate between their hands. Besides supporting collaborative multi-user settings, they proposed different hand-dependent hover techniques. Hovering with the right hand above the display triggers a marker below the hand that turns into a component-specific marking menu when it is touched. Hovering with the left hand displays an 'X' icon which deletes a component when it is touched.

The prototype by Pyryeskin et al. [18] uses light reflected from a person's palm to estimate its position in 3D space above the table based on the diffused surface illumination vision-based principle.

2.3   Mid-Air Interaction

The space above interactive multi-touch surfaces has been considered for different 2.5D and 3D user interfaces with stereoscopic display, in particular using direct touch for objects displayed on the surface as well as 3D mid-air touch for objects that are displayed with negative parallax above the surface. Bruder et al. [6] found that users tend to incorrectly perceive the 3D position of stereoscopically displayed objects with negative parallax when touching these objects by moving their finger inside their perceived 3D shape. Lubos et al. [16] showed that 3D selection performance can be greatly increased by extending the selection volume using an ellipsoid shape that is oriented towards the user's head position to account for these perceptual differences. These results are in line with results from perceptual psychology which suggest that users observing stereoscopically displayed scenes often tend to underestimate or overestimate ego-centric distances and incorrectly judge spatial relations due to visual conflicts such as occlusion or an accommodation-convergence mismatch [4, 15, 22]. Bruder et al. [5] investigated the precision and performance of 2D touch selection of stereoscopically displayed objects in comparison to 3D mid-air selection. They showed that touching on the interactive surface outperforms mid-air touch selection in a Fitts' Law experiment if the object is projected close to the surface with a distance of up to approximately 10 cm. For objects displayed farther away from the surface than this threshold 3D mid-air selection results in much higher performance in comparison to touch. In line with guidelines proposed by Schöning et al. [19] this underlines that multi-touch interaction with stereoscopically rendered objects is mainly limited to a distance of about 10 cm from the plane of the interactive surface, which we also consider to be an indicator for the typical hover space above touch-sensitive tabletops.

3 Perceptual Experiment

In this section we describe the experiment in which we analyzed the perceived affordances of hover interaction in terms of the 3D volume above rendered objects of different sizes and shapes in an interactive tabletop setup with stereoscopic display.

Based on the previous work described in Sect. 2, we explored the following expectations in this experiment: The hover space where users expect hovering effects to occur may not necessarily be oriented vertically above the object, but rather influenced by a user's head position relative to the target. Moreover, we assumed the shape of the hover volume to be influenced by the shape of the target object.

3.1 Participants

We recruited 15 participants for our experiment (11 male, 4 female), all of whom were students or professionals from the field of human-computer interaction or computer science (ages 24—54, M = 34.7, SD = 8.58, heights 1.55 m—1.92 m, M = 1.76 m, SD = .12 m). The students received class credit for their participation. Two of the participants were left handed, the remaining 13 participants were right handed. All participants had normal or corrected vision.

Using the technique proposed by Willemsen et al. [22] we measured the interpupillary distance (IPD) of each participant before the experiment (M = 6.54 cm, SD = .35 cm) and used it to calibrate the rendering for each participant.

Only one participant reported no experience with stereoscopic display and ten participants reported high or very high experience (rating scale 0 = no experience, 4 = very high experience, M = 2.80, SD = 1.21). Only one participant reported no experience with 3D computer games while ten participants reported high or very high levels of experience (rating scale 0 = no experience, 4 = very high experience, M = 2.87, SD = 1.36). The mean total time per participant, including questionnaires and instructions was about 35 min. The mean time for performing the actual experiment was about 25 min. Participants were allowed to take breaks at any time.

3.2 Material

As illustrated in Fig. 1, participants were instructed to stand at a stereoscopic multi-touch table in an upright position facing the table. A Razer Tartarus keypad was adjusted to a comfortable height for the non-dominant hand of the participant. Participants were instructed to keep their hand at that position during the experiment to confirm their selections.

The experiment was conducted with the participant wearing Samsung SSG-P51002 radio frequency active shutter glasses, a cap with an infrared (IR) marker and a glove with an IR marker at the fingertip of their dominant hand. The markers were tracked with an optical WorldViz Precision Position Tracking (PPT X4) system with submillimeter precision for view-dependent rendering and finger tracking.

The visual stimulus displayed during the experiment showed a 3D scene, which was rendered with the Unity3D Pro engine [20] with an Intel computer with a Core i7 3.4 GHz CPU and an NVidia GeForce GTX780TI.

The scene was displayed stereoscopically on a Samsung UE55F9000 TV in a height-adjustable, stereoscopic tabletop setup. The scene showed a gray brushed metal surface at the zero parallax plane and targets in a red color. For each trial, a single target was visible, either a sphere or a cube. Those shapes were chosen as they are approximations of objects typically found in user interfaces and compound objects consisting of these shapes could approximate almost any other shape.

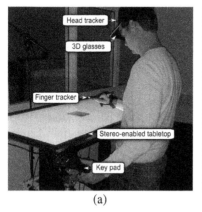
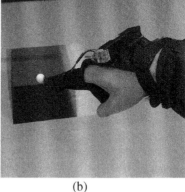

(a)   (b)

Fig. 1. (a) Participant during the experiment and (b) close-up of the participant's hand while indicating the hover volume with the tip of the index finger. The scene was displayed stereoscopically. IR markers on the head and index finger of the dominant hand were tracked. The non-dominant hand rested on a keypad.

3.3 Methods

We used a $2 \times 2 \times 6 \times 4$ design with the method of constant stimuli for the experiment trials. The two target shapes (cube, sphere), two target sizes (5 cm, 10 cm), six target positions (P0 = $(-0.2, 0, 0)$, P1 = $(0, 0, 0)$, P2 = $(0.2, 0, 0)$, P3 = $(-0.2, 0, -0.2)$, P4 = $(0, 0, -0.2)$ and P5 = $(0.2, 0, -0.2)$) and four repetitions were uniformly and randomly distributed between all 96 trials for each participant.

Each trial consisted of a single shape of one size at one of the positions being shown to the participant (see Fig. 2). The participants were instructed to think of hovering in traditional 2D user interfaces and indicate the volume where they would expect a hover effect to be triggered by moving the index finger of their dominant hand in that volume, i.e., by "drawing" the volume. During each trial, the participants indicated the hover volume for ten seconds while pressing a button on the keypad with their non-dominant hand. The non-dominant hand was chosen for this task to avoid any jittering while indicating the volume, which may be induced by pressing buttons attached to a glove on the dominant hand.

Li et al. [14] have shown an increase in performance from using the non-dominant hand for such tasks. After ten seconds the next trial started. We recorded tracking data at 30 Hz while the participant pressed the button. Each recording consisted of the participant's head and finger position.

The participants completed training trials before the main experimental phase to ensure that they understood the task correctly. The training trials differed from the main trials by showing the participants the volume which they drew to help them understand the task, while this visual feedback was excluded in the main trials, i.e., participants only saw their real hand and the virtual 3D object so as not to bias the results due to cluttering the virtual scene over time. The training trials were excluded from the analysis.

3.4 Results

We had to exclude three participants from the analysis, as they misunderstood the task and touched the 2D surface throughout the experiment instead of indicating a 3D hover volume, which was confirmed during debriefing after the experiment.

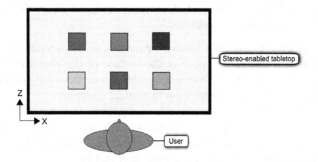

Fig. 2. Positions used to locate the objects on the tabletop surface. P0 = $(-0.2, 0, 0)$ (yellow), P1 = $(0, 0, 0)$ (magenta), P2 = $(0.2, 0, 0)$ (cyan), P3 = $(-0.2, 0, -0.2)$ (red), P4 = $(0, 0, -0.2)$ (green) and P5 = $(0.2, 0, -0.2)$ (blue). These colors are only used in the following result plots (Color figure online).

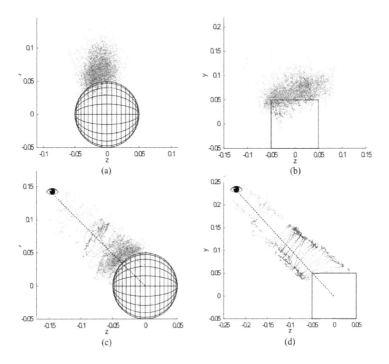

Fig. 3. Examples of the two behavior patterns in 2D coordinates with the y-axis indicating the up-direction from the tabletop at y = 0 and the z-axis indicating the direction from the participant towards the opposite side of the tabletop. (a, b) Orthogonal Hovering indicates a hover volume at the surface of the object or above it. (c, d) Line-of-Sight Hovering shows a hover volume within line-of-sight that converges towards the participant's head position. The colors represent the different tested positions of the objects on the tabletop (see Fig. 2).

Since we had four repetitions for each condition of the experiment, we pooled the results over the repetitions. We normalized the tracking data to account for the varying head positions within and between participants by normalizing head positions in target-centered coordinates (see Fig. 3). We visually analyzed the resulting coordinates and observed two main behavior patterns:

- *Orthogonal Hovering*: The first behavior pattern was characterized by seven participants indicating the hover space at the surface of the object or above it. As shown in Figs. 3(a) and (b), the horizontal width and depth of this volume increased with increasing distance to the tabletop in vertical direction.
- *Line-of-Sight Hovering*: The second behavior pattern was shown by five participants in which the hover space was tilted towards line-of-sight, i.e., the volume extended in the direction of the participant's head position instead of orthogonally from the tabletop surface as shown in Figs. 3(c) and (d).

The observed behavior patterns were consistent for each participant throughout the experiment, i.e., we did not observe any participant changing the behavior during the experiment.

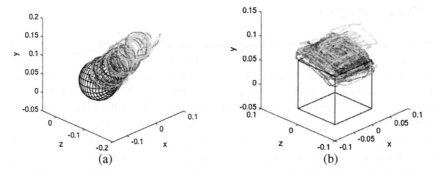

Fig. 4. Illustrations of the drawn hover volumes of participants for the (a) sphere target shape and the (b) cube target shape. The y-axis indicates the direction orthogonally to the tabletop surface at y = 0, the z-axis increases towards the opposite end of the tabletop, and the x-axis is oriented laterally to the right of the tabletop. The drawing patterns of outlining the circular or rectangular regions and then filling the regions with zigzag patterns could be observed for many participants.

We observed a difference between the cube target shape and the sphere target shape. For the sphere, all participants indicated a round hover space, often drawing circles at various distances from the object (see Fig. 4(a)). Conversely, for the cube shape, all participants indicated a rectangular hover space, often drawing a rectangular outline and then used zigzag pattern to fill the area (see Fig. 4(b)). The comments of the participants during debriefing also reflect this behavior.

3.5   Discussion

We instructed our participants to think of hovering in traditional 2D user interfaces and indicate the 3D-volume with their finger where they would expect a hover effect to be triggered. Considering this instruction, these behaviors could be explained as follows. When hovering in 2D Desktop environments, hover effects are triggered when the mouse cursor is (a) above a target object and (b) occludes the target object. Depending on the participant's understanding of 2D hovering, this has different effects on the behavior with a third, height dimension.

Indeed, the results show two groups of participants with distinct behavior patterns (Orthogonal Hovering vs. Line-of-Sight Hovering). We observed no changes in behavior for any participant during the experiment, which suggests that there are two mental models of where users expect a hover volume to be above interactive tabletops. While seven of our participants would expect a hover space to be located above a virtual object orthogonally to the display surface, five of our participants would expect the hover space to be located along the line-of-sight from the object to their head position, suggesting that they interpreted hovering as occlusion of the target object.

Additionally, we found two different hover volumes for the sphere and cube target shapes, which shows that the object's shape determines the shape of the hover volume as well. Round target shapes imply round hover volumes and angular shapes imply angular hover volumes.

4 The HoverSpace

With the results from the perceptual experiment we defined two main volumes, where participants expect hovering effects. In the following, we define a combined hover volume which we call HoverSpace. Since the volumes depended on whether the target shape was rectangular or rounded, we defined two formulas for the HoverSpace, which allow easy testing whether the tracked input object, such as the user's fingertip, is within the hover volume. The formulas are written for a left-handed Cartesian coordinate system, where the y-axis corresponds to the up-direction. Let $(x,y,z) \in \mathbb{R}^3$ be the finger position in 3D coordinates centered around the target object. Let $a \in \mathbb{R}^+$ be the scale of the target object on the x-axis, $b \in \mathbb{R}^+$ the scale on the z-axis, $c \in \mathbb{R}^+$ the scale on the y-axis and $d \in \mathbb{R}^+$ an empirically determined value defining the spread of the hover region.

Since the volumes depended on whether the target shape was rectangular or rounded, we defined two formulas for the HoverSpace, which allow easy testing whether the tracked input object, such as the user's fingertip, is within the hover volume. The formulas are written for a left-handed Cartesian coordinate system, where the y-axis corresponds to the up-direction. Let $(x,y,z) \in \mathbb{R}^3$ be the finger position in 3D coordinates centered around the target object. Let $a \in \mathbb{R}^+$ be the scale of the target object on the x-axis, $b \in \mathbb{R}^+$ the scale on the z-axis, $c \in \mathbb{R}^+$ the scale on the y-axis and $d \in \mathbb{R}^+$ an empirically determined value defining the spread of the hover region.

The HoverSpace is based on two formulas. For round shapes a paraboloid can be used which can be approximated by the following formula:

$$\frac{x^2}{a^2} + \frac{z^2}{b^2} - \frac{y}{d} \leq 0 \,\&\&\, 0 \leq y \leq 10cm$$

For rectangular shapes, the results can be approximated by a truncated pyramid and the following formula:

$$hf = \frac{y}{c}, x_{max} = lerp(a, d * a, hf), y_{max} = lerp(a, d * b, hf)$$

$$0 \leq y \leq 10\,cm \,\&\&\, x - x_{max} \leq 0 \,\&\&\, y_{max} \leq 0$$

4.1 Orthogonal Hovering

From the results of our participants who expected the hover volume to be located above the target object we determined a volume enclosing 95 % of the finger positions. The volume is oriented upwards from the target object, but the volume also expands in width and depth the higher the participant's finger was from the tabletop surface. Depending on whether the target shape was rectangular or round, we found the 95 % volume to follow a mathematical function. The region above the object is illustrated in Fig. 5.

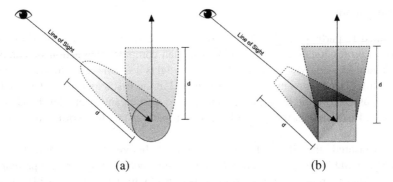

Fig. 5. Illustrations of the HoverSpace volumes in vertical direction and along line-of-sight for the two shapes: (a) For round shapes the volumes were approximated with paraboloids, and (b) truncated pyramids were used for rectangular shapes. We used d = 10 cm according to results presented by Bruder et al. [5].

For the orthogonal region, the origin of the coordinate system to transform the tracking coordinate of the finger position into for both formulas is given by the center of the object and the up axis along the display normal.

4.2 Line-of-Sight Hovering

From our participants expecting the hovering effects to occur when occluding the object along their line-of-sight, we found that the width and depth of the volume increase in size as it gets closer to the object until it covers the size of the object. The volume enclosing 95 % of finger positions is illustrated in Fig. 5. In contrast to the hover volume defined in Sect. 4.1 the size of this volume depends not only on the size of the object, but also on the distance of the head from the object. For rectangular and round shapes we found different volumes.

For line-of-sight hovering the same formulas can be used as for the orthogonal hovering. Here, the origin of the coordinate system is on the line-of-sight between the center of the object and the head position. The up axis is given by the line-of-sight. After transformation of the finger position from tracking coordinates into the line-of-sight coordinate system, the formulas can be applied.

5   Confirmatory Experiment

In this section we describe the experiment in which we compared the HoverSpace with a naive straight-up infinitely extruded outline (called Extruded in the following) approach of 3D hover volumes.

5.1   Participants

We recruited 16 participants for our experiment (11 male, 5 female), all of whom were students or professionals from the field of human-computer interaction or computer science (ages 19—36, M = 27.37, SD = 4.72, heights 1.60 m—1.93 m, M = 1.78 m, SD = .10 m). Six participants already participated in the first experiment. The students received class credit for their participation. Two participants were left-handed, the remaining 14 participants were right-handed. All participants had normal or corrected vision.

We measured the IPD of each participant before the experiment started (M = 6.61 cm, SD = .29 cm). We calibrated the system accordingly for each participant.

All participants reported at least some experience with stereoscopic display and ten participants reported high or very high experience (rating scale 0 = no experience, 4 = very high experience, M = 2.86, SD = 1.09). Three participants reported no experience with 3D computer games while ten participants reported high or very high levels of experience (rating scale 0 = no experience, 4 = very high experience, M = 2.63, SD = 1.59).

The mean total time per participant, including questionnaires and instructions was 20 min. The mean time for performing the actual experiment was about 15 min. Participants were allowed to take breaks between the conditions.

5.2   Material

The setup in the confirmatory experiment was the same as in the experiment reported in Sect. 3. The setups differed only in the visual representation. The scene showed a gray brushed metal surface at the zero parallax plane and targets were shown in a gray color. For each trial, six target objects were visible, either a round button, a round knob, a slider or a rectangular button, as illustrated in Fig. 6. Those shapes were chosen as they represent objects that we often find in practical applications for tangible user interfaces. When a participant reached with the index finger within the hover volume of an object during the experiment, the object either highlighted red (interpreted as the incorrect target) or green (interpreted as the correct target).

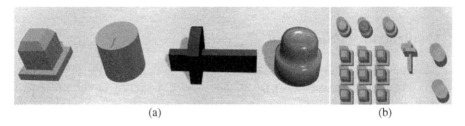

(a)   (b)

Fig. 6. (a) Illustration of the used target shapes and the colors in the confirmatory experiment. From left to right: rectangular button and round knob in grey, red rectangular slider, green round button. (b) Illustration of an example interface (Color figure online).

5.3   Methods

We used a 2 × 4 × 2 × 6 design with the method of constant stimuli for the experiment. We considered two hover volumes: HoverSpace vs. Extruded. The four target shapes (round button or knob, rectangular slider or button), two target sizes (2.5 cm or 5 cm), and six repetitions were uniformly and randomly distributed between all 48 trials in each hover condition for each participant. The hover volume condition was counterbalanced between participants, i.e., half the participants started with the Extruded condition and the other half with the HoverSpace condition.

Each trial consisted of six instances of the same shape of one size at different positions being shown to the participant. The positions were arranged in a grid representing the participant's interaction space, such that they were able to reach them comfortably. The sizes of the objects, at 2.5 cm diameter and 5 cm diameter resemble the typical button size for a display of that size, and double the size, to allow a comparison between different sizes, respectively. The grid was spaced so that the objects did not overlap at any time. The participants were instructed to find the green object by hovering over it with the index finger of their dominant hand and press a button on the keypad with their non-dominant hand when they were within the hover volume.

During the experiment, the participants saw their real hand and the six virtual objects. In the HoverSpace condition, we used the functions described in Sect. 4 and determined whether the participant's finger was in an object's hover volume. In the Extruded condition, we set the y-coordinate of the finger to the target object's height and used the corresponding equation for a 2D approximation of the object's outline. For the round objects we used the equation for an ellipse and for the rectangular condition the equation for a rectangle. This effectively creates an infinite volume, which means that the Extruded condition extended higher compared to the HoverSpace and its height of 10 cm (see Sect. 4). The objects were colored grey when the user's finger was outside the hover volume. When the finger was inside an incorrect target's hover volume, the object turned red. When the finger was in the correct target's hover volume, the object turned green as shown in Fig. 6. After pressing the button the next trial began.

All participants were instructed to complete the task as fast and as precise as possible. The first dependent variable was the selection time, i.e., the time from the start of the trial until the participant confirmed the selection with the press of a button. The second dependent variable was the error rate, i.e., the amount of times the participant pressed the button without being within the correct hover volume.

The participants completed supervised training trials before the experimental phase to ensure that they understood the task correctly. The trials differed from the actual trials in that they allowed the participants to familiarize themselves with the two different hovering conditions. The training trials were excluded from the analysis.

Subjective Questionnaires. To collect subjective impressions we utilized a comparative AttrakDiff questionnaire, which measures hedonic quality and attractiveness [11]. Following an initial demographic questionnaire, after half the trials, the participants had to take a break, answer an AttrakDiff questionnaire and then continue with the other condition. After the second condition, they filled in the second part of the AttrakDiff questionnaire and a further questionnaire directly asking them to judge which technique they preferred and why they chose that technique.

Hypotheses. Based on the results of the perceptually-inspired experiment discussed in Sect. 3, we evaluated the following hypotheses:

- H1: For the HoverSpace condition the mean selection time is lower than for the Extruded hover volume.
- H2: For the HoverSpace condition the mean error rate is lower than for the Extruded hover volume.
- H3: The participants prefer the HoverSpace over the Extruded hover volume.

5.4   Results

In the following section we summarize the results of the confirmatory experiment. We analyzed the results with a repeated measure ANOVA at the 5 % significance level. Degrees of freedom were corrected using Greenhouse-Geisser estimates of sphericity when Mauchly's test indicated that the assumption of sphericity had been violated. Since we found no difference between the results for the two round shapes, nor between the two rectangular shapes, we pooled the data.

Selection Time. The results for the selection time are shown in Fig. 7(a). The results show that the selection time differs significantly between the Extruded (M = 3.09, SD = 1.31) and the HoverSpace (M = 2.90, SD = 1.35) conditions (F(1,15) = 7.955, p < .05, η_p^2 = .347). As expected, we found a significant influence of the target scale on the selection time (F(1,15) = 16.294, p < .001, η_p^2 = .521). We did not find a significant

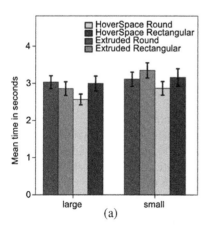
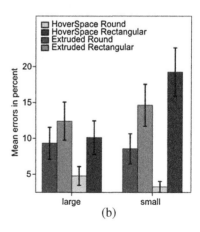

Fig. 7. Plots of the pooled results of the confirmatory experiment. The x-axes show the target scales and the y-axes show the (a) mean time in seconds and (b) the mean errors in percent. The bar plots are grouped by the hover condition and the round condition. The vertical bars show the standard error.

influence of the target shape on the selection performance (F(3,45) = 2.46, p = .075, η_p^2 = .14). We found a significant interaction effect between the hover condition and the round condition (F(1,15) = 9.256, p < .05, η_p^2 = .382). Post hoc tests with Bonferroni correction for the interaction effect between the hover and the round condition showed significant differences only between the Extruded-rectangular (M = 3.11, SD = .61) and HoverSpace-round (M = 2.72, SD = .53) conditions (T(15) = 3.164, p < .05), between the Extruded-round (M = 3.07, SD = .62) and HoverSpace-round conditions (T(15) = 4.229, p < .05), and between the HoverSpace-rectangular (M = 3.08, SD = .31) and HoverSpace-round conditions (T(15) = 3.240, p < .05).

Errors. The results for the error rate are shown in Fig. 7(b). The results showed no significant difference in error rate between the Extruded (M = .06, SD = .24) and the HoverSpace (M = .05, SD = .21) conditions. We found a significant influence of the round condition on the errors (F(1,15) = 10.392, p < .05, η_p^2 = .409). We found no significant influence of the hover condition (F(1,15) = .775, p = .392, η_p^2 = .049) or the scale (F(1,15) = 3.629, p = .076, η_p^2 = .195). We found a significant interaction effect between the scale and the round condition (F(1,15) = 7.304, p < .05, η_p^2 = .327). Post hoc tests with Bonferroni correction for the interaction effect between the scale and the round condition showed significant differences only between the big-round (M = .03, SD = .06) and small-rectangular (M = .10, SD = .12) conditions (T(15) = 3.264, p < .05), as well as between the small-rectangular (M = .10, SD = .12) and small-round (M = .02, SD = .04) conditions (T(15) = −3.178, p < .05).

Selection Distribution. We evaluated how often participants selected an object in the HoverSpace condition while being with their index finger in the Orthogonal or Line-of-Sight volumes (see Sect. 4). The distribution was approximately 23 % only in the Orthogonal volume, 7 % only in the Line-of-Sight volume, and 65 % in the overlap region of both volumes. Approximately 5 % of all selections were errors. In the Extruded condition, approximately 94 % were within the vertically extruded region and approximately 6 % of all selections were errors.

Subjective Questionnaires. The results of the AttrakDiff questionnaire show that pragmatic quality, i.e., an indication of whether the user is assisted by the product, reaches an average value overall. In comparison, pragmatic and hedonic qualities of the HoverSpace are higher than of the Extruded hover volume. The HoverSpace also has a smaller confidence interval for PQ and HQ, indicating a greater level of certainty on the users. In terms of the overall means, the HoverSpace approach is located in the above-average region with an overall impression of the approach as attractive (Fig. 8). We asked the participants which of the techniques they preferred, either the first or the second one they tried. As the experiment was counterbalanced, the results were mapped towards the HoverSpace or Extruded condition. The results show a preference of the HoverSpace (rating scale 1 = Extruded, 5 = HoverSpace, M = 3.44, SD = 1.55).

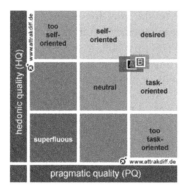

Fig. 8. Average values and confidence rectangles for the AttrakDiff questionnaire of the two conditions: **A** for the Extruded approach and **B** for the HoverSpace.

5.5   Discussion

The results of the confirmatory experiment showed that the HoverSpace outperformed the Extruded approach considering the selection time, which implies a higher overall performance, considering that we did not find a significant difference between the similar error rates. This confirms our hypothesis H1, but not H2. Considering the limited size of the HoverSpace, albeit wider than the infinite Extruded approach, the lower selection time implies that the perceptually-inspired hover volume is a valuable improvement over vertically extruded hover regions.

The results from the subjective questionnaires support our hypothesis H2, as they show that the participants subjectively preferred the perceptually-inspired HoverSpace over the Extruded approach. We received multiple comments such as "The second technique [HoverSpace] was much more intuitive and more precise compared to the first one." These comments further support this hypothesis. However, some participants thought the Extruded approach was more precise and preferred it over the HoverSpace. This might be caused by the fact that the HoverSpace volumes for different target objects overlapped when they were located close together, causing two targets to change color at the same time. To disambiguate such multiple selections in future implementations we suggest to prioritize selections in Orthogonal hover volumes compared to selections in Line-of-Sight hover volumes considering the larger number of participants in the experiment described in Sect. 3 whose mental model matched these hover volumes.

6   Guidelines

Hovering in interactive tabletop environments allows effective decluttering of interfaces. Our analysis of the perceived spatial affordances of such hover interaction has shown that perceptually-inspired hover volumes can increase the performance, as well as the subjective attractiveness of interfaces. In the following, we summarize the lessons learned:

We observed two mental models for hovering in our stereoscopic tabletop environment. The first mental model was characterized by users expecting hovering effects to occur when their hand is right above the object on a line along the display normal, and the second is characterized by users occluding the object based on their line-of-sight. The orthogonal hovering is relatively close to the naive, straight-up extruded outline solution usually implemented in related work.

We suggest a combination of both of these approaches to provide a technique valid for most users. However, our results in the confirmatory experiment suggest that only seven percent of the selections were in the line-of-sight volume. This leads to the conclusion that the line-of-sight volume should be provided when available, but could be left out when head-tracking is not available, e.g., in tabletop setups with monoscopic display.

We suggest the following guidelines for hovering in tabletop environments:

- G1: A combination of an orthogonal region and a line-of-sight region provides the best performance for hovering tasks.
- G2: Without head-tracking, using an orthogonal region with increasing width depending on the height from the object provides acceptable performance.

7   Conclusion

Due to recent technological advances, the combination of touch interaction on interactive surfaces with spatial interaction above the surface of a stereoscopic display has become feasible. In this paper we identified a way to improve the interaction in this holistic design space by conducting a perceptual study and evaluating the results to define a perceptually-inspired hover volume called the HoverSpace. We confirmed the advantages of this HoverSpace in an experiment and found a significant improvement in performance compared to the traditional approach. Finally, we discussed guidelines for the development of future touch-sensitive interfaces.

In the perceptual experiment we identified two mental models that users exhibit for hovering in stereoscopic 3D environments, which are grounded in the different interpretations of 2D hovering as bringing a mouse cursor over an object or occluding an object with a cursor, respectively. Our results show that both interpretations have direct implications for the design of hover interaction in the 3D space above interactive tabletops.

Future research may investigate whether there are similar differences in other 3D interaction techniques derived from 2D Desktop interfaces. Additionally, future work may focus on the impact of the different parameters of the HoverSpace and determine the best possible values with the smallest necessary volume to reduce overlapping HoverSpace volumes. In particular, the difference between the round and rectangular target shapes could be investigated further to determine whether a mean between these two shapes could improve the HoverSpace. Furthermore, an investigation of training effects may show how long users need to adapt to different types of hover volumes.

References

1. Annett, M., Grossman, T., Wigdor, D., Fitzmaurice, G.: Medusa: a proximity-aware multi-touch tabletop. In: Proceedings of the ACM UIST, pp. 337–346. ACM (2011)
2. Benko, H., Wilson, A.D., Baudisch, P.: Precise selection techniques for multi-touch screens. In: Proceedings of the SIGCHI CHI, pp. 1263–1272. ACM, New York (2006)
3. Bernstein, J.T., Amm, D.T., Leung, O., Mullens, C.T., King, B.M., Land, B.R., Cutler, R.T.: Touch and hover sensing, uS Patent App. 12/501,382. 10 July 2009
4. Bruder, G., Steinicke, F., Stuerzlinger, W.: Effects of visual conflicts on 3D selection task performance in stereoscopic display environments. In: Proceedings of the ACM 3DUI, pp. 115–118 (2013)
5. Bruder, G., Steinicke, F., Stuerzlinger, W.: To touch or not to touch? comparing 2d touch and 3d mid-air interaction on stereoscopic tabletop surfaces. In: Proceedings of the ACM SUI, pp. 1–8. ACM Press (2013)
6. Bruder, G., Steinicke, F., Stuerzlinger, W.: Touching the void revisited: analyses of touch behavior on and above tabletop surfaces. In: Winckler, M. (ed.) INTERACT 2013, Part I. LNCS, vol. 8117, pp. 278–296. Springer, Heidelberg (2013)
7. Buxton, W.: A three-state model of graphical input. In: Human-computer interaction-INTERACT, **90**, pp. 449–456, Citeseer (1990)
8. Echtler, F., Huber, M., Klinker, G.: Shadow tracking on multi-touch tables. In: Proceedings of AVI, pp. 388–391. ACM, New York (2008)
9. Grossman, T., Hinckley, K., Baudisch, P., Agrawala, M., Balakrishnan, R.: Hover widgets: using the tracking state to extend the capabilities of pen-operated devices. In: Proceedings of the SIGCHI CHI, pp. 861–870. ACM, New York (2006)
10. Han, S., Park, J.: A study on touch & hover based interaction for zooming. In: CHI 2012 Extended Abstracts on Human Factors in Computing Systems, pp. 2183–2188. ACM (2012)
11. Hassenzahl, M., Burmester, M., Koller, F.: Attrakdiff: ein fragebogen zur messung wahrgenommener hedonischer und pragmatischer qualität. In: Proceedings of the Mensch & Computer, pp. 187–196. Springer (2003)
12. Hilliges, O., Izadi, S., Wilson, A.D., Hodges, S., Garcia-Mendoza, A., Butz, A.: Interactions in the air: adding further depth to interactive tabletops. In: UIST 2009: Proceedings of the ACM UIST, pp. 139–148. ACM (2009)
13. Leap Motion Inc: Leap Motion (2012). http://www.leapmotion.com/
14. Li, Y., Hinckley, K., Guan, Z., Landay, J.A.: Experimental analysis of mode switching techniques in pen-based user interfaces. In: Proceedings of the SIGCHI CHI, pp. 461–470. ACM (2005)
15. Loomis, J., Knapp, J.: Visual perception of egocentric distance in real and virtual environments. In: Hettinger, L., Haas, M. (eds.) Virtual and Adaptive Environments, pp. 21–46. Erlbaum, Mahwah (2003)
16. Lubos, P., Bruder, G., Steinicke, F.: Analysis of direct selection in head-mounted display environments. In: Proceedings of the IEEE 3DUI, pp. 1–8. IEEE (2014)
17. Microsoft: Kinect (2012). http://www.microsoft.com/en-us/kinectforwindows/
18. Pyryeskin, D., Hancock, M., Hoey, J.: Extending interactions into hoverspace using reflected light. In: Proceedings of the ACM International Conference on Interactive Tabletops and Surfaces, pp. 262–263. ACM (2011)
19. Schöning, J., Steinicke, F., Krüger, A., Hinrichs, K., Valkov, D.: bimanual interaction with interscopic multi-touch surfaces. In: Gross, T., Gulliksen, J., Kotzé, P., Oestreicher, L., Palanque, P., Prates, R.O., Winckler, M. (eds.) INTERACT 2009. LNCS, vol. 5727, pp. 40–53. Springer, Heidelberg (2009)

20. Unity Technologies: Unity3D (2015). http://www.unity3d.com/
21. Valkov, D., Giesler, A., Hinrichs, K.H.: Imperceptible depth shifts for touch interaction with stereoscopic objects. In: Proceedings of the SIGCHI CHI, pp. 227–236. ACM (2014)
22. Willemsen, P., Gooch, A., Thompson, W., Creem-Regehr, S.: Effects of stereo viewing conditions on distance perception in virtual environments. Presence Teleoperators Virtual Environ. **17**(1), 91–101 (2008)
23. Zilch, D., Bruder, G., Steinicke, F., Lamak, F.: Design and evaluation of 3d gui widgets for stereoscopic touch-displays. In: Proceedings of the GI-Workshop VR/AR, pp. 37–48 (2013)

In-Situ Occlusion Resolution for Hybrid Tabletop Environments

Jan Riemann[✉], Mohammadreza Khalilbeigi, and Max Mühlhäuser

Technische Universität Darmstadt, Darmstadt, Germany
{riemann,khalilbeigi,
max}@tk.informatik.tu-darmstadt.de

Abstract. In this paper we explore the use of in situ occlusion resolution in mixed physical/digital tabletop scenarios. We propose the extension of back-projected tabletops with interactive top-projection to turn the physical object's surface into peripheral displays. These displays are used to resolve occlusion in situ without the need to use additional tabletop display space and keeping the spatial perception of the occluded objects. We contribute a visualization concept and a set of interaction techniques for in situ occlusion resolution and easy access to occluded objects. The techniques are implemented in a system named ProjecTop, which is evaluated in an quantitative user study. The study results highlight how top-projection can be beneficially used. We conclude with a set of design implications derived from the study's results.

Keywords: Interactive tabletops · Occlusion awareness · Hybrid interaction · Peripheral displays · Multitouch

1 Introduction

Tabletop computers are going to play an important role in future offices due to dropping prices and technological advances. When integrated within the normal office furniture, their table like form factor affords the usage as normal table, e.g. additional materials like printed documents, laptops, books etc. are placed and used concurrently on its interactive surface.

Fig. 1. ProjecTop system visualizing the occluded digital objects

The presence of physical objects on tabletops poses several challenges: The first is that it considerably decreases the screen real-estate for interaction with digital objects. Not only the footprint of physical objects obstructs the display, but also casual arrangement of them on the surface makes the - still visible - display areas hard to use. This becomes even worse for tall physical objects (e.g. high stacks) that shadow even more display area from the user's perspective. A second important challenge is that the physical objects may partially or

© IFIP International Federation for Information Processing 2015
J. Abascal et al. (Eds.): INTERACT 2015, Part III, LNCS 9298, pp. 278–295, 2015.
DOI: 10.1007/978-3-319-22698-9_18

entirely occlude digital objects, resulting in losing awareness about occluded objects. Further, accessing them becomes cumbersome.

Work is emerging to address parts of these problems: detecting the footprint of physical objects [2] and avoiding occlusion [1]. Other researchers address the problem by providing support for staying aware of and accessing digital objects [3, 6, 8]. The typical approach is that the occluded objects are transformed into icons or other content-wise reduced forms and visualized next to the occluding object. While this pioneering and motivating work established first design principles to mitigate the problem of physical occlusion in hybrid settings, it is not clear how these approaches extend to more cluttered workspaces where many physical objects consume considerable space on the tabletop display, which is the user's primary interaction surface.

We go beyond existing work by extending the interaction and display spaces to the surface of the physical objects using additional top-projection facilities on a back-projected tabletop system to resolve occlusion. The tabletop provides the primary high-resolution interaction surface for the user to work on while the top-projection provides a secondary class of "peripheral" displays on the physical objects' surface. These peripheral displays are used to solve the aforementioned problems. By using the object's surface as secondary display, we do not need to consume additional space on the tabletop screen. Another advantage is that the spatial layout can be left unchanged, as the visualization can be shown at the occluded object's exact location.

In this paper, we contribute a set of integrated interaction concepts and visualization techniques that leverage the underlying two-class display idea for in situ occlusion resolution in hybrid environments. The design of our techniques is grounded on an initial user study. All presented techniques are coherently implemented in a fully functional occlusion support system, named ProjecTop, allowing the users to fluidly interact in a realistic hybrid tabletop setting.

Our second contribution is a user study formally evaluating our approach in a real hybrid setting. The goal was to assess the potential of top-projection in hybrid settings in general and for occlusion management in particular. Based on the results, we present design implications for hybrid tabletop systems extended with top-projection. We believe that the results are not only relevant in the context of occlusion but also in general for the use of top-projection to project additional self-contained content on physical objects.

The outline for the rest of the paper is as follows: We start with a review of the related work. We then present an initial user study followed by the design of the ProjecTop system based on the study results. Next, we present the user study evaluating the ProjecTop system and conclude with design implications derived from the study.

2 Related Work

Our work mainly relates to two research fields - namely augmented desktops and physical occlusion - which are discussed in the following:

2.1 Augmented Desktops

Effort has been made to augment paperwork with digital projection: The DigitalDesk [22], FACT [11] and Paper-Top [13] are systems which project onto printed documents, for example allowing the user to interactively add digital content [11, 13, 22], show animations [13] or do highlighting [11]. The EnhancedDesk [10] uses a projector to display related digital content (e.g. interactive simulations) next to physical documents. However, these systems aim at augmenting paper documents with additional digital facilities and do not take into account self-contained digital objects. Other examples are the Augmented Surface system [16], which allows digital objects to "leave" devices like laptops by means of top-projection on desk and wall surfaces, or Pictionaire [4] which is a projected tabletop system to integrate digital and physical media. Projection on physical objects is used by Pictionaire to facilitate tracing of digital content into sketchbooks by projecting the original digital content on the book. There are also some systems, like PaperLens and spatially aware tangible displays [17–19], which use top-projection and passive devices to extend the interaction space from the tabletop's surface to the space above the table. This allows for example browsing three dimensional information spaces in a natural way.

While these systems allow the user to circumvent occlusion by physical objects due to the possibility of flexibly shaped display areas [1], their inherent ability to project on the occluders' surface or by using computer vision techniques to move the display around physical objects, these systems have some drawbacks: They either avoid projecting on physical objects and lose display space where physical objects are placed. Or, they do not take into account physical objects and project unaltered content on them, basically ignoring the presence of objects which possibly renders the information on the object itself unusable. Another common problem to all systems that use top-projection as their primary means of display is that they are prone to occlusion by the users' body parts. The user causes shadowing when body parts like hands or the head come into the projection frustum. Therefore, we use top-projection only as a secondary display for occlusion resolution. The primary content is displayed on the back-projected tabletop display which is not prone to these problems.

2.2 Physical Occlusion on Tabletops

Occlusion has been widely studied as it is a common problem - even in physical-only settings. Iwai et al. developed the limpid desk [5] which allows for ad hoc transparentization of stacks of physical objects to browse them. Underlying objects are projected on the topmost object if the user wants to look at them. However they investigated physical-only settings which have the inherent advantage that the presence of physical objects is more visible due to the height of the objects than it is for digital items. Our work extends this approach to digital items on a hybrid interactive tabletop.

Steimle et al. [20] as well as Khalilbeigi et al. [7] conducted studies to gain an understanding on how physical-only interaction transfers to mixed digital-physical interaction scenarios on interactive surfaces. They found out that concepts common in the physical world, like stacking, are also applied to hybrid settings by the studies' participants. Therefore the problem of physical/digital occlusion can be assumed to be an important factor for the usability of such systems.

Freeman et al. [2] developed a concept for finding free space on tabletops in order to avoid occlusion by moving objects to free areas. Avoiding occlusion is working fine in settings with much free space available and the objects need to be moved only a bit. However, in highly cluttered environments, where no near-by free space is available, it leads to significant reorganization of the users workspace, which might not be desired. Other research [21] also suggests, that users do not need any reactive occlusion support, as (unwanted) occlusion seldom occurs. Mainly because users arrange their workspace in advance to avoid it or the system can do it by relocation. However, their system did not provide any occlusion support, therefore users might have avoided occlusion by themselves due to the lack of support rather than because they don't do it in general. Also, the setting of a lab bench is rather special and probably not representative for e.g. normal office work. Besides avoiding occlusion, there are concepts to deal with it: Tumble! Splat! by Ramos et al. [15] solve the problem of awareness and access for digital/digital occlusion in drawing applications. Systems like SnapRail [3], occlusion management techniques by Javed et al. [6] or ObjecTop [8] by Khalilbeigi et al. provide means to the user to interact in hybrid settings without losing the awareness of occluded objects but without limiting the user, for example through avoiding occlusion by relocating occluded items. This is done by using interactive proxy objects, e.g. tiny icons representing occluded objects on unoccluded space, allowing for access and perception. However, while helpful for the user, these techniques all consume additional display space on the tabletop. This is not an issue as long as only a low amount of the display is covered, but it might become a problem if there is not much display space left to display the visualization.

3   Initial Study

Study Design. ProjectTop resolves occlusion using the surface of physical objects as additional display. In order to appropriately top-project digital content on such complex surfaces with various textures, we conducted a user study with 8 participants (2 female, aged 26.5 on average). The goal of this study was to find a representation of occluded objects that conveys as much information as possible while being acceptable for the user. In particular, we wanted to see which properties of the underlying objects are important to the user. We therefore employed three visualization levels, showing different characteristics of the represented object: Low (location only), Mid (location, orientation and type) and High (location, orientation and content).

Apparatus and Layout. The study was conducted using a LCD-based tabletop with a top-mounted projector. To implement the three visualization levels, we chose a small red dot (the most minimalistic visualization possible) for the "Low"-level, an icon for the "Mid"-level and a miniature version for the "High"-level. These visualizations were projected on a set of physical documents of different types (pure text, text + image, notepad). To see, whether the location of the projection matters, we projected them at two different locations (in-place and moved to the content-free border of the document close to the original position). This leads to a total of 3 visualizations × 2 locations = 6 trials per participant.

Task. A set of documents with top-projected content was presented to the participants. In order to force engagement with these documents, the participants had to answer questions related to the documents' content. To find out whether top-projection interferes with interacting with documents, the questions had to be answered in writing on a notepad which also had top-projected content on it. The set of documents was changed for each trial. The study lasted about 20 min per participant. After each trial, the participants rated the visualization regarding the perceived clutter, usefulness, interference between physical and digital content (on a 5 point Likert scale), as well as acceptability of the projection (0 (never) to 10 (continuously)) in the working and storage area.

Results. We performed a 2-way ANOVA on the data, Greenhouse-Geisser correction was used in case of violation of sphericity.

The placement of the visualization had significant influence on the perceived clutter ($F_{1,7} = 25$, p = .002), the interference (physical: $F_{1,7} = 22.9$, p = .002, digital: $F_{1,7} = 17.64$, p = .004) and the acceptability of projection in the working area ($F_{1,7} = 21.99$, p = .002). There was no significant difference for the storage area ($F_{1,7} = .13$, p = .732) or the helpfulness ($F_{1,7} = 2.03$, p = .197). In the significant cases, the users slightly favored the projection at the free spot (marginal means, free-spot/in-place, SE in brackets: clutter: 1.8[.27]/2.6[.19], phys. interference: 1.9 [.28]/2.9[.36], dig. int.: 1.7[.27]/2.5[.28], accept. work. area: 7.3[.64]/6.2[.56]). For the acceptability in the storage area, the means were 9.0[.37]/8.96[.35]. While certainly less acceptable, even in working areas, the acceptability of top- projection is more on the acceptable side (>5.5).

The different visualization had significant influence on the perceived clutter ($F_{2,14} = 19.21$, p < .001), the digital interference ($F_{1.2,8.2} = 14.04$, p = .001), the helpfulness ($F_{2,14} = 22.53$, p < .001) and the acceptability of projection in the working area ($F_{2,14} = 11.47$, p = .001). Again, there was no significant difference for the storage area ($F_{2,14} = 2.44$, p = 0.15) or the physical interference ($F_{2,14} = .07$, p = .84). As expected, the dot visualization introduced minimal clutter ($\mu = 1.4$, SE = .175) and digital interference ($\mu = 1.3$, SE = .18), however, it was not very helpful ($\mu = 1.75$, SE = .31). The icon and miniature visualization introduce more clutter (min.: $\mu = 2.75$, SE = .31, icon: $\mu = 2.56$, SE = .27), but are perceived as much more helpful (min.: $\mu = 4.25$, SE = .21, icon: $\mu = 3.63$, SE = .28). All three visualizations received values above 5.5 for the acceptability in the working area and above 8.7 for the storage area, leading to the conclusion that they are all acceptable for most users.

Based on these results, we developed a set of visualization and interaction techniques for hybrid occlusion resolution using top-projection named ProjecTop.

4 ProjecTop

The underlying idea of ProjecTop is to exploit the physical occluder's surface to extend the display and interaction spaces of tabletops in a hybrid physical-digital setting. To do so, we augment back-projected or active LCD based tabletops with projection and depth camera facilities that allow projecting digital content on the surface of physical objects (as peripheral display) and interaction with these projections using direct multitouch gestures.

While we use a rather complex setup for our implementation (see Fig. 9), the advances in miniaturization of sensors and projectors will enable more compact and ergonomic implementations in the future (for instance as an integrated

Fig. 2. Lamp enhanced tabletop

desk-lamp, c.f. Figure 2, similar to LuminAR [12]). In the following, we describe visualization and interaction techniques supported in ProjecTop (Fig. 1).

4.1 Representing Digital Objects

Based on the study results, we opted for the icon as the default representation. The reason behind this is that the icon has been shown to be acceptable and provides sufficient level of detail about occluded items while introducing less visual clutter to the workspace [6, 8]. For ProjecTop, we further extend the icon representation from the study by adding an outline visualization showing the occluded object's outline (see Fig. 3). The reason for adding the object's outline is that thereby, even more information can be conveyed: Not only the objects position, orientation and type are visible, but also the object's size and possible z-layering are immediately visible to the user. This allows the user to quickly see whether a relevant object - for example a long e-mail - is under a physical object without having to take any physical action (see Fig. 3(a)). Also, previous research [8] shows that users tend to prefer moving lightweight objects instead of using the provided system support. The spatial awareness (position, size and z-layering are visible) provided by this visualization gives them a hint where the occluded objects are, allowing a more directed and efficient movement of the occluder. Another argument for using the outline element in the visualization is that it allows to "complete" objects in partial occlusion situations (e.g. only half of the object is underneath a physical one) as shown in Fig. 3(b).

The ProjecTop system starts to visualize the occlusion when a meaningful part of a digital object is underneath a physical object. This threshold ensures that digital objects

(a) direct overview   (b) partial occlusion   (c) overlapping

Fig. 3. Visualization overview

which are, for instance, only with the tip of a corner under an physical object, do not cause disturbing projection artefacts.

Physical objects do not always occlude digital content fully, but partially. This might even be a wanted case of occlusion, as only a part of the occluded object is actually needed, e.g. a small figure on a large page. In such situations, the ProjecTop approach has several advantages over tabletop-based approaches [3, 6, 8] which use proxy objects like halos or icons on the tabletop display. These approaches require to define a point where the transition between showing the actual object and showing the icon representation happens (e.g. if a digital object is occluded by 50 %, the icon is shown instead of the object). However, it is not clear, when the user actually wants this switching to happen: As mentioned, it might be useful and wanted to have only a part (e.g. 10 %) of a technical figure looking out underneath a physical object, while for other objects, an earlier transition is desired (e.g. if 20 % are occluded). Additionally, when the switching occurs, there is a notable visual break when the large object changes to a tiny icon. In contrast, ProjecTop allows a continuous transition between fully occluded and fully visible without any distracting abrupt change in the visualization as both styles can coexist in a meaningful way, as the outline can complement the still visible part.

In case of multiple overlapping objects being occluded, ProjecTop visualization conveys their z-order in a natural way, as the outlines occlude each other just like the represented objects do. The aforementioned smooth transition helps to identify the z-order even for two partially occluded items if the overlap happens under a physical object as shown in Fig. 3(c).

The visualization is not only a static means to provide awareness about hidden objects, but also an interactive means to enable occlusion resolution without having to interact with the physical occluder. Besides retrieving the digital object from underneath the physical one, ProjecTop provides a set of multitouch gestures to interact with the occluded digital objects, even though the occluder. These techniques are explained in the following section.

4.2   Interacting with Occluded Objects

In order to provide a consistent interface, ProjecTop allows standard object manipulation (moving, rotating, etc.) not only on the tabletop's display but also on the surface of physical objects. This allows for instance to naturally manipulate an occluded object "through" the occluding object. A short single finger tap gesture allows to change the z-order of digital objects by making the tapped one the foremost. This gesture is also supported on the tabletop surface as well as on the physical objects. To support immediate access to and fluent organization of digital objects in hybrid settings, we designed three techniques described in the following:

Hold-To-Peek is a quick way of glimpsing at occluded objects. When selecting and holding an occluded object with one finger for a short amount of time, the occluding physical object becomes "transparent" by filling the outline representation with the underlying object's actual content. This allows users to see through the occluder and look at the digital item. When lifting the finger, the object returns to its default outline

Fig. 4. Hold-To-Peek   **Fig. 5.** Semantic-Pinch

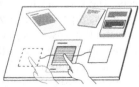

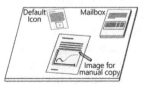

Fig. 6. Direct HyperMove   **Fig. 7.** Manual Hypermove   **Fig. 8.** Semantic-Pinch use

representation (see Fig. 4 for an example) This technique can be further extended by replacing the purely visual fade-in with a semantic fading, where gradually more information gets revealed as the user holds longer.

This approach has several advantages over the prior approaches that are based on pulling the icons out from underneath the occluder: Firstly, tapping and holding is a very fast gesture, as it does not require any further movement. Secondly, the gesture can be performed either on the occluder or on the tabletop, which mitigates the problem of the tabletop surface being inaccessible (e.g. between two tall objects). As a result of showing the occluded object in-place, there is also no additional free display space needed next to the occluder, which is beneficial in very cluttered settings.

SemanticPinch provides a permanent access to higher levels of detail about the occluded object. Similar to the typical pinch-to-zoom gesture, SemanticPinch is used to change the representation of an occluded digital object on a physical one (see Fig. 5): As the user "zooms in", more and more detail about the object is revealed. Contrary to the state-of-the-art semantic zooming facilities for occlusion [8], the visualization remains in its current semantic zoom representation when the user lifts the fingers. This way, the user is able to control the amount of information he wants to receive about an object permanently.

Using this technique, users can maintain a more detailed view on occluded objects. Practical uses-cases are for example an occluded mailbox which the user can semantically zoom in to view the last n received mails instead of just a mailbox icon. Due to the top-projection, he has an always-on-top mailbox overview. Another use-case would be tracing digital objects to copy them on physical paper: The user can place the digital object, occlude it with a sheet of paper and then semantically zoom in until the full object is shown, allowing him to trace it using a pen. See Fig. 8 for an illustration.

Moving objects is a key action for workspace organization and well supported on digital tabletops. With the addition of physical objects, moving digital objects becomes cumbersome: The direct moving path might be obstructed by a physical object, requiring the user to either move the physical object or drag the digital one around the physical one. In order to better support these cases, we developed HyperMove.

HyperMove is an extension of the moving gesture supported on conventional multitouch surfaces and is not bound to the tabletops display, but extends the interaction space onto the surface of physical objects. ProjecTop supports two variants of HyperMove: manual and direct. The manual version extends the conventional dragging to be used across physical objects: The user can for instance start dragging a digital object on the screen and move it across a printed page while searching for a suitable place. This variant is particularly useful if the user does not know the exact place where he wants the object and if there are only flat objects in the path.

The direct version uses a bi-manual gesture to move digital items over large distances without having to drag them: The user references the desired position of the object by a static tripod-gesture (similar to teleport in [8]) with one hand and can then move digital objects immediately to this location by performing a single finger flick gesture with the other hand on them. Again, ProjecTop allows this gesture to be performed on the tabletop as well as physical objects (see Figs. 6 and 7). Besides supporting conventional moving tasks, this gesture allows for more advanced an quick organization, like piling several digital objects under a stack of physical ones.

5   Implementation

All techniques described above are implemented in a system C# using DirectX. It runs on a Samsung SUR40 tabletop system with a Full HD screen resolution of 1920x1080. The raw infrared image from PixelSense is used to do a shadow tracking of physical objects on the table's surface. In addition, fiducial tag markers are used for identifying physical objects. ProjecTop uses a standard Full HD projector mounted above the tabletop to realize the top-projection. To align the projection with the tabletop coordinate system and thereby allow precise projection on the physical objects, a one-time calibration is needed if the table or projector are moved. The touch input is provided by the SUR40 for

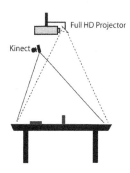

Fig. 9. Lab setup for prototype

the tabletop surface, and by a depth camera (Microsoft Kinect) based touch recognition framework for the passive physical objects. Our frameworks approach is an extended version of the approach used by for dSensingNI [9]. We added the ability to allow object and touch recognition in areas where the background image contains unknown values and simple background subtraction does not work.

6 User Study

The overarching goal of the study was to find out how ProjecTop's features, i.e. the in-place resolution and the visibility of the spatial layout perform under different clutter levels. Performance in this context mainly refers to the time that users need to find an occluded object and the effort required for doing so (e.g. the number of interactions with physical objects).

Based on prior studies [6, 8], we decided to compare the top-projection based ProjecTop approach with a system named "Baseline", that relies purely on the tabletop's display. Baseline consists of two well-established occlusion support techniques: occluded objects are visualized as icons around the occluder to provide accessibility and a glowing [6] visualization surrounding the occluding object to provide general awareness. This way we can ensure generalizability and comparability of our study's results. Additionally, we did not impose any restrictions on the interaction with the physical objects to force usage of the digital occlusion resolution techniques. The users are allowed to lift or move physical objects if they prefer to do so over using the provided system support in both systems throughout the study.

As we know from previous work, the usage and performance of occlusion related techniques is dependent on the amount of clutter of the tabletop [8]. To see whether this has any impact in a top-projection scenario, we had two conditions (low and high clutter) in our evaluation, differing in the number of physical and digital objects present on the tabletop. We rank the clutter level of hybrid tabletop settings as a function of the number of digital objects on a tabletop and the amount of occluded display surface. In this experiment, for the low clutter conditions, we used 10 digital objects (of which at least 5 were initially occluded) and 3 physical objects. This choice lead to about 40 % occluded display area. The high clutter condition consisted of 15 digital objects (10 were occluded) and 5 physical objects leading to about 60 % occlusion.

6.1 Apparatus and Material

We conducted the study using the lab hardware setup described in the implementation section. As physical objects, we used the following items: A thick book (20 by 24 cm with 4 cm height), a standard DIN A5 paper notepad, a printed A4 document, a cardboard box sized approximately A5 with a height of 3 cm and a heavy small high box (7 by 7 cm with a height of 14 cm). To have different surface textures for the projection, the document was printed with a lighter texture on it, the book was chosen to have a darker one. The small box

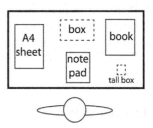

Fig. 10. Initial setup. The dashed objects were only present in high clutter conditions.

and the cardboard box were only present in the high clutter conditions. The other objects were present in both, high and low clutter, conditions.

We chose the objects to be representative for an office desk with respect to size and ease of moving them. As the size of the tabletop is limited and the display could be dam aged when high loads are placed on it, we had to abstain from other common objects like monitors, or a full keyboard. The initial physical layout for the study can be seen in Fig. 10.

As for digital objects, we chose a set of photos, documents and virtual Post-it notes. For each of these type, different categories existed, e.g. for the documents, there were documents about persons, movies, universities, etc. The objects were randomly chosen from the pool and placed randomly across the tabletop surface at the beginning of each trial.

6.2   Task

The experiment consisted of a search task in which the participants had to find and count a set of digital target objects, for example the number of documents about movies. The targets were mixed with other digital objects of different types or topics (distractors). All target objects were initially hidden under physical objects.

6.3   Hypothesis

Compared to Baseline, we expected that ProjecTop reduces the time needed to find a specific object as, in most situations, the occlusion can be directly resolved without having to perform a move gesture (e.g. for a semantic zoom) but rather a single tap-and-hold. Due to the in-place occlusion resolution, we assumed that the users are much more unlikely to actually drag out objects from underneath the occluder, as inspecting the full object is directly possible. Additionally, the interaction with physical objects should be reduced as ProjecTop provides an easy way to see where an occluded object is placed before lifting or moving the physical occluder. Therefore these actions can be carried out more efficiently. In sum, the hypotheses to be examined were:

- H1: ProjecTop requires less time to find and access objects
- H2: ProjecTop reduces the number of full object pull-outs (the occluded object is fully moved to unoccluded space)
- H3: ProjecTop reduces the number of object interactions and the distance objects are moved

6.4   Experiment Design

The experiment was designed as a two interface (Baseline and ProjecTop) × two clutter levels (Low and High) within subjects experiment. The presentation order for the four conditions was counterbalanced. For each condition, there were five repetitions with different types (documents about movies, images of persons, …) and numbers (one to three) of targets. For each condition, the order of the target types for the five trials was randomly assigned for each participant. Prior to the each set of trials, the users got a short introduction on the current interface and task and had some time to play around

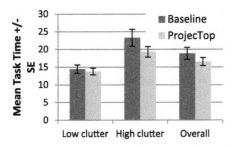
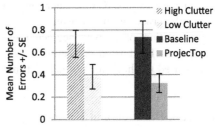

Fig. 11. Average trial duration by interface   **Fig. 12.** Average number of counting errors per trial by clutter level (left) and by interface (right)

with the system until they felt comfortable using it. The users where then asked to perform the counting task as accurate and fast as possible.

The main measurement for the task was the completion time that was measured by pressing the space bar of a keyboard within the participants' arm reach when starting and after finishing the counting. The number of interactions with physical objects as well as their movement distance was logged. For the digital objects the number and type of special interactions, like pulling out from underneath an occluder, was logged. The number of targets determined by the participants was recorded to determine the error-rate made by the participants. The participants advanced to the next trial without having been told if they were right, in order to not influence their behavior (e.g. becoming faster or slower).

After each condition, the participants had to fill in a NASA-TLX [14] questionnaire to measure the perceived workload. At the end of each session, the participants were interviewed in a semi-structured way to gather additional subjective feedback. We put an emphasis on the appropriateness of the projection during the interview. The whole sessions were recorded on video and lasted about one hour.

6.5   Participants

17 participants (15 male, 2 female, all but 2 right-handed) aged between 21 and 46 ($\mu = 27.588$, $\sigma = 5.657$) were recruited from the local university. There was no compensation provided. All participants had previous experience with touch interfaces and all except three participants had previous experience with interactive tabletops.

There was a total of 17 participants × 2 interface × 2 clutter levels × 5 repetitions = 340 trials

7   Results and Discussion

After preprocessing of the recorded trial data (e.g. removing outliers more than three standard deviations away from the mean), 9 trials had to be removed due to errors in time measurement. To analyze the data of the remaining 331 trials, we used a 2-way repeated measures ANOVA. There was no significant influence of the presentation order of the tasks for any measure, e.g. any learning effect on the interface. Therefore, the presentation order was neglected in the following analysis. For all pair-wise comparisons, Bonferroni correction was applied where necessary. The Shapiro-Wilk test was used to check for normal distribution and ensure applicability of ANOVA.

7.1   Task Duration and Errors

The analysis of the measured trial time revealed that the interface as well as the clutter level had significant influence. ProjecTop (μ = 16.5 s, SE = 1.7) performed significantly (F1,16 = 6.09, p = 0.025) faster than Baseline (μ = 18.9 s, SE = 1.1), see Fig. 11. The clutter level also had a significant (F1,16 = 34.52, p < 0.001) influence on the trial time (μ = 14.1 s, SE = 1 for low clutter, μ = 21.3 s, SE = 1.9 for high clutter). Additionally, there was a significant effect of interface × clutter on the completion time (F1,16 = 6.67, p = 0.02). Pairwise comparison revealed, that ProjecTop performed significantly faster under the high clutter condition (p = 0.017). For the low-clutter condition, the difference was not significant (p = 0.29).

Interestingly, when looking at the average number of wrong answers given by the participants, there was also a significant ($F_{1,16}$ = 8.209, p = 0.011) difference between ProjecTop and Baseline in favor of ProjecTop (see Fig. 12 right). The influence of the clutter level was also significant ($F_{1,16}$ = 4.68, p = 0.046) showing a higher number of errors for high clutter conditions as expected (see Fig. 12 left). There was no significant effect of interface × clutter on the number of errors.

These results show that ProjecTop performs faster than Baseline, especially in highly cluttered environments. This supports H1. Interestingly, despite being faster, the participants made significantly less mistakes (reporting a wrong target count) using ProjecTop than they did with Baseline. One reason for this might be that with Baseline, icons which were shadowed by a thick or high object were not visible from the users point of view. Therefore; there was a higher chance that those are missed (leading to more errors) or users needed to take special care of them by explicitly looking behind objects (leading to additional time). ProjecTop inherently circumvents this problem as the visualization is right on the occluder rather than behind it.

7.2   Interactions with Objects

When analyzing the number of interactions with physical objects, it turned out, that the interface had a significant influence on the number of interactions ($F_{1,16}$ = 9.668, p = 0.007) with physical objects and the distance physical objects were moved ($F_{1,16}$ = 5.72, p = 0.029). In ProjecTop conditions, the number of interactions was slightly higher with an average of 1.38 interactions per object, whereas Baseline had an average of 1.07. The same holds for the distance objects were moved: Baseline conditions had an average distance of 62.99 mm per object - ProjecTop conditions had 96.55 mm. Hence, H3 is rejected. There was no significant effect of the clutter level or interface × clutter.

Interestingly, even though the amount and distance objects were moved was higher with ProjecTop, it was less time consuming. A possible explanation is the spatial awareness provided by ProjecTop's visualization. It gives the users a strong visual clue of the spatial layout of the occluded digital objects before interacting (e.g. moving or lifting) with the physical occluder. As a result, no additional time is needed to interpret the layout underneath the occluder.

With respect to H2; it turned out that the number of full object pull-outs was a bit higher with ProjecTop (10.62 for Baseline and 11.62 with ProjecTop). However, with $F_{1,16} = 0.73$ and a resulting significance of $p = 0.407$ we assume that the interface had no real influence on the number of objects pulled out. Analysis of the recorded video data revealed that most users tended to lift most of the physical occluders before they finish, thereby "resolving" the occlusion for all underlying digital objects. Therefore, H2 is rejected.

7.3   Task Load Index

The analysis of the NASA TLX Questionnaire revealed that the interface had no significant influence on the measured categories (see Fig. 13 for an overview). There was also no significant effect of interface × clutter except for the perceived effort ($F_{1,16} = 4.848$, $p = 0.043$): Baseline has values of 9.82 for the high clutter condition and 6.18 for low ($p = 0.011$). In contrast, Projec-Top has 7.71 for high and 7.12

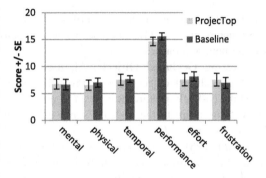

Fig. 13. Average trial duration by interface

for low clutter respectively ($p = 0.365$). The clutter level had significant influence on all measures except performance ($p = 0.17$), with mental demand ($p = 0.005$), physical demand ($p = 0.037$), temporal demand ($p = 0.012$), effort ($p = 0.01$) and frustration ($p = 0.055$) being lower for the low clutter conditions as one would expect.

7.4   User Feedback

The participants' feedback in the post-interviews regarding top-projection varied: Three users found the ProjecTop visualization to be *"chaotic"* (P11) compared to the baseline. A few participants explicitly criticized the interference between projected digital and physical text on the objects, which both get unreadable if they overlap. However, most participants really liked top-projection *"ProjecTop's projection on objects is very cool"* (P10), some even wanted the full content of digital objects to be always projected without user interaction (P10, P15, P16, P17), instead of the icons.

P12 found ProjecTop to be *"clearer [than baseline] with many objects"* and others stated that they had difficulties to obtain an overview in the Baseline condition (e.g. P15: *"Did I already take a look at that icon or not?"*).

Top-projection A common statement was that top-projected visualization should only be used for the storage area, but not for the working area (e.g. P12: "Projection is only good in storage areas and not for the working area, because one concentrates there on specific objects and doesn't want to overlook the mass of objects"). At the same time, the concern was raised that the question of where to draw the border between working and storage area is difficult to answer. To resolve this problem, users suggested a differentiation by focus, so that physical objects the user interacts with do not get top-projection, while the others do (P2, P10). An alternative suggestion was to vary the brightness of top-projection, instead of deactivating it, so that for objects in focus, the projection gets darker to improve readability of the physical content (P15). P16 suggested a combined Baseline/ProjecTop system where the system decides whether objects are suitable for top-projection (then using ProjecTop) or not (using Baseline style). The user should then, however, be able to switch between the styles for specific objects manually. In the context of a combined system, P2 wanted to have the Hold-To-Peek gesture for the icons in Baseline, so the actual object gets top-projected when touching its icon. Overall, it seems beneficial to combine both approaches.

Accessing Occluded Objects. All users found accessing occluded object through ProjecTop easy. The Hold-To-Peek gesture was even found to be sufficient to complete the task by some users, e.g. *"ProjecTop was often sufficient to see what's underneath"* (P6). However, there occurred problems in case of digital-digital occlusion, which is currently not resolved by ProjecTop. In case of one digital object being fully occluded by another under a physical object, the occlusion was reflected by ProjecTop's visualization, making the bottom digital object inaccessible. Baseline's icon representation

Fig. 14. Differently colored outlines for categorization

inherently resolves this occlusion, as the icons do not overlap. However, ProjecTop could be extended to provide access in such cases, too. Additionally, P14 suggested to add different outline colors to group objects into categories and further speed-up finding objects as shown in Fig. 14.

Spatial Awareness. In general, the participants found ProjecTop's spatial awareness useful, especially if they wanted to lift the occluder to access one or more occluded objects: *"Spatial awareness was very helpful, I could look at the physical object and directly saw where the objects are, with Baseline I had to look around the [physical] object to see where [digital] objects are."* (P15). Besides the concerns regarding interference, there were no negative comments on it. Touch on objects Touch on arbitrary physical objects was strange to two users: P4 found *"touching flat objects more intuitive than thick objects, as flat one are closer to the screen which is naturally interacted using touch. For thick or uneven objects, it was strange to touch the surface in order to interact."* P1 said that, *"for thick objects, there is a problem if a gesture* *leaves the object, for instance when dragging out an object from underneath a book, as the touch surface is not continuous at the books edge. "*. The other participants were positive about it, so it can be assumed to be an appropriate way of interacting with top-projected content.

8 Implications

Based on the study results, we propose three main implications for informing the design hybrid tabletops augmented with top-projection:

How to Resolve Occlusion? Top-Projection and In-Situ or on The Tabletop Display and Off-Place? The study showed that, in general, top-projection is a suitable means to extend the display and interaction spaces in hybrid settings and particularly to resolve physical/digital occlusion. However, its use has to be considered carefully to support the user without distracting him or hindering his work. As a result, it cannot be applied to every object to avoid conflicts with the user's task and needs. One should therefore decide on a per-object basis whether to use top-projection or not. This decision is influenced by two main factors: The user's current task and preferences on one side and the occluders properties on the other.

The first factor is driven by the user's needs during a task, e.g. top-projection on a document the user currently reads is clearly unwanted. However, reading and actively working with objects mainly happens in the working area of the table. One can use the knowledge about the users working area to automatically switch to top-projection when an object is within this area, only using top-projection within the storage areas, as P12's comment suggested.

The second factor is due to the fact that objects are not suitable for projection and/or interaction. This can either be because they very dark or strongly textured, making the projection unrecognizable, or because the objects use touch as input modality (e.g. keyboard or tablet), which would interfere with the user wanting to interact with the projection. Again, switching to a tabletop-based representation is a possible solution. The system can be enabled to recognize common unsuitable objects and do the switching automatically.

Besides these two factors which can be considered programmatically, it is sensible to provide the user a means of individually controlling top projection, so he can turn it on or o for specific objects at will. Also, some users said they would prefer to have a gesture to globally toggle top-projection. Then, they can use top-projection like an expose mode when the need an overview without being distracted otherwise.

Is Spatial Awareness Useful? Despite the higher movement count of physical objects and a large number of interactions, ProjecTop was significantly faster in the high clutter condition. Video analysis confirmed that users often lifted all objects in Baseline and ProjecTop conditions prior to finishing the task in order to check for missed objects. Probably, even if unconscious, the spatial awareness in ProjecTop facilitates this process as participants already knew the underlying layout, leading to the faster completion times and less errors. It is therefore important to provide such visual clues, even if users don't consciously use them and keep interacting with the physical objects to resolve occlusion.

How to Deal with Touch Across Tall Objects? A problem with expanding the interaction space onto the physical objects is the incontinuity of the touch surface, two participants brought up: The steep edges of physical objects make smooth touch interactions impossible, as the user has to lift his finger in a step like manner to always be on the touch surface. A possible solution to mitigate this problem can be a kind of hover-touch, which allows to continue the move while having the finger in the air. This enables a smoother transition between the surfaces, as the user can start lifting the finger before he reaches the object's edge.

9   Conclusion

Solving the problems hybrid tabletop settings pose to interaction and UI design is one key aspect to the success of tabletops in everyday environments. For instance in offices, interactive table would not only be used on its own when integrated with the office's furniture and therefore being used like a conventional desk. Physical objects which are placed on the table are - unlike objects in the context of tangible user interfaces, which are part of the interface itself – not part of the actual user interface, making them a foreign object to the interface.

We presented ProjecTop, an in-place physical/digital occlusion resolution system. It does not only circumvent occlusion by using the tabletop's display, but also uses the physical objects surface in order to do so. The formerly foreign object is made part of the interface by using it as an additional interactive display surface to resolve the occlusion situation in place, therefore not consuming additional display space on the high-resolution tabletop display. We further reported an evaluation of the ProjecTop concept, showing that the top-projection approach is not only beneficial for the resolution of occlusion related problems like awareness and accessing, but also to be a valuable addition to interactive surfaces if used advisedly. As the qualitative feedback showed, the spatial awareness is perceived as useful by the participants. Future studies should be conducted to further explore this aspect.

Acknowledgements. This work was partially supported by the ICT R&D program of MSIP/IITP. [13-921-03-001, Development of Smart Space to promote the Immersive Screen Media Service]

References

1. Cotting, D., Gross, M.: Interactive environment-aware display bubbles. In: Proceedings of the UIST, pp. 245–254. ACM, New York (2006)
2. Freeman, E., Brewster, S.: Messy tabletops: clearing up the occlusion problem. In: CHI EA, pp. 1515–1520. ACM, New York (2013)
3. Furumi, G., Sakamoto, D., Igarashi, T.: Snaprail: a tabletop user interface widget for addressing occlusion by physical objects. In: Proceedings of the ITS, pp. 193–196. ACM, New York (2012)

4. Hartmann, B., Morris, M.R., Benko, H., Wilson, A.D.: Pictionaire: supporting collaborative design work by integrating physical and digital artifacts. In: Proceedings of the CSCW, pp. 421–424. ACM, New York (2010)
5. Iwai, D., Sato, K.: Limpid desk: see-through access to disorderly desktop in projection-based mixed reality. In: Proceedings of the VRST, pp. 112–115. ACM, New York (2006)
6. Javed, W., Kim, K., Ghani, S., Elmqvist, N.: Evaluating physical/virtual occlusion management techniques for horizontal displays. In: Campos, P., Graham, N., Jorge, J., Nunes, N., Palanque, P., Winckler, M. (eds.) INTERACT 2011, Part III. LNCS, vol. 6948, pp. 391–408. Springer, Heidelberg (2011)
7. Khalilbeigi, M., Steimle, J., Mühlhäuser, M.: Interaction techniques for hybrid piles of documents on interactive tabletops. In: CHI EA, pp. 3943–3948. ACM, New York (2010)
8. Khalilbeigi, M., Steimle, J., Riemann, J., Dezfuli, N., Mühlhäuser, M., Hollan, J.D.: Objectop: occlusion awareness of physical objects on interactive tabletops. In: Proceedings of the ITS, pp. 255–264. ACM, New York (2013)
9. Klompmaker, F., Nebe, K., Fast, A.: dSensingNI: a framework for advanced tangible interaction using a depth camera. In: Proceedings of the TEI, pp. 217–224. ACM, New York (2012)
10. Koike, H., Sato, Y., Kobayashi, Y.: Integrating paper and digital information on enhanceddesk: a method for realtime finger tracking on an augmented desk system. ACM TOCHI 8(4), 307–322 (2001). ACM, New York
11. Liao, C., Tang, H., Liu, Q., Chiu, P., Chen, F.: Fact: fine-grained cross-media interaction with documents via a portable hybrid paper-laptop interface. In: Proceedings of the ACM MM, pp. 361–370. ACM, New York (2010)
12. Linder, N., Maes, P.: Luminar: portable robotic augmented reality interface design and prototype. In: Adjunct Proceedings of the UIST, pp. 395–396. ACM, New York (2010)
13. Mitsuhara, H., Yano, Y., Moriyama, T.: Paper-top interface for supporting notetaking and its preliminary experiment. In: IEEE SMC, pp. 3456–3462 (2010)
14. NASA Ames Research Center, Moffet Field: Nasa tlx (1988)
15. Ramos, G., Robertson, G., Czerwinski, M., Tan, D., Baudisch, P., Hinckley, K., Agrawala, M.: Tumble! splat! helping users access and manipulate occluded content in 2d drawings. In: Proceedings of the ACM AVI, pp. 428–435. ACM, New York (2006)
16. Rekimoto, J., Saitoh, M.: Augmented surfaces: A spatially continuous work space for hybrid computing environments. In: Proceedings of the CHI, pp. 378–385. ACM, New York (1999)
17. Spindler, M.: Spatially aware tangible display interaction in a tabletop environment. In: Proceedings of the ITS, pp. 277–282. ACM, New York (2012)
18. Spindler, M., Martsch, M., Dachselt, R.: Going beyond the surface: Studying multilayer interaction above the tabletop. In: Proceedings of the CHI, pp. 1277–1286. ACM, New York (2012)
19. Spindler, M., Stellmach, S., Dachselt, R.: Paperlens. In: Proceedings of the ITS, pp. 69–76. ACM, New York (2009)
20. Steimle, J., Khalilbeigi, M., Mühlhäuser, M., Hollan, J.D.: Physical and digital media usage patterns on interactive tabletop surfaces. In: Proceedings of the ITS, pp. 167–176. ACM, New York (2010)
21. Tabard, A., Gurn, S., Butz, A., Bardram, J.: A case study of object and occlusion management on the elabbench, a mixed physical/digital tabletop. In: Proceedings of the ITS, pp. 251–254. ACM, New York (2013)
22. Wellner, P.: Interacting with paper on the digitaldesk. Com. ACM 36, 87–96 (1993). ACM, New York

MovemenTable: The Design of Moving Interactive Tabletops

Kazuki Takashima[1(✉)], Yusuke Asari[1], Hitomi Yokoyama[2],
Ehud Sharlin[3], and Yoshifumi Kitamura[1]

[1] Research Institute of Electrical Commnication, Tohoku University, Katahira,
Aobaku, Sendai 9808577, Japan
{takashima,arthur,kitamura}@riec.tohoku.ac.jp
[2] Institute of Engineering, Tokyo Univeristy of Agriculture and Technology,
Koganei, Tokyo 1848577, Japan
hitomi-y@cc.tuat.ac.jp
[3] Department of Computer Science, University of Calgary,
2500 University Drive NW, Calgary, AB T2N 1N4, Canada
ehud@cpsc.ucalgary.ca

Abstract. MovemenTable (*MT*) is an exploration of moving interactive tabletops which can physically move, gather together or depart according to people's dynamically varying interaction tasks and collaborative needs. We present the design and implementation of a set of *MT* prototypes and discuss a technique that allows *MT* to augment its visual content in order to provide motion cues to users. We outline a set of interaction scenarios using single and multiple *MTs* in public, social and collaborative settings and discuss four user studies based on these scenarios, assessing how people perceive *MT* movements, how these movements affect their interaction, and how synchronized movements of multiple *MTs* impacts people's collaborative interactions. Our findings confirm that *MT's* augmentation of its visual content was helpful in providing motion cues to users, and that *MT's* movement had significant effects on people's spatial behaviors during interaction, effects that peaked in collaborative scenarios with multiple *MTs*.

Keywords: Human-robot interaction · Social interfaces · CSCW

1 Introduction

Interactive surfaces such as tabletops and large interactive displays provide a collaborative focal point, allowing people to gather around them and to engage in various tasks, individually or as a group. By dynamically changing their locations around interactive surfaces people can engage in tasks, change their role in a collaborative setting, protect their privacy, and disengage from a task by simply stepping away from the surface [8, 13]. These benefits of interactive surfaces are founded on the ways people use furniture and tables for thousands of years, augmenting the classic table with the additional advantages of computation and interactive visualization [13, 21]. More than a decade ago ConnecTables presented interactive displays that can be

© IFIP International Federation for Information Processing 2015
J. Abascal et al. (Eds.): INTERACT 2015, Part III, LNCS 9298, pp. 296–314, 2015.
DOI: 10.1007/978-3-319-22698-9_19

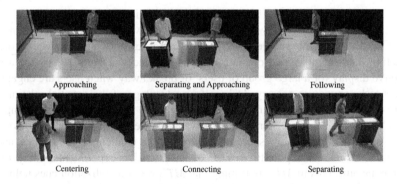

Fig. 1. *MovemenTables*

merged, manually, in order to affect the workspace and the interaction around it [20]. The premise is that changing the physicality of the interactive spaces we provide users will impact their interactive experience and affect the quality of their collaboration. We pursue this vision by proposing interactive surfaces that can automatically deform, move, connect and disconnect, changing their size, location and shape according to users' need. Recently, TransformTable explored interactive surfaces that can deform in order to address different tasks and collaborative needs [18]. In this paper we propose interactive surfaces that can automatically change their positions in order to address different tasks and collaborative settings, and present a design exploration of this vision.

Our exploration is based on a set of practical prototypes we call MovemenTables (Fig. 1). MovemenTables (*MT*) can move, rearrange, connect and disconnect in various forms according to task and needs. *MT*'s movements can follow users' requests, or be mediated by collaborative or social need, and autonomously initiated.

Realizing *MT* required us to tackle three main challenges.

(1) Technical implementation of *MovemenTable*. We implemented two *MT* prototypes, *MovemenTable* Senior and *MovemenTable* Junior, following a human-robot Interaction (HRI) design approach. In the technical sense *MT* can be viewed as a robotic interactive tabletop that autonomously moves, can be tracked and benefits from some level of situational awareness of its environment [4].

(2) Designing motion cues with tabletop content. In order to be more socially acceptable to the people interacting with it, *MTs* should provide simple cues regarding their movements, clearly expressing their intent to start moving, to turn, or to stop. Previous research shows that people can infer goal and intent from non-verbal motion cues [3, 6, 7]. This tendency to relate social intent to even abstract motion cues was later explored in HCI and HRI (e.g., [11, 19]). *MTs* are employing a similar approach, communicating their physical locomotion intentions using motion stylization of the interactive visual content the display. In essence, *MT* is using its tabletop visual content as if it is an animated cartoon character, styling, squashing, stretching and augmenting the visual content in order to communicate its locomotion intent.

(3) *MT*'s user experience. Ultimately, *MT*'s goal is to impact users' interactive social experiences. Provided with sufficient social awareness, *MT*s can attempt to support, and even guide people's social interactions by moving, connecting or disconnecting. For example, two or more *MT*s may connect in order to provide a wide interactive display for a large group of users, or break away when users are engaged in different tasks or require privacy. *MT* can take advantage of their spatial relationships and proxemics [5, 8] to people in order to socially guide the interaction, for example by approaching a reluctant user, or provide privacy to one group of people by avoiding others. While our work stop short of tackling these challenges in practice and in naturalistic setting, we report the results of an extensive experimental study of the fundamental attributes of *MT*, confirming that *MT*'s motion stylization cues help users infer its movement intention (study 1), that *MT*'s basic spatial movements are recognizable and socially acceptable by users (study 2), and that the basic movements of a single or of multiple *MT*s impact users' spatial behaviors and perspective around the *MT*s in interactive and collaborative settings (study 3 and 4).

This paper reports how we pursued the aforementioned three *MT* research threads, the insight gained on the concept of automatically moving tabletop interfaces, and the remaining challenges.

2 Related Work

2.1 Social Interactions and Tabletops

The physicality of tabletop interfaces was shown to affect the social interaction between users, for example by influencing people's personal spaces and their spatial arrangements around the surface (e.g., territoriality [16], group coupling [21]). The design of better collaborative tabletop workspaces was shown to be affected by the table and group size [13]. While these effects were observed and reflected upon, static tabletop interfaces are not capable of dynamically changing their physicality and cannot physically affect the spatial behaviors of people interacting with them.

In collaborations, workspace dynamic connections have been well researched with personal tabletop [20] and personal tablets [9]. ConnecTable [20] is a manually movable personal tabletop display, motivated by the simple social observation that people move closer to each other when engaged in discussions. Two ConnecTable displays can be seamlessly coupled in order to create a larger display workspace, or can be detached to provide two separate interaction spaces. TransformTable is a self-actuated shape-changing tabletop display enabling basic deformations of its interactive surface according to task and interaction settings, but with no locomotion capabilities [18]. *MT* is extending these past efforts by integrating locomotion capabilities in interactive tabletops, and examining how their intentional movement affects people's spatial behaviors and experience during collaborative interaction. *MT*'s dynamic spatial relationships with users closely relates to research on spatial relationships between displays, interfaces and people, for example proxemics interactions [8] and F-Formation [9]. The concept of space-aware interactive tabletops which detect and sense their users was explored in static tabletop interfaces (e.g., [1]).

2.2   Human-Robot Interaction and Robotic Tables

MT is practically a robotic tabletop interface. Interaction between people and robots was shown to follow behavioral and social spatial interpersonal principles, such as proxemics [14] and the design of *MT* and its movements is informed by these themes. *MT* augmentation of its physical movements using classic cartoon art and motion stylization techniques [7, 10], allows it to express its locomotion intentions. Animation and cartoon art techniques were previously introduced to HRI (e.g., [19, 22]), though *MT*'s adaptation of these principles to interactive tabletops is, as far as we know, new in its transformation of the tabletop visual content into an implicit animated character providing motion cues to the user.

Past research in robotic interfaces proposed the concept of robotic tables. For example, [15] implemented multiple table robots that could autonomously change their positions and arrangement according to different tasks. The project was focusing on actuating the classic table furniture, and did not address interactive tabletops, motion cues, or the collaborative tasks that tabletop interfaces afford.

3   MovemenTable

We designed two types of *MovemenTable* prototypes: *MovemenTable* Senior (*MTSr.*) and *MovemenTable Junior (MTJr)*. *MTSr* is more robust, providing a larger interactive space for small group collaboration and implemented using an internal rear-projector, while the smaller *MTJr* is designed for personal use, and is implemented using a commercial touch display and a Roomba for its locomotion.

The *MT* prototypes are being controlled by an off-board server that communicates with the *MT*s and handles their movements. The server synchronizes the *MT*s coordinated actions, for example connection or separation of two *MT*s. The server also helps easy administration of the *MT* Wizard of Oz (WoZ [12]) algorithms we employed when evaluating the tabletops.

3.1   MovemenTable Senior

MTSr is a wheeled robotic interactive tabletop display (Fig. 2a), 96 × 96x100 cm (WxDxH) in size. The physical dimensions of *MTSr* were chosen to allow four adults to comfortably interact with the tabletop. The interactive surface is a typical FTIR tabletop with rear projection, using a 40', 850 × 850 mm screen, with maximum

(a) *MovemenTable Senior*   (b) *MovemenTable Junior* and its tabletop view

Fig. 2. *MovemenTable* **prototypes**

projection area of about 800 × 600 mm, and 4:3 aspect ratio. The projector is fed by an external PC using a wireless HDMI connection. *MTSr* requires an external power supply to drive the projector and is carrying a power extension cord as it moves about. *MTSr*'s locomotion is controlled by an onboard PIC microcontroller, which communicates with an external PC through Bluetooth and manages the motor driver. *MTSr* translates and rotates using a traditional differential two wheeled robot at the bottom of the table enclosure. *MTSr* controls its translation, with speeds of around 0.3 m/sec, and rotation, with speeds of around $\pi/4$ rad/sec. The location and the orientation of *MTSr* and its users are being tracked using a motion capture system.

3.2 MovemenTable Junior

MTJr is a smaller robotic table that is designed for personal use. It carries a commercial touch display (27 inch full HD, 1980 × 1080 pixels display, IIyama ProLiteT27), controlled by a laptop and buttery within the *MTJr* enclosure. *MTJr* is completely wireless and carries its own standalone battery power supply. For locomotion, *MTJr* uses a Roomba with Bluetooth receiver (RombaSCI), mounted below the *MTJr* wheeled alumni frame box enclosure (67 × 42x90 cm WxDxH, in dimension, see Fig. 2b) enabling movement capabilities which are identical to *MTSr*. *MTJr*'s maximum speeds are 0.5 m/sec in translation and $\pi/3$ rad/sec in rotation. In our fourth study (described in Sect. 6.2, below) we explored fundamental *MT*'s connecting and separating movements using two *MTJrs*.

3.3 Visual Motion Cues

To provide users with motion cues about the *MT*s movements and spatial intentions we implemented an augmentation of the *MT*'s physical movements with visual motion cues (Fig. 3). While other motion cue modalities can be implemented, the current prototype of *MT* was designed so it will be as true as possible to its tabletop metaphor, rather than becoming, for example, a speaking or arms waving robot. *MT* is using its current visual tabletop content to create a set of implicit animated characters that convey its locomotion intentions via non-verbal motion cues. In principle *MT*'s motion cues can incorporate a rich variety of motion stylization and animated cartoon art techniques, for example, *MT* could use different motion cues to express different emotive motions such as hesitation, determination, shyness, or submission [23]. Our current *MT* prototype provides motion cues only for basic straight movement, using

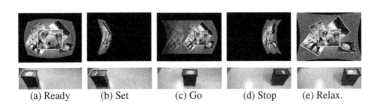

| (a) Ready | (b) Set | (c) Go | (d) Stop | (e) Relax. |

Fig. 3. Motion cures by animated tabletop content

five movement phases: *ready, set, go, stop* and *relax*. When the *MT* is about to move it generates motion cues for the five movement phases by capturing its current visual tabletop content and using it as an implicit animated character. The visual content will then be used to generate the different animated motion stylizations, which are informed by animation techniques such speedlines [10] and squash-and-stretch [7]. Below we briefly discuss the implementation of the five movement phases based on the cartoon squash-and-stretch [7] steps (Fig. 4).

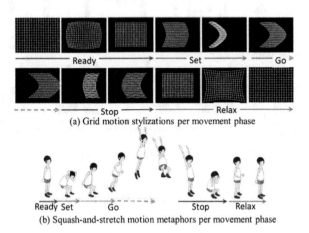

(a) Grid motion stylizations per movement phase

(b) Squash-and-stretch motion metaphors per movement phase

Fig. 4. Squash-and-stretch motion stylization

Ready. *MT* disables the touch input on its interactive surface and freezes the screen content. The screen content is captured as an image and mapped onto a 20 × 15 points grid (Fig. 3a). Following that, the image, using the point grid, dynamically deforms, contracting onto itself and shrinking slightly over two seconds in a sequence that suggests concentration and preparation for oncoming events. A side effect of the *ready* shrinking is that it frees screen space which subsequent movement phases use for their motion stylizations (e.g. drawing speed-lines).

Set. This motion cue was designed to generate anticipation to movement towards a specific direction. The squash cue [7] and the level of exaggeration, provide indication of the intended movement direction, as well as a sense of the expected distance (Fig. 3b). The duration of the compression animation is 500 ms, and the compressed form is kept for another 200 ms before moving to the next motion cue.

Go. This phase initiates and augments *MT*'s actual physical movement towards its intended direction, as shown at the *Set* phase. As *MT* starts to move the tabletop image is quickly stretched and deformed into an arrow-like shape, pointing towards the physical movement direction (Fig. 3c). *Go* also includes dynamically moving speed-lines and shadows [10] which are overlaid behind the arrowed image to further augment *MT*'s physical movement, stopping only when *MT* reached its destination.

Stop. As soon as *MT* reached its destination it physically stops, with its visual cues showing a squashed animation of the visual content, communicating exaggerated deceleration in the direction of the previous movement trajectory, and then recovery, the entire *Stop* animation sequence is about 400 ms in length (Fig. 3d).

Relax. Following the exaggerated *Stop* deceleration, *MT* presents a slow recovery cue, with the screen leisurely stretched back to its full screen version, in a 2 s animation. During *Relax* the touch input on the screen is re-enabled. The *Relax* cue is designed to clearly show that *MT*'s

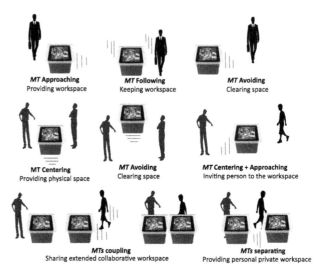

Fig. 5. Interaction scenarios of *MovemenTables*

physical movements are all done, prompting users to reengage with the tabletop interactive content (Fig. 3e).

4   Interaction Scenarios with MovemenTables

In this section we assume that *MTs* is provided with sufficient social and situational awareness of the users surrounding it, e.g., their position, orientation, group size, and some low-level of insight on their overall interactive goal and social engagement. While these assumptions are currently not realized in our *MT* prototypes, we believe they can become feasible, and they are useful in allowing us to consider the design of *MT*'s interactive scenarios. Figure 5 shows some examples of *MT*'s fundamental potential applications. As shown in Fig. 5 upper row, *MT*'s approaching movement can invite a specific person (e.g., a shy or reluctant user) and provide her with access to a digital workspace at her position. *MT* also can keep the workspace close to a moving person by following their movements or moving out of her way when the interaction is over by avoiding movements.

Figure 5's middle row shows basic usage examples of a single *MT* working with a group of people. Similarly to the single user case, *MT*'s approaching and avoiding movements affects the group's physical workspace, and may change their task-flow and group dynamics. For example, *MT*'s centering movement between two people can physically emphasizes their work or conversational space, providing a shared physical and interactive surface, or *MT* clearing the shared space can indicate the ending of a task. Following, *MT*'s movements, if supported by sufficient situational awareness of the group (e.g., [4, 8, 9]) can assist and augment face-to-face collaboration.

Figure 5's lower row presents a simple example of how a synchronized group of *MTs* can support users' collaboration. For example, two or more *MTs* may connect in order to provide a wide and shareable interactive display for a large group of users, or break away to provide individual workspaces when users are engaged in different tasks or require privacy. We envision that these *MTs'* movements can be actuated by user's explicit commands, by implicit inputs like proxemics and F-Formations, or autonomously based on the task phases.

In summary, *MT's* autonomous movements, given sufficient situational awareness, can physically create and change its users' workspaces adapting them according to the task-flow, and potentially helping users improve task efficiency, and allowing them to feel more comfortable during different phases of a dynamic task. The following sections describe our exploratory evaluations of the fundamental attributes of *MT*, how *MT's* movements are recognized by users based on the motion cues, and how users spatial behaviors and space awareness are impacted by *MTs* basic movements.

5 Understanding of *MT's* Motion Cues

We conducted two observation studies to investigate whether tabletop users can infer, understand and socially relate to *MT*'s basic movements based on its motion cues. The first study focused on *MT*'s straight movement and examined whether observers could anticipate *MT*'s locomotion intention based on the motion cues it displays. The second study investigated whether observers can infer the social essence of *MT* movements. We used single *MTSr* for both of observation studies, allowing participants to perceive *MT's* movements along with their associated motion cues.

5.1 Study1: Linear Movement

Goal. Our first study was set to examine if *MT*'s motion cues are comprehensible, and whether they can help people anticipate *MT's* locomotion intent prior to its actual movement.

Method. This study was conducted in a 5 m x 5 m experimental room. We recruited fourteen participants from the local university (six male, eight female, average age: 21.9) who were not informed of *MT*'s locomotion capabilities. We used two *MT*'s conditions in a within-subject design study: animated motion stylization (AMS); and *MT* without the motion stylization for baseline, presenting a static image while its moving (SI). The order of the conditions was counterbalanced. For each condition, *MT* displayed the visual content shown in Fig. 3, and moved back and forth twelve times along a 3 m straight line. Each participant observed the movements from approximately one meter away from the line-of-movement. Afterwards each answered a questionnaire about *MT*'s movements using a 5 Likert scale (1: disagree, 5: agree), and was interviewed.

Result and Discussion. We confirmed the overall tendency of the obtained Likert-scale data fits normal distribution and analyzed the data with one-way ANOVA. Unsurprisingly, *MT*'s motion cues made sense to participants, and they reported understanding the coupling of the animated visual content with the table's physical movement and movement intentions in the AMS condition compared to reporting inability to infer *MT* movements in the SI condition. More interestingly, participants reported higher awareness of the screen visual content in the AMS condition (4.57 when answering "I paid attention to the screen") than in SI condition (3.43) ($p < .05$). They reported surprise when *MT* moved for the first time in both conditions, with average rating of 2.71 and 3.42 for AMS and SI respectively ($p > .05$), meaning that AMS did little to diminish the surprise effect of an interactive tabletop move for the first time. Overall the results show that *MT*'s animated motion stylization significantly prompted users to look at the screen content, and helped them infer the table's movement and its direction prior to the actual movement.

When asked to reflect on the AMS motion cues, most participants remembered the first three phases (Fig. 3a, b and c), and could map them to the metaphor of crouching to *set* before starting to move. Particularly, participants liked the arrow-shaped *Go* stylization (Fig. 3c), which received a relatively high score of 3.58 when answering "I felt that the animated screen content supported the table physical movement". While the *Stop* phase (Fig. 3d)) was successful in reflecting *MT*'s reaching its end of movement (4.07 for AMS), the *relax* phase (Fig. 3e) was less effective in expressing that *MT* relaxes, with AMS of 1.86 for "I felt the table becomes relaxed when it stopped." while SI was 1.36 ($p > .10$).

During the interview many participants reiterated that the integration of physical and visual elements on *MT* was providing efficient cues for the table's movement intentions. The interview provided many positive comments on *MT* and on its use of AMS: e.g., "funny", "interesting", or "useful device that extends classic furniture".

5.2   Study 2: "Social" Movements

Goal. Our second observation study examined how observers recognize and understand *MT*'s basic social behaviors when it was moving by itself, or when it was moving in relation to actors. This study was conducted with identical experimental setting and with *MT* providing AMS motion cues in all the conditions.

Method. Ten participants (four males and six females, average age: 22.5) in a within-subject design following six *MT* movement conditions. Participants were not informed of *MT*'s locomotion capabilities. In every movement condition, participants were asked to observe *MT*'s movement for 30 s from 1 meter away from the movement range. Participants were then asked to reflect on their experience via a GodSpeed questionnaire [2], reflecting on five HRI perceived aspects of a robot: anthropomorphism, animacy, likability, perceived intelligence, and perceived safety. We used GodSpeed, a standard qualitative HRI evaluation tool, in order to evaluate user's perceptions and social acceptance of *MT*'s social movements, and to reflect on how these can scale to the perception of *MT* as a social agent. Each dimension was evaluated using 5 points scale. Some of *MT*'s movements were done in relations to actors; the six conditions were presented in a customized counterbalanced order among participants. Below we outline the different *MT*'s movements examined in the study:

Stand – MT was located at the center of the room, not displaying any visual content on its surface and not moving.

Move – MT displayed a static image on its surface and moved randomly within the room.

MT Move – MT randomly moved within the room while displaying motion cues.

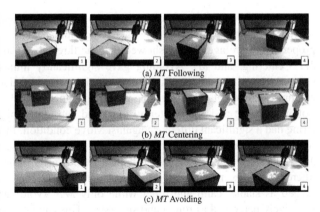

(a) *MT* Following

(b) *MT* Centering

(c) *MT* Avoiding

Fig. 6. *MT* social movements in study 2

MT Following –MT automatically followed an actor who was walking freely in the room (MoCap tracked). It was demonstrated several times for duration of around 30 s. (Figure 6a).

MT Centering –MT located itself, with motion cues, at the central position between the two actors, simulating a basic social behavior of *MT* suggesting its physical workspace to collaborating users. It was demonstrated several times for duration of around 30 s. (Figure 6b).

MT Avoiding – MT continuously kept away from the moving actor as long as possible within the room (Fig. 6c).

In all six conditions *MT*'s initial location was at the center of the room and its *MT's* movements were initiated by the actor's movements.

Result and Discussion. In addition to the Godspeed HRI questionnaire, we also asked participants to reflect on their understanding of *MT*'s movements by selecting descriptors from six candidates. Overall, as we expected, participants correctly understood the meaning and intentions of *MT's* social movements. For example, *MT* Following condition was accurately judged as "Table is following a person" and *MT* Centering condition was correctly recognized as either "Table is following" or "Table is approaching to be used". On the other hand, *MT* Avoiding condition was not always (5/10 participants) recognized correctly by participants. The reason could be that participants were less inclined to infer an unhelpful movement of a tabletop interface escaping its user, or from lack of agility in the *MTSr* movements when trying to avoid the approaching actor.

We confirmed normal distribution of the obtained 5 scale data and used one-way ANOVA and Bonfferoni test to compare the average scores of the six conditions for each GodSpeed dimension. For anthropomorphism, the overall scores for all conditions were less than the neutral (e.g., 2.1 for Stand, 1.7 for Move, 2.5 for Animation and *MT* Move, 2.7 for *MT* Avoiding) while only the *MT* Following condition provides a high score of 3.4 (with significant difference than Stand and Move). This result reflected on overall weak perception of *MT* as having human-like attributes. Animacy is the property of alive agent. This showed that the three social movements, *MT* Following, *MT* Centering, and *MT* Avoiding gave significantly higher scores of 3.7, 3.6, 3.5 respectively, than others. Similar perceptions were found in the interviews, for example, "like creature" "The table was suggesting its workspace". For likeability, *MT* Following (3.7) and *MT* Centering (4.0) had substantial high scores. Here, *MT* Centering had a significant difference against Move condition. In Perceived intelligence, we obtained similar tendency to the Likeability in which the scores of *MT* Following and *MT* Centering were larger (sig. diff than Stand). The dimension of Perceived safety offered complex results, our brief summary shows that the static conditions were judged as stable, calm and quiet while only *MT* Avoiding, a social movement was negatively perceived as rough and supersize. This can be also explained by the clumsy movements of *MTs* in this condition, which can also be fixed with minor technical improvements.

In summary, the basic social movements of *MT* were recognizable by participants. Also, from Godspeed, the *MT* Following and *MT* Centering were perceived as socially acceptable with the impressions of intelligent agent, likable and safe. This is an interesting finding that shows *MT* can be adopted to various social settings.

6   Impact of *MT* on Interaction and Collaboration

The two observation studies established an understanding of two important aspects of how people perceive *MT's* movements. We were also interested in exploring how users behave and change their interaction flow in order to adapt to the dynamically changing workspace afforded by *MTs*. Therefore, we conducted two interactive studies (study 3 and 4) that asked participants to perform a collaborative task with a partner using *MT*, allowing us to probe some of the social and collaborative aspects of interaction with a moving interactive tabletop. *MTJrs* were used for studies 3 and 4 because they incorporated a more sensitive multi-touch display, and their compact enclosures was more convenient, stable and safe when investigating MT's movements during user interaction.

Our two interactive studies were designed as an early reflection on the interaction scenarios described in Sect. 4, taking a simplified approach to reflect on some of the fundamental aspects of group interaction with automatically moving tabletop interfaces. While the participants were asked to perform valid tasks on the tabletop, *MT's* movements were basic, and initiated by a simple WoZ [12] algorithm.

6.1   Study3: Single *MT* Single User

Goal. This study examined how the movement of a single *MT* can impact interaction. *MT* performed a set of basic movements, but this time with a participant being part of the interaction scene, not merely observing from the sidelines.

Method. Twelve participants (8 males and 4 females, average age: 21.8) from local universities participated in this study, which took place in the same experimental room as studies 1 and 2. Participants were provided with a simple *MT*-based tool and a generic picture browsing task: *MT* displayed an interactive picture browser that allowed participants to browse pictures presented on the tabletop surface. The browser (Fig. 2b) consisted of two views: pictures thumbnails were shown at the left half of the screen, while the right half presented a preview window showing a larger version any of one of the thumbnail pictures. The interface was populated with twenty contemporary pictures relating to popular topics such as sports, politics, and hobbies. The participants could select any of the thumbnails which will in-turn populate the preview window.

Participants were not provided with any specific instructions on how to use the tool, or *MT* and were Mo-Cap tracked as they moved through the experiment room. Each task was short, around 40 s long, allowing the participant to engage with the tabletop task and with a different movement by *MT*. This study was conducted with a within-subject design that examined impact of the following *MT's* movement conditions; static, approaching and avoiding (Fig. 7). The order of the conditions was counterbalanced among participants. All the *MT* movements in this study included motion cues on its display. The three conditions below were run by the study administrator using a simple WoZ algorithm. The three conditions below were run by the study administrator using a simple WoZ algorithm. The conditions and method of this study were based on the basic movements of *MT* shown in Fig. 5's upper row where *MT* is approaching a person in order to engage her in interaction or *MT* is avoiding the participant, disengaging from interaction.

Static – A reference condition; *MT* was located around the center of the room, and remained static, running the picture browser tool on its surface (Fig. 7a).

Approaching – *MT* was initially located around 2 meters off the room center. Ten seconds after the task started *MT* initiated approaching movement, towards the center of the room and the participant (Fig. 7b). *Avoiding* –*MT* was initially located at the center of the room. Ten seconds after the task started, *MT* initiated a movement away from the center of the room, and the user (Fig. 7c).

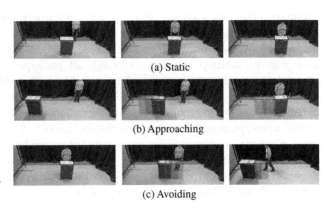

(a) Static

(b) Approaching

(c) Avoiding

Fig. 7. Single *MT* interactive study

Results and Discussion. The qualitative analyses were performed based on questionnaire asking participants to rate their experience using a 5 scale Likert. We also conducted a post-interview and a grounded theory [17] video coding behavioral analysis.

Participants in general accepted the automatic movements of *MT* and had positive reactions to the motion cues on the *MT* tabletop. Participants reflected on the importance of timing when triggering *MT's* movements during interaction.

We coded the participants' spatial actions and behaviors, reflecting on the three movement conditions and analyzed our coded events by a comparative analysis relating to our control factors. We compared the coded events numbers in relation to the movement condition in which they occurred and the timing of the event relatively to the movement (i.e., before, during and after table movement). Below we briefly highlight our main findings regarding participants' spatial behaviors:

- All participants approached *MT*. About 30 % of the participants followed *MT's* in its avoiding movement.
- Following *MT's* movement, participants frequently moved and looked around.
- All participants touched *MT's* surface and interacted with the tabletop picture browser significantly more after *MT*'s movement compared to before its movement (in touch/min).
- Some participants were visibly surprised with *MT's* first movement, but this effect disappeared in the following movements.

Generally, and surprisingly to us, our statistical analysis of questionnaire results were overall flat: participants remained relatively neutral, or just below neutral, regarding their *MT* experience, and there were no meaningful differences in ratings between the conditions. From interviews, a possible explanation for these findings emerged: participants who were left alone with the moving *MT* were not sure about the purpose of the task, which lacked by design social context. Several potential applications were suggested in the interview, for examples a "seller robot", "domestic robot for elder persons", or that *MT* will be "useful in hospital, classroom, and office meeting" etc.

Summary. The video coding showed that participants interacted with the visual content on *MT's* surface, and that their interactions with *MT* were significantly altered after *MT's* movement occurred, causing people to follow *MT* spatially, and interacting more with its tabletop interface. Although all participants accepted that *MT* had potential, the questionnaire results did not indicate clear differences between *MT's* movement conditions. Our assumption is that when evaluated by a single user in the current study setting and thus taken out of the collaborative context, *MT* becomes 'just' a robot, a perception which diverts from the social role it was design to serve, helping a group of people as a dynamically moving and changing interactive surface. While we do not argue that the results of single *MT* with a single user are not valid, they do highlight *MT* limitations, and point to its true potential serving a group of collaborative users, which we explore in the following study.

6.2   Study 4: Multiple *MT*s Multiple Users

Goal. Our 4th study was probing a more holistic *MovemenTable* vision: what will be the impact of a group of *MT*s who are dynamically changing users' interactive collaborative workspace? For simplicity, we studied synchronized physical connections and separations of two *MTs* and investigated how these movements affect two users' spatial behaviors, workspace awareness and interactions during collaborative tasks over the *MTs*. The purpose of this study is also to understand basic effects of *MTs* by using a simplified WoZ study design with timed-movement of *MTs* during users' collaborative task, which will offer fundamental key findings of how people react to changing workspace by *MTs*.

Method. Participants were the same group of 12 university students recruited for study 3, paired into six teams, and located in the same *MT* experimental settings (Fig. 8). The teams members knew each other. Based on their experience in study 3 team members were aware of *MT*'s locomotion abilities, and knew how to use the interactive picture browser on its surface. This method allows us to see more realistic social experiences by multiple *MTs* movement in the study 4, rather than seeing fundamental or first-time reaction of the *MTs*' automatic movements, which was already observed in Study 3. We conducted a within-subject study with the following four conditions using a customized counter balance order among teams.

Connected –Two *MTs* were arranged side-by-side around the center of the room (Fig. 8a). Each display surface ran a standalone picture browser. *MT* remained static throughout the condition.

Separated –Two *MTs* were placed 1.8 meters apart from each other (Fig. 8b). The distance was sufficient for participants to maintain privacy as they interact with *MT*. *MT* remained static throughout the condition.

Connecting –Two *MTs* were placed 1.8 meters apart (Fig. 8c) and started to move towards each other 30 s into the interactive task.

Separating –Two *MTs* were connected to each other at the center of the room (Fig. 8d) and departed to different directions of the room 30 s into the interactive task, stopping when they were 1.8 meters apart from each other.

The connecting and separating conditions allowed us to test how *MT* intentional dynamic changes to the workspace, moving from a unified large interactive space to two distributed smaller ones affect the collaborating users, reflecting on basic collaboration themes such as individual vs. collaborative, or private vs. shared data access. For each condition, participants were instructed to

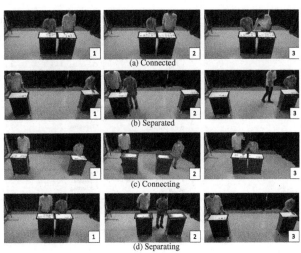

Fig. 8. Multiple *MTs* for multiple users study

collaboratively create a story on the *MT* based on pictures they selected individually. The pictures followed a different theme for each of the four conditions (e.g., pictures relating to sports, hobby etc.), which were presented in a balanced order to the different teams. The task was completed once participants reported that their collaboratively created story is ready. This simple task was designed because we were interested in how users interaction, behaviors are affected *MT*'s movement during typical collaboration that requires both touch interaction and some discussions with partner. The two dynamic conditions of connecting and separating included motion cues in all *MTs* movements.

Results and Discussion. We probed the impact of the four movement conditions on participant's behaviors and interactions using a questionnaire, video coding, and post-interviews. Regarding analysis of questionnaire, we used ANOVA and Bonfferoni test for normal distribution data while we used Freedman test in the case that data does not have normality. Table 1 details how the different conditions were rated on the questionnaire, showing only questions (designated by Q below) that reflected significant difference between the movement conditions. The results demonstrate that most participants thought of following the *MTs* movements (Q1), and were affected by the changes of their collaborative workspace due to *MT* movements. For example, *MTs* connecting guided the two participants to spatially get closer to each other, spatial behavior that could trigger discussion of the task within the team (Q2). On the other hand, the *MTs* moving away from each other would cause participants to finish their chat (Q3). Participants were collaborating closely on their team tasks in the connection and connecting conditions (Q4) while separation from their partner caused them to pursue a separate task, for example picture browsing on the tabletop instead of the requested story composition (Q5, weak effect). Q6 showed an interruption effect by *MTs*. The separating and connecting conditions disturbed team collaboration; however, this negative effect was arguably not high, with ratings close to neutral.

Table 1. Study 4 questionnaire results

	Question	Condition	Score	Sig.
1	I wanted to follow the table	Connected	1.4	
		Separated	1.9	
		Connecting	4.1	
		Separating	4.2	
2	I thought to start talking with partner	Connected	2.7	
		Separated	2.9	
		Connecting	4.1	
		Separating	3.5	
3	I thought to finish talking with partner	Connected	1.5	
		Separated	1.2	
		Connecting	1.3	
		Separating	2.4	
4	I thought to do the task together	Connected	4.5	
		Separated	3.4	
		Connecting	4.1	
		Separating	3.3	
5	I thought to do the task separately	Connected	2.3	
		Separated	2.8	
		Connecting	2.2	
		Separating	3.3	
6	The table movement disrupted our task	Connected	1.3	
		Separated	1.3	
		Connecting	2.4	
		Separating	3.6	

In the video coding, we compared the number of participants' spatial actions to the movement condition in which they occurred, and to the timing of the event relatively to the movement (i.e., before, during and after *MT* movement). Our main findings are:

- All participants approached *MTs* and touched their surfaces during collaboration.
- About 70 % participants followed the *MTs'* movements and changed their positions accordingly. This is encouraging since we did not provide any instruction on the *MTs* movements or on how to react to them. The participants that did not follow "their" *MT* when it separated remained with their teammate's *MT*, sharing it after it stopped its movement.
- While there was no accidental collision between participants and *MTs*. 16 % of the participants had at some point to visibly back out of the *MTs* trajectory.
- Participants pointed their finger at the partner's table. This effect was more evident in connected and connecting, and grew more especially after the connecting movement in frequency of interactions, touch/sec.
- Frequencies of gestures such as nodding, hand waving, pointing and looking at the partner significantly increased after the *MTs* separated.

Summary. The collaborative workspace was significantly influenced by the *MTs'* physical connecting and separating movements, strongly impacting the collaborative and spatial behavior of participants. Our findings suggest that *MTs'* connecting can lead a more focused collaboration in a shared space, allowing teams to work closely together on a task, possibly so than in the connect condition with its preexisting larger surface. *MTs* separating on the other hand led to a more individual work style, with teams keeping apart and focusing less on their collaborative task. While this influence was generally perceived positively it is important to note that our study was not done on a naturalistic settings, and it remains to be seen how *MT's* movements will affect users in actual workspaces.

A technical limitation emerged from *MT's* physical bezels limited the ability of two *MTs* to connect into a single unified and unobscured surface. A study design limitation was recruitment of our participants who are aquatinted. On one hand, this is a clear bias, on the other; it did allow us to observe more natural and dynamic collaboration in the study teams. Given the preliminary nature of our study, being the first examination of multiple moving interactive tabletops with multiple users, we preferred this approach, but it leaves the question of *MT's* potential social impact on users who do not know each other unanswered.

7   Discussion

All our prototypes, *MTSr* and *MTJr* functioned well in our four WoZ studies, moving around the environment, tracked and controlled with the aid of a MoCap system, providing continuously the interactive surface function, and the motion cues visualizations augmenting their movements. However, more work needs to be done to improve the technical aspects of *MT*: using a bezel-less tabletop, allowing seamless merger of several *MTs*, improving *MT's* motion agility to support more accurate movements during multiple *MTs* synchronization, and developing algorithms for autonomous and safety *MT* behaviors.

We are quite satisfied with *MT's* motion cues technique, using the tabletop visual content as an implicit animated character according to *MT's* movement. People found *MT's* non-verbal motion cues helpful and were successful in inferring *MT's* movement intention, direction and distance based on its squash-and-stretch and speedlines motion cues. Using of the tabletop content to create animated motion cues maintains continuity of content on the tabletop surface, and does not move too far from the metaphor of an interactive tabletop, which may not be the case if the tabletop will provide motion cues using voice or physical robotic arms waving. We are planning to explore the abundance of other expressive motion cues, inspired by the rich possibilities afforded by cartoon art and animation.

Our interactive studies demonstrated that multiple *MT's* movements had strong impact on user's spatial behaviors and interactions. This effect was most impressive in synchronized movements of multiple *MTs* in collaborative scenarios. These finding are encouraging and point to the potential contribution *MTs* can have on affecting and guiding social and collaborative interactive settings. While our current findings are limited to WoZ experimental settings, the potential shown through our studies offer several steps and directions of future work. It would be interesting to explore practical performances of *MTs* in a targeted context by comparing with manually moving tabletop (e.g., [20]). We also plan to explore *MTs* autonomous control by leveraging situational awareness tracking technologies, instead of the WoZ study. Based on study 4 findings we are able to pursue larger and more complex *MT* spatial arrangements for example moving beyond simple connections to L- and U- shape table arrangements, deploying *MTs* in large spaces and social functions, applying more advanced algorithms, such as flocking, for grouping/ungrouping of a large number of *MTs*, and providing *MTs* with tools for better situational group awareness of their environment and users.

Finally, we are hoping to assess *MTs'* effect more and more in the wild, following at the beginning a few simple scenarios. Grabbing attention of passersby and enticing to interact is a fundamental challenge in interactive public displays. While our work still stop shorts of introducing automatically moving interactive tabletops into realistic public settings we think that *MT* has the potential to provide a novel solution to this basic public display challenge.

8   Conclusion

We presented an exploration of *MovemenTables (MTs)*, moving interactive tabletops designed to affect their workspace and collaborative settings by changes to their spatial position and arrangement. We implemented two types of *MT* prototypes and designed animated tabletop content as motion cues that help *MT* users infer the tabletop locomotion intentions. We evaluated the prototypes via a set of user studies, based on several simple interaction scenarios. Our findings demonstrate that moving interactive tabletops can be accepted by users, and can influence their spatial behaviors. Our studies of a group of *MTs* also suggest that *MT's* fundamental movements, such as approaching a user, centering between two collaborating users, or connecting and separating have substantial impact on users' spatial behaviors and on their workspace awareness. The current findings motivate our future *MT* effort towards designing and testing more realistic collaborative scenarios. As part of our future work we will be designing proof-of-concept *MTs* that will guide users interactions and will probe the impact the dynamically changing interactive surfaces' location and size have on the collaborative task and the quality of the interaction.

Acknowledgments. This work was supported in part by JSPS KAKENHI Grant Number 26730101, by an NSERC Discovery Grant, and the Cooperative Research Project of the Research Institute of Electrical Communication, Tohoku University.

References

1. Annett, M., Grossman, T., Wigdor, D., Fitzmaurice, G.: Medusa: a proximity-aware multi-touch tabletop. In: UIST 2011, pp. 337–346 (2011)
2. Bartneck, C., Kulic, D., Croft, E., Zoghbi, S.: Measurement instruments for the anthropomorphism, animacy, likeability, perceived intelligence, and perceived safety of robots. Int. J. Soc. Robot. **1**(1), 71–81 (2009)
3. Blythe, P., Todd, P. Filler, G.: How motion reveals intentions: categorizing social interactions, In: Simple Heuristics that Make us Smart, pp. 257–285. Oxford Univsity Press, The ABC Research Groupxv (1999)
4. Drury, J.L., Scholtz, J. Yanco, H.A.: Awareness in human-robot interactions. In: SMC 2003, pp. 912–918 (2003)
5. Hall, E.: The Hidden Dimension. Doubleday, Newyork (1966)
6. Heider, F., Simmel, M.: An experimental study of apparent behavior. Am. J. Psychol. **57**, 243–259 (1944)
7. Kwon, J., Lee, I.: The squash-and-stretch stylization for character motions. TVCG **18**(3), 488–499 (2012)
8. Marquardt, N., Greenberg, S.: Proxemic interactions: from theory to practice. Synthesis Lectures on Human-Centered Informatics. Morgan & Claypool Publishers, San Francisco (2015)
9. Marquardt, N., Hinckley, K. Greenberg, S.: Cross-device interaction via micro-mobility and f-formations. In: UIST 2012, pp. 13–22 (2012)
10. Masuch, M., Schlechtweg, S., Schulz, R.: Speedlines–depicting motion in motionless pictures. In: SIGGRAPH 1999, Abst. 277 (1999)
11. Mutlu, B., Forlizzi, J., Nourbakhsh, I., Hodgins. J.: The use of abstraction and motion in the design of social interfaces. In: DIS 2006, pp. 251–260 (2006)
12. Riek, L.: Wizard of Oz Studies in HRI: a systematic review and new reporting guidelines. J. Human-Robot Interaction **1**(1), 119–136 (2012)
13. Ryall, K., Forlines, C., Shen, C., Morris, M.: Exploring the effects of group size and table size on interactions with tabletop shared-display groupware. In: CSCW 2004, pp. 284–293 (2004)
14. Satake, S., Kanda, T., Glas, D., Imai, M., Ishiguro, H., Hagita, N.: How to approach humans? –strategies for social robots to initiate interaction. In: HRI 2009, pp. 109–116 (2009)

15. Sawada, Y., Tsubouchi, T.: Autonomous re-alignment of multiple table robots. In: ICRA 2010, pp. 1098–1099 (2010)
16. Scott, S., Carpendale, S., Inkpen, K.: Territoriality in collaborative tabletop workspaces. In: CSCW 2004, pp. 294–303 (2004)
17. Strauss, A., Corbin, J.: J. Basics of qualitative research techniques and procedures for developing grounded theory. Sage Publications, Inc., Thousand Oaks (2015)
18. Takashima, K., Aida, N., Yokoyama, H., Kitamura, Y.: Transfomtable: a self-actuated shape-changing digital table. In: ITS 2013, pp.179–188 (2013)
19. Takayama, L., Dooley, D., Ju, W.: Expressing thought: improving robot readability with animation principles. In: HRI 2011, pp. 69–76 (2011)
20. Tandler, P., Prante, P., Müller-Tomfelde, C., Streitz, N., Steinmetz, R.: Connectables: dynamic coupling of displays for flexible creation of shared workspaces. In: UIST 2001, pp.11–20 (2001)
21. Tang, A., Tory, M., Po, B., Neumann, P., Carpendale, S.: Collaborative coupling over tabletop displays. In: CHI 2006, pp.1181–1190 (2006)
22. Young, J. Xin, M., Sharlin, E.: Robot expressionism through cartooning. In: HRI 2007, pp. 309–316 (2007)
23. Young, J., Sharlin, E., Igarashi, T.: Teaching robots style: designing and evaluating style-by-demonstration for interactive robotic locomotion. Hum. Comput. Interact. 28(5), 379–416 (2013)

If You Are Happy and You Know It, Say "I'm Here": Investigating Parents' Location-Sharing Preferences

Paolo Massa[✉], Chiara Leonardi, Bruno Lepri, Fabio Pianesi, and Massimo Zancanaro

Fondazione Bruno Kessler, Trento, Italy
{massa, cleonardi, lepri, pianesi, zancanaro}@fbk.eu

Abstract. A diary approach was used to explore location-sharing preferences of 126 parents with young children with the goal of investigating which elements play a role in their decision to share their location. During a 3-week user study, we daily collected parents' preferences of location sharing along with data related to the physical and social context, their interest in socializing with other parents and their emotional states. Our analysis points out several insights for this previously underexplored user group. In particular, our results suggest a relative greater importance of the context, both physical and social, with respect to individual traits such as personality, trust dispositions, and demographic characteristics. Moreover positive and negative emotions seem to influence the intention to share location information in a peculiar way: positive moods like happiness seem to encourage private sharing with selected people such as partner, relatives, friends and nearby parents, yet, when parents experience a negative mood, such as being worried, angry or sad, their intention to share publicly on the web is higher.

Keywords: Parents · Location sharing · Day reconstruction method

1 Introduction

In the last years, there has been a growing interest in investigating preferences regulating location-sharing behavior. The decision to share own location is a complex and dynamic phenomenon that depends on a number of factors such as the target of the disclosure and hence the interpersonal relationship between the discloser and the target of disclosure [6, 33]; the physical, the social and the emotional context [6, 16, 29, 31]; the motivation for sharing such information [3, 31] as well as personality and other individual traits of the discloser [15].

The user population usually investigated in literature is young adults and students that are likely to have peculiar values, privacy attitudes, lifestyles and needs [3, 17]. Hence, these studies mostly consider places related to student life (cafeteria, canteen, library, etc.). There is a pressing need to understand location privacy behaviors across a wider population [2]. In order to contribute on the discussion about this phenomenon, we focus on a different target group: parents with young children.

© IFIP International Federation for Information Processing 2015
J. Abascal et al. (Eds.): INTERACT 2015, Part III, LNCS 9298, pp. 315–332, 2015.
DOI: 10.1007/978-3-319-22698-9_20

Indeed, parents display several critical aspects that may differentiate their attitudes and possible usage of location sharing services from students. First, the social context is far more complex because of the presence of children and the extra-work time of parents is mostly spent with children. This means that parents' sociability is highly determined by children needs and this fact often turns leisure activities to a mix of leisure and family duties [8]. Second, the stress of juggling child rearing responsibilities with the demands of work impacts on the usage of time and makes time scheduling activities between parents a very complex activity [7]. Finally, parents' experience of public spaces is different from that of other target groups such as students mainly because of safety issues [35].

Parents and families are receiving growing attention in the HCI community and studies highlighted how social media are becoming essential for parents to keep in contact and ask/give advices and support to other parents [22]. In a recent study, Gibson and Hanson [11] discussed how new mothers use Facebook to avoid social isolation and improve their confidence. The transition to parenthood is actually a gratifying although stressful experience and social connectedness is expected to heavily impact on the quality of life of both parents and children [9, 21]. While parents' online sociability is receiving a growing attention [11], few studies explored how offline interaction may be encouraged through digital technologies. Recently, Leonardi et al. [16] showed a positive attitude of parents toward location sharing services that may facilitate ad hoc encounters between nearby parents and the exchange of information about places as trigger for further offline meetings.

In this paper, we report a comprehensive user study that involved 126 parents with young children aged 0 to 10. The age range was set to include infancy to middle childhood because in this phase parents' life is driven by children needs more than their own [36]. Parents' preferences of location sharing were collected through a Day Reconstruction Method (DRM) for 3 weeks. Participants were asked each evening to describe a place they have visited during the day, along with the social, emotional and physical context, their interest in socializing with other parents in that place and their willingness to disclose own location with different targets.

The main contributions of this paper are a number of insights on the intention to share the physical location through mobile devices for the previously underexplored user group of families with young children. In particular, the study highlights interesting opportunities for location-sharing applications showing situations in which parents may be interested in sharing own location:

1. The relative greater importance of the context (presence of other people, current mood, type of place) with respect to individual traits (e.g., personality, trust dispositions, and demographic characteristics);
2. The special roles played by the partner and the children as social contexts;
3. The different effects of positive and negative emotions on intention to share location with different targets: positive mood seems to encourage sharing location with specific people (partner, other family members, friends but also nearby parents) while negative mood seems to encourage it with everyone, i.e. publicly on the web.

Understanding parents' needs for socialization and their location sharing preferences is of paramount importance to eventually design appropriate services for this user group. Still, this paper focuses on the analysis of the conditions that influence the decision to share and it does not aim at discussing design issues.

2 Related Works

Several researchers have shown the potential but also the risks associated with applications that exploit location for improving social contacts in the offline world [see for example 32; 30]. A survey by Lindqvist [18] shows that 30 % of participants had met new people with the use of Foursquare and some of them have even used Foursquare for the purpose of dating or developing a romantic relationship. Toch [32] discussed how the so-called "nearby applications", which support ad hoc encounters with strangers, introduce social opportunities but also new challenges related to physical risks, emotional harm and social embarrassment. The target group of parents with young children are likely to share the general attitude toward the use of "nearby applications" but the specific characteristics might be quite different because of their specific social needs.

Disclosing own location is an action that combines high risks with a number of benefits and studies have shown how different factors came into play to explain people preferences toward disclosing or not these sensitive information. Xie et al. [34] investigated how different contextual factors affect users sharing preferences. They found that emotion is a useful predictor for sharing behavior followed by companion and time: people tend to share much more with family and friends when they are in a positive mood. The role of emotional context is also highlighted by Consolvo [6] that reported participants were most willing to disclose their location when they were depressed or happy and that they disclosed least often when angry. Wiese et al. [33] studied the willingness to share in 21 ubiquitous scenarios by using observed and non-observed data and found that closeness with the person target of the location sharing is the strongest predictor. The characteristics of physical location also play an important role; Toch et al. [32] found that users were more comfortable in sharing their location when they are at places visited by a large and diverse set of people. Again, the target group of families with young children may share the regulating role of emotions but the way it impacts on the decision may be influenced by their peculiar social pressures and social needs. A recent paper [23] included parental status as a control variable in their investigation on adoption of location-sharing social networks (LSSN) such as Foursquare. Authors found that the intention to use LSSN is explained mostly by a communication style personality trait they called "for your information" [23]. They also found that respondents who have children are more likely to be FYI communicators.

Other studies have identified cultural and gender differences concerning information disclosure behaviors. Lin [17] compared Chinese and American participants' attitudes and found that Chinese participants seem more conservative. They also reported cultural differences in disclosing location at "home" and at "work" and gender differences: Chinese female participants were more conservative than Chinese male while they did not find differences in sharing between US male and female but they found that US female participants show different attitudes with different recipients: a more open attitude toward close friends and friends on social network while they are more conservative with University community and advertisers.

Prior work has also investigated the role of an individual's stable psychological attributes - e.g. personality traits - to explain information disclosure behavior. Korzaan et al. [15] explored the role of the Big5 personality traits [12] and found that Agreeableness has a significant influence on individual concerns for information privacy. Junglas et al. [13] and Amichai-Hamburger and Vinitzky [1] also used the Big5 personality traits and found that Agreeableness, Conscientiousness, and Openness affect a person's concerns for privacy. More recently, Quercia et al. [26] found weak correlations among Openness to Experience and, to a lesser extent, Extraversion and the disclosure attitudes on Facebook. However, other studies targeting the influence of personality traits did not find significant correlations [28]. In 2010, Lo [19] suggested that Locus of Control could affect an individual's perception of risk when disclosing personal information: internals are more likely than externals to feel that they can control the risk of becoming privacy victims, hence they are more willing to disclose their personal information [19]. Although in this respect our target population might not differ from other groups, in our study, we analyzed the effect of personality traits because their effects are still much debated.

3   The Study

The study was conducted within the Mobile Territorial Lab[1], a joint initiative created by Telecom Italia, Telefonica, MIT Media Lab and Fondazione Bruno Kessler. One of the goals of the Mobile Territorial Lab is to design and test new services in real-life scenarios. In this sense, participants are involved in co-creating and exploring breakthrough scenarios, innovative concepts and novel systems. The living lab is a permanent community of 150 families with young children located in the Trentino area, North East Italy. It has been running since November 2012. Participants were recruited using a snowball sampling approach where existing study subjects invite future subjects from their acquaintances. Participants receive some benefits (usage of a smartphone and some monthly credit for voice, sms and internet) in exchange for releasing their data usage and other information for studies focused on human-behavior analysis and human-computer interaction. The participants did not receive any further compensation for the present study.

3.1   Participants

The study involved 126 participants of the community. They were 77 mothers (61 %) and 49 fathers (39 %) with an age ranging from 28 to 50 years (mean = 39.3, std = 4.1). 91 % of the participants lived with a partner and 88 % are families with both parents working (dual-earner couples). The participants had an average of 1.79 children

---

[1] http://www.mobileterritoriallab.eu

(std = 0.67). They held a variety of occupations and education levels, ranging from high school diplomas to PhD degrees. All were savvy smartphone users.

3.2 Procedure

All the participants of the living lab were contacted to offer participation in this study by informing them on the purposes and the procedure. All the 126 people who volunteered were recruited.

The study lasted for 24 days in April 2014. We used the Day Reconstruction Method approach (DRM, [14]) to collect data about the sharing preferences of the participants. Every evening participants received an email and a notification on their smartphone containing a link to a personalized survey they could fill using a browser (see Fig. 1). The survey contained a list of places in which the participant has remained

Fig. 1. A snapshot of the personalized daily survey for the DRM that participants received on their smartphones.

during the day for more than 15 minutes, along with the arrival and exit time. The locations tracked by the positioning system of participants' smartphones were aggregated using the same algorithm used in [17] and [4]. They were presented both as a map and as a list.

Every day, participants were asked to choose the place that was the most relevant for them as parents; we decided to let participants choose just one place rather than ask them about any place to reduce the cognitive effort of filling the survey every night. Furthermore, we asked them to select the place most relevant for them as parents because we wanted to focus our study on decision making related to parenting and not with other roles that people may have during the day (professional, friends, etc.) Participants also had the possibility of entering a place not in the list, in case the location tracking of the smartphone did not work correctly during part of the day. Then participants had to fill a number of questions about the chosen place aimed at assessing their sharing preferences as well as some features of the context. The questionnaire can be read at http://bit.do/DRM_en.

A pre-study questionnaire was administered exploring perceived social support and the sense of community. Other previously collected information related to individual traits was used (see next section).

Sharing Preferences and Contextual Variables Collected Through DRM. Participants sharing preferences and socialization needs related to the specific place they chose each day through the DRM were investigated in terms of:

- *Intention to share the physical location:* participants were asked to imagine they had a way to share their location using the smartphone and we asked them their agreement with the statement: "In that moment, I would have shared my position with (group)". Precisely we asked about 5 different groups: (1) the partner ("In that moment, I would have shared my position with my partner"), (2) relatives ("grandparents, uncles, …"), (3) friends, (4) other parents who were nearby at that moment (1 Km radius) or (5) everyone by making it publicly available on the web. These were 5 different 5-point Likert scales.
- *Need for socialization* (5-points Likert) as the degree of agreement with the statement: "I would have liked to meet other parents".

The context related to the chosen place was modelled in terms of three dimensions that emerged as important in literature (see above) and in our previous study [16].

- *Type of place:* the participants were asked to describe the place (for example, playground and mall). The descriptions were then coded into 8 categories expressing functional values: home, work, house of other people (relatives or friends), recreational (such as playground, cinema, theme park, etc.), commercial (shops, malls, etc.), health (doctor, hospital, etc.), religion (church, etc.) and education (kindergarten, school and school-related activities).
- *Social context:* the participants were asked to report with whom they were ("I was alone", "with at least one of my children", "with my partner", "with relatives", "with friends"; "with other parents"). Multiple options were possible.

- *Mood*: they reported the magnitude of different moods as they were feeling them during the time spent in the place. We followed Kahneman [14] to model affective experience: the dimension measured with 5-point Likert scale had the following items: Happy; Warm/Friendly; Enjoying myself; Frustrated/Annoyed; Depressed/ Blue; Hassled/Pushed around; Angry/Hostile; Worried/Anxious; Tired.

All the previous information about the chosen place was mandatory and so was completely filled by each participant.

Individual Characteristics. As already explained, we also asked participants to fill an initial questionnaire. Our goal was to investigate the importance of perceived social support in relation to location sharing so we used:

- The *Interpersonal Support Evaluation list (ISEL)* [5] to gather information about participants' social support, defined as the various resources provided by one's interpersonal ties. The questionnaire provides a measure of the overall perceived support and the measure of four separate functions of support: appraisal support, self-esteem support, belonging support, tangible support.
- The *Brief Sense of Community Scale (BSCS)* [25] to measure attitudes toward the community. The sense of community refers to the fundamental human phenomenon of collective experience and includes four different dimensions: needs fulfillment (a perception that members' needs will be met by the community), group membership (a feeling of belonging or a sense of interpersonal relatedness), influence (a sense that one matters in a community), and emotional connection (feeling of attachment).

Moreover, as additional individual traits, we also considered other measures that were available about each participant from the living lab: since they are considered stable traits, we did not administer them again for the study.

- The *Big Five personality traits (Big5)* [12] cover the traditional dimensions of Extraversion, Neuroticism, Agreeableness, Conscientiousness and Openness. We measured this scale by means of the BFMS [12] questionnaire, which is validated for the Italian language [24].
- *Locus of Control (LoC)* [19], a psychological construct measuring whether causal attribution for subject behavior or beliefs is made to oneself or to external events and circumstances. The LoC measures whether the outcomes of a set of beliefs are dependent upon what the subject does (internal orientation) or upon events outside of her/his control (external orientation).
- Finally, we collected information about the participants' *Dispositional Trust* [27]: in this perspective, trust is considered as a form of personality trait, defining interpersonal trust as a generalized expectancy that the words or promises of others can be relied on. In our study, we used Mayer and Davis's Trust Propensity Scale (TPS) [20].

4 Results

In total, 3024 evening questionnaires were sent to the 126 participants and 2504 have been filled (83 %). The minimum number of filled survey per participant is 6 and the maximum is 24 with an average of 19.87 surveys per participant (standard deviation = 4.82).

4.1 Descriptive Statistics

The intention to share the location was higher toward the partner (mean = 4.19; std = 1.32), followed by relatives (mean = 4.02; std = 1.37), friends (mean = 3.31; std = 1.47), nearby parents (mean = 2.62; std = 1.46) and everyone (i.e. publicly on the web; mean = 1.61; std = 1.16); see Fig. 2. The mean for the need of socialization was 2.99 (std = 1.48).

With regard to the social context, the participants reported they were with at least one of their kids (86 %), with the partner (50 %), with other family members (22 %), with other parents (13 %), with friends (13 %), and very rarely alone (8 %), see Fig. 3. As already said, multiple conditions were possible.

For what concerns the places, two categories represent, not surprisingly, the majority: recreational places (34.3 %) followed by the home (31.2 %); then house of other people (14.0 %) and commercial (6.4 %), education (4.5 %), work (3.9 %), health (1.8 %), religion (1.4 %). The remaining 2.5 % (63 places) was not identified under any of the previous categories and was labeled as other places, see Fig. 4. It is important to note that we explicitly asked the participants to select a place that was particularly relevant for them as parents.

In general, the places chosen by our participants were associated with high levels of positive emotions and low levels of negative emotions: happy (mean = 4.12; std = 0.92), friendly (mean = 3.92; std = 1.05), fun (mean = 3.62; std = 1.22), daunted (1.35; std = 0.74), frustrated (mean = 1.39; std = 0.80), angry (mean = 1.27; std = 0.64),

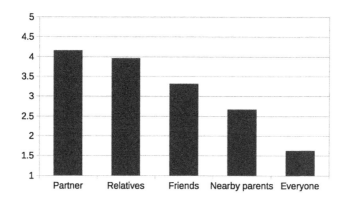

Fig. 2. Intentions to share with different target groups (means of 5-point Likert scale)

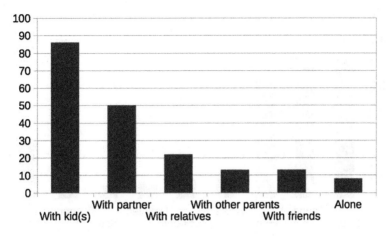

Fig. 3. Distribution of social context (in %).

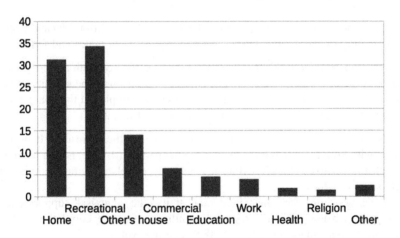

Fig. 4. Distribution of the types of places (in %).

worried (mean = 1.48; std = 0.9049), sad (mean = 1.29; std = 0.69), tired (mean = 2.27; std = 1.20), see Fig. 5.

Data Analysis. In the following subsections, we analyze the associations between location sharing preferences (with partner, relatives, friends, nearby parents, and everyone) and need for socialization on one side, and individual traits, physical context, emotional context, and social context on the other side. We report results that are significant with a level of significance of $p < .05$.

Sharing Preferences and Individual Traits

Gender. Contrary to other studies [17], the analysis of our data does not suggest any gender difference along the sharing preferences dimensions. An ANOVA run using

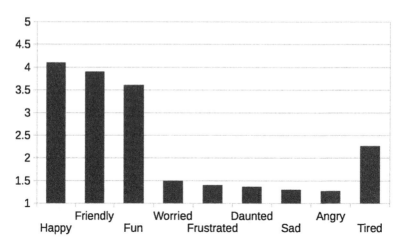

Fig. 5. Distribution of emotions (means of 5-point Likert scale)

gender as a factor on the need for socialization and the various location sharing preferences did not reveal any significant difference between males and females.

Personality and other individual traits. We computed the correlation among each of the means of the 6 sharing preferences and subjects' scores on the personality and other individual traits described above. For these analyses, we employed the non parametric Spearman's Rho method with a level of significance of $p < .05$.

Of the Big5 traits, only Consciousness produced significant results. It positively correlated with both the intention to share with the partner (0.199) and the intention to share with the relatives (0.197), while it negatively correlated with the intention to publicly share (–0.208).

For what concerns the other individual traits, the appraisal support and the self-esteem dimensions of ISEL revealed significant negative correlations with the intention to publicly share (–0.203 and –0.202, respectively).

The traits above denote individuals who can be defined as balanced: higher score on Consciousness suggest thorough and careful personalities while Self-esteem and Emotional Stability is usually associated with positive behavior. Our results suggest that conscientious, thorough and careful people focus their sharing behavior on family members, avoiding doing so with the wide public. People who are not comforted in their self esteem by their social network and/or do not feel enough support from it, in turn, have a greater tendency to share their location with everyone on the Web.

No significant associations were found with Locus of Control and Dispositional Trust.

Sharing Preferences and Physical Context. The types of places indicated by subjects were coded from their descriptions in the daily surveys. The resulting categories are the following ones: home, work, house of other people (relatives or friends), recreational, commercial, health, religion and education.

The association between type of place and our six dependent variables were investigated by means of a series of linear mixed models to flexibly account for the repeated measure nature of our data (the id of the participant is the random effect). The variables are not normally distributed but linear mixed models are robust with this regard [10]. For each model, we used location = Home as basic category. Table 1 reports the significant effects we found, i.e. the raw coefficients of the linear mixed models ($p < .05$). Positive coefficients are reported in green and negative ones in red.

The need to socialize negatively associates with work as compared to home, suggesting that our subjects have less need to socialize for what concerns family aspects in the work environment than at home. All the other places show positive correlations but the health-related places, hinting at a greater need for socialization in public spaces than at home. It is worth noting than the quite high effect of educational places are likely due to the fact that the vast majority of such cases consist of situations in which parents are waiting for their children at school exit, among many other parents, and in fact the effect of sharing location with nearby parents is one of the highest (0.72) and the need for socialization with other parents is the highest (1.03).

Similar patterns, though restricted to fewer places, emerge for the sharing preferences: in particular, sharing with partners, relatives, parents and friends increase when at the houses of other people or in recreational places with respect to home. The intention to share with the wider public, in turn, is lower in a commercial place than at home.

Sharing Preferences and Emotional Context. Linear mixed models were also used to investigate the associations between mood (Kahneman's dimensions of affective experience) and sharing preferences. Table 2 reports the significant effects found ($p < .05$).

Quite generally, positive mood tends to positively associate to (and presumably encourage) the need for socialization and all the sharing intentions (see the highlighted top-left rectangle in Table 2) The pattern for negative moods is less clear: it does not associate to the need to socialize; it negatively associate with sharing within the family

Table 1. Significant relations and their magnitude for the mixed models that relates sharing preferences and type of place (all the effects reported are significant for $p < .05$)

		WORK	HOUSE (others)	RECRE-ATIONAL	COMMER-CIAL	HEALTH	RELIGION	EDUCATION
	NEED TO SOCIALIZE	-0.33	0.38	0.96	0.28		0.76	1.03
INTENT TO SHARE LOCATION	PARTNER		0.25	0.33	0.23			
	RELATIVES		0.31	0.33				0.27
	NEARBY PARENTS			0.77			0.66	0.72
	FRIENDS		0.3	0.76				0.31
	PUBLIC			0.16	-0.28			

Table 2. Significant relations and their magnitude for the mixed model that relates sharing preferences and emotions (all the effects reported are significant for p < .05)

| | | POSITIVE MOODS | | | NEGATIVE MOODS | | | | | |
		HAPPY	FRIENDLY	FUN	WORRIED	FRUS-TRATED	DAUNTED	SAD	ANGRY	TIRED
	NEED TO SOCIALIZE	0.34	0.43	0.24						-0.06
INTENT TO SHARE LOCATION	PARTNER	0.26	0.27	0.20	-0.14	-0.14	-0.12	-0.13		
	RELATIVES	0.35	0.45	0.27	-0.09	-0.07		0.10		
	NEARBY PARENTS	0.22	0.30	0.22	0.13	0.16	0.20	0.30	0.23	0.10
	FRIENDS	0.30	0.45	0.45			0.11	0.17	0.09	
	PUBLIC	0.09	0.08		0.31	0.34	0.38	0.36	0.44	0.17

circle; it positively associates with sharing with nearby parents, the general public and, at least for some components, it positively associates also with sharing with friends. However, even if all the reported relations are statistically significant, it might be more informative to focus on larger coefficients, for example, higher than 0.2, that is for which an increase of 1 in the corresponding emotion has an increase of 0.2 in the related willingness to share location and hence a stronger effect. If we limit to those stronger relations, we observe that an increase in negative emotions has an increase in willingness to share the location publicly on the web, with everyone, while the effect for two positive emotions and tiredness is very limited (see the highlighted bottom-right group of cells in Table 2).

Sharing Preferences and Social Context. As mentioned before, sociality is modeled by means of whom the person is with: on his/her own (alone), with children, with the partner, with relatives, with other parents and with friends. Participants could indicate, for the chosen place and time, one or more options.

The associations with our dependent variables were investigated through linear mixed models, each including all the independent variables (the dimensions above) treated as binary factors. The significant effects (p < .05) are reported in Table 3.

Being with the partner negatively associates with the need of socialization and with the intention to share the physical location with other parents. No other significant effects of this independent variable are found. In the end, being with the partner does neither encourage socialization nor sharing.

Instead, being with one' children and/or other parents positively associates with both the need of socialization and the intention to share location with other parents. Being with relatives seems to have a similar but somehow smaller effect and it seems restricted to the family context only.

Table 3. Significant relations and their magnitude for the mixed model that relates sharing preferences and social context (all the effects reported are significant for $p < .05$)

		ALONE	with KIDS	with PARTNER	with RELATIVES	with OTHER PARENTS	with FRIENDS
	NEED TO SOCIALIZE		0.58	-0.26		0.77	
INTENT TO SHARE LOCATION	PARTNER				0.24	0.18	
	RELATIVES		0.20		0.48		
	NEARBY PARENTS		0.23	-0.23		0.51	
	FRIENDS				0.24		0.44
	PUBLIC						

The relation between the intention to share location with friends and the social context is less clear: it positively correlates with being with friends and with relatives but the effect is not significant for the childcare-related activities (being with children, with partner and with other parents). It may suggest that our subjects clearly separate childcare from being with friends and while in the latter context they feel more appropriate sharing their location while in the former they tend to focus on childcare social relations.

It is worth noting that publicly sharing location does not associate with any social context and that being alone does not associate with any sharing preference or need to socialize. As it turns out, location sharing preferences are associated with only truly social contexts.

5 Discussion

In this section, we summarize the main findings of our study and compare them with related works' results.

There is need to socialize with other parents. The mean of the expressed need to socialize related to the 2504 chosen places is 2.99 which, in the Likert scale 1–5, is precisely in the middle indicating a varied and open perspective on this basic issue, especially considering its standard deviation which is 1.48. However there are large and significant coefficients related to specific contexts, which indicate larger or smaller need to socialize in specific cases. With regard to the physical context, being in places related to education has a large and positive effect on the need to socialize: parents waiting for their children outside schools or kindergardens are more willing to socialize with other parents. A similar large effect occurs for recreational places such as playgrounds: while children play, parents could be more open to chat a bit with another parent. With regard to emotional context, unsurprisingly, parents report a higher need to socialize when they are happy, friendly and having fun. The social context also features interesting insights: the need to socialize with other parents is higher when the parent is with their kids or when he or she is already with other parents. On the contrary, when the parent is with the partner, the need to socialize with other parents is reduced indicating what can be a private family moment. These insights suggest that there are indeed situations in which parents experience a larger need to socialize with other parents and these are opportunities for services designed to enable and facilitate offline encounters.

Closer relationship, higher sharing. As expected, sharing is higher the closer the social relationship is: partner, relatives, friends, nearby parents, and finally everyone. This confirms [33] which found closeness being the stronger predictor for willingness to share location.

Demographic characteristics do not matter. Contrary to other studies [17], we did not find any statistically significant influence of gender on location sharing preferences.

Individual characteristics do not matter a lot. In general, personal traits do not influence too much the need for socialization and the sharing intentions. The only aspects that seem to matter are those related to psychological stability: Consciousness, Self-esteem and support from the group. More stable individual tends to share more with family and less with the web and vice versa.

Previous studies on the influence played by individual traits (usually personality traits and LoC) on privacy dispositions and disclosure behaviors have provided contrasting evidence: some of them found small correlations [19, 26, 30], while Schrammel et al. found no correlations [28]. Page and colleagues [23] found that a specific individual characteristics, the FYI communication style, predicts the adoption of location-sharing social networks and also that parents are more likely to be FYI communicators.

Our results seem to shed some new lights on this aspect but further studies are needed to better understand whether the effect we found is typical of parents and parent-related sharing or more general.

The context does matter. A more relevant impact seems to be played by the context in which the decision to share is considered: the physical context as well as the social one.

About the physical context, it seems that at working place the need for socialization is lower. This, at least partially, confirms [18] which found that shared locations might be those seen as somehow interesting (it is worth remembering that our participants were instructed to select the place on the relevance as parents). Another confirmation of this argument comes from the fact that recreational places are always positively associated with the intention of sharing location and with the need of socialization. This is also in line with Toch et al. [32] who found that users were more comfortable in sharing their location when they are at places visited by a large and diverse set of people. The houses of other people (other parents, relatives or friends) follow a similar pattern with the important exception that they are not shared with the wider public. This is, possibly, due to the fact that privacy concerns may arise.

For what concerns the social context, the presence of one's children or of other parents correlates with higher need for socialization. The social context has no significant effect on the willingness to share own location publicly with everyone; while being with children, relatives or other parents increase the sharing with different groups. In general, when people are with a particular member from a group (e.g., family or friends), people are more willing to disclose their location to other members in the same group. This result is in line with what was found by Xie [34].

If you are with your partner, keep it to yourself. The case in which the partner is in the social context is a special one, the socialization needs and the intentions to share physical location drop; this partially confirms the findings of Xie [34].

If you are with your children, say "we are here!" to your relatives and to other parents. Locations including children are shared only to members of the "inner" circle (relatives) or others members "thematically" connected (other parents). This confirms and qualifies [34] who found that "when people are accompanied by kids, they also become more prudent." And more selective, we might say, in choosing their sharing targets. An obvious exception to this rule is sharing with the partner: there is no need, for she/he knows.

If you are happy say it to your friends; if you are sad say it to the entire world. The emotional context also played an important role. Higher positive emotions are associated with higher need for socialization and higher intentions to share with close people (partner, relative, friends, but also nearby parents). On the other hand, there is a strong effect of negative emotions on the willingness to share location publicly on the web, with everyone. Even if on average sharing on the web was largely less popular than sharing with the partner (1.61 and 4.19 respectively, on a 5-point scale), it seems that when parents are happy or having fun they want to disclose it more to their close circles. On the other hand, when they are angry or frustrated, sad or hassled or worried, they relatively tend to disclose their location more publicly on the web, to everyone. This, again, is in line with the results of Xie et al. [34] who found that people tend to share much more positive feelings with family and friends.

6 Limitations

The study presented in this paper has some limitations. In particular, it is based on declared intentions rather than actual behavior and it is based on a reconstruction method rather than on on-the-spot survey. Moreover, we asked participants to choose the place they considered most relevant for them as parents because we wanted to focus our analysis on location sharing of parents when their main role was parent and the context parent-related. This choice might have introduced biases, such as for example the relatively small presence of work as place and the large presence of recreational places. This might also explain the large values, on average, for positive emotions and small values for negative emotions. It is possible to read online the text of the survey in order to better ponder how the survey might have influenced the collected data. We presented only places in which the participant has remained for more than 15 min by using the same method used in [17] and [4] for aggregating GPS points. This procedure excluded uses of location sharing for coordinating meetups or showing others how far you are from reaching a destination. We did so because we were interested in sharing of location for purposes related to socialization with other people or parents.

We are aware that these limitations may have somehow affected the results. Still, we believe that the data and the findings, although in need to be confirmed by further studies, may shed new lights on the important research topic of location-based applications in general and may eventually guide to design of specific technologies to support families with young children.

7 Conclusions

The overall goal of our research was to investigate the dimensions that affect the intention to share the physical location while in family-related contexts. A diary study was run for 3 weeks involving 126 participants. The main outcomes of this paper are several insights for the previously underexplored user group of families with young children. In particular, our results suggest a relative greater importance of the context (physical, social and emotional) with respect to individual traits (e.g., personality, trust dispositions, and demographic characteristics) and some different effects of positive and negative emotions on intention to share with different targets: negative mood seems to discourage sharing privately with specific groups of people and to encourage sharing with everyone publicly. These results have been compared with those of similar studies on different populations.

Acknowledgments. We thank all the participants in the study and all the reviewers for their helpful comments and suggestions. We thank the Mobile Territorial Lab for providing us support for conducting our research.

References

1. Amichai-Burger, Y., Vinitzky, G.: Social network use and personality. J. Comput. Hum. Behav. **26**(6), 1289–1295 (2010)
2. Anthony, D., Kotz, D.: Privacy in location-aware computing environments. IEEE Pervasive Comput. **4**(6), 64–72 (2007)
3. Barkhuus, L., Brown, B., Bell, M., Sherwood, S., Hall, M., Chalmers, M.: From awareness to repartee: sharing location within social groups. In: Proceedings of CHI, pp. 497–506. ACM (2008)
4. Benisch, M., Kelley, P.G., Sadeh, N., Cranor, L.F.: Capturing location-sharing preferences: quantifying accuracy and user-burden tradeoffs. Pers. Ubiquit. Comput. **15**(7), 679–694 (2011)
5. Cohen, S., Hoberman, H.: Positive events and social supports as buffers of life change stress. J. Appl. Soc. Psychol. **13**, 99–125 (1983)

6. Consolvo, S., Smith, I.E., Matthews, T., LaMarca, A., Tabert, J., Powledge, P.: Location disclosure to social relations: why, when, and what people want to share. In: Proceedings of CHI 2005 (2005)

7. Davidoff, S., Ziebart, B.D., Zimmerman J., Dey, A.K.: Learning patterns of pick-ups and drop-offs to support busy family coordination. In: Proceedings of CHI 2011, pp. 1175–1184. ACM, New York (2011)

8. Devault, M.: Producing family time: practices of leisure activity beyond the home. Qual. Sociol. 23(4), 485–503 (2000)

9. Garbarino, G., Vorrasi, J.A., Kostelny, K.: Parenting and public policy. In: Bornstein, M.H. (ed.) Handbook of Parenting Vol. 5 Practical Issues in Parenting, pp. 487–507. Laurence Erlbaum Associates, New Jersey (2002)

10. Gelman, A., Hill, J.: Data Analysis Using Regression and Multilevel/Hierarchical Models. Cambridge University Press, New York (2007)

11. Gibson L., Hanson V.L.: Digital motherhood: how does technology help new mothers?. In: Proceedings of CHI 2013, pp. 313–322. ACM, New York (2013)

12. John, O.P., Srivastava, S.: The big five trait taxonomy: history, measurement, and theoretical perspectives. In: Pervin, L.A., John, O.P. (eds.) Handbook of Personality: Theory and Research, 2nd edn, pp. 102–138. Guilford, New York (1999)

13. Junglas, I.A., Johnson, N.A., Spitzmuller, C.: Personality traits and concern for privacy: an empirical study in the context of location-based services. Eur. J. Inf. Syst. 17(4), 387–402 (2008)

14. Kahneman, D., Krueger, A.B., Schkade, D.A., Schwarz, N., Stone, A.A.: A survey method for characterizing daily life experience: the day reconstruction method. Science 306(5702), 1776–1780 (2004)

15. Korzaan, M., Brooks, N., Greer, T.: Demystifying personality and privacy: an empirical investigation into antecedents of concerns for information privacy. J. Behav. Stud. Bus. 1, 1–17 (2009)

16. Leonardi, C., Massa, P., Zancanaro, M.: I'm here with my kids: investigating location sharing preferences of parents with young children. In: Extended Abstracts CHI. ACM (2014)

17. Lin, J., Benisch, M., Sadeh, N., Niu, J., Hong, J., Lu, B., Guo, S.: A comparative study of location-sharing privacy preferences in the United States and China. Pers. Ubiquit. Comput. 17(4), 697–711 (2013)

18. Lindqvist, J., Cranshaw, J., Wiese, J., Hong, J., Zimmerman, J.: I'm the mayor of my house: examining why people use foursquare - a social-driven location sharing application. In: Proceedings of CHI 2011. ACM, New York (2011)

19. Lo, J.: Privacy concern, locus of control, and salience in a trust- risk model of information disclosure on social networking sites. In: Proceedings of Americas Conference on Information Systems (2010)

20. Mayer, R.C., Davis, J.H.: The effect of the performance appraisal system on trust for management: a field quasi-experiment. J. Appl. Psychol. 84, 123–136 (1999)

21. Meadows, S.: The association between perceptions of social support and maternal mental health: a cumulative perspective. J. Fam. Issues 32, 181–208 (2011)

22. Morris, M.R., Teevan, J., Panovich, K.: What do people ask their social networks, and why? a survey study of status message Q&A behavior. In: Proceedings of CHI (2010)

23. Page, X., Knijnenburg, B.P., Kobsa, A.: FYI: communication style preferences underlie differences in location-sharing adoption and usage. In: Proceedings of UbiComp 2013. ACM (2013)

24. Perugini, M., Di Blas, L.: The Big Five Marker Scales (BFMS) and the italian AB5C taxonomy: analyses from an emic-etic perspective. In: de Raad, B., Perugini, M. (eds.) Big Five Assessment. Hogrefe & Huber Publishers, Gottingen (2002)
25. Peterson, N., Speer, P.W., McMillan, D.W.: Validation of a brief sense of community scale: confirmation of the principal theory of sense of community. J. Commun. Psychol. 36(1), 61–73 (2008)
26. Quercia, D., Las Casas, D., Pesce, J.P., Stillwell, D., Kosinski, M., Almeida, V., Crowcroft, J.: Facebook and privacy: the balancing act of personality, gender, and relationship currency. In: Proceedings of the 6th AAAI Conference on ICWSM (2012)
27. Rotter, J.B.: A new scale for the measurement of interpersonal trust. J. Pers. 35(4), 651–665 (1967)
28. Schrammel, J., Koffel, C., Tscheligi, M.: Personality traits usage patterns and information disclosure in online communities. In: Proceedings of the 23rd ACM BCS-HCI (2009)
29. Shklovski, I., de Souza e Silva, A.: An urban encounter: realizing online connectedness through local urban play. Inf. Commun. Soc. 16, 3 (2012)
30. Staiano, J., Oliver, N., Lepri, B., de Oliveira, R., Caraviello, M., Sebe, N.: Money walks: a human-centric study on the economics of personal mobile data. In: Proceedings of UbiComp 2014. ACM (2014)
31. Tang, K.P., Lin, J., Hong, J.I., Siewiorek, D.P., Sadeh, N.: Rethinking location sharing: exploring the implications of social-driven vs. purpose-driven location sharing. In: Proceedings of UbiComp 2010. ACM (2010)
32. Toch, E., Levi, I.: UbiComp locality and privacy in people-nearby application. In: Proceedings of UbiComp, 8–12 September 2013, ACM, Zurich (2013)
33. Wiese, J., Kelley, P.G., Cranor, L.F., Dabbish, L., Hong, J.I., Zimmerman, J.: Are you close with me? are you nearby? Investigating social groups, closeness, and willingness to share. In: Proceedings of UbiComp 2011, pp. 197–206. ACM (2011)
34. Xie, J., Knijnenburg, B.P., Jin, H.: Location sharing privacy preference: analysis and personalized recommendation. In: Proceedings of IUI 2014. ACM (2014)
35. Veitch, J., Bagley, S., Ball, K., Salmon, J.: Where do children usually play? a qualitative study of parents' perceptions of influences on children's active free-play. Health Place. 12(4), 383–393 (2006)
36. Savin-Williams, R.C., Small, S.A.: The timing of puberty and its relationship to adolescent and parent perceptions of family interactions. Dev. Psychol. 22, 342–347 (1986)

Navigation in Long Forms on Smartphones: Scrolling Worse than Tabs, Menus, and Collapsible Fieldsets

Johannes Harms[✉], Martina Kratky, Christoph Wimmer,
Karin Kappel, and Thomas Grechenig

INSO Research Group, Vienna University of Technology, Vienna, Austria
{johannes.harms,martina.kratky,christoph.wimmer,
karin.kappel,thomas.grechenig}@inso.tuwien.ac.at

Abstract. Mobile applications provide increasingly complex functionality through form-based user interfaces, which requires effective solutions for navigation on small-screen devices. This paper contributes a comparative usability evaluation of four navigation design patterns: Scrolling, Tabs, Menus, and Collapsible Fieldsets. These patterns were evaluated in a case study on social network profile pages. Results show that memorability, usability, overview, and subjective preference were worse in Scrolling than in the other patterns. This indicates that designers of form-based user interfaces on small-screen devices should not rely on Scrolling to support navigation, but use other design patterns instead.

Keywords: Navigation · Mobile · Smartphone · Form design · Evaluation

1 Introduction

Forms are widely employed as user interfaces (UIs) for data entry and subsequent editing [14, 16, 21]. Long forms are often considered a bad design practice – e.g., an empirical study [22, p. 294] and recent guidelines [2] recommend against long forms and unnecessary questions. But they cannot always be avoided due to complex application requirements [15]. This also holds for forms on small-screen, mobile devices such as smartphones. Examples of mobile apps with long form-based UIs include editing a contact in the iOS address book (43 form fields), Facebook's mobile profile page (11 collapsible fieldsets for 88 form fields), and the Samsung Galaxy system settings (4 tabs for about 380 form fields). The length of these UIs clearly indicates a need for effective navigation. This can be supported through a variety of navigation design patterns (NDPs). Popular NDPs include Scrolling, Tabs, Menus, and Collapsible Fieldsets. It is the goal of this work to compare and evaluate these four NDPs in a case study on social network profile page editing, see Fig. 1 for screenshots of the evaluated prototypes. Section 2 discusses related work with a focus on navigation within mobile UIs. Section 3 describes the case study and the empirical study design. A comparative, lab-based usability test was conducted with N = 24 participants. Evaluation results are presented in Sects. 4 and 5.

© IFIP International Federation for Information Processing 2015
J. Abascal et al. (Eds.): INTERACT 2015, Part III, LNCS 9298, pp. 333–340, 2015.
DOI: 10.1007/978-3-319-22698-9_21

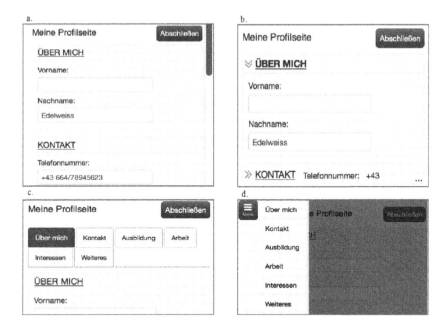

Fig. 1. Screenshots of the four navigation design patterns (NDPs) evaluated in this work: Scrolling (a) shows the entire form in a single, static view. Tabs (b) and Menus (c) provide an overview of the form schema and show details (for the selected tab or menu entry) in a spatially separated view. Collapsible Fieldsets (d) were designed as described in [15]; they employ the Focus + Context principle by surrounding detailed information at the user's focus of interest with a contextual overview.

2   Related Work

A recent overview of navigation research in HCI in mobile, wearable, embedded, 3D, and desktop information systems is provided in [19]. One branch of research has examined navigation between documents, e.g., in hypertext environments [7] and websites [20]. In contrast, research on within-document navigation investigates topics such as reading long documents [1, 9, 12], navigation in lists [11], and navigation in long form-based UIs [10, 15], as examined in this paper. Mobile UIs require special solutions for navigation – techniques for desktop computers may not be directly applicable [22]. Challenges specific to mobile navigation include smaller screen sizes, limited input devices and changing external environment [8].

Related work has presented recommendations for websites on smartphones, suggesting to keep navigation on a minimal scale to avoid using up too much screen space [17]. Existing navigation design patterns (NDPs) can be classified through concepts from information visualization [9]. Accordingly, Tabs, Menus, and Tables-of-Contents offer a spatially separated overview and detailed view. Zooming (not examined in this work) uses a temporal separation. Collapsible Fieldsets employ the Focus + Context principle, seeking to minimize the separation by combining overview and detail in a single, dynamic view. In contrast, Scrolling uses a single, static view.

Related evaluations of NDPs have compared the following usability measures: effectiveness and efficiency, errors, simplicity, comprehensibility, learnability, memorability, and user satisfaction; albeit with conflicting results, see [22] for a literature review. Scrolling is a popular NDP, but has delivered bad results for long mobile UIs [13]. Tabs are a common way to organize navigation in both desktop and mobile interfaces. They have been suggested for splitting heterogeneous content [18, p.448], but also recommended against due to poor performance in very long forms [16, p.111, 18, p.357]. Collapsible Fieldsets and Fisheye distortions employ the Focus + Context principle, which has been shown to reduce task completion time when navigating websites on small-screen devices [13]. The Fisheye distortion that is often – but not necessarily [9] – used in Focus + Context UIs has been shown to decrease targeting performance [9, 14]. Hence related work has recommended to investigate new, non-traditional, possibly non-distorted Focus + Context interaction techniques [3]. Within this direction, recent work has proposed a non-distorted, adaptive form design featuring Collapsible Fieldsets [15]; one such design is evaluated in this work with regard to small-screen devices. Menus and Tables-of-Contents are employed in many mobile apps to provide overview and detail for the primary navigation. Despite the popularity of these patterns, related research has mostly investigated Overview + Detail in a different context, namely navigation in two-dimensional map views. One study reported benefits [5], another pointed out the drawback of reduced screen size [6]. In summary, the above conflicting results indicate a need for further evaluation.

3   Case Study: Social Network Profile Forms

Social network profile pages were chosen as a case study. Many popular social networks allow users to edit their profile using a mobile app installed on their smartphone. These profile pages employ long form-based user interfaces (e.g., Facebook's profile page with 88 form fields, LinkedIn's with 43 fields) to help users provide details about themselves. Tasks comprise both initial filling and subsequent revising. In this respect profile pages are similar to forms in productivity applications and different from, e.g., registration forms and questionnaires. The forms are sparsely filled because not all fields are relevant, the frequency of use is rather low, and information is shared voluntarily at the users' discretion. Navigation is non-linear, not strictly goal-directed (compare [12] for more on goal directedness), and to some degree explorative. In contrast to other domains, no special knowledge is required to answer the questions of a profile page, making the case study suited for evaluation without interference by varying domain-specific knowledge.

The four NDPs of Scrolling, Tabs, Menu, and Collapsible Fieldsets served as test conditions, see Fig. 1a–d for screenshots. We measured efficiency, errors, memorability, perceived usability, and subjective rankings of difficulty, overview, and preference. Participants started working with one randomly assigned NDP. A subsequent first questionnaire assessed memorability (between-subject test design). They then performed three more test runs with the remaining three NDPs. The order in which NDPs were assigned was randomized to level out learning effects. This provided measures regarding efficiency and errors (within-subject test design). Lastly, participants ranked and qualitatively described the NDPs in a second post-test questionnaire and in a short, semi-structured interview (between-subject). All tests took place in a home/office usage context. Users were allowed to sit or stand and used their own smartphones to access a website running the profile page. The tasks required entry, retrieval, editing, and deletion of fictitious form data. Screen recordings and log files supported further analysis.

4   Results

This section presents quantitative and qualitative results, as assessed through a comparative usability test with N = 24 participants (f = 14, m = 10). The significance of observed differences was tested using two-sided Kruskal-Wallis H-Tests with a significance level of $p < 0.05$. We used an Exact-Methods implementation of Kruskal-Wallis when computationally possible, otherwise Monte-Carlo with 10.000 samples. Post hoc pairwise comparisons between groups were tested using Exact Mann-Whitney U-Tests. These test methods are well-suited for the lack of normality and the heteroscedasticity present in much of the data.

Efficiency. We measured the time needed for navigation by analyzing screen recordings, thus splitting total task completion time into navigation, data entry, and task comprehension. There were no significant influences of NDP on the time needed for navigation ($p = 0.170$), data entry ($p = 0.994$), and task comprehension ($p = 0.377$), see Table 1. To assert that these results are not biased by learning effects, we additionally conducted separate statistical tests for each one of the test runs 1−4, but found no significant differences. This indicates that our randomized study design worked well for eliminating learning effects.

Navigation Errors. Screen recordings were further analyzed in order to count navigation errors. This included Scrolling in the wrong direction as well as selecting the wrong Tab, Menu entry or Fieldset. We found no significant influence ($p = 0.094$) of NDP on the number of errors, see Table 2.

Memorability. The first questionnaire allowed to measure three memorability scores. Mem1 (number of correctly remembered form sections) and Mem2 (number of correctly ordered form sections) relate to how well participants remembered an overview of the form schema, whereas Mem3 (number of correct labels from the "hobbies" section) measures how well they remembered details. Test results show a significant influence of NDP on Mem1 ($p = 0.001$), but not on Mem2 ($p = 0.128$) and Mem3 ($p = 0.813$), see Table 3. Pairwise comparisons for Mem1 revealed that Menu worked significantly better than both Collapsible Fieldsets ($p = 0.009$) and Scrolling ($p = 0.002$), the latter of which performed worse than Tabs ($p = 0.041$); all other differences were insignificant.

Perceived Usability. Participants comparatively rated the usability of the four NDPs by answering System Usability Scale (SUS) [4] questions in the second post-test questionnaire (handed out upon completion of all test runs). Overall SUS scores significantly differed ($p = 0.019$) depending on NDP, see Table 4. Pairwise comparisons

Table 1. Efficiency (measured as time needed for navigation, data entry, and task comprehension) was insignificantly different depending on NDP.

Time needed for:	Navigation	Data Entry	Task comprehension
Scrolling	00:59.37 ± 00:18.56	01:25.63 ± 00:38.03	00:41.79 ± 00:15.28
Tabs	00:53.74 ± 00:30.14	01:18.93 ± 00:25.27	00:49.26 ± 00:17.77
Menu	01:05.50 ± 00:27.80	01:22.92 ± 00:32.79	00:45.04 ± 00:15.39
Collapsible Fieldsets	00:59.15 ± 00:25.00	01:18.40 ± 00:20.62	00:41.05 ± 00:13.23
H-Value, p-Value	H(3)=4.967, p=0.170	H(3)=0.83, p=0.994	H(3)=3.144, p=0.377

Table 2. Navigation errors were not significantly different depending on NDP.

Navigation Errors	Scrolling	Tabs	Menu	Collapsible Fieldsets	H-Value, p-Value
	2.50 ± 1.719	1.75 ± 2.541	1.79 ± 2.553	2.00 ± 2.377	H(3)=6.333, p=0.094

Table 3. Memorability scores depending on NDP. Mem1 (number of correctly remembered form sections) was significantly better for Menu, followed by Tabs, Collapsible Fieldsets and Scrolling. Mem2 (correctly ordered form sections) and Mem3 (correctly remembered labels in the "hobbies" section) showed no significant differences.

Memorability Scores:	Mem1	Mem2	Mem3
Scrolling	1.00 ± 1.265	3.17 ± 0.753	1.50 ± 0.548
Tabs	3.67 ± 1.966	3.67 ± 2.338	1.50 ± 0.837
Menu	4.50 ± 0.548	4.67 ± 1.633	1.83 ± 0.753
Collapsible Fieldsets	2.50 ± 1.225	4.83 ± 0.983	1.83 ± 1.169
H-Value, p-Value	H(3)=13.071, **p=0.001**	H(3)=5.616, p=0.128	H(3)=1.072, p=0.813

showed that Scrolling scored significantly worse than both Tabs ($p = 0.007$) and Menu ($p = 0.024$). We also evaluated each SUS question individually, revealing significant influences of NDP on three out of ten questions: SUS1 ($p = 0.001$, "I think that I would like to use this design frequently"), SUS5 ($p = 0.015$, "I found the various functions in this design were well integrated"), and SUS8 ($p = 0.004$, "I found the design very cumbersome to use"), see Table 4. In each of these questions, pairwise comparisons showed that Scrolling performed significantly worse than all other NDPs (p-Values between 0.000 and 0.026); all other pairwise differences were insignificant.

Subjective Rankings. Users ranked clarity of overview, perceived difficulty, and their individual preference of the four NDPs in the second post-test questionnaire. Results show a significant influence of NDP on overview ($p < 0.001$) and preference ($p = 0.001$), but not on difficulty ($p = 0.143$), see Table 5. Pairwise comparisons for both preference and overview revealed that Scrolling worked significantly worse than all of the other NDPs (all p-Values ≤ 0.001); there were no significant differences in all other pairwise comparisons.

Qualitative Feedback. Semi-structured post-test interviews asked participants to describe their experience and whether they had difficulties using the NDPs. The interviews were recorded, transcribed and analyzed using empirical codes, see

Table 6. Scrolling garnered more negative comments than any other NDP. Users criticized a lack of usability in Scrolling (N = 17 comments), stating they found it disorienting and cumbersome. In the same way, they criticized a lack of overview (N = 7). The other three NDPs received mostly positive comments regarding these topics. Tabs (N = 2) and Menu (N = 4) were criticized for hidden UI elements, i.e., the tab bar or menu button was hidden when users scrolled down. The visual design was only commented upon with regard to Collapsible Fieldsets (N = 6); some users mentioned a lack of color; others were unable to articulate more specifically what they did not like. Users also complained that Collapsible Fieldsets (N = 2) and Menu (N = 3) lacked familiarity.

Table 4. Perceived usability. Overall SUS (System Usability Scale) scores ranging from 0 to 100, the higher the better. Three individual SUS questions (ranging from 1 to 5, the higher the more agreement) showed significant differences: SUS1 ("would like to use this frequently"), SUS5 ("well integrated"), and SUS8 ("cumbersome to use").

SUS Scores:	Overall	SUS1	SUS5	SUS8
Scrolling	66.35 ± 23.751	2.33 ± 1.579	3.17 ± 1.551	3.08 ± 1.863
Tabs	83.13 ± 19.157	3.87 ± 1.191	4.29 ± 1.042	1.71 ± 1.197
Menu	80.94 ± 20.494	3.83 ± 1.167	4.25 ± 1.189	1.58 ± 1.213
Collapsible Fieldsets	78.75 ± 15.429	3.29 ± 1.429	4.17 ± 0.917	1.75 ± 0.897
H-Value, p-Value	H(3)=9.544, **p=0.019**	H(3)=15.24, **p=0.001**	H(3)=10.378, **p=0.015**	H(3)=12.751, **p=0.004**

5   Discussion

The four NDPs of Scrolling, Tabs, Menu, and Collapsible Fieldsets evaluated in this work differed regarding memorability, perceived usability (SUS), subjectively ranked overview, and user preference. There were no significant differences in measures of efficiency (time needed for task completion) and navigation errors.

Scrolling performed worse than all other NDPs in every measure with significant differences. Memorability was lower in Scrolling, indicating that users remembered the form schema less well. One possible explanation is that Scrolling required no direct interaction with form section titles, never showed all section titles at once, and thus provided less overview. This lack of overview is confirmed by qualitative results and subjective rankings. Perceived usability and user preference were also significantly worse for Scrolling. The other three NDPs performed equally well with regard to most measures, the only significant pairwise difference being higher memorability of Menu than Collapsible Fieldsets.

Results indicate that designers should not rely on Scrolling alone, but should provide an additional high-level overview of the form schema, possibly using Tabs, Menus, or Collapsible Fieldsets. We expect the results to be generalizable from our case study about social network profile pages to other scenarios with similar characteristics: Long, form-based UIs filled on small-screen devices where tasks include initial filling and subsequent revision of form data in a non-linear, not strictly goal-directed manner. Examples are forms in productivity applications, mobile app

Table 5. Subjective Rankings. Scores ranging from 1 to 4, with lower scores indicating a better overview, higher difficulty, stronger preference.

Ranking Scores:	Overview	Difficulty	Preference
Scrolling	3.63 ± 0.770	2.04 ± 1.334	3.29 ± 1.042
Tabs	1.96 ± 0.859	2.67 ± 0.917	2.29 ± 0.955
Menu	2.21 ± 1.021	2.58 ± 1.100	2.17 ± 1.049
Collapsible Fieldsets	2.21 ± 1.021	2.71 ± 1.042	2.25 ± 1.113
H-Value, p-Value	H(3)=32.854, **p< 0.001**	H(3)=5.476, p=0.143	H(3)=16.031, **p=0.001**

Table 6. Qualitative feedback from the post-test interviews. Transcriptions were coded into positive and negative statements and counted regarding the four NDPs.

Feedback:	Scrolling	Tabs	Menu	Collapsible Fieldsets
Positive	Usability (1)	Usability (11)	Usability (10)	Usability (10)
		Overview (8)	Overview (8)	Overview (9)
Negative	Lack of Usability (17)	Lack of Usability (2)	Hidden UI Elements (4)	Visual Design (6)
	Lack of Overview (7)	Hidden UI Elements (2)	Unfamiliar Design (3)	Lack of Usability (3)
				Unfamiliar Design (2)

settings, and system preferences. Future work should investigate further scenarios and other, not just form-based UIs. Also, the memorability of the various NDPs should be further examined in long-term studies.

6 Conclusion

This paper set out to compare Scrolling, Tabs, Menus, and Collapsible Fieldsets with regard to navigation in long forms on small-screen devices. A usability evaluation was performed with 24 participants in a case study on social network profile pages. Results revealed no influence of navigation design pattern on efficiency and errors, but the following measures significantly differed: memorability, perceived usability, subjectively ranked overview, and user preference. Scrolling performed worst in all of these measures. The remaining three patterns worked equally well. Qualitative results and subjective rankings provided the explanation that the more interactive patterns (i.e., Tabs, Menus, and Collapsible Fieldsets) offer a better overview than Scrolling. We conclude that designers should avoid Scrolling in favor of the other patterns when designing navigation for long, form-based UIs that users fill and edit on small-screen devices.

References

1. Atterer, R., Lorenzi, P.: A heatmap-based visualization for navigation within large web pages. In: Proceedings of the 5th Nordic Conference on Human-computer interaction: building bridges, NordiCHI 2008, pp. 407–410. ACM, New York (2008)

2. Bargas-Avila, J., Brenzikofer, O., Roth, S., Tuch, A., Orsini, S., Opwis, K.: Simple but crucial user interfaces in the world wide web: introducing 20 guidelines for usable web form design. In: Matrai, R. (ed.) User Interfaces, ch. 1. InTech (2010)
3. Bjork, S., Redstrom, J.: Redefining the focus and context of focus + context visualizations. In: IEEE Symposium Information Visualization, InfoVis 2000, pp. 85–89. IEEE (2000)
4. Brooke, J.: SUS-A quick and dirty usability scale. Usability Eval. Ind. **189**, 194 (1996)
5. Burigat, S., Chittaro, L.: On the effectiveness of overview + detail visualization on mobile devices. Pers. Ubiquit. Comput. **17**(2), 371–385 (2013)
6. Büring, T., Gerken, J., Reiterer, H.: Usability of overview-supported zooming on small screens with regard to individual differences in spatial ability. In: Proceedings of the Working Conference Advanced Visual Interfaces, AVI 2006, pp. 233–240. ACM, New York (2006)
7. Chen, C., Rada, R.: Interacting with hypertext: a meta-analysis of experimental studies. Int. J. Hum. Comput. Interact. **11**(2), 125–156 (1996)
8. Chittaro, L.: visualizing information on mobile devices. Computer **39**(3), 40–45 (2006)
9. Cockburn, A., Karlson, A., Bederson, B.B.: A Review of Overview + Detail, Zooming, and Focus + Context Interfaces. ACM Comput. Surv. **41**(1), 2:1–2:31 (2009)
10. Couper, M.P., Baker, R., Mechling, J.: Placement and design of navigation buttons in web surveys. Surv. Pract. **4**(1), 1–21 (2013)
11. Furnas, G.: A fisheye follow-up: further reflections on focus + context. In: Grinter, R., Rodden, T., Aoki, P., Cutrell, E., Jeffries, R., Olson, G. (eds.) Proceedings of the SIGCHI Conference Human Factors in Computing Systems CHI 2006, pp. 999–1008. ACM, New York (2006)
12. Guiard, Y., Du, Y., Chapuis, O.: Quantifying degree of goal directedness in document navigation: application to the evaluation of the perspective-drag technique. In: Proceedings of the SIGCHI Conference on Human Factors in Computing Systems, CHI 2007, pp. 327–336. ACM, New York (2007)
13. Gutwin, C., Fedak, C.: Interacting with big interfaces on small screens: a comparison of fisheye, zoom, and panning techniques. In: Proceedings of the Graphics Interface, GI 2004, pp. 145–152. Canadian Human-Computer Communications Society, Waterloo (2004)
14. Harms, J.: Research goals for evolving the 'form' user interface metaphor towards more interactivity. In: Holzinger, A., Ziefle, M., Hitz, M., Debevc, M. (eds.) SouthCHI 2013. LNCS, vol. 7946, pp. 819–822. Springer, Heidelberg (2013)
15. Harms, J., Wimmer, C., Kappel, K., Grechenig, T.: Design space for focus + con- text navigation in web forms. In: Proceedings of the 2014 ACM SIGCHI Symposium Engineering Interactive Computing Systems, EICS 2014, pp. 39–44. ACM, New York (2014)
16. Jarrett, C., Gaffney, G.: Forms that Work: Designing Web Forms for Usability. Morgan Kaufmann, San Francisco (2008)
17. Lobo, D., Kaskaloglu, K., Kim, C.Y., Herbert, S.: Web usability guidelines for smartphones: a synergic approach. Int. J. Inf. Electron. Eng. **1**(1), 33–37 (2011)
18. Tidwell, J.: Designing Interfaces. O'Reilly Media, Inc., Canada (2010)
19. Vainio, T.: A review of the navigation HCI research during the 2000's. Int. J. Interact. Mob. Technol. **4**(3), 36–42 (2010)
20. Weinreich, H., Obendorf, H., Herder, E., Mayer, M.: Off the beaten tracks: exploring three aspects of web navigation. In: Proceedings of the 15th International Conference of World Wide Web, WWW 2006, pp. 133–142. ACM, New York (2006)
21. Wroblewski, L.: Web Form Design: Filling the Blanks. Louis Rosenfeld, New York (2008)
22. Zhang, D., Adipat, B.: Challenges, methodologies, and issues in the usability testing of mobile applications. Int. J. Hum. Comput. Interact. **18**(3), 293–308 (2005)

Synchronising Live Second Screen Applications with TV Broadcasts Through User Feedback

Pedro Centieiro[1,2]([⊠]), Teresa Romão[1], A. Eduardo Dias[1,2],
and Rui Neves Madeira[1]

[1] NOVA-LINCS, Faculdade de Ciências e Tecnologia, Universidade Nova de
Lisboa, Caparica, Portugal
pcentieiro@gmail.com, tir@fct.unl.pt, edias@bviva.com,
rmadeira@est.ips.pt
[2] Viva Superstars Digital Media Lda, Madan Parque, Caparica, Portugal

Abstract. A common issue on live sports TV broadcasts happens when a viewer hears a neighbour screaming a goal before watching it on his TV. Similarly, viewers will also have a disruptive experience if a second screen application, designed to present information synchronised with the live TV broadcast, displays information beforehand. This paper presents a simple and universal synchronisation mechanism for second screen mobile applications, which does not rely on automatic content recognition, but rather on user feedback to help users achieve a pleasant and effective second screen experience. Results from user tests helped validate our approach, as users were able to synchronise a mobile application with a simulated live TV broadcast, with different delays.

Keywords: Second screen · Delays · Live TV broadcasts · User experience · Sports

1 Introduction

In recent years, many media devices have become a regular presence in our living rooms. This space, once used mostly to watch television, has evolved into a shared space where we use different devices like laptops, tablets, smartphones or gaming handhelds. Within this refurnished space, an innovative concept has become quite popular: the possibility to interact with the content watched on television through an additional electronic device. This concept, defined as second screen, provides several functionalities that improve the viewers' experience, usually by providing additional show-related information and access to social networks or interactive experiences, such as polls and quizzes, synchronised with the program content. In a survey conducted by Nielsen on the first quarter of 2013 [7], it was showed that nearly half of smartphone (46 %) and tablet owners (43 %) used their devices as second screens while watching TV every day, which depicts how this interaction concept is becoming widely adopted by TV viewers. Thus, it is not surprising there are mobile applications solely focused

© IFIP International Federation for Information Processing 2015
J. Abascal et al. (Eds.): INTERACT 2015, Part III, LNCS 9298, pp. 341–349, 2015.
DOI: 10.1007/978-3-319-22698-9_22

on exploiting this concept. For instance, in the world of sports there are several examples of applications that seek to enhance the viewers' experience during live broadcasted sports, usually by predicting what will happen next [8, 11].

However, since different TV providers have diverse types of connections and hardware, it is common for some viewers to get events on second screen applications that are not synchronised with the TV broadcasts. Although this issue could be solved using automatic content recognition (ACR), like audio watermarking or audio finger-printing, and inter-destination media synchronisation (IDMS), both approaches may not work on all scenarios. There is not a universal ACR solution that allows developers to synchronise any given TV show, and TV service providers with a lower broadcast delay are not interested in synchronising with others with a higher delay. These facts motivated us to implement a universal and simple interaction mechanism to allow users to synchronise second screen applications with TV broadcasts.

This interaction mechanism is named SMUF (Synchronisation Mechanism through User Feedback) and is based on the feedback given by users on how the applications' events are synchronised with the corresponding TV broadcasts. We developed a pro-totype called WeSync to evaluate how users interact with SMUF and to analyse if they are able to synchronise a second screen application with a TV broadcast using SMUF. WeSync is a mobile application that prompts users to interact on key events of a soccer match TV broadcast. When these events are not synchronised with the TV broadcast, users can give feedback on how the application is presenting the events: before or after they appear on TV. Each subsequent event is presented taking into account the feed-back previously given, in order to have the application and the TV broadcast syn-chronised. Results from user tests allowed us to gather important insights, which will contribute for future research on this area.

2   Related Work

In the context of second screen interaction, content enrichment [4] refers to the content manipulation that users can perform on either the TV or the second screen device. Several studies were conducted within this context, with second screen applications tackling different areas such as newscasts [1], TV series [6], and sports [3]. These applications seek to deliver in-sync additional content-related media, such as trivia questions, key information and predictions about future events.

When watching a TV broadcast, out of sync multimedia streams can spoil the viewer's experience. In the context of sports, Mekuria et al. [9] presented empirical evidence that relative delays encountered in digital TV degrade the soccer watching experience, especially, when there are fans close to each other (i.e., neighbours) watching non-synchronised TV feeds. Furthermore, the study conducted by Kooij et al. [5] depicts a variation of the playout delay up to 6 s in TV broadcasts, and more than one minute in some web based TV broadcasts. Within the second screen context, this can affect the user experience of viewers, particularly when receiving key events on an application before watching them on the TV broadcast. In fact, a study conducted by Centieiro et al. [3], in which users were prompted to guess if a goal would happen in the next seconds during a soccer match, showed that some users were frustrated or stressed for not being able to perform this action. This happened since the match on TV was delayed relatively to the real match and consequently to the match events on the second screen application.

It is possible to solve this issue in either two ways, without having to add or replace hardware: by using IDMS to synchronise all the viewer's televisions, or by using ACR on the TV broadcast audio to synchronise each viewer's mobile application. The goal of IDMS is to deliver the same stream for all the individuals of a group at the same time. There have been several approaches to achieve this goal, either based on reporting the media stream arrival time and buffering at the end-points [2], or doing it so at the network itself [10]. However, viewers are dependent on the TV service providers to implement these solutions, and if they do not do it the synchronisation problem will remain. Regarding ACR, there are two main methods to identify a given TV show: audio watermarking and audio fingerprinting. Audio watermarking works by adding a well-defined sound to an audio stream, in order to be detected by an algorithm. Audio fingerprinting (popularly used by Shazam) works by comparing an audio fragment to a database of unique audio fingerprints of millions of audio files. However, when there are not third-party APIs for ACR that can detect a given TV show, viewers will not be able to synchronise their applications with the TV broadcast. Furthermore, the development of an ACR system for a given TV show may result in a complex and lengthy process that developers may not wish to go through.

3 Synchronisation Mechanism Through User Feedback (SMUF)

As we mentioned before, it is easy to think of a scenario where solutions like the IDMS algorithms and ACR are not able to guarantee a synchronised experience between the TV and the second screen applications to all users. Since different users might have different TV broadcast and network delays, we argue that the solution needs to go through them. Users should be involved in the solution process, by providing feedback on their experience. Thus, we implemented a simple, universal and low-cost synchronisation mechanism called SMUF that developers can quickly add to any kind of second screen application and by which users can easily synchronize them with the TV. To evaluate how users interact with SMUF and to analyse if they can synchronise an application with a TV broadcast, we developed a prototype called WeSync.

WeSync is a mobile application that prompts users to guess the outcome of corner kicks, penalty kicks and freekicks during a soccer match. Users can also check their predictions' outcomes, as well as their friends' scores. Furthermore, WeSync also notifies users when a goal is scored (allowing them to quickly share their thoughts on social networks), or when a half starts or ends. However, when these events are not synchronised with the TV broadcast, users need to synchronise them by using SMUF, which can be done by adjusting a slider after each event occurrence (Fig. 1a). Through SMUF, users can rate their experience, providing feedback on how the application is presenting the events. Each subsequent event is presented taking into account the previously provided feedback, in order to achieve the synchronisation between the application and the TV broadcast.

An interaction walkthrough is presented to show how SMUF works on WeSync:

1. A screen appears asking users to rate their experience after completing a given interaction, such as predicting the outcome of a corner kick.
2. Users may specify that the application is synchronised by simply clicking on the "Confirm" button, or they can adjust the slider in order to select how the application behaved in comparison to the television.
3. If the user starts to adjust the slider, a text appears describing the experience rating currently selected (e.g., "Good! App is 1.5 s ahead."). Moreover, the slider changes its colour (e.g., red indicates a higher delay) and an animation starts on the upper half of the screen indicating how that given delay corresponds to the user experience. Users with a high delay can move the slider all the way to the right (max = 4 s) and, once there, if they keep their finger on the slider, the slider scale will increase allowing for a higher maximum value (4 s are added to the maximum value every 0.5 s a finger is kept on the slider). Users can touch the "Confirm" button once they are satisfied.
4. The next time a key event happens, the application will delay the request by the number of seconds chosen by the user, so it can be closer to the TV broadcast timeline. A screen will appear once again asking for his feedback (Fig. 1a) after the user finishes interacting with the key event. At this time, users can slide to the left, decreasing the delay that was set (again, a finger kept on the slider increases the minimum value, which is the delay value previously selected). Users can also slide further into the right (Fig. 1b), increasing the delay (up to a maximum of 4 s). The process will repeat until the user states that the application is synchronised, or close to it (delay < 1 s).
5. Once the users state that the application is synchronised, the application stops asking them about their experience. Then, a popup appears explaining that from now on they can adjust their experience whenever they wish, by clicking on the top-right button that just appeared at that point (Fig. 1d).

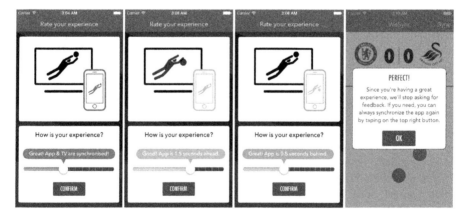

Fig. 1. (a) Iterative process of setting a delay. After setting a 3 s delay in a previous interaction. (b) Second try to set the right delay. (c) Third try to set the right delay. (d) Notification after the application is synchronised.

We designed SMUF by taking into account several facts. First, we assume that the events triggered on the second screen application are always synchronised with their real counterparts occurring on the venue where the live event is taking place. This is not just for the sake of simplicity, but it is a guideline for similar works: live second screen interactions that rely on tight synchronisation will not work correctly if they are not synchronised with the real time of the live action, or at least, the fastest TV broadcast available. If this is not the case (e.g. the human operator triggering the events on the application is watching a delayed TV broadcast), users with a TV broadcast delay lower than the operator's will get the events on the application after they have occurred on the TV broadcast, with no possibility of synchronising them.

Second, we introduced four interaction cues to facilitate the user interaction: the temporal indication, the illustrative animation, the overall colour, and the experience rating. The temporal indication aims at giving precise information on how the TV delay compares with the mobile application events (e.g. "App is 3.0 s ahead"). Some users may not be able to initially identify their exact delay, but they will gradually get closer. The remaining cues are defined according to the temporal indication value. The illustrative animation simulates the situation corresponding to the delay specified by the user, aiming at providing the user with a better perception of his choice: the key events on the mobile device are appearing synchronised with the TV, ahead, or behind it (Figs. 1a, b and c). The animation reproduces the exact temporal indication value selected by the user up to a maximum of 4 s. The use of colours allows the user to immediately recognize the current situation: green for synchronized, red for not synchronised at all and yellow for in-between situations. In order to complement this cue, we also added a popup text describing the experience rate currently selected by the user ("Great!", "Good!", "Fair.", and "Poor..."). The way that values change on both of these interaction cues were based on the work done by Mekuria et al. [9], who studied how viewers are disturbed by different TV delays.

Finally, we did not include any information regarding the live sports event, such as the match time - which could be used to compare the TV broadcast match time with the application match time to synchronise both feeds - since we wanted to have a universal synchronisation mechanism that could be deployed on any broadcast. Thus, considering that it is not certain that a well-defined cue is present on the TV broadcast to help users synchronising their applications, we designed SMUF without relying on any extra information besides the users' feedback regarding their experience.

At this stage, WeSync simulates a soccer match broadcast on a TV, by presenting different videos with several highlights. Running on an iPhone, the application presents a screen with information about the match, while waiting for events to occur. Each highlight video is streamed from the iPhone to an AppleTV connected to a TV.

4 Evaluation

We carried out a user study based on the WeSync prototype in order to evaluate the SMUF's usability and usefulness. The user tests were conducted with 30 voluntary participants (28 male and 2 female) aged 20–36 ($\bar{x} = 23.3$). The tests took place in a room at our University campus. Participants were briefed before each test session.

In each session, participants watched three 7-min highlight videos from Chelsea 4 - 2 Swansea match that took place on September 13, 2014. None of the participants had seen the match before. We edited each video to contain the same number of events. Since several TV providers have different delay values, it was set a different delay (low, medium and high, as random values in the range of 0–2 s, 2–4 s and 4–6 s, respectively) for each highlight video, based on the work by Kooij et al. [5]. A within-subject experimental design was used to evaluate the three delay scenarios and the sequence of videos and delay scenarios was counterbalanced to minimize learning effects. After watching each video, we asked participants to rate two statements in a questionnaire regarding their user experience at the start and at the end of the video. Lastly, at the end of each test session, users were asked to fill in the remainder of the questionnaire. This questionnaire was based on the USE questionnaire and was comprised of nine statements regarding general feedback about the activity, and the SMUF's interaction cues. Users rated these statements by using a five-point Likert-type scale, which ranged from strongly disagree (1) to strongly agree (5). Users were also free to write down any further suggestions and comments. Finally, we also registered all the users' interactions during each test, such as number of times SMUF was accessed, response times, delays set by users, among other important data.

Users accessed SMUF 240 times during the whole evaluation process, averaging 2.677 times per user/scenario ($\sigma = 1.43$), with 1.566 times during the low delay scenario ($\sigma = 0.78$), 2.633 times during the medium delay scenario ($\sigma = 1.16$), and 3.833 times during the high delay scenario ($\sigma = 1.31$). These data show that when the delay is lower users need to perform fewer interactions with SMUF to get the application synchronised with the TV. Since each scenario had 6 events where users could compare the application to the TV broadcast, these results are very positive. Only in high delay scenarios users needed to set a delay more than 3 times on average.

We also analysed the time duration of each user interaction with SMUF. We were interested in finding out if the users' interactions with SMUF got shorter as the number of interactions performed by them increased and they became more familiar with SMUF. In Fig. 2a, we can see that on average, during the first interaction, users took around 7 s to set a delay, but it lowered over time reaching 3.5 s on the sixth interaction (in this case we could only analysed the medium and high delay scenarios, as users did not accessed SMUF more than 4 times during the low scenario). Only on the third interaction the overall response increased, but we did not find any data that could explain these results in an objective manner. Although, we presume that, at the third interaction, users were wondering why the application was still not synchronised with the broadcast, hence the time they took to set a new delay.

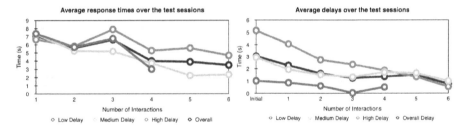

Fig. 2. (a) Average response time for all scenarios. (b) Average delays for all scenarios.

An important topic that we also investigated was the difference between the initial delays of the scenarios and the final delays achieved by the users at the end of the videos. We wanted to analyse which delay values the users were satisfied with, and whether they managed to set the application as synchronised at the end of a video. We verified that on average users ended the low delay scenario, the medium delay scenario, and the high delay scenario with 0.6 s ($\sigma = 0.63$), 1.38 s ($\sigma = 0.70$), and 1.61 s ($\sigma = 0.98$) delays. Overall, the average final delay was 1.20 s ($\sigma = 0.89$). We presume that these values could change slightly if the videos were longer – the delay difference was converging to values near or below 1 s over time as presented on Fig. 2b – as users may still try to do fine adjustments in order to reach a perfect synchronisation (ending up decreasing the average difference). In addition, we found out that on overall, only 23.76 % of users changed the delay after setting the application as synchronised, trying to achieve a perfect synchronisation.

Regarding the questionnaire, results were extremely positive when we analysed the reported user experience at the beginning and at the end of each video. As Table 1 shows, users always had a better experience by the end of the video, after using SMUF.

Table 1. Summary of the questionnaire results regarding the user experience. Low delay in green, medium delay in yellow and high delay in red (higher scores are highlighted).

Statements	Strongly Disagree	Disagree	Neutral	Agree	Strongly Agree
In the beginning, I had a good experience.	0%	3.3%	16.7%	43.3%	36.7%
In the end, I had a good experience.	0%	0%	0%	16.7%	83.3%
In the beginning, I had a good experience.	0%	6.7%	33.3%	40%	20%
In the end, I had a good experience.	0%	3.3%	0%	20%	76.7%
In the beginning, I had a good experience.	0%	36.7%	40%	16.7%	6.7%
In the end, I had a good experience.	0%	0%	6.7%	46.7%	46.7%

The remainder of the questionnaire also showed positive results. In general, participants stated that they liked to use SMUF (56.7 % agreed and 36.7 % strongly agreed) and found it easy to learn (46.7 % agreed and 50 % strongly agreed) and to use (33.3 % agreed and 56.7 % strongly agreed). The majority of the participants disagreed with the statement "I had difficulties to understand how the key events should be synchronised" (40 % strongly disagreed and 26.7 % disagreed). Finally, almost all participants stated that SMUF was useful to synchronise the application with the TV broadcast (46.7 % agreed and 46.7 % strongly agreed). These results give us a lot of confidence in applying SMUF to other kinds of broadcasts.

Next, we evaluated the different interaction cues to ascertain whether they helped the users to synchronise the application with the TV broadcast. Table 2 shows that the temporal indication and the overall colour proved to be very helpful for users to interact with SMUF ($\bar{x} = 4.47$, $\sigma = 0.57$, and $\bar{x} = 4.4$, $\sigma = 0.81$, respectively). Users also rated the illustrative animation and the experience rating as helpful ($\bar{x} = 4.0$, $\sigma = 1.08$, and $\bar{x} = 3.63$, $\sigma = 1.09$), although getting lower scores than the previous ones.

Table 2. Summary of questionnaire results regarding the questions presented at the end of each test session. Higher scores are highlighted.

Statements	Strongly Disagree	Disagree	Neutral	Agree	Strongly Agree
The temporal indication helped to synchronise the application.	0%	0%	3.3%	46.7%	50%
The experience rating helped to synchronise the application.	3.3%	13.3%	23.3%	36.7%	23.3%
The overall colour helped to synchronise the application.	0%	3.3%	10%	30%	56.7%
The illustrative animation helped to synchronise the application.	3.3%	3.3%	26.7%	23.3%	43.3%

Finally, one third of the participants mainly suggested that: the device should vibrate on whistles marking the key events; and it should be possible to access SMUF after making a prediction and while waiting for its outcome, which we agree.

5   Conclusions and Future Work

This paper presents an interaction mechanism called SMUF, which allows developers to quickly add a simple, universal and low-cost synchronisation mechanism to their second screen applications. In order to evaluate SMUF, we implemented a mobile application called WeSync, where users were prompted to synchronise different kinds of events during a soccer broadcast match. The user tests were extremely positive, validating SMUF's design and concept. Overall, participants managed to set a delay near 1 s, making WeSync almost perfectly synchronised with the TV broadcast. One of the most important results was that participants stated that they had a better user experience by using SMUF to synchronise WeSync with the videos.

In the future, we aim to solve the issues reported by the users in order to improve the user experience. We will also study how to prevent cheating during a real second screen competition. Currently, users that set up a delay higher than the real one of a TV broadcast get an advantage in predicting key events, since they see what happens on the TV before interacting on the application (happens both with SMUF and ACR). We hope that by analysing usage patterns we can prevent users from exploiting this flaw.

References

1. Blanco, R., Morales, G.D.F, Silvestri, F.: Towards leveraging closed captions for news retrieval. In: Proceedings of the WWW 2013 Companion, pp. 135–136 (2013)
2. Boronat, F., Lloret, J., García, M.: Multimedia group and inter-stream synchronization techniques: a comparative study. Inf. Syst. **34**, 1 (2009)
3. Centieiro, P., Romão, T., Dias, E.A.: From the lab to the world: studying real-time second screen interaction with live sports. In: ACE 2014, article 14. ACM (2014)

4. Cesar, P., Bulterman, D., Jansen, J., Geerts, D., Knoche, H., Seager, W.: Fragment, tag, enrich, and send: enhancing social sharing of video. J. ACM Trans. Multimedia Comput. Commun. Appl. **5**, 3 (2009)
5. Kooij, W., Stokking, H., Brandenburg, R., Boer, P.: Playout delay of TV signals: measurement system design, validation and results. In: TVX 2014, pp. 23–30. ACM (2014)
6. Nandakumar, A., Murray, J.: Companion apps for long arc TV series: supporting new viewers in complex storyworlds with tightly synchronized context-sensitive annotations. In: TVX 2014, pp. 3–10. ACM (2014)
7. Nielsen: How Second Screens are Transforming TV Viewing. http://bit.ly/1grK4R3
8. MLB Preplay. http://bit.ly/1BKVyUV
9. Mekuria, R., Cesar, P., Bulterman, D.: Digital TV: the effect of delay when watching football. In: EuroITV 2012, pp. 71–74. ACM (2012)
10. Stokking, H.M., van Deventer, M.O., Niamut, O.A., Walraven, F.A., Mekuria, R.N.: IPTV inter-destination synchronization: a network-based approach. In: ICIN 2010, pp. 1–6. IEEE (2010)
11. Viva Ronaldo. http://bit.ly/1LTsplD

UbiBeam: Exploring the Interaction Space for Home Deployed Projector-Camera Systems

Jan Gugenheimer[1]([envelope]), Pascal Knierim[2], Christian Winkler[1], Julian Seifert[3], and Enrico Rukzio[1]

[1] Ulm University, Ulm, Germany
{jan.gugenheimer,christian.winkler,
enrico.rukzio}@uni-ulm.de
[2] University of Stuttgart, Stuttgart, Germany
pascal.knierim@vis.uni-stuttgart.de
[3] European Patent Office, Munich, Germany
julian.seifert@uni-ulm.de

Abstract. Until now, research on projector-camera systems had only concentrated on user-interaction within a lab-environment. As a result of this, there are very limited insights into how such systems could be used in everyday life. It was therefore our aim to investigate requirements and use cases of home deployed projector-camera systems. To this purpose, we conducted an in-situ user study involving 22 diverse households. Several different categories were specified using a grounded theory approach; placement, projection surface, interaction modality and content/use cases. Based on the analysis of our results, we created *UbiBeam*; a projector-camera system designed for domestic use. The system has several different features including automatic focus adjustment with depth sensing which enables ordinary surfaces to be transformed into touch-sensitive information displays. We developed *UbiBeam* as an open source platform and provide construction plans, 3D-models and source code to the community. We encourage researchers to use it as a research platform and conduct more field studies on projector-camera systems.

1 Introduction

Mark Weiser's vision [24] of ubiquitous information being constantly provided to the users is not fully achievable with current technology. Even if smartphones, tablets and public displays are one step in this direction, they still lack the omnipresence and the ability to fully blend into the users environment.

Current research achieves this ubiquity by simulating omnipresent screens using projector-camera systems (e.g. [11, 26, 28–30]). Most of these projects provide valuable insights on either the interaction with the projection or on technical implementations to create more sophisticated technology. These two aspects are widely researched in the field of projector-camera systems, whereas aspects such as real-life use-cases, domestic deployments and in-situ evaluations are rare. However, projects such as IllumiRoom [14] or Lumo [1] show that the insights of home deployment and home use can be of great value for designers of projector-camera systems.

© IFIP International Federation for Information Processing 2015
J. Abascal et al. (Eds.): INTERACT 2015, Part III, LNCS 9298, pp. 350–366, 2015.
DOI: 10.1007/978-3-319-22698-9_23

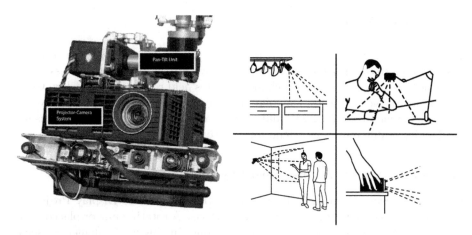

Fig. 1. The UbiBeam system in combination with the envisioned use cases for a home deployable projector-camera system

In this paper, we explore the design space of home deployed projector-camera systems by conducting an in-situ study in the homes of 22 people. Based on our insights, we build UbiBeam (Fig. 1), a small and portable projector-camera system for home deployment. We envision a future where such devices will be sold in hardware stores. They could be available in different form factors, either as a replacement for light bulbs or a simple small box which can be placed in several ways inside the users' environments to be able to blend into the household (Fig. 1). The design of these devices will not only focus on the interaction with the content but also on aspects such as deployment and portability. This work is a first step towards a greater understanding of developing home deployed projector-camera systems for end-users as it provides system and design requirements derived from results from a qualitative in-site user study.

The main contribution of this paper is a qualitative research in-situ study of domestically deployable projector-camera systems conducted by visiting 22 households with the aim of identifying design opportunities and use cases. Four main categories (*Projector-Camera Placement, Projection Surface, Interaction Modality, Projected Content/Use Case*) were identified. Based on these insights, *UbiBeam* a steerable and stand-alone projector-camera system for domestic use was designed and implemented to be able to conduct further research by deploying *UbiBeam* and collecting real usage data.

The rest of this paper is organized as follows. First, we present related work and prior research on projector-camera systems. We then report and discuss the findings on our exploratory field study. Subsequently, we illustrate how these findings can be implemented inside a projector-camera system and present our prototype *UbiBeam*. Finally we discuss our results and show future research directions.

2   Related Work

Previous related work can be categorized as follows: *mobile projector-camera systems* and *stationary projector-camera systems*. In addition we discuss work on projector-camera systems which incorporates field research approaches. General trends of pico-projectors/mobile projectors have been discussed in several overview papers, e.g. [7,12,23], and showed a promising future and increasing availability of different devices and form factors.

2.1   Stationary Projector-Camera Systems

In an earlier work, Pinhanez [19] presented the Everywhere Display Projector which can project onto several predefined surfaces. A rotating mirror placed over the projector enables a movable projection cone. In this work, challenges such as distortion, focus and obstruction were introduced and addressed.

Raskar et al. presented several concepts on geometric aware projector-camera systems for non-planar surfaces [20,22]. In a later work, Raskar et al. presented their vision of the Office of the Future. Here, they used projector-camera systems to create a spatially immersive display [21]. In more recent work, Wilson et al. focused on touch interaction with projected interfaces using a depth camera [27,28]. Furthermore, Wilson et al. introduced Beamatron, a steerable projector-camera system which uses computational techniques to capture the whole geometry of the room and superimpose graphics all over the room in real time [26]. Such steerable projector-camera systems were also researched by Butz. et al. [3] and Cauchard et al. [5]. Both showed different implementations for either a mobile or a stationary steerable projector system.

Linder and Maes introduced LuminAR, a projected augmented reality interface, which dynamically augments objects and surfaces with digital information [16]. LuminAR consists of a pico-projector, a camera and a wireless computer in a compact form factor embedded in a design similar to a desk lamp. However, Luminar is implemented as a stationary lamp which does not support portability and ad-hoc mounting. The MirageTable by Benko et al. [2] presented a setup which used a projector-camera system above a curved display which was designed to merge real and virtual worlds. The depth camera tracks the user's eyes and enables perspective stereoscopic 3D visualization to a single user.

This representative selection of prior work illustrates the lab driven research currently conducted with projector-camera systems. In this work, we draw the focus beyond the scope of instrumented lab environments and investigate possibilities for applications of projector-camera systems in-situ in potential users' homes.

2.2   Mobile Projector-Camera Systems

In contrast to stationary setups, mobile projector-camera systems face a new variety of challenges due to their mobility factor. An early work by Karitsuka and Sato [15] presented the concept of a wearable projector which created a permanent interactive display for the user on the go. Mistry and Maes (SixthSense) advanced this concept by adding gestural interaction and context-awareness. SixthSense, a portable system consisting of a projector, a camera and colored markers [17]. SixthSense enabled gestural interaction with the physical world by augmenting different objects. In OmniTouch [11], Harrison et al. mounted a projector-camera system onto the shoulder and in doing so enabled multi-touch on planar surfaces. Molyneaux et al. [18] enhanced this by enabling touch on arbitrarily shaped surfaces and also offering geometrically correct projections. Winkler et al. [29] presented AMP-D, a similar setup to OmniTouch. However AMP-D includes also the floor in front of the user as a projection display. Hence, users can transition between using a private display (hand) and public display (floor). Some research was conducted on mobile projectors which are not mounted but held by the user. Willis et al. [25] and Cao et al. [4] presented solutions on what an interaction between several mobile devices could look like.

Our work focuses on form factors which are in-between stationary and mobile projector-camera systems. We have envisioned a device which is portable but which can also be easily mounted inside a room to create a stationary interaction space.

2.3   Field Research for Projector-Camera Systems

The previously discussed work focused on either the implementation of projector-camera systems or the evaluation of individual interaction techniques. To our knowledge no exploratory study on the deployment and use of projector-camera systems in domestic environments has ever been conducted. Huber et al. conducted in LightBeam [13] a qualitative study with several researchers working on interaction techniques using a pico projector. However, the participants were all HCI researchers and were used to help explore the interaction technique. Hardy et al. [9] conducted a self experiment by using an interactive desk for one year and reported their experience. Hardy provides valuable insight into the long-term use of a projector-camera system in the work space, however a larger sample of data is still missing. WorldKit, a first step towards the deployment of projector-camera systems was made by Xiao et al. [30]. WorldKit offers similar to UbiDisplays [10] a simple framework to create quick interactive surfaces with a projector-camera system. However, the setup presented is still big and bulky and would be hard to deploy in several homes of participants. The main difference of our work is the approach of visiting users in their home environment and exploring home deployment and home usage of projector-camera systems. We based our work on the implementation and insights conducted by Gugenheimer et al. [8]. This work extends the previous by giving a deeper understanding of the design space for home deployed projector-camera systems. The study procedure and methodology is explained in full detail and the results are set in contrast to requirements for home deployed projector-camera systems. These requirements were used to build and implement *UbiBeam* which shows an example of how to implement those requirements in future projector-camera systems.

3   Design Process

In order to gain a comprehensive understanding of the requirements of home deployed projector-camera systems, we designed and conducted an exploratory field study.

3.1   Study Design

For the purpose of data analysis, we visited 22 different households and conducted semi-structured interviews. We decided to interview participants in their homes for several reasons. On the one hand, it created a familiar environment for the participant which led to a pleasant atmosphere. Furthermore, the participants were aware of whole arrangement of the rooms and could therefore provide a detailed insight into categories such as the placement of the projector-camera system and display spaces. This also allowed us to have a variety of rooms in which the participants could set up different scenarios. The rooms we covered in our study are: the living room, bedroom, bathroom, working room, kitchen and corridor.

We recruited 22 participants (10 female, 12 male) between 22 and 58 years of age (M= 29). The apartment sizes measured between 27 and 104 square meters (M= 71.68) and consisted of 1 to 4 rooms (M= 2.86). By conducting the semi-structured interview for every room, we collected 92 samples. Most participants did not live alone and shared a flat with 1 to 4 other people (M= 2.14). The majority of the participants were students with a technical background. The participants received 8 Currency as a reward.

Before the interview started the participants were introduced to the study and also received a brief introduction into ubiquitous computing and everywhere displays. The participants were all equipped with a mock up (Fig. 2) which consisted of an APITEK Pocket Cinema V60 projector placed inside a cardboard box which was mounted onto a flexible camera stand. This allowed participants to attach the mock up to almost all surfaces. The cardboard box provided illustrations of non functional input and output possibilities such as a touchpad, several buttons, a display and a depth camera. The purpose of this low-fidelity mock up was to inspire creativity in the participant's handling of the device.

The interviews were structured into three parts. First, each room of the participants home was inspected. Each participant was asked questions about how they would use the projector-camera system. Furthermore, they were asked to build a potential set-up using the mock up. There were several pre-designed non-interactive widget examples stored on the projector (watching a movie, social media, weather, cooking etc.). To avoid biasing the participants the widgets were only revealed when a participant mentioned them in their individual set-up. The second part consisted of a questionnaire about the general requirements

Fig. 2. Mock-up consisting of a projector inside a cardboard box mounted on a flexible camera stand

for a projector-camera system. The last part was a demographic questionnaire including data on the apartment. The whole process took around one hour. Even though this study was not conducted using a real projector-camera system, we argue that this resulted in more creative solutions and responses, since an actual system would have limited the participants due to the technical implementation. For this reason we intentionally used a low fidelity mock-up.

A grounded theory approach was chosen for the analysis of the data [6]. To gather the aforementioned data, we conducted semi-structured interviews with the participants and made notes, pictures and video recordings of many sessions. Two of the authors coded the data using a selective, open and axial coding approach. The initial research question was: *"How would people use a small and easy deployable projector-camera system in their daily lives? When and how would they interact with such a device, and how would they integrate it into their home?"*.

During the process we discovered that the four main categories the participants were focusing on when they handled the projector-camera system were:

Projector-Camera System placement. Where was the projector-camera system mounted inside the room? Was it placed so the participant can reach the projection or the projector-camera system? How was the projector-camera system placed: Standing on a flat surface or mounted around an object?

Projection surface. What projection surfaces did the participant choose? Was the projection horizontal (table) or vertical (wall) and how was the orientation of projector-camera system and projection surface?

Interaction modalities. What modalities were used for the input and why?

Projected Content/Use Cases. What content did the participant want to project for each specific room and which use cases were important to them?

The following subsections present the findings of our study. The numbers in brackets indicate the number of participants who performed a specific action in a particular room. We start the results with the use cases, since the other categories were mostly influenced by the content created. The placement and the projection surface both also highly influenced the interaction modalities.

3.2   Content and Use Cases

The exact use cases varied since the participants each referred to different rooms. In spite of this variation, larger concepts were able to be found in the set-ups created by the participants: *information widgets* and *entertainment widgets*.

Information Widgets. We consider information widgets as use cases in which the participant almost only wants to aggregate data. This use case was mostly mentioned in the kitchen and the corridor. These places can mostly be seen as utilitarian rooms where someone would not spend a significant amount of their free time. These rooms also usually do not offer any seating possibilities for a longer amount of time. The most common use case in the kitchen was to project *recipe* information while cooking (16). Further suggestions were *shopping lists* and *notes*. In the corridor the most frequent use cases were a *bus schedule* (5), a *calender* and a *weather forecast*. The main suggestions for the working room was an *extension of the monitor* (3). When observing these suggestions, it can be claimed that most use cases were used as an aid in finishing a specific task characteristic to the room.

Entertainment Widgets. Entertainment use-cases were mostly created in the living room, bedroom and bathroom. In the living room participants mostly created set-ups for *games* (6) and watching *television* (6). These use cases mostly took advantage of the fact that big spaces such as walls or tables were available. Having such a device, P20 also re-thought the arrangement of his living room since *"the focus does not have to be on the television anymore"*. In the bathroom several participants mentioned the boredom they experience during some tasks such as taking a shower (P7, P19), sitting on the toilet (P20) or cleaning (P19). Therefore they suggested an accompanying task such as *television* (6) or reading the *news* (5). Several participants (6) had privacy concerns in using a device with a potential camera inside their bathroom and bedroom: *"I don't want a camera where I undress myself"* (P10). For the bedroom participants created similar use cases as the living room. The most cited use cases for the bedroom was the *television* (7). Some participants (P22, P6, P5) suggested to create an *ambient* device which would project specific colors and *"moods"* suited to music. The use of the projector-camera system in these rooms highly differed compared to the kitchen, corridor and working room. Here the focus was on enhancing the free time one spends in these rooms and making the stay more enjoyable.

3.3   Placement of the Projector-Camera System

To avoid the placement of the projector-camera system being biased by the limitation of the projection size (as we expect projectors to provide much larger projections in the near future) we asked the participants to place the system anywhere irrespective of the picture size it created. In a next step the participant showed the size of the projected surface they expected from the device.

Similar to the use cases, the placement can be divided into two higher concepts: placing the device *in reach* and *out of reach*.

In reach. When placing the device either in the bedroom, bathroom or kitchen, the participants always placed the device within reaching distance. In each case the device was mounted either at waist or shoulder height. In the bedroom participants mostly attached the device to *the bed* (5). P20 took the device in their hand when lying in bed to have *"full control"* of it. One reason why participants picked the bed as a location could be that resting and sleeping is the primary purpose of this place. Furthermore, the whole room is in sight from the bed. In the kitchen the device was mostly attached to the *wall* (7) or placed on a *cupboard* (5). The kitchen and bathroom were not considered locations where a device would be permanently mounted. Therefore, participants attached it to locations they could effortlessly remove it from and carry it to a different room. In the bathroom the most preferred location was again the *wall* (7).

Out of reach. In the living room, working room and corridor participants preferred a mounting above body height. These were also rooms where participants could imagine a permanent mounting. For this reason the device was placed in a way that it could project on most of the surfaces and was *"not in the way"* (P19). In the living room the preferred location was the *ceiling* (8) and the *wall* (4). The same applied for the corridor where 8 participants tried to mount it to the *ceiling* and 4 to the *wall*. The most used location in the working room was the *ceiling* (3). In these rooms the mounting of the device was not considered an important aspect. It was almost always assumed that *"the device is somewhere where it can reach every surface"* (P22). The focus hereby was more on the projected surfaces.

3.4   Orientation and Type of Surface

To gain an impression as to where the surfaces should be and how they look like, participants removed the projector-camera system from their mounting position and placed it somewhere close by.

The participants almost exclusively chose flat and planar surfaces for each interface. At the beginning of the study each participant was informed that it is technically possible to project onto non-planar surfaces without distortion. In spite of this, only one participant expressed a desire to project onto a couch. Although the remaining participants were aware that they could project onto non-planar without distortion, they explained that they would still prefer to project onto a flat and non-planar surface: *"I prefer flat surfaces even if the projection can be undistorted otherwise"* (P1). Therefore the only meaningful

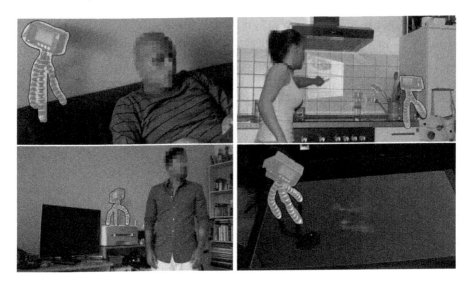

Fig. 3. Users building and explaining their setups (Mock-Up highlighted for better viewability).

classification on projection surfaces consists of a distinction between *horizontal* (e.g. tables) and *vertical* (e.g. walls) display orientation.

In the kitchen, bedroom, working room and living room horizontal and vertical surfaces were used almost equally. However in the corridor and bathroom, vertical surfaces were used more often as a result of the lack of sufficient horizontal surfaces. The most used surface in the bathroom was the *mirror* (4). However, since the projection was not working on the mirror participants projected right next to it. In the corridor almost only vertical surfaces were created either onto the *door* (5) or the wall (2). As already mentioned in the section on use cases, the corridor was used to aid specific tasks that participants commonly undertake there. In this case the situation would be *leaving the apartment*, and when leaving the apartment, seeing the bus schedule and/or weather forecast on the door seemed natural to participants. P10 was the only participant who used the floor as a projection surface to create an interactive rug.

In the living room a popular surface was the *table* (7) in the center of the room. Participants create an interactive tabletop (Fig. 3) and wanted to *"play different kinds of board games"* (P20). Furthermore, participants used the *wall* to create a large television. In the kitchen the *cabinet door* (5), the *table* (5) and the *space between stove and kitchen hood* (5) were used the most. Participants also wanted the interface either to *"follow"* (P21) or project several interfaces on different surfaces. In the bedroom the most used surface was the *wall*. Only two participants used the *ceiling* (P5, P20). The working room mostly used a *desk* (4) or the *wall* (3).

By observing these results, we have concluded that the projection surface was mostly used to support the use-case and was influenced by the room.

3.5   Interaction Modalities

The main interaction modalities participants requested were *speech recognition, touch* or a *remote control*. Other techniques such as *gesture recognition, shadow interaction* or a *laser pointer* were mentioned rarely. The interaction modality was highly influenced by the room and the primary task in there.

Given that cooking is regarded as one of the primary tasks in the kitchen, displaying the recipe would support that primary task. Many of the participants considered using touch as an input method since the projection surface they had chosen was always within their reach. However, most participants opted for a *speech* (11) input since the task of cooking involved using both hands or both hands were often dirty. Nevertheless some participants did choose *touch* (6) or a *remote control* (5) as an input modality. The same reasoning was also given in the bathroom: *"I dont want to touch having wet hands"* (P19). Therefore *speech* (3) was again the preferred input modality. One participant (P21) even mentioned that they *"do not want any input"* and only wanted to consume content.

Looking at the living room where the placement was made out of reach and the focus was on entertainment use cases, participants preferred using a *remote control* (9) or *touch* (5) to interact with the surface: *"I already use a remote control here so I want to control it with the same one"* (P19). However, a mobile phone or a tablet was often named as the remote control. The location of the surface was a big influence on the interaction. If the surface was the table, touch was preferred. If the surface was a wall the remote control was used.

Inside the bedroom, working room and corridor *remote control* and *touch* were named almost equally. Similar to the living room it was dependent on the location of the surface. When the surface was horizontal and close by, the participants preferred *touch*, but when a vertical surface was out of reach the participants preferred a *remote control*. One participant explained that his choices are mostly driven by convenience: *"You see, I am lazy and I don't want to leave my bed to interact with something"* (P22).

3.6   Derived Requirements for Prototype

After analyzing the data from the semi-structured interviews we combined the results with those of the questionnaires and derived several requirements for our prototype of a domestically deployed projector-camera system. Participants always wanted more than only one fixed surface in every room. Considering the *out of reach* placement, we concluded that the projector-camera system must be *steerable* so it can autonomous create different interfaces. The form factor was mostly dictated by the projector used. We analyzed the set-ups of the participants and found out that the distance between the device and surface was between 40 cm and 350 cm (Mdn= 200 cm). The projected surfaces sizes varied from the size of a cupboard door to a whole wall. Therefore, the projector used must be an *ultra-compact DLP* to have a high brightness at the required distance and still have a small form factor. Since participants wanted to carry the device into several rooms and have different use cases the mount must offer a *quick and*

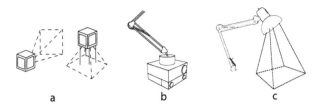

Fig. 4. Different form factors which were considered for the projector-camera system

easy deployment. A last issue which came up several times was the focus of the projector. Participants did not want to adjust the focus every time they deploy the device in a new location. Therefore an *auto focus* must be realized.

After we derived the key requirements for a device, we experimented with several form factors (Fig. 4) which could fulfill the needs of the participants. Firstly, we envisioned a small cube (a) which could be placed on flat surfaces. The two different versions were mounted on a flexible arm (b) or similar to [16] inside a lamp (c). We finally decided to use the rectangular design (b), hanging from an arm with a clamp which can be mounted on several surfaces. This design provided more freedom in terms of movement compared to the lamp approach but could still provide a motorized rotation unlike to the cube.

4   Implementation

4.1   Hardware Architecture

UbiBeam uses the ORDROID-XU as the processing unit which offers a powerful eight-core Single-Board-Computer (SBC). A WiFi-Dongle and a wireless keyboard are also connected to the SBC. The Carmine 1.08 from PrimeSence is used as a depth camera. It offers a wide range advantage for our particular user cases, such as a higher resolution in comparison to smaller Time-of-Flight cameras. Moreover, it is well supported by the OpenNI framework. As for the projector we opted for the ultra-compact LED projector ML550 by OPTOMA (a 550 lumen DLP projector combined with a LED light source). It measures only 105 mm x 106 mm x 39 mm in size and weights 380 g. The projection distance is between 0.55 m and 3.23 m. For the pan and tilt of the system, two HS-785HB servo motors by HiTEC are used. These quarter scale servos offer a torque of 132 Ncm. To be able to provide an auto focus, we attached a SPMSH2040L linear servo to the focusing unit of the projector similar to [29]. To control the actuators, an Arduino Pro Mini is used.

Focus-Adjustment. As *UbiBeam* is required to support quick switching between display positions at various distances, automatic focus adjustment is essential. All available handheld projectors only provide manual focus adjustment as this is sufficient in typical usage scenarios. The only exception, Laser Beam Steering projectors, cannot provide the required luminosity. As for the

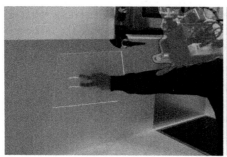

Fig. 5. Touch interaction using the UbiBeam system (UbiBeam is highlighted for better viewability).

Optoma 550ML DLP, its focus is manually adjusted via a small lever. To realise automatic adjustment of the focus, the movement of the lever is controlled with a servo (SPMSH2040L). The servo is glued to the designed servo mount. To determine the required position of the servo for a given distance, a calibration task was conducted which determined a formula which calculates a PWM signal to a particular distance with a maximum error less than 40 μs.

Pan-Tilt Unit. The pan-tilt unit is responsible for moving the depth sensing camera, the projector and the SBC. This allows *UbiBeam* to rotate along two axis and allocate the interactive projection inside this space. Each tilt and pan servo is grounded to a ServoBlocks. A ServoBlocks isolates the lateral load from the servo and increase the load-bearing. The pan servo is mounted overhead. The tilt servos is rotated by 90 degree in a vertical plane.

The final hardware construction measures 10.5 *cm* x 12.2 *cm* x 22.5 *cm* including the pan-tilt unit and weighs 996 *g* (Fig. 1). To be able to easily mount the device to a variety of surfaces we adjusted it to a Manfrotto Magic Arm. The hardware components can be bought and assembled for less than 1000 USD.

4.2 Software Implementation

Building a stand-alone projector-camera system requires a lightweight and resource saving software. We decided to use Ubuntu 12.04 on the ODROID since it also offered the most compatibility with the hardware and software. For reading RGB and depth images, OpenNI version 2.2 for ARM is used. Image processing is done with OpenCV in version 2.4.6. Visualisation of widgets is accomplished with Qt (version 4.8.2), a library for UI development using C++ and QML.

Based on our results from the interaction of the qualitative study (controlling the device by using a remote control or touch interaction), we established interaction with *UbiBeam* by following a simple concept: after running our software the projection turns into a touch sensitive interaction space. The user then creates widgets on this space (e.g. digital image frame, calendar etc.) and interacts with them via touch (Fig. 5). The orientation of the device itself is done with an Android application sending pan and tilt commands. After moving the device to a new space the auto focus and touch detection recalibrates automatically and creates a new interaction space.

Touch Algorithm. The touch detection was implemented based on an algorithm demonstrated in [27]. One of the key characteristics is that touch can be detected on any physical object without user driven calibration tasks. The touch detection developed can be divided into four parts. To begin with, the scenery is analyzed and a spatial image, the ground truth, is generated. The image retrieved is then filtered for noise and used to calculate a binary contact image while touch detection is still running. The contact image is filtered and blob detection is able to specify contact points. In the end contact points are tracked over time and turned into interaction events which in turn trigger events intended by the user. Contact points which have been specified are then classified into different touch events (*touch down, long touch, move, touch release*). The spatial ground truth image is created by a temporal filtering of 30 single depth images. Mapping the specified touch events from the camera coordinate system to the widget is required to enable interaction. Therefore, the touch event point $P(x, y)$ detected in the camera coordinate system is transformed several times until the point is located in the same coordinate systems as the widget. This whole pipeline allows for touch events to be detected on any kind of non-planar surfaces.

Picture Distortion. In order to project distortion free content onto surfaces which are not perpendicular to the device, a pre-warping of the projected content had to be done. A plane detection on the depth map was carried out in accordance with the concepts of Yoo et al. [31]. This helped to find potential projection surfaces. Four points, each situated on one of the detected planes and spanning a rectangle of the desired size were specified. Finally, the perspective projection which transforms the widget to the determined points is calculated and applied to render a corrected representation of the widget.

Developing Widgets. The framework developed enables a dynamic loading of widgets. All the complexity of the spatially aware projection, dynamic touch detection and movement of the projector-camera system are encapsulated and hidden from the view of the widget. This allows for the straight forward development of widgets. Two different possibilities are supported to create a new widget. Developers are able to implement a provided C++ interface to create a widget. Alternatively, developers can implement widgets using Qt User Interface Creation Kit (Qt Quick). It uses QML to describe modern looking, fluid UIs in a declarative manner.

5   Discussion

The in-situ user study revealed that participants preferred *entertainment widgets* for home deployed projector-camera systems. Even if the most mentioned use cases was a solely utilitarian one, the qualitative feedback showed that participants valued the benefit for entertainment more than the benefit a projector-camera system would bring for a certain task. The placement category indicated that each room would have a slightly different requirement and a final system should support mobility but also the ability to be spontaneous mounted to a free space. Therefore the interaction concept should support *in reach* (touch) and *out of reach* (remote control) functionalities. Even though, voice command was often mentioned as an interaction modality it was always combined with very specific use-cases as a cropping technique for touch interaction. The preference for flat surfaces and creating tabletop similar spaces supported the choice of touch as an interaction modality. The implementation of *UbiBeam* shows one feasible example solution for a home deployed projector-camera systems. We hope that researchers will use our description to re-implement a similar device and be able to use it as a research platform to gain insights on home deployed projector-camera systems.

6   Conclusion

With *UbiBeam* we focused on small and deployable camera-projector systems which are designed for domestic use. Albeit a large existing body of previous works on mobile projected interfaces, the requirements of domestic use had been completely neglected so far. These include portability, deployment, the selection of projection surfaces both from an interaction as well as an implementation perspective.

In this work we assessed users requirements for projected interfaces in their own homes and contexts. The presented qualitative study discovered the important categories and their interrelations that a domestically deployed projector-camera system must focus on. An example of such was that users differentiated between basic information aggregation to support a specific in task in a room and entertainment to enhance free time. Both aspects had different requirements for deployment and interaction. We discussed the several dimensions of each category and showed how they influenced each other. Based on these results, we derived requirements (Steerable, Remote Control Interaction, Touch Input Interaction, Fast Deployment, Auto Focus) for a first prototype, and explored different form factors.

The design of the *UbiBeam* prototype based on requirements derived from the study led to further insights into technical considerations and constraints. We demonstrated a possible implementation that already sufficiently delivers the required performance and accuracy. Still there is room for improvement, most notably, the size of the system should be further shrunken in the future to simplify handling and portability of the device. With projectors constantly gaining in brightness and first miniature depth cameras shortly to be introduced on the market (e.g. Googles Tango), this size reduction seems to come naturally. With releasing the *UbiBeam* framework open source[1], including a more detailed

---

[1] https://github.com/jangugenheimer/UbiBeam.

building instruction, hardware list, source code and 3D-print models for all parts, we further allow the community to easily rebuild and advance our presented prototype and its applications. We believe that this will help the community to further investigate the domestic deployment of projector-camera systems.

In the future we would like to develop several systems and deploy them in households to collect quantitative data and qualitative feedback over a longer period of time. The design of the system already facilitates running a long term study. This will provide insights into the when, why, and how the system is used.

Acknowledgements. The authors would like to thank all study participants. This work was conducted within the Transregional Collaborative Research Centre SFB/TRR 62 Companion-Technology of Cognitive Technical Systems funded by the German Research Foundation (DFG).

References

1. Lumo interactive projector. http://www.lumoplay.com/. Accessed 18 April 2015
2. Benko, H., Jota, R., Wilson, A.: Miragetable: freehand interaction on a projected augmented reality tabletop. In: Proceedings of the CHI 2012, pp. 199–208. ACM, New York, NY, USA (2012)
3. Butz, A., Krger, A., Peepholes, A., Lenses, M.: A generalized peephole metaphor for augmented reality and instrumented environments. In: Workshop on Software Technology for Augmented Reality Systems (2003)
4. Cao, X., Forlines, C., Balakrishnan, R.: Multi-user interaction using handheld projectors. In: Proceedings of the UIST 2007, pp. 43–52. ACM, New York, NY, USA (2007)
5. Cauchard, J., Fraser, M., Han, T., Subramanian, S.: Steerable projection: exploring alignment in interactive mobile displays. Pers. Ubiquit. Comput. **16**(1), 27–37 (2012)
6. Corbin, J., Strauss, A.: Basics of Qualitative Research: Techniques and Procedures for Developing Grounded Theory. Sage, New York (2008)
7. Dachselt, R., Häkkilä, J., Jones, M., Löchtefeld, M., Rohs, M., Rukzio, E.: Pico projectors: firefly or bright future? Interactions **19**(2), 24–29 (2012)
8. Gugenheimer, J., Knierim, P., Seifert, J., Rukzio, E.: Ubibeam: an interactive projector-camera system for domestic deployment. In: Proceedings of the ITS 2014, pp. 305–310. ACM, New York, NY, USA (2014)
9. Hardy, J.: Reflections: a year spent with an interactive desk. Interactions **19**(6), 56–61 (2012)
10. Hardy, J., Ellis, C., Alexander, J., Davies, N.: Ubi displays: a toolkit for the rapid creation of interactive projected displays. In: The International Symposium on Pervasive Displays (2013)
11. Harrison, C., Benko, H., Wilson, A.D.: Omnitouch: wearable multitouch interaction everywhere. In: Proceedings of the UIST 2011, pp. 441–450. ACM, New York, NY, USA (2011)
12. Huber, J.: A research overview of mobile projected user interfaces. Informatik-Spektrum **37**(5), 464–473 (2014)
13. Huber, J., Steimle, J., Liao, C., Liu, Q., Mühlhäuser, M.: Lightbeam: interacting with augmented real-world objects in pico projections. In: Proceedings of the MUM 2012, pp. 16:1–16:10. ACM, New York, NY, USA (2012)

14. Jones, B.R., Benko, H., Ofek, E., Wilson, A.D.: Illumiroom: peripheral projected illusions for interactive experiences. In: Proceedings of the SIGCHI Conference on Human Factors in Computing Systems, CHI 2013, pp. 869–878. ACM, New York, NY, USA (2013)

15. Karitsuka, T., Sato, K.: A wearable mixed reality with an on-board projector. In: Proceedings of the 2nd IEEE/ACM International Symposium on Mixed and Augmented Reality, ISMAR 2003, pp. 321– 322. IEEE Computer Society, Washington, DC, USA (2003)

16. Linder, N., Maes, P.: Luminar: portable robotic augmented reality interface design and prototype. In: Adjunct Proceedings of the UIST 2010, pp. 395–396. ACM, New York, NY, USA (2010)

17. Mistry, P., Maes, P.: Sixthsense: a wearable gestural interface. In: ACM SIG-GRAPH ASIA 2009 Sketches, SIGGRAPH ASIA 2009, pp. 11:1–11:1. ACM, New York, NY, USA (2009)

18. Molyneaux, D., Izadi, S., Kim, D., Hilliges, O., Hodges, S., Cao, X., Butler, A., Gellersen, H.: Interactive environment-aware handheld projectors for pervasive computing spaces. In: Kay, J., Lukowicz, P., Tokuda, H., Olivier, P., Krüger, A. (eds.) Pervasive 2012. LNCS, vol. 7319, pp. 197–215. Springer, Heidelberg (2012)

19. Pinhanez, C.: The everywhere displays projector: a device to create ubiquitous graphical interfaces. In: Abowd, G.D., Brumitt, B., Shafer, S. (eds.) UbiComp 2001. LNCS, vol. 2201, pp. 315–331. Springer, Heidelberg (2001)

20. Raskar, R., Brown, M.S., Yang, R., Chen, W.-C., Welch, G., Towles, H., Seales, B., Fuchs, H.: Multi-projector displays using camera-based registration. In: Proceedings of the VIS 1999, pp. 161–168. IEEE Computer Society Press, Los Alamitos, CA, USA (1999)

21. Raskar, R., van Baar, J., Beardsley, P., Willwacher, T., Rao, S., Forlines, C.: iLamps: geometrically aware and self-configuring projectors. In: ACM SIGGRAPH 2003 Papers, pp. 809–818. ACM, New York, NY, USA (2003)

22. Raskar, R., Welch, G., Cutts, M., Lake, A., Stesin, L., Fuchs, H.: The office of the future: a unified approach to image-based modeling and spatially immersive displays. In: Proceedings of the SIGGRAPH 1998, pp. 179–188. ACM, New York, NY, USA (1998)

23. Rukzio, E., Holleis, P., Gellersen, H.: Personal projectors for pervasive computing. IEEE Pervasive Comput. 11(2), 30–37 (2012)

24. Weiser, M.: The computer for the 21st Century. In: Baecker, R.M., Grudin, J., Buxton, W.A.S., Greenberg, S. (eds.) Human-Computer Interaction, pp. 933–940. Morgan Kaufmann Publishers Inc., San Francisco (1995)

25. Willis, K.D., Poupyrev, I., Hudson, S.E., Mahler, M.: Sidebyside: ad-hoc multi-user interaction with handheld projectors. In: Proceedings of the UIST 2011, pp. 431–440. ACM, New York, NY, USA (2011)

26. Wilson, A., Benko, H., Izadi, S., Hilliges, O.: Steerable augmented reality with the beamatron. In: Proceedings of the UIST 2012, pp. 413–422. ACM, New York, NY, USA (2012)

27. Wilson, A.D.: Using a depth camera as a touch sensor. In: Proceedings of the ITS 2010, pp. 69–72. ACM, New York, NY, USA (2010)

28. Wilson, A.D., Benko, H.: Combining multiple depth cameras and projectors for interactions on, above and between surfaces. In: Proceedings of the UIST 2010, pp. 273–282. ACM, New York, NY, USA (2010)

29. Winkler, C., Seifert, J., Dobbelstein, D., Rukzio, E.: Pervasive information through constant personal projection: the ambient mobile pervasive display (amp-d). In: Proceedings of the CHI 2014, pp. 4117–4126. ACM, New York, NY, USA (2014)

30. Xiao, R., Harrison, C., Hudson, S.E.: Worldkit: rapid and easy creation of ad-hoc interactive applications on everyday surfaces. In: Proceedings of the CHI 2013, pp. 879–888. ACM, New York, NY, USA (2013)
31. Yoo, H.W., Kim, W.H., Park, J.W., Lee, W.H., Chung, M.J.: Real-time plane detection based on depth map from kinect. In: Proceedings of ISR 2013, pp. 1–4, October 2013

Cue Now, Reflect Later: A Study of Delayed Reflection of Diary Events

Ming Ki Chong[1($\boxtimes$)], Jon Whittle[1], Umar Rashid[2],
and Chee Siang Ang[2]

[1] School of Computing and Communications, InfoLab21, Lancaster University,
Lancaster LA1 4WA, UK
mingki@acm.org, j.n.whittle@lancaster.ac.uk
[2] School of Engineering and Digital Arts, Jennison Building, University of Kent,
Canterbury CT2 7NT, UK
{U.R.Mir, C.S.Ang}@kent.ac.uk

Abstract. Diary studies require participants to record entries at the moment of events, but the process often distracts the participants and disrupts the flow of the events. In this work, we explore the notion of *delayed reflection* for diary studies. Users quickly denote cues of diary events and only reflect on the cues later when they are not busy. To minimize disruptions, we employed a squeeze gesture that is swift and discreet for denoting cues. We investigated the feasibility of delayed reflection and compared it against a conventional digital diary that requires users to reflect immediately at the time of entry. In a weeklong field study, we asked participants to record their daily experiences with both types of diaries. Our results show that users' preference is context-dependent. Delayed reflection is favored for use in contexts when interruptions are deemed inappropriate (e.g. in meetings or lectures) or when the users are mobile (e.g. walking). In contrast, the users prefer immediate reflection when they are alone, such as during leisure and downtime.

Keywords: Diary study · Delayed reflection · SqueezeDiary

1 Introduction

Field studies that require the full-time presence of researchers are impractical to conduct. Researchers have therefore adopted the diary method as an alternative for recording everyday behaviors of participants [11]. The method relies on participants to capture events in situ as they happen, so it requires no researcher presence and the participants provide first-hand self-reporting of their experience. Two types of diary studies exist [2]: *feedback* studies where participants answer predefined questions about events, and *elicitation* studies where participants capture media that are used as prompts for discussion in interviews.

Feedback studies enable researchers to capture immediate answers from participants. For example, in a study of understanding task switching and interruptions in the work place, Czerwinski et al. [5] asked participants to reflect while they were working. This form of immediate reflection provides the benefit that diary data is not influenced

© IFIP International Federation for Information Processing 2015
J. Abascal et al. (Eds.): INTERACT 2015, Part III, LNCS 9298, pp. 367–375, 2015.
DOI: 10.1007/978-3-319-22698-9_24

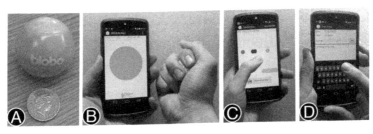

Fig. 1. Interaction of the delayed reflection diary used in our study. (A) The squeeze sensor. (B) Squeeze to record a cue. (C) Review recorded event cues. (D) Diary entry. (Source: [3])

by memory decay. However, the immediate reflection distracts participants from carrying out their main task [2].

In elicitation studies, interviews are conducted at the end of the study. Detailed infor-mation may therefore be lost due to prolonged delay, and participants' emotional responses may change over a period of time [8]. To help participants recon-struct their memories, researchers have investigated the role of different media (e.g. photographs, audio recordings, location information, and tangible artifacts) in diary studies [2] and have used lifelogging tools to support recall and reflection [6, 9, 12].

Researchers have proposed an alternative elicitation method for conducting diary studies on mobile phones [1]. The intention is to lower users' burden by allowing them to only capture "snippets of information" via text (SMS), voicemail or pictures (MMS). The users then explicitly upload the snippets onto a server for revisiting later. The snippets serve as prompts for users to complete full diary entries at a later, more convenient time. We embrace this notion of *delayed reflection*: events are first triggered and stored as cues, and reflection is carried out during users' downtime.

We adopted *SqueezeDiary*, a delayed reflection diary tool that uses squeeze ges-tures for triggering event cues [3, 4]. The application has several advantages. Squeeze is simple and quick to perform. The small form factor of the tactile sensor (see Fig. 1) enables users to squeeze it swiftly without the need for accessing the smartphone. Data is stored locally, so the system requires no explicit upload-ing of information.

In this paper, we present a comparative study between delayed reflection for elicitation and a conventional digital text diary that requires immediate feedback from users. We first present the implementation of the two diaries, and then report on our weeklong deployment of the diaries. The results reveal that users' preference in the type of diary is context-dependent. Participants reported that they would prefer to use delayed reflection for recording events when they are mobile (e.g. walking), in a social event (e.g. meeting with colleagues), or in a restricted context (e.g. attending a lecture). However, the participants would prefer to use the conventional text diary during their leisure and downtime. In this case, they can reflect and enter diary entries straightaway, so the process of triggering an event instance before entering a diary description becomes unnecessary.

Fig. 2. Screenshots of SqueezeDiary, an implementation of delayed reflection.

Fig. 3. Screenshots of text diary, an implementation of immediate reflection.

2 Diary Applications

To learn the differences between immediate reflection versus delayed reflection, we studied the use of two digital diaries: a conventional digital text diary for immediate feedback and a delayed reflection diary. Both applications are designed for recording life events/experiences that users want to keep a record of. We implemented and tested our prototypes on Nexus 4/5 smartphones running Android version 4.4.2.

We adopted SqueezeDiary [3, 4] as an application for delayed reflection (see Fig. 2). A user first squeezes a sensor to trigger the system to record an event instance, and the user later enters a description for the event retrospectively. The application uses a small tactile ball as a squeezable user interface, and it interfaces with the smartphone through Bluetooth. The sensor device can be carried in a pocket, and users can squeeze it easily when needed, without accessing their smartphone. A user triggers an event instance by simply squeezing the sensor for two seconds, and the system automatically logs the location, the timestamp and the pressure levels. Our application provides visualizations of the recorded events on a timeline (2B) and on a map (2C). The application initially provides a graphical visualization of squeeze pressure, but we abandon it as a pre-study revealed that the pressure visualization provides no help for users to recall detail memory events. The application included an interface for users to add retrospective descriptions for their recorded events (2D), and a calendar interface for selecting recorded diary entries (2E).

For immediate reflection, users provide a textual description when they add a diary entry. We implemented a simplified diary application that has only two UI options (see Fig. 3). One option is for adding a new diary entry that automatically includes GPS location and timestamp (3B). The information serves as temporal and location cues to help the users to reconstruct their episodic memory [6, 9]. The second UI option allows users to revisit and update their records (3C).

3   Diary Study

We conducted a weeklong field trial to compare the two diaries. We recruited 8 participants (3F), aged between 19 and 27 ($M = 22.25$, $SD = 3.20$). The participants were students at our institutions, from a variety of academic disciplines. They all owned a smartphone (either Android or iPhone) and self-rated as proficient smartphone users.

In the briefing we demonstrated the operations of both diary applications and also asked the participants to practice using the applications by recording sample diary entries. We explained to the participants that their task was to record instances of when they realized that they were not focusing or struggling to concentrate on their current task; for example, doing one thing but thinking about another. We selected this task because our target domains are well-being related applications, and the problem of 'doing one thing but thinking about another' is one representative of such applications. At the end of the briefing session, we gave the devices to the participants and instructed them to start recording on the next day. We also provided demonstration videos in case the participants encountered problems with using the diaries.

The recording lasted for six days. The study followed a within-group study design; half of the participants started with the squeeze diary and then switched to the text diary after recording for three days, and vice versa for the other half. During the recording period, the participants used the diary for the entire day; they started recording from the point they awoke until they retired in the evening. We instructed the participants to record instances only during weekdays when they were usually busy. To keep the participants engaged with the study, we sent an email reminder every evening [10].

After recording for six days, we invited the participants back for exit interviews; each session lasted for approximately 30 min. We used the diary entries to prompt the participants on how they used the diary applications; we also elicited qualitative feedback, as well as suggestions for improvement.

4   Results

In total, our participants recorded 120 delayed-reflection diary entries ($M = 15$, $SD = 10.70$, $Mdn = 11.5$) and 84 immediate-reflection diary entries ($M = 10.5$, $SD = 6.65$, $Mdn = 9.5$). A Wilcoxon Signed-Rank Test did not reveal a significant difference in the number of entries between the two diaries ($N(8)$, $Z = -1.47$, $p > 0.05$). Two members of our research team analyzed the collected data independently.

4.1   Reflection: Immediate vs. Delayed

We observed two types of users. One type of users found it easier to perform delayed reflection, as it allows them to continue with their primary task with minimum disruption. These users enjoyed the freedom of entering diary entries *"at [their] own pace"*. Some participants mentioned that they occasionally found it *"challenging to reflect"* on an event if it was recorded after a lengthy period or if they had a busy day. For example, there was a day that a participant was busy for four consecutive hours (attending lectures and meetings), and she had squeezed the sensor several times. During her delayed reflection, a cluster of events was shown on the timeline which confused her. She clarified by examining the locations of the events, which helped her to differentiate whether she was in a lecture or in a meeting. Our participants described that seeing a cluster of events on a timeline made them realize how much they struggled to concentrate in specific events (e.g. attending *"a boring lecture"*).

The second type of users that we observed preferred immediate reflection. These users could *"only remember the gist"* but forget the details quickly if the description was not recorded straightaway. One participant who had several part-time jobs mentioned that on a busy day he had to multitask frequently, so memories could overlap and detailed information could become vague if he did not record it immediately.

Our participants mentioned that when using the SqueezeDiary, they wrote a description immediately after they squeezed the sensor during their leisure, such as relaxing at home in the evening. In contrast, one participant used the mobile text diary for delayed reflection. He explained that he often switched his thoughts when he was changing venues between lectures, so he would not have enough time to reflect immediately and enter a description while in transit. He instead first started a diary entry with empty content, and then entered a detailed description later using the update feature.

4.2   Context Preferences

The participants preferred to use delayed reflection diary during busy working hours and in situations where using a phone was forbidden or considered inappropriate. The participants considered short notifications as acceptable (e.g. short vibrations or audio alerts on the phone for when an event cue is recorded), as it is similar to *"receiving a text"* message. However, taking out a phone and entering text would be deemed socially impolite (e.g. *"rude to enter text in front of friends"*) or inappropriate during classes and lectures. The participants reported that they usually reflect on recorded events during their breaks (e.g. long breaks between lectures or lunchtime) and in the evening.

The participants also reported that they prefer to perform immediate reflection during their leisure or downtime (e.g. resting at home), when they were not bounded by work or duties, which gave them opportunities to self-reflect. The participants also mentioned that they preferred to write diaries when they were alone, as this eliminates distractions and social awkwardness. Some participants mentioned that if they were not busy it is more convenient to "just enter diaries", without needing to first squeeze a sensor to cue an event.

Overall, our participants disliked writing diary entries when they were moving. We learned that delayed reflection is good for recording instance of events during users' busy periods, while immediate reflection is suitable for leisure situations, as the action of first cueing an event before recording a description becomes unnecessary.

4.3   Visualization

Our participants explained that the act of squeezing prompted them to consciously remember particular thoughts, and later seeing the cues of the recorded events helped them to recall those thoughts. Visualizing the cues on a timeline and on a map helped the participants to disambiguate events. They did this by correlating their daily schedules with the visualizations.

4.4   User Feedback

We also elicited general feedback on usability, alternative uses, and suggestions for improvement. One participant said that he kept the tactile squeeze ball in his trousers pocket. The "*bulginess*" reminded him to squeeze for an event. This indicates that the physicality of the sensor can act as a reminder for users to record events.

The participants reported several issues of SqueezeDiary. On several occasions users could not record due to unstable Bluetooth connection between the sensor and the smartphone. Once a connection was lost, the users needed to reconnect the devices manually. The participants suggested automatic reconnection. Battery life is another issue: leaving the sensor connected could deplete the battery overnight, which required the users to recharge the sensor when they had the opportunity during the next day. The sensor occasionally recorded false data when it was left inside a bag or in a pocket. All of these indicate that the performance of the sensor is very important. Users are sensitive to inaccurate data; false positives or missing data could render the diary ineffective. This could be explained that people use the recorded cues for assisting their recall of memory events, so some information is already embedded in their memory, which makes spotting inconsistency easy.

Suggestions include using the diaries as a reminder for tracking daily tasks. The time and location cues could improve prospective memory [13]. Suggestions for other memory aids include adding pictures and replacing text with voice narration, but some people reported that they do not like to listen to their own voices.

4.5   Post-Study Impact

After completing our study, two participants expressed that by reflecting on their recorded entries, they realized that they needed a better management strategy for multitasking. One participant noticed how much time she spent thinking about her work. Even during her downtime, she was constantly worrying about work. For instance, her diary entries include "*I couldn't sleep… thinking about how much work I need to do*" (recorded at 4:24 am); and "*packing my bags for a weekend away and thinking about whether I should with all my work*". She explained that going through the diaries made her realize that she was consumed by her work and needed a break. Similarly, another participant also reported that seeing her own diaries made her "*realize how stressed out [she was]*".

5 Discussion

From the study we learned that delayed reflection is a suitable method for people to record diaries when they are busy or in situations when they could not reflect immediately. However, there exists a trade-off of detailed information for users' convenience. Detailed information could be lost because people's memory decays due to interference over time, especially when they experience a busy day or reflect after a long period. Our study showed that location and temporal cues helped users disambiguate events; however, other studies have shown that these cues are only inferential, and they are insufficient for reconstruction of finer details [9]. For recalls of detailed memories, media elicitation techniques (e.g. recording visual cues) could be usefully combined. One way for this is to incorporate the diary application with a lifelogging camera (e.g. SenseCam [7]). The event instances could then be synchronized with the camera data to provide rich media information to help the users reflect.

Our study revealed that people have different preferences between immediate and delayed reflection. We were surprised that our participants found novel ways to use our diary applications as the other type of diary (e.g. using the update feature of text diary for delayed reflection). Hence, there is no one method that fits all; designers should consider creating diary applications that allow users to do both types of reflection, and let users decide their preferred usage.

People often reflect while they were traveling, in transit between venues, and in traffic. We should design interfaces that allow people to easily record thoughts when they are on the move. For instance, a participant mentioned that accessing his mobile phone to record a thought while riding a motorbike would be impossible. He would prefer to have sensors embedded into his gloves and use voice for recording descriptions. With the proliferation of wearable devices, we envision that in the near future we could use body-worn devices to detect users' intents to record diary events.

While automated recording devices (e.g. lifelogging cameras) generate overabundance of information, our dairy enables users to choose the moment they want to record, and the users can do it discreetly without comprising privacy.

The gesture for triggering event instances could easily be extended with multiple gestures for new interactions. For example, users can customize a particular gesture for work related entries and another gesture for family related entries, so event annotation could be done at the time of recording. Instead of using a squeeze ball, the system could adopt other devices, like a smartwatch that senses user gesture (e.g. tapping), to record event instances. Also, delayed reflection could be applied beyond the diary study method. The diary application has other use cases. For example, it could be applied as a site-tracking tool for people to keep track of where they have visited. This is particularly convenient for tourists who enjoy exploring new places. They can mark down any interesting places and later use the recorded cues to reflect on their journey.

Finally, our study recruited university students as participants; their daily activities mainly involved attending lectures and societal meetings. It would be beneficial to study whether delayed reflection helps workers (e.g. office employees) to reflect on their busy activities and find ways to improve their work-life balance.

6   Conclusion

This paper presented a weeklong in situ diary study that compared immediate reflection with delayed reflection. Our results show that people's preference is context-dependent. They preferred recording diary entries with delayed reflection during busy hours or when they cannot access their devices to provide a complete diary entry; however, the method became unnecessary during people's leisure when they are relaxed and alone.

Acknowledgement. This work is part of the Digital Brain Switch project and is funded by the EPSRC (EP/K025201/1).

References

1. Brandt, J., Weiss, N., Klemmer, S.R.: Txt 4 l8r: lowering the burden for diary studies under mobile conditions. In: Proceedings of the CHI EA 2007, pp. 2303–2308, ACM (2007)
2. Carter, S., Mankoff, J.: When participants do the capturing: the role of media in diary studies. In: Proceedings of the CHI 2005, pp. 899–908, ACM (2005)
3. Chong, M.K., Whittle, J., Rashid, U., Ang, S.A.: Squeeze the Moment: denoting diary events by squeezing. In: Proceedings of the UbiComp 2014 Adjunct, pp. 219–222, ACM (2014)
4. Chong, M.K., Whittle, J., Rashid, U., Ang, S.A.: SqueezeDiary: using squeeze gesture as triggers of diary events. In: Proceedings of the MobileHCI 2014, pp. 427–429, ACM (2014)
5. Czerwinski, M., Horvitz, E., and Wilhite, S.: A diary study of task switching and interruptions. In: Proceedings of the CHI 2004, pp. 175–182, ACM (2004)
6. Gouveia, R., Karapanos, E.: Footprint tracker: supporting diary studies with lifelogging. In: Proceedings of the CHI 2013, pp. 2921–2930, ACM (2013)
7. Hodges, S., Williams, L., Berry, E., Izadi, S., Srinivasan, J., Butler, A., Smyth, G., Kapur, N., Wood, K.: Sensecam: a retrospective memory aid. In: Dourish, P., Friday, A. (eds.) UbiComp 2006. LNCS, vol. 4206, pp. 177–193. Springer, Heidelberg (2006)
8. Isaacs, E., Konrad, A., Walendowski, A., Lennig, T., Hollis, V., Whittaker, S.: Echoes from the past: how technology mediated reflection improves well-being. In: Proceedings of the CHI 2013, pp. 1071–1080, ACM (2013)
9. Kalnikaite, V., Sellen, A., Whittaker, S., Kirk, D.: Now let me see where i was: under-standing how lifelogs mediate memory. In: Proceedings of the CHI 2010, pp. 2045–2054, ACM (2010)
10. Palen, L., and Salzman, M.: Voice-mail diary studies for naturalistic data capture under mobile conditions. In: Proceedings of the CSCW 2002, pp. 87–95, ACM (2002)
11. Rieman, J.: The diary study: A workplace-oriented research tool to guide laboratory efforts. In: INTERCHI 1993, pp. 321–326, ACM (1993)

12. Sellen, A.J., Fogg, A., Aitken, M., Hodges, S., Rother, C., Wood, K.: Do life-logging technologies support memory for the past?: an experimental study using sensecam. In: Proceedings of the CHI 2007, pp. 81–90, ACM (2007)
13. Sellen, A.J., Louie, G., Harris, J.E., Wilkins, A.J.: What brings intentions to mind? an in situ study of prospective memory. Memory 5(4), 483–507 (1997)

Tick that Box: Interactive Paper Documents

Yomna Abdelrahman[(✉)], Thomas Kubitza, Katrin Wolf,
Norman Pohl, and Albrecht Schmidt

VIS, Stuttgart University, Stuttgart, Germany
{yomna.abdelrahman,thomas.kubitza,katrin.Wolf,
norman.pohl,albrecht.Schmidt}@vis.uni-stuttgart.de

Abstract. Many documents are still printed on paper and their interaction is disconnected from the digital paper representation. Conductive ink allows to print documents with embedded electrical circuits. We developed several layouts to add interactive elements, such as tick boxes or signature fields, to paper documents. In this paper we propose several techniques to enhance classical paper documents by an additional layer of conductive ink. Through this layer the documents maintain their traditional properties and affordances but receive new interactive capabilities that transform them into smart documents. Attached tiny computing elements enable interaction with the paper, such as sensing selections on a form, detecting a signature, or traditional office equipment (e.g. paperclip). Additionally to the layout suggestions we show different ways how the computing unit can be connected to the document and how multi-page documents can be connected to a single computing unit.

1 Introduction

Printed material and paper documents still play an important role in modern work environments, including offices and fieldwork. People have well understood how to handle paper documents and many organizations have processes in place for distributing paper documents, implementing access control, or destroying copies. Further, the pen usage for annotating document is found to be the most direct, flexible and intuitive way [1]. At the same time we are more and more used to digital documents that offer a variety of functions. Hence, paperless dealing with information is highly unlikely, in our approach we investigate smart documents that use conductive ink and a computing component to reduce the gap between physical documents and digital functionality. The prototypes of smart documents we present in this paper can detect different physical interactions. Examples of these interactions are filling form elements with different pens, tearing up paper, punching holes, and stapling pages. Additionally, mechanisms for physical bookmarking and for detecting annotations are investigated. Detection of these interactions with physical documents offers means to active and responsive documents, and it allows reflecting these actions in their respective digital representations. The contribution of this paper is a set of mechanisms and layout designs that enable interaction with paper documents based on conductive ink printing.

J. Abascal et al. (Eds.): INTERACT 2015, Part III, LNCS 9298, pp. 376–383, 2015.
DOI: 10.1007/978-3-319-22698-9_25

Fig. 1. Form elements sheet demonstrating 4 mechanisms: crossing out words (a), checkboxes (b, c), signature (d), punch-hole (e), bookmarks (f), text marking (g), and staple (h).

These mechanisms are experimentally evaluated and the layout designs are provided under creative commons license.

2 Related Work

The unlikeliness of paperless office makes it the focus of researches to maintain its affordances yet augment interactivity aspects. In this section we discuss prior work in two different areas aiming to introduce interactivity to paper form using (1) camera based systems and (2) new technologies namely conductive ink to enable printed electronics.

2.1 Interactive Paper Documents

Relevant research with the aim to add and link digital value to paper documents includes work that focuses on linking the physical and digital world and enhancing the responsiveness of paper and office tools [2–4]. Through embedding cameras onto the pen [5] or above the desktop [6, 7] for capturing pen-paper interaction, or even using scanners [8]. The Anoto pen[1] contains a built-in camera to record what has been written on special paper with a preprinted pattern. Further, this pen is employed by other systems to transfer the physical editing on paper documents to the digital world [9–12]. *CoScribe* utilized it to combine work on digital and printed documents, where they used the digital pen to allow annotating, linking and tagging printed and digital documents as the pen interacts with both the printed documents and pen-sensitive displays [13]. In the *PaperProof* they extended the *iPaper* framework [4]. However, using a camera as the pen paper interaction tracking device introduced interactive aspect to the papers, however it restricted the interaction to a rather limited area in front of the camera.

---

[1] http://www.anoto.com.

2.2   Conductive Ink and Printed Electronics

Recently, different forms of conductive ink (paint, pens, and printers) became commercially available[2] and electronics can nowadays be homemade. Additionally, the vast enhancement introduced by chemical sintering [14] allowed the fast and easy use of conductive ink for drawing or printing circuits using pens or off-the-shelf inkjet printers [15, 16]. Hodges et al. [17] added interactive elements through stickers. Moreover, printable electronics have been combined with other technology as described in [18] introducing new applications.

3   Smart Printed Paper Forms

Completing a paper form using a pen is generally perceived as very natural interaction. The mechanisms we propose to turn a paper document into a smart document exploit as much as possible conventional forms, shapes, methods, and tools known from common daily routines. Those include shapes and layout known from common document forms (e.g., checkboxes), office tools such as staplers, paper-clips, hole-punchers and stamps, as well as natural interaction such as ripping a document apart.

3.1   Traditional to Digital

Certain traditional forms in paper documents can easily be transferred to conductive circuit layouts. Two examples are checkboxes and signature fields. Figure 1b–c shows two checkbox layouts that are optimized for the use with pencil or pen. Their ground electrode is arranged on the outer side which makes it easy to create multiple stacked checkbox items. The signature field (Fig. 1d) demonstrates a layout which detects whether text was written inside. Most of the layouts introduced rely on the same electrical principle: two electrodes arranged in close distance that are connected when a pencil or conductive pen crosses both, significantly reducing the resistance between them which is then measured by the computing unit. The ground electrode is however shared between all conductive elements. This principle can be also applied to detect crossed out words (Fig. 1a). A pencil is often used instead of a pen if actions (e.g., crossed checkboxes) should be reversible using a rubber. This works as well for removing pencil lines on conductive elements that again increases the resistance between two electrodes. Further, a set of conventional office tools can be involved in the interaction with smart paper documents. We found a stapler to be a surprisingly reliable tool for electrically connecting circuits on multiple pages. Figure 1h depicts a layout which targets the interconnection of circuits on multiple pages. This approach allows placing the computing unit only on one page on which all circuits run together.

---

[2] Bare paint and Circuitworks conductive pen.

Further tools are paper-clips that can be used as temporary selectors, a hole-puncher for setting the archival state of documents. Table 1 provides an overview of traditional mechanisms that can be also used to realize digital functionality.

3.2   Attaching a Computing Unit

We propose multiple mechanisms for electrically connecting a computing unit to a paper document. The connection can be either of permanent or temporal type. A permanent connection can be achieved by following the functionality of a sticker. Practically, this is realized by attaching a computing unit to a document for its whole lifespan for instance by using conductive z-tape [19]. Temporal connections can be realized in different ways:

- Clip: Attaching a clip that uses mechanical pressure for connecting a computing unit (similar to [20]). This can be a tiny paper clip as well as a clip-board with a mechanical spring holder on top.
- Hole-Puncher: Using a hole-puncher with embedded computing for reading out document information. The document information is read out in the moment of punching the paper.
- Stapler: A computing unit on flexible PCB film (such as Seeduino Film) that provides connectors that are stapled onto matching connectors on a paper document.

4   Evaluation

As a proof of concept and to evaluate our mechanisms, we conducted a user study with 12 participants (4 female, 8 male). Each participant filled in a paper form with both, a pencil and a ball-pen including: 3 checkboxes and 3 radio buttons with different gaps between the printed circuit wires sizes (0.2 mm/0.5 mm/1.0 mm), cross out 2 words written in different font sizes (Myriad Pro, bold, 16pt/24pt) and sign with her/his name on a dedicated field. The order of the writing tools was counterbalanced. We additionally asked the participants to staple 10 pages to create a conductive connection among those pages. For evaluating the mechanisms of our layout library, we measured the resistance of the connection created through the pencil/pen. While pencils have been used to draw circuits on common paper they do not work well on photo paper: Only in 15 of 108 cases the pencil created a connection with a resistance smaller than 60 MΩ (M = 38.9 MΩ, SD = 14.5). The multi-page connections created by the stapler were conductive in all 108 cases. All mean resistances using a ball-pen are in a range that can be sensed by a microcontroller. By adding an appropriate resistance (ca. 200 kΩ), a voltage divider can be built for each input mechanism. In this way the checked/signed state can be sensed using digital inputs of common MCUs. The forms used in the study was stored in a normal office environment and the measurements were retaken in 6 months and they were consistent with the previously measured ones, which implies the paper's maintainability.

5 Prototypes

As proof of concept we have created two fully functional prototypes. Each of them implements multiple mechanisms that were introduced in the last sections. Prototype 1 focuses on form elements that can detect pen-based user input on the fly. Prototype 2 demonstrates the detection of text markings, bookmarks and the interconnection of multiple pages.

Table 1. Traditional mechanisms and their mapping to digital functionality

Mechanism	Traditional function	Digital function
Check box	Selecting (multiple) items	Digitally synchronizing the selection
Radio box	Selecting an item from a list of mutually exclusive items	Synchronizing a single item selection
Signature	Assuring the correctness of content provided	Check if the signature is missing
Ripping the document	Destroying the document, making it unreadable	Deleting the digital document/marking as deleted
Paper-clip	Temporally connecting multiple pages	Temporally defining a digital state, e.g. a bookmark
Stapler	Permanently connecting multiple pages	Connecting (circuits on) multiple pages
Punched holes	Enabling to archive paper documents	Archiving the digital document
Rubber	Erasing pencil strokes	Remove electric connection created by a pencil
Crossing out words	Excluding inapplicable items/words	Selecting the non-crossed items
Text marking	Adding markers to text	Adding a marker to the corresponding digital document

5.1 Computing Unit

To measure changes in the resistance of conductive elements and to transfer this information to a host system, a computing unit and power source are required. We used the Blidgets platform that was also developed by the authors in a recent parallel project. A Blidget has the dimensions of $25 \times 25 \times 3$ mm, a weight of 3 g which makes typical handling of a paper document remains mostly unaffected. It allows instant wireless communication with computers and smartphones via Bluetooth Low Energy (LE) and it is remotely configurable. It's tiny and at footprint allows it to be easily connected to a circuit on a sheet of paper using for instance z-tape. We use a small 110mAh LiPo battery to power the device, but any power source between 1.8–4 V is sufficient. Software on a desktop computer equipped with a USB Bluetooth LE dongle allows to instantly monitor the state of all input ports of a Blidget. Those state changes are then mapped to specific actions related to the digital representation of the paper document.

The mapping of a Blidget to a digital representation is configured once through a graphical user interface on the host computer. Afterwards modifications on the paper such as checking a box, signing a field are instantly visualized in the same user interface.

5.2   Form Elements

Our single-page prototype primarily focuses on demonstrating the feasibility of conductive form elements that allow detecting user input through a pen. As depicted in Fig. 1 it is equipped with the Blidget computing unit and fully functional. Figure 1b, c shows two circuit layouts that mimic the visual layout of checkboxes. They are optimized for electrically sensing pen strokes. One computing unit port is needed for each checkbox item as well as the common ground. The distance between the checkbox electrodes in the prototype is 0.2 mm. Another forms element is to cross out items that are not applicable, Fig. 1a two electrodes are alternately connected to the letters of each item. Also, one computing-unit port is required for each element that can be crossed out in addition to the common ground. The signature field (Fig. 1d) is a specific example for a circuit layout that is intended to detect the existence of handwritten text in input fields. It requires one input port of the computing unit. Finally, a mechanism that is not related to user input with a pen is show in Fig. 1e. A simple circuit on the left of the page is intended to detect punch holes. The software on the host computer uses this information to add an "archived" tag to the digital document.

5.3   Text Markings, Bookmarks and Multiple Pages

Research shows that, particularly for reading, paper has inherent advantages over digital documents. To state only some of them, annotating paper documents with a pen is intuitive very flexible, and smoothly integrated with reading. Moreover, paper provides for two-handed interaction and navigation and for creating flexible spatial arrangements. Our second functional prototype demonstrates mechanisms for detecting text markings, setting bookmarks and interconnecting circuits on multiple pages. For detecting text markings we introduce a simple layout that consists of a vertical ground electrode and multiple vertical section electrodes. Here the idea is that a user draws a vertical line to the left and connects the electrodes at the height of the text marking. The resolution depends on the number of used section-electrodes: in our prototype 4 electrodes are used resulting in 4 sections with text markings that can be distinguished. A more advanced circuit layout would be placed within the text area (e.g. multiple rows of electrodes) to detect markings at their original spot. For detecting bookmarks we use a simple paper-clip and an area in the upper right corner. This area consists of two generous electrodes that are electrically connected when a paper clip is attached. In this particular case the traditional functionality of the paper-clip (clipping multiple pages) is ignored and instead it is used as a temporal selector. Conductive pads on the left side and staples are used to electrically connect multiple pages. As depicted in Fig. 1h 11 electrodes allow to detect 1 bookmark and 4 text marking sections per page (2 text pages and 1 page for the computing unit). One electrode is the common ground. With the rising number of pages also rises the amount of connectors needed on the left side. Here one approach is to share the same connectors between pages and introducing a mechanism that only connects the ground electrode of the active page to the computing unit. A mechanism for encoding the page number of the active page is then required as well (e.g. binary encoding).

5.4 Equipment

For the creation of all printed circuit layouts we have used a Brother DCP-J125 printer, Mitsubishi conductiveink (NBSIJ-MU01) and Mitsubishi paper (NBWF- 3GF100) optimized for high conductivity. As ball-pen we used the Mitsubishi Uniball GEL IMPACT UM-153S and for permanently connecting the computing unit to paper we used 3 M electrically vertically conductive adhesive tape 9703.

6 Conclusion and Future Work

We presented a set of mechanisms that allow adding interactivity to paper documents and maintaining their traditional properties and affordances. Our layout library allows an easy reproduction of all used circuit layouts. An evaluation provides insights into the electrical behavior of differently designed input form layouts and the reliability of stapled multi-page connections. Two functional prototypes prove the concept of multiple proposed mechanisms and demonstrate a feasible approach for attaching a computing unit. We envision more advanced layouts and mechanisms to be created. Those could be collected in a software tool that automatically adds the desired interactive elements into documents and generates multi-page layouts as well as connectors for different computing units.

Acknowledgements. The research leading to these results has partly received funding from the European Union Seventh Framework Programme ([FP7/2007-2013]) under grant agreement no 600851 and the German Research Foundation within the SimTech Cluster of Excellence (EXC 310/1).

References

1. Hansen, W.J., Haas, C.: Reading and writing with computers: a framework for explaining differences in performance. Commun. ACM **31**(9), 1080–1089 (1988)
2. Luff, P., Heath, C., Norrie, M., Signer, B., Herdman, P.: Only touching the surface: creating affinities between digital content and paper. In: Proceedings of CSCW, pp. 523–532 (2004)
3. Luff, P., Pitsch, K., Heath, C., Herdman, P., Wood, J.: Swiping paper: the second hand, mundane artifacts, gesture and collaboration. Pers. Ubiquit. Comput. **14**(3), 287–299 (2010)
4. Signer, B.: Fundamental Concepts for Interactive Paper and Cross-Media Information Spaces. ETH, Zurich (2005)

5. Arai, T., Aust, D., Hudson, S.E.: PaperLink: a technique for hyperlinking from real paper to electronic content. In: Proceedings of CHI, pp. 327–334 (1997)
6. Wellner, P.: The DigitalDesk calculator: tangible manipulation on a desk top display. In: Proceedings of UIST, pp. 27–33 (1991)
7. Newman, W., Wellner, P.: A desk supporting computer-based interaction with paper documents. In: Proceedings of CHI, pp. 587–592 (1992)
8. Heiner, J.M., Hudson, S.E., Tanaka, K.: Linking and messaging from real paper in the paper PDA. In: Proceedings of UIST, pp. 179–186 (1999)
9. Tsandilas, T., Letondal, C., Mackay, W.E.: Mus ink: composing music through augmented drawing. In: Proceedings of CHI, pp. 819–828 (2009)
10. Liao, C., Guimbretière, F., Hinckley, K., Hollan, J.: Papiercraft: a gesture-based command system for interactive paper. ACM Trans. Comput. Hum. Interact. (TOCHI) **14**(4), 18 (2008)
11. Guimbretière, F.: Paper augmented digital documents. In: Proceedings of UIST, pp. 51–60 (2003)
12. Winkler, C., Seifert, J., Reinartz, C., Krahmer, P., Rukzio, E.: Penbook: bringing pen + paper interaction to a tablet device to facilitate paper-based workflows in the hospital domain. In: Proceedings of ITS, pp. 283–286 (2013)
13. Steimle, J., Brdiczka, O., Muhlhauser, M.: CoScribe: integrating paper and digital documents for collaborative knowledge work. Learn. Technol. IEEE Trans. **2**(3), 174–188 (2009)
14. Yoshiki, T., Shino, S., Kobayashi, K.: Process for preparing conductive material. Google Patents (2011)
15. Olberding, S., Gong, N.-W., Tiab, J., Paradiso, J.A., Steimle, J.: A cuttable multi-touch sensor. In: Proceedings of UIST, pp. 245–254 (2013)
16. Karagozler, M.E., Poupyrev, I., Fedder, G.K., Suzuki, Y.: Paper generators: harvesting energy from touching, rubbing and sliding. In: Proceedings of UIST, pp. 23–30 (2013)
17. Hodges, S., Villar, N., Chen, N., Chugh, T., Qi, J., Nowacka, D., Kawahara, Y.: Circuit stickers: peel-and-stick construction of interactive electronic prototypes. In: Proceedings of CHI, pp. 1743–1746 (2014)
18. Sarik, J., Butler, A., Scott, J., Hodges, S., Villar, N.: Combining 3D printing and printable electronics
19. Kawahara, Y., Hodges, S., Cook, B.S., Zhang, C., Abowd, G.D.: Instant inkjet circuits: lab-based inkjet printing to support rapid prototyping of UbiComp devices. In: Proceedings of Ubicomp, pp. 363–372 (2013)
20. Decker, C., Beigl, M., Eames, A., Kubach, U.: DigiClip: activating physical documents. In: Proceedings of Distributed Computing System WS, pp. 388–393 (2004)

Towards Deeper Understanding of User Experience with Ubiquitous Computing Systems: Systematic Literature Review and Design Framework

Kaisa Väänänen-Vainio-Mattila[1]([⊠]), Thomas Olsson[1],
and Jonna Häkkilä[2]

[1] Unit of Human-Centered Technology, Tampere University of Technology,
Tampere, Finland
{kaisa.vaananen-vainio-mattila,thomas.olsson}@tut.fi
[2] Faculty of Art and Design, University of Lapland, Rovaniemi, Finland
jonna.hakkila@gmail.com

Abstract. Over the past decades, a plethora of innovative ubiquitous computing (ubicomp) systems have been constructed. The acceptance of the systems, however, depends on how users experience them in real contexts. While many of the ubicomp research projects include some form of user study, there is no overview of how user experience (UX) is approached in ubicomp research. To this end, we conducted a systematic literature review of ubicomp UX studies. Our findings reveal that users'experiences with ubicomp systems have often been investigated in rather lightweight ways, for example by addressing basic usability issues, collecting ratings by simple, predetermined scales, or producing descriptions of general experiences such as fun and trust. Based on the findings we argue that a deeper and more fine-grained understanding of user experience would help developing more successful ubicomp systems. We propose a ubicomp UX framework that can help design and evaluate ubicomp systems with a desirable set of target experiences.

Keywords: User experience · Ubiquitous computing · Literature review · UX design and evaluation framework

1 Introduction

The core principles of ubiquitous computing visions include the omnipresence of computing devices integrated to our everyday environments, smooth interoperability between distributed platforms, and hiding computing in the periphery of human attention [52].

Since the early days of Mark Weiser's vision, ubiquitous computing, or ubicomp, has become one of the dominating technology trends. With increasing numbers of sensor-enhanced everyday objects and infrastructures, such as smart home controls, activity tracking applications and context-sensitive mobile devices, ubicomp systems have already gained initial foothold in our environments. As a field, ubicomp research

© IFIP International Federation for Information Processing 2015
J. Abascal et al. (Eds.): INTERACT 2015, Part III, LNCS 9298, pp. 384–401, 2015.
DOI: 10.1007/978-3-319-22698-9_26

is pushing further to expand the frontiers of current solutions, and seeking ways to fulfill the promise of its visions to the users [1]. The original vision has been developed further, for example to address ubicomp which can actively engage the users in everyday interactions [46].

The promise of ubicomp includes a strong emphasis on end-user's perceptions and experiences. In order to hide the technology and make its use fluent and eventually transparent, incorporating the end-user's perspective is essential in the design of the devices, applications and services [35]. Including user experience in the design goals as well as evaluation criteria becomes essential especially when taking steps from early proof-of-concept level technical demos towards more mature prototypes and commercial products. The commercial success is in the end determined by the suitability in authentic usage situations "in the wild".

User experience (UX) as a field seeks to offer a systematic approach to design and analysis of the user's holistic experiences with the technology. As a quality attribute that is an increasingly important success factor of any interactive technology, UX has become one of the major interest areas in the field of human-computer interaction (HCI) since the early 2000's. On a general level, UX refers to users' perceptions and responses that arise in the use of an interactive system [29]. Going beyond this definition, UX covers a broad set of users' experiences based on the instrumental (pragmatic) and non-instrumental (hedonic) system qualities [24]. Instrumental qualities cover traditional viewpoints like usability and efficiency of the system but also other experiential aspects, such as supporting sense of achievement, flow and self-esteem. The hedonic aspects enable experiences related to pleasure, stimulation, social connectedness, inspiration and self-expression, for example. Many of such aspects have been acknowledged in the UX literature only recently as a result of elaborate analysis of the concept of user experience.

Understanding subjective and emotional experiences will help set meaningful and explicit targets for system design [25]. UX studies thus need to go beyond traditional usability tests and field studies where the focus is on the efficiency and ease of use of the system interaction. To provide detailed guidance for the design of experiential aspects of especially such novel and versatile technology as ubicomp, UX studies need to take into account a broad spectrum of human experiences.

Coming from different research traditions, ubicomp has roots in the engineering fields and computer science whereas UX is strongly connected with HCI, psychology and design. These two fields have not yet been fully entwined. Ubicomp is addressing paradigmatic changes on how technology is interacted with and what are the potential technology-mediated services in different surroundings. Experiential design thinking has become a prominent trend in HCI and we believe that the UX approach can bring opportunities for enticing ubicomp experiences. Deep, detailed understanding of experiences that are desirable and opportune in ubicomp is necessary to guide the design of successful ubicomp systems.

In this paper, we seek to provide understanding of the current study practices and types of UX findings in the area of ubiquitous computing research. Such overview has so far been missing. We do this by a systematic literature review and the following analysis of current state of UX research in ubicomp. Specifically, the main goals of our study were:

- to understand what kind of UX studies have been conducted in ubicomp research, and
- to understand what kind of user experience findings have been gained in the empirical UX studies of ubicomp systems.

The main contribution of this paper is the overview of the status of empirical UX research in ubicomp. Based on the findings, we argue that understanding different user experience types in more depth can give a basis to future designs of ubicomp systems. We also propose a ubicomp UX framework which can help design and evaluate successful ubicomp systems with desirable target experiences.

2 Background and Positioning of this Study

In order to understand the roots of ubicomp research, we first take a glance to the early work conducted in the field. From the early days of ubicomp, there has been an emphasis on building interactive systems and integrating existing technologies, such as sensors and location tracking, to application and device concepts that can be trialed out. Especially, the seminal work conducted in Xerox PARC in the dawn of 1990's illustrates the research approach and the motivation of bringing the ubicomp philosophy, as verbalized by Weiser [52] alive. As an example, Active Badge project [51] demonstrated and trialed in the wild the device and service for locating people in the large office and routing the telephone calls to correct locations.

Sensor data fusion and the idea of context-aware devices became integral part of ubicomp. Probably the most used definition related to context-awareness dates back to 2000 when Dey & Abowd define context as "any relevant information used to characterize an entity" [14]. Other landmark early works from ubicomp include mobile technology focused TEA project, which investigated technology enabled awareness through context recognition and device integrated sensor modules using e.g. mobile phones as platforms [48, 49]. Location-awareness became already early one of the key attributes when demonstrating ubiquitous technologies (e.g. Cybreminder reminder system [16] and the first location-aware tourist guide publicly available for city visitors, GUIDE [10]). Also new output technologies such as peripheral and public displays started to emerge (e.g. [38]). While these works already included the aspect of taking the technology out from the laboratory conditions and to the field, it is evident that the development of prototype devices and applications was conducted very much from the technical viewpoint. The central outcome of the field studies was very much to verify that the technology concept actually worked in the real world settings, rather than that it was valid for the actual end users and targeted contexts of use.

Over the years, the trend to demonstrate more complex systems and multitude of ubicomp technologies became evident. Living lab type environments such as Georgia Tech Aware Home [31] gave opportunities to evaluate the research concept in an instrumented environment but yet with authentic, real world users. Moreover, demo environments focused on a specific topic, such as shopping [34], mixing the controlled and in-the-wild research setting were set up. During past few years, sensor instrumentation in the form of smart phones has enabled data collection of numerous everyday activities even in the global scale [7].

In our research, we are especially interested in detailed understanding of user experience (UX), and how it can be applied in ubicomp system development. As was stated above, UX goes beyond the traditional instrumental aspects of conventional usability [29] and extends the focus towards hedonic and emotional aspects of interaction with the product or service [24]. Due to the maturing ubicomp technologies, more high fidelity prototypes are developed and employed in real world use. While this is happening, it becomes more relevant to investigate the user perceptions in a holistic manner in order to find solutions how to introduce the technology for larger audiences and in the real world use.

Earlier literature reviews and surveys in the area of ubicomp have mostly considered the topic from the technology point of view. These literature reviews include, for instance, surveys focusing on Internet of Things [4] or context-aware smart homes [40]. HCI-oriented surveys have been conducted on research methods in mobile HCI [32], virtual environments [8], augmented reality (AR) [17, 50] and UX study practices in general [5]. For example, Swan et al. [50] show that user experiments have been conducted only in 8 % of AR studies. Regarding ubicomp, so far no comprehensive review investigating the UX research in the field has been conducted.

3   Review of Literature of Empirical Ubicomp UX Studies

Our review process was based on iterative evaluation, filtering and analysis of literature. We started by defining and selecting appropriate sources and keywords for the survey. This was followed by a multi-phased iterative filtering of the collection of articles to meet our relevance requirements, and finally a systematic analysis of the UX related findings reported in the selected publications.

3.1   Database and Keyword Selection

We focused the search to six major publishers, digital libraries or meta search engines in the field: Scopus, Springer Link, IEEE Xplore, Science Direct, ACM, and ProQuest. These were chosen because they cover the majority of the publications in the fields of ubicomp and HCI. The query was conducted on August 21st 2014.

The initial search from each source was executed with a combination of three types of keywords, one focusing on the ubicomp system type, the second on the empirical user study and the third on the UX related terms (see Table 1). Regarding the technology, we aimed at covering keywords that represent the broad field of ubicomp. We included generic ubiquity-related terms (e.g. pervasive, ambient, everyware), recent related trends that are considered to belong to ubicomp (e.g. internet of things), as well as technologies related to interaction, such as tangibility. We focused especially on emerging ubicomp technologies, i.e. computing and interaction technologies that are relatively novel and have not yet produced well-established business, and thus would benefit from user-centric research. Consequently, we defined that pure mobile applications would not be included in the review. Only mobile systems with further ubicomp aspects, such as location sensing or other novelties were agreed to be acceptable to the sample.

Table 1. Search logic and keywords.

UBICOMP keywords (| refers to OR *operation):*
ubiquitous computing | ubiquitous system | ubiquitous service | pervasive system | pervasive computing | calm computing | smart space | smart environment | context-aware system | context-aware service | context-aware application | context-based system | context-based service | context-based application | location-aware system | location-aware service | location-aware application | proximity-based system | proximity-based service | location-based | smart device | smart object | physical computing | tangible computing | mixed reality | wearable system | wearable device | sensor-based system | ambient intelligence | internet of things | everyware

AND

EMPIRICAL keywords:
user study | field study | user trial | user evaluation | empirical study | usability study

AND

UX keywords:
user experience | experience | experiential | product experience | human experience | user acceptance | user perception | user perceptions | human factors | perceived value | customer value | emotion | emotional

---

With the second keyword type (empirical) we wanted to ensure that there would be some actual user experiences found in the ubicomp study. The focus in the UX keywords was in experiences, emotions, user perceptions and value, to cover the subjective aspects of UX and to exclude papers which focused on usability or practices of use. Narrowing down the scope already at this phase was done to avoid excessive noise in the resulted data (i.e. false positives, such as papers about ubicomp demonstrators without any experiential findings).

The initial query resulted in 1016 publications that we selected for further investigation (see Table 2 for the distribution according to the source). Instead of accepting the approximately 8500 results based on the entire publication data (including full text) we included only the search results based on the title, abstract, keywords and other metadata. This was to avoid investigation of a vast body of probably mostly irrelevant publications. We assumed that for the types of research papers we were looking for, the defining keywords would be mentioned in the abstracts, keywords or metadata. We tested this assumption by going through the Springer Link results where the search results could only be based on all article data. Only 19 of the 640 search results were

Table 2. Summary of the initial database sources and search results.

Source	# of results	Search based on
ACM	31 / 2998	Title + abstract / full text
IEEE Xplore	57 / 3313	metadata / full text
Science direct	7 / 894	Title + abstract + keywords / full text
Scopus	125	Title + abstract + keywords
Springer Link	798	All article data
ProQuest	6 / 728	metadata / all data

relevant, so we assumed that the situation would be similar also for the other sources and continued with the narrower set of papers.

3.2   Iterative Analysis and Selection of Relevant Papers

Selection Criteria.   We assessed the relevance of each paper in several phases and with three main criteria. First, the publication had to fit in the technological scope of ubicomp (e.g., not merely a mobile application or web service). Second, the research approach had to be based on an empirical study, rather than, e.g., pure literature review or a vision paper. Most of the exclusions took place based on these two aspects. Third, the UX focus determined the final relevance, based on how detailed and analytical the user study findings were.

The Process of Iterative Analysis-Based Filtering.   The first analysis phase was conducted to filter out publications that were obviously irrelevant or incomplete (missing authors, publication names or abstracts; papers from completely different disciplines, abstracts of journal and book chapters, dictionary entries). In this phase, 156 publications were excluded, remaining 860. Furthermore, majority of the duplicates were eliminated (due to the slight overlap between what sources the different search engines use). This phase was executed by one researcher.

In the second phase, a relevance inspection based on the title and abstract was conducted in parallel by three researchers. Three levels of relevance (no relevance, maybe relevant, relevant) were considered based on the abovementioned three aspects of search. This resulted in 31 relevant and 158 maybe relevant publications. The relevance requirements that excluded most of the publications in this phase were the lack of UX viewpoint or a missing empirical user study. In the third phase, we performed a cross-analysis by three researchers of eight randomly selected relevant publications by reading the publications thoroughly and inspecting the user study methodology and reported results. The aim was to refine the analysis scheme for the rest of the publications. This helped create a commonly agreed view and later systematically analyze the entire variety of relevant aspects. In the fourth phase we performed an analysis of the relevant and maybe relevant papers (189) based on the full text. This included a systematic inspection of the key criteria in each paper to determine the final relevance.

Finally, the analysis resulted in 75 relevant publications as our data set. This means that originally, based on the abstract, there were 114 publications that were thought as relevant but after reading the full text were found irrelevant. Again, the most important reasons which led to filtering out papers at this phase were the lack of empirical user study that focused on any experiential aspects and some of the systems being mere mobile applications without any aspects that could be considered as ubicomp. In addition, a few duplicates and five papers that we could not access were excluded.

Content Analysis of the Relevant Papers.   After gaining the set of 75 relevant papers, three researchers analyzed the contents bottom up from the full text, extracting items that were sought for in the research questions relating to the user study approaches and types of UX findings. Unclear items were discussed and resolved for the final classification of the found items.

4 Results

We first present an overview of the resulting 75 papers and their publication forums. A majority of the selected papers are conference papers from established fora such as UbiComp, CHI, AmI, MobileHCI, Pervasive and MUM. It is noteworthy that the set of papers represent almost 20 further conferences, relating to, e.g., entertainment technologies, assistive technologies, interactive tabletops, persuasive systems, mixed reality, and children and technology. This implies that ubicomp is indeed a broad area with a variety of subtopics and related themes, and that UX studies of ubicomp are published in both ubicomp-specific technical forums and HCI-centered forums. There are altogether 13 journal publications, seven of them from Personal and Ubiquitous Computing. Furthermore, the resulting set of publications includes six book chapters, all in books with a theme closely related to Ubicomp.

Figure 1 summarizes the publication years of the papers in our final data set. We can see that the majority of relevant user studies have emerged in the field rather recently. All the papers in the corpus, including the main categorizations, are listed at https://sites.google.com/site/ubiuxcorpus/.

The majority of the systems in the relevant papers are for everyday pragmatic (20) and leisurely (11) tasks, and for communication (13). Other intended task types include various cognitive tasks, such as learning and searching (11), transport and navigation (10), monitoring and self-reflection (9) and sports and exercise (5). The types of ubicomp technologies used are location or proximity sensing (16), smart objects (13), smart environment (11), public displays and projectors (11), context awareness and activity tracking (10), wearable technology (7), augmented/mixed

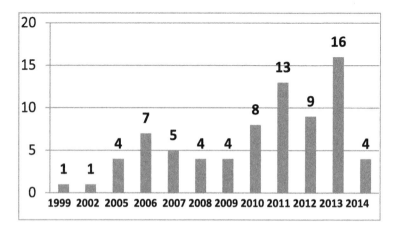

Fig. 1. Publication years of the resulting 75 publications matching the search criteria (the 2014 data is based on query performed on August 21st, 2014).

reality (7), interactive tags and near-field communication (3), cameras and object recognition (3), proactive assistants or agents (1) and novel interaction techniques (1).

In the following subsections, we present the findings from the literature review to the two key areas: (1) empirical user study approaches which have been used with ubicomp systems and (2) types of user experience findings that have been presented in the relevant literature.

4.1 Ubicomp User Experience Study Approaches

Most of the papers (47) included field studies in real contexts of use. 20 of the studies were laboratory studies. In eight of the studies, a laboratory was constructed to simulate the real context, for example a smart home. Most studies represented primarily qualitative research (37), whereas mainly quantitative approach was used in 16 papers. Many papers included both qualitative and quantitative approaches (20).

Table 3 presents key aspects of the user study approaches and methodology of the empirical user studies in the surveyed set of papers. In some cases one paper fits in several categories, increasing the total number of the papers in the table (e.g. multiple methods used). Additionally, not all papers have explicitly reported all the inspected matters (marked as "N/A").

As Table 3 shows, the data gathering methods represent traditional user study methods, based largely on interviews, questionnaires, system logging and observations. Methods suitable for long-term field studies, such as diaries and experience sampling are rare. The system logging some of the users' activities was well utilized in this set of studies.

Table 3. Distributions of data gathering methods, user representatives and use periods, and # of participants in the relevant papers.

Data gathering methods	#	User representatives	#	Use period	#
Questionnaire (paper, online)	45	System's intended target users	20	< 30 min	10
Interview (incl. group interviews)	40	High diversity or anyone available	16	30 min - 2 h	22
System logging	22	Students	11	Up to 1 day	1
Observation	12	Colleagues and other internals	5	1-6 days	7
Diaries and probes	5	Groups of (unspecified) people	4	1-7 weeks	19
Experience sampling or day reconstruction method	3	Early adopters	3	2 months or more	6
N/A	5	N/A	20	N/A	9

A majority of the papers reported studies with fewer than 30 participants (23 papers with 1-12 participants and 29 papers with 13-30 participants), which is a typical number in user studies conducted in HCI. Only 15 papers had a sample size of 30-100. The seven studies employing over 100 participants were largely using questionnaires to gather UX data (e.g. [39, 47]).

Only 14 of the papers reported a study where we interpreted the participants to represent the system's intended target users. Mostly, various kinds of "convenience samples" were used (e.g. students or colleagues) or the user representatives were not reported at all. This may naturally has an effect on the validity of the experiences that the users have with the system, as opposed to studying UX with the real users. As Table 3 shows, in this set of studies long periods (over a week) were quite common. Slight majority, however, is based on short-term studies that allow only the first-time experiences to be studied. When trying to understand the experiences beyond first-time impressions, longer periods of use increase the validity of the UX results.

4.2   Types of UX Findings

In the analysis of the papers we looked for user study results that related to experiential aspects of using novel ubicomp systems. We grouped the UX findings bottom-up into six UX finding types. Table 4 shows the distribution of the papers in these categories.

Many studies included aspects of several UX finding types, and our categorization was based on the central result type elicited from each paper (i.e., each paper is only counted once in this grouping). The types of UX findings shown in Table 4 are described below in association with example studies for each type.

Usability Findings.   Even though our filtering process aimed at excluding usability, some papers addressed usability issues labeled under the term of user experience. In this category, the user study findings focused on the traditional usability issues like efficiency and ease of use on the user interface level.

Harrison et al. [23] studied a system called UbiFit Garden which automatically infers and communicates information about particular types of user's physical activities, and reflects this on the mobile user interface. A two-phase study was conducted with altogether 40 participants in field conditions. The results reveal issues related to the system's form factor and design, power consumption, connectivity, accuracy, generalizability, and adaptability.

Table 4. Types of user experience findings in empirical ubicomp user studies.

Types of user experience findings	# of papers	Examples
Usability findings	9	[21, 23, 33]
User acceptance findings	9	[3, 30, 45]
Scaled ratings on predetermined UX aspects	14	[2, 8, 15]
Individual user comments or observations	16	[13, 26, 27]
Overall summaries about UX	23	[20, 28, 36]
Description of several UX types	4	[12, 19, 44]

Koskela et al. [33] studied a mobile, location-based music recommendation service in the restaurant context with 53 participants. The study assessed the technical feasibility of the system and general understanding of central usability factors of the service, including ease of use, effectiveness and speed of using the service user interface.

User Acceptance Findings. The papers that fell in this category contained views to the user acceptance. In some cases, Technology Acceptance Model (TAM, [15]) was used as the reference model for the analysis and to construct Likert statements; in others the issue of acceptance was addressed more as a general term to describe how users perceive the system.

Arning et al. [3] studied a location-based indoor navigation system that uses pico projectors to display additional navigation information into the surroundings. In their laboratory study of 24 participants the pico projector based solution was compared to the mobile screen. The main findings related to UX are user acceptance factors such as visibility, trust, and disorientation. A major outcome of the study is a structural model of user acceptance of the compared ubiquitous display solutions.

In the study of Portet et al. [45], a smart home environment was developed and studied in a simulated home laboratory with 8 elderly people and their family members and caretakers. The specific features studied were the voice command UI, alert messages and a shared calendar. The results show that the voice UI was acceptable to the elderly, but they were worried about their privacy and potential decrease in activity caused by the automatisation of home.

Scaled Ratings on Predetermined UX Aspects. This subset of papers used one or more scaled questions to ask the participants to rate their subjective experiences of the evaluated ubicomp system. The scales were based on predetermined experiential aspects. Ratings provide summative information about the perceived system quality but do not allow analysis or understanding of the assumed or emerging experiences.

Ecker et al. [18] developed and studied a community- and location-based persuasive game for the car context with the goal to motivate and support behavioral change towards a fuel-saving driving style. In a field study with 37 people, the results regarding driving style showed the effectiveness of the approach. In the final questionnaire, a question on "joy of use" got the highest average score of 4.5 on the Likert scale from 1 to 5. The paper concludes that the users confirmed a very positive experience with the system.

Ankolekar et al. [2] studied the performance and emotional engagement of different types of audio-based cues for directing users' attention to specific points of interest (POI) in a city. In the field study evaluation, effectiveness and affect with five types of cues were studied amongst the 15 participants. Experience sampling was used with a scale consisting of six pairs of words related to 3 dimensions of emotional response, namely pleasure, arousal and autonomy: Annoyed – Pleased; Bored – Engaged; Calm – Excited; Relaxed – Stimulated; Influenced – Influential; Guided – Autonomous. The comparison results show that musicons and mixed-modality cues create more pleasant and engaging user experience than other forms of cues.

Individual User Comments or Observations. In many studies, understanding UX itself is not the main aim of the user study but the focus is on assessing more specific aspects of the studied system. Thus, even if the paper addresses user experience, the results might contain individual findings or sporadic mentions related to how the users experienced or perceived the system.

Hoffman et al. [27] developed an in-car game that combines location-based information, AR and virtual characters. They studied how children's and parents' experiences could be supported by this game in a field study of six families (27 persons). One of the user comments with regards to UX was that capturing the game characters was fun, especially for the children. The paper concludes with key challenges for in-car game design for children.

In the first user study with SenseCam by Hodges et al. [26], a single participant suffering from amnesia was using the device in her real life, and it was compared to using a diary as a memory aid. The main result of this study is that the participant's ability to remember things increased. With regards to UX, the researchers observed reduced anxiety and increased ability to relax when using SenseCam.

Overall Summaries About UX. In contrast to the previous UX finding type, the studies belonging to this category summarize the study findings by describing certain types of prevalent experiences users have with the system. Still, these experiences are not necessarily in the core of the presentation of the findings but complement the more pragmatic and technical findings.

In their study of an interactive theatre experience for the blind and sighted, van der Linden et al. [36] had 96 participants explore the theatre space blindfolded, enhanced with a haptic mobile device. In regard to UX, they conclude that the participants' responses to the overall immersive experience were very positive, for example related to surprises while interacting in the space. The paper presents findings also related to the haptic device and arm gestures used while moving around in the space.

Holmquist et al. [28] studied Hummingbird, a location-aware system to support awareness and collaboration between people who are in the physical vicinity of each other. Based on their field studies in the office, rock festival and conference, the conclusion was that users did not find Hummingbird immediately as compelling to use in the familiar setting as in the unfamiliar settings. The summarized user experiences include the feelings of connection and comfort from others being around.

Description of Several UX Types.   Papers in this category address several specific user experience types systematically or in detail. In the reviewed papers none of the studies provided a very broad set of such experience type descriptions but the level of detail in the description of the selected ones is much higher than in the categories discussed above.

In their study of a persuasive, sensor-based bin can, Comber and Thieme [12] had 22 participants use the system for five weeks. Their findings point out several experience related areas, including self-consciousness by awareness raising and aversive feelings of guilt or shame based on the social influence arising from the system use.

Persson et al. [44] studied DigiDress, a mobile system for proximity-based social interaction in a long-term (avg. 25 days) field trial with 619 participants in the corporate office environment. The lookaround feature to identify nearby users was the most valued aspect of the system. The found experiences included fun, liveliness and social play, which all relate to the increased social awareness and interaction.

Summary. Overall, the papers found relevant in our review contained less detailed UX findings than what we originally expected. Only 4 of the 75 papers were at a level of description of the subjective user experiences that foster deep understanding of how the ubicomp systems are experienced. Most user studies in this sample are limited to more pragmatic or "lighter" forms of UX results. Such information can help assessing important aspects like the specific user interface design or measuring acceptance but they may not help in concepting and designing desirable ubicomp systems. To formulate meaningful experiential design targets for ubicomp, we argue that there is a need for more thorough and fine-grained understanding of the types of experiences and how different technology features and design solutions can enable them.

5 Discussion

The presented systematic literature review aimed at revealing the status of what kind of empirical UX studies have been conducted within ubicomp research, as well as the kinds of user experience findings these studies repor. Based on our findings it can be concluded that the subjective user experiences have been investigated in rather lightweight ways in the vast majority of ubicomp research projects. UX is an evolving concept and it has often been seen to relate to any form of user data or feedback. While general understanding of user responses and practices can be useful, we argue there is a need for more detailed understanding of UX. Thus, we have investigated UX from a viewpoint that addresses specific user experiences that go beyond the traditional pragmatic qualities of the system such as usability or usage patterns.

With regard to the user study approaches and methods, field studies have clearly been the most often used approach. Qualitative data gathering, especially interviews, has been a prominent approach in the ubicomp UX studies. Still, many studies have employed simple scales for summative evaluation based on narrow sets of experiential aspects, such as fun or sense of privacy. Furthermore, using convenience samples (often students or any accessible people) has been quite common. We propose that qualitative, open-ended methods are applied to gain understanding of the experiences of the developed ubicomp systems. The aim should be to understand the reasons for both positive and negative experiences, and ways to enable the desirable ones. These user studies should ideally be conducted with real target users, in the real contexts of use and in long-term use. These approaches will increase the ecological validity of the UX findings, and will enable transfer of the findings to the design of further, similar ubicomp systems.

The focus in this study was on the experiential aspects beyond basic usability factors, including the subjective and hedonic aspects, such as pleasure, self-expression, discovery, social connectedness, empowerment, awareness and engagement. User experiences like this have been envisioned to be probable results of the use of ubicomp systems by early visionary papers like [46, 52]. We were surprised to find very little systematic, in-depth analyses of such experiences. In many studies there are interesting findings about usage practices and design choice preferences, and these findings can be used for gaining insights of system use and needs for redesign. Still, such findings do not reveal insights to actual subjective experiences. Instead, the majority of the UX findings mention only individual, general experiences – such as fun or trust – or overall summary statements about user judgements of the system. In addition, even though we excluded mere usability studies from our selection criteria, some studies addressed usability issues, termed as UX. This illustrates the fact that the term UX is still used very loosely and often seems to refer to any form of user feedback about the system. Many systems in ubicomp are still in rather immature stage and the user evaluations bring up technical challenges, leading to unavoidable usability problems – even when the intended focus of the study would initially have been in UX. Having said that, even many of the qualitative studies seem not to have aimed at digging deep into the detailed experiences with the systems.

Then why should we gain more in-depth UX understanding for ubicomp systems? Ubicomp is maturing as a field of technology, and products and services are starting to enter the market. Human-centered design and the resulting pleasurable user experiences are becoming important competitive factors in the services offered by ubicomp systems. Designers of these systems and services can benefit from insights of the kinds of target experiences that the systems should support. The paradigmatic changes that ubicomp has to do with (e.g., implicit interaction, context awareness, proactivity and engagement [1, 46]) could allow types of user experiences that cannot be reached with other types of systems. This experience design potential deserves to be explored.

It is interesting to compare the number of papers that were relevant (75) to our review criteria (ubicomp technology + empirical user study + user experience) with all surveyed ubicomp literature. The fact that so little ubicomp literature deals with subjective, detailed aspects of UX may be because ubicomp comes largely from groups with strong technology and engineering backgrounds. Only recently have ubicomp systems started to reach such technical maturity level that it is feasible to evaluate the systems in real contexts of use, with real users. We hope that in the coming years we will see an increasing number of studies focusing on detailed understanding of a variety of UX aspects. All in all, a continuing dialogue between HCI/UX and ubicomp communities is needed to reach the ubicomp visions in the most desirable and appropriate way. For example, the HCI/UX community should provide methodologies, such as advanced simulations, to better suit the development challenges in ubicomp.

Regarding the validity of this research, literature reviews face inherent challenges regarding the coverage. Because of the keyword and database selection in this broad field, some relevant papers have probably been missed. For example, papers discussing phenomena related to UX but not with that specific term may have been left out (e.g. related to affective interaction or novel, embedded systems). Furthermore, we focused on ACM, IEEE, etc. because of their technical ubicomp relevance, and thus it is possible that we left out some relevant social science research focusing on ubicomp systems. After conducting the systematic literature review, we found some further ubicomp studies (such as [6, 9, 22]) which would have been relevant but were not found by the review because the keywords were not present in the title or abstract. We thus acknowledge that, due to limitations of keyword-based systematic searches, our literature sample omits some relevant papers in the field.

Despite the inevitable coverage challenges, we believe that the identified issues on the user study and UX finding types are sufficiently well covered to form the "big picture" of UX in research of ubicomp systems. The findings indicate trends and gaps in the research approaches that we believe that both the ubicomp and UX fields can agree with, and hence the results point out important steps towards the next, more human-centered and successful era of ubicomp research and product development.

6   Towards a Framework for Design and Evaluation of UX in Ubicomp Systems

The findings from our literature survey revealed a need for detailed understanding of user experiences when designing ubicomp systems. To theorize our findings, in Fig. 2 we propose an initial framework for how ubicomp design and evaluation could be conducted with a specific emphasis on user experience. It describes how specific experiences could serve as starting points and be matched with ubicomp technologies to drive design and evaluation of successful, human-centered systems.

An **experience category**, such as *relatedness*, can be manifested by specific experiences (X) such as social *connectedness*, *intimacy* and *nurture*. Experience categories can set design goals or targets for the design and evaluation of ubicomp system.

A **designable feature**, such as proximity view or camera surveillance, is a type of functionality which is enabled or implemented by the selected **ubicomp technologies**. Designable features should support the design goals set by the targeted experience types. The features then form the basis for the ubicomp system design.

The following examples from our data set illustrate the elements of the framework. In the study by Chi et al. [11], a cooking assistant system was built with the aim to increase the experience of *self-awareness* of the user's processes and habits. The developed system supported this by *instant feedback of own actions*, enabled by an

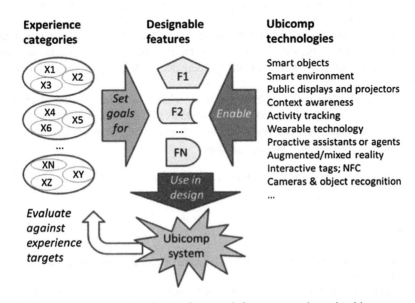

Fig. 2. An initial design and evaluation framework for user experience in ubicomp systems.

awareness display in the cooking space. Coulton et al. [14] studied a mobile outdoors game with kids and their parents. The resulting experiences were mainly about *stimulation*, and they included *fun*, *discovery* and *creativity*. The central feature of the system was a *competition to create "monsters"*, and this feature was enabled by *mobile augmented reality*.

We envision that this framework can be used and developed further in the following ways.

Experience-Driven design. In the beginning of the design process, the designer of a ubicomp system can define target user experiences based on user needs studies or experience frameworks in literature. One or several related experiences are set as design goals. The designer then chooses and designs the features and enabling technologies to fit those targets. This approach is along the lines of supporting users' feelings as in Kansei engineering [41] as well as in more recent proposals of experience-driven design [25, 37, 43].

To this end, the framework needs to be developed further by populating the experience categories with rich descriptions of a large set of experiences based on user studies of existing ubicomp systems and prototypes. The relationships between designable factors and features that affect UX in different ways need to be established. A recent example of a related framework on user experience of augmented reality is presented in [42]. In addition, further aspects affecting ubicomp UX such as relevant aesthetic and interaction design principles should be linked to the design process.

Experience Evaluation. To understand how well the system enables the experience goals and what are its experiential facets in the overall system quality, the developed ubicomp system should be evaluated against the experience targets. By evaluating the system both quantitatively and qualitatively, deep understanding of the experiential qualities of the system can be formed. Such understanding will support the further development of the system.

To this end, the framework needs to be developed to include operationalized, quantifiable evaluation metrics for the specific target experiences. Also actionable and lightweight techniques to elicit qualitative experience feedback from the end users are needed.

The proposed framework can help in gaining elaborate understanding of ubicomp user experiences and focusing on them systematically through the design process. Eventually, the framework can contribute to both empirical research as well as to the development of successful ubicomp systems.

Acknowledgement. We thank Jari Laaksonen for conducting the article database queries.

References

1. Abowd, G.D., Mynatt, E.D., Rodden, T.: The human experience. IEEE Pervasive Comput. **1** (1), 48–57 (2002)
2. Ankolekar, A., Sandholm, T., Yu, L.: Play it by ear: a case for serendipitous discovery of places with musico-ns. In: Proceedings of the CHI 2013, pp. 2959–2968. ACM (2013)

3. Arning, K., Ziefle, M., Li, M., Kobbelt, L.: Insights into user experiences and acceptance of mobile indoor navigation devices. In: Proceedings of the MUM 2012, pp. 1–10. ACM (2012)
4. Atzori, L., Iera, A., Morabito, G.: The internet of things: a survey. Comput. Netw. **54**(15), 2787–2805 (2010)
5. Bargas-Avila, J., Hornbaek, K.: Old wine in new bottles or novel challenges? a critical analysis of empirical studies of user experience. In: Proceedings of the CHI 2011, pp. 2689–2698. ACM (2011)
6. Bentley, F., Basapur, S., Chowdhury, S.K.: Promoting intergenerational communication through location-based asynchronous video communication. In: Proceedings of the UbiComp 2011, pp. 31–40. ACM (2011)
7. Böhmer, M., Hecht B., Schöning J., Krüger, A., Bauer, G.: Falling asleep with angry birds, facebook and Kindle: a large scale study on mobile application usage. In: Proceedings of the MobileHCI 2011, pp. 47–56. ACM (2011)
8. Bowman, D., Gabbard, J., Hix, D.: A survey of usability evaluation in virtual environments: classification and comparison of methods. Presence Teleoperators Virtual Environments **11** (4), 404–424 (2002)
9. Brown, B., Taylor, A.S., Izadi, S., Sellen, A., Kaye, J.J., Eardley, R.: Locating family values: a field trial of the whereabouts clock. In: Krumm, J., Abowd, G.D., Seneviratne, A., Strang, T. (eds.) UbiComp 2007. LNCS, vol. 4717, pp. 354–371. Springer, Heidelberg (2007)
10. Cheverst, K., Davies, N., Mitchell, K., Friday, A.: Experiences of developing and deploying a context-aware tourist guide: the GUIDE project. In: Proceedings of the International Conference on Mobile Computing and Networking, pp. 21–30. ACM (2000)
11. Chi, P.-Y., Chen, J.-H., Chu, H.-H., Lo, J.-L.: Enabling calorie-aware cooking in a smart kitchen. In: Oinas-Kukkonen, H., Hasle, P., Harjumaa, M., Segerståhl, K., Øhrstrøm, P. (eds.) PERSUASIVE 2008. LNCS, vol. 5033, pp. 116–127. Springer, Heidelberg (2008)
12. Comber, R., Thieme, A.: Designing beyond habit: opening space for improved recycling and food waste behaviors through processes of persuasion, social influence and aversive affect. Pers. Ubiquit. Comput. **17**(6), 1197–1210 (2013)
13. Costanza, E., Ramchurn, S.D., Jennings, N.R.: Understanding domestic energy consumption through interactive visualisation: a field study. In: Proceedings of the UbiComp 2012, pp. 216–225, Springer-Verlag (2012)
14. Coulton, P., Lund, K., Wilson, A.: Harnessing player creativity to broaden the appeal of location based games. In: Proceedings of the BCS 2010, pp. 143–150. British Computer Society, Swinton (2010)
15. Davis, F.D.: Perceived usefulness, perceived ease of use, and user acceptance of information technology. MIS Q. **13**, 319–340 (1989)
16. Dey, A.K., Abowd, G.D.: Cybreminder: a context-aware system for supporting reminders. In: Thomas, P., Gellersen, H.-W. (eds.) HUC 2000. LNCS, vol. 1927, pp. 172–186. Springer, Heidelberg (2000)
17. Dünser A., Grasset, R., Billinghurst M.: A survey of evaluation techniques used in augmented reality studies. In: Proceedings of the SIGGRAPH ASIA 2008, Courses, ACM (2008)
18. Ecker, R., Holzer, P., Broy, V., Butz, A.: Ecochallenge: a race for efficiency. In: Proceedings of the MobileHCI 2011, pp. 529–532. ACM (2011)
19. Efstratiou, C., Leontiadis, I., Picone, M., Rachuri, K., Mascolo, C., Crowcroft, J.: Sense and sensibility in a pervasive world. In: Proceedings of the Pervasive 2012, pp. 406–424, Springer-Verlag (2012)

20. Ervasti, M., Isomursu, M., Kinnula, M.: Experiences from NFC supported school attendance supervision for children. In: Proceedings of the UBICOMM 2009, pp. 22–30. IEEE (2009)
21. Fernandez, M.A., Pelaez, V., Lopez, G., Carus, J.L., Lobato, V.: Multimodal interfaces for the smart home: findings in the process from architectural design to user evaluation. In: Proceedings of the UCAmI 2012, pp. 173–180, Springer-Verlag (2012)
22. Håkansson, M., Rost, M., Jacobsson, M. Holmquist, L.-E.: Facilitating mobile music sharing and social interaction with push!music. In: Proceedings of the HICCS 2007, pp. 1–10. IEEE (2007)
23. Harrison, B.L., Consolvo, S., Choudhury, T.: Using Multi-modal sensing for Human Activity Modeling in the Real world. Handbook of Ambient Intelligence and Smart Environments, pp. 463–478. Springer-Verlag, Heidelberg (2010)
24. Hassenzahl, M., Tractinsky, N.: User experience - a research agenda. Behav. Inf. Technol. 25(2), 91–97 (2006)
25. Hassenzahl, M.: Experience Design, Technology for All the Right Reasons. Morgan & Claypool, UK (2010)
26. Hodges, S., Williams, L., Berry, E., Izadi, S., Srinivasan, J., Butler, A., Smyth, G., Kapur, N., Wood, K.: Sensecam: a retrospective memory aid. In: Dourish, P., Friday, A. (eds.) UbiComp 2006. LNCS, vol. 4206, pp. 177–193. Springer, Heidelberg (2006)
27. Hoffman, G., Gal-Oz, A., David, S., Zuckerman, O.: In-car game design for children: child vs. parent perspective. In: Proceedings of the IDC 2013, pp. 112–119. ACM (2013)
28. Holmquist, L., Falk, J., Wigström, J.: Supporting group collaboration with interpersonal awareness devices. Pers. Technol. 3(1–2), 13–21 (1999)
29. ISO 9241–210: 2010. Ergonomics of human system interaction-Part 210: Human-centred design for interactive systems. International Standardization Organization (2010)
30. Kaasinen, E., Niemela, M., Tuomisto, T., Valkkynen, P., Jantunen, I., Sierra, J., Santiago, M.A., Kaaja, H.: Ubimedia based on readable and writable memory tags. Multimed. Syst. 16 (1), 57–74 (2010)
31. Kientz, J.A., Patel, S.N., Jones, B., Price, E., Mynatt, E.D., Abowd, G.D.: The georgia tech aware home extent abstracts. In: CHI 2008, pp. 3675–3680. ACM (2008)
32. Kjeldskov, J., Paay, J.: A longitudinal review of Mobile HCI research methods. In: Proceedings of the MobileHCI 2012, pp. 69–78. ACM (2012)
33. Koskela, T., Järvinen, S., Liu, M., Ylianttila, M.: User experience in added value location-based mobile music service. In: Proceedings of the ICWS 2010, pp. 465–472. IEEE (2010)
34. Krüger, A., Spassova, L., Jung, R.: Innovative retail laboratory - investigating future shopping technologies. Inf. Technol. 52(2), 114–119 (2010)
35. Kuniavsky, M.: Smart Things: Ubiquitous Computing User Experience Design. Morgan Kaufmann, San Francisco (2010)
36. van der Linden, J., Rogers, Y., Oshodi, M., Spiers, A., McGoran, D., Cronin, R., O'Dowd, P.: Haptic reassurance in the pitch black for an immersive theatre experience. In: Proceedings of the UbiComp 2011, pp. 143–152, Springer-Verlag (2011)
37. Lucero, A., Arrasvuori, J.: The PLEX cards and its techniques as source of inspiration when designing for playfulness. Int. J. Art Technol. 6(1), 22–43 (2013)
38. McCarthy, J.F., Costa, T.J., Liongosari, ES.: Unicast, outcast & groupcast: three steps toward ubiquitous, peripheral displays. In: Proceedings of the UbiComp 2001, pp. 332–345, Springer-Verlag (2001)
39. Meschtscherjakov, A., Reitberger, W., Mirlacher, T., Huber, H., Tscheligi, M.: AmIQuin - an ambient mannequin for the shopping environment. In: Tscheligi, M., de Ruyter, B., Markopoulos, P., Wichert, R., Mirlacher, T., Meschterjakov, A., Reitberger, W. (eds.) AmI 2009. LNCS, vol. 5859, pp. 206–214. Springer, Heidelberg (2009)

40. Meyer, S., Andry Rakotonirainy, A.: A survey of research on context-aware homes. In: Proceedings of the Australasian Information Security Workshop Conference on ACSW Frontiers 2003, vol. 21, pp. 159–168, CRPIT (2003)

41. Nagamachi, M.: Kansei engineering as a powerful consumer-oriented technology for product development. Appl. Ergon. 33(3), 289–294 (2002)

42. Olsson, T.: User Expectations and Experiences of Mobile Augmented Reality Services. Doctoral dissertation, Tampere University of Technology (2012)

43. Olsson, T., Väänänen-Vainio- Mattila, K., Saari, T., Lucero, A., Arrasvuori, J.: Reflections on experience-driven design: a case study on designing for playful experiences. In: Proceedings of the Designing Pleasurable Products and Interfaces DPPI 2013, pp. 165–174. ACM (2011)

44. Persson, P., Blom, J., Jung, Y.: Digidress: a field trial of an expressive social proximity application. In: Beigl, M., Intille, S.S., Rekimoto, J., Tokuda, H. (eds.) UbiComp 2005. LNCS, vol. 3660, pp. 195–212. Springer, Heidelberg (2005)

45. Portet, F., Vacher, M., Golanski, C., Roux, C., Meillon, B.: Design and evaluation of a smart home voice interface for the elderly: acceptability and objection aspects. Pers. Ubiquit. Comput. 17, 127–144 (2013)

46. Rogers, Y.: Moving on from weiser's vision of calm computing: engaging ubicomp experiences. In: Dourish, P., Friday, A. (eds.) UbiComp 2006. LNCS, vol. 4206, pp. 404–421. Springer, Heidelberg (2006)

47. Rothensee, M.: User acceptance of the intelligent fridge: empirical results from a simulation. In: Proceedings of the IoT 2008, pp. 123–139, Springer-Verlag (2008)

48. Schmidt, A., Aidoo, K.A., Takaluoma, A., Tuomela, U., Van Laerhoven, K., Van de Velde, W.: Advanced interaction in context. In: Gellersen, H.-W. (ed.) HUC 1999. LNCS, vol. 1707, pp. 89–101. Springer, Heidelberg (1999)

49. Schmidt, A., Beigl, M., Gellersen, H.-W.: There is more to context than location. Comput. Graph. 23(6), 893–901 (1999)

50. Swan II, J.E., Gabbard J.L.: Survey of user-based experimentation in augmented reality. In: Proceedings of the Virtual Reality 2005, IEEE (2005)

51. Want, R., Hopper, A., Falcão, V., Gibbons, J.: The active badge location system. ACM Trans. Inf. Sys. (TOIS) 10(1), 91–102 (1992)

52. Weiser, M.: The Computer for the 21st Century. Sci. Am. 265(94–104), 94–104 (1991)

uCanvas: A Web Framework for Spontaneous Smartphone Interaction with Ubiquitous Displays

Tilman Dingler[✉], Tobias Bagg, Yves Grau, Niels Henze,
and Albrecht Schmidt

VIS, University of Stuttgart, Stuttgart, Germany
{Tilman.Dingler,Niels.Henze,
Albrecht.Schmidt}@vis.uni-stuttgart.de,
{tobiasbagg,grauys}@googlemail.com

Abstract. In recent years the presence of displays has become ubiquitous. They range from small-sized screens, such as smartphones or tablets to large screens as they are found in projection screens or public displays. Each display requires a unique modality of interaction, such as a dedicated input device, direct touch or does not provide any interaction at all. With the ubiquity of smartphones people carry with them a high-end interaction device that can connect to any web-connected screen. To allow quick access, we built *uCanvas* ("Ubiquitous Canvas"), a system to engage with interactive surfaces. In contrast to previous work no additional hardware is required, nor do users need to install any proprietary software. Our system runs on all current smartphones equipped with magnetometer and accelerometer, which is used to define a canvas and transmit cursor positions to a server connected to the display. To integrate interactive surfaces into applications, we created a lean Javascript library that allows publishers to specify interaction parameters (such as pointing, clicking, menu selection and text entry) by adding just a few lines of code. We built two example applications to evaluate the feasibility of the system and findings show that (1) interaction is intuitive and (2) easy to set up on the user side.

Keywords: Mobile interaction · Public display · Ubiquitous computing · Magnetometer · Pointing · Smart environments · Toolkit

1 Introduction

Mark Weiser's vision of integrating computers seamlessly into our everyday environment [8] has taken shape in a ubiquity of displays: screens are present almost everywhere in different shapes, sizes, functionality (informative vs. interactive), location and context (home, work, public). Especially public displays have been emerging in recent years being installed in airports, train stations, shopping malls as well as outside. Their primary function still lies in being a sole information display with few cases of options for user interaction. Touch-based interaction in public spaces is often limited because of screen protection (e.g. against vandalism). Hence, these displays tend to provide only unidirectional broadcast without possibilities for bidirectional

© IFIP International Federation for Information Processing 2015
J. Abascal et al. (Eds.): INTERACT 2015, Part III, LNCS 9298, pp. 402–409, 2015.
DOI: 10.1007/978-3-319-22698-9_27

interaction. In home environments on the other hand, appliances like projectors, TV or other device screens mostly lack sophisticated input capabilities beyond those of a TV remote. Meanwhile, people carry with them the most ubiquitous personal computing device: their mobile phone. Previous work has taken into account mobile phones as input devices ([1, 3]) for large screens. However, none of these techniques have been widely adopted. Often times the setup is costly and requires additional hardware infrastructure. In other cases the user interaction is cumbersome due to the fact that proprietary software needs to be installed first, which disrupts the flow from user intention to actual interaction.

To provide an easy and quick way to make any display interactive and allow spontaneous interaction for users equipped with a smartphone, we developed *uCanvas*: the system consists of three components: any kind of screen connected to the web, the user's smartphone with integrated accelerometer and magnetometer, and the *uCanvas* server. To interact with the screen, the user follows three simple steps: (1) device to screen registration is done via entering the canvas URL. (2) To calibrate the canvas, the user points the device to the screen's upper left corner, taps and releases at the bottom right corner. (3) Canvas interaction is done by simply pointing the device within the defined corners (Fig. 1). We use the phone's built-in magnetometer and accelerometer sensors to map the user's pointer to a cursor position on the screen. Additional functionality on the smartphone can be provided beyond the continuous cursor positioning: left-click, right-click, a menu or a keyboard for text entry. Multiple users can simultaneously interact with one canvas and the same canvas can be shared and displayed in multiple locations allowing remote interaction.

Fig. 1. User interacting through *uCanvas* with the game *food ninja* on a public display.

Screens that can be made interactive in this way include projected spaces, public displays, media facades, TV or smartboards, for example. In fact, any surface showing a website that is connected to the Web, can be turned into a *uCanvas*. For publishers the *uCanvas* system provides an easy way to make their content interactive: we developed a simple Javascript library, that publishers can include in their website in a few lines of code (Fig. 4 (right)). It is a low-cost solution due to the fact that no new communication protocol needs to be implemented and users can use their own devices without the need to install proprietary software. To assess the feasibility of our approach, we implemented and tested two example applications showing how through minimum effort the requirements of a quick and easy interactive canvas can be addressed, for which pointing and selection works conveniently. The contribution of this paper is 2-fold:

1. We developed a system that allows spontaneous interaction between users' smartphones and any web-connected screen via magnetometer data and
2. that provides a lean Javascript library which publishers can easily integrate to make their content interactive.

2 Related Work

Early work on managing graphic space on large displays using voice and gesture was done in 1980 by Bolt [2]: an entire *Media Room* was designed consisting of a speech recognizer and a complex system of magnetic sensor cubes to recognize pointing direction. Nowadays, there is a great body of research on the interaction with public and distant displays. The most common approach is relative and indirect pointing as well as the use of augmented reality. Ballagas *et al.* [1] make use of a phone's camera to control a mouse pointer on distant displays by using optical flow image processing. Their studies resulted in high task completion time and low scores in the subjective evaluation. Boring *et al.* [3] used the phone's keys, camera and accelerometer to move a pointer across a display. Hardy and Rukzio [5] created *Touch & Interact* where a mobile phone is used to touch a display equipped with a grid of NFC/RFID tags to perform selection tasks. A more novel approach to control appliances is taken by Derthick et al. [4]: they use a WiFi access point to display the appliance's web UI as soon as a mobile device connects to it.

There are numerous approaches to implement screen interaction, but there is still no wide-spread adoption. We think this is because costly implementations, cumbersome setup and approaches that are not designed to scale. One way to rapidly deploy a multi-touch enabled display based on projection was suggested by Hardy and Rukzio [5]. By providing a toolkit they allow designers to deploy interactive surfaces at relatively low costs. Their solution is based on the *Microsoft Kinect,* which allows the detection of touch events on the projected surface. In their case, however, additional hardware is required. Seifert et al. [7] on the other hand make use of the phone to point at remote screens. However, the setup is not trivial and cannot be integrated easily by application developers.

Our approach provides a scalable client-server solution where scale is reached by allowing a multitude of devices to be connected with multiple canvases at the same time. *uCanvas* can be deployed on any screen with a web connection and applies to a wide range of smartphones independent from the phone's platform and solely requiring access to magnetometer readings. Magnusson et al. [6] use the phone's magnetometer combined with GPS data for non-visual orientation and navigation tasks by allowing users to scan their environment by pointing. With pointing being a natural gesture we used this approach to map users' wrist movements to continuous cursor movements on the screen. In contrast to previous work our approach is optimized for setup speed and without the need for additional hardware infrastructure.

3   System Overview

uCanvas is a multi-user client-server system (Fig. 2). We distinguish between two types of clients: smartphones, which send sensor data and information about the actions to be executed (user clients), and screens connected to the server through a web browser (canvas). The *uCanvas* server routes actions from the smartphone to the connected display where the data is processed by a Javascript library. Each canvas' state is stored on the server, so a canvas can be connected at any time and retrieve its current state. Multiple user clients can be connected to one canvas instance on the server. This setup also allows for sharing a canvas across multiple locations.

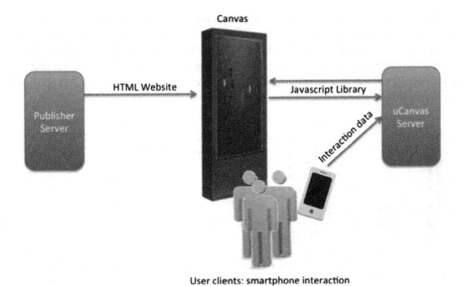

Fig. 2. A Javascript library connects publishers' content with the *uCanvas* server for interaction.

User Client. We created two versions of the user client: a native Android app that connects to the *uCanvas* server by opening a TCP connection which is kept alive, and a HTML5 client to allow platform independence and prevent users from having to download a proprietary application. It uses web sockets to keep the connection open to the server. To connect to a screen there are 3 steps: (1) the display registration, where users enter a website URL (Fig. 4 (left)) or scan a code (i.e. barcode, QR code) to get to the website corresponding to the current canvas which is delivered by the *uCanvas* server. This website contains the canvas-specific parameters which define the possible user actions (pointing, button-clicks, menu and keyboard). (2) The actual canvas needs to be calibrated: The user defines the canvas' bounding box by pointing to the left upper corner of the screen, touching a button and doing the same for the right bottom corner. At button press, the system records the readings from the magnetometer, translates them to relative coordinates and thereby defines a bounding box of the screen. Once calibrated, (3) the user can start interacting by pointing within the bounding box and executing actions on the screen.

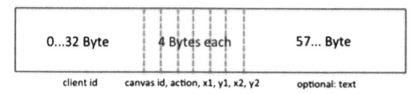

Fig. 3. Data format: Byte array with dedicated positions.

The user faces the screen during calibration and interaction. Because we are using the phone's magnetometer data, user gestures are restricted to wrist movements since lateral arm movements would distort the angle to the screen and therefore the relative position to the bounding box. To keep latency between the phone's movement and the cursor on the canvas at a minimum, the data exchange format consists of a compressed array of 56 Byte as depicted in Fig. 3.

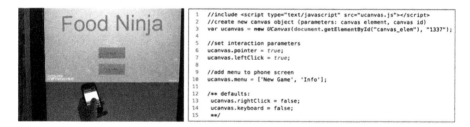

Fig. 4. *Left:* User connects to *uCanvas* by entering the canvas' URL. *Right:* Adding interactivity to the UI on the left by adding a few lines of Javascript: defining a pointer, a left-click button and a menu.

Javascript Library. This library lets publishers configure parameters for interacting with their website. It provides means to include buttons as well as a menu and keyboard. Hence, content publishers can integrate *uCanvas* into any area of their application by simply declaring which HTML canvas element shall be enhanced with interactivity. Cursor position, clicks as well as text entry are then relayed to the underlying canvas and can be processed. To equip a screen with means of interaction, content publishers follow 3 simple steps: (1) they need to register their website at our *uCanvas* server in order to retrieve a canvas id. (2) With this id, a *uCanvas* object can be instantiated on their website via Javascript. Figure 4 (right) shows how to set up a canvas in 4 lines of code that comes with pointing and click capabilities as well as with a menu. (3) Last, the corresponding canvas URL (or a corresponding barcode or QR code) needs to be displayed somewhere on the screen.

4 User Study

We implemented two example applications to evaluate the feasibility and usability of the *uCanvas* system: a game (*Food Ninja*) and an application for creating mindmaps. We recruited 10 participants (all male), mostly from the academic field, their average age being 25 (SD = 3.37). We asked participants to connect to the *uCanvas* (a projection area), calibrate their phone and to familiarize themselves with using the phone for pointing on the display, after which we randomly started with one of the example applications and asked participants to do the following tasks: (1) Mindmap application: first, we presented an existing mindmap and asked them to edit it by deleting nodes and creating new connections. As a second task participants had 4 min to create a mindmap from scratch for the topic 'vacation planning'. (2) A game application: We implemented the game *Food Ninja* where players cut fruits that fly across the screen, thereby trying to dodge the occasional bombs. Participants were asked to play 3 rounds, each round ended by contact with a bomb.

Results. We used a System Usability Score (SUS) questionnaire and the general part of the questionnaire for User Interaction Satisfaction (QUIS) to assess the usability of the interactions, followed by a semi-structured interview. Asked about interacting with the display using our system participants provided SUS scores between 67.5 and 95 with an average of 75.75 (SD = 10.48). Overall, the system received an average rating of 3.20 on the QUIS general part's 5-point scales (1 = negative to 5 = positive). Figure 5 shows the rating for the five individual dimensions.

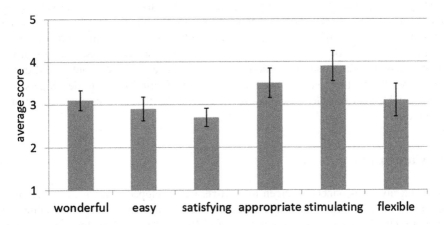

Fig. 5. The average score of the QUIS's general part (1 = negative to 5 = positive). Error bars show the standard error.

Asked what they liked about the system, participants appreciated its intuitiveness. *E.g.* P9 stated that the system is similar to the *Wii Control* and therefore easy to use. P2 further highlighted that the system is intuitive because of the pointer displayed on the screen. P3 liked that the phone's movement is directly mapped to the pointer's movement and similarly P7 stated that the system enables a very direct input. All participants but P10 and P8 criticized jerky pointer movement. P1 and P3 therefore proposed to smoothen the pointer movement, e.g. by averaging the pointer's position over a time window (P1). Other main aspects of criticism have been an observable delay in pointer movement (P2, P5, P8, and P10) and not being able to point with the whole arm but only with the wrist (P1, P6, and P7).

All participants stated that they could imagine to use the system for pointing on a public display. P1, P2, and P9 highlighted that it would particularly useful for gaming. Eight of the ten participants could also imagine using the system at home, particularly for large projected screens and multiple users (P1). Asked about further applications, we received diverse answers. Examples include using the system for presentations (P2 and P10) and games (P1, P3, P6, P7 and P9). Furthermore, they proposed the usage of *uCanvas* for distant displays that cannot be reached through touch (P4 and P9) (e.g. like ordering food from a screen at a drive-through) and, in particular, for situations that require quick access (P6 and P9).

5   Discussion

Despite occasional delays and jerkiness of the pointing activity, study participants liked the intuitive interaction and the quick setup. Even though magnetometer and the web connection sometimes behave in unreliable ways, the ease of setting up the system at any web-connected screen and the simple device registration on the user's side make the system being convenient enough for adding interaction capabilities. Since *uCanvas* is based on the phone's magnetometer data, users need to stay in a fixed position once the canvas has been calibrated. However, gyroscope and accelerometer data could be used to detect position change and adjust angels so that users can move around while interacting with the screen. The advantage of our approach is the scalability: users can interact with any size of screen ranging from Desktop screens to large screens across multiple devices. In our user study we collected solely subjective measures. Rigorous system tests including communication delays and pointer accuracy could yield quantitative results. Further, we will need to hand our Javascript library to developers and content publishers in order to collect more detailed feedback on its ease of use and integration.

6   Conclusion

To make any web-connected screen interactive, we developed *uCanvas*, a system that optimizes for easy deployment and quick user setup. Interactions include continuous pointing, clicks, menu selection and text entry. By providing a lean Javascript library we allow publishers to integrate interactive canvases into their applications with few lines of code. Using the phone's magnetometer and accelerometer allows for natural interaction without the need to install any additional software. We developed two example applications, which we tested with 10 participants to assess the ease and usability of our approach. Future work will focus on automatic canvas calibration by using, for example, highly accurate GPS locations to determine the exact user position in relation to the canvas position nearby. Hence, registration and calibration could be done automatically. Further, we are working on including gesture recognition to extend the capabilities of our Javascript library.

Acknowledgements. The authors acknowledge the financial support of the Future and Emerging Technologies (FET) programme within the 7th Framework Programme for Research of the European Commission, under FET grant number 612933 (RECALL). We further thank our study participants.

References

1. Ballagas, R., Rohs, M., Sheridan, J.G.: Sweep and point and shoot: phonecam-based interactions for large public displays. In: CHI 2005 Extended Abstracts on Human factors in Computing Systems. ACM, pp. 1200–1203 (2005)
2. Bolt, R.A.: Put-that-there: voice and gesture at the graphics interface. In: Proceedings of the 7th Annual Conference on Computer Graphics and Interactive Techniques, SIGGRAPH 1980. ACM, New York, NY, USA, pp. 262–270 (1980)
3. Boring, S., Jurmu, M., Butz, A.: Scroll, tilt or move it: using mobile phones to continuously control pointers on large public displays. In: Proceedings of the 21st Annual Conference of the Australian Computer-Human Interaction Special Interest Group: Design: Open 24/7. ACM, pp. 161–168 (2009)
4. Derthick, K., Scott, J., Villar, N., Winkler, C.: Exploring smartphone-based web user interfaces for appliances. In: Proceedings of the 15th International Conference on Human-Computer Interaction with Mobile Devices and Services. ACM, pp. 227–236 (2013)
5. Hardy, R., Rukzio, E.: Touch & interact: touch-based interaction of mobile phones with displays. In: Proceedings of the 10th International Conference on Human Computer Interaction with Mobile Devices and Services. ACM, pp. 245–254 (2008)
6. Magnusson, C., Molina, M., Rassmus-Grohn, K., Szymczak, D.: Pointing for non-visual orientation and navigation. In: Proceedings of the 6th Nordic Conference on Human-Computer Interaction: Extending Boundaries. ACM, pp. 735–738 (2010)
7. Seifert, J., Bayer, A., Rukzio, E.: PointerPhone: using mobile phones for direct pointing interactions with remote displays. In: Kotzé, P., Marsden, G., Lindgaard, G., Wesson, J., Winckler, M. (eds.) INTERACT 2013, Part III. LNCS, vol. 8119, pp. 18–35. Springer, Heidelberg (2013)
8. Weiser, M.: The computer for the 21st century. Sci. Am. **265**(3), 94–104 (1991)

Wireless Smartphone Mirroring in Video Calls

Henrik Sørensen[1(✉)], Kenton O'Hara[2], Phil Gosset[2],
and Jesper Kjeldskov[1]

[1] S+I, Aalborg University, Aalborg, Denmark
{hesor,jesper}@cs.aau.dk
[2] Microsoft Research, Cambridge, UK
oharakenton@gmail.com, a-phgoss@microsoft.com

Abstract. While screen mirroring is an integral part of many video mediated collaborations, current systems are limited in their ability to include ad hoc screen mirroring from personal devices of collocated participants on each end of a video call. In this paper we introduce a system that addresses this limitation by enabling lightweight multi-user wireless smartphone mirroring within a video call. The system enables multiple smartphones to share both digital content as well as physical artefacts when mirroring the live view from the smartphone camera feed. We present a study of the system in use for a distributed design task. The findings explore how shared access to screen mirroring facilitates a fluid switching of floor control in the meeting and smooth interleaving of individual, sub group and full group shared activities. Further, the findings highlight the importance of smartphone mobility in enabling access to screen mirroring from the sites of individual work and sites of various physical artefacts and the significance of this for the dynamics of a video mediated collaboration.

Keywords: Screen mirroring · Video conferencing · Distributed collaboration · Collocated collaboration

1 Introduction

Since the early days of video mediated communication research, there has been widespread recognition of the importance of sharing the viewing of information artefacts between distributed participants as the basis for ongoing discussion and collaboration [e.g. 2]. These shared artefacts whether physical or digital provide a common ground [1] that can be drawn attention to in the context of collaborative work. Significant research efforts within the domain of computer-supported cooperative work (CSCW) have looked to develop ways in which these artefacts can be shared and simultaneously viewed by distributed collaborators. Drawing on these efforts, many commercially available video calling solutions (e.g. Skype, Lync, Google Hangouts, and WebEx) offer some form of screen mirroring capability to support shared viewing of digital documents across distributed sites. In this paper the term *mirroring* refers to the direct duplication of one screen to another, while *sharing* is used to describe the act of visually sharing activities and digital or physical artefacts among collaborators.

© IFIP International Federation for Information Processing 2015
J. Abascal et al. (Eds.): INTERACT 2015, Part III, LNCS 9298, pp. 410–417, 2015.
DOI: 10.1007/978-3-319-22698-9_28

While screen mirroring capabilities offer important value in video mediated collaborations, the current set-ups are not without their limitations. For example, it is common in many everyday conferencing situations for one site to use a single host computer to connect to another host computer at a remote site. It is common for multiple collocated participants to be present at either site but in hosting on a single computer, the access to screen mirroring capabilities can be restricted to the person driving the host computer. While it is possible to swap control to another participant, this process is cumbersome and ultimately inhibits more casual and ad hoc artefact sharing [4, 8]. Related to this concern, these collocated participants may be working with a broader ecosystem of mobile devices such as laptops, tablets and smartphones as well as a variety of physical information surfaces like whiteboards and paper. Such personal devices have significance in that they may contain information arising from individual work performed prior to the video call as well as supporting any individual or subgroup work being performed in the meeting in parallel to the shared aspects of the work – both of these being potential contributions to subsequent shared activities in the meeting. While there are possibilities for sharing from some of these devices, the mechanisms are again cumbersome and inhibitory. For example, it is possible that these devices actively join the video meeting as an additional participant and then proceed to mirror the screen from there. But this is sufficiently effortful to be a barrier. As argued by Mueller-Tomfelde and O'Hara [5], such effort also incurs certain social consequences. Going through these processes entails "taking the floor" in a strong way in which the contributions of the sharing and talk need to be sufficient to justify the interruption. In this sense, these cumbersome processes create a social barrier to more casual sharing.

Furthermore, there are various physical constraints on the sharing opportunities within such set-ups. Elements of sharing may involve fixed wired connections such as those connecting to any shared display used within the room. Again while not insurmountable, such requirements do present certain constraints on the sharing from wherever in the room. As McGill et al. [4] highlight in relation to purely collocated settings, wireless screen mirroring can liberate collaborators from such constraints in ways that can benefit the participation dynamic of the collocated settings. Additional concerns here arise in relation to opportunities for sharing physical artefacts whether these are personally created and assembled paper documents or larger vertical surfaces such as flipcharts and whiteboards within a conference room. While there exist bespoke camera based set-ups that support aspects of this kind of sharing, what is more typical is to appropriate the existing single camera set-up already in use for the video sharing. Such cameras are either fixed to the host machine or alternatively to the front of the meeting room. In either instance such fixity of the camera offers significant limitations on the ability to use them for the sharing of physical artefacts. Smaller documents can potentially be brought to within the camera frame which is burdensome, but the fixed cameras cannot be brought to the site of their production and use at the table. For larger physical information surfaces, such as wall-based whiteboards and flip charts there is little or no opportunity to usefully bring them into the frame of the primary video camera and little opportunity to bring cameras to their location in the meeting room.

In this paper, we present work that is motivated by the key arguments and limitations of current screen mirroring capabilities discussed above. The work looks to support more ad hoc and casual screen mirroring opportunities within video calls for multiple collocated participants at either end of a remote collaboration. The aim here is to achieve this by facilitating the personal devices of all participants that are not explicitly connected as host devices within the call. Furthermore it aims to enable this to be done from wherever in the room by using wireless rather than wired based screen mirroring mechanisms. While our aims and motivations apply to a broader range of personal devices and artefacts within the meeting room ecosystem, we focus in the first instance on wireless smartphone screen mirroring. One of the key reasons for this is to enable us to further exploit the specific mobile camera capabilities of smartphones with a view to open up access to all in the room to participate in distributed sharing of the various physical information artefacts located around the room. Before presenting the system, we briefly discuss some related work to further ground the arguments underpinning the system. After presenting the system, we highlight some initial findings from a study of the system in use for a distributed collaborative activity.

2   Related Work

The sharing of screens, documents, and artefacts within collocated and distributed settings has been well documented in the CSCW literature and a comprehensive review of the various systems and nuances of particular approaches cannot be given due justice here. A good review of the key arguments can be found in the work of Tee et al. [8]. Of particular significance to our concerns here are some of the themes arising from research into Multi Display Groupware. Such efforts look to augment elements of single display groupware based collaboration with additional display devices such as personal tablets or mobile devices (e.g. [6, 10]). Of particular relevance here is the combination of personal and shared displays that acknowledge and bring together strands of individual and small subgroup work with the larger shared activities of the group as a whole (e.g. [9]).

With the emergence of commercial screen mirroring technologies in smartphones such as Miracast, Airplay and Chromecast, we are beginning to see some explorations of its use among small collocated groups of collaborators. A recent study [4] showed how multiple collocated users of these technologies self-managed the mirroring of their phones to a main display. While they used wired connections in their study, they highlighted the ways in which participation was better shared among the collaborators reducing dominance by a single person who might otherwise control the mirrored display. In our work we extend these ideas to include remote settings as well as wireless techniques for smartphone screen mirroring.

In addition to such multi-display and screen mirroring work, additional work looks to consider the potential for incorporating mobile phone camera capabilities into video call and media space set-ups. Neustaedter and Judge, for example, developed the peek-a-boo [7] concept that exploited the mobility of the camera phone to link in with a fixed media space display in the home [cf. 3].

3 System

Detailed technical details is beyond the scope of this paper, but the following provides an overview of the used technologies and the main components of the implementation. The system we developed draws together capabilities from Microsoft's Lync communication suite and Lumia Beamer screen mirroring applications. Lync is Microsoft's communication suite that supports video conferencing, instant messaging and screen sharing functionalities. While a mobile Lync client is available, it does not support distributed screen mirroring capabilities. Lumia Beamer is an application available on Nokia Lumia Phones that enables users to mirror the screen of their phone to another display through a regular web browser. By using the phone to scan a QR code presented in the browser, the application mirrors the screen of the phone in the web session. In addition, switching to the inbuilt smartphone camera application while mirroring, can effectively make the phone function as a wireless handheld web cam.

Fig. 1. The interface consists of the video conversation, a QR code for connecting mobile devices and the mirrored content.

The prototype is implemented as a desktop application using.NET 4.5 and Windows Presentation Foundation. Using the Lync SDK we developed a bespoke Lync Client into which we have wrapped key elements of the Lumia Beamer functionality. The key difference from the standard Lync desktop client is in the interface of an active video call. When a call is answered our application intercepts the conversation and presents a full screen mode containing 3 primary elements: The video conversation, a QR code for connecting the Beamer application, and an area for displaying the mirrored smartphone screen (see Fig. 1). To synchronise the mirrored view on both clients connected to a call, a lightweight machine-to-machine communication protocol (MQTT) with a publish/subscribe mechanism is used. Whenever a Lync call is accepted, each client creates an ID unique to the conversation, based on an MD5 hash of a sorted list of the Lync IDs of connected users. Each client connects to a MQTT message broker and uses the created ID as the subscription topic. When a QR code is scanned the client publishes the session URL to the conversation topic and all clients with the same ID receive the message and redirect its mirrored view to that session URL. Each time a Beamer mirroring session has been initiated, the client on which the QR code was scanned generates and presents a new unique QR code. By doing this, participants on each side of the video call always have access to start a new Beamer mirroring session.

4   Study

In order to evaluate the system in action we conducted a study of its use in a distributed collaborative task. The study consisted of 20 participants in total, organised into five different sessions with four participants in each. The participants were employees at the same company recruited on a volunteer basis. Of these, 16 were male and 4 female (average age = 29 years, SD = 4.10).

A session consisted of an introduction to the task and system, a 20 min collaborative design session, followed by a 20 min group interview. The task chosen for the design session was for participants to collaborate on a t-shirt design representing the company they work for. The task was chosen to encourage several participants to create, share and discuss both physical and digital artefacts. Participants were divided across 2 conference rooms with 3 collocated people in one room and a single person in the other. This configuration was chosen as we found the 2 × 2 configuration option to be limiting for exploring aspects of collocated interaction. As such we chose 3 people at one end to better represent these concerns in each session.

Fig. 2. Room set-up for the study

The rooms used were standard conference rooms with a large display on the front wall on which the application was presented (see Fig. 2). Each room had various vertical whiteboard surfaces on the walls. We also provided both rooms with coloured pencils, felt-tip pens, post-its, and A4 paper both blank or with pre-printed t-shirt templates. During the introduction each participant was given a Nokia Lumia phone configured to have access from the start screen to the Beamer application, Internet Explorer, Office, camera, photo gallery, and calendar. Browser history and photo gallery were cleared between sessions. Each session was video recorded using a dedicated video camera that was positioned to capture all of the collocated participants in the room and the shared display on the front wall on which the remote video of the single participant room was visible. The single person room was not video recorded but observed, to document events that might not be so apparent through the video conversation view.

The subsequent group interview sessions were used to elicit general opinions about the system as well as elaborations on specific behaviours of interest identified by the researcher observing the sessions. These interviews were video recorded and transcribed for later analysis. Over and above the in situ observations of the research, video recordings of the task sessions were subsequently revisited to allow a more detailed, reflective and systematic analysis of the unfolding collaborative action of the participants. Findings are primarily based on the observations and video recordings, but interview data have been utilised in getting a deeper understanding of particularly interesting events throughout the analysis.

5   Findings

Within the sessions, it was observed that multiple people in both locations took the opportunity to share content from their devices. The content shared included images sourced from the web, photographs taken of drawings on paper documents, photographs of whiteboards, photographs of objects captured outside the meeting room and live video images of paper documents and objects as they were being worked on or discussed and pointed to in real time.

5.1   Coordinated Organisation

Of significance here was the coordinated organisation of individual and shared aspects of the task. Individual work here took place in parallel to shared discussions happening around the shared display. For example, individuals were observed using their smartphones to search for images while not mirrored to the shared display. Once the images were located they would then mirror their display to the shared surface in order to take the floor. Likewise, design ideas were explored on paper documents in preparation for subsequent sharing via the main screen. Such preparation would often happen in parallel with another participant sharing and presenting. Some participants would prefer to utilise the live video to share design ideas with the option of quickly switching between different documents laid out on the table, by simply moving the camera around. Others would take photos as their work progressed and later share them by mirroring the photo gallery application of the smartphone. In any case, distributing the activities across multiple devices and artefacts enabled a more fluid interleaving of individual, subgroup and full group sharing activities. The preparation work meant that objects of sharing were immediately available to facilitate the social mechanisms and timings by which new ideas could be introduced to take the floor in the discussion.

5.2   Sharing Physical Artefacts

As well as sharing products of particular individual and subgroup work, what was also noteworthy was the real time sharing of work being done on paper documents and whiteboards. Here the video capabilities of the phones were used to reveal work as it was being performed. This involved some collaborative efforts with one person holding the mirrored phone to video the mark-up, gesticulation and talk around the paper in situ such that it could be shared across the two locations.

A critical feature of these interactions was the nature of mobility enabled by the wireless sharing of these images. This played out in a number of important ways. First of all, we saw how it allowed people to perform sharing activities from wherever they were seated allowing them to fluidly shift from individual to shared activities in the context of their locally assembled artefacts. Second, we saw how this mobility enabled movement around and beyond the room. For example, one participant left the meeting room to capture a photo of artwork situated in the atrium of the building. Another participant moved from their seat to the whiteboard in the room and proceeded to share a live image of the content from his camera phone while talking about it. Finally the micro mobility of the phone was exploited to achieve the fine-grained framing requirements of specific features of the work process and artefacts that were deemed useful to be shared across sites. In essence, mobility allowed participants to accommodate for features of the environment that impacted on the spatial organisation of the work.

5.3   Negotiating Control

As a final point we saw how participants were able to successfully negotiate among themselves the fluid transfer of control over the shared display. With the always-present availability of the barcode to control mirroring, participants were observed to vocalise their intention to share just prior to initiating the mirroring process. It was apparent in the timing and nature of these socially mediated requests that participants exhibited sufficient awareness of the ongoing work of the collaborating parties across sites to achieve such transitions relatively smoothly. Because there were no explicit mechanics in the application to control the flow of screen mirroring or indicate who was currently sharing content, occasionally situations would occur where multiple participants would for instance try to share content simultaneously. However, keeping negotiation of control as part of the social interaction rather than an explicit function in the application was observed to be a strength rather than a needed feature that could easily complicate frequent switching between participants.

6   Discussion

In this paper, we have presented a system to enable wireless screen mirroring from smartphones to shared displays and across distributed settings. Key here is the integration of these mirroring capabilities within a video conferencing application that lends mirroring access mechanisms both across sites and to collocated participants within a site. What we see is how this extends the ecosystem of devices from which ad hoc wireless screen mirroring can be achieved within a video call in ways that exploits their unique affordances. Of note here is the lightweight way in which the camera ecosystem of the video call can be extended through the camera capabilities of the smartphone.

The mobility of these devices means that real time capture opportunities are available in flexible sites around the distributed locations. As we saw, this enabled this functionality to be moved to the sites of interest allowing physical artefacts and the work around them to be incorporated in the distributed screen mirroring. In extending the mirroring capabilities across multiple personal devices, individuals had an additional resource through which to take control of the floor in the conversation. We saw how this facilitated parallel streams of individual and shared working and the fluid interleaving of these activities. Individuals were able to engage in their own preparatory activities with both digital and physical resources before introducing them into a more shared context for discussion. Directly mirroring personal devices such as smartphones naturally introduce privacy issues. These are outside the scope of this paper but is an interesting issue for future work. Finally, in contrast to some screen mirroring technologies that require an existing mirror connection to be first disconnected, our mechanism enabled participants to override any existing connection. This meant the opportunity to share was always available and negotiable through lightweight social mediation.

References

1. Clark, H.: Using Language. Cambridge University Press, Cambridge (1996)
2. Heath, C., Luff, P.: Media space and communicative asymmetries: preliminary observations of video-mediated interaction. Hum. Comput. Interact. 7(3), 315–346 (1992)
3. Inkpen, K., Taylor, B., Junuzovic, S., Tang, J.C., Venolia, G.: Experiences2Go: sharing kids' activities outside the home with remote family members. In: Proceedings of CSCW 2013, pp. 1329–1340. ACM Press, New York (2013)
4. McGill, M., Williamson, J., Brewster, S.: Mirror, mirror, on the wall: collaborative screen-mirroring for small groups. In: Proceedings of TVX 2014, pp. 87–94. ACM Press, New York (2014)
5. Mueller-Tomfelde, C., O'Hara, K.: Horizontal surfaces in media space assemblies. In: Mueller-Tomfelde, C. (ed.) Tabletops: Horizontal Interactive Displays, pp. 435–456. Spinger, London (2010)
6. Nacenta, M.A., Jakobsen, M., Dautriche, R., Hinrichs, U., Dörk, M., Haber, J., Carpendale, S.: The lunchtable: a multi-user, multi-display system for information sharing in casual group interactions. In: Proceedings of PerDis 2012, pp. 1–6. ACM Press, New York (2012)
7. Neustaedter, C., Judge, T.: Peek-A-Boo: the design of a mobile family media space. In: Proceedings of UbiComp 2010, pp. 449–450. ACM Press, New York (2010)
8. Tee, K., Greenberg, S., Gutwin, C.: Artifact awareness through screen sharing for distributed groups. Int. J. Hum. Comput. Stud. 67(9), 677–702 (2009)
9. Terrenghi, L., Quigley, A., Dix, A.: A taxonomy for and analysis of multi-person-display ecosystems. Pers. Ubiquit. Comput. 13(8), 583–598 (2009)
10. Wallace, J.R., Scott, S.D., Stutz, T., Enns, T., Inkpen, K.: Investigating teamwork and task work in single- and multi-display groupware systems. Pers. Ubiquit. Comput. 13(8), 569–581 (2009)

Disperse: Enabling Web-Based Visualization in Multi-screen and Multi-user Environments

Megan Monroe[(⊠)] and Casey Dugan

IBM Research, 1 Rogers Street,
Cambridge, MA 02142, US
mmonroe@us.ibm.com

Abstract. For visualization developers, the design and construction of effective applications can often feel like a war against screen space. Every now and then, developers are tasked with building a visualization that will live exclusively on a large, high-resolution display. More often than not, however, visualizations must be built to survive across the varying screen sizes of laptops, tablets, and phones. This may explain why many developers have flocked to the web, where stylesheets can easily be swapped and modified to tailor an application's look and feel to the current screen size. But that *screen* is defiantly singular. If developers want to tap into a more elaborate hardware ecosystem, they must take on the additional workload of server-side or device-specific coding. To this end, we introduce Disperse, a server-based framework that allows developers to encode multi-screen capabilities into web-based visualizations using a simple set of client-side mark-ups. The framework is intended primarily for authoring new visualizations, but can also be used to add multi-screen capabilities to existing visualizations. Disperse not only imposes minimal time and complexity overhead on the development and deployment of these visualizations, as we show through five case studies, but also allows multi-screen visualizations to be realized across any set of web-enabled devices.

Keywords: Visualization · Authoring · Multi-screen · Multi-user · Collaboration

1 Introduction

For visualization developers, every pixel counts. As datasets become larger and more complex, it is increasingly rare for a single view of the data to sufficiently address a meaningful range of the potential questions that might be explored. As a result, developers frequently build visualizations comprised of multiple linked views of the data, each designed to address a unique set of questions or contexts. This approach has been widely adopted in both research [4, 12, 23] and industry [29, 32, 35].

When a multi-view visualization is being designed specifically for a large, high-resolution display, developers have a lot of freedom in deciding how many views of the data to include and how complex those views should be. However, this luxury is rare. Most visualizations must be built without prior knowledge of the hardware on which it will be deployed. In these cases, developers must build their application to

© IFIP International Federation for Information Processing 2015
J. Abascal et al. (Eds.): INTERACT 2015, Part III, LNCS 9298, pp. 418–435, 2015.
DOI: 10.1007/978-3-319-22698-9_29

function on a standard laptop screen, which means that they must either limit the number of views that can be displayed at one time, or limit the complexity of the visualizations within those views. The ultimate design can be heavily dictated by the limited number of pixels in a typical display.

One could argue though, that pixels are never in short supply. Not every room is equipped with a wall-sized display, but walk into a typical meeting, and what do you see? There are probably between two and ten people sitting around a table, each with a laptop, a tablet, or, at the very least, a smartphone in front of them. Maybe the voices of remote collaborators emanate from the speakerphone system. There are probably computer screens in front of those people as well. In short, there are pixels everywhere! They're simply not connected in a way that is readily accessible to developers.

But all of these screens, from tablets to high-resolution displays, are connected by at least one feature, which is that they can all typically run a web browser. This is precisely why visualization developers have flocked to web development. Not only is it easy to customize the look and feel of an application based on varying screen sizes, but developers can reliably assume that their application can be quickly deployed on virtually any device. Additionally, a new fleet of approachable visualization libraries, such as Processing.js [28], D3.js [9], and Three.js [37], has made it increasingly easier to build web-based visualizations (Fig. 1).

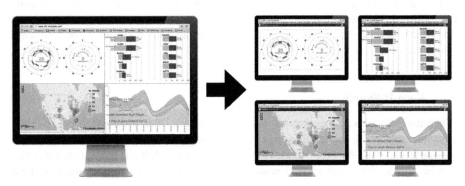

Fig. 1. The Disperse framework allows multi-view web-based visualizations to be easily split across multiple screens and multiple devices to enable more data-rich displays, provenance, and both remote and co-located collaboration.

Our goal with this work was to leverage the prevalence of web development skills, and the natural constructs of client-side programming languages to give visualization developers access to any pixels they need, regardless of what device they reside on. We introduce Disperse, a web-based framework that enables the development of multi-screen and multi-user visualizations. Disperse offers a unique set of advantages over other approaches for realizing multi-screen applications:

1. Developers are tasked only with client-side web programming. For many developers, this is well within their wheelhouse.

2. A web-based implementation means that (1) developers do not need to worry about the specific hardware configuration that their application will be deployed on and (2) end users are tasked only with opening browser windows and pointing them at the correct URLs in order to use a Disperse visualization.
3. The framework comes with history tracking and version control capabilities built in, further saving developer time and effort.

Given the complexity of executing multi-screen applications using other approaches, we argue that this is a substantial simplification of the overall process. This paper is organized as follows: in the following section, we discuss current approaches for creating and deploying multi-view visualizations. We then present the Disperse implementation, and walk through the process of building a multi-screen visualization. This is followed by five case studies that demonstrate the use of Disperse from the perspective of visualization developers. Finally, we discuss limitations and future work before a final conclusion.

2   Related Work

In 2000, Baldonado et al. advised that multi-view visualizations should be "used minimally" due to limited screen space and the increased demand they impose on cognitive attention [3]. Despite this warning, multi-view visualizations have become the norm across research and industry in order to support larger datasets and multi-faceted decisions. These visualizations typically adhere to one of the following four strategies:

2.1   Keep It Simple

When multiple views are presented on the same screen (tiled displays), users have the advantage of seeing the relationships between these views and understanding how a change to one will affect the others. However, this approach limits the screen space that can be allocated to each view. Because of this, each individual view must be kept relatively simple, limiting developers to scatterplots, line graphs, and pie charts (Fig. 2).

Fig. 2. Tableau (left) [35], QlikView (center) [29], and Spotfire (right) [32] - three of the biggest industrial visualization platforms - all allow users to create dashboards of simple views that are tiled across a single screen.

2.2   Hide and Seek

When more complex views are needed, the alternative to the above strategy is to display a single view at a time, and allow users to navigate to the additional views (navigational displays). This is usually accomplished using tabs or a menu of views [6, 15, 22, 33]. However, this strategy prevents users from seeing multiple views concurrently and directly observing how changes in one view affect the others. Obviously users can "fake" a multi-screen experience by opening independent instances of the application on different devices, and navigating to a different view on each device, but then the linking between the views is lost.

Disperse is designed to capture the advantages of both tiled and navigational displays. Developers can plan for each view to take up a full screen of its own, much like navigational displays, and users can see all of these views and the interactions between them at once, just as they can using tiled displays.

2.3   Go Big

Large, high-resolution displays offer an obvious solution for multi-view visualizations. They can display more data, more details, and provide a host of other benefits including leveraging spatial memory and facilitating collaboration [1, 38]. However, these displays are comparatively scarce. When developers build tools specifically for one of these large displays, they are essentially ruling out the use of their tool in the vast majority of collaborative, decision-making scenarios. Our goal with Disperse was to allow users to take advantage of large displays when they are present, but not be left entirely without a solution when they are not. Using Disperse, it is just as easy to position multiple views across a large display as it is to run each of those views on separate laptop screens.

2.4   Device-Sprawl

A considerable amount of previous work has focused on applications that can run across distributed user interfaces (DUI's). One of the biggest challenges of DUI's, however, is maintaining clear boundaries between development, deployment, and usage. Many efforts in this space require developers to have some understanding of the deployment environment, which can involve custom synchronization software [11, 14, 17, 34] and/or pre-determined tasks [7, 8, 16], and end users must have these environments available to them and properly configured. This can be a steep requirement for real world meetings, which get scheduled on the fly, can be brief in duration, and frequently involve non-technical users.

Much like the current trend in visualization, DUI applications are resolving these challenges by migrating to the web. Web-based DUI solutions began with efforts to facilitate collaborative browsing [5, 24] and have evolved to support more general functionality [10, 13, 39]. Badam and Elmqvist recently introduced a web-based framework that supports collaborative, multi-device interaction for single-view visualizations [2].

With Disperse, we extend this concept to multi-view visualizations, and propose an alternate strategy for allocating screen space and synchronizing interaction that is designed to require minimal additional coding effort from developers.

3   Disperse Implementation

Disperse is a server-side application that hosts other HTML code, much like the popular tool, JSFiddle [19]. Developers access the framework by either installing Disperse on the server that is currently hosting their visualization, or by uploading their code to a server that is already running Disperse. The framework is currently implemented as a J2EE Web Application, running on a Tomcat Application Server, however, this was simply the most accessible configuration available at the time of development. Disperse could just as easily be implemented in Node.js [25] or other server-side environments. The framework allows developers, using a simple set of client-side mark-ups, to split a single webpage into multiple browser windows across any set of web-enabled devices without losing the linking between these views.

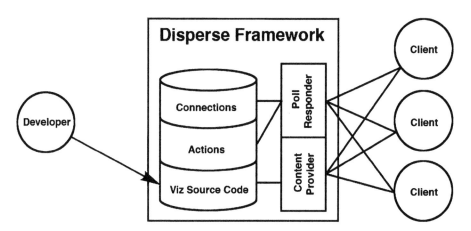

Fig. 3. The Disperse architecture consists of three data stores, which maintain (1) the source code of the multi-screen visualizations, (2) the clients that are connected to each visualization, and (3) a running list of actions that have been performed.

3.1   Visualization Development

Disperse tasks developers with two coding requirements: (1) indicate which HTML elements constitute the different views of their visualization, and (2) indicate which JavaScript functions enact meaningful changes across these views.

The first requirement is met using simple CSS identifiers. Developers must add the Disperse screen class, <div class="disperse_screen1">, to any HTML element that encapsulates a unique view of their visualization. Each element with the disperse_screen class will be able to function as a stand-alone view in its own browser window when the application is run through Disperse. Since CSS classes are additive, this class can be appended to an existing element, or it can be the sole class of a new <div> element that simply wraps around the relevant content. To further facilitate the screen-tagging process, we created two Disperse development templates, one navigational and one tiled, which come with pre-tagged disperse_screen elements in which developers can build their various visualization views (Fig. 4).

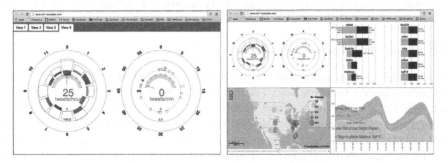

Fig. 4. We provide a tab-based, navigational template (left) and a tiled template (right), which can be used to build visualizations both within and outside of a multi-screen environment.

The second requirement that Disperse imposes on developers is to indicate which JavaScript functions propagate meaningful changes to one or more views within the application. This done by prepending the word synchronize to the function name (e.g. function synchronize_applyFilter{}). It is the actions of these functions that will be replicated across the other views (and thus screens) of the application. This function tagging can be done both at the end of development or to existing applications, however, the primary intent is for developers to build in these synchronized functions from the ground up. This allows developers to design their application around a comprehensive, yet minimal set of synchronized functions. For example, helper functions, and functions that modify a view temporarily (such as hover effects) do not necessarily need to be synchronized. The function-level synchronization also means that developers can leverage any web-based visualization libraries, including Processing.js [28], D3.js [9], and Three.js [37].

While we considered many alternate approaches for both splitting content onto multiple screens and synchronizing the actions between them, we chose this tagging approach for three primary reasons:

- It involves only client-side coding. Developers use the same set of constructs that they would use to build a single-screen application.
- The required mark-ups piggyback off the natural constructs of HTML, CSS, and JavaScript. It is difficult to imagine a discernable area of a webpage that is not encapsulated in <div> tags (or some equivalent), or a user interaction that is not routed through a JavaScript function.
- Neither the screen tags nor the function synchronization tags have any effect on the functionality of the application if it is run outside of Disperse. We wanted the same code base to function in both multi-screen and single-screen environments.

The goal of Disperse is to allow developers to construct multi-screen experiences as quickly as they can imagine them. The framework makes it extremely easy to prototype multi-screen concepts, a task that has been only minimally addressed in previous DUI efforts [5]. Developers do not need to tailor their application to a specific physical environment or implement any sort of synchronization between devices. We wanted developers to feel like adding multi-screen capabilities was just as accessible as importing a JavaScript library, much like jQuery has become a ubiquitous inclusion [18].

3.2 From Mark-Ups to Multi-screen

When end-users (clients) connect to a Disperse visualization, they are assigned a connection profile, which includes a connection ID, a branch ID (to be discussed later), the visualization ID, and a screen number. This information is maintained in the framework's "Connections" database (see Fig. 3). Disperse then serves up a webpage that includes a minimal navigation header (described in the next section) followed by an iFrame that fills the remainder of the browser window. The source code of the developer's visualization is loaded as the content of the iFrame. Since this code has been uploaded to the Disperse server, the framework can access and modify the iFrame code without violating same-origin policies.

The client page is also loaded with Disperse's two primary JavaScript libraries. The first of these libraries inspects the content of the iFrame, and hides any `dis-perse_screen` elements that do not match the screen number that is selected in the navigation header. We chose to hide (rather than remove) these elements in order to prevent potential errors from being thrown if a JavaScript function in the developer's code is looking for a removed element. The second of Disperse's JavaScript libraries searches the content of the iFrame for synchronized JavaScript functions. These synchronized functions are overridden with a new function that first runs the original function in the local iFrame, then pushes a message to the Disperse server with the client's connection profile, the name of the function that was called, and its parameters.

In turn, each connected client continually polls the Disperse server, checking for updates from other clients. When the server receives one of these updates, it is stored in Disperse's "Actions" database and delivered to all of the connected clients except for the one that originally produced it. The server also delivers updates about how many users are participating in the analysis session, which is reflected in the navigation header of all the clients. Each client then programmatically executes the prescribed JavaScript function to bring their iFrame view up to date. Because Disperse was designed specifically for conducting collaborative data analyses, there was no immediate need to optimize this update polling for high throughput situations. We envisioned a typical meeting consisting of around ten people, where the actions performed within the visualization take place at the pace of the discussion. Given that usage scenario, the current implementation has not encountered any scalability or message ordering difficulties. However, we are currently building a production-ready version of the framework that will likely adhere to an open connection architecture to better support higher throughput situations, should they arise.

In addition to the multi-screen capabilities, Disperse enables a whole host of features that would otherwise have to be implemented manually and independently by every visualization developer. For example, provenance is naturally kept during an analysis in the form of the functions that were called and the parameters that they took. This allows new users to be quickly "fast-forwarded" to the current state of the visualization. Users can also branch off into an independent exploration or return to previous steps. For example, if users notice a feature of potential interest in their view of the visualization, they can create a separate branch of the application that is not synchronized with the original branch. This is done using the branch ID field of the client's connection profile. If the user stumbles upon an interesting finding, the other users can move to this new branch and be brought up to date. Otherwise, if nothing of interest is found, the user can simply return to the original branch. This functionality is designed to mirror the Branch-Explore-Merge model described by MCGrath et al. [21]. The built-in usage tracking also means that, across multiple sessions, a complete history of the application's use is recorded, allowing for higher-level analyses of frequent/unused features as well as typical patterns of use. This data could guide the better overall design of interactive visualization tools or help to suggest potential next steps to users who are stuck in an analysis.

3.3   The Disperse Interface

For end users, deploying a Disperse visualization requires only opening browser windows and pointing them at the correct URL. Based on the URL parameters, Disperse visualizations can be opened in three different ways:

- A link to a specific screen of the visualization.
  (i.e. http://www.disperse.com/multi?id=ad762eb0&screen=5)
- A link to the visualization session, which defaults to the first screen.
  (i.e. http://www.disperse.com/multi?id=ad762eb0)
- A link to the single-screen version of the visualization, which displays the page without any of the Disperse functionality.
  (i.e. http://www.disperse.com/single?id=ad762eb0)

Once a visualization has been deployed through Disperse, users interact with the Disperse interface, which is designed to be nearly invisible to allow users to focus on the visualizations themselves. The interface consists of only a small navigation header in each browser window, as shown in Fig. 5. This header provides access to the framework's three primary features:

Fig. 5. The Disperse interface appears as a header in each browser window and includes (1) the name of the visualization that is being run, (2) a source code editor, (3) the screen layout, and (4) a branch selector (Color figure online).

Screen Layout. For every unique `disperse_screen` that developers specify in their CSS mark-ups, end users will see a unique box in the screen layout portion of the Disperse header. The view/screen that the user currently has displayed is highlighted in blue. Each box also lists the number of users that are logged into each view. Users can switch to a different view by simply clicking one of the other screen boxes in the header.

Branch Selection. The header displays the branch ID of each screen in a small, drop down menu. The initial/main branch is given an ID of 1. Users can create a new branch using the small, branch icon next to the drop down menu. When a new branch is created, it is silently added to the drop down menu, which allows users to complete work on their new branch without explicitly having to notify other users that the branch was created. Users can remove/terminate a branch only if they are the only user logged into that branch.

Source Editor. Much like the web testing tool, JSFiddle [19], Disperse allows the source code of an application to be edited within the framework itself (Fig. 6). This feature is primarily intended for developer use in finding and debugging JavaScript functions that have not been properly synchronized. However, it also allows more advanced end users to quickly reconfigure screen numbers in the CSS and turn on/off different function synchronizations. The source editor provides instructions for both of these mark-up requirements for developers to reference.

4   Case Studies

In order to understand the impact of Disperse on the visualization development and deployment process, we constructed five multi-screen and/or multi-user scenarios that were representative of Disperse's intended functionality (modeled after the evaluation in [14]). The first two of these scenarios were performed by two participants who were familiar with web development, but not with Disperse. Our goal was to observe whether these developers could grasp the fundamental building blocks of creating a multi-view visualization using Disperse. The final three scenarios, since they required a more substantial time commitment, were implemented by members of the Disperse design team. Each team member took a turn serving as the lead developer, while the other members observed the coding process and recorded any roadblocks or difficulties. All of the studies were conducted using the Google Chrome browser.

4.1   Splitting Static Content

One of the works that inspired us was the WinCuts system by Tan et al. [36], which allows users to extract any content on their screen into a separate window. The benefit is that extraneous space between relevant content can be quickly eliminated. Our first goal was to simulate this basic functionality using Disperse. To do this, we selected

Asif Rahman's visualization of publication counts over time for different topics in neuroscience and brain stimulation, which is publicly listed in the D3.js example gallery [30]. This visualization consists of five static charts, each of which fills the full height of a standard laptop screen, meaning that users must scroll to see all of the content.

For this study, the developers were asked to use Disperse to display each chart in this visualization on a separate screen. This allows each chart to be seen concurrently, and for users to quickly switch between charts. The developers had not previously seen this visualization, and had no prior knowledge of its underlying structure. However, both developers immediately opened Chrome Developer Tools and isolated the `<div>` elements that contained each chart. The developers then added the `dis-perse_screen` class to each of these five elements (Fig. 6), one using the Disperse source editor and one using their text editor of choice. The source code was then uploaded to the Disperse server.

From there, the final step was to open a browser window on four additional screens, browse to the URL of the visualization on the Disperse server, and select one of the five screens to display. Both developers were able to accomplish this in just over a minute, about the same amount of time that it would have taken to open this visualization directly on all five screens and scroll each one to a unique chart. Accomplishing this using Disperse, however, has four advantages:

- This configuration is saved, so it can be quickly recreated.
- Users can switch views in a single click, instead of having to scroll.
- Errant scrolling does not perturb the display since the other views are hidden.
- The screen numbering provides an index of which chart is being viewed.

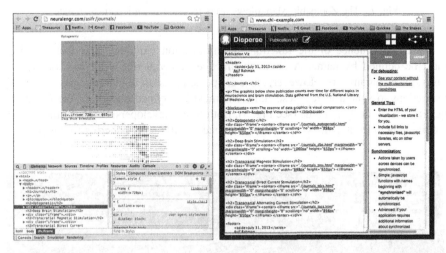

Fig. 6. Even beginner-level web developers can use Chrome Developer Tools (left) to isolate the HTML that contains relevant content. Developers can then use the Disperse source editor (right) to add screen tags and function synchronization.

4.2 Basic Interaction Synchronization

For our second case study, we wanted to capture the experience of two remote users interacting with a single view. Again, the developers were tasked with augmenting an existing D3.js example. In this case, we chose the Zoomable Map (shown in Fig. 7), which allows users to click a U.S. map in order to zoom in on a particular state [40]. To enhance this example with synchronized, remote interaction, the developers both copied the Zoomable Map source code into the Disperse source editor. First, the page element that contained the actual map was given the `disperse_screen` class. Second, the developers located the JavaScript function that was enacted when a user clicked the map, and augmented this function name with the `synchronize` identifier. These two simple edits, which took both developers only a couple minutes to complete, now allowed any number of users to synchronously interact with this visualization. For example, two users in separate cities could both log into this view. If one user clicked to zoom in on a particular state, that action would also affect the display that the second user saw. The second user could then zoom back out, and again, that action would be propagated to the view of the first user.

Fig. 7. The Zoomable Map allows users to zoom in on a particular state.

One consequence of the function synchronization requirement is that functions must be defined by name. A common practice in JavaScript is to pass anonymous functions as parameters. However, since Disperse relies on function names to identify the actions to synchronize, these functions must be defined outside of the parameter field and referenced by name (see Fig. 8). Both of the developers were informed of this requirement upfront and, as a result, neither had any difficulty adhering to this practice.

```
// Common JavaScript coding practice
maps.event.addListener('click', function(event) {
    removeStandingMarker();
    panLeft.setPosition(event.latLng);
    panRight.setPosition(event.latLng);
});
```

```
// Disperse functions must be declared by name
maps.event.addListener('click', function(event) {
    syncronize_updateLoc(event.latLng);
});

function syncronize_updateLoc(location) {
    removeStandingMarker();
    panLeft.setPosition(location);
    panRight.setPosition(location);
}
```

Fig. 8. Synchronized functions must be declared and referenced by name.

4.3 Modifying Existing Visualizations

One of the applications that motivated the development of Disperse was a web-based visualization dashboard called Social Pulse. Social Pulse performs text and sentiment analysis on the internal social media posts of our large, international organization. Its goal is to provide our human resources (HR) department with a better sense of what employees are interested in and passionate about, as determined from internal and external social media.

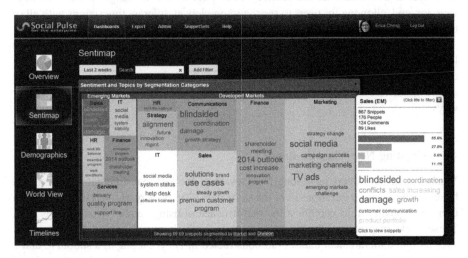

Fig. 9. Social Pulse allows uses to navigate to different views of the data using the icons on the left. However, in order to see two views side-by-side, users had to open the application in two windows, and manually set the appropriate filters in both.

The navigation-based interface provides multiple views, including a global map, colored by the average sentiment of posts from each region (chorophleth map), and a treemap, which can break down post topics by any employee demographic (such as business unit and rank within the company). Users can select from a detailed array of filtering options, such as posts from a certain time period or containing an important keyword (see Fig. 9). These filters persist as users navigate to other views. However, two aspects of Social Pulse have proved useful for analysis, but cumbersome for users to accomplish within the tool:

- Seeing different views (constrained by the same filters) side by side. For example, users frequently would like to see a particular topic both geographically (using the chorophleth map) and by business unit (using the treemap).
- Seeing the same view side by side with the same filters, but different time periods. For example, users would like to compare the topics from today to the topics from yesterday.

Because the Social Pulse filters are passed from view to view as URL parameters, the developer was tasked with creating these two additional capabilities without modifying the Social Pulse code base. This was accomplished by creating a new web page with multiple iFrames pointing to the different views of Social Pulse. Each of these iFrames was given a different `disperse_screen` class. The page included a synchronized JavaScript function that monitored the URL of each iFrame for changes to the filter parameters. When the function detected a change to the filters in one iFrame, it would update the URLs of the other iFrames to reflect the change. The developer also created a second version of this page in which changes to the time filter were ignored, allowing for users to see the same view at different timestamps with all of the other filters still synchronized.

Overall, a single day of coding yielded two much-needed extensions to a long-standing web application. Social Pulse can now be run as a multi-screen application either in a single-room environment or from opposite sides of the world, allowing our HR users to synchronously and collaboratively explore this data in new ways.

4.4 Creating New Visualizations

Visualization developers have long been aware of the fact that different visualizations better support certain questions over the same data [20]. New research also shows that a user's personality traits can affect the performance of using certain visualizations [26]. These works inspired our fourth implementation, which provides three different views over the same hierarchical dataset (all constructed in D3.js): a graph, a sunburst, and a treemap. Selecting an element in one view propagates the selection to the other views. This implementation is designed to be representative of the brushing and linking that is typically found across the views of a visualization.

From a development perspective, this implementation combined the approaches of our first two case studies. The developer used Disperse's tab-based template, so the `<div>` elements that comprised separate screens were already tagged with the `disperse_screen` class. The implementation included three synchronized functions, one to select an element of the hierarchy, one to deselect the hierarchy, and one to show the details of the selected element. Overall, the developer reported that it was not disruptive to plan function synchronization into the normal development process. Propagating changes between views inherently required special attention during development. The "synchronize" naming convention only made this thought process explicit. Additionally, the developer commented that this naming convention *helped* with general debugging because it made these critical functions extremely easy to locate through search.

In addition to observing the development process, this case study was also used observe the ease and flexibility of deploying a Disperse visualization. Our 3-view, hierarchical visualization was deployed in environments ranging from a trio of iPhones, to a wall-sized display, to combinations of the two (Fig. 10). Remote users who had been e-mailed a link to the application could immediately navigate to the URL and enact changes that could be seen by all users. Ultimately, the end user experience of deploying a Disperse visualization is virtually identical to deploying a normal web application.

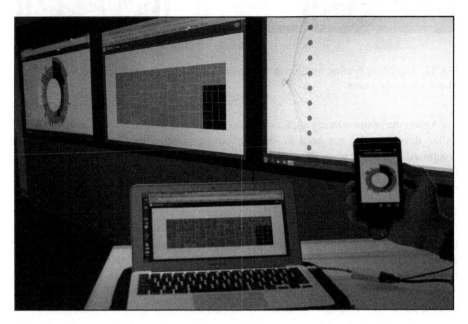

Fig. 10. Our 3-view, hierarchical visualization is deployed across five screens on three devices. First, all three views are tiled across a wall-sized display. Next, a user logs into the treemap view from a laptop. Finally, a user logs into the sunburst view from a phone browser. Now, any user can click on a component of their view and see the selection propagate to other screens.

4.5 Beyond Visualization

While Disperse was designed for the specific purpose of creating multi-screen visualizations, the framework can be used to create any sort of multi-screen web application. For our final implementation, we wanted to create an immersive experience for house hunting. The developer was asked to create an application that allowed prospective homebuyers to take a virtual walking tour of potential neighborhoods, all while maintaining their perspective of where they are on a broader scale. To do this, the developer created a three-view application that pairs a Google Map View with opposing Google Street Views (see Fig. 11). Using the list of potential properties on the Map View, the user can focus in on any property, which updates the opposing Street Views to show the property location. From there, users can use the Map View or either of the Street Views to "walk" around the neighborhood. As they do this, they can track their progress away from the original property on the Map View and see their surroundings get updated on the opposing Street Views.

Fig. 11. Our house hunting application pairs two opposing Google Street Views with a Google Map View in the center.

Again, the house hunting application was built using Disperse's tab-based template, so the developer did not need to worry about designating the `<div>` elements that comprised separate screens. However, the developer was responsible for synchronizing the appropriate JavaScript functions. This process revealed two new considerations that resulted in updates to the Disperse framework.

Embedded Synchronization. Due to the nature of the Google Street View event listeners, it was impossible to distinguish between a user generated update to the location and a programmatic update to the location. Because of this, the developer arrived at impasse where a synchronized function needed to call another synchronized function. For obvious reasons, this would set off an infinite loop of synchronizations. To account for this, Disperse was updated to detect these embedded synchronizations, and suppress their propagation across views.

Object Serialization. Disperse synchronizes views by passing JavaScript functions the same parameters that were passed by the view that initiated the update. However, JavaScript does not serialize complex objects, which is a known problem throughout the language. To account for this, Disperse needed to be updated to manually serialize objects as they pass from the client to the server. Fortunately, serialization issues are so pervasive throughout JavaScript that custom serializers have been written for many complex objects. For example, the Google Maps location object that was being used in our house hunting application already had a serializer written for it. However, handling certain complex objects that do not have an existing serializer, such as objects with recursive functions, is still an open issue.

5   Limitations and Future Work

The case studies presented above are intended to serve as a sample of potential applications that can currently be built using Disperse. However, additional work is needed to ensure that the framework can handle a more complete spectrum of multi-view visualizations. For example, we encountered a D3.js application that relied on the location of the mouse on the screen to accomplish certain animations. These parameters were so deeply embedded in the D3.js code that it was not immediately clear how to surface them for synchronization. Further work is needed to understand the benefits and limitations of Disperse across a wider range of interactive visualization environments.

Still, this work demonstrates the ability of Disperse to take advantage of multi-screen environments across a wide range of tasks. Given the positive reception of our five case study implementations across the organization, it is clear that Disperse provides a capability that is needed by users of various levels of technical expertise. To this end, our next step is to build an interface that allows less technical users to create multi-screen environments. For example, in our first case study, the developer used the Chrome Developer Tools to identify `<div>` elements that would comprise separate screens. We would like to allow less technical users to identify these elements by simply hovering over them on the page and entering the appropriate screen number. Furthermore, we would like to provide more assistance in identifying functions that need to be synchronized. Once Disperse knows which components of a web page constitute separate views, we would like to automatically generate a list of JavaScript functions that will need to be synchronized.

6   Conclusion

In this paper, we presented Disperse, a web-based framework for splitting multi-view visualizations onto multiple screens. Disperse is designed to impose minimal time and complexity overhead on visualization developers, and eliminate hardware dependencies. Furthermore, the natural functioning of the framework allows for provenance to be kept without additional programming, and for users to both branch and merge their analyses using version control. We demonstrated the use of the tool through five case studies, which highlight the role of the developer in the creation of multi-screen, collaborative visualizations applications.

More broadly, Disperse allows multi-screen visualizations to be built and deployed without drastically deviating from the process of building and deploying a normal web application. Developers build the application, and users deploy it by navigating to the appropriate URL. There does not need to be any intermediary coordination between the hardware and the software, as is the case for many current DUI environments. Additionally, any user with basic knowledge of HTML and JavaScript can use Disperse to create multi-screen environments involving basic interaction. Our future work includes making this process even more accessible for less technical users.

Finally, while Disperse was designed expressly for the purpose of creating multi-screen visualizations, we have barely scratched the surface of its ability to create multi-screen environments in general. For example, the rise of online tools for presentation-making such as Prezi [27] and Reveal.js [31] offer an opportunity for using Disperse to create multi-screen presentations. Disperse is a first step towards providing access to screen space on a broader scale, using whatever hardware is available. This, in turn, will allow us to better understand the use of these environments and effects they have on collaborative decision-making processes.

References

1. Andrews, C., Endert, A., Yost, B., North, C.: Information visualization on large, high-resolution displays: issues, challenges, and opportunities. Inf. Vis. Spec. Issue State Field N. Res. Dir. **10**, 341–355 (2011)
2. Badam, S.K., Elmqvist, N.: PolyChrome: a cross-device framework for collaborative web visualization. In: Proceedings of the Ninth ACM International Conference on Interactive Tabletops and Surfaces, pp. 109–118 (2014)
3. Baldonado, M.Q.W., Woodruff, A., Kuchinsky, A.: Guidelines for using multiple views in information visualization. In: Proceedings of the Working Conference on Advanced Visual Interfaces (AVI 2000), pp. 110–119 (2000)
4. Bernard, J., Wilhelm, N., Krüger, B., May, T., Schreck, T., Kohlhammer, J.: Motionexplorer: exploratory search in human motion capture data based on hierarchical aggregation. IEEE Trans. Visual Comput. Graphics **19**, 2257–2266 (2013)
5. Calderon, R., Blackstock, M., Lea, R., Fels, S., de Oliveira Bueno, A., Anacleto, J.: Red: a framework for prototyping multi-display applications using web technologies. In: Proceedings of the ACM International Symposium on Pervasive Displays (2014)
6. Carter, S.: Four ways to slice Obama's 2013 budget proposal. http://www.nytimes.com/interactive/2012/02/13/us/politics/2013-budget-proposal-graphic.html. Accessed 17 September 2014
7. Chung, H., North, C., Self, J.Z., Chu, S., Quek, F.: Visporter: facilitating information sharing for collaborative sensemaking on multiple displays. Pers. Ubiquit. Comput. **18**, 1169–1186 (2014)
8. Chung, H., Yang, S., Massjouni, N., Christopher Andrews, R.K., North, C.: Vizcept: Supporting synchronous collaboration for constructing visualizations in intelligence analysis. In: Proceedings of IEEE Symposium on Visual Analytics Science and Technology, pp. 107–114 (2010)
9. D3.js: Data Driven Documents. http://d3js.org/. Accessed 20 September 2014
10. Esenther, A.W.: Instant co-browsing: lightweight real-time collaborative web browsing. In: Proceedings of the World Wide Web Conference, pp. 107–114 (2002)
11. Fox, A., Johanson, B., Hanrahan, P., Winograd, T.: Integrating information appliances into an interactive workspace. IEEE Comput. Graphics Appl. **20**, 54–65 (2000)
12. Guerra-Gómez, J.A., Pack, M.L., Plaisant, C., Shneiderman, B.: Visualizing changes over time in datasets using dynamic hierarchies. IEEE Trans. Visual Comput. Graphics **19**, 2566–2575 (2013)
13. Han, R., Perret, V., Naghshineh, M.: WebSplitter: a unified XML framework for multi-device collaborative web browsing. In: Proceedings of ACM Conference on Computer Supported Cooperative Work, pp. 221–230 (2000)
14. Hartmann, B., Beaudouin-lafon, M., Mackay, W.E.: Hydrascope: creating multi-surface meta-applications through view synchronization and input multiplexing. In: Proceedings of the 2nd ACM International Symposium on Pervasive Displays (PerDis 2013), pp. 43–48 (2013)
15. Healey, C.G., Shankar, R.S.: Sentiment Viz: Tweet sentiment visualization. http://www.csc.ncsu.edu/faculty/healey/tweet_viz/tweet_app/. Accessed 17 September 2014
16. Huang, E.M., Mynatt, E.D., Trimble, J.P.: Displays in the wild: understanding the dynamics and evolution of a display ecology. In: Fishkin, K.P., Schiele, B., Nixon, P., Quigley, A. (eds.) PERVASIVE 2006. LNCS, vol. 3968, pp. 321–336. Springer, Heidelberg (2006)

17. Jettera, H.C., Michael Zöllnera, J.G., Reiterera, H.: Design and implementation of post-wimp distributed user interfaces with zoil. Int. J. Hum. Comput. Interact. **28**, 737–747 (2012)
18. jQuery. http://jquery.com/. Accessed 22 September 2014
19. JSFiddle. http://jsfiddle.net/. Accessed 17 September 2014
20. Kobsa, A.: User experiments with tree systems. In: IEEE Symposium on Information Visualization (INFOVIS 2004), pp. 9–16 (2004)
21. McGrath, W., Bowman, B., McCallum, D., Ramos, J.D.H., Elmqvist, N., Irani, P.: Branch-explore-merge: facilitating real-time revision control in collaborative visual exploration. In: Proceedings of the 2012 ACM International Conference on Interactive Tabletops and Surfaces (ITS 2012), pp. 235–244 (2012)
22. Miller, J.: Twitter Viz. http://www.twitterviz.com. Accessed 17 September 2014
23. Mühlbacher, T., Piringer, H.: A partition-based framework for building and validating regression models. IEEE Trans. Visual Comput. Graphics **19**, 1962–1971 (2013)
24. Nebeling, M., Mintsi, T., Husmann, M., Norrie, M.: Interactive development of cross-device user interfaces. In: Proceedings of the ACM Conference on Human Factors in Computing Systems (2014)
25. Node.js. http://nodejs.org/. Accessed 22 September 2014
26. Ottley, A., Yang, H., Chang, R.: Personality as a predictor of user strategy: how locus of control affects search strategies on tree visualizations. In: Proceedings of the SIGCHI Conference on Human Factors in Computing Systems (CHI 2015), To appear (2015)
27. Prezi. http://prezi.com/. Accessed 22 September 2014
28. Processing.js. http://processingjs.org/. Accessed 20 September 2014
29. QlikView. http://www.qlik.com/. Accessed 17 September 2014
30. Rahman, A.: Publications in journals over time. http://neuralengr.com/asifr/journals/. Accessed 20 September 2014
31. Reveal.js. http://lab.hakim.se/reveal-js/. Accessed 22 September 2014
32. TIBCO Spotfire. http://spotfire.tibco.com/. Accessed 17 September 2014
33. Stolte, C., Hanrahan, P.: Polaris: a system for query, analysis and visualization of multi-dimensional relational databases. In: Proceedings of the IEEE Symposium on Information Visualization (INFOVIS 2000), vol. 8, pp. 5–19 (2000)
34. Streitz, N.A., Geibler, J., Holmer, T., Konomi, S., Müller-Tomfelde, C., Reischl, W., Rexroth, P., Seitz, P., Steinmetz, R.: I-land: an interactive landscape for creativity and innovation. In: Proceedings of the SIGCHI Conference on Human Factors in Computing Systems (CHI 1999), pp. 120–127 (1999)
35. Tableau Software. http://www.tableausoftware.com/. Accessed 17 September 2014
36. Tan, D.S., Meyers, B., Czerwinski, M.: Wincuts: manipulating arbitrary window regions for more effective use of screen space. In: CHI 2004 Extended Abstracts on Human Factors in Computing Systems, pp. 1525–1528 (2004)
37. Three.js. http://threejs.org/. Accessed 20 September 2014
38. Vogt, K., Bradel, L., Andrews, C., North, C., Endert, A., Hutchings, D.: Co-located collaborative sensemaking on a large high-resolution display with multiple input devices. In: Campos, P., Graham, N., Jorge, J., Nunes, N., Palanque, P., Winckler, M. (eds.) INTERACT 2011, Part II. LNCS, vol. 6947, pp. 589–604. Springer, Heidelberg (2011)
39. Wiltse, H., Nichols, J.: PlayByPlay: collaborative web browsing for desktop and mobile devices. In: Proceedings of the ACM Conference on Human Factors in Computing Systems, pp. 1781–1790 (2009)
40. Zoomable Map. http://bl.ocks.org/mbostock/2206590. Accessed 20 September 2014

Evaluation of Distance-Aware Bimanual Manipulation Techniques for Large High-Resolution Displays

Anke Lehmann[1]([✉]) and Oliver Staadt[2]

[1] Faculty of Civil Engineering, Technische Universität Dresden,
Dresden, Germany
anke.lehmann@tu-dresden.de
[2] Institute for Computer Science, University of Rostock,
Rostock, Germany
oliver.staadt@uni-rostock.de

Abstract. In this paper we present the approach of interaction scaling. It assists users during their current tasks by adjusting interactivity depending on the user's distance to large high-resolution displays. The mapping method of interaction scaling combines the calculation of a distance-adjusted mapping factor with a manual/automatic change of precision levels. In our user study we evaluated how different accuracies, user preferences and physical navigation affect the user performance of distance-aware manipulation techniques. We used symmetric/ asymmetric bimanual manipulation techniques that were evaluated with inter-action scaling and a direct mapping approach. Further, we differentiated between coarse-grained and fine-grained accuracy of manipulation tasks. The study identified that interaction scaling improves user performance for very precise manipulation tasks. The participants were able to manipulate objects more accurately with asymmetric technique than with symmetric technique. Most participants preferred a manual switching; however, the tasks could be solved equally well with automatic switching by half of them.

Keywords: Large display · Interaction technique · 2D manipulation · Distance · Mapping factor · Control-display gain · User study · Proximity

1 Introduction

Nowadays, large high-resolution displays (LHRDs) are used in wide application areas like product engineering, geospatial imaging or scientific visualization. They combine a large physical display area with high pixel density. In addition, LHRDs change the way users perceive and interact with information as is known from small displays [1]. This has resulted in modifications of user behavior and interaction possibility. We must consider these aspects at information visualization and application of interaction techniques in LHRD environments.

For instance, physical navigation provides a natural behavior for user interaction. This means users step forwards or backwards in front of a large display to perceive detailed information or the global context of information. Similarly to visual perception

© IFIP International Federation for Information Processing 2015
J. Abascal et al. (Eds.): INTERACT 2015, Part III, LNCS 9298, pp. 436–454, 2015.
DOI: 10.1007/978-3-319-22698-9_30

tasks, different interaction tasks are performed at close-up range or at distant. These tasks require different precision and sensitivity of user input.

On the one hand, there are tasks which require fast and imprecise user input such as object movements across large distances with less effort. On the other hand, some tasks need precise and slow user input like exact object positioning despite of natural hand tremor. To overcome the human precision limit a control-display gain or mapping factor is used. For instance, a low mapping factor generates slower pointer motions in display space than the actual user input in motor space, and conversely with a high mapping factor. In general, different mapping factors were used to map the user input to coarse-grained or fine-grained virtual interaction. Therefore, we need methods to switch between these precision levels during user interaction.

Our approach of interaction scaling assists the user during his current activity by adjusting the precision of interaction depending on the user's distance to the display. This work is an extension of interaction scaling presented in [22], in which we investigate how the user benefits from a distance-aware manipulation technique. We improved the calculation of a distance-adjusted mapping factor with a switching method of precision level. The automatic change of precision levels uses an implicit granularity control via task-based and distance-adapted mapping factor. In contrast, the manual switching of precision levels uses an explicit switching between distance-adapted mapping factor and one-to-one mapping. We applied the extended interaction scaling approach to bimanual manipulation techniques; a symmetric technique which allows performing the manipulation tasks simultaneously, while the asymmetric technique differentiates between manipulation tasks. The switching methods and manipulation techniques use different interaction metaphors. For instance the manual switching and symmetric technique seems to be easy to use for novice user, whereas the others more suitable for experts. In our user study we evaluated how different interaction accuracies, user preferences and behavior of physical navigation affect the user performance of distance-aware manipulation techniques.

The contributions of our work are applying interaction scaling with task-based automatic switching of precision levels, evaluation of distance-aware manipulation techniques, and discussion of findings during distance-aware manipulation.

2   Related Work

Previous studies showed that LHRDs impact positively user performance on visualization and manipulation tasks [3, 10] and influence the user's information perception and their interaction [2, 26].

Hence, large displays require interaction techniques that support different precision of user input. The challenge is to switch between fast and precise interaction tasks that require different speed and accuracy of user input. There are several approaches that vary the mapping factor during interaction, like target-oriented techniques [6, 14], velocity-based techniques [8, 9, 11, 13, 19, 20, 23], and manual-switching methods [12, 23, 28]. However, using target-oriented methods we need knowledge about the virtual environment. Further, velocity-based approaches require device-specific calculations because of different input modalities (e.g., touchpad, laser pointer, mouse).

Esakia et al. [11] used a velocity-based touchpad in combination with an explicit switching between multiple acceleration curves by varying the number of fingers to control the cursor pointer. Thus, a larger range of dynamic mapping factors is supported.

However, using the user's distance in front of a LHRD allows to adjust the mapping factor dynamically and device-independent. Such distance-aware techniques adjust the precision of interaction according to the user's current position [7, 18, 24, 25, 27]. For instance, the interactive public ambient display [27] utilizes the user's distance to control public and personal information presentation. In [25] the user distance controls a virtual light position that affects the user's shadow cast and the positioning of virtual tools during interaction. In multiscale interaction [24] the multiscale cursor is changed based on the user's position relative to the display and re-scales the displayed data interactively.

Furthermore, LHRDs attract users to move within the physical space in front of the display (physical navigation). Related work showed that using physical navigation increases user performance on navigation and visualization tasks [1–3, 5, 18]. Jakobsen et al. [18] investigated proxemics for visualization tasks. For instance, the physical sense to abstract data was increased by using proxemics and the user's effort was reduced with proxemic-based zooming and aggregation. In [4] the authors discussed the concept of proxemic interactions in a smart living environment, for example to control a media player by implicit or explicit spatial user movements.

In previous work the user's distance was considered for selection and navigation tasks [3, 18, 20, 24]. We assume that physical navigation also increases user performance on manipulation tasks. Our objective is to find a distance-aware adjustment of interaction precision by using physical navigation in LHRD environments. Furthermore, the distance-aware adjustment should be almost device-independent.

3   Distance-Aware Interaction

As mentioned above this paper describes a further development of our interaction scaling approach (see [22]). We implemented a bimanual symmetric and asymmetric interaction technique that enables users to manipulate virtual content with the suitable accuracy in large display environments. In a preliminary study [22] we evaluated these techniques with a distance-adapted mapping method. We used continuous and discrete distance-adjusted mapping factors with pure relative mapping and compared it with an absolute (1:1) mapping. The results indicated that a distance-adapted continuous mapping factor is more suitable than discrete mapping factors. Furthermore, we investigated an interaction accuracy of 5-3 mm. Subjects were able to manipulate objects easily with absolute mapping, because the natural hand tremor was manageable. Moreover, the drift effect of relative mapping was difficult to compensate by users. We observed that interaction scaling had a positive impact on user performance (e.g., less object selection) but we did not find statistical significant results.

Based on these results we integrated a switching method to interaction scaling. We implemented a task-based automatic switching to reduce the drift effect. Some subjects requested fast object manipulation at close-up range of the display, thus, we implemented a manual switching method to support user preferences. Furthermore, we adjusted the continuous mapping functions to support user interaction with high accuracy.

3.1   2D Manipulation Techniques

In this section we shortly describe the used bimanual 2D manipulation techniques which support the fundamental manipulation tasks of selection, positioning, scaling, and rotation. We utilize an indirect interaction technique to interact from various distances. The manipulation techniques use a ray-casting technique to determine the virtual cursors of the corresponding interaction devices. We apply only the position data of the input devices (3-DOF) to calculate the virtual cursor position by using an orthographic projection. Thus, the hand tremor is invisible at the corresponding virtual cursors. The object manipulation is performed in a similar way to common two finger multitouch gestures.

The **asymmetric manipulation technique** differentiates between manipulation tasks which are performed with the dominant hand (i.e., selection and positioning) and the non-dominant hand (i.e., rotation and scaling). At selection the dominant hand's cursor is moved onto the virtual object and the selection button is pressed (manipulation start). The selected object is translated according the movements of the dominant hand. If the selection button is released the object is placed at the current cursor's position (manipulation end). To scale or rotate an object the user switches the interaction mode by pressing the manipulation button with the non-dominant hand. During the scale-rotate mode (SR-mode) the dominant hand's cursor is fixed and the object's positioning is disabled. The object can be scaled down or up by constricting or expanding the distance between the hands' cursors. To rotate the object the user changes the angle between both cursors. If the user releases the manipulation button, the SR-mode is disabled and the positioning mode is enabled again.

Guiard's framework [15] suggests that users perform fine-grained interaction tasks with their dominant hand, whereas they use their non-dominant hand for coarse-grained interaction tasks. Here, the dominant hand is used for the selection task which uses an absolute mapping (1:1) and requires precise motions. By contrast, the rotation and scaling task are supported by a distance-adjusted mapping factor why the non-dominant hand is used for it.

The **symmetric manipulation technique** uses an additional midpoint cursor between both hands' cursors to interact with virtual objects. For the selection task the midpoint cursor is moved onto the virtual object and the selection button is pressed with the dominant hand (manipulation start). The hands' cursors must be moved simultaneously according the desired direction to translate the selected object. The object can be scaled down or up by constricting or expanding the distance between the hands' cursors. At rotation task the user's hands are moved like a steering wheel. The selected object is placed on the current position of the mid-point cursor when the selection button is released. Using the symmetric technique the manipulation tasks are performed simultaneously.

3.2   Interaction Scaling

Interaction scaling defines the distance-adjusted precision of user input based on the user's physical navigation in front of a LHRD. With a distance-adjusted mapping factor we calculate the virtual motions (display pointer) based on the user's physical motions (input device) and the user's current display distance.

Therefore, we use the dimensions of the physical interaction space in front of the display wall and define special interaction ranges. In addition, these interaction ranges depend on the current LHRD configuration (e.g., dimension of display surface, pixel resolution, display alignment). We calculate different viewing distances to define the interaction ranges, when a fine-grained or coarse-grained interaction is appropriated.

The *visual acuity* is used to determine the maximum viewing distance d where a user is able to perceive objects with object size h separately [29]. By using the formula of visual angle θ (Eq. 1) we can calculate the viewing distance d_{pixel} where a user with normal vision is able to recognize individual pixels on a LHRD with given pixel pitch pp (see Eq. 2, $\theta = 1/60°$). Further, we calculate the viewing distance d_{block} where pixels are merged by doubling of pixel pitch. At this distance fine detailed information are not anymore noticeable. We determine the viewing distance d_{wall} where a user is able to see the entire display wall s (see Eq. 3).

$$\theta = 2 \arctan\left(\frac{h}{2d}\right) \tag{1}$$

$$d_{pixel} = \frac{pp}{2\tan\left(\frac{1}{120}\right)} \tag{2}$$

$$d_{wall} = \sqrt{\frac{s^2}{2 * (1 - \cos(120))}} \tag{3}$$

In order to calculate the distance-adapted mapping factor we use the following relative mapping functions.

Linear Mapping Function: A continuous linear factor is applied to the physical motions. The factor (mf) grows linearly with increasing distance to the display. At close-up and middle range a small mapping factor ($mf < 1$) is calculated. Thus, larger physical movements are needed to perform small virtual movements. At distant range a greater mapping factor is used ($mf > 1$) to support small physical movements which result in larger virtual movements.

Exponential Mapping Function: The mapping factor decreases closer to the display. At close-up range a mapping factor less one ($mf < 1$) is calculated which increases slowly. Thus, a very precise interaction is supported. At middle distance the mapping factor grows faster, accordingly smaller physical movements are needed to achieve the same virtual movements with increasing distance. At distant range a constant mapping factor ($mf \geq 1$) is used to provide coarse interaction.

We use two methods to switch the precision levels between fast, imprecise interaction (absolute mapping) and slow, distance-adjusted precise interaction (relative mapping).

Manual Switching: The user can switch between absolute mapping and relative mapping (e.g., pressing an additional button). Here, the user is able to deactivate the distance-adjusted precision at each distance.

Automatic Switching: The selection task uses an absolute mapping and the other tasks are performed with a relative mapping, i.e., a task-based method is used. Additionally, the relative mapping is preserved if the user is within the close-up range at manipulation end (current distance ≤ close-up range). If no object is selected and the user leaves the close-up range then the relative mapping is changed to absolute mapping automatically (current distance > close-up range).

Both methods use animated cursor positions to switch from relative to absolute mapping. The automatic switching requires no additional user input in contrast to the manual switching. This is useful in environments where limited user input is available.

4 User Study

We conducted an experiment to evaluate our interaction scaling techniques. Our goal was to determine how different accuracies and preferences affect user performance. We assume the user performance is increased by using interaction scaling (IS). We implemented a 2D puzzle solver application to compare the user performance with and without interaction scaling. The experiment task was inspired by a children's toy (the shape sorting cube).

The accuracy represents the tolerance range when an object is manipulated correctly to fit into its target. The experiment differentiated between big targets, objects with coarse-grained accuracy (tolerance range ± 2.5 mm), and small targets, objects with fine-grained accuracy (tolerance range ± 1 mm). Therefore, we supported an interaction at distant and at close-up range. In the experiment we had three big targets (square, circle, star) and five small targets (square, circle, star, two triangles). The targets with coarse accuracy were displayed with a thicker silhouette.

Task. The participants were asked to manipulate 2D objects to fit into their corresponding 2D targets with respect to size, position, and orientation. They had to sort eight objects with the same color like the target container (see Fig. 1). The application will only verify the object adjustment if the user drops down the manipulated object onto the desired target by releasing the selection button.

In the experiment we tested the following hypotheses for both manipulation techniques:

- **H1:** Manipulating objects is more efficient and effectively with interaction scaling than without interaction scaling.
- **H2:** There is a difference between big and small targets according to number of attempts and error rate. Furthermore, the error rate is lower with interaction scaling

than without interaction scaling for small targets. The error rate of big targets will not be affected by interaction scaling.

- **H3:** Using interaction scaling reduces the physiological effort.

4.1   Apparatus

The display wall is a 6×4 tiled display. Each tile has a resolution of 1920×1200 pixels (DELL 2709W), resulting in a total resolution of 11520×4800 pixels (55 million pixels). We used a 12-camera infrared tracking system from NaturalPoint (OptiTrack[1]) and the cameras are mounted on a suspended traverse system. The tracking volume in front of the display wall is approximately 3.8 m wide, 3.0 m deep and 3.0 m tall. The user holds a tracked Nintendo Wii Remote Controller (Wiimote) in each hand to interact with the application. We used the Wiimote's [A] button as selection button on the dominant hand (both techniques) and as manipulation button on the non-dominant hand (asymmetric technique). The Wiimote's [B] button was used as switch button on the dominant hand (both techniques). Furthermore, the user wears a tracked baseball cap to determine his current user-display distance. The test application was implemented by using the VRUI toolkit [21].

We use a tiled display wall with bezels, thus, the test application is configured in such a way that no virtual content is occluded by the bezels (see Fig. 1). The virtual objects' size was limited from 0.5 to 25.4 cm. The size limits were tested experimentally and the objects were visible from any distance. At application start the objects were generated randomly with respect to size and position without overlapping each other.

Fig. 1. Test application to evaluate distance-aware manipulation technique with a large high-resolution display.

---

[1] www.naturalpoint.com/optitrack/.

4.2 Design and Procedure

In our user study we evaluated the asymmetric technique (*asymT*) and the symmetric technique (*symT*) with two distance-adjusted mapping functions and two methods of switching the precision level as described in Sect. 3.2. Thus, we combined the linear mapping function (*lmf*) and the exponential mapping function (*emf*) with the automatic (*auto*) and the manual (*manu*) switching method.

Table 1. Five conditions evaluated in the experiment.

	Mapping function		
Switching method	Linear (*lmf*)	Exponential (*emf*)	Static (*smf*)
Automatic (*auto*)	✓	✓	
Manual (*manu*)	✓	✓	
Without			✓

These four interaction scaling conditions were compared with a static mapping function without a cursor switching method (*smf*), see Table 1. This condition used one-to-one mapping of user motion to cursor motion (absolute mapping). In our preliminary studies this baseline condition performed well. The used mapping functions are illustrated in Fig. 2. The linear and exponential mapping functions generated similar mapping factors. However, the exponential mapping function supports more precise interaction with increasing distance than the linear function.

We calculated the viewing distances to determine the close-up range (d_{pixel}: 1.03 m) and the distant range (d_{block}: 2.06 m) for exponential mapping function based on our LHRD setup (pixel pitch 0.3 mm). In our setup the viewing distance d_{wall} (2.2 m) is similar to d_{block}, thus, we only used d_{block}. For automatic switching the close-up range was defined at 115 cm approximated to d_{pixel} with an additional tolerance value to compensate users' head tremor.

The experiment was performed by each subject with both manipulation techniques to obtain sufficient experimental data. The techniques use different interaction metaphors why only one technique was performed by the user on one experimental day. Therefore, the user's time exposure was limited to 45 min per experimental day.

Each subject performed the task with all experimental conditions (within-subject design[2]). The subject has been informed which condition was activated. The condition *smf* was performed as first and last trial. The switching method was performed with both distance-adjusted mapping functions, afterwards the switching method was changed to avoid mental overload (example presentation order: *smf, auto-lmf, auto-emf, manu-lmf, manu-emf, smf*). The experimental condition was counterbalanced between the subjects.

---

[2] The experimental design was: 2 manipulation techniques (*asymT, symT*) × 2 distance-adapted mapping functions (*lmf, emf*) × 2 switching methods (*auto, manu*) + 4 baseline conditions (as first/last trial per technique, *smf*) = 12 trails per participant.

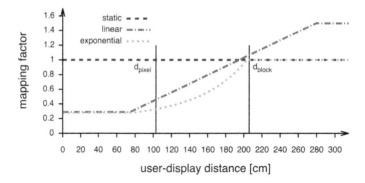

Fig. 2. Illustration of the used mapping functions within the experiment.

The experiment consist of two parts – a training phase and the test scenarios (trials). At the beginning the subjects performed a 10 min tutorial[3] to practice the interaction technique with the automatic and manual switching method. Afterwards the trail started. When the subject selected the first object the application timer was started. The subject manipulated the objects according to the current experimental interaction technique. The trial was finished if the last object was sorted correctly. The application timer was stopped and all data was written to a csv-file.

For each switching method the subject filled out the NASA task load index [16], a questionnaire to determine his physiological effort. In addition, the subject filled out a questionnaire reporting demographic information (before the study) and subjective data on his preferences (after the study). Furthermore, we captured the participant's 3D position to gain an insight into physical navigation.

Participants. The experiment had 24 voluntary participants (2 females and 22 males), whereas two male subjects could not finish the tasks, thus, they have been excluded from the data set. The participants were college students (9 subjects) or staff members (13 subjects) from the university. The ages of the participants ranged from 22 to 42 years with an average age of 30 years. One subject was a left-hander and all partici-pants reported normal vision or corrected-to-normal vision (45 %). 7 participants reported experience with interaction in LHRD environments; the remaining 15 par-ticipants reported no experience.

5   Results

This section reports the results of the experiment. We did not remove outliers from the data set to represent different user types. Hence, the precondition of normal distributed data was violated in some cases (non-parametric tests applied). In order to analyze the user performance we ran a repeated-measured ANOVA (Greenhouse-Geisser

---

[3] The tutorial used the same task, whereby the tolerance range of big/small targets was increased to ± 3.8 mm and ± 2 mm, respectively.

corrected) or a Friedman ANOVA on ranks on the dependent variables. The post hoc pairwise comparison (samples t-test or Dunn's method) was performed with Bonferroni correction.

User performance is usually assessed by efficiency, effectiveness, physiological effort, and satisfaction [17]. In our study the efficiency and effectiveness were determined by measured manipulation time, number of attempts, and error rate. The physiological effort was determined by number of button events as the user's motor effort and his subjective workload rating. The workload was determined as *Raw TLX* [16] without weighting scales. The NASA task load index (TLX) uses six subscales (i.e., mental/physical/temporal demand, performance, effort, frustration) to determine the total workload. The overall TLX workload represented the satisfaction. We used z-score transformation to combine the different metrics. Figure 3 shows the mean z-scores of efficiency/effectiveness, physiological effort, and overall user performance.

Due to the participant's expectation on first trial and his training curve on last trial, we combined both trials of condition *smf* by arithmetic averaging of measured values.

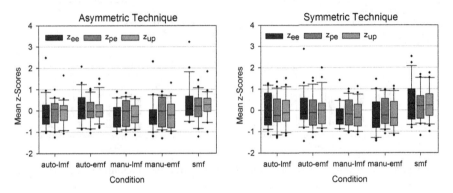

Fig. 3. User performance (z_{up}) with the sub-scales effectiveness/efficiency (z_{ee}) and physiological effort (z_{pe}).

5.1 Efficiency/Effectiveness

According to mean efficiency/effectiveness z-scores we found significant differences ($\chi^2(4)_{asymT} = 12.04$ p $= 0.017$, $\chi^2(4)_{symT} = 13.35$ p $= 0.01$). Pairwise comparison showed that the subjects were more efficient and effective with interaction scaling at *asymT* (p < 0.05, excluded *auto-emf*) and with both conditions of *manu* at *symT* (p < 0.005) compared to *smf*.

We have analyzed the efficiency/effectiveness values with respect to the different accuracies of target type. The efficiency/effectiveness of small targets differed significantly ($\chi^2(4)_{asymT} = 14.10$ p $= 0.007$ and $\chi^2(4)_{symT} = 14.66$ p $= 0.005$) between *smf* and *manu* (p < 0.05) at both techniques. We found no differences for big targets.

The used parameters of efficiency/effectiveness were analyzed in detail. We measured the total manipulation time in seconds per object, i.e., the times were added up during the object manipulation. In order to sort in an object the required attempts were counted for each object according to the target parameters (position, size, orientation). We calculated the relative error rate of the corresponding target by the average sum of failed attempts and divided by the total number of attempts. That means, the less attempts, the lower the target's error rate.

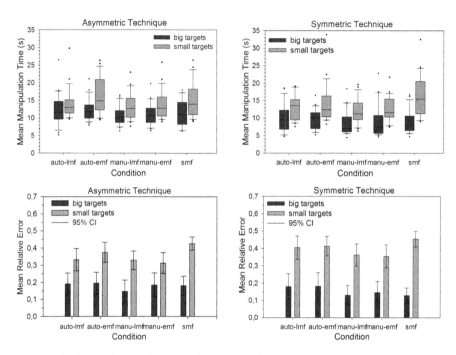

Fig. 4. Comparing manipulation time (top) and error rate (bottom) by target type.

Manipulation Time. On average, the subjects needed less time to manipulate the big targets than the small targets, as expected (see Fig. 4). For big targets we found a significant difference between the conditions ($F(4,84)_{asymT,big}$ = 2.51 p = 0.048, $\chi^2(4)_{asymT,big}$ = 9.64 p = 0.047). However, a pairwise comparison could not show which conditions are differed. For small targets we only found a significant difference at $symT$ ($\chi^2(4)_{symT,small}$ = 16.2 p = 0.003) between smf and the conditions of $manu$ (p < 0.05).

Number of Attempts. The subjects needed less attempts for the big targets than for the small targets. The number of attempts differed significantly between condition and small targets ($\chi^2(4)_{asymT,small}$ = 27.44 and $\chi^2(4)_{symT,small}$ = 19.02 p ≤ 0.001) and not significantly between condition and big targets. A pairwise comparison identified the differences of small targets between the condition smf and both conditions of $manu$ ($asymT$ and $symT$), also between smf and $auto\text{-}lmf$ ($asymT$ p < 0.005) or $auto\text{-}emf$ ($symT$ p < 0.05).

Error Rate. The lowest error rate was achieved with manual switching for big and small targets (see Fig. 4). As expected, the big targets achieved a low error rate with the static mapping function, whereas the small targets generated a higher error rate. For each condition the error rate differed very significantly between big and small targets (all p < 0.005 at *asymT* and all p < 0.001 at *symT* with Wilcoxon signed rank test). Furthermore, the error rate of small targets differed significantly between *smf* and *manu* at both techniques (p = 0.027 at *asymT* and p = 0.01 at *symT*) and between *smf* and *auto-lmf* at *asymT* (p = 0.002).

H2. We partially confirmed H2. By means of big/small targets with different accuracy we could show that accuracy affects the user performance. We found a difference according to required attempts between the targets types, whereby the big targets were solved faster. According to error rate the big targets were not affected by interaction scaling as expected. On the contrary, the error rate of small targets was affected positively by manual switching with symmetric technique. For asymmetric technique the error rate of small targets was affected positively by interaction scaling with manual switching and automatic switching with linear mapping factor. Since the exponential mapping factor decreases fast by stepping forwards, sometimes clutching was required for scaling/rotation tasks.

Table 2. Mean relative frequency distribution (x) of less attempts (≤ 2) and less error rate (≤ 20 %) by target type (with $N_{big} = 66$ and $N_{small} = 110$). Best performance results are highlighted bold.

Condition	Attempts ≤ 2		Error rate ≤ 20 %		Attempts ≤ 2		Error rate ≤ 20 %	
	$\bar{x}_{big}$	$\bar{x}_{small}$	$\bar{x}_{big}$	$\bar{x}_{small}$	$\bar{x}_{big}$	$\bar{x}_{small}$	$\bar{x}_{big}$	$\bar{x}_{small}$
auto-lmf	83,3 %	**63,6 %**	65,2 %	**42,7 %**	86,4 %	**56,4 %**	72,7 %	30,9 %
auto-emf	81,8 %	59,1 %	62,1 %	38,2 %	87,9 %	51,8 %	69,7 %	31,8 %
manu-lmf	86,4 %	60,0 %	77,3 %	41,8 %	95,5 %	57,3 %	77,3 %	32,7 %
manu-emf	80,3 %	**63,6 %**	72,7 %	**57,3 %**	89,4 %	**58,2 %**	72,7 %	**50,0 %**
smf	80,3 %	44,5 %	72,0 %	26,4 %	89,4 %	48,6 %	78,8 %	30,0 %
	asymmetric technique (*asymT*)				symmetric technique (*symT*)			

We found interesting results according to the maximum number of attempts (≤ 2) and low error rate (≤ 20 %), see Table 2. In total, at *asymT* the subjects solved 60 % of the small targets with a maximum of two attempts with interaction scaling in comparison to 45 % of small targets without interaction scaling. On the contrary, at *symT* the participants solved more than 52 % of the small targets with one or two attempts by using interaction scaling and 49 % without interaction scaling. At *symT* only about 30 % of the small targets were solved with low error rate with/without interaction scaling, excepting *manu-emf*. In particular, the participants had problems to solve the small rotated square[4]. At *asymT* over 38 % of the small targets were solved with low error rate using interaction scaling, while only 26 % of them were solved without interaction scaling. One exception was condition *manu-emf* where half of the small targets were solved with low error rate.

---

[4] This object was the smallest one with 11 mm size and 40° orientation.

H1. We partially confirmed H1. Our findings have shown participants required shorter manipulation times, less attempts and less error rate for object manipulation with both distance-adjusted mapping functions combined with the manual switching method of precision levels. In addition, the subjects performed the tasks more efficiently with automatic switching and linear mapping factor at asymmetric technique. Especially the required high accuracy of ± 1 mm benefited from interaction scaling. Nevertheless, the coarse accuracy of ± 2.5 mm supported good performance with and without interaction scaling.

5.2 Physiological Effort

The motor effort (i.e., movements of fingers and arms) differed between the manipulation techniques due to the used interaction metaphors. For symmetric technique the number of manipulation operations was equal to the number of object selections due to the simultaneous tasks. However, for asymmetric technique the number of manipulation operations were calculated from the count of object selections and the count of SR-mode activation. The total button events were counted for each trial (number of pressing switch button, select button, and manipulation button).

Button Events. At *symT* less button events were averagely needed with *auto* ($\bar{x}_{lmf} = 19$, $\bar{x}_{emf} = 20$), followed by *smf* ($\bar{x}_{smf} = 27$) and *manu* ($\bar{x}_{lmf} = 28$, $\bar{x}_{emf} = 29$). Similarly, at *asymT* less button events were averagely required with *auto* ($\bar{x}_{lmf} = 46$, $\bar{x}_{emf} = 52$), followed by the *manu* ($\bar{x}_{lmf} = 57$, $\bar{x}_{emf} = 58$) and *smf* ($\bar{x}_{smf} = 56$). The difference was significantly ($\chi^2(4)_{asymT} = 19.97$, $\chi^2(4)_{symT} = 25.05$ p ≤ 0.001). Pairwise comparisons showed that *auto* needed significantly less motor effort than *manu-emf* (p < 0.005) or *smf* (p < 0.05) at *symT*. At *asymT* the significant difference occurred between *auto-lmf* and *manu* (p < 0.01).

Workload. In general, the participants assessed that the overall workload of both manipulation techniques is roughly the same. However, the workload of *auto* was evaluated higher than *manu*. The frustration and effort were rated highest by *smf*. The participants reported a higher temporal/physical demand and frustration for *symT*, in particular with *auto*. Due to the simultaneous manipulation tasks of *symT* more physical demand was required and increased the frustration level (e.g., readjustment of scaling during positioning). In contrast, the mental demand, performance and effort were rated higher at *asymT*. Here, the switching of interaction mode required additional mental demand and effort, thus, reduced the frustration level (e.g., positioning is preserved during scaling). From the participants' point of view, the manual switching of precision levels required no additional physical/mental demand or effort.

Based on the workload results the subjective workload rating was calculated by using the scales of physical demand, mental demand, effort, and frustration.

H3. In general, the physiological effort was higher at condition *smf* compared with *auto* or *manu* (see Fig. 3). However, a significant effect was only found for *asymT* ($F(4,84)_{asymT} = 3.98$ p $= 0.005$) between *smf* and *manu* (p < 0.01) and *auto-lmf* (p < 0.05) respectively. Thus, H3 was only confirmed by asymmetric technique.

The workload of manual switching was less appraised by the subjects than for automatic or without switching. However, the number of button events was similar for automatic and without switching. Furthermore, we could not find a significant difference of physiological effort between the manipulation techniques. We assume that the higher number of button events do not affect the physiological effort at asymmetric technique.

5.3 User Performance and Preferences

User Performance. There was a significant effect of condition on user performance ($\chi^2(4)_{asymT}$ = 19.82, $\chi^2(4)_{symT}$ = 20.18 both p < 0.001) between *smf* and *manu* (see Fig. 3). At *symT* there was an additional significant difference between *smf* and *auto-emf* (all p < 0.05). We found no effect of manipulation technique and switching method. In general, the user performance was better with *manu* than with *auto* at *asymT*. This difference is due to the poor performance results of efficiency/effectiveness and the increased physiological effort on *auto*. At *symT* also *auto* obtained averagely poor performance results of efficiency/effectiveness than *manu*. However, the performance values of physiological effort are roughly the same at *symT*.

Preferences. In general, the manual switching was preferred by the participants (68 % at *asymT* and 77 % at *symT*). Furthermore, the automatic switching was preferred by 7 subjects at *asymT* and 5 subjects at *symT*. Only 3 subjects reported preferences of both switching methods for symmetric and asymmetric techniques. Further, the participants reported preferences for both manipulation techniques (i.e., *asymT* by 10 subjects, *symT* by 9 subjects, both by 3 subjects). The presentation order of techniques (experimental day 1 vs. day 2) had no impact on the participants' preferences.

The preference of switching method depends on the manipulation technique. As opposed to this, the preference of manipulation technique depends on individuals. Many participants sensed the symmetric interaction technique as intuitive, i.e., natural and easy handling, less mentally demanding. Nevertheless, the simultaneous manipulation operations complicate precise scaling and positioning at the same time. Furthermore, some users reported that they became even easier with the asymmetric interaction technique after a training period. The separation of the interaction tasks enabled more precise manipulation and they sensed this technique less physically demanding in the long term. Consequently, the automatic switching is rather preferred at symmetric technique than at asymmetric technique.

5.4 Physical Navigation

We could observe three behavior pattern according to physical navigation (see Fig. 5). First, a subject used the entire physical interaction space to manipulate the objects sequentially by stepping forwards/backwards (vertical movements). Second, a subject preferred a constant interaction distance to the display and only stepped forwards when the attempt failed (horizontal movements). Third, the subject used a strategy, while he manipulated all objects at distant and afterwards he performed a fine adjustment at close-up range (tactical movements). At asymmetric technique with automatic switching the participants using vertical movements performed the tasks more efficiently, whereas the participants using horizontal movements attained better performance results with manual switching. At symmetric technique the participants using vertical movements performed the tasks with manual and automatic switching more efficiently and effectively. However, the tactical movements benefited from static mapping function.

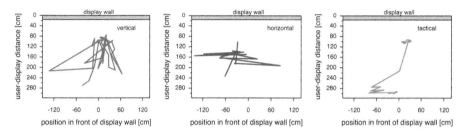

Fig. 5. The observed behavior patterns regarding to physical navigation: vertical movements (left), horizontal movements (center), and tactical movements (right).

Using the users' physical navigation profile we also identified three interaction ranges, where participants interacted frequently (i.e., close range $udd < 0.9$ m, close-middle range $udd \leq 1.5$ m, middle-distant range $udd < 2.0$ m). Far distances ($udd > 2.0$ m) were used rarely. About half of the participants interacted in close-middle range (12 subjects), whereas the remaining participants preferred close range (3 subjects) or middle-distant range (7 subjects) at *asymT* and close or middle-distant range (5 subjects each) at *symT*. We observed that subjects with close-middle range were more efficient with automatic switching. For the other preferred ranges a manual switching was more suitable. Here, clutching could reduced by using coarse-grained precision (absolute mapping) at close range. However, we could not find a relation between user performance and movements or preferred distance.

6   Discussion and Conclusion

We evaluated how different accuracies affect user performance on distance-aware bimanual manipulation techniques. To consider user preference during object manipulation, we compared a direct mapping approach with distance-adapted mapping approaches that use an automatic task-based or a manual switching method of precision levels. Table 3 outlines the main findings of our user study.

In summary, the user performance is increased by using interaction scaling in LHRD environments. The results have shown that the users are able to effectively solve fundamental manipulation tasks with distance-aware interaction techniques. In fact, interaction scaling improved the performance significantly if a high accuracy (2 mm) was required; but it has no effect at lower accuracy (5 mm). The participants were able to

Table 3. Summary of main findings.

Metric	Results

Efficiency/Effectiveness	• Improvement of efficiency/effectiveness
	  – Interaction scaling with automatic/manual switching (asymmetric technique)
	  – Interaction scaling with manual switching (symmetric technique)
	  – Accurate object manipulation with distance-aware asymmetric technique

Physiological Effort	• Workload of manual switching was less appraised in spite of significant higher number of button events (both techniques) • Higher number of button events had no effect at asymmetric technique

User performance	• High accuracy (2 mm) benefited from interaction scaling
	• Improvement of user performance
	  – Manual switching with linear/exponential mapping factor (both techniques)
	  – Automatic switching with linear mapping factor (asymmetric technique)

Preferences	• Interaction scaling with manual switching was preferred • Preference of manipulation technique depends on individuals and switching preference depends on manipulation technique

Physical Navigation	• Observation of behavior pattern (vertical, horizontal, and tactical):
	  – Distance-aware symmetric technique was efficient with vertical movements
	  – Asymmetric technique with automatic switching was efficient with vertical movements or manual switching was efficient with horizontal movements
	• Automatic switching was efficient at close-middle range and manual switching was suitable for other ranges

manipulate the objects more accurately with the asymmetric technique than with the symmetric technique. Most of the participants preferred a manual switching of precision levels; however, half of the subjects solved the tasks with automatic switching well.

Basically, the best performance results are provided by the automatic switching method with linear mapping factor at asymmetric technique. Furthermore, the manual switching method with linear or exponential mapping factor provided the best performance results for both techniques. As the manual switching of precision levels required often a minor adjustment after the coarse adjustment, a smaller (exponential) mapping factor was more efficient. At automatic switching of precision levels a continuous adjustment was performed, thus a larger mapping factor was appropriated for effective motor movements effectively (less clutching).

Based on our findings, we recommend to consider the user's preferences and navigation behavior in distance-aware interaction, such as the user's preferred distance and walk movements. In principle, the distance-adjusted mapping factor is appropriate, but the calculation should not be the same over all interaction distances. For instance, at close range the possibility of coarse precision has to be provided by manual switching of precision levels. In contrast, if the user prefers to interact at distant, then the user should reach a high precision level with a few steps closer to the large display by using an exponential mapping function.

The study has shown that the physical navigation is used differently by the users, e.g., their interaction distances vary. Our results agree with Kopper et al. [20] that users interact mainly from a constant distance during manipulation tasks (horizontal movement), but also with Ball et al. [3] that users prefer to walk during navigation tasks (vertical movements). We recommend to consider various parameters, such as parameters of the physical interaction space (e.g., input device, dimensions of interaction space), objective characteristics of the user (e.g., body size, physiological limitations), and individual subjective characteristics (e.g., preference of bimanual technique, preferred interaction distance) to define the interaction scaling.

The idea of interaction scaling with task-based automatic switching between coarse and precise interaction is only partly suitable in LHRD environments. We recommend to use a semi-automatic distance-aware approach to assist users. That means the user controls the precision of interaction and at the user's request an adjustment should be performed by the system automatically.

In our study we identified behaviors according to physical navigation. However, the behaviors were partially inaccurate. In future work we plan to investigate the user's physical navigation more detailed during object manipulation on a LHRD. Afterwards, we assume to generate user profiles that improve distance-aware interaction by considering individual properties.

Acknowledgments. This work was supported by EFRE fond of the European Community and a grant of the German National Research Foundation (DFG), Research Training Group 1424 MuSAMA. We thank our study participants and the anonymous reviewers for their valuable contribution.

References

1. Andrews, C., Endert, A., Yost, B., North, C.: Information visualization on large, high-resolution displays: issues, challenges, and opportunities. Inf. Vis. **10**(4), 341–355 (2011)
2. Ball, R., North, C.: The effects of peripheral vision and physical navigation on large scale visualization. In: Proceedings of GI 2008, pp. 9–16. Canadian Information Processing Society (2008)
3. Ball, R., North, C., Bowman, D.A.: Move to improve: promoting physical navigation to increase user performance with large displays. In: Proceedings of CHI 2007, pp. 191–200. ACM (2007)
4. Ballendat, T., Marquardt, N., Greenberg, S.: Proxemic interaction: designing for a proximity and orientation-aware environment. In: Proceedings of ITS 2010, pp. 121–130. ACM, New York, NY, USA (2010)
5. Bezerianos, A., Isenberg, P.: Perception of visual variables on tiled wall-sized displays for information visualization applications. IEEE Trans. Visual Comput. Graphics **18**, 2516–2525 (2012)

6. Blanch, R., Guiard, Y., Beaudouin-Lafon, M.: Semantic pointing: improving target acquisition with control-display ratio adaptation. In: Proceedings of CHI 2004, pp. 519–526. ACM (2004)

7. Cao, X., Balakrishnan, R.: Visionwand: interaction techniques for large displays using a passive wand tracked in 3d. In: Proceedings of UIST 2003, pp. 173–182. ACM (2003)

8. Casiez, G., Vogel, D., Balakrishnan, R., Cockburn, A.: The impact of control-display gain on user performance in pointing tasks. Hum. Comput. Interact. **23**(3), 215–250 (2008)

9. Collomb, M., Hascoët, M., Baudisch, P., Lee, B.: Improving drag-and-drop on wall-size displays. In: Proceedings of GI 2005, pp. 25–32. Canadian Human-Computer Communications Society (2005)

10. Czerwinski, M., Smith, G., Regan, T., Meyers, B., Robertson, G.G., Starkweather, G.: Toward characterizing the productivity benefits of very large displays. In: Interact 2003, pp. 9–16. IOS Press (2003)

11. Esakia, A., Endert, A., North, C.: Large display interaction via multiple acceleration curves and multifinger pointer control. Adv. in Hum.-Comp. Int. 2014, 12:12–12:12, (Jan 2014)

12. Forlines, C., Vogel, D., Balakrishnan, R.: Hybridpointing: fluid switching between absolute and relative pointing with a direct input device. In: Proceedings of UIST 2006, pp. 211–220. ACM (2006)

13. Frees, S., Kessler, G.D.: Precise and rapid interaction through scaled manipulation in immersive virtual environments. In: Proceedings of IEEE VR 2005, pp. 99–106 (2005)

14. Grossman, T., Balakrishnan, R.: The bubble cursor: enhancing target acquisition by dynamic resizing of the cursor's activation area. In: Proceedings of CHI 2005, pp. 281–290. ACM (2005)

15. Guiard, Y.: Asymmetric division of labor in human skilled bimanual action: The kinematic chain as a model. J. Mot. Behav. **19**, 486–517 (1987)

16. Hart, S.G.: Nasa-Task Load Index (NASA-TLX); 20 Years Later. Proc. Hum. Factors Ergon. Soc. Annu. Meet. **50**(9), 904–908 (2006)

17. Hornbaek, K.: Current practice in measuring usability: challenges to usability studies and research. Int. J. Hum Comput Stud. **64**(2), 79–102 (2006)

18. Jakobsen, M.R., Sahlemariam Haile, Y., Knudsen, S., Hornbæk, K.: Information visualization and proxemics: Design opportunities and empirical findings. IEEE Trans. Visual Comput. Graphics **19**(12), 2386–2395 (2013)

19. König, W.A., Gerken, J., Dierdorf, S., Reiterer, H.: Adaptive pointing – design and evaluation of a precision enhancing technique for absolute pointing devices. In: Gross, T., Gulliksen, J., Kotzé, P., Oestreicher, L., Palanque, P., Prates, R.O., Winckler, M. (eds.) INTERACT 2009. LNCS, vol. 5726, pp. 658–671. Springer, Heidelberg (2009)

20. Kopper, R., Silva, M.G., McMahan, R.P., Bowman, D.A.: Increasing the precision of distant pointing for large high-resolution displays. Technical report, TR-08-17, Computer Science, Virginia Tech. (2008)

21. Kreylos, O.: Environment-independent VR development. In: Bebis, G., Boyle, R., Parvin, B., Koracin, D., Remagnino, P., Porikli, F., Peters, J., Klosowski, J., Arns, L., Chun, Y.K., Rhyne, T.-M., Monroe, L. (eds.) ISVC 2008, Part I. LNCS, vol. 5358, pp. 901–912. Springer, Heidelberg (2008)

22. Lehmann, A., Staadt, O.: Distance-aware bimanual interaction for large high-resolution displays. In: Csurka, G., Kraus, M., Laramee, R.S., Richard, P., Braz, J. (eds.) VISIGRAPP 2012. CCIS, vol. 359, pp. 97–111. Springer, Heidelberg (2013)

23. Nancel, M., Chapuis, O., Pietriga, E., Yang, X.D., Irani, P.P., Beaudouin-Lafon, M.: High-precision pointing on large wall displays using small handheld devices. In: Proceedings CHI 2013, pp. 831–840. ACM, New York, NY, USA (2013)

24. Peck, S.M., North, C., Bowman, D.: A multiscale interaction technique for large, high-resolution displays. In: 3D User Interfaces, pp. 31–38. IEEE Computer Society (2009)
25. Shoemaker, G., Tsukitani, T., Kitamura, Y., Booth, K.S.: Body-centric interaction techniques for very large wall displays. In: Proceedings of NordiCHI 2010, pp. 463–472. ACM (2010)
26. Tan, D.S., Gergle, D., Scupelli, P., Pausch, R.: Physically large displays improve performance on spatial tasks. ACM Trans. Comput. Hum. Interact. **13**, 71–99 (2006)
27. Vogel, D., Balakrishnan, R.: Interactive public ambient displays: Transitioning from implicit to explicit, public to personal, interaction with multiple users. In: Proceedings of UIST 2004, pp. 137–146. ACM (2004)
28. Vogel, D., Balakrishnan, R.: Distant freehand pointing and clicking on very large, high resolution displays. In: Proceedings of UIST 2005, pp. 33–42. ACM (2005)
29. Ware, C.: Information Visualization: Perception for Design. Morgan Kaufmann Publishers Inc., Burlington (2004)

Should I Stay or Should I Go? Selecting Between Touch and Mid-Air Gestures for Large-Display Interaction

Mikkel R. Jakobsen[✉], Yvonne Jansen, Sebastian Boring, and Kasper Hornbæk

Department of Computer Science, University of Copenhagen, Copenhagen, Denmark
{mikkelrj,yvja,sebastian.boring,kash}@diku.dk

Abstract. Users can interact with large displays in many ways, including touch and mid-air gestures. However, it remains unclear how these ways compare and when users choose one over the other. In a first experiment, we compare touch and mid-air gestures to identify their relative performance for target acquisition. In a second experiment, participants choose freely between touch and mid-air gestures and we artificially require movement to simulate situations where mid-air is considered beneficial. Results from the first experiment show mid-air to be overall slower than touch depending on the task; in the second experiment, participants mostly chose touch in particular for selecting small targets and they rarely switched between mid-air and touch. Results also show that when faced with an increasing cost of using touch in the form of movement, participants chose mid-air over touch; touch remains as fast as mid-air on average.

Keywords: Large display · Mid-air · Touch · Freehand gestures · User study

1 Introduction

Users can interact with large displays in many ways, including through touch when being close to the display and through mid-air gestures when standing at a distance. Both touch and mid-air gestures leverage our basic human ability to point with our hands at objects of interest. Each of them has been researched in isolation [31, 38] and they have been researched in combination [24, 26, 39], but they have rarely been compared (except for specific public display scenarios [20]).

Touch and mid-air gestures seem appropriate for different tasks or situations. For working with detailed information up close with a large high-resolution display, touch requires direct interaction through physical contact, which may be faster and preferred over indirect input (e.g., using a mouse [35]). In contrast, users may want to view large displays from a distance to gain an overview. At a distance, mid-air gestures allow users to interact with targets anywhere on the display [40]. Both interaction styles may be combined to support large-display interaction, allowing users to transition between them. However, an important question remains to be answered: When do users choose one over the other? This paper aims at answering this question.

© IFIP International Federation for Information Processing 2015
J. Abascal et al. (Eds.): INTERACT 2015, Part III, LNCS 9298, pp. 455–473, 2015.
DOI: 10.1007/978-3-319-22698-9_31

Users may have different reasons for choosing to interact through touch or mid-air. First, the relative performance of touch and mid-air may influence users' choice. There are several reasons for expecting touch and mid-air to perform differently for common tasks (e.g., target acquisition): Display space and input space are unified in touch but decoupled in mid-air; touch gives tactile support, but incurs friction while dragging, in contrast to mid-air movement; mid-air gestures can be performed at a distance, but distance affects accuracy; touch is limited to display parts within arms' reach and extensive movement is required to interact with remote parts; and touch onset naturally delimits gestures, whereas mid-air gestures need an explicit delimiter (e.g., pinching). Empirical studies are needed to help understand these differences.

However, users choose to interact through touch or mid-air not only based on their relative performance. For instance, mid-air gestures might be used for a task because they require less effort, even though they might be slower or less accurate than touch. This choice may depend on the task or result out of convenience (e.g., in order to avoid repetitive locomotion). Investigating when users choose one over the other and how they switch between touch and mid-air gestures is important for understanding how and when they might be combined.

We present two experiments: (1) a controlled experiment that compares the relative performance of touch and mid-air gestures for different target acquisition tasks in which we vary target size, distance, and whether target locations are known; and (2) an experiment in which users can freely choose between touch and mid-air gestures, but are required to step away from the display at different intervals (i.e., simulating conditions that benefit from mid-air input and impose a cost on using touch). The experiments present the first empirical data on users' choice between touch and mid-air, which may help better take advantage of both types of input for wall-displays.

2   Related Work

Touch and mid-air gestures are particularly interesting input modes for interacting with large displays: they allow free movement in front of the display, can be used without a dedicated input device, and can therefore be used straight away and by several users at a time. Other input options that allow freedom of movement have been researched, including gyroscopic mice, handheld devices (e.g., smart phones [6, 25]), and tangibles [18]. However, in this paper we mainly discuss direct touch and mid-air gestures that use free hand movement. Also, while many types of gestures have been researched (e.g., for moving objects or executing commands), we focus on selection.

In the following, based on a review of literature, we discuss factors that may influence the use of, and choice between, touch and mid-air gestures. We also review research about the combination of touch input and mid-air gestures.

2.1   Touch-Based Interaction

Touch is familiar to many people and simplifies interaction on large displays (e.g., by allowing direct pointing to an object instead of moving a mouse pointer [38]). Yet, it introduces new challenges: First, finger occlusion makes accurate pointing at small targets difficult; this has been addressed through novel interaction techniques [41].

Second, touch requires users to be within reach of the point of interaction. When people want to interact with content further away on a large display, they must physically move there. Techniques such as Frisbee [19] and Drag-and-pop [4] provide access to distant content with less movement. Nacenta et al. [28] compared different techniques for reaching distant targets located on multiple displays. They found a control-display ratio of 1:1 to be preferable to amplified touch movements.

Third, content further away is not always visible when standing close to the display; close proximity makes it difficult to search the display. Although users can step back in order to get an overview, and have been found to do so [16], additional effort is required to go back to the display in order to interact. Several researchers have explored distant touch interaction that allow for overview at a distance (e.g., Touch Projector [6] or ARCPad [25]), but they require the use of a handheld device.

2.2   Mid-Air Gestures

Mid-air gestures have the advantage that users can directly point to an object, similar to touch, except that users can do so from a distance [38]. Most prominent are mid-air techniques using ray casting, which extend a finger or object with an imaginary line to determine the point of contact with the display. Early research used laser pointers to interact with distant content [28]. Later work has investigated freehand pointing [40]. Research on mid-air interaction has addressed several challenges.

First, for techniques that continuously track the user's hand, there is no differentiation between action (i.e., selecting an object) and movement (i.e., moving towards a target). Naturally, techniques that require a dedicated device can have buttons to perform selection operations. For freehand pointing, several gestures have been proposed to trigger a selection: the most often used is the pinch gesture where users pinch together index finger and thumb to trigger an action [22, 34, 42]; other techniques such as AirTap [40], ThumbTrigger [40], or SideTrigger [3] use different gestures. Techniques differ in how fingers used for ray casting (often the index finger) move during the selection gesture, which affects pointing.

Second, mid-air pointing generally suffers from low accuracy. A common cause is the natural hand tremor, which is particularly problematic for small targets at far distance [27]. Vogel et al. compensate for these problems by switching between relative pointing and absolute pointing [40]. Nancel et al. used different regions on a mobile device for different control-display ratios [29]. Relative pointing techniques can thus improve pointing accuracy, but require recalibration or clutching.

Third, users become less accurate without visual feedback even with direct pointing through ray-casting [9]. Users have to relate hand movements to on-screen cursor movement because the input space is separated from the output space [14].

2.3   Combination of Touch and Mid-Air Gestures

Having both touch and mid-air input available at the same time is feasible and earlier work has emphasized that the techniques may be integrated (e.g., [24]). Directly related to our work is the study of Schick et al. that compared a touch-and-point condition, in which participants could point at an object and hold their arm still for .25 s to select it, to a touch-only condition [37]. Touch-and-point was faster and preferred, requiring less physical effort. However, the study involved moving rather large 300×300 pixel blocks (on a 25 ppi display) and did not control for target distance. Vogel and Balakrishnan developed an ambient display that supported transitions from implicit interaction at a distance to explicit interaction through touch [39]; others have explored such transitions [23, 26]. Touch and mid-air interaction has also been unified for tabletop displays: the continuous interaction space allows moving from touch to gestures above the surface [24]; Hilliges et al. supported picking up objects for mid-air manipulation [13]. Pointable, which augments touch with in-air pointing to allow bimanual interaction with distant content, was found to perform comparable to multi-touch [3].

In sum, empirical comparisons of touch and mid-air gestures for wall-display interaction are rare. Several factors might affect how users would choose between the two modalities if both were available at the same time, but it is unclear how users choose; we have found no research on this. Thus, with this paper we aim to contribute empirical data to help understand when users choose between touch and mid-air gestures.

3   Experiment 1: Touch vs. Mid-Air

We first conducted an experiment comparing touch and mid-air for target acquisition tasks. The purpose was to obtain empirical data on user performance and satisfaction for touch and mid-air gestures that would allow us to hypothesize about when users would choose one or the other for different tasks. Our aim was not to conclude on the relative performance of touch and mid-air in general; the results do not necessarily generalize to other implementations. The experiment focused on interaction with wall-sized displays, on which mid-air gestures have been primarily used [22, 30].

3.1   Interfaces

Participants used two interfaces that implement pointing and selection using either touch or mid-air. With the *Touch* interface, a touch cursor appears when a participant's finger touches the surface, and the touch is registered as a selection. With the *Mid-air* interface, participants move a cursor on the display using ray casting similar to Vogel and Balakrishnan's technique [40]: the cursor is placed at the point where the ray cast from the tip of the user's index finger intersects the display plane. We chose ray casting because it is the "canonical pointing technique" (according to Bowman et al. [7], p. 82) and it is straightforward to use. Participants make a selection using a SideTrigger gesture [3]: while pointing, they move their thumb towards the middle finger, which is curled toward the palm (see Fig. 1–C). "Clicking" the middle finger provides kinesthetic feedback while minimizing involuntary movements of the index finger during selection [3]. We considered using the other hand to make selections, but decided against it, since touch is also (in the present experiment) a single-handed technique. We used the €1-filter [8] to compensate for jitter in cursor movements.

3.2 Apparatus

We conducted the experiment on a wall-sized display (see Fig. 1) that consists of 12 HD projectors with a total of 7680 × 3240 pixels and a resolution of around 68 pixels per inch. Touch on the display is detected through camera-based tracking. Input from six cameras, each capturing 640 × 480 pixels at 30 frames per second (fps), are processed by Community Core Vision. A custom program written in Java multiplexes the tracked touch points. The overall touch resolution is around 17 pixels per inch.

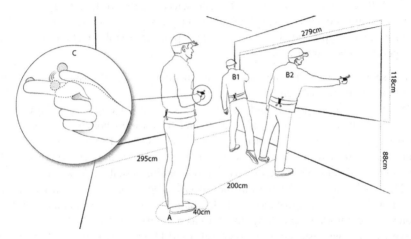

Fig. 1. Experimental setup: A–starting position for all tasks; B–maximum distance to cover in the touch condition; C–thumb trigger gesture used to make selections in the mid-air condition.

Participants were tracked using an OptiTrack motion capture system (.5 mm tracking error, 50 fps). Participants wore a baseball cap, a belt, and a glove with markers attached. This helped quantify head turning and body movement, and gave position and orientation of the hand and the position of the tips of the index finger and thumb.

3.3 Tasks

We used two types of target selection task: *Varied* and *Fixed*. Both consisted of consecutive selections of targets, typical for evaluations of input devices. Previous studies have typically chosen to either (1) vary the size and distance of targets [e.g., 21] or (2) keep the size and distance constant within a sequence (e.g., the reciprocal task [35]).

We designed our tasks to manipulate participants' ability to anticipate target locations, which may influence the relative performance of Touch and Mid-air. While participants can anticipate the next target location in a reciprocal selection task, mixing combinations of size and distance in a sequence requires them to visually search for targets, and they cannot anticipate the direction in which to move for selecting the next target. As Touch requires close proximity to the display, visual search is harder due to the limited field of view. We further expect larger anticipation effects for Touch where larger body movements are required to reach distant targets. Using both types of task helps us investigate these differences. The two tasks are as follows:

- *Varied.* Participants select 13 targets shown (as a red circle) one at a time. When they successfully select a target, the next target appears at a random location, but at a given distance from the previous target. All combinations of size and distance occur once in the sequence. The first target is always 128 pixels in diameter and placed in the center of the display.
- *Fixed.* Participants perform nine alternate selections of two targets of a fixed size, spaced a given distance apart. The current target is shown as a red circle, while the other target is represented as a gray circle. Upon successful selection of the current target, the other target turns red.

The selection of the first target marks the beginning of both tasks; only data from the following selections were used.

We also wanted to understand how the distance and size of targets influence the relative performance of touch and mid-air and thus varied both (see Table 1). We varied target size from 32 pixels to 512 pixels (1.2 cm to 18.8 cm on the display): smaller targets were deemed impractical for both Touch (due to occlusion) and Mid-air (due to limits in pointing accuracy). The corresponding visual angle was between 1.3° and 21° when standing 50 cm from the display. The visual angle of a target varies proportionally to viewing distance: A 128px target has the same visual angle at 50 cm distance ($\sim$ comfortable touching distance) as a 512px target at 2 m.

We varied target distance from 768 pixels to 6144 pixels, which is 10 % to 80 % of the display width, and 31° to 132° visual angle viewed from 50 cm distance.

Participants were allowed to move around freely in both interface conditions. We considered restricting movement in the Mid-air condition, but since movement is required for Touch, we allowed movement so as to make the conditions more similar. However, participants started each task from a fixed position (Fig. 1–A). For Mid-air participants could thus move in order to point more accurately; moving changes the control-display ratio, which depends on both the viewing distance and viewing angle.

3.4   Participants

We recruited 19 volunteers (14 male), 19–36 years old ($M = 26$), to participate; all but two were right handed. Participants received an equivalent of €25 as compensation.

3.5   Experimental Design

The experiment used a within-subjects design with interface (Mid-air, Touch), task type (Varied, Fixed), target size (3 levels), and target distance (4 levels) as factors. For each interface, participants performed a series of tasks for both task types. The order of interface was counterbalanced across participants to compensate for learning and fatigue. For both task types, participants performed 8 repetitions for each of the 12 combinations of size and distance. Participants thus performed 8 Varied tasks (8 × 12 = 96 timed targets) and 12 Fixed tasks (12 × 8 = 96 timed targets). Altogether, the experiment gave data from 19 participants × 2 (interfaces) × 2 (task types) × 3 (target sizes) × 4 (target distances) × 8 (repetitions) = 7296 target selections.

3.6   Dependent Variables and Data Collection

As dependent variables we measured accuracy, target selection time, subjective satisfaction, and preference. We also collected data on participants' physical movement in order to describe how participants performed the tasks using the two interfaces.

- *Accuracy:* We calculated the error rate as percentage of targets that were not selected on the first attempt; outside-target selections do not cause the next target to appear, only a correct selection does.
- *Target Selection Time:* We split the elapsed time into a pointing phase (time spent approaching the target) and a selection phase (time spent touching or making a selection gesture on target). For Mid-air, we determined when the cursor had first entered the target; as a proxy for the cursor in the Touch condition, we orthogonally projected participants' index finger onto the display plane.
- *Subjective Satisfaction:* We used 12 questions from the ISO 9241-9 device assessment questionnaire [11] including questions on fatigue. We changed the anchors of questions from "too low"/"too high" to "appropriate"/"inappropriate" as we believe that the original anchors were confusing (i.e., what is too low fatigue?).
- *Physical movement:* We quantified participants' locomotion (from belt position), head turning, and hand movements necessary for selecting targets. Our measures of movement were calculated from our tracking data, which we filtered using the Douglas-Peucker algorithm (1 cm tolerance) to compensate for jitter.

Table 1. Target sizes and distances. Visual angle is at a 50 cm distance to the display.

	Target sizes			Distances between targets			
pixels	32	128	512	768	1536	3072	6144
cm	1.2cm	4.7cm	18.8cm	28cm	56cm	112cm	224cm
visual angle	1.3°	5.3°	21°	31°	59°	96°	132°

3.7   Procedure

We first introduced participants to the experiment and calibrated the system. For calibration, we asked participants to raise their hand in a pointing gesture with their thumb touching the knuckle of their curled middle finger (Fig. 1–C), and repeat this gesture a number of times. This was captured to build a template for the selection gesture. Participants then did five practice tasks with each interface. Participants operated both interfaces using their preferred hand; we automatically verified that touch events were produced by the gloved hand. The introduction took around 15 min.

Before each task, we asked participants to stand at the starting position 2 m away from the center of the display (Fig. 1–A); an on-screen indication helped them find the position; when in position, the first target was shown. Participants selected the first target to begin the task. Participants were asked to select targets as quickly as possible, while maintaining high accuracy. Participants could rest after each task. Once they completed all tasks with one interface, they were handed the questionnaire.

After completing all tasks, participants were asked to explain which interface they preferred. The experiment lasted around an hour on average for each participant.

3.8   Hypotheses

We expected that the different control-display ratios of touch and mid-air would result in a speed-accuracy tradeoff. Moreover, mid-air should generally be slower, as input space and output space are decoupled and users therefore must relate movements to the visual feedback. We hypothesized the following:

- Touch is faster and less error-prone than mid-air for subsequent targets close to each other on the display. Compared to mid-air, direct coupling of motor space and display space gives users direct feedback on interaction as it occurs.
- Mid-air is faster for distant targets as users can cover any distance to a target solely through arm/hand/finger movements. For touch, in contrast, distant targets require extensive body movements, which are slower.
- Mid-air is slower for small targets, because the higher control-display ratio makes pointing more difficult; users may need to move closer to point more accurately.
- Touch performs relatively worse for Varied tasks, especially with large distances and small targets, because visual search is harder due to the limited field of view.

3.9   Results

We report results based on the estimation approach [10], that is, as effect sizes with confidence intervals following the latest recommendations from the APA [1]. We report geometric means, as they predict population means of completion times more reliably than other metrics [36], and 95 % confidence intervals. Note that geometric means may lead to asymmetric confidence intervals.

Accuracy with Touch and Mid-Air. We observed a high error rate (M = 25 %) affecting both Touch (M = 16 %) and Mid-air (M = 34 %). As shown in Table 2, the error rate depends on task type, target distance, and target size. Small targets were particularly difficult to select and produced high error rates with both interfaces (Touch: M = 39 %, Mid-air: M = 59 %); these error rates are consistent with previous studies of touch (29 % for 1.26 cm targets, 19–57 cm distances [33]) and mid-air (56 % for 1.6 cm targets, 134–402 cm distances [40]). However, error rates for larger sizes are higher than expected. We identified 3 % of the errors as due to participants making selections far from the target or where a "double-selection" was made within 200 ms after a successful selection. When we compare selection times below, we only analyze trials where targets were successfully selected in the first attempt (N = 5450).

Target Selection Time with Touch and Mid-Air. Interface has a clear effect on selection time: Participants spent 40 %, CI [29 %, 52 %] more time selecting targets with Mid-air (M = 1698 ms, CI [1570 ms, 1863 ms]) than Touch (M = 1214 ms, CI [1111 ms, 1327 ms]). This is in line with our expectation of mid-air being generally slower because of the decoupled input and output spaces.

We see from Fig. 2 that the mean selection time is higher for Mid-air for both task types, but that the difference is larger for Fixed tasks (1.6 times, CI [1.45, 1.77]), where target placement was predictable, than for Varied tasks (1.22 times, CI [1.1, 1.35]), where targets appeared in random locations. This difference in ratios is likely because searching for randomly appearing targets is easier when using Mid-air at a distance from the display.

Table 2. Error rate across target size (rows) and distance (columns) for the two interfaces and task types.

	Mid-air					Touch				
Fixed	768	1536	3072	6144	M	768	1536	3072	6144	M
32	41%	51%	55%	68%	54%	27%	30%	32%	41%	32%
128	16%	26%	34%	42%	29%	1%	2%	2%	7%	3%
512	9%	11%	14%	23%	14%	1%	1%	1%	1%	1%
Varied										20%
32	60%	66%	65%	68%	65%	36%	45%	48%	51%	45%
128	36%	34%	33%	41%	36%	8%	6%	11%	17%	10%
512	12%	15%	20%	27%	19%	2%	7%	4%	9%	6%

One reason for the relatively poor performance of Mid-air is difficulties with the thumb trigger gesture. We occasionally had to recalibrate the trigger gesture during the experiment (mostly due to a shifted glove) in order to ensure correct recognition of selections. For Mid-air, a relatively large amount of time (M = 26 %, CI [24, 30]) is spent selecting the target after having pointed at the target.

Fig. 2. Average target selection times showing main effects for interface and task type.

Effects of Distance and Size. We expected the relative performance between Touch and Mid-air to depend on target size and distance. Figure 3 shows selection times as the ratio of Mid-air to Touch; a ratio larger than 1 means that Mid-air is slower. The figure shows that the main effect of interface holds for most of the tested conditions: ratios are larger than 1 for 21 out of 24 (task type × size × distance) combinations.

The advantage of Touch diminishes with increasing distances, in particular when targets cannot easily be reached without much body movement (cf. Figure 1–B1/B2). Mid-air even performs better than Touch for the combination of largest targets at the farthest distance, although the ratio is relatively small (0.89 times, CI [0.82, 0.97]).

Contrary to our expectations, there seems to be less variation in task completion times for randomly placed targets (the Varied task) than for reciprocal placements (the Fixed task). For small targets, the results are less reliable due to high error rates for these targets. Still, the overall trend is clear that Touch performs well for selections across short distances, which require little or no locomotion.

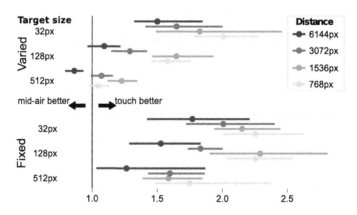

Fig. 3. Selection times for the two interfaces as the ratio of Mid-air to Touch (x-axis) for all combinations of target size (y-axis) and distance (color). A lower ratio means that Mid-air is better. Error bars show the 95 % confidence interval for bootstrapped effect sizes [9].

Physical Movement. As expected, more movement was required for Touch than for Mid-air (see Fig. 4). For Touch, participants naturally have to move their body to bring their hand within physical reach of the target on display: they moved their hand 237 cm on average to reach targets at the largest distance of 224 cm. For Mid-air, targets can be selected from a distance with arm and hand movements only.

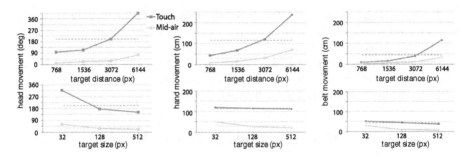

Fig. 4. Mean physical movement for Touch (dark blue) and Mid-air (light blue) across different target distances (top) and sizes (bottom) (Color figure online).

Movement increased with larger distances for both interfaces (Fig. 4, top), but in particular for Touch ($M = 115$ cm vs. $M = 33$ cm for Mid-air, at the largest distance) as participants moved their whole body in order to get in a position to better reach the target. On average, participants moved more and approached the display more for small targets (Fig. 4, bottom). Also, participants moved sideways in order to gain a better visual angle, and therefore had to move more if they were closer to the display.

Participants also turned their head much more for Touch ($M = 201°$) than Mid-air ($M = 92°$). The field of view is limited when being close to the display and visual search for targets is likely more time consuming. This impacts only the Varied task, which explains the difference in relative performance between the two interfaces for the two task types.

Subjective Satisfaction and Preference. Participants gave Touch more positive scores on 6 out of 12 questions about subjective satisfaction (see Fig. 5). Interestingly, participants reported higher wrist and finger fatigue for Mid-air than for Touch, which contradicts movement data. Holding the hand and fingers in a static mid-air pointing gesture seems to be more straining than more dynamic movements for touch input.

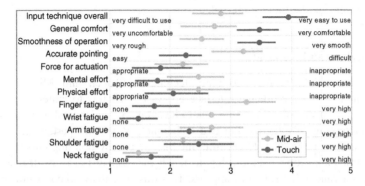

Fig. 5. Bootstrapped confidence intervals for ratings on questions about subjective satisfaction.

Twelve participants preferred Touch, seven preferred Mid-air (not significant by X^2-test). Participants hinted at the reasoning behind their preferences in their comments. Participants explained that Touch was accurate and reliable (9 participants), but that the requirement for moving was taxing (4). Mid-air was thought to give an overview and made it "easy to see targets" (5) and required less walking (4), but accuracy was low particularly for small targets (10).

4   Experiment 2: Movement Costs and User Choice

Our second experiment investigated which input modality users choose when both mid-air and touch are available. We were interested in how the introduction of conditions under which mid-air input is thought to be beneficial (e.g., backing away to overview a display [30] or use a keyboard [22]) affects performance, preference, and choice of interface: we simulated these conditions by artificially requiring movement.

4.1   Hypotheses

Our first hypothesis was that participants overall would choose touch over mid-air. This hypothesis is based on the results of Experiment 1, which showed that touch performs the best except for one distance/size combination. However, about a third of the participants preferred mid-air input in Experiment 1, which suggests that they might choose mid-air interaction. Due to the cost of switching and incurred performance degradation for some targets, we still expect touch to be chosen overall.

Our second hypothesis for the experiment was exploratory. We investigated how manipulating the cost of location-dependent input (such as touch) changes performance and preference. We introduced a backing-up request, requiring participants to move to a particular place in the room. This request abstracts situations where users have to move during or in-between interaction (e.g., to type on a keyboard, write on paper, consult with peers, or get an overview); earlier work has thought that mid-air might be beneficial in such situations (e.g., [22, 30]). Our expectation was that—with an increasing cost associated with location-dependent input (i.e., having to walk back and forth between touch and backing-up requests)—mid-air would be chosen more often, perform better, and be more preferred.

4.2   Interface and Apparatus

Our interface combines the two input techniques (Touch and Mid-air) used in Experiment 1: The experimental interface allows participants to either touch or, at a distance, point in mid-air. We found this to be simple to understand and thus decided against attempting to integrate the two techniques. When the participant's hand or index fingertip is more than 20 cm from the display the ray-pointing cursor is shown. As the participant's finger approaches to touch the display (<15 cm distance, using hysteresis tolerance) that cursor disappears. This was done to avoid confusion about the cursor being shown while interacting with the display through touch.

4.3   Tasks

We used only the Fixed task from Experiment 1, for which there was the greatest performance benefit for touch input, in order to reduce the length of the experiment and the risk of tiring participants. We used the same target sizes (3 levels) and target distances (4 levels) as in Experiment 1.

The *backing-up request* required participants to move to a 40 cm-wide circular area located 2 m away from the display (see Fig. 1–A). The request abstracts situations in large-display interaction where users have to move away from the display, for example to gain an overview or to access a keyboard in a particular location. We considered asking participants to type on a keyboard, but since we were only interested in the consequent effects of having to move away from the display, we decided against introducing an arbitrary task. The request was signaled by a message on the display asking participants to move to the location: this message was removed when the participants had stayed in the area for 500 ms (as determined by the tracked position of the head). We varied the frequency of backing-up requests as follows: *Absent* (no requests, corresponding to Experiment 1), *Infrequent* (a third of the trials), and *Frequent* (half of the trials). Requests were made after randomly determined trials.

4.4   Participants

We recruited 10 volunteers (5 female), 18–47 years old (M = 24), to participate; all were right handed. Participants received an equivalent of €25 as compensation.

4.5   Experimental Design

We varied backing-up requests within participants; size and distance were also varied within participants as in Experiment 1. We varied the order of levels of backing-up request across participants using a Latin square. Participants performed 8 repetitions for each combination of size and distance, for a total of 96 timed targets. Altogether, the experiment gave data from 10 participants × 3 (backing-up request frequencies) × 3 (target sizes) × 4 (target distances) × 8 (repetitions) = 2880 target selections.

4.6   Dependent Variables and Data Collection

We collected task time, error rate, data on whether selections were done with touch or mid-air gestures, and participants' preference for either touch or mid-air gestures.

4.7   Procedure

The calibration and instructions were as in Experiment 1. Participants first performed four practice tasks with each input type to familiarize themselves with them; then they performed eight practice tasks (four with infrequent and frequent backing-up requests, respectively) where they could freely choose and switch between touch and mid-air. Participants selected the first target to begin a task. In order to avoid bias against touch input, participants did not have to stand 2 m away from the display to start each task, as was required in Experiment 1. After completing a task, they could rest and move freely in order to use either touch or mid-air gestures to begin the next task. The backing-up request required participants to move to the location 2 m away from the center of the display (see Fig. 1–A), as described above. After standing there for 500 ms participants could select the next target. After completing all tasks, participants stated which interface they preferred. The experiment lasted 45 min on average.

4.8 Results

Choice of Input. Overall, participants completed 978 trials with touch (34 %) and 1902 trials with mid-air gestures (66 %). Touch was the most often used when backing-up requests were absent, see Fig. 6 (top row). This supports our first hypothesis. However, we had not expected mid-air to be chosen so often (42 % of trials). We had hypothesized that the cost of using touch, which was imposed by the backing-up requests, would lead mid-air to be chosen more often. There was a significant association between backing-up requests and input used, $X^2(2) = 393.8$, $p < .001$. Indeed, with more frequent requests, mid-air was chosen more often (83 % of trials for frequent requests).

The question then is whether target size and distance had an effect on choice? Figure 6 (middle rows) shows how often touch and mid-air were chosen for different target sizes. It seems choice of input depends on target size. For medium-sized and large targets, touch and mid-air were used equally often when requests were absent, whereas almost all selections were done using mid-air when requests were frequent. Participants chose to use mid-air surprisingly often for selecting small targets, which are particularly challenging with mid-air, even in absence of backing-up requests. Figure 6 (bottom rows) suggests that distance had less effect on participants' choice of input.

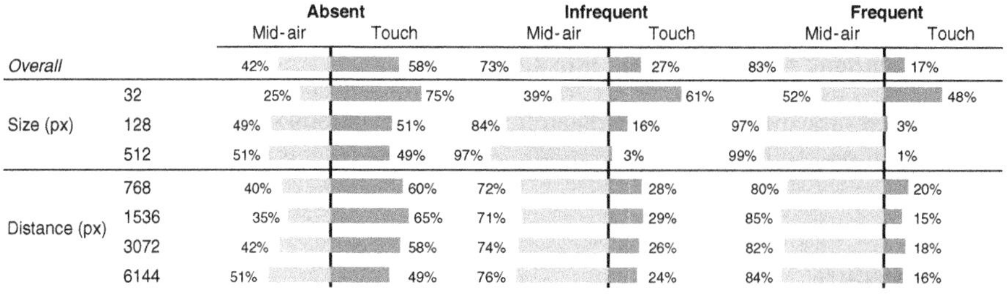

| | | Absent | | Infrequent | | Frequent | |
		Mid-air	Touch	Mid-air	Touch	Mid-air	Touch
Overall		42%	58%	73%	27%	83%	17%
	32	25%	75%	39%	61%	52%	48%
Size (px)	128	49%	51%	84%	16%	97%	3%
	512	51%	49%	97%	3%	99%	1%
	768	40%	60%	72%	28%	80%	20%
Distance (px)	1536	35%	65%	71%	29%	85%	15%
	3072	42%	58%	74%	26%	82%	18%
	6144	51%	49%	76%	24%	84%	16%

Fig. 6. Frequency of trials made with each input mode for each condition.

Switching Input: Staying or Going. Participants switched between using touch and mid-air for 158 (out of 1902) target selections, altogether, of which 67 times were associated with a backing-up request. After backing up, they switched to using mid-air 70 % of the times; the remaining times they walked back to use touch (85 % of which were for small targets). Considering that 840 backing-up requests were made, participants were prone to stay at a distance from the display. Also, 32 switches to using mid-air were not associated with a request. We saw no instances of alternating between using touch and mid-air for consecutive target selections.

Table 3. Mean target selection times after having used the same mode of input as for the previous selection (i.e., not switched) and having switched from another mode of input.

	Not switched			Switched			
Size (px)	32	128	512	32	128	512	*M*
Midair	5341	2323	1362	7914	2714	2581	**2570**
Touch	2786	1138	885	8725	6806	10799	**2565**
M	**3805**	**2055**	**1276**	**8500**	**3981**	**2897**	**2568**
N	870	918	934	90	42	26	2880

The frequency of switches depends on the frequency of backing-up requests in the task: Participants switched more often (.61 times on average) when requests were infrequent than when they were absent or frequent (.32 and .39 times, respectively), which suggests that participants were more challenged in making the tradeoff between staying and using mid-air or going back to the display in order to use touch.

Task Time. We hypothesized that mid-air would perform better with increasing cost of location-dependent touch input: the backing-up requests penalize touch because participants must spend time walking *back* to the display (in the following analysis of target selection times we exclude time spent backing up). Generally, it takes time to switch between the two modes of input, which impacts both mid-air and touch. As can be seen in Table 3 (rightmost column), the overall mean selection time (which includes selections with errors) is comparable for Mid-air and Touch. However, selection times depend much on whether participants switched from another input mode.

Preference. Seven out of ten participants preferred mid-air gestures (cf. only seven out of 19 in Experiment 1). It seems that with an increasing cost of touch, by way of movement induced by the backing-up requests, mid-air becomes preferable. As benefits of mid-air, seven participants mentioned the lack of a need to move (e.g., "little movement required") and the ease of selecting distant targets (e.g., "much easier to click dots that are far apart"). Five participants liked touch for being precise.

5 Discussion

Summary of Results. Touch was between 22 % and 60 % faster than mid-air in Experiment 1. Selection with touch was uncomplicated and had lower error rates. Touch also scored higher than mid-air on several aspects of satisfaction. Touch performance suffered when a target's size and position could not be anticipated; participants turned their head much more, presumably searching for targets. In Experiment 2, touch was as fast as mid-air on average, even with the requirement to do additional movement.

Mid-air was slow and error-prone in Experiment 1. In Experiment 2 mid-air was also slow compared to touch, but users chose it frequently, especially when they were asked to back away, and almost exclusively for selecting medium-sized and large targets (97 %–99 %). Preferences also shift between the two experiments: 7/10 preferred mid-air with backing-up requests in Experiment 2 versus 7/19 in Experiment 1. Mid-air required less movement and was therefore liked.

Interpretations of Results. The results can be interpreted in several ways. First, the results suggest a place for mid-air interaction. While touch is hard to compete with, mid-air seems to work well and to be chosen by users in situations where earlier work has suggested that it is beneficial (e.g., walking to type on a keyboard [22]). Further, users might choose to manipulate even small targets from a distance when they do not need to inspect them in detail up close: Participants in Experiment 2 chose mid-air for over half of the smallest targets with frequent backing-up requests. This calls for accurate mid-air pointing techniques. These are key implications of the present study.

Second, the results seem to present a new case of performance-preference dissociation; several studies in usability research have shown that people are not necessarily performing best with the interfaces they prefer [15, 31]. Mid-air might benefit from the principle of least effort: users prefer not to move, even if small targets are hard to select at a distance. Similarly, a study found users largely preferring virtual navigation over locomotion for a classification task using a gyroscopic mouse, despite possible performance benefits of locomotion [17]. Public display research has also presented subjective feedback that suggests users might minimize physical effort [20].

Third, the viewing angle and distance to the display has played an important role in earlier work when users need to overview [2] or make visual comparisons [5] of data on large displays. Here, we show it is also important for choice of input mode. The benefit of mid-air, in part, comes from the lower need to visually scan or to move in order to point at far-between targets, when users stand at a distance.

Limitations and Future Work. Several limitations of the study and avenues for future work are clear. First, the high error rates of the study are a concern. Even if comparable to earlier studies (e.g., [40]), investigating interaction techniques that may reduce them is crucial. Many such techniques exist [12, 41] that could be adapted and tested for mid-air. Improving the trigger implementation could also reduce error rates.

Second, we studied just one task, pointing, but other tasks also need studying. Users' performance with and choice between touch and mid-air gestures may look quite different for other types of task (steering, manipulation of data, etc.), and for collaborative tasks in particular, which is an important use case for large displays.

Third, we artificially manipulated participants to move to a distant location. A next step for research is to study both realistic tasks and cognitively demanding tasks that benefit from using the display from a distance (e.g., overview of information) and from off-loading cognitive effort into physical movement. Such studies might see users choose differently between touch and mid-air gestures.

Acknowledgements. This work has been supported in part by the Danish Council for Strategic Research under grant 10-092316.

References

1. American Psychological Association. The Publication manual of the American psychological association (6th edn.). Washington, DC (2010)
2. Ball, R., North, C., Bowman, D.A.: Move to improve: promoting physical navigation to increase user performance with large displays. In: Proceedings of CHI. ACM, pp. 191–200 (2007)
3. Banerjee, A., Burstyn, J., Girouard, A., Vertegaal, R.: Pointable: an in-air pointing technique to manipulate out-of-reach targets on tabletops. In: Proceedings of ITS. ACM, pp. 11–20 (2011)
4. Baudisch, P., Cutrell, E., Robbins, D., et al.: Drag-and-pop and drag-and-pick: techniques for accessing remote screen content on touch-and pen-operated systems. In: Proceedings of INTERACT, pp. 57–64 (2003)
5. Bezerianos, A., Isenberg, P.: Perception of visual variables on tiled wall-sized displays for information visualization applications. IEEE Trans. Vis. Comput. Graph. (Proc. InfoVis.) **18** (12), 2516–2525 (2012)
6. Boring, S., Baur, D., Butz, A., Gustafson, S., Baudisch, P.: Touch projector: mobile interaction through video. In: Proceedings of CHI, pp. 2287–2296. ACM (2010)
7. Bowman, D.A., McMahan, R.P., Ragan, E.D.: Questioning naturalism in 3D user interfaces. Commun. ACM **55**(9), 78–88 (2012)
8. Casiez, G., Roussel, N., Vogel, D.: 1 € Filter: a simple speed-based low-pass filter for noisy input in interactive systems. In: Proceedings of CHI, pp. 2527–2530 (2012)
9. Cockburn, A., Quinn, P., Gutwin, C., Ramos, G., Looser, J.: Air pointing: design and evaluation of spatial target acquisition with and without visual feedback. Int. J. Hum. Comput. Stud. **69**(6), 401–414 (2011)
10. Cumming, G.: The new statistics: why and how. Psychol. Sci. **25**(1), 7–29 (2014)
11. Douglas, S.A., Kirkpatrick, A.E., MacKenzie, I.S.: Testing pointing device performance and user assessment with the ISO 9241, Part 9 Standard. In: Proceedings of CHI, pp. 215–222. ACM (1999)
12. Grossman, T., Balakrishnan, R.: The bubble cursor: enhancing target acquisition by dynamic resizing of the cursor's activation area. In: Proceedings of CHI, pp. 281–290. ACM (2005)
13. Hilliges, O., Izadi, S., Wilson, A.D., Hodges, S., Garcia-Mendoza, A., Butz, A.: Interactions in the air: adding further depth to interactive tabletops. In: Proceedings of UIST, pp. 139–148. ACM (2009)

14. Hinckley, K., Wigdor, D.: Input technologies and techniques. In: Sears, A., Jacko, J.A. (eds.) The Human-Computer Interaction Handbook: Fundamentals, Evolving Technologies and Emerging Applications. CRC Press, Boca Raton (2011)
15. Hornbæk, K., Law, E.L.-C.: Meta-analysis of correlations among usability measures. In: Proceedings of CHI, pp. 617–626. ACM Press (2007)
16. Jakobsen, M.R., Hornbæk, K.: Up close and personal: collaborative work on a high-resolution multitouch wall display. ACM Trans. Comput. Hum. Interact. **21**(2), 11:1–11:34 (2014)
17. Jakobsen, M.R., Hornbæk, K.: Is moving improving? Some effects of locomotion in wall-display interaction. In: Proceedings of CHI, pp. 4169–4178. ACM (2015)
18. Jansen, Y., Dragicevic, P., Fekete, J.-D.: Tangible remote controllers for wall-size displays. In: Proceedings of CHI, pp. 2865–2874. ACM (2012)
19. Khan, A., Fitzmaurice, G., Almeida, D., Burtnyk, N., Kurtenbach, G.: A remote control interface for large displays. In: Proceedings of UIST, pp. 127–136. ACM (2004)
20. Kurdyukova, E., Obaid, M., André, E.: Direct, bodily or mobile interaction?: comparing interaction techniques for personalized public displays. In: Proceedings of MUM, pp. 44:1–44:9. ACM (2012)
21. Mahyar, N., Sarvghad, A., Tory, M.: A closer look at note taking in the co-located collaborative visual analytics process. In: IEEE VAST, pp. 171–178 (2010)
22. Markussen, A., Jakobsen, M.R., Hornbæk, K.: Vulture: a mid-air word-gesture keyboard. In: Proceedings of CHI, pp. 1073–1082. ACM (2014)
23. Marquardt, N., Ballendat, T., Boring, S., Greenberg, S., Hinckley, K.: Gradual engagement: facilitating information exchange between digital devices as a function of proximity. In: Proceedings of ITS, pp. 31–40. ACM (2012)
24. Marquardt, N., Jota, R., Greenberg, S., Jorge, J.A.: The continuous interaction space: interaction techniques unifying touch and gesture on and above a digital surface. In: Campos, P., Graham, N., Jorge, J., Nunes, N., Palanque, P., Winckler, M. (eds.) INTERACT 2011, Part III. LNCS, vol. 6948, pp. 461–476. Springer, Heidelberg (2011)
25. McCallum, D.C., Irani, P.: ARC-Pad: absolute + relative cursor positioning for large displays with a mobile touchscreen. In: Proceedings of UIST, pp. 153–156. ACM (2009)
26. Müller, J., Bailly, G., Bossuyt, T., Hillgren, N.: MirrorTouch: combining touch and mid-air gestures for public displays. In: Proceedings of MobileHCI, pp. 319–328. ACM (2014)
27. Myers, B.A., Bhatnagar, R., Nichols, J., et al.: Interacting at a distance: measuring the performance of laser pointers and other devices. In: Proceedings of CHI, pp. 33–40. ACM (2002)
28. Nacenta, M.A., Gutwin, C., Aliakseyeu, D., Subramanian, S.: There and back again: cross-display object movement in multi-display environments. Hum. Comput. Interact. **24**(1–2), 170–229 (2009)
29. Nancel, M., Chapuis, O., Pietriga, E., Yang, X.-D., Irani, P.P., Beaudouin-Lafon, M.: High-precision pointing on large wall displays using small handheld devices. In: Proceedings of CHI, pp. 831–840. ACM (2013)
30. Nancel, M., Wagner, J., Pietriga, E., Chapuis, O., Mackay, W.: Mid-air pan-and-zoom on wall-sized displays. In: Proceedings of CHI, pp. 177–186 (2011)
31. Nielsen, J., Levy, J.: Measuring usability: preference vs. performance. Commun. ACM **37**(4), 66–75 (1994)
32. Olsen, D.R., Jr., Nielsen, T.: Laser pointer interaction. In: Proceedings of CHI, pp. 17–22. ACM (2001)
33. Pedersen, E.W., Hornbæk, K.: An experimental comparison of touch interaction on vertical and horizontal surfaces. In: Proceedings of NordiCHI, pp. 370–379. ACM (2012)

34. Pierce, J.S., Forsberg, A.S., Conway, M.J., Hong, S., Zeleznik, R.C., Mine, M.R.: Image plane interaction techniques in 3D immersive environments. In: Proceedings of I3D, p. 39–ff. ACM (1997)
35. Sasangohar, F., MacKenzie, I.S., Scott, S.D.: Evaluation of mouse and touch input for a tabletop display using fitts' reciprocal tapping task. In: Proceedings of HFES, vol. 53, no. 12, pp. 839–843 (2009)
36. Sauro, J., Lewis, J.R.: Average task times in usability tests: what to report?. In: Proceedings of CHI, pp. 2347–2350. ACM (2010)
37. Schick, A., van de Camp, F., Ijsselmuiden, J., Stiefelhagen, R.: Extending touch: towards interaction with large-scale surfaces. In: Proceedings of ITS, pp. 117–124. ACM (2009)
38. Swaminathan, K., Sato, S.: Interaction design for large displays. Interactions 4(1), 15–24 (1997)
39. Vogel, D., Balakrishnan, R.: Interactive public ambient displays: transitioning from implicit to explicit, public to personal, interaction with multiple users. In: UIST 2004: Proceedings of UIST, pp. 137–146. ACM (2004)
40. Vogel, D., Balakrishnan, R.: Distant freehand pointing and clicking on very large, high resolution displays. In: Proceedings of UIST, pp. 33–42. ACM (2005)
41. Vogel, D., Baudisch, P.: Shift: a technique for operating pen-based interfaces using touch. In: Proceedings of CHI, pp. 657–666 (2007)
42. Wilson, A.D.: Robust computer vision-based detection of pinching for one and two-handed gesture input. In: Proceedings of UIST, pp. 255–258. ACM (2006)
43. Wilson, A., Shafer, S.: XWand: UI for intelligent spaces. In: Proceedings of CHI, pp. 545–552. ACM (2003)

Funky-Design-Spaces: Interactive Environments for Creativity Inspired by Observing Designers Making Mood Boards

Andrés Lucero[(✉)]

Mads Clausen Institute, University of Southern Denmark, Kolding, Denmark
lucero@acm.org

Abstract. Research in surface computing has traditionally been driven by technology. A project that explored ways to provide support for professional users in their work with novel technology by focusing on people instead is presented. A co-design approach was applied by systematically involving end users (i.e., industrial designers) throughout the design process. In a series of activities with fifty designers, the creation of mood boards was identified as an important task for them, and studied in depth. The *funky-design spaces* vision of a holistic design studio housing interconnected tools that support the creation of mood boards was co-designed, brought to life in two prototypes, and evaluated with designers. The results suggest these environments could stimulate designers to break away from their desks and encourage collaboration with more people.

Keywords: Design practice · Creativity · Co-design · Tabletops · Displays

1 Introduction

The field of human-computer interaction (HCI) has been investigating how people interact with computer systems at work, at home, and more recently in open public spaces, in an attempt to help people achieve their goals. Within HCI, researchers have already identified the potential behind interactive horizontal (e.g., DigitalDesk [27], ReacTable [11]) and vertical surfaces (e.g., DynaWall [23], ambient displays [25]) as a more natural and familiar setting to design collaborative interactions. Research in this area has traditionally been driven by technology.

A research project that explored ways in which novel technologies can provide support for professional users (i.e., industrial designers) in their work is presented. A co-design approach was applied by systematically involving fifty practicing designers throughout the design process in a series of activities. First, cultural probes [8] were used to understand design practice and identify an important task for designers (i.e., mood-board making). Second, retrospective interviews based on contextual inquiry [10] were carried out in the Netherlands and Finland to understand what the creation of mood boards entails. Third, designers were invited to co-design workshops (i.e., *dialogue-labs* [16]) in both countries to collaboratively create novel tools that support the creation of mood boards. Finally, designers were invited to prototype

© IFIP International Federation for Information Processing 2015
J. Abascal et al. (Eds.): INTERACT 2015, Part III, LNCS 9298, pp. 474–492, 2015.
DOI: 10.1007/978-3-319-22698-9_32

evaluations of two resulting tools from the co-design sessions (i.e., the Funky Coffee Table [14] and Funky Wall [15]). The structure of the paper is as follows. First, two studies on design practice and mood board creation are presented. Next, the results of co-design workshops are introduced, which lead to the *funky-design-spaces*. Then, the two resulting tools and the outcome of a joint evaluation are presented. Finally, limitations of this work and future improvements are discussed, followed by conclusions.

2 Design Practice

With the aim to get a broad understanding of design practice and identify an important activity that could be supported by novel technologies, a first study with industrial designers was conducted. The study took place in design studios and looked into what designers do there, their activities, the places and objects they use in the practice of industrial design. There are many studies of design practice, focusing on different design disciplines and specific stages of the design process. These include studies with knitwear designers to facilitate communication within design teams [6], and of how product designers keep their informal collections of visual material [12].

2.1 Method, Participants and Procedure

The method used was design probes [8]. Regarding its main characteristics, probes: (1) are based on user participation by means of self-documentation, (2) look at the user's personal context and perceptions, and (3) have an exploratory character [18]. One main advantage of applying probes includes collecting participant data over an extended period of time (e.g., one week), which in turn allows people to reflect on what they are being asked and the answers they have provided on the previous days.

The probes study was conducted in the Netherlands with 10 practicing industrial designers. All participants had at least two years of design practice experience (nine years on average), with varying educational level (university or academy), age (between 24 and 50), and gender (6 male, 4 female). A wide variety of work contexts was obtained, ranging from an office in a large company, to freelance work performed at home, and sometimes combined with part-time teaching at a university.

Participants worked on the probes in their design studio and home for a period of one week (i.e., seven consecutive days) and freely chose the starting day. The probe kit contained a design-studio diary including: (1) a timeline to probe the daily thoughts and activities of the participants, (2) closed questions covering different aspects of routines, collaboration, and use of technology, (3) open questions to make people tell stories and express their opinions, (4) a map to allow for self-expression, and (5) a drawing exercise (i.e., *ideal design studio*) to probe the dreams and aspirations of the participants. The kit also included a single-use camera (i.e., 36 exposures) to illustrate interesting activities, places and objects, and a 'Picture Record Table' to keep track of their pictures. Two researchers processed the data from the diaries and cameras (i.e., 200 photos) for interpretation. General findings were formulated and presented back to the participants during a workshop to triangulate the interpretation.

(a)   **(b)**

Fig. 1. a) Designing behind a standing desk. b) Bookshelves filled with magazines for inspiration, including a special box with magazines to make mood boards.

2.2   Findings

From the probes, a set of possible research directions connected to supporting creativity and finding inspiration in the early stages of the design process was deduced.

- **Supporting flexibility in creation.** Designers stressed the importance of working with their hands in the early stages of the design process. Designers prefer the naturalness of using pen and paper and thus keep a sketchbook at hand to make notes and bring their ideas to life. Work related to the creation phase is mostly performed away from the computer, as designers need tools that provide flexibility. This extends to their workplace, where designers want to decide how and where they work (Fig. 1a), and prefer not being tied to their computers or (indoor) physical spaces.
- **Finding inspiration.** This is important for designers. It is a way to forget about work for a while, allowing them to approach design problems from a different perspective with a fresh mind. Designers have different ways to find inspiration (e.g., browsing magazines and the web, reading books, visiting fairs, meeting people). Taking short breaks to perform physical activities both inside and outside the design studio can also be beneficial (e.g., playing darts or football at the office, taking a bicycle ride in town, walking the dog). Designers keep special areas in their studios where they can stick sketches, photos and project printouts, keep their collections of magazines, or relax for a while. Having a view on the outside world to observe people and life also creates an inspiring atmosphere inside the design studio.
- **Mood boards.** Designers mentioned the creation of mood boards as an important activity for their work. One designer described herself as a *mood board designer,* and kept special magazines to make her mood boards with (Fig. 1b). Mood boards (Fig. 2a, b) are an idea development tool consisting of visually stimulating images from magazines affixed to an A0 foam board, and which are used by designers and their clients to share their different views that emerge from the design brief [17].

The creation of mood boards was selected for further research, as it had not been sufficiently studied in design research despite its importance for designers. Furthermore, mood boards shared characteristics with the other findings: they are created in the early stages of the design process, by designers manipulating physical images, away from computers, and they force designers to move about their design studio.

(a)   **(b)**

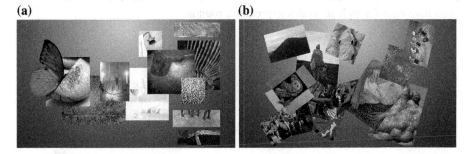

Fig. 2. Two mood board examples [17]: a) exploring the use of other senses than just sight for interaction. b) The five roles that mood boards play at the start of the design process.

3   Mood Boards

After identifying the creation of mood boards as an important task for designers, an empirical study of how experienced designers from different design disciplines (i.e., fashion, textile and industrial design) use mood boards as part of their work was conducted. Earlier studies on mood boards have concentrated on understanding the role that mood boards play in design education [7, 19]. In doing so, these studies have been mostly looking at design students and how they create and perceive mood boards. One notable exception is Eckert and Stacey [6] who analyzed the use of mood boards to study the role played by sources of inspiration in the knitwear industry.

3.1   Method, Participants and Procedure

The type of study conducted was retrospective interviews based on contextual inquiry [10]. The retrospective interviews were conducted in the Netherlands and Finland with 14 practicing designers who regularly use mood boards as part of their work. All participants except one had at least ten years of design practice experience (14 years on average), with varying education level (university or academy), background (4 textile designers, 4 industrial designers, 3 fashion designers, 2 designers, and 1 stylist/photographer), age (between 35 and 45), and gender (9 female and 5 male). Three of them worked in large companies (i.e., Nokia and Stockmann), six of them worked in small design firms that they owned, and the rest did freelance work at home for large companies (e.g., Nike, SNCF, Rukka, Luhta, Pentik).

The retrospective interviews were planned for a total of two hours in the participants' workplace. Participants freely described between two and five of their previous projects for which they had used mood boards. Designers took the role of experts and guided the interviewer (the author) through different aspects of each mood board such as its purpose, the client's expectations, and the making process. There were no pre-defined sets of questions for the interviewer to ask, allowing for a more informal discussion to flow. Affinity diagramming [10] was used to analyze the data from the retrospective interviews. The interviewer plus two researchers first independently made notes as they watched the 14 interview videos, and then collaboratively analyzed the qualitative data through several interpretation rounds.

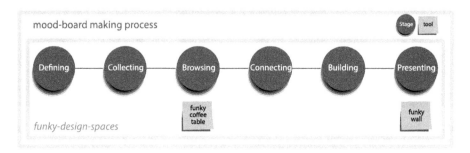

Fig. 3. The mood-board making process and the two support tools that were created. The Funky Coffee Table and the Funky Wall provide support for two stages of the process, i.e., browsing and presenting. The *funky-design-spaces* support the entire process creating mood boards.

3.2   Findings

Five Roles. Five roles that mood boards play in the early stages of the design process were identified [17]. First, mood boards play a *framing* role by defining the limits of the design task, which includes both problem setting and problem solving. Second, mood boards assist in the transmission of a mindset or vision by *aligning* the different stakeholders and getting them on the same wavelength. Third, mood boards support designers in visually researching apparently conflicting or contradicting ideas or *paradoxing*. Fourth, mood boards play an *abstracting* role by allowing designers to juxtapose both concrete and abstract imagery depending on the project and client. Finally, mood boards play a *directing* role by setting a trajectory for future design efforts. A mood board was created to communicate these five roles to different stakeholders (Fig. 2b) [17].

The Mood-Board Making Process. Six stages of the mood board making process were also found (Fig. 3). First, in *defining*, designer and client hold meetings where the client tries to express through words their rough ideas for a product or service, while the designer attempts to understand (and shape) what the client has in mind. Second, the designer begins by roughly *collecting* images that reflect the client's vision from magazines, the Internet, and occasionally their own personal collection of images (Fig. 4a). Third, once the designer feels they have enough (visual) material to work with, they will move on to *browsing*. Here the designer can spend a considerable amount of time pre-selecting images that will help them build a story or say something about the target audience, product, or company they are designing for. Fourth, through *connecting*, the designer sorts the pre-selected images in a simple and flexible way by assigning them to piles (usually up to 30 images per topic or idea). Fifth, the designer starts *building* the mood board by thinking how they want to arrange the images and create different layouts. In the final sixth stage, *presenting*, designer and client meet face-to-face to share and discuss the intended story behind the mood board (Fig. 4b). The designer creates a single large mood board or a series of smaller booklets for their clients to keep and share with stakeholders.

(a)   (b)

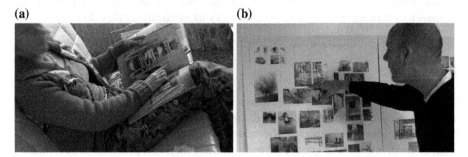

Fig. 4. a) A designer in her studio browsing images while seated on a couch by a coffee table. b) A designer guiding their client through the presentation by means of an explanation.

3.3   Considerations for a Mood-Board Making Tool

Based on the main aforementioned mood board interview findings, six considerations for a mood-board making tool were identified. Also, two mood boards were created to help communicate some of these findings to different stakeholders (Fig. 2a, b).

- **Support Idea Development.** Mood-board making entails a series of steps occurring both before and after building the mood board itself. *New tools should support idea development through all six stages of the mood board making process, rather than only focus on the creation of the artifact.*
- **Encourage Two-Way Communication.** Mood boards create the conditions for both designer and client to have a productive discussion together. *New tools should en-courage two-way communication allowing the designer to present the mood board, see how the client perceives it, have a discussion, and get feedback on the artifact.*
- **Involving the Senses.** Designers involve all five senses (plus their intuition) to create a mood board (e.g., they like the touch and smell of different paper types). However, mood-board creation on computers is currently restricted by the visual nature of the artifact. *New tools should encourage using other senses than just sight for interaction.*
- **Holistic Interactive Space.** Mood-board making is a dynamic and iterative process where designers must often switch activity and place. *New tools should create a holistic interactive design space consisting of several interconnected tools that together support the mood-board making process.*

- **Merging With the Real Context.** The process of making mood boards takes place at different locations inside and outside the design studio. *New tools should merge with the real context of the activity by considering both place and the relaxed (e.g., image browsing on a couch) or formal (e.g., meeting or presentation) nature of the activity.*
- **Flexible and Intuitive Interaction.** For creativity-related activities, designers prefer working with their hands using simple tools (e.g., pen and paper), and using their hands collaboratively (e.g., knife and fork). *New tools should provide flexible and intuitive interaction through hand movements and other modalities (e.g., speech), allowing designers to perform tasks as naturally as they do now.*

4 Co-design

Co-design activities with practicing designers and researchers were organized to collaboratively develop future ways of creating mood boards with novel technologies. Practitioners from different fields of research and design have understood the importance of involving diverse groups of users in the generation phase of novel artifacts, products and services, and thus facilitating participation has become one of the cornerstones of co-design [4]. Underpinning this approach is the supposition that stakeholders, including users, can contribute productively through involvement in the design process since they bring privileged insights into the domain that designers are trying to address and the ways in which future products and services may fit into and affect that domain. Within this field, there exists a variety of methods, techniques and events intended to inspire design participants and scaffold collaborative ideation and concept development. Such methods include inspiration card workshops [9], design games [3], and contextmapping [22].

4.1 Method, Participants and Procedure

The method used was *dialogue-labs* [16]. *Dialogue-labs* and its three structuring elements (i.e., *process, space* and *materials*), provide a structured way of generating ideas through a sequence of co-design activities. The *process* provides a clear step-by-step procedure for a two-hour idea-generation session in which participants work in pairs. The *space* is carefully crafted to align content to different locations, inspire participants and encourage them to move around the room. Finally, the *materials* are the means for participants to build a design language of their own and to provide different entry points to the design problem.

Seven *dialogue-labs* sessions were conducted in the Netherlands and Finland with 14 practicing designers, experienced mood-board makers, some of which had previously participated in the probes study (n = 1) and the retrospective interviews (n = 3). All participants had at least five years of design practice experience (ten years on average), with varying education level (university or academy), age (between 28 and 46) and gender (7 male, 7 female).

Each *dialogue-labs* session was planned for a total of two hours and involved four people; two designers plus two researchers who acted in a double role of facilitator/designer. Based on the findings from the previous studies with practicing designers (i.e., probes and retrospective interviews), activities and locations of the *dialogue-labs* environment were aligned according to the six stages of the mood-board making process (Fig. 3). The physical space was further designed to look and feel like a design studio (including working tables, chairs, a laptop, magazines, drawing materials, a large screen for presentation, and a sofa). Participants formed pairs, with at least one domain expert in them, and were then asked to think of unusual ways to support the process of making mood boards with novel technologies. At the end of each session, the quality of the resulting ideas was collectively assessed. Participants rated each idea on a seven-point Likert scale (where −3 was very bad, +3 was very good, and 0 was neutral). The most promising ideas (i.e., mean rating ≥2.5) are presented below.

4.2 Ideas

Layered Table. This tool consists of a set of adjustable multi-purpose surfaces (e.g., table, wall). Different surfaces can be used to keep a collection of materials, to make a selection of materials, to put the discarded material (e.g., garbage surface), or to build the mood board. Materials can easily be shared between surfaces. These surfaces stimulate designers to be standing in an active attitude to be able to easily and rapidly share materials between surfaces. Mood boards can be built on a horizontal surface, be put up on a vertical surface to check and share the results, and back down on the horizontal surface for adjusting. Surfaces with discarded material can inspire and be a starting point for other designers working on a different project.

Mood Sketching. This tool (Fig. 5a) supports the designer's creative impulses by allowing them to create several mood boards in a very quick and inexpensive way. Designers use a phone or tablet to intuitively sketch different moods by selecting, moving, rotating, and enlarging images on the screen. The sketched mood board is then shared and put up on a digital wall so that colleagues can comment on them. At this point, the mood board looks pixelated when enlarged for display, but it is only a sketch. When designers are happy with a few mood sketches, the materials used in them pop up on a large horizontal table in full resolution for fine-tuning and to create a final mood board.

Living Mood Board. The living mood board is a tool that makes mood boards become interactive living objects that provide inspiration and surprise. The designer creates a core mood board with a few basic elements, and then adds alternative images, movies or sounds for each basic element. The mood board is displayed on a wall and changes over time by reacting to context (e.g., the number of people around, the amount of light in the room, or if it has remained unchanged for some time). The tool and other colleagues can also suggest new content related to the basic elements to challenge the designer. The living mood board provides inspiration for its creator and other designers by catching their attention and defining the atmosphere they work in.

Presentation Recorder. This tool (Fig. 5b) helps client and designer interactively communicate and later remember ongoing discussions. The tool captures the presentation given by the designer and shares it with the client to also involve them in the process. It becomes some kind of contract with the agreement to follow a given path for the remainder of the project. This pre-editing tool only captures movements and sounds to see the discussion (i.e., no video, no faces). The client can then take specific things of the presentation, point at them and change them. The tool takes snapshots of the different stages of the discussion. Mood-board making becomes a closer cooperation between the designer and the client who work as a team.

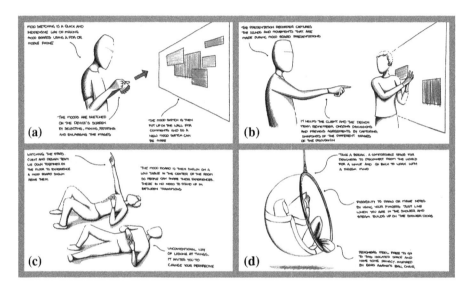

Fig. 5. The main ideas from the co-design sessions: a) in Mood Sketching designers use mobile devices to impulsively create several mood boards and put them up on the wall for feedback. b) Presentation Recorder captures sounds and movements made during a presentation, serving as a reminder of previous agreements. c) Watching the Stars is an invitation for designers and their clients to experience mood board presentations in a different way. d) Take a Break responds to the designers' need for a comfortable place where they feel free to rest and unwind for a while.

Watching the Stars. This tool (Fig. 5c) is an open invitation to experience mood boards in a new way. Client and designer let go of their inhibitions and lie down together on the floor (or on Japanese Tatami mats) in a completely different sensorial experience. The tool projects the mood board on the ceiling for a few minutes, allowing people to immerse themselves into the mood board as they observe in silence. Lying on the floor creates a more relaxed and intimate setting, almost like a personal cocoon. After witnessing the mood board, people sit around a low round table in the center of the room on which the mood board is projected while it slowly rotates to provide different views. After discussing and sharing their experiences of what they have seen, the mood board can be put up on the ceiling or down on the table once again for further discussion.

Take a Break. This tool (Fig. 5d) responds to the designers' need to have a space where they can momentarily disconnect from work, do something in there, and come back with a fresh mind. This comfortable space creates a feeling of disconnection from the world, similar to that of taking a shower or lying flat in bed. Designers feel free to go to this isolated space for a creative moment of doing nothing, while having some privacy and not being disturbed by others. An inspiration for this space could be Eero Aarnio's Ball Chair (1966), described as a "room within a room with a cozy and calm atmosphere, protecting outside noises and giving a private space for relaxing."

Fig. 6. The *funky-design-spaces* are located in a natural surrounding where designers can disconnect from the world by, for example, going into the deep woods. Large windows provide a direct view on the natural surroundings and allow natural light to energize designers.

4.3   Funky-Design-Spaces

The *funky-design-spaces* is a vision for a new holistic design studio, a comfortable environment that facilitates creative thinking in designers. During the co-design sessions, designers expressed the need to have easily convertible flexible spaces that support different mood-board making activities. The *funky-design-spaces* consist of interconnected tools that encourage breaking the rhythm [12] and stimulate designers to perform activities away from their desks. The co-design teams suggested a mentality change for their work culture where they would have the mental freedom to go outside during work hours to find inspiration or simply to take a break.

The *funky-design-spaces* are set in natural surroundings (Fig. 6) where designers can disconnect from the world and come back with a fresh mind. For example, designers can go into the deep woods or walk along the canal during work hours to re-energize. The dome-like shape of the environment is an open invitation to leave behind current conceptions of what a design studio is and think of new inspiring buildings that house the *funky-design-spaces*. Within this larger context, a houseboat on the canal or a greenhouse in the forest could become good examples of design studios that house the *funky-design-spaces*. Large windows provide a direct view on the natural surroundings and allow natural light to energize designers.

Once inside (Fig. 7), the *funky-design-spaces* create a relaxed and comfortable atmosphere where designers can engage in individual activities as well as creative collaboration. Designers feel that they belong to a larger team but they can also have a moment for themselves when needed. Adjustable multi-purpose surfaces can be used to easily display and share information. These surfaces can be assigned for different uses.

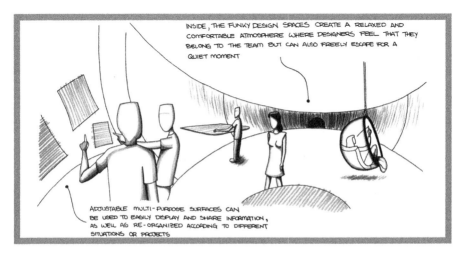

Fig. 7. The *funky-design-spaces* create a relaxed and comfortable atmosphere where designers can engage in individual activities as well as creative collaboration. Adjustable multi-purpose surfaces are used to easily display and share information.

Storing and moving information between these different tools or spaces should also be made in a simple way to avoid breaking the creative process (Fig. 8). Designers have a ball that they can bounce on a surface (e.g. wall) to collect information that is being displayed there. Then, designers can move to any other surface (e.g. table) and then roll the ball on the surface to display the contained information (e.g. images, audio, text, etc.).

5   Interactive Support Tools

To test the ideas behind the *funky-design-spaces*, two prototypes (i.e., the Funky Coffee Table [14] and Funky Wall [15]) were developed and evaluated with designers.

STORING AND MOVING INFORMATION BETWEEN FUNKY
DESIGN SPACES IS ACHIEVED IN A VERY SIMPLE WAY
TO AVOID BREAKING THE CREATIVE PROCESS

DESIGNERS USE A BALL THAT THEY JUST BOUNCE ON THE WALL
TO COLLECT THE INFORMATION AND THEN ROLL THE BALL ON
ANOTHER SURFACE TO DISPLAY THE CONTAINED IMAGERY

Fig. 8. Sharing information between the different *funky-design-spaces* is done in a simple way to support the natural creative flow. Designers have a ball that they can bounce on a wall to collect the information and then can move to a table and roll the ball on it to display the contained imagery.

5.1   Intuitive Interaction

Intuitive interaction is proposed as a perspective on providing interactive support for professional users in their work, and it consist of four parts. First, it allows people to simply walk up to and start interacting with a tool using their current skills and knowledge on the task that is being supported. There are no hidden functions, menus or complex actions to be learned, and thus engaging with the system just makes sense to them. Second, it allows designers to use their hands as the main input mechanism for activities that involve creation, through asymmetric two-handed interaction. Designers wear custom-made Lycra® gloves that contain sensors to detect hand gestures. Speech provides an alternative to interact with the tools. Third, it takes use contexts into account or the ability of the tools to merge with the existing possibilities of a design studio environment. Finally, the orthogonal distance from a surface (or 'z') is introduced as a cue for interaction, to generate extra interaction space, or to hide and reveal different functions of the tools.

5.2   The Funky Coffee Table

The Funky Coffee Table [14] is an interactive tabletop tool that supports image *browsing* (Figs. 3, 4a). A number of tabletop systems have been designed to support image browsing and sharing. The Personal Digital Historian [21] is a tabletop pen-based system that helps people construct, organize, navigate and share digital collections in an interactive multi-person conversational setting. SharePic [1] is a multi-touch, gestural, and collaborative digital photograph sharing application for a tabletop, which was strongly influenced by the way physical photographs are handled and placed on physical tables. Cabinet [12] helps designers collect and organize visual material for inspiration. Other authors [28, 20] have studied the general application of hand gestures and movements to support human-computer interaction.

Design. Three main principles guided its design. First, the interaction was set around a coffee table to encourage image searching in a relaxed setting (Fig. 9a). A long rect-angular IKEA coffee Table (120 × 40 × 40 cm.) was used, onto which three images were simultaneously projected to allow designers to discover, compare, and make connections between the materials. Second, the tool encourages designers to work using hand movements to pre-select images. Finally, to reduce the desk clutter that results from cutting out dozens of pictures from magazines (Fig. 4a), the space above the work surface has been extended for interaction and divided into multiple interaction layers [24]. Piles of images can be created in two layers above the table, which can be promptly consulted for an updated overview of the selection process.

(a)   **(b)**

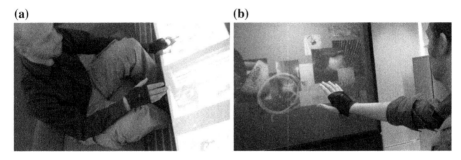

Fig. 9. a) In the Funky Coffee Table, designers use their hands to store images in layers above the table. b) Funky Wall uses hand gestures, body position, and speech to support presentations.

Interaction Techniques. There are two ways to browse images on the Funky Coffee Table. Designers can flip to the next or previous three images in the collection by placing their hand at table level and performing a short and quick diagonal movement to the left or to the right. The change of pages is accompanied by a page-flipping sound. Designers can also flick the collection by performing a longer and slower flip gesture, which triggers continuous image scrolling (without friction). The direction and speed of flicking are mapped to the direction and rate at which the images scroll. Continuous scrolling without friction was chosen to avoid fatigue while browsing large image collections. Tapping on the table stops continuous scrolling.

The Funky Coffee Table also allows creating, reviewing and arranging two soft piles of images using layers above the digital table. To put an image in a soft pile, the designer must place their dominant hand over an image at table-level and quickly move it upwards orthogonally with respect to the table surface. Depending on the highest point reached by the hand while performing the gesture, the image is placed into soft-pile A (30–50 cm) or B (50–70 cm). To review soft-pile contents, the designer must place their non-dominant hand above the table inside the range for layer A or B. Finally, to arrange soft piles, the designer must first use their non-dominant hand to locate the image and put their dominant hand on top of the image at the same orthogonal height as the non-dominant hand to activate it. By moving the dominant hand, the selected image can then be put into another soft-pile or removed from the pile.

5.3   The Funky Wall

The Funky Wall [15] is a wall-mounted display tool that supports *presenting* mood boards (Figs. 3, 4b). Clark and Brennan [5] have extensively studied the relation between gestures and speech, and the role of gestures in human communication. Von Hardenberg and Bérard studied bare-hand human computer interaction, focusing on static hand postures to issue a command, and fingers for pointing [26]. Vogel and Balakrishnan [25] studied shared interactive public displays that support the transition from implicit to explicit interaction. Hand gestures and touch were used for explicit interaction, while body orientation and location played part in implicit interaction. Charade [2] allows presenters to use free-hand gestures to control a remote computer display, while also using gestures to communicate with the audience.

Design. Three main principles guided the design of the Funky Wall. First, four ranges of interaction are used depending on the designer's proximity to the wall display [25]: *showing, contemplating, replaying*, and *exploring*. Different tool functionalities are available to people (e.g., designer or client) in each range. Second, the designer records their presentation by gesturing and explaining in front of the screen, using their hands to point or outline specific areas of the mood board. The tool automatically records three essential aspects of the mood board presentation (i.e., gestures, speech, and visuals, which are used to split the presentation into a number of meaningful segments by looking into hand location, gesture acceleration, and speech pauses. Third, the tool supports two-way communication between designer and client by allowing them both to provide input by creating a presentation, and to share their thoughts by providing feedback. For this type of communication to happen, two Funky Walls are needed, one for the designer and another one for the client.

Interaction Techniques. In the first range of interaction (i.e., *showing*), the designer records a presentation by standing in front of the wall display at close range (<0.5 m) and then simply gesturing and speaking next to the mood board. The tool overlays white traces of the hand gestures made by the designer, at 30 % opacity to allow good visibility of the mood board. Traces gracefully degrade to 25 % opacity after 10 s to make recent traces more prominent than older ones.

The next three ranges of interaction provide different ways to review the presentation contents. In *contemplating*, spectators (i.e., the designer or client) assess the mood board by standing away from the wall display (>2 m), for a more comfortable and clean overview. In *replaying*, spectators play back the entire presentation by approaching the wall display (1.5–2 m). Raising the dominant hand results in displaying a static representation of all gestures made during the presentation, semitransparent on top of the mood board. Raising the non-dominant hand triggers the complete recorded speech. By putting both hands together, the recorded speech is played and the transparent dynamic gestures unfold as the presentation progresses. In *exploring*, spectators browse specific parts of the presentation by taking one step closer towards the wall display (0.5–1.5 m). Pointing with the dominant hand to a given area in the mood board shows a static representation of the traces made in that area (Fig. 9b). These overlaid traces of gestures serve as guides for retrieval. The tool highlights both the explanations made by the designer just before (i.e., in white) and immediately after (i.e., in black) the currently selected gesture. Putting both hands together triggers the dynamic gestures together with its corresponding spoken explanation.

Implementation. Both prototypes were set up using a desktop PC, connected to a top-down projector displaying a 120 × 40 cm (1272 × 424 pixels) image on a white IKEA Table (120 × 40 × 40 cm) for the Funky Coffee Table, and to a back-projection screen of 200 × 150 cm (1024 × 768 pixels) for the Funky Wall. Both PCs also controlled an InterSense IS-600 ultrasonic tracking system to detect hands. Participants wore custom-designed Lycra® gloves that contained the sensors (Fig. 9a, b). Both applications were written in C# and used OpenGL for visualization purposes.

5.4   Method, Participants, Procedure

Prototype evaluations of both tools were conducted in the Netherlands with nine practicing designers, some of which had previously participated in the probes study (n = 1), the retrospective interviews (n = 2), and the co-design workshops (n = 3). The participants had at least five years of design practice experience (13 years on average), with varying education level (university or academy), age (between 31 and 46), gender (7 male, 2 female), and handedness (7 right, 2 left). The evaluations were conducted individually and lasted on average one hour.

In the first part of the evaluation participants experienced both tools in counterbalanced order (i.e., five began with the table and four with the wall). Participants were asked to perform simple tasks such as change pages, start and stop scrolling, create piles and rearrange piles using 30 images for the Funky Coffee Table, and make a new mood board presentation, and explore an existing one for the Funky Wall (20 min. per tool). In the second part of the evaluation, participants were asked to share their views on the *funky-design-spaces*, specifically on the idea of supporting the process of making mood boards by having distributed interconnected tools (10 min.). Earlier studies where designers evaluated either tool are reported elsewhere [14, 15].

5.5 Findings

Participants agreed with the vision of a holistic design studio housing interconnected tools that stimulate designers to break away from their desks. Designers also reflected on how these spaces could and should encourage collaboration with more people, not just designers: *"The problem of [working] in front of a computer is that you are on your own. (...) Someone else could be sitting here (points) and another one there (points), and all could be browsing simultaneously. (...) You could use these (tools) for focus groups (...) so it's not just designers that can use it. It would also be a way to [bring] the world of the designer closer to the user." [P1] "You could use the table to browse images and magazines in less solitude. The same goes for the wall." [P6]*

Regarding the use of the orthogonal distance from the interactive surface for interaction, participants identified both positive (i.e., extra space) and negative aspects (i.e., lack of physicality) of interacting in open space (i.e. midair). Regarding asymmetric two-handed interaction, designers found similarities between the tools and the use of one hand to select and the other hand to perform an action: *"Although I want to have less chaos in my office, (...) at the same time I still want to see (how big) the pile of images is (...) and then move towards the screen where I make (the mood board). So for me it still needs to have the physical world that I have but you translated it into another physical world into using distance as a cue for interaction and I like that. Maybe I am missing the physicality of it (in midair). In a way the table is already a touch screen so it comes very close to what I want." [P4] "(Using hand gestures) feels good for me because it's a bit the same with (triggering sounds on the wall) and the table where you choose a layer with one hand and activate with the other." [P6]*

The table and wall prototypes running alongside each other allowed participants to get a glimpse of and imagine how the tools might work together. Designers reflected on how information might be transferred from one tool to another: *"I see this table in a meeting room for example (...) so you can make groups of images and then you put them on the wall and the (groups of) images appear there (...) on the wall. So it's like a selecting table." [P1] "If you have places within one room, it should be easily shareable and also somehow clear what the other is trying to communicate to you in any stage of the mood board making process." [P3]*

6 Discussion

6.1 Supporting the Remaining Stages of the Mood-Board Making Process

The full *funky-design-spaces* vision was inspired by and provides support for the six stages of the mood-board making process (Fig. 3). However, the two prototypes developed only support two stages of the process (i.e., *browsing* and *presenting*). To obtain a full understanding of the impact of the proposed holistic environment, four tools that support the remaining stages of the mood-board making process would need to be co-designed and evaluated (i.e., *defining*, *collecting*, *connecting*, and *building*). All six interconnected tools would need to be evaluated alongside each other to check whether people might naturally group back some of these tools together, so that instead of six tools, designers might only require four. Participants made some comments during the evaluations of the tools that might lead in this direction.

6.2 Virtual Space Above Versus Around the Table

Setting the interaction above the table created a problem in terms of the mental model we were trying to introduce. When rearranging an image pile, the action space is set in mid-air (i.e., holding both hands above the table to access a layer and interact with an image), while the perception space is located at table-level (i.e., image projected on the table). Participants instinctively tried to grab the projected image at table-level instead of layer-level. One way to circumvent this problem is to use 'y' instead of 'z' as a cue for interaction. Each row of images corresponding to one magazine or pile would be browsed horizontally using 'x', and then designers could use 'y' to move to other groups of images or magazines. Alternatively, marking menus [13] could be used to assign different actions to the eight points of the compass. East (E) and West (W) would correspond to browsing backward and forward (as is currently), while the remaining six cardinal (i.e., North or N, South or S) and ordinal (i.e., NE, SE, SW, and NW) directions could be used to put images in piles. For novice users, pressing and waiting would display a discoverable menu as a reminder of the different options available. These eight directions fall within the capacity of short-term memory and therefore can be remembered and learned very quickly. The actions can be performed almost automatically with eyes closed so that the attention is always on the work. Another improvement for the Funky Coffee Table could be to retrieve the layer contents using one's fingers by indicating the number of the layer on the table or the direction where the layer is located by pointing to it.

6.3 Proximity-Based Interaction

Using the distance from the vertical display in the Funky Wall allowed designers to easily reveal different parts of the tool. However, participants mentioned some difficulties in knowing which range of interaction they were in (i.e., *showing, contemplating, replaying, exploring*) solely based on visual aspects, due to a lack of other feedback. This happened especially when designers would walk closer or further away from the tool without performing any hand gestures (i.e., keeping their hands in a resting position next to their body). One way to tackle this issue could be to add an extra sensor that would only track the designer's position with respect to the screen independent from hand gesturing. Another alternative would be to use other motion sensing devices (e.g., Kinect), which might allow us to design a different set of gestures to select and trigger different parts of the presentation by doing quick movements in mid-air pointing towards as specific sound or part of the presentation. Audio transitions could also indicate moving from one range of interaction to another.

7 Conclusions

This paper presents an example of surface computing support using a co-design approach by systematically involving end users throughout the design process. In a series of activities with fifty designers (i.e., probes study, retrospective interviews, co-design workshops, and prototype evaluations) the *funky-design-spaces* vision of a holistic design studio housing interconnected tools for creativity was arrived at by observing designers making mood boards. Evaluations suggest these environments could improve creativity and encourage collaboration, however more tools are needed to fully test the vision. Future research includes developing tools for all stages of the mood-board making process, and evaluating them in a design studio for a longer time.

References

1. Apted, T., Kay, J., Quigley, A.: Tabletop sharing of digital photographs for the elderly. In: SIGCHI Conference on Human Factors in Computing Systems, pp. 781–790. ACM (2006)
2. Baudel, T., Beaudouin-Lafon, M.: Charade: remote control of objects using free-hand gestures. Commun. ACM **36**(7), 28–35 (1993)
3. Brandt, E., Messeter, J.: Facilitating collaboration through design games. In: 8th Conference on Participatory Design, pp. 121–131. ACM (2004)
4. Brandt, E., Johansson, M., Messeter, J.: The design lab: re-thinking what to design and how to design. In: Binder, T., Hellström, M. (eds.) Design Spaces, pp. 34–43. Edita, Helsinki (2005)
5. Clark, H.H., Brennan, S.E.: Grounding in communication. Perspect. Socially Shared Cogn. **13**(1991), 127–149 (1991)
6. Eckert, C., Stacey, M.: Sources of inspiration: a language of design. Des. Stud. **21**(5), 523–538 (2000)
7. Garner, S., McDonagh, D.: Problem interpretation and resolution via visual stimuli: the use of 'mood boards' in design education. Art Des. Educ. **20**(1), 57–64 (2001)
8. Gaver, B., Dunne, T., Pacenti, E.: Design: cultural probes. Interactions **6**(1), 21–29 (1999)
9. Halskov, K., Dalsgård, P.: Inspiration card workshops. In: 6th Conference on Designing Interactive Systems, pp. 2–11. ACM (2006)
10. Holtzblatt, K., Wendell, J., Wood, S.: Rapid Contextual Design. Morgan Kaufmann, Burlington (2005)
11. Jordà, S., Geiger, G., Alonso, M., Kaltenbrunner, M.: The reacTable: exploring the synergy between live music performance and tabletop tangible interfaces. In: 1st International Conference on Tangible and Embedded Interaction, pp. 139–146. ACM (2007)
12. Keller, I., Sleeswijk Visser, F., van der Lugt, R., Stappers, P.J.: Collecting with cabinet: or how designers organise visual material, researched through an experiential prototype. Des. Stud. **30**(1), 69–86 (2009)
13. Kurtenbach, G., Buxton, W.: The limits of expert performance using hierarchic marking menus. In: INTERACT 1993 and CHI 1993 Conference on Human Factors in Computing Systems, pp. 482–487. ACM (1993)
14. Lucero, A., Aliakseyeu, D., Martens, J.B.: Augmenting mood boards: flexible and intuitive interaction in the context of the design studio. In: International Workshop on Horizontal Interactive Human-Computer Systems, pp. 147–154. ACM (2007)

15. Lucero, A., Aliakseyeu, D., Overbeeke, K., Martens, J.B.: An interactive support tool to convey the intended message in asynchronous presentations. In: International Conference on Advances in Computer Entertainment Technology, pp. 11–18. ACM (2009)
16. Lucero, A., Vaajakallio, K., Dalsgaard, P.: The *dialogue-labs* method: process, space and materials as structuring elements to spark dialogue in co-design events. CoDesign **8**(1), 1–23 (2011)
17. Lucero, A.: Framing, aligning, paradoxing, abstracting, and directing: how design mood boards work. In: Designing Interactive Systems Conference, pp. 438–447. ACM (2012)
18. Mattelmäki, T.: Design Probes. Aalto University, Espoo (2006)
19. McDonagh, D., Denton, H.: Exploring the degree to which individual students share a common perception of specific mood boards: observations relating to teaching, learning and team-based design. Des. Stud. **26**(1), 35–53 (2005)
20. Quek, F., McNeill, D., Bryll, R., Duncan, S., Ma, X.F., Kirbas, C., McCullough, K.E., Ansari, R.: Multimodal human discourse: gesture and speech. ACM Trans. Comput. Hum. Interact. (TOCHI) **9**(3), 171–193 (2002)
21. Shen, C., Lesh, N. B., Vernier, F., Forlines, C., Frost, J.: Sharing and building digital group histories. In: Computer Supported Cooperative Work, pp. 324–333. ACM (2002)
22. Sleeswijk Visser, F., Stappers, P.J., Van der Lugt, R., Sanders, E.B.: Contextmapping: experiences from practice. CoDesign **1**(2), 119–149 (2005)
23. Streitz, N.A., Geißler, J., Holmer, T., Konomi, S., Müller-Tomfelde, C., Reischl, W., et al.: i-LAND: an interactive landscape for creativity and innovation. In: SIGCHI Conference on Human Factors in Computing Systems, pp. 120–127. ACM (1999)
24. Subramanian, S., Aliakseyeu, D., Lucero, A.: Multi-layer interaction for digital tables. In: 19th Symposium on User Interface Software and Technology, pp. 269–272. ACM (2006)
25. Vogel, D., Balakrishnan, R.: Interactive public ambient displays: transitioning from implicit to explicit, public to personal, interaction with multiple users. In: Annual ACM Symposium on User Interface Software and Technology, pp. 137–146. ACM (2004)
26. Von Hardenberg, C., Bérard, F.: Bare-hand human-computer interaction. In: Proceedings of the 2001 Workshop on Perceptive User Interfaces, pp. 1–8. ACM (2001)
27. Wellner, P.: Interacting with paper on the DigitalDesk. Commun. ACM **36**(7), 87–96 (1993)
28. Wexelblat, A.: An approach to natural gesture in virtual environments. ACM Trans. Comput. Hum. Interact. (TOCHI) **2**(3), 179–200 (1995)

Kwento: Using a Participatory Approach to Design a Family Storytelling Application for Domestic Helpers

Kakit Cheong$^{(\boxtimes)}$ and Alex Mitchell

Department of Communications and New Media,
National University of Singapore, Singapore, Singapore
{kakit,alexm}@nus.edu.sg

Abstract. The recording and sharing of family stories remains an important part of what it means to be a "family". While there is prior research into supporting storytelling for families living apart, there remains a gap in understanding and supporting family storytelling for migrant workers. To address this gap, we explored how technologies could be designed for domestic helpers. Nine domestic helpers were recruited and divided into three design teams. The participatory design sessions and cultural probe findings led to the design of *Kwento*, a prototype mobile application that uses prompts to encourage helpers to reflect upon their personal experiences.

Keywords: Family storytelling · Migrant workers · Participatory design · Cultural probes

1 Introduction

There are various reasons for families, especially families living apart, to share stories. In addition to maintaining close bonds and helping family members to make sense of difficult or traumatic experiences, stories are also a key way for family members to share significant personal experiences that they hope will be remembered and retold. Traditionally, these stories have been shared face-to-face. However, in recent times, more families are geographically distributed for a variety of reasons.

For example, in Singapore, many families with two working parents employ female domestic helpers to perform duties such as cleaning the house, taking care of children or elderly family members, cooking and grocery shopping [1]. Unlike other migrant workers who are employed in the construction or manufacturing industries, these women work as "live-in" maids and are required to stay with their employers. As a result, these women often spend many years working in challenging environments. Prior research shows that such helpers are typically restricted in terms of access to information and communication technologies [2]. Most helpers are also only given one "rest-day" every week or fortnight, and are discouraged from taking part in social activities outside of the house. Given these conditions, these women may not have sufficient opportunities to share about their lives with their families.

© IFIP International Federation for Information Processing 2015
J. Abascal et al. (Eds.): INTERACT 2015, Part III, LNCS 9298, pp. 493–500, 2015.
DOI: 10.1007/978-3-319-22698-9_33

This raises the question: how can technologies be designed to help families living apart to share significant personal experiences? To address that, our paper focuses on the design of a mobile application that supports family storytelling for a specific group: migrant domestic helpers in Singapore.

2 Related Work

Related work includes the use of technologies by migrant families, and the design of systems to support family storytelling. We now briefly survey this work.

2.1 Use of Technologies by Migrant Families

There has been a considerable amount of research that investigates how migrant families make use of information and communication technologies (ICTs) to stay in touch. A study by Wong-Villacres and Bardzell examined the role that technologies play in supporting long-distant relations between migrant parents and left-behind children in developing countries like Ecuador. They found that due to their separation, such families lacked common experiences resulting in children desiring a "private channel for communication" [3].

Lu Pan et al. also sought to uncover how migrant workers in China made use of ICTs to communicate with their left-behind children. Their study revealed that the mobile phone remains as the primary communicative device for such families. Additionally, the study also showed that both parents and children expressed a strong desire for more in-depth interactions, for example, more than half of the children interviewed said they wanted to share about events at school or at home [4]. As a final example, Oduor et al. present an exploratory qualitative study on how technology supports family communication in different parts of Kenya. Similar to the other papers, they found that communication for such families typically revolves around "economic support, life advice and the everyday coordination of activities", leaving such families with limited opportunities for the sharing of personal experiences [5].

2.2 Systems Supporting Family Storytelling

There is also existing research on family storytelling systems that can be categorized into two groups: synchronous storytelling systems and asynchronous systems.

Studies in the first group often focus on supporting synchronous storytelling over video-chats. An advantage of such systems lies in how video communication is currently able to replicate the experience of face-to-face communication to a large extent. For example, a study by Ames et al., found that video-chat allows users to express themselves with facial emotions, hand gestures and other non-verbal cues. In addition, the study showed that video-chats were often set up in such a way that the screen was broadcast into a room, allowing different family members to enter or leave the conversation [6].

The second group of studies focuses on supporting asynchronous family storytelling. These studies typically acknowledge that coordinating a time for both parties may prove challenging. For example, one study observed a tension between generations as grandparents claimed they were reluctant to share stories with their children as they did not want to bother them. In response, the study proposed a system that allowed for grandparent to record their stories, which their children or grandchildren could view at their own convenience [7].

3 Research Focus

While there has been extensive research on how migrant families use ICTs to communicate, these studies do not focus specifically on how such families use ICTs to share stories. At the same time, while there have been prior studies on supporting family storytelling, these systems do not consider the specific circumstances faced by migrant domestic helpers. This paper therefore poses the following question: how can we design a family storytelling system that addresses the needs of domestic helpers?

4 Methodology

For this study, nine domestic helpers were recruited via snowball sampling from two local churches. We made use of snowball sampling, as it is a useful technique for reaching difficult to locate participants like migrant workers. In addition, given the sensitive nature of some personal experiences, it was important for the researchers to build rapport with the community before the women would agree to the study. All of the participants were females, 26–39 years old, and from the Philippines. In terms of working experience, some had worked in Singapore for a few months while others had worked for 10 years.

We divided the participants into three design teams, each consisting of three participants. Collaboration with the participants took place over three sessions, each lasting between an hour and ninety minutes: (1) a focus group, (2) a design session and (3) an evaluation session. The entire study took place over a period of four months.

As none of our participants had any design experience, we began the focus group with an explanation of the concept of participatory design. Drawing upon prior research, our study defines participatory design as "a democratic approach to design by creating a platform for active end-user participation in the design process" [8]. To encourage active participation, we stressed that all aspects of the proposed solution would be open to the participants' suggestions and feedback. Following this, participants were asked to share how they currently made use of technology to share stories with their families, and any problems they faced. They were then asked to discuss their initial ideas for possible solutions. Finally, the participants were provided with a cultural probe pack consisting of a Polaroid camera and writing material and given between two weeks to capture significant personal experiences for discussion in the design session. As Gaver explains, cultural probes are designed to provoke inspirational responses and provide fragmentary clues about their lives making them valuable in inspiring design ideas that could enrich people's lives [9]. More importantly, given the participants' work environment, we felt that probes would allow us to gather tacit information in an unobtrusive manner. We shared suggestions for use of the camera, such as capturing significant people, places or events in their lives. At the same time, we stressed that such suggestions were for inspiration only and that the women could be as creative as they wanted.

During the design session, participants were asked to present the photos and the stories they recorded using the probes. Next, they were asked to group their photos to uncover dominant themes. We also paid attention to the intended audiences of the stories and how the women hoped to share their experiences. After this, the participants were shown three existing storytelling applications[1] to familiarize them with common features and interfaces. The remainder of the session was devoted to coming up with usage scenarios and features for the proposed solution. With the exception of the first group, the other two groups were presented with the design ideas proposed by the previous groups and asked to critique and build upon these designs. It is important to note that this critique was done only after each team had finished proposing their ideas. We chose to adopt this "mixing ideas" technique as it remains a useful way of merging individual ideas into larger, collaborative ideas [10].

Between the second and third session, a low-fi mockup of the prototype was put together by the researcher, which was then evaluated by the design teams in the final session. During the evaluation session, participants interacted with the mock-up and provided feedback on the system. For example, to evaluate the usefulness of the reflective prompts, participants were asked to create a story using one of the prompts. Prompts that were deemed unsatisfactory were then removed.

Following the sessions, the researchers carried out inductive coding on the researcher notes taken during the sessions, as well as on the probe pack materials gathered by participants. As Seidman points out, inductive coding is useful for condensing raw textual data into a brief summary format and to establish clear links between research objectives and the summary findings from the raw data [11]. From this, we were able to sort low-level codes into broader themes. For instance, *suggestion, topic, inspiration* were grouped into the theme of *prompts or triggers*.

Having described our study procedures, in the following sections we will present the key findings from the focus group, followed by the results of the design and evaluation sessions.

5 Challenges Faced by Domestic Helpers

The focus group was intended to introduce participatory design to the helpers. In addition, we wanted to examine the specific challenges faced by such women when trying to share stories about their lives and explore possible technological solutions.

---

[1] Storehouse (https://www.storehouse.co/).
   Touch & Tell (http://www.touchandtell.net/).
   Storyworth (https://www.storyworth.com/).

First, participants shared that their current working conditions did play a role in preventing them from sharing stories with their families. For example, helpers said that they were expected to work an average of ten to fourteen hours a day, making it difficult to communicate with their families. Some helpers were also restricted in their access to technology, with employers choosing not to provide them with access to the household Wi-Fi.

Next, the focus group findings support prior literature which point out that migrant workers tend to prioritize hearing updates about their families [5]. As such, they often have limited opportunities to share about their own experiences, despite the fact that they have a strong desire to.

Finally, the findings suggest that these women currently perceive themselves to be unable to **"do more"**. As one participant shares, *"every day we do the same things, clean the house and take care of the children. If we go out, it's to church or to send money, so quite hard to think of stories to share"* (Participant 2). Interestingly, the cultural probes strongly suggest that this perception may not always be accurate. For example, after using the probes, the same participant shared that the activity was able to motivate her to reflect and find significance in some of her daily activities. For instance, she showed us a picture of a bus, explaining: *"when I first come here, I always lost and I will get very scared. Now I know this bus go where and I am happy that I learnt to be strong... when my daughter wants to work overseas, I will share such experiences to teach her"*.

6   Design Requirements

Beyond the challenges faced by such women in the focus group, the participatory design and evaluation sessions uncovering requirements for our proposed design solution. Two themes emerged from the coding process: the need for a system that is both safe and suitable for use in the participants' working environment, and the need for prompts or triggers to encourage reflection and storytelling. We now discuss the design requirements implied by these two themes.

6.1   Systems that Are "Safe and Suitable for Work"

The first requirement that emerged from the design sessions was for the proposed solution to be both practical and suitable for their work environments. Therefore, taking into consideration that they have limit access to technology, the design teams suggested a mobile application. As previously mentioned, the mobile phone remains the primary and often, only communication device for such workers. The participants also pointed out that most helpers are reliant on pre-paid data cards that they have to purchase every month. As such, they are not willing to use applications or services which required them to be online all the time. Participants also acknowledged that given their working hours, they would only be able to spend between fifteen to thirty minutes a day to record their personal experiences. This suggests that the system should reduce the time taken to record a story.

The participants also expressed that it was important that they would have complete control over the audience of the recorded stories. As one participant shares, "*I used to share on Facebook, but one day, I see my employer there also. After that I change my account name and don't post anymore*" (participant 8). Another woman added, "*Facebook all that is too open, I am not happy to share about my problems with everyone, just my sister and some close friends*" (participant 5). As a result, the mobile application the participants proposed allows users to share their stories with a closed network of family members and confidants.

6.2   Prompts or Triggers

Another theme we identified was the difficulty of thinking of what personal experiences to record. To address this, the design teams suggested a system that could prompt or guide the users on possible stories to record and save. Based on the design sessions, we propose two types of prompts to aid users: (1) reflective prompts and (2) meta-cognitive prompts.

Our participants shared that when using the cultural probes, some were initially unsure of what to record. In response, they would speak with other members of the team to "*be inspired*". Additionally, we noticed that the participants often relied on asking one another questions to determine what experiences would be worth sharing. Examples of such reflective prompts include questions like "What was the first meal you had in Singapore?" and "What is something you wish you had known about Singapore before leaving the Philippines?" Apart from these text prompts, participants suggested that previously taken photos could also be used to encourage reflection. For example, a participant mentioned how she went through her entire phone media library to determine what types of stories to write. Prior studies have also shown the value of using photos to support everyday reminiscence [12].

Interestingly, a study by Nuckles et al. found that meta-cognitive prompts were effective in optimizing journal writing by students. As they explain, such prompts can be conceived of as "strategic activators" given how they encourage "learning strategies that the learners are in principle, capable of, but do not spontaneously demonstrate, or demonstrate to an unsatisfactory degree". We feel meta-cognitive prompts will help to change users' perception that they are not able to "do more" [13].

7   Proposed System: *Kwento*

We now describe our low-fi prototype that emerged from the participatory sessions. *Kwento* (Tagalog for story) is a mobile application that is specifically designed for use by helpers to create and record personal experiences without Internet connectivity. To minimize the amount of data used, users can choose to upload or download their stories on their rest days when they are able to access free public Wi-Fi. The story creation page has also been designed to reduce the amount of time needed to record a story. For example, users can choose to import or take new photos with their phones. From there, users can type out or voice-record their stories.

The main feature of the application lies in the implementation of prompts to encourage self-reflection (see Fig. 1a, b). Each time a helper logs in she is free to choose from two types of reflective prompts: (1) a question or (2) a randomly selected image. The reflective questions were taken directly from the sessions to ensure other helpers would find such topics relevant. Acknowledging that some users prefer more open-ended prompts, users can also choose to receive a randomly selected photo taken from their phone. From there, they are encouraged to examine the photo or image and reflect if there is an interesting experience worth sharing.

To address the perception issue, we also included meta-cognitive prompts (see Fig. 1c). As Efklides and Vauras explain, metacognition refers to the "knowledge and awareness of one's cognitive processes and ability to actively control and manage those processes" [14]. To support this awareness, when a user saves her story the application asks her what problems she faced when writing the story, and then provides relevant suggestions when she starts writing her next story. The design teams feel that such prompts will assist the user to be aware of which aspects of the story recording and sharing they find difficult. More importantly, these prompts may guide users to think of strategies to overcome these difficulties. For example, if the user feels that her stories are too short, she can indicate this, and the application will prompt her to include more details from similar experiences in her next story.

Fig. 1. Low-fi prototype showing (a) text-based prompt, (b) photo prompt and (c) meta-cognitive prompt

8   Conclusions and Future Work

In this paper, we have presented the findings from our study investigating the family storytelling needs of migrant domestic helpers in Singapore. The results of the focus groups strongly suggest that such women perceive themselves to be "unable to share more" as a result of their work environments, despite the fact that they do, indeed, have stories to tell. Through the participatory design sessions, we were able to collaborate with the intended end users to design a low-fi prototype. The next step will be to build the full application. Once completed, the system will be deployed with a new pool of participants to evaluate the strengths and limitations of the system.

Acknowledgements. This research is supported by the National Research Foundation, Prime Minister's Office, Singapore under its International Research Centre @ Singapore Funding Initiative and administered by the Interactive & Digital Media Programme Office.

References

1. Quek, K.M.-T.: The evolving challenges of modern-day parenthood in Singapore. Parenting Across Cultures, pp. 145–161. Springer, Berlin (2014)
2. Yeoh, B.S., Soco, M.A.: The cosmopolis and the migrant domestic worker. Cultural Geograph. **21**(2), 171–187 (2014)
3. Wong-Villacres, M., Bardzell, S.: Technology-mediated parent-child intimacy: designing for Ecuadorian families separated by migration. In: CHI 2011 Extended Abstracts on Human Factors in Computing Systems, pp. 2215–2220. ACM, Vancouver, BC, Canada (2011)
4. Pan, L., et al.: An exploration on long-distance communications between left-behind children and their parents in China. In: Proceedings of the 2013 Conference on Computer Supported Cooperative Work, pp. 1147–1156. ACM, San Antonio, Texas, USA (2013)
5. Oduor, E., et al.: How technology supports family communication in rural, suburban, and urban Kenya. In: Proceedings of the 32nd Annual ACM Conference on Human Factors in Computing Systems, pp. 2705–2714. ACM, Toronto, Ontario, Canada (2014)
6. Ames, M.G., et al.: Making love in the network closet: the benefits and work of family videochat. In: Proceedings of the 2010 ACM Conference on Computer Supported Cooperative Work, pp. 145–154. ACM, Savannah, Georgia, USA (2010)
7. Bentley, F.R., Basapur, S., Chowdhury S.K.: Promoting intergenerational communication through location-based asynchronous video communication. In: Proceedings of the 13th International Conference on Ubiquitous Computing. ACM (2011)
8. Wakil, N., Dalsgaard, P.: A Scandinavian approach to designing with children in a developing country - exploring the applicability of participatory methods. In: Kotzé, P., Marsden, G., Lindgaard, G., Wesson, J., Winckler, M. (eds.) INTERACT 2013. LNCS, vol. 8117, pp. 754–761. Springer, Heidelberg (2013)
9. Gaver, B., Dunne, T., Pacenti, E.: Design: cultural probes. Interactions **6**(1), 21–29 (1999)
10. Guha, M.L., et al.: Mixing ideas: a new technique for working with young children as design partners. In: Proceedings of the 2004 Conference on Interaction Design and Children: Building a Community, pp. 35–42. ACM, Maryland (2004)
11. Seidman, I.: Interviewing as Qualitative Research: A Guide for Researchers in Education and the Social Sciences. Teachers college press, New York (2012)
12. Peesapati, S.T., et al.: Pensieve: supporting everyday reminiscence. In: Proceedings of the SIGCHI Conference on Human Factors in Computing Systems, pp. 2027–2036. ACM, Atlanta, Georgia, USA (2010)
13. Nuckles, M., et al.: Short-term versus long-term effects of cognitive and metacognitive prompts in writing-to-learn. In: Proceedings of the 8th International Conference on International Conference for the Learning Sciences - Volume 2, pp. 124–131. International Society of the Learning Sciences, Utrecht, The Netherlands (2008)
14. Flavell, J.H.: Metacognition and cognitive monitoring: a new area of cognitive–developmental inquiry. Am. Psychol. **34**(10), 906 (1979)

Paper or Pixel? Comparing Paper- and Tool-Based Participatory Design Approaches

Matthias Heintz[(✉)], Effie Lai-Chong Law, and Samaneh Soleimani

University of Leicester, University Road, Leicester LE1 7RH, UK
{mmh21, ss887}@leicester.ac.uk, elaw@mcs.le.ac.uk

Abstract. Traditionally, in participatory design (PD) workshops, pens and paper are often used by participants to provide their design ideas. However, using a software tool to gather their feedback can have certain advantages. While some attempts to develop such tools have been undertaken, the basic question whether the tool-based approach is better or worse than its paper-based counterpart in terms of the quality of feedback gathered is rarely explored. We aim to address this research question by conducting three PD workshops with the paper-based and tool-based approach. In addition to the findings about the comparability of the two approaches, one of our main contributions to the future research on this question is the development of the coding scheme CAt+. It enables systematic comparisons of PD data collected with different methods and aims to support designers and developers to exploit PD results.

Keywords: Participatory design · Paper-based · Tool-based · Coding scheme

1 Introduction

Participatory design (PD) is a broad research area regarding the inclusion of prospective users in the design and development process for various physical as well as digital systems, products, and services [1–3]. The goal is to gather their insights and input, especially design suggestions. There exists a proliferation of PD approaches, methods, techniques, and tools, for example: an expert designer co-creates with a single user to create a 3D mock-up from scratch using clays; a researcher elicits feedback on a simple 2D paper mock-up from a group of users using coloured pens [4]. In this paper, we present our research study on PD for "webapps", a collective term we use to refer to a variety of web-based applications, websites, and online portals.

With prevalent PD techniques (see [4] for an overview) feedback is typically elicited from participants in the form of verbal comments and sketches with the help of different materials and props such as storyboards, post-it notes, paper mock-ups, and acetates (see [5] for details). Using a software tool for PD instead, enables the user to interact with a prototype directly, creating a more realistic and engaging experience (e.g. [7–11]). This could result in more feedback of possibly better quality, as compared to the paper-based approach. In addition, applying a software tool for data gathering can be advantageous for the data analysis, i.e. digitalisation of PD data at the time of

© IFIP International Federation for Information Processing 2015
J. Abascal et al. (Eds.): INTERACT 2015, Part III, LNCS 9298, pp. 501–517, 2015.
DOI: 10.1007/978-3-319-22698-9_34

capturing can enhance the effectiveness and efficiency of data processing (e.g. mitigating data loss; enabling software-supported data analysis).

However, there are also some constraints for using a software tool as compared to using pen-and-paper, e.g. computer access is needed; drawing on paper is more natural than on a screen [6].

When comparing the two approaches for PD, amount and quality of feedback is the most important aspect. Accordingly, we formulate two research questions (RQ):

RQ1:   To what extent is the number of comments captured by tool-based PD activities on a specific webapp different from that by their paper-based counterparts?

RQ2:   How are the comments captured by tool-based PD activities on a specific webapp qualitatively different from those by their paper-based counterparts?

The specific webapp for which our PD activities have been performed is a web-based portal under development in the European Go-Lab project. The goal of this project is to develop a portal [12] and online tools to facilitate the integration of online labs in science lessons. PD activities on the associated mock-ups have been performed with the target groups of the project, namely teachers and students from primary schools up to universities. According to the IBF Participatory Continuum Model [13] our PD activities lean towards the informant design [5]. When participants are used as informants for design decisions it is a normal PD practice to develop initial mock-ups and utilise them to gather user feedback and ideas. Specifically, myBalsamiq, the web-version of the prototyping software Balsamiq, which can be used to create interactive mock-ups from predefined or custom shapes (see Sect. 3.1 for details), has been selected as the tool for our PD activities, because the mock-ups had been created with this tool. Therefore the results from the PD sessions would directly be visible and integrated in the design environment. Designers could not only instantly see it but also use it as a base or an input for the next re-design iteration. To further support the decision to use myBalsamiq for the PD activities and not only rely on the designers' choice of software tool, as it might be very good for design work but inappropriate for PD activities, we additionally performed a tool evaluation. From the results the use of myBalsamiq can also be inferred (see Related Work section for details). As it is not clear yet if the tool usage leads to results comparable to using the conventional way of gathering the feedback on paper, we aimed to answer the two research questions stated above to justify applying the tool over using paper in order to benefit from the described advantages. But it also goes the other way around: We are aware of some of myBalsamiq's shortcomings (e.g. the requirement for an Internet connection) and the question then becomes if paper is an appropriate way to be used as a back-up, e.g. in case of very limited Internet access.

To answer the two RQs, it is crucial to have a coding scheme for analysing and comparing PD user comments, thereby allowing systematic comparisons of the cross-media results (paper vs. digital). As such a scheme is lacking in existing literature, we have been motivated to develop one, which we named CAt+, to fill the gap. It comprises one Categorisation and three Attributes (Impact, Specificity, Uniqueness). By rating comments based on those attributes, it allows quantifying and assessing qualitative characteristics of PD comments and thus enables a more thorough comparison (see Sect. 5 for details). The coding scheme has been developed with generalizability in mind to enable other PD professionals to apply it for coding their participants' feedback. Although this generalizability of CAt+ is yet to be established, it can be considered as advancing a critical step for this specific area of PD data analysis. In this study we focus on the use of the coding scheme to compare data collected using the two different methods. In our future work, we will validate the impact of the scheme on enabling designers and developers to make sense of user feedback and implement changes.

2   Related Work

Some studies (e.g., [14, 15]) compare paper- and tool-based approaches to collect user input empirically in contexts other than but somehow related to PD, including software inspection [16] and multimedia design [17]. These comparison studies focused mostly on quantitative results (e.g., the number of defects found during inspection; task completion time) and on subjective opinions of the participants about the use of a tool versus the use of paper for performing specific tasks. However, they hardly compared the quality of the results (except [17] where the richness of the user-generated screens was evaluated to some extent).

The drawbacks of exclusively quantitative (or qualitative) approaches are increasingly recognized in the field of HCI (e.g., [18]). For instance, the total number of user comments cannot tell whether the comments address the content or the user interface design and interaction concept of the system evaluated. One of the challenges of qualitative analysis is the identification or development of a viable coding scheme.

Various coding schemes have been developed for a variety of topics, ranging from user comments on machine learning [19], over student comments on the teaching performance of professors [20] to YouTube comments [21]. Reference [22] applied PD in a school setting to plan and improve lessons together with students and developed a coding scheme to code the spoken comments made during discussions. As those schemes are tailored to specific topics and use cases, they are not general enough to be applied directly to coding comments from different domains, e.g. PD user comments on webapp design.

While paper-based approaches remain commonly used for PD of webapps, some research efforts have been undertaken to mimic properties of paper in software tools suitable for PD by supporting graphical as well as textual feedback. One of them is GABBEH [23], an electronic paper prototyping tool which enables users to comment on the current design. Another one is DisCo [24] an online tool supporting PD workshops where adults and children collaborate. However, GABBEH only works with the DENIM tool [25] and DisCo is not yet publicly available for use.

To the best of our knowledge, no study has been conducted to compare systematically a paper-based and tool-based approach to determine to what extent software tools can be used to support or even replace paper-based PD activities. This gap has motivated us to conduct such a study.

The first and foremost step of the planned study was to identify an appropriate paper-based approach and software tool to use. As our target group involves children (students) as well as adults (teachers), we decided to choose a paper-based approach appropriate for children, and the Layered Elaboration approach [26] was proved to serve this purpose (see Sect. 3.1 for details). It was shown that this approach could somehow be evolved into an online tool (DisCo, see above). However, the results gathered with DisCo were not yet compared to those gathered with the paper-based Layered Elaboration approach.

Given the constraints of DisCo and GABBEH, we had to find an appropriate tool to compare with the Layered Elaboration approach. The use of myBalsamiq by the mock-up designers was a strong argument to also use it for PD. But for a proper comparison of paper- and tool-based method, a sound tool selection is necessary. To guide this, ten requirements (six user-based and four developer-based) were gathered from three main sources: a literature review (especially [2, 4, 5]), end-user survey results, and unstructured interviews with main developers of the portal. The requirements scoped our search that resulted in 21 tools of which only two can fulfil most of the ten requirements: *Appotate* and *MyBalsamiq*, with the latter having the higher maturity and usability (details are reported in [27]). Therefore myBalsamiq was chosen for comparing the effectiveness of the paper-based and tool-based PD approach in terms of the quality of feedback elicited.

3   Design of Empirical Study

3.1   PD Study with Interactive Mock-Ups

With the Balsamiq software, three mock-ups were created that shared the same basic structure but differed in the complexity of the learning content to address students of different academic levels (Fig. 1).

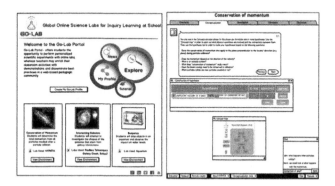

Fig. 1. Mock-ups of the portal: homepage (left) and a webpage with learning content and tools provided by the teacher for students (right).

The PD work of the Go-Lab project has been implemented with two approaches: (1) tool-based with interactive mock-ups and (2) paper-based with printouts of those mock-ups. Details are described in the following.

Paper-Based: Layered Elaboration is a more recent paper-based prototyping technique [26], which is simple to apply, and has the feature of keeping the initial prototype and comments from an iterative process intact. By overlaying different acetate sheets for the same mock-up printout, researchers can identify, for instance, which features have most frequently been commented on. The process starts by providing each individual or a small group of participants with a usage scenario, a set of ordered numbered printouts of the mock-up, a clipboard, and acetate sheets. Participants are asked to read through the scenario, put one acetate sheet on a printout, one after the other following the given order of printouts, and then provide feedback by annotating the acetate sheets with text and sketches, while working through the scenario on their own pace within a 45- or 60-minutes timeslot.

Tool-Based: Participants are provided with computer access and work individually or in a small team of two or three people. They are introduced to the mock-up and then shown how to modify the mock-ups using different options provided in the myBalsamiq editor (Fig. 2). As with the paper-based approach participants are given a usage scenario specific to the mock-up to follow and are asked to give feedback while following the scenario. As the tool adds the user feedback elements in a transparent layer on top of the prototype, leaving the original prototype intact, it is comparable to the layered elaboration approach. Among the feedback options there are yellow "virtual sticky notes", which are added to the prototype by dragging them from the menu, to give textual feedback. Such notes are also commonly used in paper-based PD methods [28]. As with the paper-based method the participants progress through the scenario on their own pace within a 45- or 60-minute timeslot.

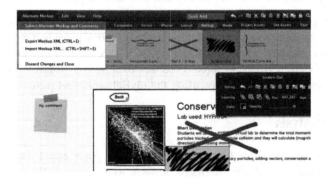

Fig. 2. The main feedback functions of myBalsamiq (screenshot of myBalsamiq taken and included with the permission of Balsamiq studios, LLC)

3.2 Participants and Procedure

The mock-ups were used in PD workshops in two schools in a European country (School 1 and School 2) and in an international teachers programme in Europe (Teachers Programme) to gather ideas for the improvement of the prototypes and data for the comparison of the paper-based and tool-based approach. The workshops were started with two presentations (i.e. one briefly on the project and one on the PD process), followed by about a one-hour session of hands-on activities with the mock-ups.

School 1: The first PD workshop took place in a high school. Thirteen science students (mean age: 17 years old) were randomly divided into two groups with six using the Layered Elaboration approach (paper-based) and seven using myBalsamiq (tool-based). Two researchers were present to provide support, and each observed one of the two student groups.

The Layered Elaboration technique is typically applied on a group basis and with young children, albeit being applicable to other age groups as well. Because of the low number of participants, they did not work in groups at this event but gave feedback individually, to maximize the number of datasets, with no intention to use it as an intervention variable to compare the results from the two settings. Although the Layered Elaboration approach was altered slightly in this case, this did not affect the comparability of the data collected with the two PD approaches, as the participants using the tool to give feedback also did not work in groups at this event.

School 2: The second PD workshop took place in an elementary (or primary) school. The procedure was the same as in School 1, except having the students working in groups instead of individually, thus following the Layered Elaboration approach as initially described. 28 students (mean age: 10 years old) were randomly assigned to one of the approaches; 13 (in three groups of three and two groups of two) used the paper-based approach and 15 (in five groups of three) used the tool-based approach to give feedback. Because of the larger number of participants four researchers (two per group) were present this time, observing and providing support.

Teachers Programme: The third PD workshop was organized as one of the activities in a programme for international high school teachers. It took place in a research institute in Europe and involved 51 science teachers from 29 countries worldwide. The participants were split in groups of three. Feedback data from 8 groups working with the paper-based approach and 6 groups using the myBalsamiq tool were collected.

4   Data Analysis

All data were digitalised for further analysis. For the paper-based data, a set of the mock-up printouts and all the annotated acetates were scanned. With the use of the Gimp software the acetate part was removed from the scanned images, making the area where there was no drawing transparent again. Then all feedback from a single session was digitally layered onto the scanned mock-ups (Fig. 3).

For further data analysis, all comments, including textual and graphical, were recorded in Microsoft Excel sheets with two columns. The first one labelled "source" contains "participant and screen ID" allowing the retrieval of the original feedback from the digital files. The second column records the textual user comment enhanced with researcher-generated details to make it easier to understand (e.g. description of the position or target) or a description of the drawing. Comments covering several ideas were split into individual rows during this step to prepare for further analysis.

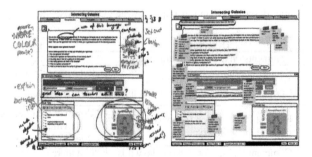

Fig. 3. Superimposed feedback gathered using the paper- (left) and tool-based (right) approach.

5   Origin and Description of Coding Scheme CAt+

Each user comment was coded by two HCI researchers (i.e. fully crossed design [29]) with about two and six years of experience in usability research. Content analysis was applied to generate categories while coding [30]. Both researchers coded the comments in chunks of about twenty, introducing new category identifiers and definitions where necessary. To make sure that all comments were coded appropriately, earlier comments were revisited whenever a new category was introduced. The results were then compared and in case of discrepancy the researchers discussed till a consensus was reached.

Classifying comments based on their content can help to get an idea about the information contained, but not necessarily enables the comparison of the two approaches used to create the comments. For instance, comments on design are not necessarily "better" than comments on functionality; on this basis no conclusion can be drawn which approach is "better". Hence, a broader set of codes with meaningful ratings on the measurable quality of feedback such as specificity (the more specific, the better) was needed. Based on the literature on user defect classification systems (e.g. [31]) and downstream utility (supporting developers in addressing user feedback, e.g. [32]), we identified the following three major attributes: Impact – the extent to which the mock-up will be changed by addressing the idea expressed in the comment; Specificity (regarding target, reasoning, and solution) – the detailedness and thoroughness of the comment in terms of explicitly stating the target, reasoning, and possible solution to make an improvement; Uniqueness – the distinctiveness of the idea expressed in the comment. The initial coding scheme containing categorisation was thus completed by including those Attributes with values and definitions.

Accordingly, we name the coding scheme CAt+: **C**ategories plus **At**tributes, with the **plus** of Attributes compared to other coding schemes that only apply Category (or content) based coding.

5.1   Categories

Table 1 shows the categories of CAt+. Each rating is composed of a sub-category together with the main category, e.g. "Content-Add" (i.e. no feedback is just rated as "Content").

Table 1. Name, description, and example for each category of the rating scheme.

Category	Description	Example
Content	Comments on the learning material.	
Add	Request for more	"Put some text on this page."
Amount of text	Comment on the number of words used	"Shorten the text."
Change	Request for alteration (i.e. what is written), including typos	"However the questions don't seem to link in with the overall subject of the page."
Language	Comment on the wording (i.e. how it is written)	"Use more child friendly language."
Missing description	Request for explanation	"Unclear what to do with these questions."
Positive statement	Supportive comment	"I like the idea of having a video"; "Helpful instructions"
Remove	Request for deletion	"You don't need it to say in three minutes"
Terminology	Comment on only single words and their definition	"What does Buoyancy mean?"
Design	Comments on the visual appeal of the mock-up.	
Add	Request for new graphical elements or sound	"add crashing sounds"
Colourful	Comment on the colour or aesthetics	"The tabs could be more colourful."
Friendly layout	Comment on the suitability for children	"Kid friendly layout"
Negative statement	Criticism	"I do not like how the lines meet, it looks messy."
Not specific	General comment without detailed information	"Nothing to grab my attention."
Positive statement	Supportive comment	"Good use of colour to engage the students."
Screen layout	Comment on the positioning, order and size of elements on the page	"Make this bigger to fill the page?"
Terminology	Comment on only single words	e.g. button labels: "Complicated word ["Conceptualization" tab]"
Text layout	Comment on the format (size, style, colour, etc.) of the writing	"Better font, bigger font."
Remove	Request for deletion	"Don't need this [Page 2/2]."
Visual	Comment on the form/shape/sharpness of elements other than text and images	"... a different symbol could be used."
Functionality	Comments on interactivity of the mock-up.	
Add	Request for more things to do (e.g. buttons or apps)	"Maybe include zoom in and out buttons [...]."
Missing description	Request for explanation	"What is this for? [Resize element on video]"
Positive statement	Supportive comment	"Good system dragging and getting the answer."
Remove	Request for deletion	"I don't think you will need the calculator."
Picture	Comments on the pictures in the mock-up.	
Layout	Comment on the positioning, order and size of pictures on the page	"... have bigger pictures so you can see better"

(Continued)

Table 1. (*Continued*)

Missing description	Request for explanation (including all "picture unclear" comments)	"Try to describe the photos more so we know what they are."
Unknown	Comments of which the coders could not make sense or it was not clear how to address this comment (e.g. could be redesign or adding content or functionality).	
Not under-standable	Comments of which the coder could not make sense	"Isn't the video"
Unreadable	Comments which or important parts of which could not be deciphered.	
Irrelevant	Comments not related to the mock-up itself	"less scribleing (sic!) [feedback to scratched out feedback from another participant]"

5.2   Attribute: Impact

The impact rating specifies how much of the user interface would change if this comment is addressed. Its possible values from 0 to 4 are defined as follows:

- No changes suggested (code: '0'). There is nothing which could have an impact on the mock-up if implemented (e.g. "good idea").
- Change affecting one element (code: '1'). As implementing the suggested changes would only influence a small part or a single element, the impact of this comment on the whole prototype is small (e.g. "the next [button] needs to be in a different colour to make it clearer.").
- Change affecting several elements (code: '2'). As multiple parts of a mock-up page would change if this feedback is addressed, the impact of this comment is medium (e.g. "Do titles for pictures and stuff").
- Change affecting the page on a level larger than element (code: '3'), e.g. by adding/removing an element to/from the page, which would cause a change of the layout of the other elements as well. As significant parts or even the whole mock-up page would change if this suggestion is implemented, the comment is rated as having a high impact (e.g. "Add some thing (sic!) here [white space on the right].")). If the comment does not specify an element, it is assumed that the whole webpage is the target and thus affected (e.g. "More colour").
- Change affecting several pages (code: '4'). As implementing the changes suggested in this comment would change various parts of the whole prototype, its impact is rated as very high (e.g. "log out option").

5.3   Attribute: Specificity

The specificity of a comment indicates how detailed the feedback is. This influences how easily and fast the designer or developer can assess and address the feedback. If the target (e.g. an interface object) is specified, the developer is able to identify which part of the mock-up should be changed. If the reasoning for a comment is given, the developer may find a solution, even if none has been specified by the participant. If a solution is specified by the participant the developer can decide to implement it or take it as further guidance in finding a feasible solution. If such information is not specified, it might still be possible and reasonable for the designers or developers to make an educated guess. But if the informativeness of a comment is too low, even guessing might not be possible.

Accordingly, a Specificity rating consists of six sub-ratings based on the three aspects of the comment discussed: Target, Reasoning, and Solution, and if they are stated or guessable. The aspects "Target/Reasoning/Solution stated" can have the value 0, 0.5 or 1. If the respective information is given explicitly in the feedback, the rating is 1. If it is somewhat clear what the participant means, the rating is 0.5. If no information is given, the rating is 0. The aspects "Guessability of Target/Reasoning/Solution" have been introduced to rate if this information can be guessed (1) or not (0). If it is not necessary to guess this information (most of the time because it has been clearly stated), this aspect is rated as 1 (i.e. "it is guessable").

5.4   Attribute: Uniqueness

Each idea or issue is either coded as 1 if it has not been mentioned before or as 0 if it is a duplicate. By adding up the coding over all comments, the number of distinct comments can be known.

6   Results and Discussion

6.1   RQ1: The Number of Comments

Through the PD activities, 701 valid comments (720 in total of which 19 were not related to the mock-up, e.g., a participant wrote a message to the researchers on the acetate "Sorry about my messy handwriting!") were given by participants using the paper-based approach. 190 valid comments (191 in total of which one was unrelated to the mock-up) were gathered using the tool-based approach.

When comparing the number of valid comments per individual or per group, the paper-based approach resulted in more than twice (School 2: 15.2 compared to 7.0) or even three times (School 1: 51.0 compared to 15.1; Teachers Programme: 27.0 compared to 8.3) as many comments per individual/group as did the tool-based approach. Due to the limited space, Table 2 only shows the results grouped by the main categories. Table 3 shows the percentage (to account for and offset the vast difference in number of results gathered with paper and tool) distribution of comments to categories for the three PD events, for the categories with a difference in the percentage values larger than 5 % between the paper-based and tool-based approach in at least one event.

Summing up, the empirical data of all the three PD workshops with students and teachers indicate that the paper-based approach was much more effective in terms of eliciting comments.

When looking at the percentage results per category presented in Table 3 most of the differences between paper and tool in one event are contradicted by the results of

Table 2. Number of comments per participant (School 1) or group of participants (School 2, Teachers Programme) for each of the main categories and in total.

| Main category | Comments per participant/group | | | | | |
| | School 1 | | School 2 | | Teachers programme | |
	Paper	Tool	Paper	Tool	Paper	Tool
Content	8.5	3.0	3.7	3.6	13.1	5.8
Design	14.5	8.0	6.3	0.8	4.4	1.0
Functionality	21.0	2.7	2.3	1.4	5.9	1.2
Picture	0	0.3	0.5	0.4	1.9	0
Unknown	6.7	1.1	1.8	0.8	0.8	0.2
Irrelevant	0.3	0	0.6	0.0	1.1	0.2
Total	**51.0**	**15.1**	**15.2**	**7.0**	**27.0**	**8.3**

Table 3. Distribution of comments to categories (with a difference of more than 5 % between paper and tool for at least one of the three result sets) in both Schools and the Teachers Programme (in %).

| Category | Percentage of comments | | | | | |
| | School 1 | | School 2 | | Teachers programme | |
	Paper	Tool	Paper	Tool	Paper	Tool
Content	16.8	19.8	25.3	51.4	50.7	71.4
Add	5.3	11.3	6.8	2.9	27.5	26.5
Language	1.3	0	5.8	14.3	1.9	4.1
Remove	0.3	0	1.6	0	1.0	6.1
Terminology	3.0	0	4.2	22.9	2.4	8.2
Design	28.6	52.8	43.2	11.4	16.4	12.2
Colourful	5.9	9.4	8.4	2.9	1.4	0
Text layout	1.3	11.3	12.1	0	4.3	2.0
Functionality	41.4	17.9	15.8	20.0	22.7	14.3
Add	23.7	9.4	3.2	17.1	7.7	14.3
Missing description	6.9	3.8	11.1	2.9	7.7	0
Picture	0	1.9	3.7	5.7	7.2	0
Missing description	0	0.9	3.7	5.7	6.3	0
Unknown	13.2	7.5	12.1	11.4	2.9	2.0

another event. Thus no advantage for paper or tool can be identified for most of the categories. Two exceptions are "Functionality – Missing description" and Unknown, where on a percentage basis (far) more comments have been created when the paper-based method was used to gather the feedback as when the tool-based method was used. For the missing description of functionality this might be explained by the paper being non-interactive and presenting the mock-up out of context (e.g. not on a computer screen; not in a browser). Thus users might have a harder time to identify the functionality of screen elements and therefore give the feedback that a description would be needed. The differences in "Unknown" can be partly explained by unreadable comments but more often by comments on the paper, where the target was unclear and therefore the problem could not be understood. We assume this happened less with the tool, because to give textual feedback there, the participants had to put a yellow sticky note, which they mostly put onto the screen element causing the issue, thus at least giving a hint regarding the target.

6.2   RQ2: The Quality of Comments

All comments categorized either as 'irrelevant' or 'unknown' (either not understandable or unreadable) were removed from further analysis, as they do not contain useful information for the designers and developers. Therefore 809 comments (632 paper- and 177 tool-based) were further analysed with regard to the three Attributes of CAt+.

Impact. As presented in Table 4, most of the changes proposed by the participants have an Impact of either 1 or 3 – affecting a single element or the whole page. This might imply that the participants tended to perceive the mock-up from a holistic perspective, although they zoomed in to explore specific elements (e.g. the next button) in detail. Regarding the comparison of paper and tool it can be seen that paper elicited (slightly) more feedback coded as 1 as compared to the tool results with this impact coding. Participants being more willing to give feedback on small details with paper, might imply that giving feedback with the tool needs slightly more effort, which was more likely spent on ideas with bigger impact.

Table 4. Distribution of Impact rating (in %).

Impact	Percentage of further analysed comments					
	School 1		School 2		Teachers programme	
	Paper	Tool	Paper	Tool	Paper	Tool
0	15.9	10.2	9.6	0.0	7.5	6.3
1	28.4	22.5	40.7	32.3	32.3	27.1
2	1.5	1.0	7.2	25.8	9.5	14.6
3	35.2	58.2	31.1	32.3	32.8	33.3
4	18.9	8.2	11.4	9.7	17.9	18.8

Specificity. Table 5 presents the percentage of results where the corresponding sub-rating was clearly stated. When looking at the Target it can be seen that this is more specific in paper-based comments than tool-based. This may be explained by the fact that paper allows for a variety of ways to highlight a target (e.g. by drawing a circle around or an arrow pointing towards something, or by underlining text), where the tool used in the evaluation was restricted to a predefined set of feedback elements. Users mainly attached virtual sticky notes, which might explain the lower precision and could be approached by enhancing the functionality of the tool.

On the other hand the use of sticky notes might explain the higher specificity of the Reasoning found for the tool-based comments, as the text field on the note might have invited the participant to further elaborate.

Table 5. Comments coded as very specific for each sub-rating (in %).

	Percentage of further analysed comments					
	School 1		School 2		Teachers programme	
	Paper	Tool	Paper	Tool	Paper	Tool
Target	86.1	65.3	78.0	61.3	83.6	68.8
Reasoning	23.7	41.8	26.8	32.3	32.3	45.8
Solution	26.8	20.4	6.6	22.6	40.8	41.7

Uniqueness. To determine how many duplicated ideas have been generated with the paper- and tool-based approach, the comments have been rated based on their uniqueness. The results are shown in Table 6.

When comparing the percentage of duplicates in the paper- and tool-based results, it can be noticed, that it is mostly higher for paper. If one assumes that there is a limited pool of possible ideas the participants can come up with, the higher total number of comments for paper also explains the higher percentage of duplicates as it becomes less likely to come up with a unique idea with an increasing number of comments. The exception of this for School 1 might partly be explained by having the highest number of comments for the tool-based method throughout the three events, but is still unexpected.

Table 6. Results of the Uniqueness rating.

	School 1		School 2		Teachers programme	
	Paper	Tool	Paper	Tool	Paper	Tool
No. of comments	264	98	167	31	201	48
No. of **unique** comments	225	80	137	30	178	47
% of duplicates	14.8	18.4	17.9	3.3	11.4	2.1

Inter-rater Reliability. As two researchers were involved in coding the participants' comments, weighted Cohen's kappa [33] was calculated to determine the inter-rater reliability for the different coding criteria. For the Categorization the weight was determined based on the agreement about the main- and sub-category. If only the sub-category differed, a weight of 1 was used (as there was at least agreement about the main category of the comment), if the main category differed, a weight of 2 was applied. For Impact and Specificity, the weight has been determined by the difference between higher and lower value. For Uniqueness, the standard weight was used. For all ratings the value of Weighted Cohen's kappa was above 0.7, ranging from 0.72 (for Uniqueness) to 0.88 (for Specificity – Solution). Although the kappa rating magnitude guidelines in the literature are inconsistent (e.g. [34, 35]), with all values being above 0.7 we are still confident that our results are reasonable or even good.

Pearson's $\chi 2$ Analysis of Category Rating. Some inferential statistics on the results were performed to check whether the observed differences are significant. As we have categorical data, we used Chi square tests [36] to verify the null hypothesis (H_0):

H_0: the number of comments in each of the coding dimensions (categories, impact, specificity, uniqueness) is independent of the method used to elicit and capture them (paper or tool).

Table 7 shows the results. To get expected values larger than 5 (as required by the Chi square test, e.g. [37]) it was necessary to combine some of the results. For categories Picture, Unknown, and Irrelevant were combined to "Other". For Impact 0, 1, and 2 were combined to "less than page level" and 3 and 4 to "page level and above". For Specificity the results were combined into three groups, very specific (two or more sub-ratings that are very specific), specific (one sub-rating that is very specific), and unspecific (no sub-rating that is very specific). For Uniqueness no combination was possible, therefore the result for School 2 is included in Table 7 although the requirement for Chi square was not met, as the expected value for "not unique" in "tool" was less than 5 (~ 4.85). A Fisher's Exact test has therefore been performed for the latter, confirming the rejection of H_0 in this case.

As can be seen in Table 7 the results are only affirmative for Categories and Specificity ratings. For Categories, H_0 has to be rejected, meaning that the different methods influence the number of comments in different categories. For Specificity, H_0 is not rejected, meaning that the specificity of a comment is independent from the method used for feedback gathering. For Impact and Uniqueness the results of the Chi square tests are ambivalent.

Table 7. $\chi 2$ values for independence of number of comments per rating dimension of CAt+ on method (for all three events). Shading of cells indicates, where H_0 was rejected. *Contains one expected value less than 5!

	School 1	**School 2**	**Teachers Programme**
Categories	$\chi 2$ (3, n=412)=27.19, p<.001	$\chi 2$ (3, n=233)=15.51, p<.05	$\chi 2$ (3, n=266)=8.41, p<.05
Impact	$\chi 2$ (1, n=362)=4.32, p<.05	$\chi 2$ (1, n=198)=0.004, p>.05	$\chi 2$ (1, n=249)=0.03, p>.05
Specificity	$\chi 2$ (2, n=362)=3.52, p>.05 (ns)	$\chi 2$ (2, n=198)=1.96, p>.05 (ns)	$\chi 2$ (2, n=249)=4.44, p>.05 (ns)
Uniqueness	$\chi 2$ (1, n=362)=220.24, p>.05 (ns)	$\chi 2$ (1, n=198)=4.30, p<.05 *	$\chi 2$ (1, n=248)=20.57, p<.001

7 Conclusion and Future Work

When comparing the number of comments given, one can easily recognize that the paper-based approach created much more results than did the tool-based approach, even after normalizing it based on the number of participants or groups using the respective approach. The answer to RQ1 is then clear. One reason for this difference lies in the tool chosen for the evaluation. During the PD sessions with the students and teachers, it showed that some usability problems of myBalsamiq had undermined the efficiency of giving comments.

The results of the descriptive statistics suggest that no consistent trends or meaningful patterns in terms of the qualitative differences of the comments (i.e., Categorization and three Attributes) can be observed. The answer to RQ2 remains ambivalent.

Nonetheless, the number of students and teachers involved in the current study was relatively small. We are aware of this limitation. More studies, involving more participants would be needed to further substantiate the results presented in this paper.

Given the vast difference in number of comments gathered and the dependence of feedback gathered on the method used (at least for categories), we have to conclude that myBalsamiq cannot be used to replace the paper-based method. This interesting finding and the advantages we see in using a tool, have motivated us to develop a more usable PD online tool that can enhance the value of Participatory Design in general and be a valid substitute for the currently conventional and common paper-based method, to be confirmed by further evaluations.

Furthermore, our coding scheme CAt+ for PD data analysis can be useful for other researchers in this field and future comparison studies. Furthermore, we will focus not only on using the coded results to compare paper- and tool-based performance but also demonstrating how the coding can be applied by developers and designers to make better sense of user feedback and address it more effectively. For instance, sorting the list of comments in descending order of Impact or Specificity rating could support them in dealing with the most important feedback first. This approach can also be automated as a kind of tool-supported content analysis in the future.

In summary, with the groundwork built as reported in this paper, our future work will comprise three main strands: (i) To further validate and substantiate our coding scheme CAt+ in different settings (i.e., co-located, distributed, individual, group-based) involving different stakeholders (teachers, students, researchers, designers, developers); (ii) To evaluate the downstream utility of coded PD results by examining whether and how such results support a development team in their redesign work; (iii) To develop a usable PD online tool enabling participants to give comments with ease and even fun.

Acknowledgements. This work was partially funded by the European Union in the context of the Go-Lab project (Grant Agreement no. 317601) under the Information and Communication Technologies (ICT) theme of the 7th Framework Programme for R&D (FP7). This document does not represent the opinion of the European Union, and the European Union is not responsible for any use that might be made of its content.

References

1. Greenbaum, J., Kyng, M.: Design at Work: Cooperative Design of Computer Systems. Erlbaum, Hillsdale (1991)
2. Muller, M.J.: Participatory design: the third space in HCI (revised). In: Jacko, J., Sears, A. (eds.) Handbook of HCI, 2nd edn. Erlbaum, Hillsdale (2007)
3. Schuler, D., Namioka, A. (eds.): Participatory design: principles and practices. CRC Press (1993)
4. Sanders, E.B.N., Brandt, E., Binder, T.: A framework for organizing the tools and techniques of participatory design. In: Proceedings of the 11th Biennial Participatory Design Conference, pp. 195–198 (2010)
5. Walsh, G., Foss, E., Yip, J., Druin, A.: FACIT PD: a framework for analysis and creation of intergenerational techniques for participatory design. In: Proceedings of CHI 2013, pp. 2893–2902. ACM (2013)
6. Weibel, N., Signer, B., Norrie, M.C., Hofstetter, H., Jetter, H.C., Reiterer, H.: PaperSketch: a paper-digital collaborative remote sketching tool. In: Proceedings of the 16th International Conference on Intelligent User Interfaces, pp. 155–164. ACM (2011)
7. Lin, J., Newman, M.W., Hong, J.I., Landay, J.A.: DENIM: finding a tighter fit between tools and practice for Web site design. In: Proceedings of the SIGCHI Conference on Human Factors in Computing Systems, pp. 510–517. ACM (2000)
8. Rogers, Y., Sharp, H., Preece, J.: Interaction Design: Beyond Human-Computer Interaction. Wiley, Hoboken (2011)
9. Sundar, S.S., Oh, J., Bellur, S., Jia, H., Kim, H.S.: Interactivity as self-expression: a field experiment with customization and blogging. In: Proceedings of the SIGCHI Conference on Human Factors in Computing Systems, pp. 395–404. ACM (2012)
10. Teo, H.H., Oh, L.B., Liu, C., Wei, K.K.: An empirical study of the effects of interactivity on web user attitude. Int. J. Hum. Comput. Stud. **58**(3), 281–305 (2003)
11. Zhao, L., Lu, Y.: Enhancing perceived interactivity through network externalities: an empirical study on micro-blogging service satisfaction and continuance intention. Decis. Support Syst. **53**(4), 825–834 (2012)
12. Govaerts, S., et al.: Towards an online lab portal for inquiry-based STEM learning at school. In: Wang, J.-F., Lau, R. (eds.) ICWL 2013. LNCS, vol. 8167, pp. 244–253. Springer, Heidelberg (2013)
13. Read, J.C., Gregory, P., MacFarlane, S.J., McManus, B., Gray, P., Patel, R.: An investigation of participatory design with children – informant, balanced and facilitated design. In: Interaction Design and Children, pp. 53–64 (2002)
14. Hundhausen, C., Trent, S., Balkar, A., Nuur, M.: The design and experimental evaluation of a tool to support the construction and wizard-of-oz testing of low fidelity prototypes. In: IEEE Symposium on Visual Languages and Human-Centric Computing, VL/HCC 2008, pp. 86–90 (2008)
15. Segura, V.C.V.B., Barbosa, S.D.J., Simões, F.P.: UISKEI: a sketch-based prototyping tool for defining and evaluating user interface behavior. In: Proceedings of the International Working Conference on Advanced Visual Interfaces, pp. 18–25. ACM (2012)
16. MacDonald, F., Miller, J.: A comparison of tool-based and paper-based software inspection. Empirical Softw. Eng. (Kluwer Academic Publishers) **3**, 233–253 (1998)
17. Bailey, B.P., Konstan, J.A.: Are informal tools better?: comparing DEMAIS, pencil and paper, and authorware for early multimedia design. In: Proceedings of the SIGCHI Conference on Human Factors in Computing Systems, pp. 313–320. ACM (2003)

18. Law, E.L.-C., van Schaik, P., Roto, V.: Attitudes towards user experience (UX) measurement. Int. J. Hum. Comput. Stud. **72**(6), 526–541 (2014)
19. Stumpf, S., Rajaram, V., Li, L., Burnett, M., Dietterich, T., Sullivan, E., Drummond, R., Herlocker, J.: Toward harnessing user feedback for machine learning. In: Proceedings of the 12th International Conference on Intelligent User Interfaces (IUI 2007), pp. 82–91. ACM, New York, NY, USA (2007)
20. Kindred, J., Mohammed, S.N.: "He will crush you like an academic ninja!": exploring teacher ratings on Ratemyprofessors.com. J. Comput. Mediated Commun. **10**, 00 (2005)
21. Madden, A., Ruthven, I., McMenemy, D.: A classification scheme for content analyses of YouTube video comments. J. Documentation **69**, 693–714 (2013)
22. Könings, K.D., Brand-Gruwel, S., van Merriënboer, J.J.: An approach to participatory instructional design in secondary education: an exploratory study. Educ. Res. **52**, 45–59 (2010)
23. Naghsh, A.M., Andy, D.: GABBEH: a tool to support collaboration in electronic paper prototyping. In: CSCW 2004 the ACM Conference on Computer Supported Cooperative Work, Chicago, USA (2004)
24. Walsh, G., Druin, A., Guha, M.L., Bonsignore, E., Foss, E., Yip, J.C., et al.: DisCo: a co-design online tool for asynchronous distributed child and adult design partners. In: Proceedings of International Conference on Interaction Design and Children (IDC 2011), pp. 11–19. ACM (2012)
25. Newman, M.W., Lin, J., Hong, J.I., Landay, J.A.: DENIM: an informal web site design tool inspired by observations of practice. Hum. Comput. Interact. **18**(3), 259–324 (2003)
26. Walsh, G., Druin, A., Guha, M.L., Foss, E., Golub, E., Hatley, L., …, Franckel, S.: Layered elaboration: a new technique for co-design with children. In: Proceedings CHI 2010, pp. 1237–1240. ACM (2010)
27. Heintz, M., Law, E.L.-C., Govaerts, S., Holzer, A., Gillet, D.: Pdot: participatory design online tool. In: CHI 2014 Extended Abstracts on Human Factors in Computing Systems, pp. 2581–2586. ACM (2014)
28. Druin, A.: Cooperative inquiry: developing new technologies for children with children. In: Proceedings of CHI 1999, pp. 592–599. ACM Press (1999)
29. Hallgren, K.A.: Computing inter-rater reliability for observational data: an overview and tutorial. Tutorials Quant. Methods Psychol. **8**(1), 23–34 (2012)
30. Krippendorff, K.: Content Analysis: An Introduction to Its Methodology, 2nd edn. SAGE, London (2004)
31. Vilbergsdottir, S.G., Hvannberg, E.T., Law, E.L.-C.: Assessing the reliability, validity and acceptance of a classification scheme of usability problems (CUP). J. Syst. Softw. **87**, 18–37 (2014)
32. Hornbaek, K., Stage, J.: The interplay between usability evaluation and user interaction design. Int. J. Hum. Comput. Interact. **21**, 117–123 (2006)
33. Fleiss, J.L., Cohen, J.: The equivalence of weighted kappa and the intraclass correlation coefficient as measures of reliability. Educ. Psychol. Measur. **33**, 613–619 (1973)
34. Altman, D.G.: Practical Statistics for Medical Research. Chapman and Hall, London (1991)
35. Fleiss, J.L., Levin, B., Paik, M.C.: Statistical Methods for Rates and Proportions, 3rd edn. Wiley, Hoboken (2003)
36. Maltby, J., Liza, D.: Early Success in Statistics. Pearson Education, New York (2002)
37. McDonald, J.H.: Handbook of Biological Statistics, 3rd edn. Sparky House Publishing, Baltimore (2014)

Participatory Design in Practice

The Case of an Embroidered Technology

Laura Cortés-Rico[1]([⊠]) and Giovanny Piedrahita-Solórzano[2]

[1] Pontificia Universidad Javeriana, Bogotá, Colombia
cortes-laura@javeriana.edu.co
[2] Politécnico Grancolombiano, Bogotá, Colombia
gapiedrahita@poligran.edu.co

Abstract. This paper presents a project for the social development of ICTs, which used a participatory design approach and sought to have a high social impact on a community of craftswomen (embroiderers from Cartago, Colombia). Participating in this project implied active dialogue with the community to recognize the knowledge of each participant and achieve culturally relevant representations materialized in technological artifacts. We posit dialogue, representation and recognition as key elements for developing successful participatory design. In practice, this was achieved through an iterative, incremental and open-ended methodology, whose main feature was engagement by doing. This process of design allowed engineers to recognize the craftswomen's traditional knowledge and allowed craftswomen to be less afraid of technology. The main resultant artifact was a tangible user interface that facilitates dialogue between fashion designers and embroiderers in the process of designing new embroidery patterns. This and other artifacts that emerged from the activities and dialogues, the level of engagement of the participants, and the convergence points discovered between embroidery and technology, lead us to conclude that the process presented here can be replicated with other craft communities, to reinforce these communities and assist them in generating innovation in their processes and products.

Keywords: Participatory design · Crafts · Embroidery · Representation · Dialogue · Recognition · Tangible user interfaces and social technologies

1 Introduction

Pérez-Bustos and Franco-Avellaneda outlined the idea of designing an ICT inspired by embroidery as an approach to enhancing embroidery as it is practiced in Cartago, Colombia [1]. They presented their intention to reinforce the making of embroidery as "an expression of caring practices aimed to build self-knowledge." Although Cartago is nationally recognized for its embroidery, the embroiderers themselves experience precarious conditions and their craft is often an informal and secondary labor. Because of this, Pérez-Bustos and Franco-Avellaneda proposed that ICT could be an appropriate tool to make the artisans' material conditions and core skills more visible to those unfamiliar with this kind of craft work.

© IFIP International Federation for Information Processing 2015
J. Abascal et al. (Eds.): INTERACT 2015, Part III, LNCS 9298, pp. 518–525, 2015.
DOI: 10.1007/978-3-319-22698-9_35

The creation of such a social ICT implied a project developed using a participatory design (PD) approach, to make possible the "dialogue between technological knowledge and different kinds of traditional wisdom" [1]. PD not only means involving the prospective users of a new technology in specifying requirements, and testing and gathering reactions to it, but giving users the role of co-designers. Choosing a PD approach for the project implied taking into account the care practices and the moral and pragmatic issues outlined in [1]. According to Carroll [2], users not only have the right to be included in the design process (moral proposition), but their inclusion leads to a more successful outcome (pragmatic proposition).

This project, "Embroidering self-knowledge: Systematization of experiences and participatory design of weaving as a caring practice in Cartago, Valle, Colombia",[1] began in January 2014 and will take two years. It is focused on *calado*, a particular type of embroidery made in Cartago.[2] It involves the participation of a group of people with diverse forms and areas of knowledge: the authors -electronic engineers-, ethnographers, software and information professionals, a collective of *caladoras* (embroiderers), fashion designers and educators. As the various research team members came to the project with different notions about PD, it was necessary to establish basic concepts and understandings at the start in order for the activities to be meaningful and successful. This included coming to a common understanding of PD concepts and adapting our ways of communicating and engaging with the other members.

In this paper we present the development of the project, which had an emphasis on engagement through doing. We outline how we achieved participation by involving ourselves in the others' and our own practices, and how this participation led us to a knowledge dialogue between tradition -embroidery- and innovation -technology-. This technological design was strongly related to activity theory [3] and phenomenology [4] as the theoretical foundations. Firstly, this was because of the continuous subject-object interactions that we were involved in, mainly in hands-on workshops, and secondly, because of the central role of our bodies, through which we explored, learnt, dialogued, and recognized the practices of the communities involved in the design.

2   Guidelines

The moral and pragmatic issues of the PD process set a very strong guideline for the team: each member had to become involved in the knowledge domain of the others. This involvement entailed the design of activities to learn *calado* techniques, the design of patterns, as well as basic concepts of electronics. Sabiescu and Memarovic [5] outline the potential challenges facing PD processes, some of which our team encountered: a knowledge gap between participants, renegotiation of design methods and reformulation of design goals, as well as the challenge of defining common boundaries for all of the research team and enabling the *caladoras* community to

---

[1] Funded by COLCIENCIAS, Pontificia Universidad Javeriana and Politécnico Grancolombiano.

[2] *Calado* is made by removing threads from a fabric with warp and woof and then embroidering the fabric again with new threads, typically of the same color as the original fabric.

become conscious of their role as peer participants in the research. Coping with these challenges implied reconfiguring our ideas about the design of technology, because of the many heterogeneous actors identified in the process who played a dual role, both as potential users and as designers of the technology. Configuring the project to give responsibility to users was important in order to make sure that the designed technology would have a real impact and would lead to new ways of conceiving the practices both of making embroideries and of designing technology [6]. As a result of this configuration, three strongly articulated processes were established in order to achieve a successful PD: self- and mutual recognition, dialogue and representation.

– *Self-and mutual recognition.* This indicates the process whereby each member of the team reflects on and comprehends who s/he is and what s/he does, and who each other member of the community is and does; this leads to the realization of what can be done as a single community.
– *Dialogue.* Within the team, participants in each knowledge area have their own codes with which to represent what they do and know, and to communicate effectively with their peers; for example, software modeling languages in the developers' community. Dialogue in a PD process, however, should allow each member to communicate ideas in a common language for all the team, and then find convergence points where all of the participants have the same core understanding.
– *Representation.* This process is possible when the participants are able to suggest and discuss design ideas because they have a sufficient interpretation of the others' and their own knowledge. It implies wishing and giving form to ideas as tangible objects that reflect diverse opinions, and are relevant and useful for the communities involved. It also means finding suitable ways to present them to others.

3   Participatory Design in Practice

In our context, PD was achieved through a methodology that included a series of activities aimed at facilitating self- and mutual recognition, dialogue and representation. These activities allowed the encounter between diverse actors at different moments of the project. In addition, these encounters allowed the co-creation of innovative and culturally representative artifacts.

3.1   Methodology

Methodologically, this project was organized using four iterative, incremental and open-ended milestones to achieve a successful technological design: recognition and reflection, ideation, prototype and experimentation (Fig. 1). Iterative means that the design process requires more than one cycle of going back and forth, and that there is a connection between milestones. This connection implies that there has to be reflection on all ideas prototyped and experimented, which includes recognizing how the different stakeholders react to prototypes and how this reaction reshapes the research. Incremental in this case does not refer to an incremental artifact, but to an incremental way

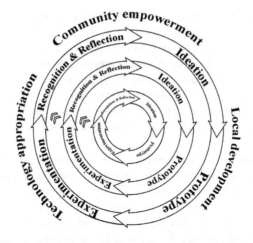

Fig. 1. Methodology followed in participatory design

of better representing the communities involved in the design. It means that the greater the immersion in the project, the easier it is for ideas to become culturally relevant artifacts. The step between one cycle and the next occurs when the design sees a significant change: an addition or removal of previous ideas; or the outcome that some ideas are justifiably swept out of the boundaries of the project, or new ideas are swept in [7]. Ideas swept out of the project boundaries may become counter-examples, helping to recognize issues within the communities or the technology itself. Finally, aiming for open-ended milestones considers that results are not just finished artifacts but an empowerment of the community, which eases the appropriation of the designed technologies and the local development of new sustainable social technology. Empowerment and appropriation lead to a process of continuous design while the artifacts are being used [8].

3.2 Milestones

– *Recognition and reflection* implied continuous active observation and receptive listening, involvement in one another's practices, as well as analysis of related work. This was accomplished through ethnography, hands-on workshops, surveys, meetings and informal chats. Through ethnography, the academic community recognized that in Cartago, *calado* embroidery and design are understood as completely separate forms of knowledge. *Calado* is usually associated with tradition and commonly used and done by elders, while design is related to young people and innovation. This recognition was the motivation for creating a technology that could bridge the gap between the design and making of *calado*.
– *Ideation* was based on desiring, proposing, discussing and negotiating ways in which technology could be woven into the context. In this case, we travelled through many ideas, from the desire for an artifact in order to smell, taste and listen

to embroidery patterns, to more realistic ideas such as representing stitches in a way that would allow users to explore new possibilities with them.

- *Prototype* refers to the act of giving form to ideas. This form is a representation of an idea that allows people in the team to express, communicate, share, manipulate, modify, transform and discuss thoughts [9]. In our project, one of the engineers had the idea that a *calado* stitch could be expressed as a drawing. The resulting prototype was a set of sketches made with different color pencils representing physical constraints of the materials, as well as the form that this stitch would have in an embroidery.
- *Experimentation* indicates the scenario in which prototypes were manipulated by all members of the team. This milestone is mainly focused on sensitizing participants to use their hands to explore, learn and test prototypes, and is thus strongly connected to reflection [3, 4]. In relation to the prototype mentioned above, when embroiderers experimented with the sketches they did not feel motivated to translate them into *calado*. They argued that though they could be embroidered as *calado*, they would not look like it. Reflecting on this, we realized that the novelty in *calado* is not in the design of new stitches, but in the way in which existing ones are combined.

3.3 Activities

The aforementioned milestones are ways of viewing the methodology, not of partitioning it. To illustrate this proposition, below we present some of the main types of activities developed in the project, which served the purposes of more than one milestone in a non-linear way.

- *Hands-on workshops* were spaces where participating communities could interact through the making of some of their practices. They were focused on: (i) allowing the academic community to recognize some of the processes involved in the design and craft of *calado* in Cartago, (ii) allowing embroiderers to get in touch with some technological issues that are close to embroidery and distant to automation,[3] and (iii) allowing the complete team to use the prototypes generated during the project. Hands-on workshops involved active dialogue, embodied learning [10] and the manipulation of materials used by the different collectives in their areas of practice (Fig. 2).
- *Discussion sessions* were spaces in which to talk about diverse issues surrounding the project. These sessions were aimed at socializing the systematization of the fieldwork, collectively clustering information, brainstorming, organizing incoming work and even telling anecdotes in familiar encounters.
- *External dialogues* were activities where the team had encounters with other people and conducted research outside of the boundaries of the project. They allowed us to know about and connect to related work, to talk to experts in knowledge areas not present in our team, to share the advances of our research and to listen to external opinions.

---

[3] Embroiderers were very afraid of technology because it was understood as a way of eliminating the craft through automation.

Fig. 2. E-embroidery workshop: using embroidery and electronic materials like conductive thread, we embroidered a crafted Christmas manger with illumination and interactivity.

3.4 Results

We consider that the process of designing technology in a participatory way constituted a result in itself. Two main achievements support this statement: (i) embroiderers managed to be less afraid of technology and to think of convergence points between embroidery and technology that are different to automation, and (ii) technology professionals recognized the potential, complexity and transformative capability of knowledge associated with embroidery.

Another result are the two technological artifacts that represent us as communities involved in the design. The first is a lighted embroidery hoop designed in recognition of the delicacy required to embroider *calado*, a craft that cannot be done with poor illumination. This artifact represents an innovation in the process of making embroideries in Cartago and has modified -and been modified by- the ongoing practices of embroiderers: to avoid shadows cast by the embroiderers' hands on the fabric, craftswomen started to use the hoop upside down, so having the light on top (Fig. 3A). The second artifact is a Tangible User Interface (TUI) that mediates dialogue between fashion designers and *caladoras* in the process of designing *calado* patterns. This TUI represents our recognition of the need to reduce the aforementioned gap between the design and making of *calado*, and a way of reinforcing and making visible the embroiderers community.

The TUI has two components: digital and physical. The digital one is a computational representation of stitches; its development required an embodied learning of *calado* [4, 10], continuously doing and undoing the labor with our hands, and developing a close relationship with materials from both *calado* and electronic development [3] (Fig. 3C). The physical dimension of the TUI represents our comprehension that a new *calado* pattern emerges from combinations of existing stitches, and not from new ones. In this sense, with the TUI components, a fashion designer can take a tangible stamp to print a representation of a stitch onto the digital representation of the fabric shown on a tablet (Figs. 3C and D). The most interesting part is that after many prototypes, the technical solution for tangibles was literally embroidered: we used conductive thread to embroider tags on the stamps, making them recognizable on the capacitive screen using pattern recognition algorithms (Fig. 3B).

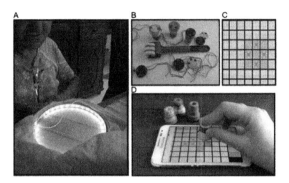

Fig. 3. A. An embroiderer using the lighted embroidery hoop upside down. **B.** Embroidered tangibles with conductive thread used to stamp digital representations of stitches onto a capacitive surface. **C.** A simple *calado* pattern designed with the TUI. **D.** A user stamping a stitch onto a smartphone screen.

4   Reflections and Conclusions

Participation was accomplished to the extent that dialogue between the different communities in the research project was achieved. A horizontal dialogue allowed negotiations and tensions to be easily translated into design decisions. Our most significant dialogue was non-verbal and took place mainly in the hands-on workshops. These activities were focused on self- and mutual recognition, and on seeking the participatory creation of representative artifacts. We also realized that the design was incrementally achieved by thinking ideas collectively, giving them a form, experimenting with them and then reflecting on the process.

Actively involving communities facilitates their empowerment, their appropriation of designed artifacts and also makes possible the local development of new sustainable social technology. Giving embroiderers and fashion designers the role of co-designers offered a more realistic interpretation of the way in which technology involves users: through use, artifacts both modify and are modified by ongoing practices [8]. The plurality and heterogeneity within and between the participating communities in our project led us to conclude that PD does not necessarily imply the complete involvement of all actors in every task, all the time. Limited resources, geographical distance and specialized languages make such participation impossible. Instead, we argue that recognition, dialogue and representation, as presented in our work, are key elements for collectively materializing relevant artifacts as synergies of multiple kinds and forms of knowledge.

We found out that crafts and technology design share a material dimension in which interacting through doing makes possible the creation of representative artifacts. This creation is achieved when each member is involved in the practices of other collectives within the research team, which generates connections between tradition and innovation, enriching craft without replacing the human role. In our project, getting involved in one another's practices enabled engineers to be more reflective about the complexity of the knowledge in the hands of embroiderers, but also revealed to *caladoras* connections between their knowhow and technology that differed from automation. These results may encourage the replication of the presented process with other craft communities, as a way of bringing innovation into their own processes and products.

References

1. Pérez-Bustos, T., Franco-Avellaneda, M.: Embroidering self-knowledge: systematization of experiences and participatory design of weaving as a caring practice in Cartago, Valle, Colombia. In: Proceedings of the 13th Participatory Design Conference: Short Papers, Industry Cases, Workshop Descriptions, Doctoral Consortium Papers, and Keynote Abstracts, vol. 2, pp. 99–102. ACM, New York, NY, USA (2014)
2. Carroll, J.M., Rosson, M.B., Carroll, J.M.: Participatory design in community informatics. Des. Stud. 243–261 (2007)
3. Kaptelinin, V.: Activity theory. In: The Encyclopedia of Human-Computer Interaction, 2nd Ed. The Interaction Design Foundation, Aarhus, Denmark (2014)
4. Winograd, T., Flores, F.: Understanding Computers and Cognition: A New Foundation for Design. Addison-Wesley Longman Publishing Co. Inc., Boston (1987)
5. Sabiescu, A.G., Memarovic, N.: Participatory design for cultural representation: a cultural transparency perspective. In: Kotzé, P., Marsden, G., Lindgaard, G., Wesson, J., Winckler, M. (eds.) INTERACT 2013, Part IV. LNCS, vol. 8120, pp. 611–618. Springer, Heidelberg (2013)
6. Gonzalez, R., Dahanayake, A.: Responsibility in user participation in information systems development. In: Presented at the 18th Annual IRMA International Conference, Vancouver, Canada (2007)
7. Midgley, G., Munlo, I., Brown, M.: The theory and practice of boundary critique: developing housing services for older people. J. Oper. Res. Soc. **49**, 467–478 (1998)
8. Orlikowski, W.J.: Using Technology and Constituting Structures: a Practice Lens for Studying Technology in Organizations. Resources, Co-Evolution and Artifacts, pp. 255–305. Springer, London (2008)
9. Watson, M.C.: Listening in the Pakal controversy: a matter of care in Ancient Maya studies. Soc. Stud. Sci. **44**, 930–954 (2014)
10. Klemmer, S.R., Hartmann, B., Takayama, L.: How bodies matter: five themes for interaction design. In: Proceedings of the 6th Conference on Designing Interactive Systems, pp. 140–149. ACM, New York, NY, USA (2006)

Better Than You Think:
Head Gestures for Mid Air Input

Katrin Plaumann[1(✉)], Jan Ehlers[2], Florian Geiselhart[1],
Gabriel Yuras[2], Anke Huckauf[2], and Enrico Rukzio[1]

[1] Institute of Media Informatics, Ulm University, Ulm, Germany
{katrin.plaumann,florian.geiselhart,
enrico.rukzio}@uni-ulm.de
[2] Institute of Psychology and Education, Ulm University, Ulm, Germany
{jan.ehlers,gabriel.yuras,anke.huckauf}@uni-ulm.de

Abstract. This paper presents a systematical comparison of pointing gestures in the context of controlling home appliances in smart homes. The pointing gestures were conducted with head, hand, arm and a computer mouse serving as baseline. To the best of our knowledge, we are the first to report on such a systematical comparison of the mentioned modalities. Our results indicate that although being overall slower and more inaccurate than hand and arm gestures, head gestures are more suitable for mid air input than previous research indicated. We show that disadvantages like slowness and inaccuracy can be compensated by a larger target size. In addition, head gestures have the largest learning effect. Considering our results and the possibilities head gestures would provide in daily life, we recommend thinking of head gestures as a feasible input modality besides hand and arm gestures.

Keywords: Pointing gestures · Smart home · Head gestures · Comparative study

1 Introduction

In recent years, smart homes have gained more and more attention from the research community. Due to the increased accessibility of low cost sensors like the Microsoft Kinect and other depth cameras, the vision of a ubiquitous gestural interface for smart homes increasingly becomes a reality. Accordingly, mid air interaction has been a big topic in recent research [1, 4, 6, 10, 12–14, 16, 19, 20, 23].

However, all the aforementioned projects have in common that they focus on gestures performed with the complete or at least part of the arm. In contrast, little research has been done to analyse the feasibility of head gestures as an appropriate alternative. The few research projects covering head gestures are mostly motivated by impairments of users whereby head-based interaction is the only possible form of mid air interaction [9, 11]. Other projects simply focused on the detection of head gestures [8]. However, little is known about the performance of head gestures compared to gestures performed with arm or hand.

We consider this an issue for smart homes interaction research, since head gestures could be useful in many scenarios, including working, cooking and leisure activities.

© IFIP International Federation for Information Processing 2015
J. Abascal et al. (Eds.): INTERACT 2015, Part III, LNCS 9298, pp. 526–533, 2015.
DOI: 10.1007/978-3-319-22698-9_36

For example, imagine typing a letter on your PC at late afternoon. As it turns dark, you would like to turn the light on. Instead of moving your hand away from the keyboard, performing a gesture, and moving your hand back to the keyboard, all needs to be done is moving your head in the direction of the lamp. In this scenario, it is not even necessary to interrupt your writing. The same goes for adjusting the heat of the oven while chopping vegetables, and turning the music off while reading a book: using head gestures, it could still be possible to control home appliances with no (or just a very short) interruption of the main task. Appliances could be controlled directly or through a graphical interface. Graphical interfaces could be displayed either on an ambient display or projected near the device.

To find out more about the performance of head movements in comparison to hand and arm gestures, we designed and conducted a study, which is, to the best of our knowledge, the first to give insights on the relative performance of head, hand and arm gestures, compared to mouse input as a baseline. We consulted pointing gestures due to their simplicity; such movements are not bound to a certain context and occur frequently in our daily communication. In addition, pointing gestures can be used for a variety of functions, such as turning on and off any device, selecting devices and things, and interacting with graphical interfaces. So far, most research comparing different mid air input techniques has focused on comparing movements of parts of the arm [2, 3, 5, 20].

Our main contributions in this paper therefore are (1) a quantitative evaluation of pointing performance across different modalities and (2) a relative comparison showing the differences between pointing modalities.

2   User Study

2.1   Participants

We invited 37 participants (six male; mean age: 22 (SE: 0.58)) to take part in our user study. All participants were students of the local universities psychology department; two of them were left-handed. All participants received course credits for their participation.

2.2   Study Design

The participants' task was to point at several targets. The configuration of the targets is shown in Fig. 1. The layout was designed in consideration of the recommendations by Soukoreff and MacKenzie [22]. As depicted, 17 targets were arranged. The centre target is further referred to as home. The remaining 16 circles result from the combination of the independent variables direction (up, down, left and right), size (small and large), and distance to home (short and long). The diameter of the small targets was 3.6 cm and 11 cm for the large targets. The shorter distance was 18 cm from the centre of home to the centres of the targets-to-reach and 54 cm for the longer distance. The resulting indexes of difficulty according to [22] were 1.4, 2.6, and 4 bits. Pointing tasks were performed in a seated position, central to and with 2.5 m distances to the projected targets.

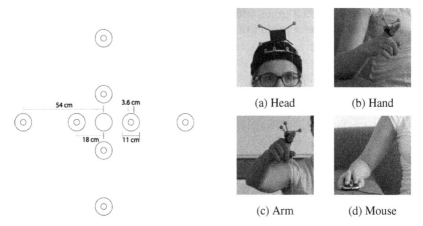

Fig. 1. Target configuration: 16 targets, two sizes and distances to the centre target ("home") as well as four directions. At each position, both small and large targets are depicted.

(a) Head   (b) Hand

(c) Arm   (d) Mouse

Fig. 2. The four input modalities head hand, arm, and mouse.

The participants' task was to select the currently presented target in less than three seconds by moving a cursor from home (middle) to the currently visible target. Thereby a dwell time of 0.6 s had to be completed for successful selection (the dwell time was included in the maximum selection time). As a proper selection mechanism is needed to avoid the Midas Touch problem, we used dwelling. Dwelling does not need a second input modality like buttons or voice commands, and according to [21], is a proper selection technique for mid air interaction especially concerning users' perceived quality and selection accuracy. The order of target appearance was randomized; a complete round was composed of all 16 targets, whereby only home and the respective target circle were visible. For each modality, every participant passed 10 rounds. A target circle appeared when the cursor rested on home and disappeared after the feedback was given. If a target was successfully selected, it was marked green and a success tone was played. Otherwise, the target was marked red and an unpleasant no-success tone resounded.

Using this set-up, we compared the four input modalities head, hand, arm and mouse as depicted in Fig. 2. Head pointing was achieved by moving the head. To point with their hand, participants placed their elbow on an armrest. Arm pointing was performed out of the shoulder joint with the complete arm outstretched. As surface for the mouse, an armrest was used. Every participant had to use all four input modalities for all target sizes, distances and directions, resulting in a $4 \times 2 \times 2 \times 4$ factorial within subject design. The order of the modalities was counterbalanced. As dependent variables we measured "time to succeed": the duration it took to successfully select an envisaged target, starting when the target appeared and ending when the target was successfully selected (only successful selections were used); and "success rate": the amount of successfully selected targets among all presented targets.

2.3   Procedure

After explaining the background, purpose and course of the study, participants signed an informed consent. Every participant was given time to acquaint with all input modalities. When the participants felt ready, we started with the first modality as described above. When the modalities changed, participants where given as much time as they needed to familiarise with the new input technique. During the course of the study, participants could take breaks at any time.

2.4   Gesture Recognition

To recognise the head, arm and hand movements, we used the marker based optical tracking system OptiTrack [18] because of its accuracy. Participants wore either a cap or a finger ring (depending on the tested input modality); both were equipped with retro-reflecting markers, as can be seen in Fig. 2. The markers were tracked with eight cameras, places around the sitting position of the participants. The system was calibrated as suggested by the manufacturer, resulting in millimeter accuracy. For each wearable, a rigid body was defined. To calculate the coordinates of the cursor participants had to move, ray casting was implemented. Therefor, the position of the particular rigid body and its orientation were retrieved using the NatNetSDK [17]. The position of the rigid body served as the starting point of the ray, while the rigid bodies' orientation defined the direction of the ray. To avoid natural hand tremor to disturb the cursor position, the 1 €-Filter [7] was implemented. The intercept was set to 0.6 while beta was set to 0.04.

2.5   Results

Overall Results. Figure 3 shows the resulting "time to succeed" and "success rate" for each modality. As can be seen, mouse was the fastest input modality (m = 1524.6 ms, SE = 17.45), followed by arm (m = 1790.0 ms, SE = 21.93), hand (m = 1795.9 ms, SE = 26.93) and head (m = 2042.2 ms, SE = 17.46). The same pattern can be observed for the success rate, with mouse being the most successful (m = 99.6 %, SE = 0.24) followed by arm (m = 91.4 %, SE = 0.91), hand (m = 87.9 %, SE = 2.03) and head (m = 76.7 %, SE = 1.75).

Due to inhomogeneity of variances, a Friedman test was used to compare time to success and success rates of the four input modalities. The Friedman test revealed that both "time to succeed" and "success rate" differ significantly ($X^2(3)$ = 95.23, p < 0.01 and $X^2(3)$ = 84.34, p < 0.01 respectively). Regarding the time to succeed, a pairwise comparison of all modalities with t-tests (normality was assured by Shapiro-Wilks tests) showed that except for hand and arm, the differences between all modalities are significant (p < 0.001). To pairwise compare the success rate, Wilcoxon-Sign-Rank tests were used since the data was not normally distributed. As with the time to succeed, the only not significant (p < 0.01) difference was between hand and arm.

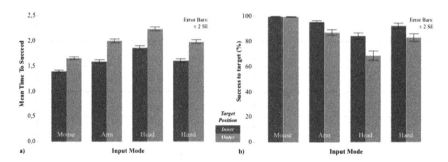

Fig. 3. Mean time to succeed (a)) and success rate (b)) for targets with short (inner) and long (outer) distance to home.

Results According to Distance from Centre. As expected, targets within the short distance from the centre were faster and more accurately selected than the targets within the longer distance. This holds true for all input modalities. Figure 4 shows the mean time to succeed and the success rate for targets with short and targets with long distance to the centre.

Results According to Target Size. Figure 4 shows the mean times to succeed and the mean success rates. For the mean times to succeed, the same pattern as described above could be found, with mouse being the fastest modality followed by hand, arm and head for both target sizes. The main difference is that larger targets could be selected faster than smaller ones, as expected. The same is true for the success rates for the smaller targets. The success rates for the larger targets, however, deviate from this pattern in two ways. First, all success rates are rather high with above 96 %. Second, although a Friedmans test showed that the input modalities differ significantly ($X^2(3) = 82.85$, $p < 0.001$), there is no significant difference between the success rate for head gestures and the success rate for hand gestures, as pairwise comparisons with Wilcoxon Sign Rank tests showed.

Figure 4 also shows that the reaction of ponderous effectors (like head) to an increased index of difficulty is stronger, as proposed in [15].

Learning Effects. Figure 5 shows the success rate for each of the ten rounds for all target sizes, large targets and small targets. As can be seen, the improvement is especially high for head gestures.

During the ten rounds of our study trial, participants improved their success rate in head pointing from 66.9 % in the first round to 78.6 % in the last round. For small targets, this increase was even higher, from 41.4 % to 61.7 %. A Friedmans test revealed that the overall differences among the pointing modalities are significant ($p < 0.001$). A pairwise comparison with Wilcoxon Signed Rank tests showed that the differences between mouse and head, hand and arm respectively were significant ($p < 0.05$).

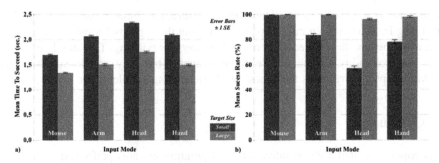

Fig. 4. Mean time to succeed (a)) and success rate (b)) for large and small targets.

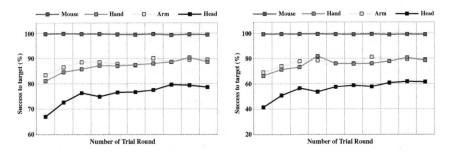

Fig. 5. Accuracy for all four modalities for every round for all target sizes (a)), and small targets (b).

3 Discussion

A key finding of the presented study is the performance of head-based pointing gestures. Although being the slowest and most error-prone pointing modality (compared to the overall results), the performance difference to selection gestures based on head, hand or arm movements is smaller than expected (time to succeed: 268.2 ms and 253.7 ms respectively, success rate: 14.4 % and 11.2 % respectively). Furthermore, head pointing can be comparably successful, if an appropriate target size is available. Despite being labeled "large" and "small" the current target sizes are in fact rather small. With 11 cm in diameter, the large circles are comparable to the size of most modern light switches. Our results showed that at this size, head pointing can be compared to hand pointing and hast a relatively high success rate. It should also be considered that mid air interaction is predominantly used over certain distances; consequently, active selection fields in smart home environments have to feature an appropriate extent to ensure smooth and trouble-free interaction.

We also observed learning effects among all mid air interaction modalities, with head-based pointing featuring the largest performance increase. It is obvious that new input techniques (in this case head pointing) lead to difficulties, particularly at the beginning and that subjects will initially perform worse compared to more usual movements (e.g. mouse input). However, the current learning results indicate, that practicing head-based pointing behaviour brings out the capacity for quick and precise interaction beyond the conventional motor pathways for pointing. This should not only open the possibility for alternative input channels but may enable simultaneous working steps and bypasses the necessity of interrupting parallel tasks.

4   Conclusion

This paper presented a comparative study of pointing gestures performed with head, hand, arm and mouse pointing gestures. We systematically compared all three modalities in a pointing task with regard to "time to succeed" and "success rate". The intresults indicated that head-based pointing gestures can perform almost equally well compared to arm or hand movements; always assuming that targets feature an appropriate size. Furthermore, target selection performance over an extended period exhibited a steeper learning curve for head-based movements in comparison to the alternative input modalities.

Considering the presented results and the current state of research regarding head gestures, we strongly recommend thinking of head gestures as a feasible alternative or at least additional way to interact in future smart home applications.

Acknowledgements. This work was conducted within the project "Gaze- and Gesture-Based Assistive Systems for Users with Special Need" funded by the BMBF and was supported by the Transregional Collaborative Research Centre SFB/TRR 62 Companion Technology for Cognitive Technical Systems funded by the DFG.

References

1. Anastasiou, D., Jian, C., Zhekova, D.: Speech and gesture interaction in an ambient assisted living lab. In: SMIAE 2012, pp. 18–27. Association for Computational Linguistics (2012)
2. Balakrishnan, R., MacKenzie, I.S.: Performance differences in the fingers, wrist, and forearm in computer input control. In: CHI 1997, pp. 303–310. ACM (1997)
3. Boyle, J.B., Shea, C.H.: Wrist and arm movements of varying difficulties. Acta psychologica **137**(3), 382–396 (2011)
4. Brown, J.N.A., Kaufmann, B., Huber, F.J., Pirolt, K.-H., Hitz, M.: … Language in their very gesture" first steps towards calm smart home input. In: Holzinger, A., Pasi, G. (eds.) HCI-KDD 2013. LNCS, vol. 7947, pp. 256–264. Springer, Heidelberg (2013)
5. Cao, X., Villar, N., Izadi, S.: Comparing user performance with single-finger, whole-hand, and hybrid pointing devices. In: CHI 2010, pp. 1643–1646. ACM (2010)
6. Caon, M., Yue, Y., Tscherrig, J., Mugellini, E., Abou Kahled, O.: Context-aware 3D gesture interaction based on multiple kinects. In: AMBIENT 2011, pp. 7–12 (2011)
7. Casiez, G., Roussel, N., Vogel, D.: 1€ filter: a simple speed-based low-pass filter for noisy input in interactive systems. In: CHI 2012, pp. 2527–2530. ACM (2012)
8. Galanakis, G., Katsifarakis, P., Zabulis, X., Adami, I.: Recognition of simple head gestures based on head pose estimation analysis. AMBIENT **2014**, 88–96 (2014)
9. Gray, J.O., Jia, P., Hu, H.H., Lu, T., Yuan, K.: Head gesture recognition for hands-free control of an intelligent wheelchair. Ind. Robot Int. J. **34**(1), 60–68 (2007)

10. Grosse-Puppendahl, T., Beck, S., Wilbers, D., Zeiß, S., von Wilmsdorff, J., Kuijper, A.: Ambient gesture-recognizing surfaces with visual feedback. In: Streitz, N., Markopoulos, P. (eds.) DAPI 2014. LNCS, vol. 8530, pp. 97–108. Springer, Heidelberg (2014)

11. Hirsch, M., Cheng, J., Reiss, A., Sundholm, M., Lukowicz, P., Amft, O.: Hands-free gesture control with a capacitive textile neckband. In: ISWC 2014, pp. 55–58. ACM (2014)

12. Kim, D., Kim, D.: An intelligent smart home control using body gestures. In: ICHIT 2006, pp. 439–446. IEEE (2006)

13. Kim, H.J., Jeong, K.H., Kim, S.K., Han, T.D.: Ambient wall: smart wall display interface which can be controlled by simple gesture for smart home. In: SIGGRAPH Asia 2011 Sketches, p. 1. ACM (2011)

14. Kosunen, I., Jylha, A., Ahmed, I., An, C., Chech, L., Gamberini, L., Cavazza, L., Jacucci, G.: Comparing eye and gesture pointing to drag items on large screens. In: ITS 2013, pp. 425–428. ACM (2013)

15. Langolf, G.D., Chaffin, D.B., Foulke, J.A.: An investigation of Fitts' law using a wide range of movement amplitudes. J. Mot. Behav. **8**, 113–128 (1976)

16. Lin, C.-Y., Lin, Y.-B.: Projection-based user interface for smart home environments. In: COMPSACW 2013, pp. 546–549. IEEE (2013)

17. NaturalPoint Inc.: NatNet SDK. https://www.optitrack.com/products/natnet-sdk/ (2015). Accessed 24 March 2015

18. NaturalPoint Inc.: OptiTrack. https://www.optitrack.com/ (2015). Accessed 24 March 2015

19. Neßelrath, R., Lu, C., Schulz, C. H., Frey, J., and Alexandersson, J.: A Gesture Based System for Context–Sensitive Interaction with Smart Homes. In Ambient Assisted Living pp. 209-219, 2011. Springer.

20. Sambrooks, L., Wilkinson, B.: Comparison of gestural, touch, and mouse interaction with Fitts' law. In: OzCHI 2013, pp. 119–122. ACM (2013)

21. Schwaller, M., Lalanne, D.: Pointing in the air: measuring the effect of hand selection strategies on performance and effort. In: Holzinger, A., Ziefle, M., Hitz, M., Debevc, M. (eds.) SouthCHI 2013. LNCS, vol. 7946, pp. 732–747. Springer, Heidelberg (2013)

22. Soukoreff, R.W., MacKenzie, I.S.: Towards a standard for pointing device evaluation, perspectives on 27 years of Fitts' law research in HCI. Int. J. Hum. Comput. Stud. **61**(6), 751–789 (2004)

23. Vatavu, R.-D.: A comparative study of user-defined handheld vs. freehand gestures for home entertainment environments. J. Ambient Intell. Smart Environ. **5**(2), 187–211 (2013)

Enhancing Pinch-Drag-Flick Paradigm with Two New Gestures: Two-Finger-Tap for Tablets and Tap&Tap for Smartphones

Alessio Bellino[(✉)]

University of Milano-Bicocca, Viale Sarca 336/14, Milan, Italy
bellino@disco.unimib.it

Abstract. The mobile versions of services such as Google Maps or Open Street Maps allow the exploration of maps on smartphones and tablets. The gestures used are the pinch to adjust the zoom level and the drag/flick to move the map. In this paper, two new gestures to adjust the zoom level of maps (but also of images and documents) are presented. Both gestures – with slight differences – allow the identification of a target area to zoom, which is enlarged automatically up to cover the whole map container. The proposed gestures are added to the traditional ones (drag, pinch and flick) without any overlap. Therefore, users do not need to change their regular practices. They have just two more options to control the zoom level. One of the most relevant and appreciated advantages has to do with the gesture for smartphones (Tap&Tap): this allows users to control the zoom level with just one hand. The traditional pinch gesture, instead, needs two hands. According to the test results on the new gestures in comparison with the traditional pinch, 30 % of time is saved on tablets (Two-Finger-Tap gesture) whereas 14 % on smartphones (Tap&Tap gesture).

Keywords: Zoom · Map · Touch · Smartphone · Tablet · Gesture

1 Introduction

Currently, one of the most common activities performed by users in their mobile devices is the exploration of large 2D spaces such as maps, pictures and websites. In these devices, the use of zoom and drag is frequent because they usually have small screens. One of the most used multi-touch paradigms devoted to the 2D navigation is the Pinch-Drag-Flick because of its simplicity and effectiveness: pinch to zoom and drag-flick to pan. In spite of these advantages, the paradigm presents some drawbacks: fingers hinder the screen visualization [14] and the pinch is difficult to perform with just one hand when it comes to smartphones [13]. These disadvantages have fostered the development of several alternatives to navigate which, for instance, use different gestures [3] or extend the interaction to the side [12] or the back of the device [14].

In this paper, two new gestures are presented. These are added to the traditional paradigm Pinch-Drag-Flick without replacing it. Furthermore, they do not require specific hardware. One gesture is designed for tablets whereas the other for smartphones. Particularly, the latter allows the usage of smartphones with just one hand, unlike the

© IFIP International Federation for Information Processing 2015
J. Abascal et al. (Eds.): INTERACT 2015, Part III, LNCS 9298, pp. 534–551, 2015.
DOI: 10.1007/978-3-319-22698-9_37

traditional Pinch-to-Zoom in which both hands are required: one to hold the smartphone and the other to act on the screen. The new gestures were evaluated qualitatively and quantitatively with 18 users. In addition, a speed test between the traditional pinch and the new gestures was carried out with the aim to understand and evaluate the design qualities of the new gestures. A 'strict' comparison between the new gestures and the traditional ones does not make sense because there is no any overlap between them. The more traditional user, in fact, can use the new gestures in addition to the Pinch-Drag-Flick paradigm. Any comparison would be probably useless, unless users are not willing to change their regular practices. Changing users' behavior is a more complex and hard challenge than any speed test.

2   Related Work

The Pinch-Drag-Flick paradigm is used frequently nowadays, therefore, no explanation would be required. Nevertheless, since an integration to the aforementioned paradigm has been designed, some details are provided when the new gestures are explained (3.3). This section, instead, is focused on spatial input-based interactions and some alternatives to the traditional Pinch-Drag-Flick paradigm. In [5], one of the first spatial input-based technique used on mobile devices is presented. This technique is driven by the see-through interfaces [2] metaphor, in which the interaction with the real world is performed by moving the device around. A recent study (2014) [13] presents a similar approach: moving the device leftwards, rightwards, upwards and downwards the pan is performed; moving the device away or bringing it closer, the zoom out or zoom in is performed respectively. The performances of spatial input interaction shown in [13] regarding time of zoom on 2D spaces (such as maps) are better than pinch. Their research is focused on smartphones and tablets as in the present study. However, the devices used in [13] were modified with infrared led lights. Through these, IR-cameras in the environment detect the movements of the device. Smartphones and tablets require, thus, modifications and additional hardware to work. Yet, the gestures proposed in this paper do not need neither modifications in the devices nor the use of ad hoc hardware. Another kind of zoom – which also exploits the device movements but it cannot be considered a real spatial input – is the Tilt-to-Zoom [7], which allows the adjustment of the zoom tilting the smartphone detecting its movements through the accelerometer. The spatial input approaches, unlike the touch input (of which the Pinch-Drag-Flick is the main one), require the movement of the device around the physical space. Therefore, the movements increase significantly (3D physical space versus 2D small screen) and different kinds of movements are required (arm versus hand/fingers) [13].

The aim of this research is not to debate about which the best approach is. Some studies have proven that there are not clear advantages for the spatial input-based approach ([6, 10]). Other recent studies have revealed that there are some improvements, and combining spatial input and touch input may be useful (i.e. the first one for navigation whereas the second one for the selection) [13]. From a more social viewpoint, the use of the spatial input could be amusing sometimes. There could be other instances, instead, in which users do not feel like using the spatial input and the Pinch-Drag-Flick paradigm is more appropriate (e.g., when users prefer to be in a fixed position). Anyways, the Pinch-Drag-Flick paradigm is deep-rooted in the market and abandoning it is as difficult as changing the users' practices (think of Dvorak keyboard). Coming back to touch interaction, some alternative paradigms are Slider, CycloStar [9] and Fat Thumb [3]. The first one, coming from desktop computers, is not common in touch devices. However, it allows the zoom adjustment by moving the slider upwards or downwards. The second [9] works by moving the finger in circles on the device screen: clockwise to zoom in and anticlockwise to zoom out. The third [3] lets users adjust the zoom by means of the contact area of their thumbs with the screen: with slight pressure, the contact area is small and the pan is allowed by moving the finger. On the contrary, with high pressure, the contact area is larger and the zoom adjustment is allowed. In this case, the zoom speed depends on the size of the contact area of the thumb. All these paradigms allow the zoom usage with just one hand. In [3] a comparison among Tilt-to-zoom [7], Slider, CycloStar [9] and Fat Thumb [3] was made and the latter is the faster.

Some commercial software for desktop computers implement another way of zoom quite interesting for this research: identifying an area by means of selection, it will be enlarged automatically up to cover the dimension of the window container. This zoom is called in different ways: Marquee Zoom in Adobe Acrobat X[1] and Zoom Window in Autodesk AutoCAD.[2] Moreover, a patent that uses a similar zoom principle was registered [4]. The two new gestures presented in this paper use an approach similar to this kind of zoom for desktops.

3   Gesture Definition

3.1   Two-Finger-Tap for Tablets

The gestures designed for tablets, namely Two-Finger-Tap, let users zoom in by tapping the screen with two fingers suitably spaced.

Figure 1 displays the whole zoom process: in the first step, users tap with two fingers the target area to be zoomed. In the second step, the algorithm identifies the area comprehended between the fingers (ideally, it may be a circle), which is enlarged automatically up to cover the map container as shown in step 3. The process is iterative: after the first zoom, the user can continue to zoom in starting again from the first step. In order to zoom out, the traditional pinch-out has to be used as shown in Fig. 2.

3.2   Tap&Tap for Smartphones

The gesture was designed to be used holding the smartphone with just one hand interacting with the thumb. This choice was made to favor the users who prefer to use the smartphone with just one hand (around 49 %) [8]. The traditional pinch, instead,

---

[1] http://help.adobe.com/en_US/acrobat/X/pro/using/WS58a04a822e3e50102bd615109794195ff-7aec.w.html.

[2] http://knowledge.autodesk.com/support/autocad/learn-explore/caas/CloudHelp/cloudhelp/2015/ENU/AutoCAD-Core/files/GUID-66E7DB72-B2A7-4166-9970-9E19CC06F739-htm.html.

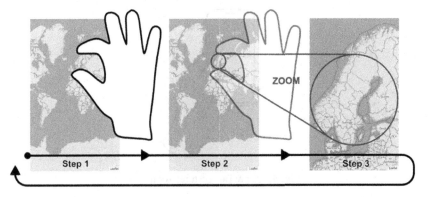

Fig. 1. Two-Finger-Tap gesture: zoom in.

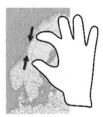

Fig. 2. Two-Finger-Tap gesture: zoom out.

compels users to employ both hands: one to hold the smartphone and the other to interact with the map on the screen.

The gesture, namely Tap&Tap, let users zoom in by touching in fast sequences two different points of the map. As in the previous process, the target area identified between the two points is enlarged automatically up to cover the map container (Fig. 3). The one-hand usage is also kept to zoom out: users have to scroll the thumb from the left edge of the screen as shown in Fig. 4.

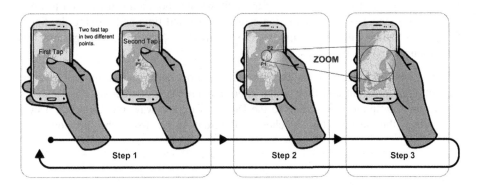

Fig. 3. Tap&Tap gesture: zoom in.

Fig. 4. Tap&Tap gesture: zoom out.

3.3   Compatibility: New Gestures and Pinch-Drag-Flick

The Two-Finger-Tap gesture comes into conflict with the gesture set of some commercial software for map navigation (i.e. Google Maps or Apple Maps): in their implementation, a tap with two fingers is used to zoom out one level in opposition to the traditional double tap (which is used to zoom in one level). At any rate, that gesture is unknown by users (none of the users who took the test was acquainted with it) and seems not to be that useful because it is similar to the traditional pinch-out (beyond the fact that two hands are needed in smartphones). Other frameworks for map navigation (e.g. Open Street Maps or Leaflet), in fact, do not implement that gesture. Moreover, neither Google mentions that gesture in the tips&trick official area.[3] For these reasons, that gesture is not taken into account in the following discussion.

In order to understand the mechanisms through which the integration with the Pinch-Drag-Flick paradigm is designed without overlapping, a review of the traditional gestures is presented here:

1. Pinch: it allows the zoom adjustment by touching the screen with two fingers expanding/shrinking them (Fig. 5 line A).
2. Drag: it allows the pan of the map by moving the finger in all directions (Fig. 5 line B).
3. Double-Tap: it allows the zoom in with just one hand by using a double tap. The zoom starts from the point tapped (Fig. 5 line C).
4. DoubleTap-and-Hold + Vertical-Drag: it allows the zoom adjustment with just one hand by tapping twice, holding the screen the second time and moving the finger upwards (zoom out) or downwards (zoom in) (Fig. 5 line D). This gesture was introduced by Google Maps.

The proposed gestures look like some of the aforementioned gestures. However, they are quite different and their usage is not ambiguous. In particular, the Tap&Tap gesture for smartphones is similar to the Double-Tap. Anyway, the Tap&Tap occurs only when the second tap touches a different point from the previous one

---

[3] https://support.google.com/gmm/answer/3273126.

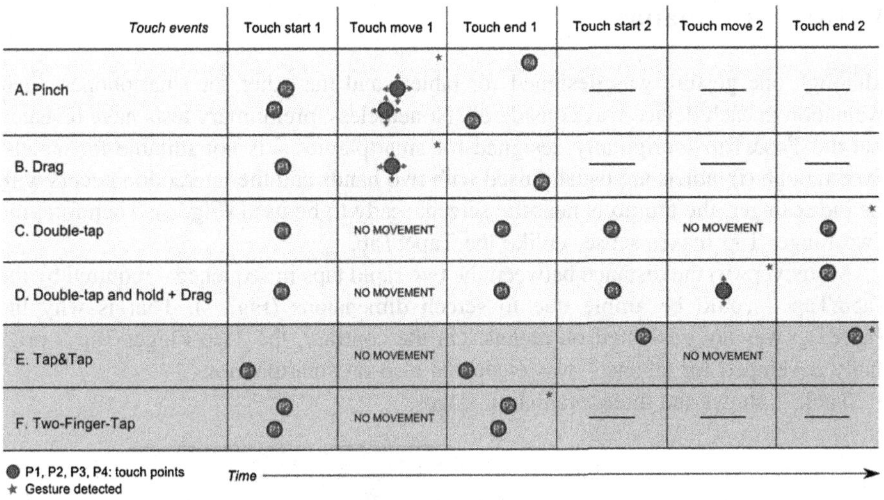

Touch events	Touch start 1	Touch move 1	Touch end 1	Touch start 2	Touch move 2	Touch end 2
A. Pinch	P2 / P1	✦ (movement)	P4 / P3	—	—	—
B. Drag	P1	✦ (movement)	P3	—	—	—
C. Double-tap	P1	NO MOVEMENT	P2	P3	NO MOVEMENT	P4 ✦
D. Double-tap and hold + Drag	P1	NO MOVEMENT	P4	P1	✦ (movement)	P2
E. Tap&Tap	P2 / P1	NO MOVEMENT	P1	P2	NO MOVEMENT	P2 ✦
F. Two-Finger-Tap	P2 / P3	NO MOVEMENT	P5 / P4 ✦	—	—	—

● P1, P2, P3, P4: touch points   Time ──────────────────────────────▶
✦ Gesture detected

Fig. 5. Touch detection algorithm. P1, P2, P3 and P4 indicate four different touch points on the screen. The red star indicates the moment in which each gesture is detected. Touch start indicates the moment in which fingers touch the screen; touch move indicates the moment in which fingers are moving on the screen; touch end indicates the moment in which fingers release the screen. Some gestures can be detected only repeating the process start/move/end. For example, the required sequence for 'DoubleTap-and-hold + Drag' is 'touch start', 'no movement' and 'touch end' (first tap) and continuing 'touch start', 'a movement' and 'touch end' (second tap-hold + drag [-and release]). In this example, the gesture is detected (it starts to work) when 'touch move 2' occurs.

(Fig. 5 line E), whereas the Double-Tap occurs only when the two taps touch the same point (Fig. 5 line C). Going on, the Two-Finger-Tap gesture is similar to the pinch. Anyway, the Two-Finger-Tap occurs only when fingers remain fixed on the screen and are released immediately after (Fig. 5 line F), whereas the pinch occurs only when fingers move on the screen expanding or shrinking (Fig. 5 line A, see touch move 1). The entire gesture set in Fig. 5, without producing any overlap, lets users increase their possibilities to choose the most appropriate gesture in any conditions (tablets, smartphones, one-hand usage, two-hands usage). In this discussion, the Tap&Tap zoom-out gesture (Fig. 4) was not taken into account: since only the edge of the screen is involved (Bezel Swipe [11]), there is not any overlap.

Finally, the conceptual differences between the pinch and the new gestures are clarified in order to better understand their nature. The pinch is 'incremental': the zoom adjustment works continuously following the finger movements. The new gestures are 'fit-area-to-container': the identified area comprehended between two points of the map is automatically enlarged up to cover the map container (like Adobe Acrobat X and Autodesk AutoCAD previously mentioned in the related work).

4   User's Evaluation

Although one gesture was designed for tablets and the other for smartphones, their evaluation in each device was considered. Nonetheless, preliminary tests have revealed that the Tap&Tap – originally designed for smartphones – is not suitable for tablets. Even though (i) tablets are usually used with two hands and the interaction occurs with the index finger, the thumb is near the screen, ready to be used (Fig. 6). Therefore, the Two-Finger-Tap makes sense, unlike the Tap&Tap.

Moreover, (ii) the distance between the two rapid taps in sequence – required by the Tap&Tap – could be ample due to screen dimensions (Fig. 7). That is why the Tap&Tap was not evaluated on tablets. On the contrary, the Two-Finger-Tap – originally developed for tablets – was evaluated also on smartphones.

Table 1 shows the three evaluation stages.

Fig. 6. Even if the index finger is normally used for interaction on tablets, the thumb is usually near the screen, ready to be used.

Fig. 7. The distance between taps could be too long to make the interaction usable.

Table 1. Stages for gesture evaluation through questionnaire.

Tablet	Smartphone	
Two-Finger-Tap (stage one)	Tap&Tap (stage two)	Two-Finger-Tap (stage three)

4.1   Representative Population

The evaluations involved a 22–42 age group of 18 users (one of them was a woman) split in five age brackets (Fig. 8A).

All users asserted they use touch devices regularly (Fig. 8C). 10 out of 18 users asserted they use the smartphone with just one hand regularly, whereas the others with two hands or sometimes with one hand and sometimes with two hands (Fig. 8B). 10 users asserted they could need to use maps with one hand frequently, seven users do rarely and one user never had the need of using maps with just one hand (Fig. 8D). Four users asserted they use maps daily, 10 users do weekly, three users do monthly and one user sometimes a year (Fig. 8E).

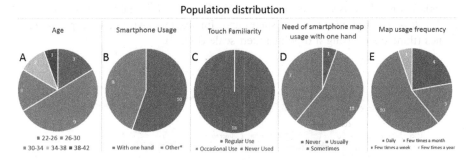

Fig. 8. Representative population. *Other indicates sometimes with one hand and sometimes with both hands.

4.2   Hardware and Software Employed

In order to carry out the tests, a smartphone Motorola Moto G (4-inch with Android OS) and a tabletop Lenovo Flex 2–15 (15-inch with Windows 8 OS) were used. The smartphone was used in portrait mode whereas the tabletop in landscape mode. The prototype works in both devices in the same way and was developed in HTML5, JavaScript and CSS3 redesigning Leaflet,[4] an open source library for maps management optimized for mobiles (maps are provided from Open Street Maps). Both devices display the prototype at full screen through Google Chrome browser (in the respective versions for Android and Windows 8).

Further details on the implementation are presented in [1].

4.3   The Test Procedure

The tests were carried out in a lab of the university. First of all, users watched an introductory video in which gestures were described while working. After that, the first stage was the test of the Two-Finger-Tap on the tabletop, followed by the test of the Tap&Tap (second stage) and the Two-Finger-Tap (third stage) on the smartphone (see Table 1). For each stage, the following tasks were carried out: starting from the whole world, it was requested to: (1) zoom in up to Sardinia (Italian island) (2) go back, (3) zoom in up to Paris, (4) go back, (5) zoom in up to Madrid, (6) go back, (7) zoom in up to the United Kingdom, (8) go back, (9) zoom in up to a city chosen by the user and (10) go back.

At the end of the three stages, answering a questionnaire was requested.

4.4   The Questionnaire

The questionnaire is composed by four sections. In the first, the users' information was gathered (see Fig. 8). In the following three sections (which correspond to the three

---

[4] http://leafletjs.com.

stages), it was asked users to evaluate the Two-Finger-Tap on tablets (first stage), the Tap&Tap on smartphones (second stage) and, finally, the Two-Finger-Tap on smartphones (third stage) using a 6-point Likert scale (Fig. 9).

Fig. 9. Section of the questionnaire regarding the evaluation given for each gesture. *The full sentence for useful is: "Useful, the gesture is a good alternative to the traditional pinch".

4.5 Time Measurement

At the end of the questionnaire (to avoid possible biases), it was asked users to take a speed test (composed by 20 tasks) in order to measure the execution times of zoom with the new gestures in comparison with the traditional pinch. The software calculated the execution times automatically.

4.6 Correlation Analysis

A correlation analysis was carried out using Spearman's rho test.

4.7 Qualitative Analysis

After the time measurements, it was asked users to provide an opinion regarding the new gestures promoting a discussion.

5 Experimental Results

5.1 Questionnaire

A binomial test was conducted on the data gathered from the Likert scale for each stage. Values from 1 to 3 were considered negative whereas values from 3 to 6 were considered positive (see Fig. 9).

The binomial test results on Two-Finger-Tap gesture for tablets (first stage) show clear positive tendencies ($p < 0.05$) for usability (proportion .17 vs. 87, $p = 0.008$), naturalness (proportion .17 vs. 83, $p = 0.008$), convenience (proportion .22 vs. 78, $p = 0.031$), and usefulness (proportion .22 vs. 78, $p = 0.031$). Regarding precision (proportion .28 vs. 72 $p = 0.096$), it is not possible to establish any clear positive tendency ($p > 0.05$). A summary of the results is displayed in Fig. 10 through box-plots with mean (red) and mode (blue).

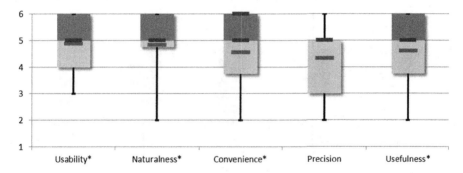

Fig. 10. Two-Finger-Tap evaluations on tablets.

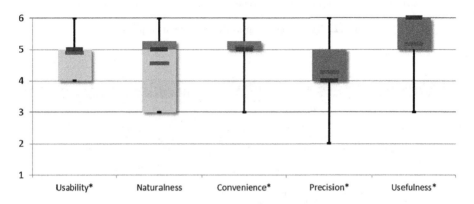

Fig. 11. Tap&Tap evaluations on smartphones.

The binomial test results on Tap&Tap gesture for smartphones (second stage) show clear positive tendencies ($p < 0.05$) for usability (proportion .00 vs 1.00, $p < 0.001$), convenience (proportion .06 vs. 94, $p < 0.001$), precision (proportion .17 vs .83, $p = 0.008$) and usefulness (proportion .11 vs. 89, $p = 0.001$). Regarding naturalness (proportion .28 vs. 72 $p = 0.096$), it is not possible to establish any clear positive tendency ($p > 0.05$). A summary of the results is displayed in Fig. 11 through box-plots with mean (red) and mode (blue).

The binomial test results on Two-Finger-Tap for smartphones (third stage) do not show clear positive tendencies in any of the variables ($p > 0.05$): usability (proportion .44 vs. 56, $p = 0.815$), naturalness (proportion .44 vs. 56, $p = 0.815$), convenience (proportion .61 vs. 39, $p = 0.481$), precision (proportion .50 vs. 50, $p = 1$), and usefulness (proportion .50 vs. 50, $p = 1$). A summary of the results is displayed in Fig. 12 through box-plots with mean (red) and mode (blue).

In the light of the results previously presented, the Two-Finger-Tap for tablets and the Tap&Tap for smartphones are appreciated by users. Moreover, as expected, they are considered as a good alternative to the traditional pinch. For the Two-Finger-Tap for smartphones, such negative results were not expected. Anyway, evaluations lower than the Tap&Tap were predictable.

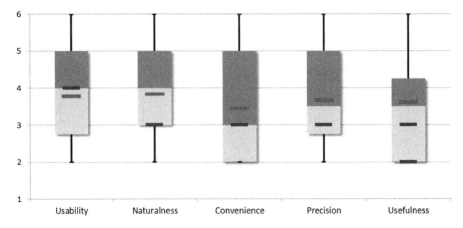

Fig. 12. Two-Finger-Tap evaluations on smartphones.

	Tablet (two stages)		Smartphone (three stages)		
	Pinch	Two-Finger-Tap	Pinch	Tap&Tap	Two-Finger-Tap
Sicily	Z=-2.896; p<0.004*		Z=-2.591; p<0.010* (Pinch–Two-Finger-Tap); Z=-1.851; p<0.064 (Pinch–Tap&Tap)		
	3909 (SD=1000)	2375 (SD =1051)	3924 (SD=893)	3285 (SD=947)	3083 (SD=874)
Bicocca	Z=-2.722; p<0.006*		Z=-3.114; p<0.002* (Pinch–Two-Finger-Tap); Z=-2.809; p<0.005* (Pinch–Tap&Tap)		
	8802 (SD=1822)	6644 (SD=2871)	8683 (SD=1466)	7531 (SD=1673)	7095 (SD=1745)
Denmark (part of)	Z=-3.027; p<0.002*		Z=-2.025; p<0.043* (Pinch–Two-Finger-Tap); Z=-1.807; p<0.071 (Pinch–Tap&Tap)		
	3760 (SD=1170)	2173 (SD=1167)	2921 (SD=800)	2405 (SD=695)	2555 (SD=538)
Berlin	Z=-2.853; p<0.004*		Z=-2.417; p<0.016* (Pinch–Two-Finger-Tap); Z=-2.853; p<0.020* (Pinch–Tap&Tap)		
	5814 (STD=2506)	4141 (SD=2331)	4953 (SD=1247)	4192 (SD=1005)	4226 (SD=1074)
Total time	Z=-3.680; p<0.001*		Z=-3.506; p<0.001* (Pinch–Two-Finger-Tap); Z=-3.462; p=0.001* (Pinch–Tap&Tap)		
	22186 (SD=4994)	15334 (SD=4995)	20482 (SD=2721)	17414 (SD=2595)	16960 (SD=3092)

Fig. 13. Stages of tests for speed evaluations (average in milliseconds on 18 users with its standard deviation). The distribution of each new gesture (Two-Finger-Tap and Tap&Tap) in each device was compared with the ones of the traditional pinch evaluating, using the Wilcoxon signed rank test, whether they are statistically different.

5.2   Zoom Speed Measurement

After the questionnaire, each user performed 20 tasks (split in five stages, two for tablets and three for smartphones, see Fig. 13) devoted to the time measurements of the pinch in comparison with the new gestures.

For each stage, the tasks executed by users consisted in zooming inside a rectangle that identified a fragment of the world established by the experimenter. In any case, the zoom started from the whole world (Fig. 14, left). The first task consists in zooming inside the rectangle (53122 km^2) that comprehends Sicily (Fig. 14, task 1) an Italian island. The second task consists in zooming inside the rectangle (4.5 km^2) that comprehends Bicocca (Fig. 14, task 2), a neighborhood of Milan. The third task consists in zooming inside the rectangle (121820 km^2) that comprehends the eastern part of the

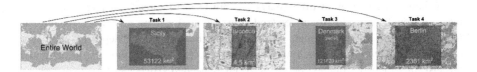

Fig. 14. Tasks for speed tests.

Denmark (Fig. 14, task 3). The fourth task consists in zooming inside the rectangle (2361 km^2) that comprehends Berlin (Fig. 14, task 4). The average time on the 18 users was calculated both for smartphones and tablets for each place and every gesture (gray rows in Fig. 13). The total time, for each gesture, was calculated summing the execution times of each place (the red row in Fig. 13).

Since the new gestures do not hinder the usage of the traditional ones, a comparison between the execution times of the new gestures with the traditional pinch, would be probably useless. Therefore, the aim of this comparison is to understand better how the new gestures work. Since some of the data was not normally distributed (Shapiro-Wink test), the non-parametric Wilcoxon signed rank test is used to evaluate whether two distributions are statistically different.

The average zoom speed with Two-Finger-Tap on tablets is 15334 ms (SD = 4995) whereas with the traditional pinch is 22186 ms (SD = 4994). The new gesture Two-Finger-Tap on tablets saves 30 % of time. The difference between distributions is significant (Z = −3.680; p < 0.001). The average zoom speed with Tap&Tap on smartphones is 17414 ms (SD = 2595) whereas with the traditional pinch is 20482 ms (SD = 2721). The new gesture Tap&Tap on smartphones saves 15 % of time. The difference between distributions is significant (Z = −3.462; p = 0.001). The average zoom speed with Two-Finger-Tap on smartphones is 16960 ms (SD = 3092) whereas with the traditional pinch is 20482 ms (SD = 2721). The new gesture Two-Finger-Tap on smartphones saves 17 % of time (even though this gesture is not that appreciated by users as shown in Fig. 12). The difference between distributions is significant (Z = −3.506; p < 0.001).

See Fig. 13 for the average of the execution times, standard deviations and comparisons among places. Significant differences between distributions are marked with an asterisk.

Discussion. Little relevance is given to the speed tests results in this study. Actually, on tablets, the Two-Finger-Tap has a moderate advantage in comparison with the pinch. Regarding smartphones, the 15 % of time saved given by the Tap&Tap does not seem to be that relevant for users. Taking into account the absolute times shown in Fig. 13, in the best of the cases, an advantage of around 2 s is given by the new gestures. These advantages seem to be irrelevant in the regular use of maps. At any rate, there are other relevant factors to highlight; besides the little advantages in terms of execution time, the new gestures are considered useful by users because they allow the zoom adjustment in an alternative and effective way. In particular, the advantages of the Tap&Tap are related to the employment of just one hand with execution times comparable with the traditional pinch.

Although the execution time analysis is not used to spread out inexistent advantages, it could be useful to understand more about the new gestures. Actually, an improvement of execution times directly proportional with the depth of zoom was expected. This hypothesis was rejected by the results shown in Fig. 13. In particular, the task in which the highest depth of zoom is needed (Bicocca, 4.5 km^2) does not display better results than the task in which the lowest depth of zoom is needed (Denmark, 121820 km^2). For example, the Two-Finger-Tap on tablets saves 24 % of time on the task of Bicocca and 42 % on the task of Denmark. These results are contradictory considering the initial expectations. An explanation is given by a further time execution analysis.

5.3   Further Time Execution Analysis

The execution times previously presented were calculated considering the sum of the times in three different phases:

1. The zoom phase occurs when the map is enlarged or stretched (Fig. 15A).
2. The drag[5] phase occurs when the map is moved centering the target area to zoom (Fig. 15B).
3. The planning phase occurs when users (release the finger from the screen – Fig. 15C – and) plan the next action (another zoom or drag phase). The planning usually also includes the time needed by the system to load new tiles.[6] In fact, if the map is not refreshed, users cannot plan the next action easily (unless they go blindly, remembering the place locations even when the map is not loaded yet).

Fig. 15. Three zoom phases: zoom (A), drag (B) and planning (C).

This section shows how different gestures employ time considering the aforementioned phases. In general, both the new gestures let users save time on the zoom and drag phases whereas the execution time of the planning phase increases (unlike the expectations). Figure 16 shows that every difference among zoom, drag and planning

---

[5] The more skilled users who use the traditional pinch are usually able to merge the zoom and the drag phase. In other words, they are able to zoom and move the map at the same time. Anyway, it is not always convenient and/or possible when the target area to zoom is near the border of the screen. Therefore, also for the more skilled users, some movements of the map (drags) are essential.

[6] http://wiki.openstreetmap.org/wiki/Tiles.

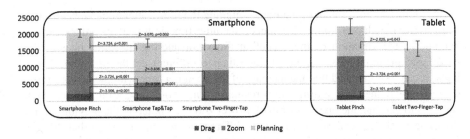

Fig. 16. Comparison among the execution time of each gesture phase with Wilcoxon signed rank test results: drag in blue, zoom in green and planning in yellow. Error bars denote standard deviations (95 % CI) on the total time (drag + zoom + planning).

time for each gesture is significant (p < 0.05): also in this case, the non-parametric Wilcoxon signed rank test is used to evaluate whether two distributions are statistically different.

To begin with, the results on smartphone are presented. The average time of drag on the pinch is 2221 ms (SD = 955), on the Tap&Tap is 1140 ms (SD = 777), whereas on the Two-Finger-Tap is 821 ms (SD = 510). The average time of zoom on the pinch is 12750 ms (SD = 1824), on the Tap&Tap is 4444 ms (SD = 1588), whereas on the Two-Finger-Tap is 8362 ms (SD = 1569). The average time of planning on the pinch is 5510 ms (SD = 2191), on the Tap&Tap is 11829 ms (SD = 2628), whereas on the Two-Finger-Tap is 7776 ms (SD = 2692).

Then, the results on tablet are presented. The average time of drag on the pinch is 1497 ms (SD = 1797), whereas on the Two-Finger-Tap is 381 ms (SD = 468). The average time of zoom on the pinch is 11722 ms (SD = 2220), whereas on the Two finger-Tap is 4416 ms (SD = 1256). The average time of planning on the pinch is 8965 ms (SD = 3016), whereas on the Two-Finger-Tap is 10536 ms (SD = 4133).

Figure 16 shows the histograms of the total execution times (the same of the red row in Fig. 13) for each gesture: the drag phase is colored in blue, the zoom phase is colored in green and the planning phase is colored in yellow.

Discussion. With the new gestures, in comparison with the pinch, it was expected: (1) a strong reduction of the drag time, (2) a strong reduction of the zoom time (because it is automatic, performed by the prototype using a fast animation), (3) a substantial equality of the planning time. The drag time of the new gestures, on every device, decrease as expected (−48 % for Tap&Tap for smartphones, −63 % for Two-Finger-Tap for smartphones and −74 % for Two-Finger-Tap for tablets). The zoom time of the new gestures, on every device, decreased as expected (−65 % for Tap&Tap for smartphones, −34 % for Two-Finger-Tap for smartphones and −62 % for Two-Finger-Tap for tablets). The planning time of the new gestures, on every device, had a significant increase (+114 % for Tap&Tap for smartphones, +41 % for Two-Finger-Tap for smartphones and +17 % for Two-Finger-Tap for tablets). Reflecting on this increase, the hypothesis is that users get lost due to the automatic zoom of the new gestures. Thus, it takes them more time to understand (1) where they are and (2) what to do (planning the next action). In the traditional pinch, instead, the zoom follows the movement of the fingers guiding the user's attention, so that users are more aware of what is going on. Hence, planning time is lower. In order to test the hypothesis, the variation of the execution times considering the three phases (drag, zoom, and planning) was examined according to different depths of zoom. Accordingly, it can be confirmed that the increase of the planning time with the new gestures is the reason why the save of time – in percentage terms – on the task on Bicocca (higher zoom) is lower than the one on Denmark (lower zoom) as noted in the previous section. Zooming in on Bicocca, in fact, requires different zoom sequences; so that, the planning time increases, probably, because users feel more disoriented due to the repeated zoom sequences. This way, as shown in Fig. 17, the advantages related to the higher zoom speed of the new gestures are partially lost due to the lower planning speed. Figure 17 shows the example of tablets but the same also occurs with the new gestures for smartphones. In any case, the planning time is likely to decrease if users get used to working with the new gestures.

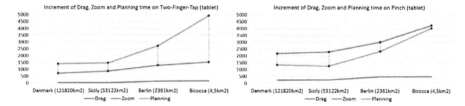

Fig. 17. Drag, zoom and planning time comparison according to Two-Finger-Tap and Pinch on tablets. In the graphic about the Two-Finger-Tap gesture (left), the increase of the gap between zoom and planning (black dotted line) is directly proportional to the zoom level (having a low zoom time but a high planning time on the Bicocca task). On the contrary, in the graphic about the traditional pinch (right) the gap is substantially constant.

5.4 Correlation Analysis

41 correlations were found using Spearman's rho test. The more interesting ones are presented in this section. Correlations regarding the Two-Finger-Tap for smartphones are not put forward because it was not appreciated by users and the available space is not enough.

Age and need of using maps with just one hand are moderately inverse correlated ($r = -590$, $p = .010$), therefore, the youngest users show a tendency towards the usage of maps with just one hand. In addition, frequency of usage of maps is slightly correlated with the need of using maps with just one hand ($r = 475$, $p = .046$). This means that providing a gesture that can be used with just one hand could be useful for those who use maps very often.

As expected, the usefulness of the gesture Tap&Tap is moderately correlated with the need of using maps with just one hand ($r = .619$, $p = .006$). The usefulness of the same gesture is also moderately correlated with the frequency of usage of maps (r = .603, p = .008). If this gesture were implemented in commercial software, people would probably use it.

The execution time of Tap&Tap on smartphones is moderately correlated with their convenience (r = .580, p = .012). This is interesting because the users took the speed test only after the questionnaire. This means that the (fast) users thought they were fast also before the direct comparison with the pinch.

Other two noteworthy correlations are: (1) the execution time of the pinch gesture on smartphones and the execution time of the Tap&Tap gestures on smartphones are moderately correlated (r = .507, p = .032); (2) the execution time of the pinch gesture on tablets and the execution time of the Two-Finger-Tap gestures on tablets are moderately correlated (r = .697, p = .001). These two correlations mean that fast (or slow) people with the traditional pinch gesture are fast (or slow) with the new gestures too. Thus, the new gestures are practical to use. In fact, also in the case of a strong experience with the pinch (fast usage), the introduction of the new gestures seem to be favorable (people who are fast with the pinch are fast with the new gestures too).

Another moderated correlation (r = .692, p = .001) was found between the execution time of the Two-Finger-Tap on tablets and the execution time of the Tap&Tap on smartphones.

Several significant correlations were also found between questionnaire variables of the same gesture: they were expected, they do not seem to be very interesting and other details are not shown.

5.5 Qualitative Analysis

After the speed test, users have provided their opinions regarding the new gestures. The most significant ones are translated and discussed here.

P. "If I had taken the questionnaire after the speed test, I would have changed a lot of answers. I understood the pinch is an old and uncomfortable gesture. The Tap&Tap on smartphones is more comfortable and I would really like the gesture to be implemented in existent applications". This user was so enthusiastic that he was willing to look for other participants for the study. Besides that, his opinion is interesting because the evaluations on the questionnaire, probably, would be better after the speed test (in which the execution time of the pinch was compared with the one of the new gestures). Moreover, this comment confirms that doing the speed test after the questionnaire was a good choice in order to avoid bias.

C. "I had the need to zoom with one hand and I noted that Google Maps was the first which implemented a similar possibility. Nevertheless, your gesture is more precise and fast". This comment proves that the need to zoom with just one hand is very relevant for some users (he had looked for this option). In addition, after the test, the user said to a friend that this test had surprised him.

G. "I do not have a tablet but I prefer the Two-Finger-Tap to the pinch". This comment is not the only instance in which a similar idea was expressed. Moreover, some of the users who own tablets have also provided the same opinion.

V. "Why did you not implement the Tap&Tap on tablets too? In my opinion, it is the best in any case. I have never liked the pinch, it is uncomfortable, sometimes it works badly and I am not able to go where I want. The Tap&Tap, instead, is more precise because it allows the identification of the target area I want to zoom". Undoubtedly, the Tap&Tap was very appreciated. At any rate, the reasons why it was not tested on tablets was explained. After that, the experimenter asked to try the Tap&Tap on tablets and the users realized that it was not as advantageous as it seemed.

E. "The Two-Finger-Tap works very well, but I am not sure that it is useful on smartphones because the screen is too small". There were not big doubts regarding the success of the Two-Finger-Tap on tablets. However, these such negative results were not expected on smartphones (other users had also expressed the same).

P. "Even though the Two-Finger-Tap on tablets seems to be faster, the pinch is more amusing". Usually the 'fun effect' decreases over time. Probably, the user does not use the pinch very often and its evaluations are still influenced by the 'fun effect'. At any rate, it indicates that the Two-Finger-Tap (but probably also the Tap&Tap) is not perceived as amusing.

D. "The Two-Finger-Tap on smartphones does not seem that useful. If I want to zoom deeply, keeping the fingers too close is not possible because, sometimes, the gesture does not work. The pinch is better. On smartphones, instead, the Tap&Tap is very useful if I have to use the smartphone with just one hand. On the contrary, I continue to prefer the pinch". The user perceives the usefulness of the Tap&Tap, nevertheless, he prefers the traditional pinch (the comment is not isolated; the pinch is preferred also by other users).

R. "The gestures I tried are useful only if I have to zoom deeply. Otherwise, I think using the traditional pinch is better". The user was deceived by the same expectations rejected and discussed in Sect. 5.3 regarding the execution speed of the gestures when the zoom is deep. At any rate, the user would continue to prefer the traditional pinch.

As seen, the users' opinions are quite different. There are enthusiastic users and more traditional ones who are not willing to change their practices. Anyway, when the users realized that the new gestures were added to the traditional pinch without replacing it, they perceived them as very positive.

6   Conclusions

In this paper, two new gestures that enhance the Pinch-Drag-Paradigm were presented. All in all, the evaluations were very positive. The most noteworthy advantage is related to the Tap&Tap that can be used with just one hand. Both gestures can be implemented easily with few changes in existent software: around 50 lines of code [1] were enough to redesign Leaflet, the base framework used to develop the prototype presented in this paper. The implementation of the presented gestures in free and/or commercial software could not be so unfeasible.

Acknowledgments. Thanks to Daniela Bascuñan, linguist, for helping me to translate this paper. Thanks to Giorgio De Michelis and Flavio De Paoli, my PhD supervisors, for their human and academic support. Thanks to Lorenzo Fusco, physicist, for some pieces of advices on the statistical analyses.

References

1. Bellino, A.: Two new gestures to zoom: enhancing online maps services. In: Proceedings of the Companion Publication of the 24rd International Conference on World Wide Web Companion. International World Wide Web Conferences Steering Committee, May 2015
2. Bier, E.A., Stone, M.C., Pier, K., Buxton, B., DeRose, T.D.: Toolglass and magic lenses: the see-through interface. In: Proceedings of SIGGRAPH 1993, pp. 445–446. ACM (1993)
3. Boring, S., Ledo, D., Chen, X., Marquardt, N., Tang, A., Greenberg, S.: The fat thumb: using the thumb's contact size for single-handed mobile interaction. In: Proceedings of MobileHCI 2012, pp. 207–208. ACM (2012)
4. Engholm, K.A., Demory, M.D.: Touch zoom in/out for a graphics display. U.S. Patent No. 6,642,936. 4 Nov 2003
5. Fitzmaurice, G.W., Zhai, S., Chignell, M.: Virtual reality for palmtop computers. ACM Trans. Inf. Syst. **11**(3), 197–218 (1993)
6. Hansen, T.R., Eriksson, E., Lykke-Olesen, A.: Mixed interaction space - expanding the interaction space with mobile devices. In: Proceedings of HCI 2006, pp. 365–380. Springer, London (2006)
7. Hinckley, K., Song, H.: Sensor synaesthesia: touch in motion, and motion in touch. In: Proceedings of CHI. ACM (2011)
8. Hoober, S.: How do users really hold mobile devices? UX Matters Web Site http://www.uxmatters.com/mt/archives/2013/02/how-do-users-reallyhold-mobile-devices.php (2013). Accessed 14 Jan 2015
9. Malacria, S., Lecolinet, E., Guiard, Y.: Clutch-free panning and integrated pan-zoom control on touch-sensitive surfaces. In: Proceedings of CHI, pp. 2615–2624. ACM (2010)
10. Pahud, M., Hinckley, K., Iqbal, S., Sellen, A., Buxton, B.: Toward compound navigation tasks on mobiles via spatial manipulation. In: Proceedings of Mobile HCI 2013, pp. 113–122. ACM (2013)
11. Roth, V., Turner, T.: Bezel swipe: conflict-free scrolling and multiple selection on mobile touch screen devices. In: Proceedings of the SIGCHI Conference on Human Factors in Computing Systems, pp. 1523–1526. ACM, April 2009
12. Spelmezan, D., Appert, C., Chapuis, O., Pietriga, E.: Side pressure for bidirectional navigation on small devices. In: Proceedings of MobileHCI, pp. 113–122. ACM (2013)
13. Spindler, M., Schuessler, M., Martsch, M., Dachselt, R.: Pinch-drag-flick vs. spatial input: rethinking zoom & pan on mobile displays. In: Proceedings of the 32nd Annual ACM Conference on Human Factors in Computing Systems, pp. 1113–1122. ACM, April 2014
14. Wigdor, D., Forlines, C., Baudisch, P., Barnwell, J., Shen, C.: Lucid touch: a see-through mobile device. In: Proceedings of UIST 2007, pp. 269–278. ACM (2007)

Estimating Production Time of Touchless Hand Drawing Gestures

Orlando Erazo[1,2]($\boxtimes$), José A. Pino[1], and Pedro Antunes[3]

[1] Department of Computer Science, University of Chile, Santiago, Chile
{oerazo,jpino}@dcc.uchile.cl, oerazo@uteq.edu.ec
[2] Escuela de Informática, Universidad Técnica Estatal de Quevedo,
Quevedo, Ecuador
[3] School of Information Management, Victoria University of Wellington,
Wellington, New Zealand
pedro.antunes@vuw.ac.nz

Abstract. Quantitative user models such as CLC, Isokoski's and KLM have been used to estimate the production time of mouse and pen interactions (pointing, clicking, selecting, drawing, writing). In this paper, we assess if these models can be adapted to estimate the production time of touchless hand gestures (air figures of letters and numbers). New parameters were added to the existing models with empirical values drawn from experiments with users. Two metrics were used to evaluate model quality: strength of the relationship between estimated and observed times, and percentage root mean square error. The obtained results support the hypothesis that CLC, Isokoski's and KLM can be adapted to touchless hand gestures. The paper contributes with model modifications and parameters required to estimate the production times of touchless hand gestures.

Keywords: Touchless hand gestures · Natural user interfaces · Predictive evaluation · User models

1 Introduction

Hardware devices such as Kinect, Leap Motion and Myo have contributed significantly to the emergence of a new class of graphical user interfaces labeled as Natural User Interfaces (NUIs), which most distinctive characteristic is using touchless hand gestures as a new interaction modality. Besides the obvious advantages in entertainment, NUIs are also becoming increasingly popular in fields such as education [1] and healthcare [2]. However, depending on each particular application, hand gestures may be very taxing on production time, i.e. the time spent by users engendering interactions with an application's user interface. This situation leaves user-interface designers with the difficult task of evaluating which touchless hand drawing gestures are most adequate and how they can be tailored to a user-interface under construction to optimize production time.

Considering the logistic difficulties of doing tests with real users, regarding planning, timing, laboratory setup, recruiting, and conducting experiments, a reasonable

© IFIP International Federation for Information Processing 2015
J. Abascal et al. (Eds.): INTERACT 2015, Part III, LNCS 9298, pp. 552–569, 2015.
DOI: 10.1007/978-3-319-22698-9_38

assumption is that user-interface designers may find value in instead adopting predictive evaluation. Predictive evaluation provides quantitative indications on how users may perform based on user models instead of real users, thus easing the abovementioned logistic problems.

Of course a consequence of adopting predictive evaluation is that we need quantitative user models. Although some quantitative models have already been proposed that include gestures [3, 4], they do not support the estimation of production time. However, an extensive body of research in quantitative user models for pointer- and pen-based gestures has already been developed. One of the most influential instances is the KLM (Keystroke Level Model) model originally proposed by Card, Moran and Newell and extended by others [5–7]. Another notable example is Fitts' Law [8], which has been widely used to estimate physical and virtual pointing [9–12].

Some interactions like pointing, clicking and selecting can be done both with a mouse and in the air using hand gestures, and therefore can be modeled using KLM and Fitts' Law, as demonstrated by [9–12]. However, more complex interactions such as drawing characters, numbers and figures require either extending the existing models with new parameters or developing whole new user models. Considering this landscape, the generic goal of the research reported in this paper is to extend the existing models to encompass hand gestures. More specifically, our goal is to extend the CLC (Curves, Line segments and Corners) [13], Isokoski's [14] and KLM [5] models to estimate the production times of touchless hand gestures. Our research is restricted to gestures performed by young adults in normal health conditions, with basic or no experience with touchless interactions, and using the dominant hand (fingers are not considered). The gestures of interest consist of drawing in the air figures or shapes such as letters or numbers.

2 Related Work

A commonly accepted strategy to evaluate the usability of a user interface is to use modeling techniques. This strategy presents the advantages of neither depending on real users nor requiring usability experts to participate in the evaluation process.

Models can vary in detail and complexity, ranging from *descriptive models*, which provide a framework for designers to delineate and reflect on usability problems, to *predictive models*, which use mathematical expressions for estimating user performance [15]. Unlike the descriptive category, predictive models can be used to objectively estimate the required time for performing a set of user interactions. Likewise the descriptive category, predictive models can be applied at early design stages, before starting to develop the real user interface.

Some notable user models have been proposed in the research literature. One of the most known and cited models is Fitts' Law [8], which allows estimating the time to point at a target based on the object size and distance. Taking into account that Fitts' Law is not adequate for certain types of tasks, and based on it, Accot and Zhai [16] proposed the "steering law" for trajectory-based tasks. This model allows predicting the time to navigate through a two-dimensional tunnel, but it may not be adequate to analyze the trajectory of touchless hand gestures when there are no visual guides.

An alternative was proposed by Isokoski [14], who introduced a conceptually simple model that predicts production time for unistroke interactions done by expert users. According to this model, a gesture is first decomposed into a number of "needed straight-line segments" which are then counted to estimate the overall time-complexity of the gesture. The number of considered segments is the minimum necessary to make the gesture recognizable. Additionally, it is assumed that drawing a straight-line segment takes a constant time.

By comparing the model with real-user interactions, Isokoski [14] measured the *strength of the relationship between estimated and observed times* (usually noted as R^2) to be <0.85. The *percentage root mean square error* (usually noted as %RMSE) of these measures was 30 % [14].

Although the definition of "needed straight-line segments" is ambiguous [13, 17] (a procedure describing the reduction of gestures with curves into straight lines is missing), Isokoski's model seems conceptually easy to extend to hand gestures because it requires estimating the constant time to produce a straight line gesture segment from experimental data.

Cao and Zhai [13] suggested a model to estimate the production time of single pen-stroke gestures. The model considers three features found in pen-stroke gestures: Curves, Line segments, and Corners (the reason why the model is referred to CLC).

For any gesture, the production time is calculated by summing up the estimated time durations of all gesture segments (see formula 1 below). The estimated production times of Curve and Line are defined in formulas 2 and 3. (Formula 4 can be used instead of formula 3.) The Corner, which is an abrupt change in stroke direction, was discarded by Cao and Zhai after empirical studies showed its insignificant impact on production times [13].

The CLC model reveals a strong relationship between estimated and observed times ($R^2 > 0.90$). Even though the model has been used in several research studies (e.g. [17, 18]), we do not have evidence that it has been used beyond pen-stroke gestures.

$$T = \sum T(line) + \sum T(corner) + \sum T(curve) \qquad (1)$$

$$T(curve) = \frac{\alpha}{K} r^{1-\beta} \qquad (2)$$

$$T(line) = mL^n \qquad (3)$$

$$T(line) = aL + b \qquad (4)$$

Where: α is the sweep angle; r is the radius of the arc; β and K are empirical constants. L is the length of the line; a, b, m and n are empirical constants.

Another well-known user model is the Keystroke Level Model (KLM) [5]. KLM defines a set of primitive operations: key press (K); point (P); button press (B); hand movement between keyboard and mouse (H); Drawing (D); and mental preparation (M). For each primitive operation, empirical studies with various types of users allowed to determine the respective average production time constant. The D primitive is the only one relevant to this study, even though it has several constraints worth noticing:

drawing is done with the mouse, it only concerns straight-line segments, and it is assumed to be done on a square grid with 0.56 cm. According to KLM, the production time of a drawing interaction is defined as a linear function of the number of segments (n_D) and the total length (l_D) of all segments (see formula 5) [5].

$$D(n_D, l_D) = an_D + bl_D \tag{5}$$

Where: a and b are constants ($a = 0.9$ and $b = 0.16$ in the original KLM version [5]).

All in all, the Isokoski's, CLC and KLM models advocate: (1) decompose a gesture either into a series of straight-line segments (Isokoski's and KLM) or into a series of curved and straight-line segments (CLC); (2) use a set of formulas and parameters to calculate the production time of each segment, adding them to obtain the overall production time of a gesture; and (3) derive the parameters from empirical studies with various users, so that the formulas adjust to reality. Nevertheless specific parameters for touchless hand gestures do not currently exist and will have to be further researched. We detail that process in the following section.

3   Hypotheses and Research Design

As mentioned above, there is no evidence that the three described models may be used for touchless hand gestures. Therefore, the following hypothesis should be tested:

H1: CLC, Isokoski's and KLM models can be adapted to predict the production time of hand gestures.

The starting point to test this hypothesis is the definition of formulas. Either the original formulas can be applied to hand gestures or they have to be extended to encompass the new conditions imposed by hand gestures. Hence, we introduce a first step in our study where the formulas are evaluated and adapted if necessary. This step is shown in Table 1 (step 1) and denoted as "An" (A - Adaptation).

After adapting the formulas, it is necessary to define new parameters for hand gestures. The second step requires carrying out several experiments with real users (En in Table 1, step 2; E - Experiment) and then tuning the parameters so the models may reflect the users' performance.

At this point, the models should be ready to use. However, we still have to consider the quality of the estimations. Thus, we have to evaluate the models, that is, to verify the second hypothesis:

H2: The adapted models can predict the production time of hand gestures with acceptable quality.

We will test this hypothesis using the two metrics also adopted by Cao and Zhai [13], considering both the strength of the relationship between estimated and observed times (R^2), and percentage root mean square error (%RMSE). Furthermore, we will consider that a model has acceptable quality if R^2 and %RMSE are proximate to the values obtained by Cao and Zhai [13]: $R^2 > 0.90$ and %RMSE < 30 %.

Table 1. Research design: adaptations of models (A) and experiments (E).

| | Models | | |
Steps	CLC	Isokoski's	KLM
1. Definition of formulas	A1	A2	A3
2. Estimation of parameters	E1	E1	E2
3. Evaluation of models	E2	E2	E3

H2 must be tested with a set of experiments with real users (E*n* in Table 1, line 3). With a careful experimental setup, some of the experiments required to test H1 can also be used to test H2. That is the reason why we see in Table 1 that E1 and E2 are shared by steps 2 and 3. This is possible because: (1) the parameters required by CLC and Isokoski's models can be tuned using the same experiments; and (2) we use two different sets of users in E1 and E2, so that the users being used to tune a model can be reused to validate another model, but one set of users is not simultaneously used to tune and validate the same model.

In the remainder of this section we give more details about the experimental setup. The validation of H1 and H2 is discussed in detail in the following sections using the stepwise structure described in Table 1.

3.1 Apparatus and Method

The hardware setup for the experiments consisted of notebook, Kinect sensor and TV screen mounted in a controlled laboratory setting. The notebook was equipped with an i7 processor and 8 GB of RAM. The Kinect sensor was used with a refresh rate of 30 fps, connected to track users' hand position and recognizing gestures, placed at a height of 0.9 m and below the TV screen. The TV screen had 42 in, 1360×768 px resolution. The participants stood in an uncluttered space, 2.5 m away from the Kinect sensor.

A custom software tool (Fig. 1) was developed for precisely controlling the experiments. The tool was developed using MS Visual C# and Kinect for Windows SDK V1.8 on Windows 7. The tool logged time marks and hand coordinates while a participant performs a gesture. The Dynamic Time Warping algorithm [19] was used for gesture recognition. The tool's interface consisted of an augmented video blending user interface controls and the real environment. Augmented video was adopted in order to avoid participants' distractions while performing the tasks. For instance, a person may judge his/her movements based on a hand cursor and try to make adjustments [20], especially because of the sensor noise [10, 12, 21] which should be avoided. We fine-tuned these experimental conditions through a set of trial experiments.

The tool had two additional software modules focused on gesture analysis. The first module allowed recording gestures (Fig. 1a), while the second one was able to reproduce every user-generated gesture using segmentation and logged hand coordinates (Fig. 1b).

Each gesture instance was segmented in the phases proposed by [22] to measure the production times of gestures. More specifically, the measured stroke-phase time was

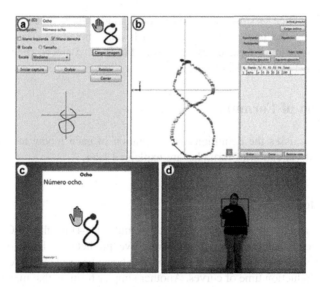

Fig. 1. Interface of the experimental software.

defined as corresponding to production time, which does not account for the time spent by the participants in other gesture phases.

The participants in the experiments were University students (33 in total, aged between 17 and 28) invited by email, social networks, etc. The participants were not paid for their participation. Written informed consents were obtained before starting each experiment. A student was allowed to participate in a single experiment.

Before the experiment, each participant received written instructions and an explanation about the research goals. Then, the participant performed some training gestures guided by the software. When the participant indicated s/he was ready, more specific instructions appeared on the TV screen using a PowerPoint slideshow. Enough time was allowed to read the instructions. The instructions required that every gesture should be done inside a red box (gesture input area or gesture space, see Fig. 1d), having approximately the same size, and balancing speed and accuracy. (The tool adjusted the size of the input area according to the size of the required gesture.) The instructions also noted the participants should use the dominant hand, and should start (preparation phase [22]) and finish (retraction phase [22]) a gesture with both hands in a relaxed position below hips.

The tool immediately started the data acquisition phase after displaying the instructions. The tool was programmed to randomly pick a gesture within a gesture set and display it for 2 s (Fig. 1c). The gesture image was displayed along with a name and a very short description. After the 2 s period, the description disappeared, the red box was displayed, and the participant's gesture was collected (Fig. 1d). When the gesture was correct, the tool displayed a green check and moved on to the next gesture. When a gesture was wrong, a red-cross mark was displayed, the input was discarded, and the participant had to re-enter the gesture.

Besides a practice session, every experiment included three blocks with gestures to be performed by the participants (e.g. a block only including straight lines). The specific characteristics of these blocks are defined in Sects. 5 and 6. The tool included a resting period between blocks of gestures.

4 Definition of Formulas

This section discusses the definition and adaptation of each model to hand gestures. The tuning and validation of formulas are explained later.

4.1 CLC Model

Although Cao and Zhai [13] adopted several formulas (1–4) for the CLC model, there are other options that might be used to improve predictions. Based on regression analysis (discussed later), we suggest that formula 6 can be used instead of formula 2 to estimate the production time of curves. Another simpler formula that may be applied to curves, which Cao and Zhai did not test, is a linear function of the curve's radius and angle (formula 7). These two formulas may contribute to reduce the %RMSE of CLC, but they should be tested against the original one.

$$T(curve) = \frac{\alpha^a}{K} r^{1-\beta} \qquad (6)$$

$$T(curve) = mr + n\alpha \qquad (7)$$

Where: α is the sweep angle; r is the radius of the curve; a, β, K, m and n are empirical constants.

4.2 Isokoski's Model

Given the conceptual simplicity of Isokoski's model [14], we consider it may be straightforwardly adapted to hand gestures. Formula 8 may be applied bearing in mind that hand gestures will be reduced into a sequence of straight lines and an empirical constant is necessary to estimate the time taken to generate every straight line. This reasoning has two implications. First, Isokoski did not provide a constant time for performing a straight-line segment, so we have to estimate that constant. Second, Isokoski' does not provide a clear procedure to reduce curves into straight lines, which may range between 1 (too much error) and an arbitrary large number (less error but more difficult to calculate). We adopt the procedure suggested by Vatavu et al.: "if the angle α inscribed by an arc was greater than 270° use 3 segments; if $\alpha < 120$° use 1 segment; otherwise use 2 segments" [17] (p. 97).

$$T = \#segments * constant\_time \qquad (8)$$

4.3   KLM

As already mentioned, we are only using the D operator of KLM, and hence using formula 5 to estimate production time of hand gestures. Analyzing the original definition in detail [5], we note that formula 5 may not be applicable to gestures with curves and corners. We suggest that curves be approximated to straight-line segments by applying the procedure adopted by Vatavu et al. [17] (p. 97). Regarding corners, we suggest counting the number of corners (n_C) multiplied by an empirical constant, as shown in formula 9.

$$D_c(n_D, l_D, n_C) = an_D + bl_D + cn_C \qquad (9)$$

Where a, b and c are empirical constants.

5   Estimation of Parameters

In this section we give further insights about formulas 6–9 delineated above. The discussion is organized in two steps. In the first step, we describe the experiments (E1 and E2, see Table 1) conducted to obtain empirical data about user's hand gestures. In the second step we present the final formulas with the estimated empirical constants.

5.1   CLC Model

Experiment. We repeated most of the experimental process described by Cao and Zhai [13] using hand gestures to obtain empirical constants for formulas 2–4, 6 and 7. Experiment E1 involved gathering data for three gesture components: straight lines, curves and corners. This experiment then implied configuring the tool discussed in Sect. 3 to request participants to produce variations of these individual gesture components (see below). Each participant would produce the same gesture three times in order to increase precision. Trying to avoid learning and/or sequence effects, the order of components was counterbalanced.

Various lengths ($L = \{0.4, 0.6, 0.8\}$ meters in motor space) and orientations (0, 45, 90 and 135° counterclockwise) were tested when producing straight lines. For curves, various radiuses ($r = \{0.2, 0.3, 0.4\}$ meters in motor space) and sweep angles ($\alpha = \{90, 180, 360\}$ degrees) were tested. Start angle (90°) and direction (clockwise) were treated as control variables for curve gestures. Various corner angles ($\theta = \{45, 90, 135\}$ degrees) and directions (CW and CCW) were tested to produce corners. Length was kept constant (0.6 cm in motor space). Twelve persons participated in E1 (mean age 21y, $\sigma = 2$).

Results. In general, the results obtained from E1 for the CLC model have similar significance to those obtained by Cao and Zhai [13], which provides a first indication that CLC can be used for estimating production time of touchless hand gestures. In detail:

Straight Lines. We observed statistically significant differences when measuring production time and varying length ($F_{2,22} = 10.47, p < 0.05$) and orientation ($F_{3,33} = 2.92$, $p < 0.05$). No significant length × orientation interaction effects were found ($F_{6,66} = 0.32$, ns). Figure 2 shows the relation between length and production time for each orientation. We note that Cao and Zhai [13] did not take into account orientation in their estimations because its effect was considered smaller than length. We made the same decision due to the similarity of our results, but we also computed the correlation coefficients to confirm it. We found no correlation between orientation and time production ($r = -0.022$). Finally, performing regression analysis of our experimental data, we obtained the empirical constants shown in formulas 10 and 11.

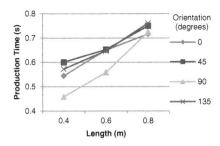

Fig. 2. Straight line production time.

$$T(line) = 0.486 \, L + 0.345 \quad \left(R^2 = 0.796\right) \tag{10}$$

$$T(line) = 0.803 \, L^{0.442} \quad \left(R^2 = 0.746\right) \tag{11}$$

Where L and T are given in meters and seconds respectively.

Curves. As we expected, measured differences in production time were statistically significant for both radius ($F_{2,22} = 12.33, p < 0.05$) and angle ($F_{2,22} = 110, p < 0.05$). We found significant radius × angle interaction effects ($F_{4,44} = 3.72, p < 0.05$). Figure 3 shows the relation between sweep angles and production time for each orientation radius. After performing regression analysis with our experimental data, we obtained formulas 12–14 below.

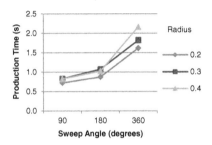

Fig. 3. Curve production time.

$$T(curve) = \frac{\alpha}{1.939} r^{1-0.711} \tag{12}$$

$$T(curve) = \frac{\alpha^{0.615}}{1.249} r^{1-0.711} \quad (R^2 = 0.919) \tag{13}$$

$$T(curve) = 1.338 \, r + 0.236 \, \alpha \quad (R^2 = 0.942) \tag{14}$$

Where α, r and T are given in radians, meters and seconds respectively.

Corners. Following Cao and Zhai's method, we computed the "net contribution time" of corners [13]. Thus, for our experimental data and using the average time to perform a line 0.6 cm long (see Table 2): *T(corner) = sample production time – 2 * 0.627* (seconds).

The measured differences in production time were statistically significant for corner angle ($F_{2,22} = 6.49$, $p < 0.05$), but not for direction ($F_{1,11} = 2.05$, $p > 0.05$). We found no significant angle × direction interaction effects ($F_{2,22} = 0.24$, ns). Taking into account that the average *T(corner)* seems to fluctuate around zero (Fig. 4), we made a deliberate simplification (formula 15): to omit corners in the model (Cao and Zhai [13] made the same decision). Although these results confirm previous preliminary findings, which postulate that corners have influence on production time of hand gestures [4], we think further research is necessary to adequately model the impact of corners in hand gestures.

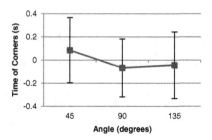

Fig. 4. Net corner time contribution. Error bars indicate 1 SD.

$$T = \sum T(line) + \sum T(curve) \tag{15}$$

5.2   Isokoski's Model

Experiment. As mentioned above, data obtained from experiment E1 was reused to build an estimation model based on Isokoski's proposal [14]. Although Cao and Zhai [13] state that a constant time model should be invalidated, we nevertheless decided to build this model because of its conceptual simplicity. An average time was calculated for each straight line produced by the participants in the experiment (Table 2). Moreover, we estimated a fourth value to evaluate the model with a smaller straight-line segment (0.2 m). These times must be verified for selecting the best one by using different gestures (see next section).

Results

Table 2. Constant times for Isokoski's model.

Straight line lengths, L(m)	Observed time, t(s)	SD(s)
0.2	0.442	NA
0.4	0.544	0.111
0.6	0.627	0.180
0.8	0.738	0.219

5.3   KLM

Experiment. Taking into account that experiment E1 is focused on curves, straight lines and corners, we had to perform another experiment (E2) to estimate the empirical constant for the D operator of KLM, given that it is based on the number of segments and the total length of all segments. The experiment consisted of drawing 14 gestures[1] (Fig. 5) in random order. Gestures were performed inside the gesture space, which was a 0.6 m square. Twelve persons took part in E2 (mean age 23y, $\sigma = 2$).

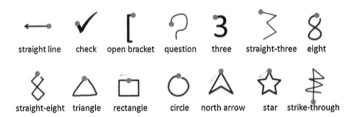

straight line   check   open bracket   question   three   straight-three   eight

straight-eight   triangle   rectangle   circle   north arrow   star   strike-through

Fig. 5. Gestures used in experiment 2.

Results. The procedure adopted by Card et al. [5] for drawing straight-line segments (formula 5) was tested with hand gestures. This means that gestures with curves ("question", "three", "eight" and "circle", in Fig. 5) were not used to build the model. The number of segments (n_D) of each gesture produce by participants in the experiment was counted and the total length (l_D) of each gesture was computed (geometrically). Formula 16 was obtained by performing regression analysis. The resulting R^2 value was high (0.988), but we thought the model could still be improved. We obtained a

---

[1] The green point indicates the start of the gesture. Strike-through was selected from [17].

higher R^2 value (0.99, see formula 17) considering the number of corners and using formula 9. (Corners were counted depending on the gesture start point.)

$$D(n_D, l_D) = 0.386n_D + 0.349l_D \quad (R^2 = 0.988) \tag{16}$$

$$D_c(n_D, l_D, n_C) = 0.223n_D + 0.297l_D + 0.173n_C \quad (R^2 = 0.99) \tag{17}$$

Formula 16 was then tested to estimate the production times of the four gestures with curves shown in Fig. 5, which had not been previously used to estimate the empirical constants (condition D in Fig. 6). Additionally, formula 17 was tested with and without corners (conditions D_c and D_c*). The obtained results for these three conditions are shown in Fig. 6. These results indicate that these models can also be applied to gestures with curves.

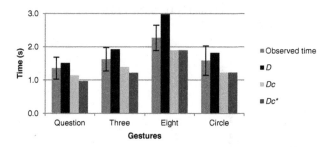

Fig. 6. Comparison of observed and predicted times of 4 gestures with curves using the D, D_c and D_c* conditions. Error bars indicate 1 SD.

6   Evaluation of Models

The production times of real hand gestures must be compared against predicted values in order to evaluate the adapted models. We tried to reduce the number of experiments to a minimum and thus, we decided to reuse data from experiment E2 to evaluate the adapted CLC and Isokoski's models, whose parameters were developed from E1 using a different cohort and different gestures. Regarding the evaluation of the adapted KLM model, a new experiment had to be setup (E3), since E2 was used to estimate the parameters for this model.

6.1   CLC Model

Formula 15 was suggested to estimate production time using the CLC model, with the provision that formulas (10–14) can be considered options for measuring straight-lines and curves, respectively. Six possibilities can be analyzed to identify the best estimation approach by combining these formulas.

The results obtained from E2 are shown in Table 3 for the six formula combinations. We note that some R^2 values are lower than the baseline (Cao and Zhai's results [13]), but the obtained %RMSE values are better. Furthermore, the differences between estimates are relatively small. The best results are obtained using the linear model for straight lines (formula 10) and the modified model for curves (formula 13). Figure 7 displays the predicted versus observed data using this formula combination.

Table 3. Comparison of CLC model predictions.

Formulas	R^2	%RMSE
(15), (10) and (12)	0.834	18.8
(15), (11) and (12)	0.779	18.8
(15), (10) and (13)	**0.859**	**15.7**
(15), (11) and (13)	0.810	15.7
(15), (10) and (14)	0.849	16.9
(15), (11) and (14)	0.798	16.9

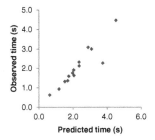

Fig. 7. CLC model prediction.

6.2   Isokoski's Model

E2 also allowed validating the Isokoski's model expressed in formula 8 with the empirical constants defined in Sect. 5.2. The obtained results, shown in Fig. 8, suggest that selecting a constant straight-line length of 0.4 m gives the least estimation error. Figure 9 shows the relationship between predicted and measured production times for the suggested straight-line length ($R^2 = 0.935$, $L = 0.4$ m, $t = 0.544$ s).

Finally, we compared the measured production time with the best results estimated by the CLC and Isokoski's models (Fig. 10). Isokoski's model is slightly better than CLC, but the difference is quite small to choose the best one. Also, we note the worst predictions were made for gestures "three" and "eight", which are outside ±1 SD.

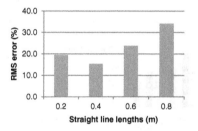

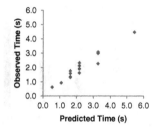

Fig. 8. Comparison of Isokoski's model prediction errors.

Fig. 9. Isokoski's model prediction.

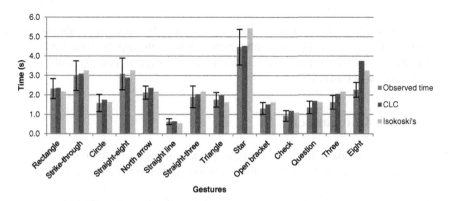

Fig. 10. Comparison of observed and predicted times using both CLC and Isokoski's models. Error bars indicate 1 SD.

6.3 KLM

Experiment E3 was set up in a similar way to E2. Nine participants (mean age 21y, $\sigma = 3$), performed the 6 gestures[2] shown in Fig. 11.

Fig. 11. Gestures used in E3.

Stroke times were compared against predicted values using formulas 16 and 17. Before applying the formulas, gestures with curves ("5", "E" and "steep-hill") were reduced into straight lines. Additionally, formula 17 was calculated with and without corners (D_c and $D_c{}^*$ conditions). For instance, gesture "E" was evaluated using 1 and 0 corners. The obtained results are shown in Fig. 12.

---

[2] The green point indicates the start of the gesture. Steep-hill was selected from [17].

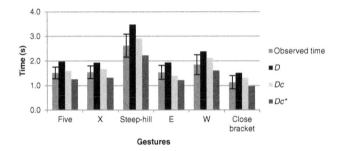

Fig. 12. Comparison of observed and predicted times for experiment E3 using D, D_c and D_c^* conditions. Error bars indicate 1 SD.

The highest R^2 (0.995) value was observed for the D condition, while the lowest (0.947) was observed for D_c, even though they were quite approximate. Since the % RMSE was favorable to the D_c condition (10.4), we suggest that D_c could be considered the best one overall.

7   General Comparison

In this section we finally compare the three models, using again the data collected in experiment E3 and focused on the formulas and empirical constants that produced the best estimates.

Table 4 shows the selected formulas and quality of estimates using the two quality criteria adopted by this study. Figure 13 provides a more detailed comparison using the

Table 4. Comparison of the three models.

Model name	Formulas	R^2	%RMSE
CLC	(15), (10) and (13)	0.996	25.7
Isokoski's	#segments* 0.544	0.881	25.7
KLM (D_c)	(17)	0.947	10.4

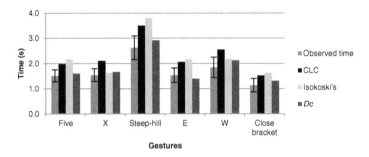

Fig. 13. General comparison of observed and predicted times using CLC, Isokoski's and KLM models. Error bars indicate 1 SD.

observed and predicted production times for the six gestures used to evaluate the estimation models. The highest R^2 value was obtained for the CLC model, but the differences to KLM (D_c condition) are quite small. On the other hand, the lowest % RMSE was obtained with KLM (D_c). Consequently, we suggest using KLM (D_c) to predict the production time of hand gestures.

8 Discussion and Conclusions

In this paper we analyze three estimation models for predicting the production time of users' interactions with other types of user interfaces. We extend these models to hand gestures. Empirical experiments were accomplished to tune and validate the models. The quality of the estimates was evaluated using two criteria: strength of the relationship between estimated and observed times, and percentage root mean square error. In a broad perspective, we can conclude that the three models can be used with hand gestures, which confirms hypothesis H1. Furthermore, we provide new or updated formulas and empirical constants required to use the models with hand gestures.

The constant-time estimation model, which was proposed by Isokoski for unistroke writing [14], is the simplest model. This model is very easy to use because it reduces gestures to straight-line segments, counts them, and uses a constant multiplier that reflects the average time necessary to produce a straight-line segment. The constant multiplier depends on the constant length assigned to a segment.

According to our results, if gestures are drawn inside a square gesture space with 0.6 m sides, acceptable results can be achieved with a segment that is 0.4 m long. Conversely, the simplifications required by this model lead to erroneous estimations when using variable gesture spaces (i.e. making gestures of different sizes).

An alternative approach, which we also analyzed, consists in using the CLC model, which breaks down gestures into curves, lines and corners [13]. This model avoids reducing curves and corners to straight-line segments.

We provide new or updated formulas and empirical constants required to use the CLC model with hand gestures. Moreover, our experiments indicate that corners influence production time and therefore should not be neglected. Additionally, slightly different formulas were evaluated, leading us to suggest a new formula for estimating the production time of hand gestures using CLC.

The KLM model also reveals easy to adapt to hand gestures, because it is only based on the number of straight-line segments and the total length of a gesture. Conversely, this strategy also reveals a limitation because KLM's D operator does not take into account other components like corners and curves. Trying to overcome these limitations, we included corners as a third parameter in KLM's estimation formula. The experimental results indicate these modifications provide good results.

Gestures with curves were analyzed as if they were straight lines and with the options of counting or not the number of corners. The obtained results show that counting corners improves the quality of the estimation. Consequently, the adapted KLM formula we suggest counts the number of segments, the total length and the number of corners of a gesture.

Regarding the experiments, we should note the following. First, we could observe a relatively high variation of gesture production times among participants. Although we did not compute a global or final value, the coefficient of variation is, on the average, about 30 %. Second, the models were adapted and evaluated only using the gestures' stroke phase, even though they could also be analyzed taking into account a more comprehensive view (e.g. [22]). Third, the gestures used in our experiments were performed using only the dominant hand, although users may perform gestures with the other hand [23]. This constraint may have an effect on the estimates (e.g. [12]).

The model we suggest as the best to estimate production time of hand gestures obtained $R^2 \geq 0.947$ and %RMSE = 10.4, which are better than the ones obtained by Cao and Zhai [13] for single pen-stroke gestures. Regarding hypothesis H2, we observe it is validated for the CLC and KLM (D_c condition).

We expect to conduct more evaluations in the future with more users and more gestures. We also consider studying other hand gesture types like hover, tap and swipe.

Acknowledgments. Orlando Erazo appreciates the financial support provided for this research by SENESCYT, Ecuador.

References

1. Blum, T., Kleeberger, V., Bichlmeier, C., Navab, N.: mirracle: An augmented reality magic mirror system for anatomy education. In: 2012 IEEE Virtual Reality Short Papers and Posters, pp. 115–116. IEEE Press (2012)
2. Erazo, O., Pino, J.A., Pino, R., Fernández, C.: Magic mirror for neurorehabilitation of people with upper limb dysfunction using kinect. In: 47th Hawaii International Conference on System Sciences, pp. 2607–2615. IEEE Press (2014)
3. Barclay, K., Wei, D., Lutteroth, C., Sheehan, R.: A quantitative quality model for gesture based user interfaces. In: Proceedings of OzCHI 2011, pp. 31–39. ACM Press, New York (2011)
4. Erazo, O., Pino, J.A.: Estimating the difficulty of touchless hand gestures. IEEE Lat. Am. Trans. **12**, 17–22 (2014)
5. Card, S., Moran, T., Newell, A.: The keystroke-level model for user performance time with interactive systems. Commun. ACM **23**, 396–410 (1980)
6. Holleis, P., Otto, F., Hussmann, H., Schmidt, A.: Keystroke-level model for advanced mobile phone interaction. In: Proceedings of CHI 2007, pp. 1505–1514. ACM Press, New York (2007)
7. Erazo, O., Pino, J.A.: Predicting task execution time on natural user interfaces based on touchless hand gestures. In: Proceedings of IUI 2015, pp. 97–109. ACM Press, New York (2015)
8. Fitts, P.M.: The information capacity of the human motor system in controlling the amplitude of movement. J. Exp. Psychol. **47**, 381–391 (1954)
9. Pino, A., Tzemis, E., Ioannou, N., Kouroupetroglou, G.: Using kinect for 2D and 3D pointing tasks: performance evaluation. In: Kurosu, M. (ed.) HCII/HCI 2013, Part IV. LNCS, vol. 8007, pp. 358–367. Springer, Heidelberg (2013)
10. Sambrooks, L., Wilkinson, B.: Comparison of gestural, touch, and mouse interaction with Fitts' law. In: Proceedings of OzCHI 2013, pp. 119–122. ACM Press, New York (2011)

11. Schwaller, M., Lalanne, D.: Pointing in the air: measuring the effect of hand selection strategies on performance and effort. In: Holzinger, A., Ziefle, M., Hitz, M., Debevc, M. (eds.) SouthCHI 2013. LNCS, vol. 7946, pp. 732–747. Springer, Heidelberg (2013)
12. Zeng, X., Hedge, A., Guimbretiere, F.: Fitts' law in 3D space with coordinated hand movements. In: Human Factors and Ergonomics Society Annual Meeting. SAGE Publications (2012)
13. Cao, X., Zhai, S.: Modeling human performance of pen stroke gestures. In: Proceedings of CHI 2007, pp. 1495–1504. ACM Press, New York (2007)
14. Isokoski, P.: Model for unistroke writing time. In: Proceedings of CHI 2001, pp. 357–364. ACM Press, New York (2001)
15. MacKenzie, I.S.: Motor behavior models for human-computer interaction. In: Carroll, J.M. (ed.) HCI Models, Theories, and Frameworks, pp. 27–54. Morgan Kaufmann, San Francisco (2003)
16. Accot, J., Zhai, S.: Beyond Fitts' law: models for trajectory-based HCI Tasks. In: Proceedings of CHI 1997. ACM Press, New York (2001)
17. Vatavu, R.-D., Vogel, D., Casiez, G., Grisoni, L.: Estimating the perceived difficulty of pen gestures. In: Campos, P., Graham, N., Jorge, J., Nunes, N., Palanque, P., Winckler, M. (eds.) INTERACT 2011, Part II. LNCS, vol. 6947, pp. 89–106. Springer, Heidelberg (2011)
18. Tu, H., Ren, X., Zhai, S.: A comparative evaluation of finger and pen stroke gestures. In: Proceedings of CHI 2012, pp. 1287–1296. ACM Press, New York (2012)
19. Senin, P.: Dynamic time warping algorithm review. Information and Computer Science Department, University of Hawaii at Manoa Honolulu (2008)
20. Sutter, C., Müsseler, J., Bardos, L., Ballagas, R., Borchers, J.: The impact of gain change on perceiving one's own actions. In: Mensch and Computer, pp. 147–156 (2008)
21. Livingston, M.A., Sebastian, J., Ai, Z., Decker, J.W.: Performance measurements for the Microsoft Kinect Skeleton. In: 2012 IEEE Virtual Reality Short Papers and Posters, pp. 119–120. IEEE Press (2012)
22. McNeill, D.: Guide to gesture classification, transcription, and distribution. In: McNeill, D. (ed.) Hand and Mind: What Gestures Reveal about Thought, pp. 75–104. The University of Chicago Press, Chicago (1992)
23. Annett, M., Bischof, W.: Your left hand can do it too! investigating intermanual, symmetric gesture transfer on touchscreens. In: Proceedings of CHI 2013, pp. 1119–1128. ACM Press, New York (2013)

The Costs and Benefits of Combining Gaze and Hand Gestures for Remote Interaction

Yanxia Zhang[1]([✉]), Sophie Stellmach[2], Abigail Sellen[3],
and Andrew Blake[3]

[1] Lancaster University, Lancaster, UK
yazhang@lancaster.ac.uk
[2] Microsoft Corporation, Redmond, USA
sostel@microsoft.com
[3] Microsoft Research, Cambridge, UK
{asellen,ablake}@microsoft.com

Abstract. Gaze has been proposed as an ideal modality for supporting remote target selection. We explored the potential of integrating gaze with hand gestures for remote interaction on a large display in terms of user experience and preference. We conducted a lab study to compare interaction in a photo-sorting task using gesture only, or the combination of gaze plus gesture. Results from the study show that a combination of gaze and gesture input can lead to significantly faster selection, reduced hand fatigue and increased ease of use compared to using only hand input. People largely preferred the combination of gaze for target selection and hand gestures for manipulation. However, gaze can cause particular kinds of errors and can induce a cost due to switching modalities.

Keywords: Hand gestural interface · Gaze interaction · Mid-air gestures · Remote interaction · Large display · Smart living room

1 Introduction

With advances in sensing technologies, people can now interact in much richer ways with computer systems without the need for physical contact or manipulation of devices. Free hand gestures, such as those enabled by the Kinect depth-sensing camera, have already been shown to be an effective method of input for games and interactive television applications on displays at a distance. This raises the question of whether other input modalities which support interaction at a distance, such as eye gaze, can further enhance the way we interact remotely. One reason for this is that many applications performed on a large screen over a distance often involve manipulating contents of the entire screen space, which can be widely dispersed [1]. Because people instinctively look at objects of interest, gaze has been shown to be an efficient modality for targeting remote objects [2–6]. In addition, gaze often precedes a manual action [7] suggesting that we could exploit the combination of these two modalities for more efficient methods of interaction. For example, it suggests that gaze might be used for selection of a target object followed by hand gestures to operate on that object.

© IFIP International Federation for Information Processing 2015
J. Abascal et al. (Eds.): INTERACT 2015, Part III, LNCS 9298, pp. 570–577, 2015.
DOI: 10.1007/978-3-319-22698-9_39

Recent work has highlighted the potential of combining gaze and hand gestures for fast and accurate *point and drag* interactions [8], and enabling more attentive and immersive 3D UI interactions [9]. While this work focused on examining speed and accuracy, many other aspects of integrating gaze with hand gesture input for remote large screen interactions are still not well understood. To further explore how people perform and perceive the combination, we ask what benefits gaze might bring to gestural interaction from the user's perspective. We also investigate any potential costs that are incurred by adding gaze as a second modality.

In order to address these questions, we constructed a photo sorting task involving the fast assignment of multiple objects spread out across a large screen to different "piles" or destinations. This task, which involves selection of remote target objects followed by a limited set of repetitive actions on those objects, has been shown to be representative of common tasks that users would want to carry out on large screens [1].

We compared users' experience of two interfaces for this task: one which represents the status quo for device-free remote interaction such as gaming, namely using gestures only *(hand-only),* and another which works across modalities (*gaze-hand*). In the cross modality condition, we assigned gaze and hand gestures in what we surmised would be the optimal way for such a task. Based on the prior work mentioned above, we reasoned that gaze would be best for target selection (of relatively large targets), while hand gestures would be good for expressive but not necessarily precise manipulation. In this case, gestures are used to "fling" photos to different piles, an action which involves coarse-grained (as opposed to fine-grained) control.

2   User Study: Photo Sorting

In this study, our goal was to examine the effect of integrating gaze into a remote, gestural interaction task in terms of both performance and subjective experience. We hypothesized that: (1) the combination of gaze pointing and hand gestures will give rise to faster task completion than sorting with gesture only; and (2) using gaze will introduce an extra mental load due to the need to work across modalities during the task. We made no a priori predictions about subjective experience.

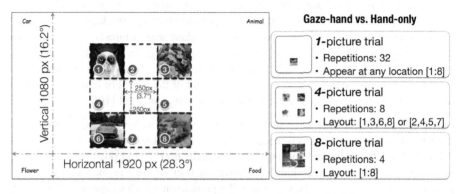

Fig. 1. User interface (left) and study design (right)

2.1   Task and Design

The photo-sorting task required repetitive selection followed by quick gesture commands on the selected items (see Fig. 1). The participants' task was to classify displayed photos into four categories labeled in diagonal corners (animal, car, flower and food), as accurately and as quickly as possible.

We used a 2 × 3 within-subjects design for factors *technique {gaze-hand, hand-only}* and *number of pictures presented {1, 4, 8}* at a time (Fig. 1). We varied the number of pictures presented in any trial reasoning that this might emphasize any differences between the two techniques: selecting amongst 8 possible targets instead of focusing on one at a time might show bigger advantages for the gaze-hand condition, for example.

In total, each session required a subject sorting 192 pictures, 96 for gaze-hand and 96 for hand-only. The order of presentation of the *technique* was counterbalanced and the order of the *number of pictures presented* was randomized among three blocks. Each block consisted of sorting 32 pictures displayed one, four or eight at a time.

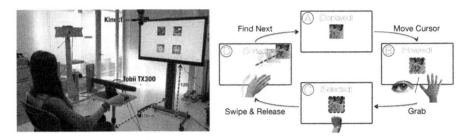

Fig. 2. Our setup: a user sat in front of a large screen using a combination of gaze and hand gestures for photo sorting. After acquiring a photo by either gaze or hand (B), users grabbed (C) and swiped it to diagonal directions (D).

2.2   Setup and Procedure

Participants and Apparatus. We recruited 15 participants (5 female), with a mean age of 26.7 years (SD = 4.5), who had little experience with eye tracking or motion and hand tracking applications. Participants sat on a chair with armrests at a distance of 2.4 m in front of a 55-inch (121 cm × 68.5 cm) display (Fig. 2). To capture gaze input, we used a Tobii TX300 at a sampling rate of 60 Hz. We positioned a Kinect sensor at a height of 1.8 m above the ground and 1.5 m in front of the user. For hand tracking, we used a fast random forest-based hand state classification method [10].

Procedure. After practicing the first technique encountered for approximately 5 min, participants were randomly presented with a set of 32 pictures, either 1, 4 or 8 pictures at a time (Fig. 2(A)). In the hand-only condition, the user's hand position was mapped to a screen cursor; in the gaze-hand condition, the user's gaze was mapped to a screen cursor for selection instead. To confirm to the participant which image was about to be selected, the cursor-overlaid image was highlighted with a gray border after 150 ms (this is the "hover state", Fig. 2(B)). Thereafter, in both conditions, the user confirmed the selection by a hand grab gesture, indicated by the border color switching from gray to black ("select state", Fig. 2(C)). (Note that we deliberately decided against using gaze dwell time to confirm selection. Short dwell durations can induce the "Midas Touch" problem [2, 5, 11] where users can easily mis-select items when they only intend to look at an image, while long dwell durations can yield lower task performance and user satisfaction, as they are slow and disruptive.) The user then sorted the photo (in both conditions) by swiping their hand diagonally (Fig. 2(D)). We used four diagonal hand swipe directions to assign categories. Once a swipe was detected, the photo flew to one of the screen corners with swoosh sound effect.

Participants filled out a questionnaire after each technique was completed. During the study, participants were allowed to take a short break after each experiment block. At the end of the entire session, we also conducted interviews to collect feedback. Each session lasted for approximately 1 h.

Dependent Variables. We logged three variables (Fig. 2): **T** the overall selection time, defined as the time between states A to C for single picture trials and from D to C for multiple picture trials; The time **T** can be further divided into: T_1 the time from initial movement of the cursor, starting from picture being presented to confirmation of the hover state, and T_2 the time between hover confirmation and selection using the grab gesture (B to C). Swipe time (from C to D) was assumed, and was indeed found to be, similar across conditions. In addition, sorting errors were logged.

3   Results

3.1   Overall Selection Time (T) per Picture

The time to select a picture was faster with gaze-hand than hand-only (shown by a significant main effect of technique on T, $F_{1,14} = 32.4$, $p < 0.0001$), being on average 0.33 s faster per picture (Fig. 3(A)). There was also a significant main effect of the number of pictures on T ($F_{1.3,18.25} = 28.8$, $p < 0.0001$), with the overall selection time increasing as the number of pictures increased. There was no interaction between technique and number of pictures on T ($F_{2,28} = 0.346$, $p = 0.71$).

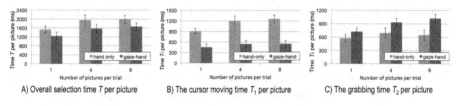

Fig. 3. Different average performance time for each technique and number of pictures presented at a time (mean ± 95 % CI).

3.2   Cursor Moving Time (T₁) and Grabbing Time (T₂) per Picture

Despite the overall difference in T or selection time, it is more instructive to break this down into two components.

Time to move the cursor to a hover state (T_1) was significantly faster (by on average 0.61 s) with gaze-hand than with hand-only ($F_{1,14} = 308.9$, $p < 0.0001$). There was also a significant main effect of the number of pictures on T_1 ($F_{1.39,19.39} = 14.18$, $p < 0.001$) but as Fig. 3(B) shows, there was also a significant interaction between technique and number of pictures ($F_{2,28} = 5.99$, $p < 0.01$) which suggests this effect is due an increase in T_1 as the number of pictures increased in the hand-only technique.

When we look at T_2, the time from hover to select, we see a very different story. Here the hand-only technique was faster than gaze-hand ($F_{1,14} = 47.33$, $p < 0.0001$), being on average 0.25 s faster per picture (Fig. 3(C)). Number of pictures again gives rise to a main effect ($F_{2,28} = 21.87$, $p < 0.0001$) but again it is made more difficult to interpret due to a significant technique by number of pictures interaction ($F_{2,28} = 6.06$, $p < 0.01$). This indicates that this time it is the gaze-hand condition that accounts for this increase and not the hand-only condition.

3.3   Sorting Accuracy and Error Analysis

We analyzed the sorting accuracy per block ($N = 32$) (see Table 1). The success rate is generally high for all trials. Error analysis revealed that users made significantly more mistakes in the 8-picture trials in the gaze-hand condition than hand-only ($t(14) = 2.902$, $p < 0.012$).

Table 1. Average sorting accuracy (mean ± std) of the 15 participants made for each block.

	Gaze-hand	Hand-only	Paired samples t-test
One	92.1 % ± 6.0 %	93.3 % ± 3.9 %	$t(14) = 1.000$, $p = .334$
Four	91.7 % ± 5.7 %	93.3 % ± 4.1 %	$t(14) = 1.035$, $p = .318$
Eight	90.0 % ± 7.4 %	95.4 % ± 3.1 %	$t(14) = 2.902$, $p = .012$

There were many kinds of errors. Most were incorrectly sorted images due to swiping in the wrong direction (categorization errors). Some were due to the way the system was configured, or the peculiarities of the interaction. For example, this included triggering a swipe response when returning the hand to the resting position or not completely releasing a grabbed picture.

However, the lower accuracy in the 8-picture condition of the gaze-hand technique is probably explained by difficulty in coordinating gaze and gesture. For example, in the 4- and 8-picture trials, participants occasionally performed a swipe as their eyes prematurely moved ahead to the next image - the eyes "jumping the gun" before the hand had finished its work, which is similar to the synchronization problem identified in prior work [11]. Further, the logged gaze data revealed that neighboring pictures in the gaze-hand condition, largely in 8-picture trials, distracted some participants. During selection, their gaze shifted between the selected and the adjacent image, resulting in incorrectly sorting the wrong object. Participants' feedback in post-task interviews suggested that both of these kinds of errors occurred when they tried to speed up their performance, which in turn caused them to slow down to be more careful.

3.4 User Experience and Preferences

The questionnaire data indicate only two significant differences across techniques. First, hand fatigue was rated significantly higher with the hand-only technique than gaze-hand ($Z = -2.751$, $p < 0.01$). Most participants (10/15) commented on this. For example, one said, *"holding the arm high in mid-air is tiring"* and *"[with gaze] I could rest my hand and use my hand only for sorting"*.

Second, participants felt that the hand-only technique was easier to learn than the gaze-hand technique ($Z = -2.309$, $p < 0.05$). Though participants were positive about the combination of gaze for selection and hand for grasping and throwing, they felt the gaze-hand combination was something that required time to get used to. Despite this, when we tested for learning effects over trials, we found no evidence of differences between gaze-hand and hand-only techniques.

Finally, participants rated which technique they preferred and the perceived speed and accuracy in the sorting task (Fig. 4). Thirteen users preferred the gaze-hand technique: although they found both techniques *"intuitive"*, some felt that the gaze-hand technique was *"less demanding"* (4/15) and *"easier to use"* (10/15), primarily due to less physical fatigue and fast and accurate gaze selection.

Further explanation for this can be found in the interview data. For example, one participant said, *"I am pretty confident with the gaze to select pictures, as what I looked at was what I wanted to select"*. In contrast, users felt that positioning the cursor on top of a picture using the hand was trickier, as it required constant checking and it was difficult to control the cursor accurately on a 2D screen while moving their hands freely in 3D space.

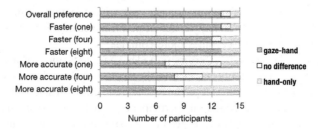

Fig. 4. Participants' technique preference, perceived speed, and accuracy in sorting as rated at the end of the experiment.

4 Discussion

4.1 The Benefits of Combining Gaze and Hand Gestures

Our results show improvements in both speed and user experience when we add gaze to hand gesture input in this remote interaction task. Previous work showed that gaze is faster than the hand for pointing and positioning a single target [8]. Our study expands on this showing that the speed advantage of gaze persists when used for target selection and when combined with gesture in a single technique. More than this, it persists in the context of multiple targets and indeed becomes more pronounced as the number of targets increases. This was shown in our analysis of T_1, the time to move the cursor, which increased significantly for the hand-only technique with more targets, but which did not increase when gaze directed the movement of the cursor. This explains the overall speed advantage for the task of image selection.

The majority of participants also perceived the gaze-hand technique as faster than hand-only, and users' subjective feedback further confirmed the fact that gaze complements gestural interaction when it comes to indicating objects of interest on a large screen. Here, users explained that hand gestures alone were slow, tiring, and inaccurate compared to incorporating gaze into the technique.

Taken together, this suggests that the combination of gaze and hand gestures is particularly well suited for applications that involve repetitive manipulation of multiple objects. Here, gaze selection can be both faster and reduce hand fatigue, especially when the task requires frequent pointing. Of course, arm fatigue could be even further reduced by attending to the ergonomics of the hand gestures too, such as designing them to require minimal effort, providing arm support and so on.

4.2   The Costs of Combining Gaze and Hand Gestures

Although participants indicated that they preferred the gaze-hand condition and reported little trouble with eye-hand coordination, the performance data (T_2) shows that it actually took longer to switch from gaze-hover to hand-select, than it did to transition from hand-hover to hand-select. Further, this effect was made worse as the number of targets to choose from increased. This may be because multiple targets increased visual distraction, delaying the ability for participants to confirm that the hovered object was indeed the intended target. This was not the case with selection within modality. In other words, there is a cross-modality speed of performance cost here, which may only be amplified as the interface becomes more complex.

Added to this, the analysis of errors provides some indication of accuracy issues induced by the mixed modality interaction. Sometimes it was clear that participants were visually distracted by adjacent pictures, leading to errors in selection. Other times, especially in the 8-picture condition, participants sometimes moved their gaze too quickly in advance of completing a gesture, causing errors. Participants were very aware of these synchronization errors and said that this was further amplified when they wanted to be fast. In other words, while gaze was often a fast way to reach the next target, the cost was that users had to wait for the hand to finish the previous manipulation. Solving this problem through good design starts by recognizing this problem.

Participants' feedback also suggests that working across modality was more difficult to learn than the single modality technique. While we might expect that these cross-modality costs would disappear with practice, we found no obvious learning effects during the course of the study. It may be that longer-term use is needed to investigate these aspects.

However, it is notable that despite the costs we outline above, participants said that overall they preferred the gaze-hand technique and expected it would be *"more productive"* in the long run. So clearly, these judgments are weighing up the benefits against the costs we have highlighted.

5 Conclusion

In this paper, we investigated both the costs and benefits of combining gaze and hand gestures for remote interaction. Our work contributes to a better understanding of how users perceive this input combination, and shows that gaze can complement free-hand gestural interfaces if the task is designed appropriately. Despite the costs, users mainly prefer the combination of gaze and gesture, but designers must take account of the kinds of errors that users can make and expect that such techniques may be initially perceived as more difficult to learn.

References

1. Vogel, D., Balakrishnan, R.: Distant freehand pointing and clicking on very large, high resolution displays. In: Proceedings of UIST 2005, pp. 33–42. ACM (2005)
2. Sibert, L.E., Jacob, R.J.K.: Evaluation of eye gaze interaction. In: Proceedings of CHI 2000, pp. 281–288. ACM (2000)
3. Zhai, S., Morimoto, C., Ihde, S.: Manual and gaze input cascaded (MAGIC) pointing. In: Proceedings of CHI 1999, pp. 246–253. ACM (1999)
4. Zhang, Y., Bulling, A., Gellersen, H.: SideWays: a gaze interface for spontaneous interaction with situated displays. In: Proceedings of CHI 2013, pp. 851–860. ACM (2013)
5. Stellmach, S., Dachselt, R.: Look and touch: gaze-supported target acquisition. In: Proceedings of CHI 2012, pp. 2981–2990. ACM (2012)
6. Turner, J., Alexander, J., Bulling, A., Schmidt, D., Gellersen, H.: Eye pull, eye push: moving objects between large screens and personal devices with gaze and touch. In: Kotzé, P., Marsden, G., Lindgaard, G., Wesson, J., Winckler, M. (eds.) INTERACT 2013, Part II. LNCS, vol. 8118, pp. 170–186. Springer, Heidelberg (2013)
7. Pelz, J., Hayhoe, M., Loeber, R.: The coordination of eye, head, and hand movements in a natural task. Exp. Brain Res. **139**, 266–277 (2001)
8. Kosunen, I., Jylha, A., Ahmed, I., An, C., Chech, L., Gamberini, L., Cavazza, M., Jacucci, G.: Comparing eye and gesture pointing to drag items on large screens. In: Proceedings of ITS 2013, pp. 425–428. ACM (2013)
9. Yoo, B., Han, J-J., Choi, C., Yi, K., Suh, S., Park, D., Kim, C.: 3D user interface combining gaze and hand gestures for large-scale display. In: Proceedings of EA CHI 2010, pp. 3709–3714. ACM (2010)
10. Keskin, C., Kıraç, F., Kara, Y.E., Akarun, L.: Hand pose estimation and hand shape classification using multi-layered randomized decision forests. In: Fitzgibbon, A., Lazebnik, S., Perona, P., Sato, Y., Schmid, C. (eds.) ECCV 2012, Part VI. LNCS, vol. 7577, pp. 852–863. Springer, Heidelberg (2012)
11. Kumar, M., Paepcke, A., Winograd, T.: EyePoint: practical pointing and selection using gaze and keyboard. In: Proceedings of CHI 2007, pp. 421–430. ACM (2007)

Sharing Wishes on Public Displays: Using Technology to Create Social Places

Vinicius Ferreira[✉], Junia Anacleto, and Andre Bueno

Advanced Interaction Laboratory - LIA, Department of Computing,
Federal University of São Carlos – UFSCar, São Carlos, Brazil
{vinicius.ferreira,junia,andre.obueno}@dc.ufscar.br

Abstract. We present a public-display-and-mobile-based digital art installation named WishBoard that translates the essence of a chalk-and-wall based art installation called 'Before I Die' into a technological communal expression. Our studies show that public sharing of personal wishes leverage the connection inside a community, creating a feeling of neutral ground for gathering, giving a sense of third place independent of physical constrains, named thirdplaceness. The installation allows people to freely express their wishes, with certain personalization, and provides a public visualization of all shared wishes promoting face-to-face conversations. We conducted two deployments using our installation in a 'socially abandoned' space. Analyzing the shared wishes content and people's behavior when observing the wishes popping up on the public displays, we were able to notice the essential role that public displays combined to mobile devices interaction can play in creating a community meeting place when providing a way for self-expression.

Keywords: Self-expression · Socialization · ICT interactive installation · Art installation · Public display in social spaces · Wishboard · Thirdplaceness

1 Introduction

Expression of thoughts, preferences, and feelings is a common and habitual practice among human beings. This expression reveals people's internal attributes, such as preferences, beliefs, and values. In Western culture, self-expression is valued as a powerful sign of individual freedom in which involves projecting one's own thoughts and ideas into the world [21]. With the rise of social media, new possibilities of expression and communication are emerging. People can keep in touch with friends and family on-the-go through their mobile devices creating new social practices. However, supporting traditional social interaction (face-to-face) is still an important issue in order to support local communities and to avoid its fragmentation [7]. Community fragmentation is a problem that has been increasing due to urbanization and decline of places outside work or family-based communication contexts. Such places, described as third places, provide the feeling of inclusiveness and belonging to a community. Coffee shops, pubs, and squares are typical examples of third places. These places have an important role in promoting quality of life for individuals reinforcing in their regulars the sense of community [34]. According to Sarason [40], sense

© IFIP International Federation for Information Processing 2015
J. Abascal et al. (Eds.): INTERACT 2015, Part III, LNCS 9298, pp. 578–595, 2015.
DOI: 10.1007/978-3-319-22698-9_40

of community is "the perception of similarity to others, an acknowledged interdependence with others, a willingness to maintain this interdependence by giving to or doing for others what one expects from them, and the feeling that one is part of a larger dependable and stable structure". This sense has two dimensions: territorial and relation [29]. The territorial dimension has relation with the territory, shared space, and proximity. However, not all cases constitute a community, the relational dimension is also essential. The relational dimension includes factors of nature and quality of relationships.

In order to support such sense of community, we translated the essence of a chalk-and-wall based art installation called Before I Die [10] that promotes self-expression through public sharing into a mobile-device-and-public-display based art installation named WishBoard. This public sharing can leverage the feeling of a neutral ground for gathering and, consequently, a sense of third place independent of place constrains, defined as thirdplaceness and discussed in Sect. 3.

Several studies have used public displays and/or interactive art installations to design a space for self-expression and socialization. In these studies, they found that public displays and interactive art installations can foster civic engagement, place attachment and community awareness [10, 12, 17, 27, 28, 39]. Moreover, such spaces give people a place and a chance to expose their inner thoughts and feelings in order to express their individuality [7].

In this context, our goal was to understand if a digital art installation, called WishBoard, which allows self-expression, combining interaction between mobile devices and public displays, can support community awareness and thirdplaceness experience. This paper focus on the impact the system had on the sense of community by promoting thirdplaceness in a place that is not a third place, which it differs from others [12, 17, 29]. To address this, we conducted an empirical study at a workplace to investigate the experience in-the-wild and observe cultural trails in anonymous posts shared. As a result, we believe that public sharing represents a promising model for mobile social collaboration in promoting and reinforcing the sense of community.

2 Self-Expression Supporting the Sense of Community

According to Kiesler and Sakumura [20] when people express their thoughts, using words, they may feel more committed to their thoughts and bound by them. They explain that expressing involves aspects of selfhood. Furthermore, the self-perception theory [5] suggests that observing their actions and behaviors is a key way for people to be aware of their own internal states.

Designing tools for self-expression in public spaces has an important role for people in a community, remembering and celebrating their own culture [7]. This public authoring enriches the space by sharing local information, knowledge and experiences [23]. In order to improve people's engagement with their community, interactive public displays and public art installations are mechanisms widely used. Several studies show that public displays can promote place attachment, community awareness, co-located interactions and technology-supported relationships. In addition, public displays can foster face-to-face human interaction and encourage collaboration among community members [1, 10, 12, 17, 27, 28, 31, 39]. Furthermore, public art installations can give people the opportunity to express their individuality and aspirations with their community, improving or creating relationships between them [7]. Regarding to design tools for self-expression, several studies have focused on elements for self-representation in online environments [8, 27]. Although, more means to express this dynamic and innate nature of self-expressions in public spaces are essential.

In this context, we have used an interactive art installation that promotes self-expression in a community exploring the interaction between mobile devices and public displays. In addition, this installation creates a space for people to freely socialize supporting the sense of community belonging and thirdplaceness experience, beyond architectural and temporal restrictions.

3   Beyond Third Places

Third places are places where people gather and enjoy each other's company. Oldenburg [34] describes third places as a means of 'keeping in touch with reality' promoting intimate personal ties outside the home (first place) and workplace (second place). In order to be a third place, the place has to be a neutral ground where everyone is free to come and go, and also, welcome without caring about the individual's status in the society. There is lively conversation inside and it is easy to access. Moreover, there are regulars who shape and bring the place to life, attracting newcomers. The place has no extravagances and the mood inside is playful. Summarizing, it is a home away from home for their regulars [34]. Within these descriptions, ethnographic studies of virtual environments such as chat rooms, multi-user environments and bulletin board systems suggest those settings can often function as a third place [18, 42]. However, these virtual environments differ from third places in respect of the 'realness' of the interaction or dependence upon simulation [44]. According to Doheny-Farina [11], a third place cannot exist separate from a locality. For him, this occurs for the reason that a 'third place exists only in comparison to its neighborhoods, to local work, play and family life, to the institutions and formal rituals that encompass daily life'.

Perhaps as a reaction to the disappearance of third places in the physical world, people found in virtual environments their third place [1]. These virtual environments have provided opportunities for people with similar interest to meet both in cyberspace and in face-to-face fostering elements of third places [35]. Nevertheless, both public places (such as third places) and more private or exclusive places have importance in the personal and collective value of social capital [36]. Taking the absence of such informal public spaces, companies spread the idea that their stores are third places, e.g., Starbucks and Applebee's. Despite that, these companies fail to meet many aspects of third places and rarely do patrons engage others in lively, extended and informal interaction [19]. For Oldenburg [34], third places are about civic responsibility and localized community maintenance and revitalization. On the other hand, Starbucks prefers an interpretation of 'third-place-ness' restricted to customer satisfaction, not civics [46]. This interpretation of 'third-place-ness' involves a set of characteristics of a third place that are often at odds with the social needs of a third place. Considering the need for promoting the sense of being in a third place not limited to architectural constrains of a third place, we prefer the definition of thirdplaceness as the 'event' of achieving the third place's characteristics in a certain place and time.

Thirdplaceness is constructed and sustained through experiences and interactions with and in the place. The thirdplaceness experience can transform a place in a third place-like permanently or just for that period. For example, in a 'happy hour' can occur thirdplaceness giving people the temporary sense of being in a third place. In third places, thirdplaceness occurs very often maintaining and reinforcing in the community this sense of third place. Such places are democratic and accessible, allowing people to discuss politics, the last football game, or the next music festivals, strengthening the notion of community in those people. However, a room full of individuals talking is not a third place [34]. Thirdplaceness has been observed in ethnographic studies, describing that third places can have an emergent nature happening in spontaneous, sporadic and nomadic way, and even in unexpected places, e.g., in a sidewalk [9, 30].

Aiming at observing thirdplaceness supported by technology, we designed a technological art installation, called WishBoard [13], in a 'socially abandoned' space. WishBoard creates a favorable space for occurrence of the sense of being in a third place, independent of where and when, a thirdplaceness.

4   ICT for Self-Expression and Contemplation - WishBoard

WishBoard [13] is an interactive art project that invites people to share their individual aspirations with the community. The installation gives people a reason and an opportunity to express openly their thoughts and feelings in a public and common space. WishBoard offers a space for self-reflection, which differs it from similar works, for example, The Facebook Wall [4] as seen in Fig. 1a, and others, such as, CitySpeak [25], TextTales [3], and Discussions In Space (DIS) [41], that encourage civic engagement through the reflection about the community problems. WishBoard also differs from other installations, such as, "A Wall of Wishes" [43] and Wishing Wall [15] (see Fig. 1(b) and (c)) in the way of engaging people by asking them to complete a fixed prefix about their expectations for the future and presenting the wishes.

WishBoard translates the essence of Chang's installation [10], consisting of five screens presenting the sent wishes dynamically and the inspiration considered imaginary and dreams, as present in Fig. 2, leveraging discussions and socialization. Every time a wish is sent, WishBoard creates a typographic art animation displaying the wish on the screens. After that, the sentence 'flies through the clouds' and joins the other sent wishes giving a certain sense of community belonging.

Chang [10] built a public art installation in which people could reflect their aspirations for a life that has an end. The installation consists of a wall painted in black stenciled with a grid of the sentence "Before I die I want to...". Chang observed that the space, once abandoned, became a meeting point in the neighborhood, as shown in Fig. 3. Moreover, Before I Die affords people to socialize, collaborate, appropriate the space and use, share democratically the space, and express their feelings considering the finitude of life [10].

Fig. 1. Installations that promote self-expression: (a) The Facebook Wall [4], (b) "A Wall of Wishes" [43], and (c) Wishing Wall [15].

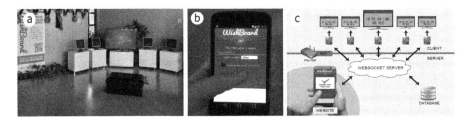

Fig. 2. (a) WishBoard installation, (b) mobile user interface, and (c) the system architecture. Users send an anonymous wish accessing the WishBoard website through their mobile devices. Once this wish is sent, the WishBoard system presents it with an animation on the screen using a WebSocket server to synchronize all screens and exploring the potential of HTML5 and CSS3.

Fig. 3. A Before I Die installation and people writing on the wall their wishes related to what they want to do before they die [10].

Translating the essence of an art installation needs to consider cultural issues and adaptations for the new context [13]. WishBoard has some adaptations maintaining the proposal of sharing in a public space, promoting individual reflection, supporting self-expression (without identification), and allowing variations (remixes) adapting to other contexts, as presented in Fig. 4.

Fig. 4. Comparing Before I Die and WishBoard in order to: a) write a message (chalk vs. phone); b) personalize the message (color chalk vs. color font); c) read messages (blackboard vs. public screen).

Before I Die [10] aims at contemplating death to make lives meaningful. On the other hand, WishBoard celebrates life reflecting about expectations for the future. WishBoard also has a keyword-based filter to unsuitable sentences due to the experience reported by Chang [10] about people writing bad things. Such corpus demands future analysis.

5 Study Design

Aiming at investigating the audience behavior, we carried out an in-the-wild study using the WishBoard installation in order to analyze collected messages comparing with the Before I Die installation. According to Rogers [37], this kind of study involves deploying new technologies in real-world conditions to observe the real-use of these technologies by people in their real context of use. We conducted this investigation dividing into two deployments using the WishBoard allowing us collect data from messages, spontaneous comments and video recordings filming both the users and the installation. Besides that, one observer was present, in a strategic place, taking field notes without disturbing the normal characteristics of the space. The advantage of using observations, taking notes and recording video, is that users behave most natural making the findings ecologically highly valid. On the other hand, a concern about the privacy of users is required.

In both deployments, we used the lobby of the Department of Computing at [*Federal University of São Carlos*], attracting passersby to interact with the installation. In addition, the installation was set following the model of central and peripheral attention [32] and observations done in our previous work. Furthermore, that space is a transitional and socially non-used space, as well as, the space in the first Before I Die installation. Taking the advantage of the festive spirit around the New Year, in the first deployment, we used the prefix 'For next year I want …'. And, in the second deployment, conducted in April, we adapted the prefix to 'For this year I want …'. In both deployments, the installation was available for five days.

In order to create an inviting place and to allow people to interact with the WishBoard, we provided a beanbag (giving a space to sit, talk, and send wishes) and information about how to interact with the installation, as presented in Fig. 5. Wireless signal was available for people to submit wishes accessing a website with a QR code or a tiny URL.

We have used the department' mailing list for informing people of the installation, collecting of data, presence of cameras, and the privacy policies. In addition, before posting a phrase, the system presented to user the ethical agreement on keeping the anonymity of senders and use the content for research only. Moreover, we did not request register information from the participants, e.g., name and email.

Fig. 5. People hanging out observing displayed wishes (a, b, c) and (d) using cellphone to interact with the WishBoard public display.

6 Behavior Discussion and Wishes Analysis and Cultural Findings

Aiming at observing the impact of the WishBoard deployments in supporting community awareness and thirdplaceness experience, we gather all collected data and we started an investigation of the audience behavior and also the content shared on the displays discussing our findings.

6.1 Understanding the Audience Behavior

In public space, the efforts in evaluation have been on identifying humans and clustering behaviors aiming at finding unusual behaviors that may help to model human interactions. Automated methods from computer vision as systems to track people sometimes can help in identifying people and audience behavior. However, uncontrolled environment and complicated scenes can decrease the accuracy of these systems [45]. In this work, we manually analyzed fifty hours of recording from both deployments, captured by two cameras, making annotations, coding, and then summarizing the results. Inter-rater reliability was substantial (Cohen's Kappa = 0.75) [24]. We observed the aspects described by Alt et al. [2] basing on a literature survey and their expertise on evaluating public displays installations. The aspects were audience behavior around the installation, effectiveness of the installation, social interaction among users, users' acceptance by engaging and inviting others, and people's concerns about their privacy. For each aspect, we observed some variables comparing the results with the reported in the Before I Die [10] discussing the findings.

Audience Behavior. In order to understand how people behave around the installation, we examined our annotations and then we reviewed the recording for a better comprehension. In WishBoard, we observed that users felt engaged in posting a message when they were in a group, about 68 % of the messages. Groups formed around the screens started a competition for the most creative message. We noticed many situations in which the audience around the installation progressively increased forming a sociable 'buzz' in the area, creating the Honey-pot effect [8]. Sometimes people stopped late and had to walk back trying to explore/understand more. This effect, known as Landing effect [33], occurred more often when there was no one in the installation or people were in a hurry noticing something different on site.

During the experiment and the analysis, we found in few moments people appropriating the installation. According to Salovaara et al. [38], appropriation refers to the creative ways in which people adapt and repurpose technologies to serve their own goals. In WishBoard installation, people subverted, in a few situations, the installation proposal by sending messages for the immediate present instead of future. For example, '*Para o próximo ano eu quero um café*' (In English: 'For next year I want a coffee'). People began to exchange messages to each other and to joke with each other, e.g. '*Para este ano eu quero que o Lucas realmente trabalhe*' (In English: 'For this year

I want that Lucas works really hard'). People sent emoticons and internet slang expressions, e.g., '*hauhauhau*' to express laughs, commonly used by Brazilians.

In the Before I Die, it was common people see drawings on the wall, such as, hearts, stars and rainbows. In addition, people wrote wishes for the present, e.g., in Berlin, a man wrote on the wall that he wanted to eat a strawberry cake and then immediately he entered in the nearest café [10].

These findings suggest that, in public spaces, installations must be prepared for the Honey-pot effect and the Landing effect. In addition, tools for self-expression need to allow appropriation of use, which may be a sign of new uses for the installation, reflecting the necessities of some users. Furthermore, allowing appropriation of use plays an essential role in designing tools for self-expression.

Display Effectiveness. Attracting attention with interactive installations is not easy. In public spaces, this is more challenging due many other objects strive for the user's attention [33]. Analyzing the footage, we observed if people looked at the installation, how many stopped and how long they stayed on site, and how many started interacting with the installation sending a message in front of the screens.

In the WishBoard installation, it was evident the passersby turning their head to the installation area attracted by the screens. Some people kept on walking looking at the displays and some people mentioned curiosity in testing the system. In the first deployment, about thirty percent of the passersby stayed in the installation and more than half of these people remained there for more than one minute [13]. In the second one, about one quarter of the passersby stayed in the installation and about sixty percent of these people remained there for more than one minute. We counted approximately 325 users sending messages in front of the screens.

According to Chang [10], with the first Before I Die wall, people paid closer attention to the abandoned house. People started to know more about the place, once forgotten, asking others what happened there and where the house's owners were living.

For achieving effectiveness, attractiveness plays an important role drawing audience attention and engaging them to use the installation, having correlation with to the chosen location for the deployment and the ease of access to the place. However, display effectiveness raises the question of whether the system is sustainable for gaining feedback from the public beyond the novelty factor of the technology.

Social Impact. Aiming at observing how an interactive installation could foster social interaction, we analyzed the video recordings and the annotations aiming at finding social experiences promoted by the installation.

Fig. 6. User greeting an acquaintance while he was using the installation.

In both deployments, people used the WishBoard space, never used before except to cross the hall, to gather, to introduce themselves, and to talk about their common interests. People democratically shared devices, the pouf and even the floor. The wishes leveraged discussions and sometimes laughs. For example, a group of professors began discussing the wishes shown on the displays and guessing who sent those wishes showing interest in knowing more about the community. We observed people experiencing unexpected encounters with their acquaintances as shown in Fig. 6. The place became a space for students, professors, employees and visitors to share playful conversations. For example, a group of students was asking the results of the exams for a professor and this professor answered sending a message for them saying to stop annoying him with the following sentence '*Para o próximo ano eu quero que os alunos me deixem em paz!!!*'(In English: 'For next year I want that the students leave me alone!!!').

Similarly, in Before I Die people began to use that space to introduce themselves. People started to talk about what they read on the wall and to laugh together.

Regarding to public displays, they can give people a chance to socialize taking the advantage of the Honey-pot effect [8]. Our findings support the notion of community, constructed and sustained through experiences and interactions with and in the place. Besides that, self-expression and information provided by these public displays leveraged discussions.

User Acceptance. Designing engaging systems, which make the users feel invited, interested and encouraged to interact, is very challenging. Engaging people to use continually the installation is still more difficult to achieve. These regulars are important shaping the "tone" of the place [34]. Reviewing the videos, we observed these regulars considering, in this work, as people who used the installation more than twice and also invited others to use it.

In the first deployment, we already had identified about seven regulars [13]. In the second deployment, we found four regulars. Figure 7 shows some of these regulars.

In several Before I Die installations, it was evident the presence of regulars [10]. Regulars bring the place to social life maintaining the playful mood [34].

Privacy Concerns. Regarding to privacy concerns, the wishers were anonymous, and we observed how people perceive privacy issues reviewing videos, annotations, audience comments.

In WishBoard, we noticed many situations in that people wanted to show their message to others, pointing to their message or even calling someone to see their

Fig. 7. Regulars using the WishBoard in different moments engaging other users in using it and starting a conversation about something shared on the screens in a process of socialization.

message. For example, a user called a girl friend who was passing by and sent the following phrase for her: 'For the next year I want < girl's name > finishing her PhD!!!'. She smiled and raised her hands celebrating, as shown in Fig. 8a. Some people took photo of the message, as present in Fig. 8b. In the comments from the audience, people said that they perceived that it was not possible to identify their anonymous wishes, making the use of the system comfortable for them. Nobody expressed any privacy concerns.

Similarly, in the Before I Die some people took photos in front of the installation and showed their message to others. Furthermore, some people reported that the anonymous nature of the contribution could allow shy people to express themselves [10]. This anonymous nature of wishes creates a neutral and leveler ground for all users without caring about the individual's status in community [34].

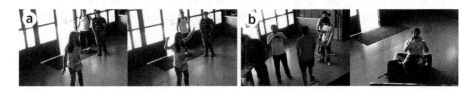

Fig. 8. (a) User celebrating a message sent for her and (b) users taking pictures of the messages.

6.2 Observing Thirdplaceness Supported by ICT

Several studies have been focusing on observing how ICT can support communities or socialization in third places [12, 17, 28]. According to Oldenburg [34], a real third place is a community-meeting place where the owner plays a key part in creating social connections by welcoming strangers and introducing them to the regulars. Such places are conversational zones where people can talk freely, openly, and entertain without care about their social status. In our study, we aimed at observing the occurrence of thirdplaceness in a place augmented by ICT that is not a third place. For this, we reviewed the videos, the annotations, and the comments listing our findings related to thirdplaceness for each characteristic of third places. In order to achieve thirdplaceness these characteristics are essentials:

- Neutral ground: People need to feel free to express their thoughts and opinions. Promoting tools for self-expression can support to achieve this feeling. Moreover, we observed in comments that the anonymity can comfort audience giving them a chance to express themselves.
- Leveler: People might have the same privileges and opportunities to express themselves or to participate of the activities in such place. Similarly as for neutral ground, anonymity can give the leveler awareness. This leveler awareness was present on the messages sent. Students, professors, employees and visitors used the installation sharing democratically their thoughts.
- Conversation: The experiences and interactions with and in the place can empower relationships and promote place attachment. We observed that ICTs can promote

activities among its users such as competitions, and provide information that can leverage discussions and conversations. Besides that, people had a chance to socialize taking the advantage of the Honey-pot effect [8].

- Accessibility and accommodation: The place needs to be easy to access and comfortable. In order to promote the feeling of fulfilled needs in the occupants, allowing appropriation of use plays an essential role. In the comments, people said the WishBoard was ease to use and accessible providing information and Wi-Fi signal allowing users to interact with it. Regarding to the few non-users of smartphones, we observed people sharing their devices and a tablet was available in the second deployment. After the installation, the department perceived the lack of accommodation and installed chairs around the department providing more comfort for all.
- Having regulars: Regulars bring the place to social life making newcomers welcomed and shaping the "tone" of a place. We noticed that themes or activities can also support to shape the "tone" [30], but people will appropriate the space according to their needs or possibilities.
- Low profile: The place needs to provide some comfort for their occupants, but this cannot be the main reference of the place. People are the main reference of a place that promotes thirdplaceness. We observed people sharing the space, the pouf and even the floor enjoying each other's company and having playful conversations.
- The mood is playful: The mood is not hostile and people always try to find ways to maintain their spirit high, even when few people want to bring this feeling down. In the WishBoard, people maintained a lively mood avoiding sharing unsuitable things. We also observed people very excited in seeing their messages on the screens, sharing smiles and laughs.
- A home away from home: People often have the relative feelings of warmth, possession, and belonging of being in their own homes. People can feel a piece of themselves is rooted in the space through their collaboration sharing a message shown on the screens.

Thirdplaceness is the 'event' of achieving these third place's characteristics in a certain place and time. Furthermore, this emergent nature transforms the concept of third place, making it independent of architectural constrains. This thirdplaceness experience can transform a place in a third place-like permanently or just for that period. However, in a third place will always occur thirdplaceness.

6.3   Finding Cultural Trails in Anonymous Posts

Hofstede et al. [16] defines culture as "the collective programming of the mind that distinguishes the member of one group or category of people from others". Several studies have been analyzed culture from data on the Web [14]. According to Garcia [14], making analysis of culture can benefit cultural social studies and the understanding on how culture affects user behavior giving insights to the designers. In addition, this analysis can model differences and similarities between cultures leading to serendipity by the discovery of unexpected data [14]. However, our work differs from those cultural researches due to restricted data.

We plan to analyze a set of phrases without related personal information (e.g., gender and age) or systematized correlations (e.g., replies). For that reason, we propose to conduct a language dependent analysis using: the classification used in the Before I Die, the Affective Norms for English Words, the Hofstede's cultural dimensions, and morphologic analysis. Our goal is to find cultural trails considering the 391 messages collected by WishBoard.

Classifying the Messages. Aiming at understanding the topics shared in the Wish-Board, we performed a classification. In our previous work [13], we classified the 244 messages collected in the first deployment into the themes presented in 'Before I Die, the book' [10]: helping others, love, well-being, celebrities, fame, family, religion, wealth, work, travel, outer space and sex. Moreover, we introduced three new themes: study, humor and politics. For each sentence, we classified in at least one of these themes. For sentences classified by the coders in different categories, we made decisions about the category chosen. In this work, we did the same for the second deployment comparing with Before I Die. In this analysis, we had a good inter-coder reliability (Cohen's Kappa = 0.61).

Our findings show that the both deployments had a similar pattern, suggesting their preferred topics. People discussed about ongoing Brazilian soccer championship, upcoming episodes of their favorite TV series and movies, their wishes for love, peace and success. Comparing the results of Before I Die with the WishBoard results there is also a similar pattern, as presented in Fig. 9.

Regarding to the sentences, there was a match between WishBoard and Before I Die. For example, people want to live intensely, lose weight, find a love, be rich and visit other countries. The mains topics discussed for each theme in the WishBoard were: (1) Love: find a love and declarations of love; (2) Well-being: things that make them happy (e.g., parties); (3) Celebrities: soccer, sayings, music lyrics, movies, and games; (4) Fame: be heard and have their wishes coming true; (5) Family: Friendship; (6) Wealth: be rich, win the lottery, and bought things; (7) Work: fewer meetings, bureaucracy, and scholarship; (8) Study: disciplines course, improving their grades, and getting a scholarship to study abroad; (9) Travel: travel more, visit other countries; (10) Sex: metaphors to reference women private parts; (11) Politics: be president and belong to some political party; (12) Humor: nonsense things and jokes. Analyzing the WishBoard messages inside the themes, the posts were casual, interesting, funny, poetic and sometimes heartbreaking. For example, in the well-being theme, people want more smiles, to live in a world without wars, to be a Jedi, to achieve nirvana and to fix everything wrong in his/her life.

Affective Analysis. In order to analyze the aspects of affectiveness, we adopt the correspondent Affective Norms for English Words (ANEW) for our language – Brazilian Portuguese. The Affective Norms for English Words (ANEW) consists of a set of 1034 words, including verbs, nouns, and adjectives, based on a tri-dimensional perspective of emotions (valence, arousal, and dominance) [22]. The Brazilian version of these norms, called ANEW-Br, provides affective norms only for valence (which ranges from pleasant to unpleasant) and arousal (which ranges from calm to excited) scales to judge the emotionality [22]. Aiming at analyzing the audience mood through their sent wishes, we used ANEW-BR to calculate the valence and the alert. For each

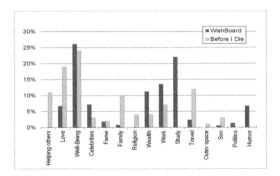

Fig. 9. Comparing the concentration of messages in WishBoard and Before I Die. Observing the graph, there is a higher expression about study, work and wealth in the WishBoard, what not happen with Before I Die. We believe that is because aspects related to the place context may lead people to think and talk more about related themes, in this case a workplace for some and study place for others. On the other side, there is a bigger concentration of phrases about love, travel, helping others, family and religion in the Before I Die, once it promotes a reflection about the end of life leading people to express religious values and feelings for family.

variable, we have used the average value. For the valence, this analysis consists in for each phrase we sum up all values of valence of words dividing it by the total number of occurrence of words. For example, in the phrase: '*Para este ano eu quero um bom emprego*' (in English: 'For this year I want a good job'). Excluding the prefix 'For this year I want' we found two valence instances: good (*bom*) and job (*emprego*). Their valence values are respectively 8.19 and 7.31. Summing the values of the valences of the words and dividing by the amount of occurrence of words in the text, which in this example was 2: (8.19 + 7.31) ÷ 2 = 7.75 that means use of positive words. In order to calculate the alert, we proceed in the same way, but using the values for alert. Furthermore, we normalized all sent messages correcting typos manually. This process of normalizing phrases, transforming text into a single canonical form, can be (semi-) automatic using a parser.

Considering the collected phrases, we found a higher occurrence of valence between 7.20 and 8.75, and a concentration of alert between 3.36 and 5.45, suggesting that people used positive words, as shown in Fig. 10. According to Kristensen et al. [22] positive words have the valence values higher than six and the alert values lower than five (V ≥ 6; A ≤ 5); negative words have the valence values lower than four and the alert values higher than five (4 > V < 6); neutral words have valence value between four and six (V ≤ 4; A > 5). Regarding to unsuitable sentences, people took care of the WishBoard installation maintaining its high spirits. In addition, we had only five blocked messages by being potentially offensive. In Before I Die installations, people also tried to maintain the mood of the installation by erasing bad things and filling with good things. These findings suggest that perhaps we need to explore ways to allow and to engage the community in managing their own messages in future work.

Individualism Cultural Dimension. In order to observe the Hofstede's cultural dimensions in the collected messages. We chose to measure the dimension of individualism of our audience due the restriction of our data. However, we still need to understand how to measure others dimensions with this set of data. For Hofstede et al. [16], individualism (IDV: high vs. low) can measure the level of integration into a group. Individualist societies (high IDV) represent loose ties between individuals basing on meritocracy and competition with other individuals. Collective (low IDV) societies represent individuals strongly integrated, extending sometimes the notion of family. However, the individualism dimension is not a dichotomous variable. This dimension ranges between 0 (lowest) and 100 (highest). For this work, we divided the dimension of individualism into four categories: collective, for a group of people, for other person, and individual. These categories ranges from low individualism to high individualism. For example, we classified 'For the next year I want more compassion among people' as collective and 'For the next year I want to be rich' as individual. For each sentence, we classified in at least one of those categories.

Analyzing the individualism in the collected phrases, we had an acceptable inter-coder reliability (Cohen's Kappa = 0.67). We found in the average that 60 % of the messages were for individual interests, followed by 12 % for other person, 18 % for a group of people, and 9 % for collective. These results indicate a prevalence of individualism in the messages. We believe this occurred due the proposal of the installations, which it was a self-reflection about their future filling the prefix 'For next year, I want …' or 'For this year, I want …'.

Morphologic Analysis. In this section, we discuss a form of morphologic analysis that can be performed (semi-) automatically using a Part Of Speech Tagger (POS-Tagger). This analysis has an objective of creating clusters for further interpretation. Aiming at analyzing tendencies in the messages, we used the PALAVRAS parser [6] for Portuguese on the collected messages with the typos already corrected. After that, we created clusters with the adjectives found in the results. Observing the clusters formed, we found that, in both deployments, about 20 % of the messages had superlative and comparative adjectives, predominating 'more' and 'better' words. Interestingly, in a manual analysis, we found that 24 % of the messages had metaphors. Optimistic words

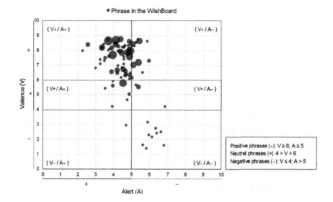

Fig. 10. Concentration of phrases in the WishBoard regarding to their valence and alert. The higher concentration of phrases on the top-left area indicates bigger number of positive phrases.

such as more and better can be related with the proximity and the start of a new year which it makes people thinking positively and optimistically. In addition, Brazilians are known by their playful nature and easygoing personality, what can justify the large number of statements related to metaphors, jokes, music and poetry.

7   Conclusion

In this paper, we demonstrate the relevance of supporting self-expression in public spaces through an interactive art installation, entitled WishBoard, at a workplace. This installation creates an environment to people express their thoughts, feelings, and aspirations. During the deployments, people shared the environment, once socially forgotten, using to discuss various topics and enjoying each other's company. The installation gave people a chance to socialize taking the advantage of the Honey-pot effect and provided information that leveraged conversations reinforcing their notion of community. Our study found that, by allowing this expression, offers the neutral ground to people express freely their individuality. In addition, we showed the importance of allowing appropriation of use in self-expression. In order to verify cultural trails in anonymous messages, we described a model to categorize, to analyze emotion related information, to verify the level of individualism in Hofstede's cultural dimensions, and to realize a morphologic analysis. Overall, it validates our previous work [13] reinforcing the essential role that public displays and mobile devices can play in providing an accessible mean for people express their individuality.

As part of our future work, we hope to extend our evaluation methods exploring the potential of quantitative methods developed from the field of psychology, such as the "Sense of Community Index" [26]. Furthermore, we also hope to explore this technology intervention to support a sense of community in further different settings.

Acknowledgments. We thank all the participants and our sponsors Boeing, FAPESP and CAPES.

References

1. Agren, P.O.: Virtual community life: a disappearance to third places for social capital. In: Proceedings of the 20th Information Systems Research Seminar in Scandinavia (IRIS 20) "Social Informatics", pp. 683–694. Department of Informatics, University of Oslo, Oslo (1997)
2. Alt, F., Schneegaß, S., Schmidt, A., Müller, J., Memarovic, N.: How to evaluate public displays. In: Proceedings of the ACM International Symposium on Pervasive Displays 2012, p. 17. ACM (2012)
3. Ananny, M., Strohecker, C.: TexTales: creating interactive forums with urban publics. In: Handbook of Research on Urban Informatics: The Practice and Promise of the Real-Time City, IGI Global, Hershey, PA (2009)

4. Bahr, E.: Why internet companies are linked to some of the happiest employees and customers (2013). http://www.electronicproducts.com/Computer_Peripherals/Systems/Why_Internet_companies_are_linked_to_some_of_the_happiest_employees_and_customers.aspx

5. Bem, D.J.: Self-perception theory. In: Berkowitz, L. (ed.) Advances in Experimental Social Psychology, vol. 6, pp. 1–62. Academic Press, New York (1972)

6. Bick, E.: PALAVRAS: a Constraint Grammar-Based Parsing System for Portuguese. In: Beber Sardinha, T., São Bento Ferreira, T. (eds.) Working with Portuguese Corpora. Bloomsbury, London (2014)

7. Brenny, S., Hu, J.: Social connectedness and inclusion by digital augmentation in public spaces. In: 8th International Conference on Design and Semantics of Form and Movement (DeSForM 2013), pp. 108–118, Philips, Wuxi (2013)

8. Brignull, H., Rogers, Y.: Enticing people to interact with large public displays in public spaces. In: Proceedings of the IFIP International Conference on Human-Computer Interaction (Interact 2003). IOS Press (2003)

9. Calderon, R., Fels, S., de Oliveira, J., Anacleto, J.: Understanding NUI-supported nomadic social places in a Brazilian health care facility. In: Proceedings of the 11th Brazilian Symposium on Human Factors in Computing Systems, Brazilian Computer Society, pp. 76–84 (2012)

10. Chang, C.: Before I Die. St. Martins Griffin, London (2013)

11. Doheny-Farina, S.: The Wired Neighborhood. Yale University Press, New Haven (1998)

12. Farnham, S.D., McCarthy, J.F., Patel, Y., Ahuja, S., Norman, D., Hazlewood, W.R., Lind, J.: Measuring the impact of third place attachment on the adoption of a place-based community technology. In: Proceedings of the ACM SIGCHI Conference on Human Factors in Computing Systems, pp. 2153–2156. ACM (2009)

13. Ferreira, V., Anacleto, J., Bueno, A.: Translating art installation into ICT: lessons learned from an experience at workspace. In: Proceedings of the 32nd ACM International Conference on The Design of Communication CD-ROM (SIGDOC), p. 11. ACM (2014)

14. Garcia, R.: On the quest of discovering cultural trails in social media. In: Proceedings of the 6th ACM International Conference on Web Search and Data Mining, pp. 747–752. ACM (2013)

15. Guljajeva, V., Canet, M.: Wishing wall (2014). http://devart.withgoogle.com/#/project/16494767

16. Hofstede, G., Hofstede, G.J., Minkov, M.: Cultures and Organizations: Software of the Mind: Intercultural Cooperation and Its Importance for Survival, 2nd edn. McGraw-Hill, New York (2004)

17. Hosio, S., Kukka, H., Riekki, J.: Social surroundings: bridging the virtual and physical divide. IEEE Multimedia 17(2), 26–33 (2010)

18. Kendall, L.: Hanging Out in the Virtual Pub: Masculinities and Relationships Online. University of California Press, Oakland (2002)

19. Khermouch, G., Veronsky, F.: Third places. Brandweek 36(11), 36–40 (1995)

20. Kiesler, C.A., Sakumura, J.: A test of a model of commitment. J. Pers. Soc. Psychol. 3, 349–353 (1966)

21. Kim, H.S., Sherman, D.K.: "Express yourself": culture and the effect of self-expression on choice. J. Pers. Soc. Psychol. 92, 1 (2007)

22. Kristensen, C.H., Gomes, C.F., Justo, A.R., Vieira, K.: Normas brasileiras para o affective norms for English words. Trends Psychiatry Psychother. 33, 135–146 (2011). http://dx.doi.org/10.1590/S2237-60892011000300003

23. Lane, G., Thelwall, S., Angus, A., Peckett, V., West, N.: Urban Tapestries: Public Authoring, Place and Mobility. Proboscis, Southampton (2005)

24. Landis, J.R., Koch, G.G.: The measurement of observer agreement for categorical data. Biometrics **33**(1), 159–174 (1977)
25. Lévesque, M., Bélanger, L., Lewis, J.. p2P: Cityspeak's reconfiguration of public media space. Wi. J. Mob. Digi. Comm. Net. **1**(1), 1–11 (2006)
26. Long, D.A., Perkins, D.D.: Confirmatory factor analysis of the sense of community index and development of a brief SCI. J. Commun. Psychol. **31**(3), 279–296 (2003)
27. Martin, K., Penn, A. Gavin, L.: Engaging with a situated display via picture messaging. In: Proceedings of CHI 2006 Extended Abstracts on Human Factors in Computing Systems, pp. 1079–1084. ACM Press, New York (2006)
28. McCarthy, J.F., Farnham, S.D., Patel, Y., Ahuja, S., Norman, D., Hazlewood, W.R., Lind, J.: Supporting community in third places with situated social software. In: Proceedings of the 4th International Conference on Communities and Technologies, pp. 225–234. ACM (2009)
29. McMillan, D.W., Chavis, D.M.: Sense of community: a definition and theory. J. Commun. Psychol. **14**(1), 6–23 (1986)
30. Memarovic, N., Fels, S., Anacleto, J., Calderon, R., Gobbo, F., Carroll, J.M.: Rethinking third places: contemporary design with technology. J. Commun. Inf. Special Issue on Urban Planning and Community Informatics (2014)
31. Memarovic, N., Langheinrich, M., Alt, F.: The interacting places framework: conceptualizing public display applications that promote community interaction and place awareness. In: Proceedings of the International Symposium on Pervasive Displays, p. 7. ACM, (2012)
32. Müller, J., Alt, F., Michelis, D., Schmidt, A.: Requirements and design space for interactive public displays. In: Proceedings of the International Conference on Multimedia, pp. 1285–1294. ACM (2010)
33. Müller, J., Walter, R., Bailly, G., Nischt, M., Alt, F.: Looking glass: a field study on noticing interactivity of a shop window. In: Proceedings of the ACM SIGCHI conference on Human Factors in Computing Systems, pp. 297–306. ACM (2012)
34. Oldenburg, R.: The Great Good Place: Cafes, Coffee Shops, Bookstores, Bars, Hair Salons, and Other Hangouts at the Heart of a Community. Marlowe, New York (1999)
35. Pasick, A.: More than love to be found on networking sites. Reuters (2004). http://usatoday30.usatoday.com/tech/webguide/internetlife/2004-02-25-online-networking_x.htm
36. Putnam, R.: Bowling Alone: The Collapse and Revival of American Community. Simon & Schuster, New York (2000)
37. Rogers, Y.: Interaction design gone wild: striving for wild theory. Interactions **18**(4), 58–62 (2011)
38. Salovaara, A., Höök, K., Cheverst, K., Twidale, M., Chalmers, M., Sas, C.: Appropriation and creative use: linking user studies and design. In: Proceedings of CHI 2011 Extended Abstracts on Human Factors in Computing Systems, pp. 37–40. ACM (2011)
39. Salvador, T., Sherry, J.W., Urrutia, A.E.: Less cyber, more cafe: enhancing existing small businesses across the digital divide with ICTs. IT for Development (2005)
40. Sarason, S.B.: The emergence of a conceptual center. J. Commun. Psychol. **14**(4), 405–407 (1986)
41. Schroeter, R.: Engaging new digital locals with interactive urban screens to collaboratively improve the city. In: Proceedings of the ACM 2012 Conference on Computer Supported Cooperative Work, pp. 227–236. ACM (2012)
42. Schuler, D.: New Community Networks Wired for Change. ACM Press/Addison-Wesley Publishing Co., Reading (1996)
43. The Highpoint Wishing Wall (2013). http://highpoint.com.au/Community/Wishing-Wall
44. Turkle, S.: Virtuality and its discontents: searching for community in cyberspace. The American Prospect, 24, 50–57 (1996)

45. Yan, W., David A.F.: Learning the behavior of users in a public space through video tracking. In: Application of Computer Vision, 2005, WACV/MOTIONS 2005, vol. 1, Seventh IEEE Workshops on vol. 1, pp. 370–377. IEEE (2005)
46. Walker, R.: Crossfire. The New York Times Magazine (2010). http://www.nytimes.com/2010/03/28/magazine/28FOB-consumed-t.html

Social Interaction Design Patterns for Urban Media Architecture

Luke Hespanhol[1]([⊠]) and Peter Dalsgaard[2]

[1] Design Lab, Faculty of Architecture, Design and Planning,
The University of Sydney, Sydney, NSW 2006, Australia
luke.hespanhol@sydney.edu.au
[2] CAVI and PIT, Aarhus University,
Helsingforsgade 14, 8200 Aarhus N, Denmark
dalsgaard@cavi.au.dk

Abstract. Media architecture has emerged as a relevant field of study within HCI since its inception at the turn of the century. While media architecture has the potential to radically affect the social space into which it is introduced, much research in the field was initially carried out through experimental installations in public spaces, often with higher emphasis on examining the properties of this novel type of interface, rather than examining the impact it had on the social context. In this paper, we look back at the field and analyze interactive urban media architecture covering a period of fifteen years of practice with a particular emphasis on how installations have influenced modes and patterns of social behaviour. We classify nine representative installations according to their physical layout, interaction strategies and types of interface. We focus on how these installations were perceived and used by their respective audiences and outline six modes of social interaction that unfold with these installations. From this analysis, we derive seven social interaction patterns, which represent different strategies for designing and employing media architecture to influence social interaction.

Keywords: Social interaction · Media architecture · Media façades · Urban HCI · Responsive environments · Proxemics

1 Introduction

Media architecture is an emergent field in the intersection of HCI, design, architecture, urban planning, art and sociology. While the use of media technologies in architecture has a long history – exemplified by the neon signs at Times Square in New York dating back to the 1920s – the field we know as media architecture emerged when designers and architects began to embed digital technologies, in particular displays, into the built environment. Decreasing prices of important media architecture components, such as display and sensor technologies, has led to uptake in industry, and it is now a prominent feature in many cities in the world. Simultaneously, the interest in media architecture has grown in the HCI community, and in addition to a dedicated conference series [17], media architecture research is represented at many HCI conferences,

J. Abascal et al. (Eds.): INTERACT 2015, Part III, LNCS 9298, pp. 596–613, 2015.
DOI: 10.1007/978-3-319-22698-9_41

including INTERACT. Typical of emergent disciplines related to HCI, the initial focus in many academic contributions was on technical aspects and the potentials of this novel form of interface. To the extent that social aspects of media architecture have been examined, it has primarily been in relation to specific installations. From these contributions, it is clear that social aspects play a very large role in how media architecture is perceived and used, and that interaction designers working in media architecture need an understanding of both technical and social dimensions to develop successful installations.

In this paper, we therefore offer an overview and analysis of social interaction in media architecture through a comparison of nine representative cases from the relatively brief history of the field. We combine the findings on social interaction from each original case study to offer two complementary contributions: firstly, a framework outlining six different modes of social interaction in relation to media architecture: *appreciation, self-expression, playfulness, collective narratives, triangulation,* and *negotiation of space*; secondly, a set of seven social interaction design patterns for media architecture, which represent different strategies for designing media architecture to achieve specific types of social interaction: *shadow playing, remote control, smooth operator, soapbox, amusement park, swarm,* and *automatic gate.*

The intended audience of the paper is HCI researchers working within the field of media architecture, who may employ the framework and design patterns, examine the relations between the technical and social aspects of media architecture and to categorise and analyse further installations. In addition, the social interaction design patterns may be of value for HCI practitioners, since they indicate specific strategies for developing media architecture installations.

2 Background: Social Interaction and Media Architecture

Goffman's seminal works in the dynamics of interaction in public spaces and the consequent impact on human social behaviour provide a suitable framework for analysis of urban interventions with media architecture. In *Relations in Public* [9], Goffman classifies agents in a social context as being either 'singles' (individuals by themselves) or in a 'with' (two or more individuals together). Such a configuration has direct implications on the relationship between the various individuals in a public space: for example, people generally feel more comfortable with approaching 'singles' than groups. Likewise, individuals in a 'with' relationship would behave differently than they would if they were singles in the same space.

The notion of *design patterns*, inspired by the work of Alexander [1], provides a frame for our analysis, which at the same time is directed towards applying insights in practice. Alexander's patterns for architecture were developed from studies of architectural practice and history, describing recurring configurations of the built environment that over the course of time had proven to have specific effects, such as courtyards as places that facilitate gatherings and social exchanges. Likewise, in the mid-90s, Gamma et al. [8] – the so-called *Gang Of Four (GoF)* – inspired by Alexander's work, adapted the concept of patterns to software engineering. By presenting a series of design patterns as reusable solutions for recurrent software development problems, their work underpinned the wide adoption of object-oriented programming and paved the way for greater reusability and scalability of computer systems. While the history of media architecture is much shorter, we can nevertheless begin to derive recurring patterns for social interaction. As in the works by Alexander and the GoF, these patterns can serve as strategies for designers of future media architecture installations.

Social aspects of media architecture have been addressed in many existing contributions; however, they have mainly addressed phenomena and design strategies in singular or few cases. For example, Dalsgaard and Halskov [6] propose that designers can work towards 'situational interaction flexibility' as a strategy for allowing people to ease in and out of specific social configurations around installations; however, this has not yet been replicated. Some social aspects discussed in the literature have started out as singular observations, and have since then been found to hold across different cases. The 'honeypot effect' [4], which proposes that the presence of people interacting with an installation will entice new users to start interacting to a higher degree than if nobody was using it, is one such aspect that has been observed in multiple cases. This is related to the observation by Mueller et al. [18] that many people notice the interactive potentials of a media architecture installation by observing other people interacting with it. Yet, an analysis of the recurring patterns of social interaction posed by media architecture design solutions is still lacking in the literature. Our approach in this paper has been to derive social interaction modes and patterns across a range of cases, with respect to common design variables such as layout of the public space and strategies for interaction and feedback. To the extent that existing literature corroborates our findings, we will discuss these in the relevant parts of the analysis.

3   Methodology

Our approach to analysing social interaction design patterns is based on a study of nine prominent examples of media architecture. We based the selection of works on two main design factors common to any responsive media architecture installation in public space: (a) the type of interface; and (b) the public space layout. We describe below each of those factors, the selection process and the steps taken in our analysis.

3.1   Types of Interfaces

Hespanhol and Tomitsch [12] argue that interactive behaviour around urban media architecture may emerge intuitively as a product of its level of accessibility and the type of feedback it offers, therefore leading to particular modes of social interaction. Analysing a variety of responsive public spaces, they propose a classification of interfaces into three types: performative, allotted and responsive ambient. *Performative* interfaces are defined as those where the interactive zones are well delimited, yet restricted to a small number of participants, resulting in a natural division of the public into 'performers' (active participants) and 'spectators' (passive participants). *Allotted* interfaces share the same basic characteristics as performative ones, however are large enough to accommodate a population of participants, so that each no longer has full visibility of the interface. Instead, participants operate locally on their own section of the interface, with interaction therefore distributed across the environment. The third category, *responsive ambient*, refers to urban interfaces which track and react to the presence of people, however offer indirect and generic feedback rather than responding to specific individuals.

We employ this classification in our analysis since it offers a framework for understanding how the design of media architecture may influence the social behaviours of the local public. To that end, we include in our analysis a selection of works that represent a balance of the different types of interfaces (see Table 1).

3.2 Types of Spatial Layouts

In categorising and analysing the spatial layouts, we employ two categories: (1) plaza, and (2) thoroughfare. These are based on the concepts of "spatial nodes" and "links" (respectively), as described in urban planning works such as Hillier & Hanson's *The Social Logic of Space* (1984) [13]. We define a *plaza* as a wide, open public space where a large number of citizens potentially congregate, facilitating social encounters as well as passive social practices as people watching or even loitering. A *thoroughfare*, by contrast, is a transit area connecting plazas, therefore characterized by the continuous flux of passers-by walking from one destination to another. In our selection, the plaza examples outweigh the thoroughfares; this is representative of the fact that media architecture is more often placed in such settings.

3.3 Selection of Case Studies

We adopted the large survey on media architecture by Haeusler et al. [11], as well as more recent literature, as departing points for our selection process. The former showcases 33 international contemporary media façades, while from the literature we singled out another 17 works, resulting on a total sample of 50 installations. From this sample, we made a selection based on the following criteria: the works should span from early examples of media architecture to newly launched works; they should range from small-scale installations to building-sized ones; they should represent a scope of uses from research experiments and artistic interventions over civic participation projects to commissioned works; they should employ a range of interaction technologies; and they should have different spatial layouts.

Within that framework, and to the extent possible, we gave preference to works we had the chance to visit in situ, either on their original setup (*Aarhus By Light* [6], *Solstice LAMP* [12], *Interference* [15], *The Climate on The Wall* [6] and *Chromapollination* [12]) or as a subsequent iteration (*SCSD* [2]), since those could offer us first hand access to evaluate the social interaction impact on their visitors. The selection of remaining works was largely determined by the availability in the literature of an in-depth account of their social interaction dynamics. Due to length constraints, we decided to include only three more representative works (*MyPosition* [22], *Body Movies* [16] and *iRiS* [3, 23]), limiting the number of case studies presented in this

Table 1. Media architecture installations.

Type of interface	Name	Location (Year)	Displaying technology	Interactive technology	Spatial layout	Interaction	Feedback
Performative	SCSD	Sao Paulo, Brazil (2013)	Hi-res LED façade	RFID card readers	Plaza	Console	Direct
	MyPosition	Berlin, Germany (2013)	Projections	IR cameras	Plaza	Full body	Direct
Performative/ Allotted	Aarhus by Light	Aarhus, Denmark (2008)	Hi-res LED façade	IR cameras	Plaza	Full body	Direct
	Body Movies	Rotterdam, Netherlands (2001)	Projections	Cameras	Plaza	Full body	Direct
Allotted	Solstice LAMP	Sydney, Australia (2013)	Projections	IR cameras	Plaza	Full body	Direct
	iRiS	Linz, Austria (2010)	Low-res LED façade	Smartphones	Plaza	Mobile	Direct
Allotted/ Responsive ambient	Interference	Kolding, Denmark (2014)	LED wall panels	IR sensors	Thoroughfare	Full body	Direct
	The Climate on The Wall	Aarhus, Denmark (2009)	Projections	Webcams	Thoroughfare	Full body	Delayed
Responsive ambient	Chromapollination	Sydney, Australia (2012)	LED mesh, fibre optics	Ultrasound motion sensors	Thoroughfare	Full body	Delayed

paper to nine. While it is important to acknowledge the limitations inherent to this selection process, we will argue that our analysis can provided the basis for further identification of social interaction patterns in urban media architecture. The balance between the different types of interfaces and spatial layouts adopted as selection criteria provides a representative sample of the works found both in the comprehensive field survey by Haeusler et al. [11] as well as in more recent literature.

3.4   Analytical Approach

We have examined the academic contributions describing each installation, the types of interfaces and spatial layouts that it represents and, to the extent that this is described in the literature, the designers' intentions with regards to affecting and/or shaping social interaction. That analysis led us to define six recurring modes of social interaction. By further observing the ways those have been recurrently combined across the selected works, we then identified seven distinct strategies, here labelled design patterns, commonly implemented in the installations to elicit intended modes of social interaction.

4   Case Studies

The goal of this section is to present a sample of previous and current works in the field (9 in total), illustrating various approaches to augmenting the urban environment. We describe each in regards to (1) the types of interfaces, interactive strategies and spatial layouts; and (2) how social interactions unfolded around it.

4.1   Smart Citizen Sentiment Dashboard (SCSD)

The *Smart Citizen Sentiment Dashboard* (SCSD) [2] introduced the notion of media architectural interfaces (MAIs), a design approach where a tangible user interface

(TUI), positioned on public space, functions as a mediator for people to interact with content in a media façade (the carrier). The TUI was an analogue console allowing users to select one of five discussion topics (environment, transport, safety, public space and housing), and use radio frequency identification (RFID) cards to select among three different moods: happy, indifferent or sad. RFID cards are used in many cities as digital tickets for the public transport system and building access, and thus constitute a familiar instrument for interaction with the urban realm; the design goal, therefore, was to opportunistically intervene in the social situation of people walking along a busy street for a brief civic poll.

SCSD was deployed in 2013 to the very large (3700 sqm.) media façade of a commercial building in the largest avenue of Sao Paulo, Brazil, running for three weeks. Due to the scale of the façade and the narrow available space in the sidewalk in front of it, the TUI was positioned across the avenue in a small square near the entrance to the local metro station. A variety of emerging behaviour by passers-by and participants could be observed. A large proportion (28 %) explored the interface playfully, expressing conflicting moods to the same topics. The majority (72 %) of participants, however, did express meaningful opinions. Awareness about the visualisations was also verified across the broader surrounding space, with a particular prevalence of people taking photos of the façade. According to the authors, however, given the small scale of the TUI compared to the high visibility of the façade, it was clear that most passers-by were unaware of the mechanisms of interaction or even the meaning of the façade graphics, rather enjoying them as visually appealing ambient art.

4.2 MyPosition

MyPosition [22] is a system designed for civic participation in public spaces. It consists of a polling interface back projected into a 5×2 m canvas, integrated to depth-cameras used to track passers-by. The interface displays a polling question at the top and graphics depicting a 4-point scale: '*strongly agree*', '*agree*', '*disagree*' and '*strongly disagree*'. Each section consists in a visualisation of the votes it has received, each vote displayed as a colourful tile. When a participant is detected in the area in front of the screen, the section corresponding to the position they occupy is animated to indicate preference. They can then vote by positioning themselves along the display in front of a desired section and raising their arms for 2s, during which a dwelling animation is displayed as feedback. Only one participant can interact with the system at any given time. After a vote is cast, a new tile is added to the chosen option. Three modalities of visual feedback are available: (1) identical tiles for all participants; (2) each tile with the participant silhouette; (3) each tile with the participant image captured by the cameras.

The system was deployed as a field study for a week in 2013, at the cafeteria foyer in a large university in Berlin, Germany. It revealed that the playfulness of the interface was not a hindrance to participation, with people interviewed stating they actually meant the answers they gave. Notably, when participants were identified (i.e. their votes were displayed as tiles containing their images) interaction events decreased and were more evenly distributed across the four options, which might be due to an increased accountability regarding the votes cast. In a broader sense, however, the authors' observed social interaction across the whole precinct, beyond the direct interaction zones: there was a considerable level of discussion, social learning and teaching as well as nudging among the public [22]. The display was not only noticed but also successfully promoted active discussion about the proposed topics.

4.3 Body Movies

Body Movies [16] is an interactive installation by artist Rafael Lozano-Hemmer. Large-scale portraits of people are projected onto an urban wall, blanked by strong white lights. As passers-by walk and position themselves in front of the lights, they cast their shadows onto the wall and reveal the images underneath.

Since its first inception in 2001 at the V2 Grounding, Rotterdam, The Netherlands, *Body Movies* has been exhibited multiple times worldwide. Social interaction generally emerges with ease, prompted by the familiarity of shadow playing – the work has famously attracted large crowds, with people readily congregating in front of the exhibition wall and moving around the space in order to cast shadows of different sizes. Notably, however, interaction through the shadow playing itself often becomes the greatest appeal of the work, as opposed to the unveiling of the underlying images, as per the artist's original concept [5]. Rather than detracting from the experience, such a spontaneous manifestation actually enriches it, not only by allowing individuals and small groups of friends to express themselves playfully in public, but also reportedly bridging the social gap between non-acquaintances. As it is typical of performative scenarios, interaction unfolds mainly in the area directly in front of the projections, via *triangulation* [19]: people communicating through their representations on the façade. Conversely, the spots along the periphery of the space turn into *comfort spaces* [7] where passive appreciation and social commentary can take place.

4.4 Aarhus By Light

Aarhus By Light [6] was an interactive media façade created in 2008 with 180 square meters of semi-transparent LED screen, distributed in a non-rectangular pattern behind the glass front wall of the Musikhuset in Aarhus, Denmark. The façade faced a public park where interactive zones were clearly identified by colourful mats placed on pathways leading to the venue. *Aarhus By Light* was one of the first public interfaces designed to support a "walk-up-and-use" experience, enabling full body interaction with a media façade via computer vision. It was designed so that passers-by in the park or going to the Musikhuset could quickly figure out the mechanisms of interaction by providing them with a clear and direct feedback in the shape of their silhouettes magnified and integrated with the visual graphics in the façade. When no person interacted with the installation, the façade displayed small, animated social creatures moving through it. When individuals were detected, the creatures would become aware of their presence, come closer to their silhouettes and start playing with them.

Social interaction unfolded seamlessly, with both individuals and groups interacting via their representations on the allotted façade. The work also managed to successfully address the various regions of proxemics around the venue: people walking along the streets around the park would become aware of the Musikhuset by observing both the animated façade and the crowd gathering in front of it; people in the park would engage both in active and passive interaction with the work, and those inside the venue could watch the animations in the façade from behind, highlighting the building itself as destination. The work successfully fulfilled its goal of transforming a whole urban precinct and the social dynamics around it with interactive technology.

4.5   Solstice LAMP

Solstice LAMP [12] was a large-scale interactive installation developed by the Design Lab, University of Sydney, Australia, for the 2013 edition of the local Vivid Sydney festival. The work was designed to reactivate a normally underused square facing a 100 m tall skyscraper in the centre of the city. It consisted of two sections: (1) two interactive rectangular zones in the building forecourt, delimited by projections on the floor; and (2) laser projections on the entire building façade, derived from the inter-action unfolding at the forecourt. Equipped with overhead depth-view cameras and data projectors, the installation tracked people within the interactive zones and projected halos around their bodies. If people got close enough, their halos would merge as a feedback to the fact they were then a single entity. During a period of one minute, each halo would become increasingly brighter and eventually pop, moving away from their hosts towards the building and then up towards the top of the building. At that point, a new interactive cycle would start at the forecourt. People could enter the interactive zones from all directions and the work would respond to as many participants as it could fit simultaneously, characterizing the interface as allotted [12].

Interaction with the work varied across demographics and different situations. The authors observed three main social interaction patterns: (1) children attracting adults; (2) tentative single 'exploration' versus expansive group 'performance'; (3) "body gloss". The first refer to the fact children would readily break into interaction upon reaching the environment, with many parents noticeably observing them 'trying' the environment before joining them in. The second points to the remarkable difference between the observed behaviour of individuals and that of groups engaging in inter-action: when the space was already full of other people by the time they start inter-acting, participants tended to demonstrate restrain and self-consciousness. However, when engaging with the work as part of a larger group of friends, they would try expansive movements like dancing, jumping or even running around. Finally, the third pattern was the amplification of what Goffman termed 'body gloss' [9], i.e. a visual reinforcement of personal space, here prompted by the projected graphics rather than emphatic body language: people not acquainted to each other would often apologise when their halos merged, even without any physical touch actually happening.

4.6   iRiS

iRiS [3, 23] is a system for remote interaction with a media façade via an application running on a smartphone, which allows participants to visualize the façade on their devices, superimposed with a user interface for drawing over the image. It identifies the colour selected by the user and the region of the image they are drawing over and turns the corresponding pixels in the façade accordingly. Multiple users can interact simultaneously with the façade, which is shared on a first-come, first-served basis.

The work was trialled at the Ars Electronica Festival 2010, in Linz, Austria, running at the exterior walls of the Ars Electronica Center. Evaluation conducted by the authors found that participants perceived the façade as (1) easy-to-learn, but also that (2) it might leave users unaware of the actions of others [3]. Concurrent users could see multiple actions unfolding on the screen, but were not always able to see who was responsible for them. Likewise, access to the interface was also sometimes denied to new users. The lack of social protocol for such an unfamiliar public space would often lead to user frustration when participants were not acquainted with each other.

4.7 Interference

Interference [15] is a permanent interactive installation by Danish company Kollision in a tunnel for pedestrians and bicycles under an avenue in Kolding, Denmark. Opened in 2014, it consists of colourful light panels installed along the walls of the underpass, equipped with a series of trip-wire infrared sensors. Passers-by are detected as they move, with the light panels in front of them turning on in response. The light effects follow the direction of their movement, progressively illuminating the way ahead. If many people occupy the tunnel at the same time, the same interaction pattern is applied simultaneously to each of them, resulting in a fleeting social interaction that amplifies their awareness of each other: if people are moving in the same direction, whoever is in front is "warned" about the presence of those coming behind; if they move in opposite directions, their light beams collide in anticipation of their physical encounter. The social experience of sharing the public space is thus highlighted by the mutual interference of the light patterns created by each individual.

4.8 The Climate on the Wall

The Climate on the Wall [6] was an installation conceived to be in operation during the climate conference Beyond Kyoto, in Aarhus, Denmark, in 2009. It consisted in a large projection on a wall of the Ridehuset, a prominent historical building in a busy intersection in the centre of the city. The projection would show falling speech bubbles containing terms employed in the ongoing climate debate. Dedicated software used cameras installed along the façade to detect people going through the sidewalk. They could then 'grab' a word, carry it along and reposition it on the wall, thus contributing to the climate debate by forming phrases expressing their views. The interface was perceived as playful and occasionally passers-by would stop by and interact with the projections. More often then not, however, implicit or inadvertent interaction [18] would take place: people would unwillingly engage in interaction just by walking passed the wall, with some noticing they had carried a speech bubble along with them only after it had already happened. The lack of proper grammar seemed to hinder the formation of coherent sentences but, most importantly, the best spot to observe the evolution of graphics on the screen was from the opposite side of the street – i.e., by people watching the façade, not those actually interacting with it. Despite the general awareness about climate debate sparked by the installation, the social conversation via the media façade seemed to have felt short of expected [6].

4.9   Chromapollination

Chromapollination [12] was a responsive ambient sculpture developed as an urban activation study by the Design Lab, University of Sydney, Australia, for the 2012 edition of the local Vivid Sydney festival. The public space was an underutilised thoroughfare beneath an elevated highway in the centre of the city. The installation consisted of three large-scale sculptures of beds of dandelion flowers, embedded with fibre optics and ultrasound motion detectors. Above, a triangular LED ceiling seamlessly connected the sculptures. As people walk through and around them, their movement was detected, creating 'digital wind' – a stream of light flowing overhead from one flower bed to another, carrying the colour of the source dandelion to be mixed with that of the target, which would then be 'pollinated' by changing colour. Responses to the detected movement were, by design, subdued and delayed, in order to avoid people interacting for too long and cluttering the public thoroughfare. Most commonly, couples or small groups of friends and families would stop for close appreciation and photos of themselves near the work, while 'singles' would usually observe and take photos or videos from a relative distance.

5   Analysis

From the juxtaposition of the key features of the nine installations summarised in Table 1, certain recurrent design strategies and resulting forms of social interaction can be identified. For example, most urban interventions designed for performance (e.g. *Body Movies*, *Aarhus By Light* or *Solstice LAMP*) are placed in urban spaces that can be characterized as plazas, while responsive ambient media architecture (such as *Interference* or *Chromapollination*) has been often used as a way to enhance the experience of thoroughfares. Likewise, full body interactions are clearly more effective to entice explicit and inadvertent interaction as a way to facilitate collective participation, leveraging from established norms of social behaviour in public spaces [18]. Allotted interfaces making use of full body interaction, in particular, reduce the social pressure and risk of embarrassment by allowing a larger number of people to perform simultaneously. In that sense, they can be considered as a less disrupting intervention on the dynamics of the social space, while still supporting both direct interaction among people and indirect interaction via triangulation [19] through the interfaces. Consoles (as used in *SCSD*) and mobile devices (as in *iRiS*) both constitute TUIs functioning as mediators to the interaction with the media architecture.

5.1   Social Interaction Modes

By comparing the installations and analysing how the social interaction unfolded around them, we propose that six modes of social interaction are present in the cases: (1) appreciation, (2) self-expression; (3) playfulness; (4) collective narratives; (5) triangulation; and (6) negotiation of space. These modes can be further grouped into three broader categories: appreciation and self-expression into *spectacle*; playfulness and collective narratives into *creativity*; triangulation and negotiation of space into *conversation*. Table 2 displays how each mode maps to the media architecture installations considered in our analysis. We discuss each of these categories below, and will later reference them to derive social interaction design patterns.

Spectacle. Creating spectacle is inherent to media architecture, especially when it is interactive. Just like street performers, media architecture disrupts the normal flow of urban activities, turning passers-by into spectators and, depending on its nature, active performers. Accordingly, we can consider two aspects of the spectacle offered by media architecture: *appreciation* (i.e. the passive spectatorship of the urban intervention) and *self-expression* (active interaction via performance or casting of votes, for example). As Table 2 indicates, although all works analysed prompted public appreciation, not all of them led to self-expression. Noticeability of the interaction zones is critical for active participation, particularly in regards to the spatial ratio between those zones and the media architecture. As pointed out by Fischer and Hornecker [7], for media façades the display space – i.e. the space around the façade where people can see it – is often much larger than the interactive zones, making it difficult for distant observers to perceive the interactive nature of the work. Installations such as *Body Movies*, *Aarhus By Light* and *MyPosition*, for example, successfully addressed this problem by positioning the interactive zones in prominent, wide and therefore very visible areas right in front of their façade. The interactive console used in *SCSD*, however, was much harder to be spotted amidst the busy urban environment of the large avenue in Sao Paulo. Equally important to making the interactive zone visible to potential participants, however, is to position it so that the feedback provided by the architecture can clearly communicate its intention: direct and uniquely addressed to an individual, if to convey agency and identity; or delayed and defused across the space if to communicate ambient response. While *MyPosition*, for example, was highly successful in its use of feedback to communicate interactivity to casual passers-by, guiding them through the various steps required for voting via the interface, *The Climate on the Wall*'s feedback was more visible to spectators on the other side of the street than to the actual (and often unaware) participants near the façade.

Embodied allotted interfaces, such as *Solstice LAMP* and *Interference*, offer a neat solution for both problems: they are wide enough to be noticed from a distance and, for having the interactive zone largely coinciding with the media architecture itself, they make the effects of participation obvious to participants. Moreover, at a closer distance, visibility is equally given to the environment *and* the people within it, highlighting their roles as agents over the immediate urban space. Such increased tangibility results in an additional benefit: learnability by demonstration. As pointed out by Mueller et al. [18],

Table 2. Social interaction modes mapped to the media architecture installations.

Type of interface	Name	Spatial layout	Interaction	Feedback	Spectacle — Appreciation/discussion	Spectacle — Self-expression	Creativity — Playfulness	Creativity — Collective narratives	Conversation — Triangulation	Conversation — Negotiation of space
Performative	SCSD	Plaza	Console	Direct	√	√				
Performative	MyPosition	Plaza	Full body	Direct	√	√				
Performative/ Allotted	Aarhus by Light	Plaza	Full body	Direct	√	√	√	√	√	
Performative/ Allotted	Body Movies	Plaza	Full body	Direct	√	√	√	√	√	
Allotted	Solstice LAMP	Plaza	Full body	Direct	√	√	√	√	√	√
Allotted	iRiS	Plaza	Mobile	Direct	√	√	√		√	
Allotted/Responsive ambient	Interference	Thoroughfare	Full body	Direct	√		√		√	√
Allotted/Responsive ambient	Climate on The Wall	Thoroughfare	Full body	Delayed	√		√			
Responsive ambient	Chromapollination	Thoroughfare	Full body	Delayed	√					

√ Aspect observed in the installation.

many people notice interactivity by observing other people interacting. Allotted interfaces, being able to accommodate a large number of simultaneous participants, are therefore highly effective in promoting social interaction, creating a positive feedback loop whereby many people interacting make even more people not only aware of the interaction but also able to readily join in. The shared interface also helps to reduce the fear of public embarrassment [21] that can potentially hinder participation by people less comfortable to perform in public.

Creativity. While media architecture can be subject to appreciation and lead to individual self-expression, it is not necessarily playful or able to accommodate simultaneous interaction by multiple agents. *SCSD* and *MyPosition* are examples of works intentionally designed to be predominantly functional (albeit enjoyable) and restricted to individual interaction. Interactive public art and urban activation projects (such as *Aarhus By Light, Solstice LAMP, Interference* and *Body Movies*), on the other hand, often rely on *playfulness* to subvert ordinary street practices. As Huizinga [14] pointed out, play is a cultural construct perceived as not "real" or "ordinary" life; it refers to activities that are intrinsically motivated, situated outside of everyday life and with no direct benefit or goal. By enabling a playful situation, interactive media architecture can achieve a relaxation of the established social norms, easing the constraints for social encounters to emerge. When the interface also allows for simultaneous interaction by multiple people, *collective narratives* may emerge out of the constraints and suspension of disbelief posed by the responsive environment, akin to what is observed in alternative or mixed reality games [20].

Conversation. As Goffman [10] pointed out, when faced with an unfamiliar social setting, people scan each other for clues about what the appropriate behaviour is. In the case of interactive public environments, unless the rules are explicitly stated via call to actions [22] they often end up emerging on the spot and collectively as people try to make sense of an otherwise unusual situation. This process of sensemaking often emerges among strangers as a consequence of *triangulation* [19], a social situation where conversation is started out of mutual interest in the content itself displayed by the interface. In that sense, allotted interfaces may have different results depending on how much visible participants are to each other: *iRiS*, although playful and enabling self-expression, was occasionally perceived as frustrating since participants could not always see physically who they were interacting with on the screen. In *Solstice LAMP* and *Interference*, on the other hand, participants were always on sight of each other and therefore *negotiation of space* unfolded according to established social norms. Technology, in those cases, supported and promoted social interaction through the mutual awareness of other people in the space.

5.2   Social Interaction Design Patterns

When compared with the interaction strategies and spatial layouts of the selected media architecture installations, the social interaction modes discussed above indicate a series of recurring strategies employed by the designers. We propose that those strategies can be characterised as *social interaction design patterns* for eliciting specific forms of crowd behaviour and, as a consequence, the social identity of the public space. In that sense, our proposed patterns are conceptually closely related to Alexander's pattern language for architecture [1] than to the software design patterns proposed by the GoF [8], consisting in reusable strategies to use digital media for designing the interaction among people and between them and their surrounding built environment. From Table 2, we derived the patterns by grouping either recurring layout factors (i.e. spatial layout, interaction strategy and type of feedback) or social interaction modes. We then named each pattern by using metaphors to familiar concepts that operate in a similar fashion, with corresponding social reactions.

Grouping recurring layout factors (Table 3, left) produced three patterns: (a) *Shadow Playing;* (b) *Remote Control*; and (c) *Smooth Operator*. Grouping the social interaction modes (Table 3, right) produced further four patterns: (a) *Soapbox*; (b) *Amusement Park*; (c) *Swarm*; and (d) *Automatic Gate*. Figure 1 summarises the proposed patterns, which can be construed as design strategies for prompting specific forms of social interaction. Below, we discuss each pattern and its effects on social interaction.

Shadow Playing. This pattern captures the recurrent combination of full-body interaction and direct feedback (Table 3, left). It prescribes the use of full body interaction and immediate visual feedback to create a 1-to-1 relationship between individuals and their graphical representation in the media architecture (as in *Body Movies*, *Aarhus By Light* and *Solstice LAMP*). Previous studies have found that *shadow playing* is an effective way to communicate interactivity to passers-by via inadvertent interaction, with mirror images, in particular, being more effective than silhouettes and avatars [18]. By minimizing noise and latency on the communication, the interface enables a high sense of agency and identity among participants, who feel like they are controlling the

Table 3. Patterns derived from layout factors (spatial layout, interaction and feedback), on the left, and social interaction modes (spectacle, creativity and conversation), on the right.

Type of interface	Name	Spatial layout	Interaction	Feedback	Spectacle		Creativity		Conversation	
					Appreciation/discussion	Self-expression	Playfulness	Collective narratives	Triangulation	Negotiation of space
Performative	SCSD	Plaza	Console	Direct						
	MyPosition	Plaza	Full body	Direct						
Performative/Allotted	Aarhus by Light	Plaza	Full body	Direct						
	Body Movies	Plaza	Full body	Direct						
Allotted	Solstice LAMP	Plaza	Full body	Direct						
	iRiS	Plaza	Mobile	Direct						
Allotted/Responsive ambient	Interference	Thoroughfare	Full body	Direct						
	Climate on The Wall	Thoroughfare	Full body	Delayed						
Responsive ambient	Chromapollination	Thoroughfare	Full body	Delayed						

Remote Control   Soapbox
Shadow Playing   Amusement Park
Smooth Operator   Swarm
Automatic Gate

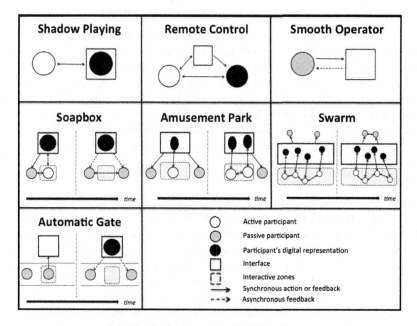

Fig. 1. Social interaction design patterns.

media content directly. Social interaction therefore unfolds both in the physical and digital environments simultaneously, via triangulation (and possibly negotiation of space) between individuals and their "projected selves". Apart from spectacle, this pattern often entails playfulness and enables the emergence of collective narratives, with multiple rows of participants tending to form around the interactive zones [18]. For that reason, this pattern typically requires a plaza spatial layout, so that multiple participants can be accommodated, allowed to move freely and have good visibility of their digital representations on the media architecture.

Remote Control. In this pattern, a tangible user interface (TUI) is employed as a mediator between the public and the media architecture [2], usually in a plaza spatial layout (for the same reasons as *Shadow Playing*). Two opposite design strategies have traditionally been adopted: centralised remote controls (such as the console used in *SCSD*) or distributed portable devices (often mobile devices, as in *iRiS*). In both cases, discoverability about the interactive aspects of the architecture becomes a recurrent challenge: how to easily communicate to the public they can use smartphones to interact with the content on the façade, or indicate the existence and location of a mediating console? Both scenarios also pose trade-offs for the design. Interaction via mobile devices allows simultaneous participation, but negotiating time on the interface may be problematic; moreover, it is usually pre-empted by the system itself rather than a result of a tacit social agreement between the participants – who, by the way, often cannot see each other. Interaction via a centralised TUI, on the other hand, solves such an accessibility problem, however eliminates the possibility of more elaborate social interaction to unfold via triangulation with the media architecture.

Smooth Operator. This pattern describes the delayed feedback to full-body tracking unfolding in a thoroughfare, responding to movements of passers-by in a covert way (Table 3, left). While affected by the presence of passers-by, a *smooth operator* does not respond direct to them, and therefore is perceived as an independent entity, not controlled by the public (or at least not entirely). Typically, its responses to inputs from the public is delayed and, often, not in their field of view (e.g. the landing effect [18] verified in *Chromapollination* and *The Climate on the Wall*). Smooth operators are normally designed for thoroughfares and regions of intense pedestrian traffic, raising awareness about the public urban space yet without compromising the flow of people through it.

Soapbox. As shown in Table 3, right, this pattern represents installations enticing predominantly individual expression and its appreciation, but with little playfulness, collective narratives or direct social conversation. Its goal is to offer an opportunistic encounter whereby citizens can informally express their opinions about a local topic without too much disruption to their daily activities. Public consultation can therefore happen in a lightweight yet regular basis, providing local government with invaluable feedback without excessive interference on the social dynamics of the community. As such, soapboxes tend to be designed for quick but reliable individual interaction, and seem to be more effective when ludic elements are downplayed – in other words, they benefit from a lack of playfulness, increasing the focus on their actual functionality. Yet, as in any interface, user experience should be taken into account. For example, according to the designers of *MyPosition* the interface was deliberately designed to create a good balance between playful interaction and meaningful participation. The goal was to enable incidental interaction leading to an enjoyable voting experience, yet avoiding the inadvertent interaction observed in *The Climate on the Wall* [22].

Amusement Park. The *amusement park* is an urban media architecture installation that promotes a wide array of social interaction, reaching out to all three proposed domains: spectacle, creativity and conversation (Table 3, right). On those settings, there is not only individual self-expression and its appreciation by bystanders, but also collective play leading to co-created narratives, mediated via triangulation with the media architecture and, occasionally (as it is the case of embodied allotted interfaces, such as *Solstice LAMP*), negotiation of the physical space during the experience. It is characterized for being a disruptive urban intervention that captures the attention of passers-by and turns some of them into performers, while others participate passively as spectators. As a playful environment, it entices suspension of disbelief and, consequently, subversion of pre-established social norms, with new ones defined on the spot as a result of the social interaction itself. Performative and allotted interfaces are the most effective choices for designing *amusement parks*.

Swarm. This pattern refers to environments where people interact via triangulation with the architecture, negotiating the physical space in the process (Table 3, right). A *swarm* is an allotted interface built upon full body interaction. Generally deployed to plazas, it consists in an interface large enough to accommodate many simultaneous participants, each involved in embodied interaction with their own section of the interface. Feedback is such that participants are continuously aware of both their own representation on the interface and those of the peers in their immediate vicinity. Consequently, local actions of one individual may imply in reactions by their immediate neighbours, which will then somehow impact their own neighbours, in a process resembling a swarm of insects or school of fishes. Works like *Solstice LAMP* and *Interference* are good examples of swarms, successfully assisting the autonomous negotiation of space by participants by making use of technology to create 'body gloss' [9] (i.e. the emphasis and exaggeration of bodily presence). In addition, the social relationships among participants may also be highlighted by the feedback they receive. For instance, *Solstice LAMP*'s feedback mechanism of merging halos when people got close enough to each other indicated the transition between a state where people were perceived by the environment as separate individuals (or 'singles', as defined by Goffman [9]) to a scenario where they could be socially characterized as a group (in a 'with'). As observed, people would often adjust their behaviour as a result of the new social configuration.

Automatic Gate. As indicated in Table 3, right, this pattern describes environments with varying levels of playful feedback and appreciation yet no room for self-expression or collective narratives. An *automatic gate* is a media architecture installation implemented in thoroughfares and areas of high pedestrian activity, which people attend to with peripheral attention. It is characterised by being strongly blended into the built environment, to the point of being almost integrated to it. It responds to pedestrians in a subtle, seamless and non-disruptive way, changing the environment appearance either in front or behind them. *Interference* and *Chromapollination* – enhancing pedestrianised areas without structurally altering them – constitute good examples. In other cases, however, such a pattern emerges unintentionally: for example, when interaction fails to be understood or noticed, the work may be inadvertently interpreted as ambient, as was the case with *The Climate on the Wall*.

6   Conclusion

Successful media architecture combines insights into technical, architectural and social issues. While the field is still relatively new, patterns in how these three aspects can be combined to elicit specific types of behaviour and use are emerging. Our focus has been to understand how different technical and architectural configurations – here labelled types of interfaces and spatial layouts – can lead to specific modes of social interaction, and whether there are recurring strategies for bringing about these social modalities. We find that the field, albeit still in the making, is mature enough to identify recurring design strategies for designing media architecture and analyse the effect they have had on the social aspects in the locations in which they were introduced. Through an analysis of nine media architecture installations that are representative of the field, we have thus identified six distinct modes of interaction, ranging from appreciation to creative expression and dialogue. In continuation, we have identified seven recurring design patterns, which have been employed as strategies to bring about specific modes of social interaction. While these contributions build on analyses of works selected to represent the scope and diversity of media architecture thus far, we do not consider the list of modes and design patterns of social interaction to be exhaustive. A clear limitation lies in our selection of works, which we have limited in order to provide enough details to make the function and purpose of the installations clear; it is plausible that a different or more expansive selection of works could lead to further examples of modes and patterns. Indeed, we would welcome additions to this work, and we expect new modes and patterns to emerge as media architecture continues to evolve. Another limitation in our methodology is that since we have strived to include installations that show the diversity of media architecture, the sample size is not large enough to indicate if specific design patterns are statistically more prevalent or successful. However, this initial identification of social modes and design patterns may lay the ground for more detailed analyses of strategies for influencing and developing modes of social interaction. In addition, we hope that the identification of design patterns can be valuable for interaction designers of future media architecture installations, who strive to bring about specific modes of social interaction.

References

1. Alexander, C.: A Pattern Language: Towns, Buildings, Construction. Oxford University Press, Oxford (1977)

2. Behrens, M., Valkanova, N., gen. Schieck, A.F., Brumby, D.P.: Smart citizen sentiment dashboard: a case study into media architectural interfaces. In: Proceedings of PerDis 2014, Copenhagen, Denmark (2014)
3. Boring, S., Gehring, S., Wiethoff, A., Blöckner, M., Schöning, J., Butz, A.: Multi-user interaction on media facades through live video on mobile devices. In: Proceedings of CHI 2011, Vancouver, BC, Canada (2011)
4. Brignull, H., Rogers, Y.: Enticing people to interact with large public displays in public spaces. In: Proceedings of INTERACT 2003, Zurich, Switzerland (2003)
5. Bullivant, L.: Responsive Environments: Architecture, Art and Design. V&A, London (2006)
6. Dalsgaard, P., Halskov, K.: Designing urban media façades: cases and challenges. In: Proceedings of CHI 2010, Atlanta, GA, USA (2010)
7. Fischer, P.T., Hornecker, E.: Urban HCI : spatial aspects in the design of shared encounters for media façades. In: Proceedings of CHI 2012, Austin, TX, USA (2012)
8. Gamma, E., Helm, R., Johnson, R., Vlissides, J.: Design Patterns: Elements of Reusable Object-Oriented Software. Addison-Wesley, Reading (1995)
9. Goffman, E.: Relations in Public. Penguin, Harmondsworth (1972)
10. Goffman, E.: The Presentation of Self In Everyday Life: The Overlook Press, New York (1973)
11. Haeusler, M., Tomitsch, M., Tscherteu, G.: New Media Facades: A Global Survey. Avedition, Ludwigsberg (2012)
12. Hespanhol, L., Tomitsch, M.: Strategies for intuitive interaction in public urban spaces. Interact. Comput. (2015). doi:10.1093/iwc/iwu051
13. Hillier, B., Hanson, J.: The Social Logic of Space. Cambridge University Press, Cambridge (1984)
14. Huizinga, J.: Homo Ludens: A Study of the Play Element in Culture. Beacon Press, Boston (1955)
15. Kollision: Interference (2014). http://kollision.dk/en/interference. Accessed 8 January 2015
16. Lozano-Hemmer, R.: Body Movies. Relational architecture 6 (2001). http://www.lozano-hemmer.com/body_movies.php. Accessed 13 January 2015
17. Media Architecture Biennale. http://mab14.mediaarchitecture.org
18. Mueller, J., Walter, R., Bailly, G., Nischt, M., Alt, F.: Looking glass: a field study on noticing interactivity of a shop window. In: Proceedings of CHI 2012, Austin, TX, USA (2012)
19. Memarovic, N., Langheinrich, M., Alt, F., Elhart, I., Hosio, S., Rubegni, E.: Using public displays to stimulate passive engagement, active engagement, and discovery in public spaces. In: Proceedings of MAB 2012, Aarhus, Denmark (2012)
20. Rettberg, S.: Collective knowledge, collective narratives, and architectures of participation. In: Proceedings of Digital Arts and Culture Conference, Copenhagen, Denmark (2005)
21. Rico, J., Jacucci, G., Reeves, S., Hansen, L.K., Brewster, S.: Designing for performative interactions in public spaces. In: Proceedings of UbiComp 2010, Copenhagen, Denmark (2010)
22. Valkanova, N., Walter, R., Vande Moere, A., Müller, J.: MyPosition: sparking civic discourse by a public interactive poll visualization. In: Proceedings of CSCW 2014, Baltimore, MD, USA (2014)
23. Wiethoff, A., Gehring, S.: Designing interaction with media façades: a case study. In: Proceedings of DIS 2012, Newcastle, UK (2012)

Thinking Like Disney: Supporting the Disney Method Using Ambient Feedback Based on Group Performance

Sarah Tausch[1]([✉]), Fabius Steinberger[1,2], and Heinrich Hußmann[1]

[1] Media Informatics Group, University of Munich (LMU), Munich, Germany
{sarah.tausch,hussmann}@ifi.lmu.de,
fabius.steinberger@qut.edu.au
[2] Urban Informatics Research Lab, Queensland University of Technology,
Brisbane, Australia

Abstract. The Disney method is a collaborative creativity technique that uses three roles - dreamer, realist and critic - to facilitate the consideration of different perspectives on a topic. Especially for novices it is important to obtain guidance in applying this method. One way is providing groups with a trained moderator. However, feedback about the group's behavior might interrupt the flow of the idea finding process. We built and evaluated a system that provides ambient feedback to a group about the distribution of their statements among the three roles. Our preliminary field study indicates that groups supported by the system contribute more and roles are used in a more balanced way while the visualization does not disrupt the group work.

Keywords: Collaborative creativity · Disney method · Feedback · Group mirror · Tabletop display

1 Introduction

Collaborative creativity (also called social creativity) is a common way to find novel ideas and can be used as an important part of problem solving. Fischer [1] describes this concept as interplay of spatial, temporal, conceptual and technological aspects. These dimensions can be interpreted as barriers but at the same time introduce opportunities for the design of socio-technical systems.

Large displays that blend into the environment are one way of supporting collaborative processes, realizing the concept of ubiquitous computing. Displaying ambient information on such screens during group work shifts the focus from human-computer interaction to technologically mediated human-human interaction. In particular, group mirrors can facilitate this approach. These are systems that support collaboration by reflecting certain aspects of group work to the group [2], for example by visualizing speaking times on a peripheral display.

Our approach investigates the combination of creativity and group mirrors. As such, we aim to create unobtrusive, ambient support for creative group work. Previous research has mainly focused on the influence of feedback about individual performance

© IFIP International Federation for Information Processing 2015
J. Abascal et al. (Eds.): INTERACT 2015, Part III, LNCS 9298, pp. 614–621, 2015.
DOI: 10.1007/978-3-319-22698-9_42

on collaborative processes. Despite several positive effects, this kind of feedback can lead to social pressure or frustration among group members [3, 4]. In contrast to previous research, our system visualizes group performance rather than individual performance. Specifically, we intend to investigate if this kind of feedback supports performance while being less disruptive and reducing social pressure.

We further explored if our system supports a particular creativity technique, the Disney method. This method uses three different roles – dreamer, realist and critic – to allow various perspectives on one topic. In a preliminary field study we investigated if our system improves performance without causing disruptions and if all roles are equally made use of, which is a key element of the Disney method.

2 Related Work

There is a tremendous amount of literature on creativity, its background and computer support for creativity (cf. overview by Sternberg [5]). We will restrain on discussing creativity support for co-located collaboration. Most tools supporting co-located creative group work use large interactive displays integrated into tables and walls. Hilliges et al. [6] for instance combined both display types to build a socio-technical environment for brainstorming. WordPlay [7] uses speech recognition and a multi-touch keyboard for the input of ideas on a table. The influence of feedback during brainstorming has been investigated for instance by Paulus and Dzindolet [8] who could show that information about performance of other groups can influence participation behavior.

Balancing participation is the main goal of several group mirrors. The Meeting Mediator [9] and a tool of Schiavo et al. [4] use private displays to visualize feedback about visual attention from and to others. Most group mirrors however use large displays, such as Reflect [3], a system that displays speaking times in form of colored LEDS integrated into a table. The Second Messenger [10] and the Conversation Clock [11] are visualizations of speaking times and speaking turns, while the latter is a bit more complex as it includes the history and indicates overlapping speech. Finally, Groupgarden [12] is a metaphorical visualization supporting brainstorming with different designs for table and wall displays.

3 Using the Disney Method for Evaluating App Ideas

Dilts [13] describes a collaborative creativity technique called the Disney method that is based on Walt Disney's way of working and thinking. He assumes that the success of Disney originates from using three conceptual positions. This can help group members to think both about both novel ideas as well as critical aspects.

In our study, conducted in a university course for app development, we explained the roles of the Disney method using examples to help teams in the development and evaluation of app ideas. In the following, we will describe the original interpretation of the roles as well as the way we used them. Notably, all roles were used at the same time to preserve the natural flow of the discussion rather than establishing constraints.

Dreamer. Originally, the dreamer's aim is to produce new ideas and goals. Given a task or challenge, it answers the question "what" and provides a vision. In our use case, the dreamer puts forward ideas regarding the design of the user interface and user experience as well as potentially new features.

Realist. Originally, the realist aims at concretizing the ideas of the dreamer. It answers the question "how". For our use case, the realist evaluates the ideas of the dreamer in respect of feasibility, originality, and significance.

Critic. Originally, the critic identifies issues and addresses constraints. It answers the question "why". For our use case, the critic challenges the concepts and detects errors.

4   Design and Implementation

A challenge for groups using the Disney method is remembering the roles and integrating them into the creative process. In particular, this is difficult for novices. Furthermore, participants often shy away from the critic role, especially when group members know each other and have to challenge their colleagues' concepts and ideas. We considered these obstacles in the design of our group mirror application.

Four aspects were most important throughout designing the group mirror: (1) the information the system reflects to the group; (2) the visualization; (3) the colors that are used in the visualization; and (4) the placement of the group mirror.

Information. The key element of the Disney method is the use of different roles. Accordingly, the main goal of the group mirror is to encourage groups in using these roles in a fairly balanced way. To support this, the system displays how many statements by a certain role have been made. Implicitly, the overall amount of contributions is visible as well. Displaying the distribution of roles instead of the amount of contributions of individual participants shifts the focus from comparing individual performance to emphasizing team performance. The rationale behind this design decision was to avoid putting pressure on individuals.

Visualization. The visualization consists of three circles, each representing one role. To allow everyone a good view regardless of angle or seating position, we used circles which can easily be compared in size from every position around the table. At the beginning of the discussion, the three circles are equally small. For each new contribution, a small circle moves from the edges of the display to the middle and joins one of the circles in the center (see Fig. 1, left and Fig. 2). Using a combination of simple, colored shapes to visualize the amount of contributions resembles the information decoration approach [14], as it balances aesthetical and informational quality.

Colors. The three roles are represented with colors. Green represents the dreamer, yellow the realist and red the critic. Dilts did not assign colors to the roles, however, using colors makes it easier to perceive information on a peripheral display. Additionally, the circles are labelled with the role names. On the one hand, this assisted participants in remembering the roles and, on the other hand, it made the group mirror accessible for color-blind participants.

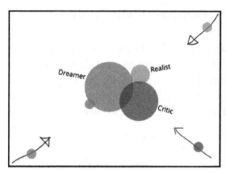

Fig. 1. Left: This sketch shows that with each contribution, a small circle moves to the center and joins the circle of its corresponding color. Right: The group sat around the group mirror that was positioned horizontally on the table.

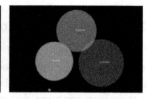

Fig. 2. These screenshots of the group mirror application show (a) how the visualization looks at the start of the group discussion, (b) how a balanced role distribution might look like, and (c) how the visualization could look like at the end of a session.

Placement. Collaboration is a complex task and nonverbal communication such as eye contact, gestures and body language help group members to effectively communicate. Our group mirror therefore follows a calm technology approach [15]. It is designed to stay in the periphery of the attention and to provide feedback to the group in an unobtrusive way to not disrupt communication and to keep the naturalness of the creative group work. We decided to position the group mirror display horizontally on a table (see Fig. 1, right) by lying a 24 in. display flat on a table. In a previous study, Tausch et al. [12] compared a wall version with a table version. Results indicate that feedback on a wall produced less pressure. However, participants perceived the feedback on the table to support collaboration and communication better than the visualization on the wall. As our goal was to accommodate for a natural communication flow, we chose a tabletop setting.

The group mirror application was implemented using Processing and can therefore be executed on Mac OS X, Windows and Linux. In our study, the application ran in full screen mode on an external monitor. The visualization can be controlled via keyboard input. The keys A, S and D signify the three Disney roles. When one of these keys is pressed, the circle of its corresponding role will increase in size. In our experiment, a person who was not participating in the discussion controlled the system.

5   Description and Results of a Preliminary Field Study

We conducted a preliminary field study to investigate the effects of our group mirror on the creative process. Our hypotheses are: (1) The amount of contributions is higher when using the group mirror; (2) the amount of statements by the three roles is more evenly balanced when the group mirror is used; (3) the group mirror does not disrupt the group discussion; and (4) the group mirror does not add additional social pressure.

5.1   Participants

16 participants took part in the study. All participants were media informatics students between 20 and 25 years, 5 were female. They were all participants of a course on iOS app development. Most of the participants were novices to the Disney method, only one person knew the method before the study.

5.2   Method and Procedure

We chose to conduct a field study instead of a lab study, on the one hand, because group mirrors have mostly been studied in lab environments to date and, on the other hand, to increase external validity [16]. The study was conducted using the Wizard of Oz technique, meaning that a person sitting next to the groups classified the contributions of the participants and operated the system while the group was not aware of it.

The study took part as an intermediate step of the practical course. Beforehand, participants had developed app ideas in groups of four over a period of three weeks. During the study, each group presented their app idea. After each presentation, the Disney method was used to discuss one app idea for 10 min. As such, four discussions were conducted in total. Participants were divided into two groups, one with support of the group mirror, one without, called baseline in the following. In each of these two groups, six students discussed the idea.

The team that had just presented their idea did not take part in the discussion but listened and took notes. The combinations of participants within the two groups were changed after every discussion to reduce the influence of group dynamics and opinion leaders. All sessions were audio- and video-recorded. Questionnaires were handed out after each session, containing 5-point Likert scales. Results are reported using three categories; 1 and 2: disagreement; 3: neutral; 4: agreement.

5.3   Results

We evaluated the study based on application logs, video observations and questionnaire responses. In the following, we will report our results with respect to the previously raised hypotheses.

Quantity of Contributions. In the condition that included usage of the group mirror, participants voiced more contributions (132 in total) than without group mirror (79 in

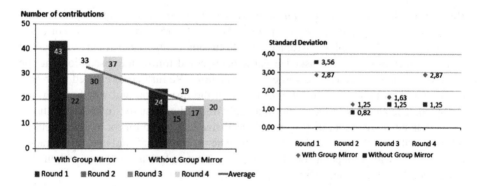

Fig. 3. Left: The number of contributions was higher with group mirror than without. Right: The standard deviation of the different Disney roles was lower in round 1 and higher in round 2, 3 and 4 with group mirror.

total). On average, 33 contributions (SD = 9.055) were stated with and 19 statements (SD = 3.916) without visual feedback (see Fig. 3, left). A dependent t-test shows a significant difference (p = 0.013).

Role Distributions. We evaluated how evenly the statements of the three Disney roles were balanced for each session. Specifically, we compared the distributions of the number of statements in each role from their mean. This basically means that we calculated the standard deviation. In three of the four rounds, the standard deviation was lower without group mirror (see Fig. 3, right), however, without a significant difference. It has to be considered, though, that the number of contributions was higher with group mirror and therefore a higher standard deviation is to be expected.

Looking at the distribution of the roles over all rounds, we can see that with group mirror, 33 % of all contributions were dreamer contributions, 39 % realists and 28 % critics. Without group mirror there were 39 % contributions using the role of the dreamer, 36 % realists and 25 % critics. The absolute numbers are shown in Fig. 4. This suggests that the use of the seemingly more difficult roles of the realist and the critic have been particularly supported by the group mirror.

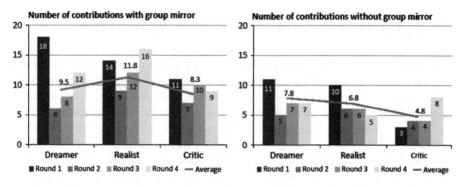

Fig. 4. The number of contributions is higher for all Disney roles with group mirror.

Disruption. Results of the questionnaires indicate that participants did not perceive the group mirror as disrupting. On a 5-point Likert scale, 15 participants did not agree when asked if the display disrupted the discussion, only one person was neutral regarding this aspect. When asked if participants could follow the discussion and the display, 13 participants agreed, while 3 were neutral. We furthermore asked after both conditions if participants were able to focus on the discussion and whether they felt disrupted. The answers to these questions only differed minimally. In both conditions, 15 participants agreed that they were able to focus with group mirror, one felt neutral, whereas in the baseline one did not agree. In general, participants did not feel distracted a lot, neither with group mirror (13 disagreed, 2 neutral, 1 agreed) nor without (14 disagreed, 2 neutral, 2 agreed).

Social Pressure and Stress. We further asked participants if they felt stressed. Results indicate that people did not perceive themselves as stressed, neither with group mirror (13 disagreed, 2 neutral, 1 abstention) nor without (16 disagreed). When asked about feeling observed, people disagreed or were neutral, both with group mirror (11 disagreed, 5 neutral) and in the baseline (13 disagreed, 3 neutral). When asked if participants perceived others as opponents, answers differed between the group mirror condition (13 disagreed, 1 neutral, 2 agreed) and the baseline (13 disagreed, 3 neutral).

Lastly, we asked participants which condition they preferred. 14 stated that they liked the session with group mirror more, one participant was indifferent and one preferred the discussion without group mirror.

5.4   Discussion of Results

We could observe that the distribution of ideas of the three Disney roles differed between both conditions. In the baseline, the role of the critic was used the least. This might be imputable to the fact that participants knew each other and their task was to challenge their colleagues' ideas. The group mirror does not provide any guidance, for example by giving explicit advice to the group. In contrary, it simply shows how often the different roles have been used and thereby implicitly suggests to use the roles in an equilibrated way. Yet, the group mirror had an influence on role distribution and could for instance achieve that the underrepresented role of the critic was used more often than without group mirror.

6   Conclusion

In this paper we presented a novel group mirror supporting collaborative creativity and a preliminary field study investigating the effects of the system, providing a basis for next iterations of the group mirror. While designing this group mirror, we aimed to support creativity through subtle and unobtrusive feedback. The approach we chose was to provide feedback about the group performance rather than comparing individual performance. The results of our preliminary study indicate that this type of feedback has a positive impact on the participants' motivation. The overall number of contributions was increased while negative effects such as disruption or stress did not increase. For future work it could be interesting to evaluate the relations to the other group members in more details, as our results indicate a difference between both conditions in this regard.

We furthermore have been exploring an interactive tool supporting the Disney method. This will allow us to investigate the differences between an interactive system with more explicit guidance with the subtle and unobtrusive group mirror presented in this paper. As a next step, we plan to compare a group mirror showing individual performance with a visualization that only reflects the group's performance. The idea is to explore if this feedback system can also support other collaborative processes, for example a balanced contribution of all participants.

References

1. Fischer, G.: Social creativity: turning barriers into opportunities for collaborative design. In: Proceedings of the Eighth Conference on Participatory Design: Artful Integration: Interweaving Media, Materials and Practices, pp. 152–161. ACM (2004)
2. Jermann, P., Soller, A., Muehlenbrock, M.: From mirroring to guiding: a review of state of the art technology for supporting collaborative learning. In: European Conference on Computer-Supported Collaborative Learning, pp. 324–331 (2001)
3. Bachour, K., Kaplan, F., Dillenbourg, P.: An interactive table for supporting participation balance in face-to-face collaborative learning. Learn. Technol. 3, 203–213 (2010)
4. Schiavo, G., Cappelletti, A., Mencarini, E., Stock, O., Zancanaro, M.: Overt or subtle? Supporting group conversations with automatically targeted directives. In: Proceedings of IUI, pp. 225–234. ACM (2014)
5. Sternberg, R.J.: Handbook of Creativity. Cambridge University Press, Cambridge (1999)
6. Hilliges, O., Terrenghi, L., Boring, S., Kim, D., Richter, H., Butz, A.: Designing for collaborative creative problem solving. In: Proceedings of C&C, pp. 137–146. ACM (2007)
7. Hunter, S., Maes, P.: WordPlay: a table-top interface for collaborative brainstorming and decision making. In: Proceedings of ITS, pp. 2–5 (2008)
8. Paulus, P.B., Dzindolet, M.T.: Social influence processes in group brainstorming. J. Pers. Soc. Psychol. 64, 575–586 (1993)
9. Kim, T., Chang, A., Holland, L., Pentland, A.: Meeting mediator: enhancing group collaboration using sociometric feedback. In: Proceedings of CSCW, pp. 457–466. ACM (2008)
10. DiMicco, J.M., Pandolfo, A., Bender, W.: Influencing group participation with a shared display. In: Proceedings of CSCW, pp. 614–623. ACM (2004)
11. Bergstrom, T., Tony, B., Karrie, K.: Conversation clock: visualizing audio patterns in co-located groups. In: Proceedings of HICSS, pp. 78–87 (2007)
12. Tausch, S., Hausen, D., Kosan, I., Raltchev, A., Hussmann, H.: Groupgarden: supporting brainstorming through a metaphorical group mirror on table or wall. In: Proceedings of NordiCHI, pp. 541–550. ACM (2014)
13. Dilts, R.: Strategies of Genius. Meta Publications, Capitola (1995)
14. Eggen, B., Van Mensvoort, K.: Making sense of what is going on "around": designing environmental awareness information displays. In: Markopoulos, P., De Ruyter, B., Mackay, W. (eds.) Awareness Systems, pp. 99–124. Springer, London (2009)
15. Weiser, M., Brown, J.S.: Designing calm technology. PowerGrid J. 1, 75–85 (1996)
16. Rogers, Y.: Interaction design gone wild: striving for wild theory. Interactions 18, 58–62 (2011)

Eery Space: Facilitating Virtual Meetings Through Remote Proxemics

Maurício Sousa$^{(\boxtimes)}$, Daniel Mendes, Alfredo Ferreira,
João Madeiras Pereira, and Joaquim Jorge

INESC-ID Lisboa/IST, Technical University of Lisbon, Lisbon, Portugal
{antonio.sousa,danielmendes,
alfredo.ferreira}@ist.utl.pt,
{jap,jaj}@inesc-id.pt

Abstract. Virtual meetings have become increasingly common with modern video-conference and collaborative software. While they allow obvious savings in time and resources, current technologies add unproductive layers of protocol to the flow of communication between participants, rendering the interactions far from seamless. In this work we introduce Remote Proxemics, an extension of proxemics aimed at bringing the syntax of co-located proximal interactions to virtual meetings. We propose Eery Space, a shared virtual locus that results from merging multiple remote areas, where meeting participants' are located side-by-side as if they shared the same physical location. Eery Space promotes collaborative content creation and seamless mediation of communication channels based on virtual proximity. Results from user evaluation suggest that our approach is sufficient to initiate proximal exchanges regardless of their geolocation, while promoting smooth interactions between local and remote people alike.

Keywords: Remote Proxemics · Virtual meetings · Collaboration

1 Introduction

When people get together to discuss, they communicate in several manners, besides verbally. Hall [5] observed that space and distance between people (proxemics) impact interpersonal communication. While this has been explored to leverage collaborative digital content creation [7], nowadays it is increasingly common for work teams to be geographically separated around the globe. In fact, through appropriate technology, it is possible to see and hear others, making it easier to communicate at a distance.

The newest videoconferencing and telepresence solutions support both common desktop environments and the latest mobile handheld technologies. However, despite considerable technological advances, remote users often feel neglected due to their limited presence [8]. Moreover, although verbal and visual communication occur naturally in virtual meetings, other modes of engagement, namely proximal interactions, have yet to be explored. This is unfortunate, since proxemics can enable many natural interactions obviating the need for cumbersome technology-induced protocol.

In this work, we introduce *Eery Space* as a virtual construct to bring remote people together and mediate natural proxemics interactions between participants as if they

© IFIP International Federation for Information Processing 2015
J. Abascal et al. (Eds.): INTERACT 2015, Part III, LNCS 9298, pp. 622–629, 2015.
DOI: 10.1007/978-3-319-22698-9_43

were in the same physical place, a mechanism which we call *Remote Proxemics*. To this end, Eery Space allows us to merge different rooms into one virtual shared locus were people can meet, share resources and engage in collaborative tasks.

Building on the notion that people do not need hyper-realistic awareness devices, such as virtual avatars, to infer the presence of others [9] and engage in natural social behavior, Eery Space employs an iconic representation for remote people. Also, to facilitate virtual meetings, we propose novel techniques for person-to-person and person-to-device interactions. We adopt a multiple interactive surfaces environment, which comprises an ecosystem of handheld devices, wall-sized displays and projected floors.

2 Eery Space

We propose an approach to bring geographically distant people together into a common space, and to provide feedback for participants in a virtual meeting in order to be able to proximally interact. We call this common space *Eery Space*. Given that people are distributed across similar rooms in different locations, Eery Space attempts to consolidate these in a common virtual locus, while providing new opportunities for interaction and communication between participants. In this way, people equipped with personal handheld devices can meet and share resources regardless of where they are.

Instead of placing users in front of each other, as is typical of commercial applications and other research works [2, 3], we place both remote and local people side-by-side, similar to Cohen et al. [4]. Unlike the common interactions with remote people using the mirror metaphor, Eery Space provides remote participants with a sense of being around local ones in a shared space. This creates and reinforces the model of a shared meeting area where proxemic interactions can take place. Moreover, each person gets assigned a definite position and a personal location within Eery Space. Allowing both local and remote people to collaborate by relating to their personal spaces strengthens the notion that everyone is treated similarly as if they were all physically co-located.

2.1 Social Bubbles

Hall's [5] model of proxemic distances dictates that when people are close to each other they can interact in specific ways. Within a proxemic social space, people do interact in a formal way, typical of a professional relationship. In contrast, the personal space is reserved for family and friends, and people can communicate quietly and comfortably. Yet, as described by Hall [5], these distances are dynamic. Friendship, social custom and professional acquaintanceship can decrease interpersonal distances [10]. We adapted these concepts to Eery Space, using a device we call *Social Bubbles*.

Inside Eery Space, interactions are initiated by analyzing the distribution of people within the shared virtual space. People having a private conversation or involved in the same task usually get closer, and, therefore, we create social bubbles using a distance metaphor. People naturally create a bubble, where they can meet, share resources and

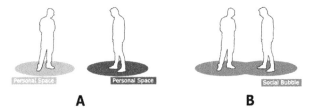

Fig. 1. Social Bubbles: (A) While distant from one another, (B) A social bubble happens when people's personal spaces intersect.

engage in private conversation, by coming sufficiently close to each other. A social bubble appears through the intersection of two or more personal spaces, as depicted in Fig. 1, implicitly capturing the intention of people to perform a collaborative task.

This formulation allows people motivated to initiate collaboration to easily create proximal interactions adopting a distance inside their social space, without needing to enter the other person's personal space. In our work, we considered personal space as a circle 0.6 m in radius. Thus two people can create a social bubble by approaching the other within 1.2 m. Destroying bubbles is analogous to creating them - a social bubbles ceases to exist when its participants move apart.

2.2 Remote Proxemics

Remote Proxemics aims to harness natural interactions that occur between co-located people and make these available to meeting participants who are not physically in the same room. In this way, all interactions within Eery Space work similarly for local and remote people. The success of our approach is to ensure that both local and remote people are always present and positioned side-by-side, so that participants can create social bubbles in a similar way, regardless of whether they are or not in the same room. Since Eery Space defines an environment with multiple people and devices, we have grouped these interactions into: person-to-person, involving people and their own mobile devices; and person-to-device, between people and shared devices.

Person-to-Person Interactions: When people come together and create a social bubble, different tools become available to support collaborative tasks, as person-to-person interactions. These interactions include both the participants and their personal handheld devices, as depicted in Fig. 2A. Since verbal communication is a key element to the success of virtual meetings, participants can both talk to and listen to other people inside their bubble. When people establish a social bubble, their handheld devices automatically open a communication channel to local and remote participants alike. This channel is closed when the bubble is destroyed. Similarly and simultaneously, if there is a shared visualization device, such as a wall display, the handheld devices of participants in the same social bubble can be synchronized to the common visualization. At this stage, participants can engage in a collaborative session around the shared visualization, either by discussing or by collaboratively creating content.

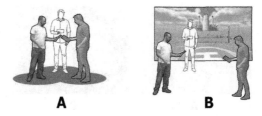

Fig. 2. Remote Proxemics: (A) Two local people and one remote (in white) engage in collaborative work in a social bubble. (B) The remote participant acts as the moderator.

Person-to-Device Interactions: The Eery Space may feature shared devices, such as wall displays and tabletops to support shared visualization and collaborative settings.

In our work, we explored the latter kind, as shown in Fig. 2(B). Due to their large dimensions, these displays can provide a visualization surface to serve many people at the same time, and make the information under analysis accessible to all. Naturally, large displays should be located at the same virtual position across all remote areas that make up Eery Space, to ensure a consistent visualization to all participants. When a participant establishes a close proximity relationship with the display, he/she becomes moderator. In Eery Space, moderators have a special authority that allows them to control the common visualization on all shared displays, either local or remote, by mirroring actions performed on the handheld device. We define moderator space as the area within a distance of 1.5 m away from the wall display, analogously to the place normally occupied by a person giving a talk to an audience. The role of moderator can only be handed over when the person assuming this role abandons the moderator space, leaving it available for another participant who wishes to take over. Furthermore, when a meeting participant becomes a moderator, a channel for speech communication is opened so that they can address all.

3 Prototype

We built a prototype system to prove that remote proxemics are possible and that Eery Space is an effective approach to manage interactions between participants as if all were in the same room. Our prototype employs multiple Microsoft Kinect depth cameras to locate people indoors in a non-intrusively fashion, while dealing with body occlusions. In this section, we describe the awareness techniques we implemented to provide appropriate feedback for interactions between participants. We opted to develop a scenario to design and review 3D CAD models in the oil and gas industry.

Floor Circles: In the Eery Space prototype, every local and remote participant has a representative projected circle on the room's floor, as depicted in Fig. 3A. All circles are unique, corresponding to a single person, and are distinguished from each other by a name (the participant's identity) and the user's unique color. These circles track a person's position within Eery Space, in order to visually define the participant's personal space, thus making all people aware of others. Thus floor circles provide the

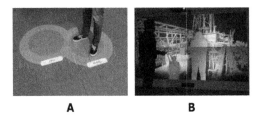

Fig. 3. Awareness techniques: (A) Floor circles. Remote and local users establish a social bubble. (B) Wall shadows depict two users. The larger shadow is the moderator.

necessary spatial information for participants to initiate and be aware of proximity interactions. In addition, projected circles depict a user's proxemic zones. The inner circle, with a radius of 0.3 m, matches the participant's intimate space. The outer ring, depicts the personal space, with a radius of 0.6 m. When people come together to start a social bubble, the circles on the floor depict the status of their Social Bubble, by matching the personal space color of the bubble participants, while maintaining the user's color in their intimate space. The social bubble receives a color which averages the color of its members. This guarantees that the bubble color is unique and unmistakably different from other content on the floor.

Intimate Space: We designed Eery Space keeping each person's personal locus in mind. Every user has their own space assured, even if they are not in the same physical room. To prevent users from invading another user's intimate space, we provide haptic feedback by vibrating their handheld device, when this happens. Participants can then quietly adjust their positions without interrupting the main meeting, since this technique does not use audio or visual cues. This way, each user's intimate space is preserved and made visible at all time to all participants, so that they can interact with it.

Wall Shadows: Additionally, and since we included large wall displays in our prototype, every person gets assigned a representative shadow on the wall display, distinguished by a name and a unique color, as shown in Fig. 3B, similarly to the work of Apperley et al. [1]. This allows for a quick recognition of all meeting's participants. The location of the shadow reflects a distance from the person to the wall to give a sense of the spatial relationship between a person and the interactive surface. Wall shadows take in consideration an imaginary directional light source placed at infinity and oriented towards the wall display, with an inclination of 45 degrees. Thus, the nearest user to the wall will have a shadow covering more area than the others. A much larger shadow also makes clear who the moderator is.

4   Evaluation

We conducted a user evaluation to assess the interactions within the Eery Space, both with local and remote people. In our experiment, subjects were invited into the room with the main setup, while a remote user was in a room equipped with a lighter version with one Microsoft Kinect, one display showing the floor projection and a smartphone.

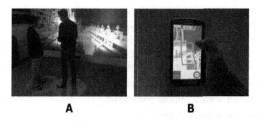

Fig. 4. Evaluation: (A) Test user interacting with the local participant during the evaluation session. (B) Handheld Client. User engaged in a sketch collaborative task.

Each participant received a smartphone running the handheld device client. Figure 4A shows our experimental setup. Participants were asked to perform collaborative sketching, (see Fig. 4B) task with both local and remote people. To verify if subjects react to the presence of other remote people, their intimate space was purposely invaded to assess their reaction. The users were also asked to synchronize the visualization on the wall with the smartphone, by assuming the role of moderator.

All participants in this evaluation were randomly selected and were mainly students of our educational institution. The set of test users was comprised of 12 participants, one of which was female, and all with a college degree and with ages between 18 and 24 years old. Furthermore, every test user had no previous experience with our work.

4.1   Results and Discussion

Since the main objective of this evaluation was to demonstrate the feasibility of remote proxemics by maintaining an adequate level of awareness of the people that are remote, the analysis of the results is divided into *Proxemics Analysis* and *Awareness Analysis*. The data gathered were obtained from a Likert scale with 6 values. Table 1 summarizes the responses obtained from the questionnaire regarding those aspects.

Proxemics Analysis: Participants' preferences regarding proxemics interactions are related to how easy it was to perform proximal interactions with both local and remote people, and also the ability to interact with the wall display. The latter, poses a conscious decision to become the moderator of the virtual meeting. The presented data suggests that it was easy to assume the role of moderator. According to the *Wilcoxon Signed Ranks* test, applied to the first and second questions ($Z = -1.890$, $p = 0.059$), there are no statistically significant differences between starting an interaction with the other participants, despite their local or remote statuses. This leads us to conclude that, in Eery Space, interacting with remote people is not that different than local interactions. This result is encouraging as it shows that remote proxemics are in fact possible and do not add obstacles in the course of virtual meetings. In the evaluation sessions, participants did not demonstrate any difficulty in repositioning themselves to establish social bubbles in the collaborative tasks, although three users took a little while (around five seconds) to remember how to become the moderator.

Table 1. Questionnaire's results (median and interquartile range): proxemics overview (questions 1 to 3) and awareness overview (questions 4 to 10).

It was easy to...	Median (IQR)
...control what is shown on the wall display	6 (1.25)
...start an interaction with a local participant	6 (0)
...start an interaction with a remote participant	6 (1)
...see who is present at the meeting	6 (0)
...see where each participant is	6 (1.25)
...see who is controlling the wall display	6 (0.25)
...see that I'm interacting with other people	6 (0.25)
...see which participant I'm interacting with	6 (1)
...see that I'm in the intimate space of another local participant	6 (0)
...see that I'm in the intimate space of another remote participant	6 (0)

Awareness Analysis: For awareness, the data shows that people in the virtual meeting can relate to the presence of remote participants. Despite some dispersion in the data (question 5) user preferences suggestion that the location of remotely located people is easily perceived. We can safely deduce that participants in the virtual meeting are always aware of the people involved. One of the requirements of our approach is the preservation of the intimate space of remote people. This design principle is required to impose their presence, while fostering remote interactions by establishing social bubbles. The *Wilcoxon Signed Ranks test* applied to the questions 6 and 7 (Z = 0.000, p = 1.000) shows no statistically significant difference between local and remote people, suggesting that test users were aware when their intimate space intercepted others'. Curiously, while performing the collaborative task, three test users made a point of informing the remote participant of his infringement on their personal space during the smartphone-enabled conversation, before readjusting their position. Every subject changed their positions, during the intimate space invasion task, responding to the haptic feedback from the handheld device. Despite that, four users first complained that the remote participant was invading their intimate space, and only then proceeded to readjust their positions. In general, participants were aware of the presence of the remote participant and reacted accordingly.

5 Conclusions and Future Work

Results from our evaluation show the promise of Remote Proxemics, since we were able to achieve interactions between local and remote people. We believe that the work here described extends proxemic interactions to augment the presence of remote users in virtual collaborative settings to address commonly-raised concerns. Furthermore, our results apply even in the absence of commonly explored devices such as avatars and eye contact. We will assess whether f-formations [7] and gradual engagement [6] can enrich remote interactions in Eery Space.

Acknowledgements. This work was partially supported by the Portuguese Foundation for Science and Technology (FCT) through the projects TECTON-3D (PTDC/EEI-SII/3154/2012), CEDAR (PTDC/EIA-EIA/116070/2009), doctoral grant SFRH/BD/91372/2012 and by national funds through FCT with reference UID/CEC/50021/2013.

References

1. Apperley, M., McLeod, L., Masoodian, M., Paine, L., Phillips, M., Rogers, B., Thomson, K.: Use of video shadow for small group interaction awareness on a large interactive display surface. In: Proceedings of the Fourth Australasian User Interface Conference on User Interfaces 2003, vol. 18, pp. 81–90. Australian Computer Society, Inc., February 2003
2. Beck, S., Kunert, A., Kulik, A., Froehlich, B.: Immersive group-to-group telepresence. IEEE Trans. Vis. Comput. Graph. **19**(4), 616–625 (2013)
3. Benko, H., Jota, R., Wilson, A.: MirageTable: freehand interaction on a projected augmented reality tabletop. In: Proceedings of the SIGCHI Conference on Human Factors in Computing Systems, pp. 199–208. ACM, May 2012
4. Cohen, M., Dillman, K.R., MacLeod, H., Hunter, S., Tang, A.: Onespace: shared visual scenes for active freeplay. In: Proceedings of the 32nd Annual ACM Conference on Human Factors in Computing Systems, pp. 2177–2180. ACM, April 2014
5. Hall, E.T.: The Hidden Dimension. Doubleday, New York (1966)
6. Marquardt, N., Ballendat, T., Boring, S., Greenberg, S., Hinckley, K.: Gradual engagement: facilitating information exchange between digital devices as a function of proximity. In: Proceedings of the 2012 ACM International Conference on Interactive Tabletops and Surfaces, pp. 31–40. ACM, November 2012
7. Marquardt, N., Hinckley, K., Greenberg, S.: Cross-device interaction via micro-mobility and f-formations. In: Proceedings of the 25th Annual ACM Symposium on User Interface Software and Technology, pp. 13–22. ACM, October 2012
8. Neyfakh L.: My day as a robot, May 2014. http://www.bostonglobe.com/ideas/2014/05/10/day-robot/6UAMgmUFn0mZhoMS8vy0GK/story.html
9. Reeves, B., Nass, C.: The Media Equation: How People Treat Computers, Tele-vision, and New Media Like Real People and Places. Cambridge Univ Press, Cambridge (1996)
10. Sommer, R.: Personal space in a digital age. Handbook of Environmental Psychology, pp. 647–660. Wiley, New York (2002)

Author Index

Printed in the United States
By Bookmasters